D0910267

Praise for
Conquering Cancer: Volume One
50 Pancreatic and Breast Cancer Patients on
The Gonzalez Nutritional Protocol

From the first time that I met Dr. Nick Gonzalez, I was impressed by his level of integrity and caring. It was clear that he was always extremely devoted to the individual needs of his patients. The patients whom I met all seemed very confident in the care that they received. It impressed me that the results of his nutritional treatment indicated that many of his patients were doing better than their predicted life expectancy.

Julian Hyman, MD, Hematologist and Oncologist, St. Luke's-Roosevelt Hospital, NYC

—❦—

Conquering Cancer reveals an approach to cancer treatment that squarely challenges what is offered by orthodox medicine. Anyone seeking a broader view of cancer treatment should study Dr. Gonzalez's compelling case histories. This book is a powerful legacy to a compassionate man dedicated to unraveling the cancer mystery.

David Perlmutter, MD, FACN, Author, #1 New York Times Bestseller,
Grain Brain: The Surprising Truth about Wheat, Carbs, and Sugar—Your Brain's Silent Killers

—❦—

Dr. Nicholas Gonzalez was a well-trained and compassionate physician, whose meticulous efforts resulted in documented benefits for scores of patients that were far superior to chemotherapy. As detailed in *What Went Wrong*, his attempt to prove this was sabotaged by vested interests intent on preserving profits and reputations. However, as these fifty pancreatic and breast cancer best case reports prove, Nick will be vindicated. His legacy lives on, and will stimulate others to investigate novel approaches that are designed to improve patient care, rather than corporate profits.

Paul Rosch, MD, MA, Chairman of the Board of the American Institute of Stress
Clinical Professor of Medicine and Psychiatry, New York Medical College

—❦—

This new book by Nicholas J. Gonzalez, *Conquering Cancer: Volume One*, describes case studies of successful treatment of cancer by The Gonzalez Protocol. This pioneering study is based on the insights of the Scottish embryologist John Beard, who first introduced the concept of the enzyme therapy of cancer in 1902. Inspired by Beard's concept, Dr. Gonzalez developed his successful protocol for cancer treatment, as illustrated by these extraordinary case studies. The Gonzalez Protocol is in accord with the discovery of abnormal homocysteine metabolism in malignant cells, which explains the molecular basis for successful treatment of cancer by pancreatic enzyme therapy.

Kilmer McCully, MD, Author of *The Heart Revolution* and Pioneer of the Homocysteine Theory

Conventional oncology delivers a verdict of pancreatic cancer as the onset of doom—pancreatic cancer patients rarely survive one year after diagnosis. Breast cancer patients tend to survive longer, but often succumb after many months of debilitating treatment. The late Nicholas Gonzalez, MD, got true lasting results with these cancers … even to the point of cure. Based on the pioneering research of Dr. John Beard, his protocol uses proteolytic enzymes, diet, and detoxification with impressive success. *Conquering Cancer* provides a roadmap for doctors and patients who want something other than chemotherapy and radiation—and not just ephemeral hope but lasting success.

Sally Fallon Morell, President, the Weston A. Price Foundation

Conventional cancer care is failing. With flagging long-term outcomes, debilitating side effects, and prohibitive cost, it is time to revisit the nosology, science, and clinical approach to oncology. Dr. Nicholas Gonzalez did just this. For twenty-eight years, he treated patients with radiographically confirmed terminal cancers and degenerative diseases and brought them to states of vitality that exceeded what has ever been documented in the published literature. The magnitude of paradigm-shifting relevance in this work is evidenced by how many industry-influenced journals closed their doors to the publication of his patient reports. The cases in this compendium demand a reckoning with the claims of allopathic medicine. With his nutrition-based approach, strategic supplementation, and detoxification, this non-pharmaceutical approach yielded life-saving, imaging-confirmed results that will leave you picking your jaw up off the ground. His indebted patients pepper the globe, to this day, awakened to the unimaginable healing power of natural medicine. The course of my life, personally, and as a practitioner, was changed forever when I learned of these survivors and the simplicity and elegance of this model of care.

Kelly Brogan, MD, Author of
A Mind of Your Own: A Revolutionary Approach to Treating Depression—Without Drugs

I have interviewed Nick Gonzalez for three of my books. We have spent hundreds of hours talking to one another. Something he told me early on has stayed with me to this day: "Cancer is manageable; if you give it what it wants, it will leave you alone." I asked, "What does it want?" He said, "It wants good nutrition and a detoxed body." Of course there is more to it than that but in essence: he cleans you out and feeds you right. He *manages* cancer. I am a friend, colleague, and patient. When I was diagnosed, a mastectomy was recommended for my cancer. Suddenly I went from interviewer to patient. The best decision I ever made was to eschew Standard of Care, allopathic medicine and follow the Gonzalez non-drug protocol. Nick does not use the word "cure" but I can. Today, I have NED . . . "no evidence of disease." I feel great, am perfectly healthy, have great energy, and am in the best shape of my life. I attribute my recovery to Nick Gonzalez.

Suzanne Somers, Entertainer and Author of Twenty-Six Books, Including
Knockout: Interviews with Doctors Who Are Curing Cancer and
How to Prevent Getting It in the First Place

Excerpt Book Reviews
Conquering Cancer: Volume One

The Man Who Cured the Most Lethal Cancers

"Nicholas Gonzalez, MD, was one of the most compassionate, intelligent, and skilled physicians the natural healing world has ever known. Nick was known as the doctor who put "incurable" cancer patients into full remission, with many still alive today, sometimes decades after being told they only had months to live. And what was even more miraculous about this man's work was that he did it entirely with natural approaches. This is why I am excited to announce that dozens of his most miraculous cancer patient cases studies are now available…"

Sayer Ji, Founder, GreenMedInfo.com

The Man Who Conquered Cancer

"What if there were already a cure for most cancers but no one knew about it?…These are remarkable case histories that illustrate the power of a holistic program to bring healing to people whose disease would usually be fatal…(it) is not a "how to" book to help practitioners learn how to implement the Gonzalez Protocols, which are complex. However, the case histories it presents should inspire health professionals and the public alike to invest the time and money that it will take to allow this successful treatment approach to flourish."

Katherine Smith, Editor, The New Zealand Journal of Natural Medicine

"The 50 case reports of breast and pancreatic cancer in **Conquering Cancer**…reflect an impressive accumulation of a quarter century's worth of evidence of the value of Dr. Gonzalez's approach to treating cancer. The research and writing were an ambitious undertaking, and the writing of the book was over ten years in the making. It is a serious effort, and the care and attention to detail, as well as the success of the therapy itself, are clearly apparent…For the open-minded clinician and medical researcher, and the serious student of innovative natural approaches to treating disease, Conquering Cancer Volume One is a major contribution to the medical and scientific literature and will, I am confident, take its place along with other notable ground breaking works of the past."

Peter Chowka, Journalist, The Townsend Letter

Other Books by Nicholas J. Gonzalez, MD

The Trophoblast and the Origins of Cancer

One Man Alone: An Investigation of Nutrition, Cancer, and William Donald Kelley

What Went Wrong: The Truth behind the Clinical Trial of the Enzyme Treatment of Cancer

Nutrition and the Autonomic Nervous System—The Scientific Foundations of The Gonzalez Protocol

Conquering Cancer: Volume One—50 Pancreatic and Breast Cancer Patients on The Gonzalez Nutritional Protocol

Praise for Other Books by Nicholas J. Gonzalez, MD

The Trophoblast and the Origins of Cancer
"Everyone interested in cancer, of how medical research should work, should read this book."
—J.P. Jones, PhD, retired VP of research and development, the Procter & Gamble Company

What Went Wrong: The Truth behind the Clinical Trial of the Enzyme Treatment of Cancer
"This tragic tale tends to support a growing suspicion that the cancer cartel of organizations, government agencies, and vested interests is devoted more to preserving their enormous profits and reputations than to the prevention and cure of cancer."
—Paul J. Rosch, MD, president, the American Institute of Stress; clinical professor of medicine and psychiatry, New York Medical College

Nutrition and The Autonomic Nervous System: The Scientific Foundations of The Gonzalez Protocol
"The only nutrition book you will ever need…Dr. Gonzalez did a fabulous job taking the key principles from the research of each of these doctors (Kelley, Pottenger and Gonzalez) and putting it into a very readable and understandable format that can be consumed by a lay person. This is a must read for anyone who is serious about applying nutritional principles for optimizing health."
—S. Walker, Amazon Review

For more information,
visit The Nicholas Gonzalez Foundation website at
www.dr-gonzalez.com.

Conquering Cancer

Volume Two

62 Patients on

The Gonzalez Protocol

NICHOLAS J. GONZALEZ, MD

Notice

This book is intended for general informational purposes only, not as a medical manual. The materials presented in no way are meant to be a substitute for professional medical care or attention by a qualified practitioner, nor should they be construed as such. Always check with your doctor if you have any questions or concerns about your condition or before starting or modifying a program of treatment. New Spring Press LLC and the author(s) are not responsible or liable, directly or indirectly, for any form of damages whatsoever resulting from the use (or misuse) of information contained in or implied by this book.

Introduction Copyright © Colin A. Ross, MD
Copyright © 2017 Nicholas J. Gonzalez, MD
A Case of Insulin-dependent Diabetes Copyright © 2016 InnoVision Professional Media

All rights reserved. No part of this publication may be reproduced or transmitted in any form whatsoever without the written permission of the publisher. For information, write to: New Spring Press LLC, 340 East 57th Street, New York, NY 10022 USA

Book design by Deborah Tremper, Six Penny Graphics LLC
Cover photograph © David Meardon. Used with permission.

Publishing and editorial team: Author Bridge Media, www.AuthorBridgeMedia.com
Project Manager and Editorial Director: Helen Chang
Editor: Katherine MacKenett
Publishing Manager: Laurie Aranda
Publishing Assistant: Iris Sasing

Publisher's Cataloging-in-Publication
(Provided by Quality Books Inc.)

Gonzalez, Nicholas J., 1947–2015 author.
Conquering cancer / Nicholas J. Gonzalez. -- First
    edition.
     volumes cm
    Includes bibliographical references.
    CONTENTS: Volume one. 50 pancreatic and breast cancer
patients on the Gonzalez nutritional protocol -- Volume
two. 62 cancer patients on the Gonzalez protocol.
    ISBN 978-0-9821965-5-7 (hardcover : volume 1)
    ISBN 978-0-9985460-2-5 (hardcover : volume 2)
    ISBN 978-0-9821965-7-1 (e-book : volume 1)
    ISBN 978-0-9985460-3-2 (e-book : volume 2)

    1. Cancer--Alternative treatment--Research--United
States. 2. Cancer--Patients--United States--Biography.
3. Cancer--Alternative treatment--Case studies.
4. Pancreas--Cancer--Patients--Case studies. 5. Breast--
Cancer--Patients--Case studies. 6. Cancer--Patients--
Case studies. 7. Biographies.   I. Title.

RC271.A62G66 2016   616.99'406
                      QBI16-900025

Printed in the United States of America

Dedication

To my patients, whose courage inspired me every day.

Nicholas J. Gonzalez, MD

Contents

⸻

Acknowledgments

—◆—

The ***Conquering Cancer*** case history series (Volume One and Two) was written by Dr. Gonzalez in his lifetime over the course of nearly 10 years. New Spring Press has posthumously published these two volumes, totaling 112 cases of evidence based scientific documentation.

Thank you Colin A. Ross, MD for your expert medical editing and guidance throughout the preparation of this second volume. As I often tell you, you are indeed a gift from God.

As Nick's colleague, Linda L. Isaacs, MD, provided insight into these case histories. She assisted by completing some of Dr. Gonzalez's case reports and providing a few of her own case reports utilizing the protocol.

Dr. Gonzalez developed a partnership with his patients, as The Gonzalez Protocol requires a special type of commitment and diligence. Nick often told patients that all they had to do was follow their program and he would worry about their cancer. Thank you to all of Dr. Gonzalez's patients and their support system of friends and family members.

These 62 case reports span Dr. Gonzalez's entire medical practice of nearly 30 years. During this time Nick employed many wonderful and devoted staff members including: Mary, Brigitte, Ingrid, Josette, Leslie, Mary Ann, Nancy, Avery, Rasheda, Christina, Cristina, Chelsea, Angela, Emily, Andrea, Mayra and Mireille.

Thank you to the staff of editing and proofreading experts at Author Bridge Media.

As awareness of the effectiveness of The Gonzalez Protocol continues to expand around the world, the work of The Nicholas Gonzalez Foundation's devoted board grows increasingly important. I greatly appreciate their commitment to Dr. Gonzalez's legacy and the future of this extraordinary medical treatment.

Finally, I'd like to extend a personal thank you to the hundreds of Nick's colleagues, patients and their families and friends who have reached out to me since Nick's death in July 2015 to offer their support. I will be forever grateful for your letters, cards, emails, prayers, gift baskets, donations and genuine love for my late husband, Dr. Nick Gonzalez.

Mary Beth Gonzalez

Introduction to Volume Two

— ∿ —

The cases in this volume provide evidence of the effectiveness of The Gonzalez Protocol. One case—Patient RG, with mesothelioma—is instructive. While being treated by Dr. Gonzalez, Patient RG was enrolled in a trial of photodynamic therapy at the National Cancer Institute (NCI), an experimental treatment that failed to help anyone. The photodynamic therapy, which involved a major surgical procedure, was provided to Patient RG at the NCI in April 1992.

By August 1994, Patient RG was the only surviving patient out of forty entered into the trial of photodynamic therapy. He survived for seven years from initial diagnosis, despite erratic compliance with the Gonzalez nutritional regimen, and died on the table during debulking surgery in February 1999, a procedure Dr. Gonzalez considered unnecessary. The trial of photodynamic therapy was never published, and the study was shut down and the research team disbanded.

Only one patient out of forty in the NCI trial—Patient RG—survived longer than two years, and he survived seven years. He was the only patient on The Gonzalez Protocol. The interest shown in The Gonzalez Protocol by the NCI as a result? Zero. In fact, the NCI, to this day, discredits the protocol on its website.[1] In a similar study during the same time period, conducted from 1993 to 1996, twenty-five mesothelioma patients received standard treatment plus photodynamic therapy, compared with twenty-three patients receiving only standard treatment. The photodynamic patients had a median survival of 14.4 months, compared with 14.1 months for the standard treatment patients, a difference that is not clinically or statistically significant.[2]

---

1   Colin A. Ross, "Methodological Flaws in the Chabot Trial of Pancreatic Enzymes for Pancreatic Cancer," *ARC Journal of Cancer Science* 1 (2015): 1–4; Colin A. Ross, "The Trophoblast Model of Cancer," *Nutrition and Cancer* 67 (2015): 61–67.

2   H. I. Pass et al., "Phase III Randomized Trial of Surgery with or without Intraoperative Photodynamic Therapy and Postoperative Immunochemotherapy for Malignant Pleural Mesothelioma," *Annals of Surgical Oncology* 4 (1997): 628–33.

Given the cases in this volume and two accompanying books,[3] plus a prior case series published by Gonzalez and Isaacs[4] and a case series from the practice of Dr. Gonzalez's mentor, Dr. Kelley,[5] there is now overwhelming published evidence of the effectiveness of The Gonzalez Protocol at the level of replicated large cohort studies. This is classified as Level II evidence by the United States Preventive Services Task Force.[6]

It is time to invest serious resources in studies of The Gonzalez Protocol and the trophoblast model of cancer, as I discuss in my Introduction to Volume One of *Conquering Cancer*. This should include basic science research on the mechanisms of action of the pancreatic enzymes, animal studies, and human trials. The Gonzalez Protocol should be accepted within mainstream medicine and should be available as a treatment option for cancer patients everywhere. A lot of work will be required to get there, but this wonderful gift to the human race should not be forgotten.

I have included some foundational references for the nutritional aspects of The Gonzalez Protocol, which are discussed in the accompanying book, *Nutrition and the Autonomic Nervous System*. The cases in *Conquering Cancer: Volume Two* are organized according to a model described in detail in *Nutrition and the Autonomic Nervous System*. Based on work by Pavlov,[7] Funkenstein,[8] Gellhorn,[9] Pottenger,[10] Price,[11] and Kelley, The Gonzalez Protocol assigns each patient a diet and supplements based on his or her nutritional subtype. The nutritional subtype is derived from analysis of the person's autonomic balance.

3 Nicholas G. Gonzalez, *Conquering Cancer Volume One: 50 Pancreatic and Breast Cancer Patients on The Gonzalez Nutritional Protocol* (New York: New Spring Press, 2017); Nicholas G. Gonzalez, *Nutrition and the Autonomic Nervous System: The Scientific Foundations of The Gonzalez Protocol* (New York: New Spring Press, 2017).

4 Nicholas G. Gonzalez and Linda L. Isaacs, "Evaluation of Pancreatic Proteolytic Enzyme Treatment of Adenocarcinoma of the Pancreas, with Nutrition and Detoxification Support," *Nutrition and Cancer* 33 (1999): 117–24.

5 Nicholas G. Gonzalez, *One Man Alone: An Investigation of Nutrition, Cancer, and William Donald Kelley* (New York: New Spring Press, 2010).

6 United States Preventive Services Task Force, *The Guide to Clinical Preventive Services: Report of the United States Preventive Services Task Force*, 3rd ed. (New York: International Medical Publishers, 2002).

7 I. P. Pavlov, *Conditioned Reflexes* (New York: Dover Publications, 1984).

8 D. H. Funkenstein, S. H. King, and M. E. Drolette, *Mastery of Stress* (Cambridge, MA: Harvard University Press, 1957).

9 Ernst Gellhorn, *Autonomic Imbalance and the Hypothalamus* (Minneapolis: University of Minnesota Press, 1957); Ernst Gellhorn, *Principles of Autonomic-Somatic Integrations: Physiological Basis and Psychological and Clinical Implications* (Minneapolis: University of Minneapolis Press, 1967).

10 Francis M. Pottenger, *Pottenger's Cats: A Study in Nutrition* (Lemon Grove, CA: Price-Pottenger Nutritional Foundation, 1983); Francis M. Pottenger, *Symptoms of Visceral Disease: A Study of the Vegetative Nervous System in Its Relationship to Clinical Medicine* (London: Forgotten Books, 2015).

11 Weston A. Price, *Nutrition and Physical Degeneration* (Lemon Grove, CA: Price-Pottenger Nutritional Foundation, 2009).

According to the model, some individuals are sympathetic dominant, others are parasympathetic dominant, and others are balanced. The nutritional needs of the person vary by subtype, but so too do the types of cancers the person is most prone to develop. According to the model, sympathetic-dominant individuals are more likely to develop solid tumors, including cancers of the breast, lung, stomach, colon, pancreas, liver, uterus, ovaries, and prostate. Parasympathetic-dominant individuals, on the other hand, are more likely to develop immune system cancers, including leukemia, lymphomas, multiple myeloma, sarcomas, and melanoma.

Like all aspects of The Gonzalez Protocol, the nutritional subtypes component can be formulated as a set of scientifically testable hypotheses. That formulation of the nutritional subtypes element of the model is in development and will be provided elsewhere.

Colin A. Ross, MD

Introduction

⸻

The Gonzalez Protocol and Cancer

In my office, I offer The Gonzalez Protocol, an aggressive nutritional program for treatment of advanced cancer and a variety of other serious illnesses, ranging from chronic fatigue to multiple sclerosis. Whatever the underlying problem, this therapy involves three basic components: *individualized diets, individualized supplement protocols,* and *intensive detoxification.* The prescribed diets can range from vegetarian raw foods to an Atkins-type red meat approach. The supplement programs are equally as varied, involving vitamins, minerals, and trace elements in various forms and various doses, as well as glandular and enzyme products, each chosen to meet a particular need in each individual patient. The detoxification routines, often the most misunderstood component of the therapy, consist of coffee enemas and a variety of other techniques that actually have been adapted from the orthodox medical literature. I believe these procedures help the body neutralize and excrete the multitude of waste products produced during routine metabolism and, in the case of cancer patients, from tumor lysis.

Though I treat many diseases, I am perhaps best known for my work with advanced cancer. For patients suffering malignancy, The Gonzalez Protocol relies on large doses, spread throughout the day, of orally ingested pancreatic enzymes derived from a pig source. Though I believe the diets, vitamins, minerals, and trace elements help improve tissue and organ efficiency, in this therapy it is the pancreatic enzymes that target and kill cancer cells.

The enzyme treatment of cancer has a long history, beginning with Dr. John Beard, professor at the University of Edinburgh, who in 1902 first proposed that the pancreatic proteolytic enzyme trypsin might represent a powerful anticancer tool. Beard, an embryologist by training and interest, detoured into cancer research as a result of his studies of the mammalian placenta and its similarity to malignant tumors.

Beard was the first to report that in many respects the placenta in its early form behaves like a tumor. It begins growing as a very undifferentiated offshoot from the primitive embryo and then quickly invades the mother's uterus, much as a tumor infiltrates host tissue in any organ. Initially, the cells of the placenta proliferate almost without control, as tumors were known to do even in Beard's day, and it quite efficiently produces a dense blood supply—a requirement for any rapidly growing malignancy, as angiogenesis research today has made very clear.

As normal development proceeds, however, at some predetermined point the placenta transforms from a highly invasive, rapidly growing, blood vessel–producing tumor-like tissue, to the noninvasive, nonproliferating, mature organ. The only difference between the placenta and a malignant growth, Beard claimed, was that the placenta knows when to stop growing and tumors don't.

Dr. Beard eventually concluded that the key to the change lay in the embryonic pancreas. As witnessed in every species he studied, the day the placenta stops its cancer-like invasion of the mother is the very day the embryonic pancreas becomes active and begins pouring out enzymes.

Even in Beard's day, more than one hundred years ago, the main categories of pancreatic enzymes had already been identified: the proteolytic, or protein-digesting component; the lipases, which hydrolyze triglycerides; and the amylases, responsible for cleaving complex carbohydrates into simple, easily usable sugars. Physiologists of the time thought all three groups were active only in the duodenum, where the enzymes continue the breakdown of food arriving from the stomach. But Beard effectively provided the data to illustrate that above and beyond this function, trypsin, the main proteolytic enzyme, served to control placental growth and prevent the tissue from invading beyond the uterus as a true cancer might.

Beard then proposed that because the early placenta behaves much as a tumor does; because under the microscope its cells even look like undifferentiated, primitive neoplastic cells; and because pancreatic enzymes forcefully regulate its growth and development, these very same enzymes could be, and in fact must be, the body's main defense against cancer and would be useful as a cancer treatment.

Dr. Beard first tested his thesis in the one animal tumor model available at the time, the Jensen's mouse sarcoma. He injected an extract of trypsin into mice growing such cancers, and the tumors regressed.[1] Subsequently, during the first decade of the twentieth century, a number of physicians interested in Beard's hypothesis began, under his direction, to use injectable pancreatic enzymes to treat their human cancer patients. The successes were published in the

---

1 John Beard, "The Action of Trypsin upon the Living Cells of Jensen's Mouse-Tumor," *British Medical Journal* 4 (1906): 140–41.

major medical journals of the day, including *The Journal of the American Medical Association*[2] and *The British Medical Journal*.[3] I have read as many of these documents as I have been able to track down, and they remain to me compelling reports of patients surviving advanced cancer, such as one with a fungating sarcoma of the jaw, well beyond any chance of surgical cure, whose tumor under enzyme therapy regressed, then fell off.[4] The patient thereafter lived a normal, cancer-free life. Other articles described patients with metastatic colorectal[5] and uterine cancer,[6] as deadly today as in Beard's time, evidently disease-free after the enzyme treatment—all carefully documented and appropriately presented in the scientific literature.

The enzyme thesis, and the supporting animal and laboratory data, provoked an enormous and angry backlash against Beard and his followers. The Scotsman was vilified in editorials in medical journals, mocked in the newspapers, and belittled at scientific conventions. But Beard fought back in articles and letters to the editor, and in 1911, he published *The Enzyme Treatment of Cancer*,[7] a monograph outlining his decades of research and his promising and compelling results. However, despite such efforts, interest in Beard's thesis gradually petered out, and when he died in 1924, he died frustrated, angry, and ignored, his therapy already considered no more than a historical oddity.

After Beard's death, periodically other physicians and scientists rediscovered his work and kept the idea alive. During the 1920s and 1930s, a St. Louis physician, Dr. F. L. Morse, reported that he had successfully treated a number of advanced cancer patients with pancreatic enzymes. When he presented his well-documented findings to the St. Louis Medical Society in 1934—a proceeding published in the *Weekly Bulletin of the St. Louis Medical Society*[8]—his colleagues attacked rather viciously. One physician at the session, a Dr. M. G. Sleek, remarked, "While I heartily agree with Dr. Allen when he strikes the note of encouragement, I recoil at the idea of witlessly spreading the hope of a cancer cure which is implicit in the remarks of Dr. Morse this evening."

During the 1960s, the eccentric dentist Dr. William Kelley again rediscovered Beard's forgotten work and developed his own variation of enzyme treatment. In addition to large doses of orally ingested pancreatic enzymes, Kelley's program included individualized diets and supplement

---

2   James T. Campbell, "Trypsin Treatment of a Case of Malignant Disease," *Journal of the American Medical Association* 48 (1907): 225–26.

3   A. Cutfield, "Trypsin Treatment in Malignant Disease," *British Medical Journal* 5 (1907): 525.

4   John Beard, *The Enzyme Treatment of Cancer* (London: Chatto and Windus, 1911), 209.

5   Margaret A. Cleaves, "Pancreatic Ferments in the Treatment of Cancer and Their Role in Prophylaxis," *Medical Record* 70 (1906): 918.

6   F. B. Golley, "Two Cases of Cancer Treated by the Injection of Pancreatic Extract," *Medical Record* 70 (1906): 918–19.

7   Beard, *Enzyme Treatment of Cancer*.

8   F. L. Morse, "Treatment of Cancer with Pancreatic Enzymes," *Weekly Bulletin of the St. Louis Medical Society* 28 (1934): 599–603.

protocols, as well as detoxification routines. Dr. Kelley came to fame at a time of great repression organized against alternative medicine in general, and particularly against anyone suggesting that a nutritional treatment might have benefit against advanced cancer. Kelley was at particular risk because as a dentist, he was not legally entitled to treat cancer in the first place. He was repeatedly attacked in the press, vilified as a "quack," and investigated by numerous government agencies.

He was thrown in jail as a public menace, had his dental license revoked for five years for practicing medicine, spent his earnings defending himself against government assaults, and saw his family life fall apart. But he, like Beard, never relented, and he survived because his successes created an extraordinary word-of-mouth network that brought an endless stream of patients to his Grapevine, Texas, and later his Winthrop, Washington, offices.

I met Dr. Kelley by chance during the summer following my second year of medical school. At that time, he seemed completely modest and unassuming, seeking only to have his work properly evaluated so that if the approach had merit, it might become more widely accessible to patients in need. I was fortunate to have as a mentor at Cornell Medical College the late Robert A. Good, MD, PhD, who encouraged a review of Kelley's cases. Dr. Good, then president of the Sloan Kettering Research Institute, was the most published author in the history of the biomedical sciences, the "Father of Immunology," as the *New York Times* described him, the man who performed the first bone marrow transplant in history.

Under Dr. Good's direction, I began a student project evaluating Dr. Kelley's patients, methods, successes, and failures. Dr. Good told me that even if Kelley proved to be a fraud, I would learn much medicine from a project of my own choosing, developed out of my own enthusiasm.

Despite the eccentricities in Kelley's behavior that would only worsen until his death in 2005, I quickly found evidence of what appeared to be patient after patient with appropriately diagnosed, biopsy-proven advanced and even terminal cancer, who were alive five, even ten years after first beginning the enzyme therapy. What began as a mere student investigation evolved into a full-fledged research project, completed while I was a fellow in Dr. Good's group, which, after he was pushed out of Sloan, ended up in Florida at All Children's Hospital.

I eventually interviewed and evaluated more than a thousand of Kelley's patients and concentrated on a group of some 455. From this population, I wrote up in detail fifty cases, representing twenty-six different types of cancer. Even today, twenty years later, when I review my efforts, I am still impressed by Kelley's achievement. By 1986, I had put the results of my five-year investigation into monograph form and was excited by the prospect of publishing such unusual case reports and presenting the documentation for this nutritional, nontoxic treatment.

To my disappointment and surprise, despite my careful labors and serious intent, I could not get the book published either in its entirety as a monograph or as a summary journal article. The responses from editors ran the gamut from disbelief and accusations of fraud, to fear that the book would generate so much controversy that publishing careers might be ruined. No editor, even those who accepted the data as real, had the courage to take on the project.

This disappointment, our inability to get the study published, had a very damaging effect on Dr. Kelley. It appeared to him once again that all doors had closed, that his work would never be accepted for what he believed it was, a promising answer to a deadly disease. In 1986, he closed down his office and eventually disappeared from sight. After 1987, I never spoke to him again. I myself, determined to keep the enzyme therapy alive, left Dr. Good's group when I finished my fellowship and returned to New York City in 1987. I then began seeing patients myself, always with the hope of obtaining proper research support from the academic world.

In July of 1993, the National Cancer Institute (NCI) invited me to present case reports from my own practice, detailing patients with appropriately diagnosed poor-prognosis cancer who had enjoyed tumor regression or unusual survival while following my therapy. Dr. Linda Isaacs, my colleague, and I put together twenty-five cases for the session, attended by a large group of NCI scientists and lasting three hours. After the meeting, I was asked to pursue as a next step a pilot study evaluating my approach in ten patients diagnosed with advanced adenocarcinoma of the pancreas.

In such phase II studies, as they are technically called, a promising new therapy is administered to patients with an aggressive cancer for which there is no effective standard treatment. A pilot study involves no control group but can still give important information about a treatment. Because inoperable pancreatic cancer has such a grim prognosis, with an average survival in the range of three to six months, the associate director who chaired the meeting suggested that if I could get three patients to live a year, that would be a significant success. From my experience with enzymes, I expected to do even better.

We were fortunate to get funding for the study from Nestlé, the giant international food conglomerate. The then-vice president of the company in charge of research, Dr. Pierre Guesry, who had formerly been medical director of the Pasteur Institute in Paris, had learned of my work and become a supporter.

We finished the study and published the results in June 1999, in the peer-reviewed research journal *Nutrition and Cancer*.[9] We had eventually included eleven subjects, adding a patient when one dropped out. Of the eleven, all had biopsy-proven, inoperable disease; eight of the

---

9 Nicholas J. Gonzalez and Linda L. Isaacs, "Evaluation of Pancreatic Proteolytic Enzyme Treatment of Adenocarcinoma of the Pancreas, with Nutrition and Detoxification Support," *Nutrition and Cancer* 33 (1999): 117–24.

eleven had stage IV; and most had been very sick prior to consulting with us. All the patients were approved by a consulting oncologist and by the late Dr. Ernst Wynder, one of the premier cancer epidemiologists of the twentieth century.

Of the eleven patients, nine lived more than one year, five lived more than two years, four lived more than three years, and two lived beyond four years. As a point of reference, in the clinical trial of Gemzar, the latest drug approved for the disease, of 126 patients treated with chemotherapy not one lived longer than nineteen months.[10] Ours were results that had not previously been reported for the disease.

Shortly after publication of the article, the NCI approved funding for a large-scale, phase III clinical trial, again testing our enzyme approach in patients with advanced pancreatic cancer, but this time against a control group that would receive the best available chemotherapy. Eventually, the FDA approved the protocol, and the National Center for Complementary and Alternative Medicine offered to put up the required funding. Columbia University, under the chief of oncology at the time, and the chief of surgical oncology, became the supervising institution in New York, where the study would be run. Unfortunately, despite my earlier optimism, the project was sabotaged, beset by bureaucratic difficulties that are documented in my award-winning book, *What Went Wrong*.

Nonetheless, as the NCI study bogged down, my friend Dr. Guesry at Nestlé provided funding for studies to test the enzyme treatment in animal models, to provide supportive data to the human clinical trials. A group at the Eppley Cancer Institute of the University of Nebraska known for their investigations into the molecular biology of pancreatic cancer agreed to take on the challenge. Dr. Parviz Pour, the supervisor of the animal work at Nebraska, has himself developed mouse models of pancreatic cancer that are used to test promising new treatments against the disease.

In May 2004, the results of the experiments were published in the peer-reviewed journal *Pancreas*.[11] I am listed as a coauthor. In these studies, the researchers evaluated the effect of our enzymes in nude mice injected with human pancreatic cancer cells of a particularly virulent strain. These mice lack a functional immune system, so normally the tumors grow very rapidly and kill quickly. In the first study, which measured survival, the mice were divided into two groups, one receiving our enzymes, the other given no therapy. The animals treated with our enzymes survived significantly longer than the untreated control group.

10 H. A. Burris et al., "Improvements in Survival and Clinical Benefit with Gemcitabine as First-Line Therapy for Patients with Advanced Pancreas Cancer: A Randomized Trial," *Journal of Clinical Oncology* 15 (1997): 2403–13.

11 M. Saruc et al., "Pancreatic Enzyme Extract Improves Survival in Murine Pancreatic Cancer," *Pancreas* 28 (2004): 401–12.

Additionally, the enzyme mice appeared to be healthy, happy mice, even well into the study, in sharp contrast to the control mice, who were listless, inactive, bloated, and obviously quite ill. In fact, two of the mice in the treated group were doing so well they had to be sacrificed so the study could be brought to conclusion. I wonder how long they would have kept going.

In a second experiment, again the mice were divided into two groups—one administered our enzymes, the other group untreated. This time, animals were periodically sacrificed and evaluated for tumor growth. The enzymes clearly reduced the proliferation of the tumors, which in the treated mice remained small and very localized. In the controls, tumors were considerably larger and more invasive.

I want to emphasize that to me, the results are particularly significant because we have never used the enzymes to treat animals before; we decided to start at the dose per kilogram that we would normally use in humans. Inbred laboratory mice, however, metabolize most drugs far differently than we do, and normally doses much higher than what would be given humans must be administered to get an effect. Further, the experiments evaluated only the enzyme component of the treatment, not the additional vitamins, minerals, trace elements, and nutritious food we prescribe for our human patients. The animal chow also contained a fair amount of soy, which, however aggressively it may be pushed as a beneficial food, contains one of the most potent natural trypsin inhibitors known.

So I believe the results are important. As the authors wrote in the "Discussion" section, "In summary, PPE (Porcine Pancreatic Extracts) is the first experimentally and clinically proven agent for the effective treatment of PC (Pancreatic Cancer). The significant advantages of PPE over any other currently available therapeutic modalities include its effects on physical condition, nutrition, and lack of toxicity." Note that these results validate only the specific enzymes used in The Gonzalez Protocol and no other commercially available formulation.

Case Report Series

Conventional medical journals often publish case reports, that is, descriptions of individual patients whose disease might have taken an unusual course in response to some new treatment. Such "anecdotal" evidence, as it is technically called, contrasts with a controlled clinical trial, in which different treatments are given to large groups of patients with a particular illness and the results compared. Some scientists stubbornly insist that only such rigorous exercises, ideally pursued under the most stringent rules and regulations, can "prove" to everyone's satisfaction that a new treatment for a disease has any value. They often argue that case reports, these histories of individual patients, though perhaps interesting or entertaining, have little scientific merit.

My mentor, Dr. Good, one of the finest scientists of the twentieth century and the most published author in the history of medicine, always insisted that case reports, if properly written and carefully documented, can teach us much about the potential of a new approach. When I first began to evaluate Kelley's records, Dr. Good said that if I could find even one patient with appropriately diagnosed, biopsy-proven metastatic pancreatic adenocarcinoma who had lived five years under Kelley's care, he would be impressed, because no one else in medicine anywhere to his knowledge had such a case. Dr. Good's knowledge was indeed extensive, because he was at the time president of Sloan Kettering and an expert in the disease. A single example might not prove to everyone's satisfaction that the enzyme therapy had value, but it certainly should grab the attention of any fair-minded researcher.

In terms of cancer, a case report, to have value, must meet certain basic criteria:

1. The diagnosis must be confirmed by biopsy.

2. The stage must be confirmed by appropriate radiographic studies or surgical procedures.

3. The unusual response to treatment must be carefully defined, carefully explained, and carefully documented.

4. The endpoints, of most importance for cancer case reports, include objective evidence of improvement in the underlying disease, or unusual prolonged survival.

For patients with the typical solid epithelial tumors, disease regression can be verified by serial radiographic studies, such as PET or CT scans. For blood cell malignancies such as leukemia or myeloma, normalization of blood parameters, such as white count or blood protein, might be the marker followed over time.

Survival, if particularly unusual, can be a valid endpoint with or without evidence of disease regression. For this to be the chosen criterion, the patient in question must have lived far beyond the accepted medians and means for the disease. Such information on expected survival can be culled with some effort from a number of sources, both governmental and private, so comparisons can be made. The SEER (Surveillance, Epidemiology, and End Results) and American Cancer Society websites, for example, provide survival statistics, including medians and means, for many cancers. However, no precise definition of "significantly" prolonged survival really exists, so it becomes more of a judgment call in each case.

When I first presented at the NCI in July 1993, Dr. Michael Friedman, then the NCI's associate director of the Cancer Therapy Evaluation Program, said that if a patient of mine diagnosed with inoperable pancreatic cancer lived three months beyond the reported mean of six months, he wouldn't be impressed, whereas survival six months in excess of the standard averages would be meaningful. Of course, absolute values for "significance" will vary from cancer to cancer: six months of extra life might be unusual for a patient with a pancreatic neoplasm, but not so for a woman with metastatic breast cancer. In this case, two years beyond the mean would, to me, indicate an interesting response to treatment.

Traditionally, the National Cancer Institute, which sets the standards for all oncology worldwide, hasn't considered survival as a valid endpoint, only objective response as documented by radiographic or other tests. At the time I presented to the NCI in 1993, for epithelial cancers the NCI experts defined "response to treatment" as a 50 percent or greater reduction in tumor size that lasted at least four weeks. Unfortunately, as it has turned out, many chemotherapy drugs easily shrink tumors to this degree and within this time span, but the patients live no longer than if they had received no therapy. Tumor reduction, in chemotherapy studies, generally does not translate into longer life for the patient.

Though the phenomenon has long perplexed the research establishment—logically, one expects that if tumors shrink, patients should live longer—scientists now recognize that chemotherapy may kill the less aggressive population of cells and shrink tumors nicely, but then leave a small drug-resistant clone that quickly takes over and proliferates explosively. So, the selection for more virulent cells cancels out the initial benefit. In any event, I have long believed this particular definition of response, 50 percent reduction lasting four weeks, to be rather meaningless, because patients care more about their length of life, not necessarily the size of their tumors.

With The Gonzalez Protocol, I learned early on that at times tumors will reduce significantly or blood parameters will improve, to the great joy of patients, but at other times, the disease does not objectively regress, but instead stabilizes. We find patients in the "stabilized" group often survive as long as those enjoying radiographic or laboratory evidence of benefit, as long as they determinedly stick to their nutritional regimen.

During my 1993 NCI presentation, though I discussed a number of patients from my practice with documented disease reduction on standard testing, I also described several cases with long-term stabilization without proof of regression. I argued that in such instances the unusual survival should be considered as a response, regardless of what the radiographic or blood tests showed. I know if I had cancer, and had a choice between a ten-year survival but no radiographic evidence of improvement, or a six-week lifespan but impressive tumor reduction, I would choose the former within about a millisecond. Though I hardly assume my comments influenced anyone's thinking at the NCI, today the scientists there have reworked their definition of response to include not only radiographic or laboratory evidence of regression, but also significantly enhanced survival, with or without correlating "objective" documentation.

In the following case reports, I describe patients appropriately diagnosed with cancer who have survived far beyond what normally would be expected for their situation. For most, but not for all, I also provide evidence of tumor regression, often with complete resolution of their disease.

I would also like to make a point or two about my practice in general. Over the years, I have repeatedly heard the claim, from any number of sources, that I must be processing and treating thousands and thousands of new cancer patients each year. This is simply not the case, nor will it ever be, for a number of reasons. First of all, my approach to patients is extremely time consuming, requiring me to spend at least four to five hours with each new patient divided into two sessions over two separate days. My patients tend to be very sick people with often very long and complicated stories, so even basic history taking can be laborious.

Furthermore, I individualize each protocol, also a time-intensive process. Then, I must spend hours with each new patient reviewing the details of my complex therapy, which for most will be very new and often times very bewildering. Few, for example, will have experience with coffee enemas prior to meeting me.

My practice is not local in nature, and in fact most patients live some distance from New York. Consequently, I spend considerable time each day on the phone—at least two hours daily—dealing with the inevitable questions that come up regarding the protocol and its management, as well as the medical issues that my patients encounter as they fight their disease.

Because most of my patients have serious medical conditions, even office visits can run up to ninety minutes—not the ten minutes most conventional physicians might allocate. I don't have a revolving-door, assembly-line practice, nor would I want to have one. On the other hand, such time commitments reduce the number of new patients I can possibly see in any given week.

A good friend of mine, a scientist by training and a strong supporter of my work, recently remarked that I must be seeing "350–450" new cases of pancreatic cancer yearly, because I am well known for my success with this particular illness. I still don't know how he came up with these numbers, but he was completely surprised when I told him in reality we might see three to five new pancreatic patients a year, and no more. True, I do get many calls from those diagnosed with the disease, but most have already been heavily—and unsuccessfully—treated with aggressive chemotherapy and radiation. By the time they learn of The Gonzalez Protocol and call my office, most have already deteriorated into the final terminal stages of the disease and are at a point where I cannot help them.

I also want to add that a substantial number of patients, perhaps 30 percent of my total practice, come to me with noncancer problems, such as chronic fatigue, multiple sclerosis, environmental illness, and any manner of situations for which orthodox medicine offers little. The Gonzalez Protocol doesn't treat only cancer.

So, with those thoughts in mind, I present the following cancer case reports.

Nicholas J. Gonzalez, MD

A Few Dr. Gonzalez Patient Testimonials

—◆—

Breast Cancer:

"My thoughts regarding Dr. Nick Gonzalez, a man whose memory I will cherish forever. It was 1990, I was fifty years old, and my son was five. I was experiencing a burning sensation in my left breast and, upon the recommendation of a friend, I consulted a "breast specialist." I remember feeling petrified as I sat alone in an examining room, waiting for the doctor. The clack of her high heels preceded her entrance into the room. When she came in she told me her name, read the form I had filled out, and proceeded to examine my breasts. I couldn't help but notice that her perfectly manicured apple red nails were glistening from the bright overhead lights. She was silent until the brief examination was completed, at which time she told me she wasn't concerned with my left breast but that in the right breast she felt some lumps. "You need a mammogram and a biopsy," she said, standing in front of me without making eye contact and with her arms folded across her chest. See my secretary…she'll make the appointments. Then she left the room.

Dr. Nicholas J. Gonzalez was everything this person wasn't, both as a human being and as a doctor. More than a quarter of a century has passed since I have been following The Gonzalez Protocol. In the ensuing years, I was able to see my son graduate from lower school, high school, college, law school and I plan to attend his wedding in August of this year. Personally, I earned a Master's Degree, developed a new career, and have enjoyed a myriad of other life experiences. It is because I have "lived" Nick's protocol that I am alive all of these years. I think of him every day of my life, and always will."

—Margo Marin

—✥—

Lyme Disease:

"It has been almost three and one half years since (my daughter) Lindsay was stung by a bee carrying Lyme and that she was bedridden for over two years. I dare to think where our family and our beloved daughter would have been today if we hadn't met you (Dr. Gonzalez). I am so very grateful for your guidance, empathy, knowledge, and the enormity of your journey as a doctor. All words of thanks feel so trite, the magnitude of Lindsay's wellness so great…Lindsay will tell you that she would go through the entire experience again, if she knew that she would end up as solid, both emotionally and physically…I worry about what would happen to so many that are so ill and pray for your wellness and safety. You are a blessing."

—*Amy Goldman*

—✥—

Tourette's Syndrome:

"Just by sheer luck, I ran into a woman who had begun seeing Dr. Nicholas Gonzalez in New York who treated cancer and other degenerative illnesses alternatively. Tragically, he passed away a year ago. I've been on his program since 1993. It allowed me to go to grad school, be successful in my field, have girlfriends, and have good relationships with my friends.

Tourette's may be partly genetic… but you have to treat your body in a way that functionally makes sense. When you nourish your body and detoxify and get an understanding of nutrition in a functional way, it does marvelous things. Most of my ticks started going away. My cognitive functioning started improving, my hair started growing again. Tourette's may be partly genetic, but in its expression it is thoroughly dependent on its environment. You have to treat your body in a way that functionally makes sense. Don't eat crap. Don't breathe crap. Don't sleep next to crap—not with your cellphone next to your head nor with a person who doesn't treat you well."

—*Eric Gault*

—✥—

"It has been our greatest privilege to be patients of Dr. Nicholas Gonzalez for almost twenty years. He was a Hero to our family. We admired him and were intrigued by his bravery. Dr. Gonzalez stood by his wisdom and courageously supported and deeply cared for his patients. There was never a time that we didn't learn volumes of new information when we met with him, and he empowered us to develop healthy balanced bodies within the framework of each of our different metabolic types.

From the moment we met Dr. Gonzalez we knew that our health care was in the hands of an expert. We adored spending time with him during each of our visits, reviewing our progress on the program and working through different health concerns if applicable. Regular life interfered with our annual visits, and some years we had to miss our appointments with him. It was always a disappointment, because we loved spending time in Nick's presence, talking to him, and getting the evaluation and results of our progress on his program. We were supported to live a healthy lifestyle, eat organically, juice regularly, detox daily and take supplements, and we tried to follow this closely.

For over twenty years, our parents were also patients of Dr. Gonzalez, following diligently as "well patients"; they loved Nick, kept up an active lifestyle and never needed prescription medication of any kind until they reached almost 90. We all want that don't we?

Our family are some of the biggest fans of Nicholas Gonzalez, and he will always be alive in our hearts and lives. It is still unbelievable to us that he is not here and that we are not going to be able to see him again. We are excited to have his newest book, a compilation of his wisdom available to us. *Nutrition and the Autonomic Nervous System: The Scientific Foundations of The Gonzalez Protocol* offers insight into the brilliance of a humble man, a visionary and proves why we must keep his therapy alive. Dr. Nicholas Gonzalez changed our lives!"

—*Katherine and Steve Zeiser*

PART I:

Sympathetic-Dominant Cancers

ADENOID CYSTIC CANCER

Case 1: Patient CC
An 18-Year Survivor

Patient CC was seventy-seven years old when he passed away from adenoid cystic carcinoma of the trachea with metastases to the lung. He had had a history of cigar smoking but had been in good health when he developed the sensation of a nodule on the left side of his throat in 1977. His physician thought the symptoms were insignificant, and no diagnostic tests were pursued. Over the following three years, the sensation gradually worsened. When Patient CC developed wheezing and dyspnea on exertion, he returned to his physician, who initially told him he had emphysema and arthritis of the neck but finally referred him to a pulmonologist, who suspected a chronic infection and prescribed various antibiotics and other medications for a year, with no effect.

Finally, Patient CC was referred for a CT of the trachea in June 1981, which revealed a large tumor of the tracheal wall at the level of the thoracic inlet. Later that month, he underwent transcervical and transthoracic resection of the trachea with primary anastomosis and suprahyoid laryngeal release. Pathological examination showed adenoid cystic carcinoma. He subsequently received 6,000 rads to the tumor bed.

Patient CC then did well until November 1987, when a routine chest X-ray demonstrated multiple pulmonary nodules. A CT scan showed bilateral hilar adenopathy and multiple pulmonary nodules bilaterally. A needle biopsy of a lesion in December 1987 revealed metastatic adenoid cystic carcinoma. At that time, Patient CC's doctors told him and his wife that he might live another six months to a year, two years if he was fortunate.

Patient CC learned of my work and was first seen in my office in May 1988. At that time, he had no complaints and was on no medications. His examination was notable only for psoriasis. He began his nutritional protocol soon after seeing me. Initially, he was highly compliant, but then in April 1989 at an office visit he reported that he was missing doses of the pancreatic enzymes, the cornerstone of the method I use, and cheating on his diet, eating at fast food restaurants. However, he was feeling quite well. At a subsequent visit in November 1990, according to my office notes, he was "at best vaguely following the diet," and missing at least one of his daily doses of enzymes regularly.

In August 1992, a chest X-ray showed that his pulmonary metastases had increased in number and size. However, he was feeling very well and had already outlived the dismal prognosis his physician had given him when his pulmonary metastases were discovered. From that point on, he decided to dispense with any follow-up testing.

Over the next several years, he came in for office visits every one to two years, less frequently than I would have liked. He always reported excellent compliance with the detoxification routines such as the coffee enemas, which made him feel better. He reported fairly good compliance with the supplements but continued to have frequent dietary lapses. Interestingly, his psoriasis, which had been a significant complaint when he was first seen, gradually resolved. In a visit in April 1996, he stated that he felt "fantastic" and was "biking for miles." On many of his visits, he marveled about how he had been told he had two years to live back in 1987.

In August 1997, he developed widespread musculoskeletal pain. After a bone scan showed no evidence of spread of his cancer, he was found to have a high erythrocyte sedimentation rate. He improved his dietary compliance while continuing his nutritional protocol, and his symptoms started to improve. Nonetheless, he received a short course of prednisone for possible polymyalgia rheumatica. In an office visit in May 1998, he reported he was once again feeling wonderful, and the musculoskeletal pain never recurred.

In visits in 1999 and in 2001, he continued to report cheating on the diet and less than 100 percent compliance with his supplements. Then in February 2003, during routine cataract surgery, a very small mass was noted on ultrasound in the tissue by the right eye, 2 × 5.5 × 3.5 mm. Both his ophthalmologist and I suggested follow-up imaging studies, but he refused, because he felt well. Around the same time, he decided to call the doctor who had given him the bleak prognosis in 1987, and he told me that the doctor was amazed that he was still alive.

I did not hear from Patient CC from mid-2003 until early 2005. At that time, I received a letter from his wife, letting me know that he had developed pneumonia in June 2004, which was treated with antibiotics. Then in January 2005, he was taken to the hospital with a high fever and low blood pressure. A CT scan showed bilateral tumors in his lungs as well as infiltrates consistent with pneumonia; no abnormalities were seen in his abdomen.

He was treated with antibiotics with improvement, and at the time his wife wrote me, he was back home and back on his protocol. I called immediately on receipt of the letter and increased his pancreatic enzyme dose. I also encouraged full adherence to all aspects of the nutritional program.

In an April 2005 office visit, he reported continued compromise with his diet but compliance with the other aspects of the protocol. His energy and stamina had improved; he was exercising and could go up the flight of stairs in his home.

Then, in February 2006, he became short of breath and was admitted to the hospital. Scans showed large pulmonary masses that had worsened from the study one year previously, as well as evidence of pneumonia. He was treated with antibiotics and inhalers. Biopsy of a lung mass confirmed metastatic adenoid cystic carcinoma, and he was seen by an oncologist, who offered chemotherapy and radiation despite what was described in the note as a "low likelihood of getting cured." According to his wife, the doctors were amazed that he was still alive eighteen years after diagnosis of metastatic disease, but they were completely dismissive of the treatment option he had chosen.

He improved enough for discharge but never returned to his baseline state, struggling with poor food intake and dehydration. Then, in April 2006, he passed away at home suddenly. His wife sent me a letter filled with gratitude for all the extra years she had been given with her husband.

In Patient CC's case, I can only speculate as to why he did not get the resolution of disease that other patients in my practice have seen. His compliance with his protocol was not perfect, as he himself admitted, and this may have meant that his cancer's growth was slowed but not stopped.

Adenoid cystic carcinoma is not a common cancer, and it can sometimes have an indolent course, but when the lung metastases were found, Patient CC's physician had no hesitation about telling him his days were numbered. In a 1996 review of similar patients, mean survival was thirty-seven months (four months to seven years) from the time of diagnosis of the pulmonary metastasis until death.[1] Patient CC lived more than eighteen years after the biopsy-proven diagnosis of pulmonary metastases from his adenoid cystic carcinoma, having received no other form of treatment besides his nutritional protocol. Despite his eventual death from his disease, Patient CC's course is certainly unusual.

---

1   D. E. Maziak et al., "Adenoid Cystic Carcinoma of the Airway: Thirty-Two-Year Experience," *Journal of Thoracic and Cardiovascular Surgery* 112, no. 6 (1996):1522–31.

BLADDER CANCER

The great majority of cancers in the urinary tract, about 95 percent, originate in the transitional cell epithelium that lines the system from the kidney pelvis to the first two-thirds of the urethra. Of these malignancies, 90 percent form in the bladder itself.

According to *Harrison's*, in 2010 70,530 new cases of bladder cancer were diagnosed in the US, with 14,680 deaths reported. Scientists link this malignancy with some certainty to cigarette smoking, considered responsible for 50 percent of all cases. The incidence shows a disparity in terms of gender, with the incidence three times higher in men than in women.[1]

At the time of diagnosis, some 75 percent of transitional cell neoplasms involve only the superficial lining of the bladder, 20 percent have penetrated into the underlying muscle, and 5 percent have already metastasized to distant sites. For superficial or minimally invasive disease, resection of the lesion via cystoscopy (insertion of a tube through the urethra into the bladder) remains the primary treatment of choice. *Harrison's* reports a recurrence rate, even for strictly superficial disease, in the range of 50 percent after surgery; in up to 20 percent of this group of patients, the cancer will advance to a more invasive stage.

Often, transitional cell carcinoma of the bladder presents in a multifocal pattern, with numerous lesions present. In this case, again surgical excision of all visible tumor remains the treatment of choice. With deeply penetrating lesions, or should the disease return repeatedly, cystectomy, complete removal of the bladder, is the preferred option.

For patients with recurrent disease, or with cancer involving more than 40 percent of the bladder, urologists recommend intravesical adjuvant drug treatment after removal of all visible or accessible tumor, involving instillation of certain medications directly into the bladder. Bacillus Calmette-Guérin (BCG), an attenuated live tuberculosis vaccine with antitransitional carcinoma action, is the most commonly recommended agent. Usually, patients undergo weekly treatments for six weeks, followed by monthly treatments for a year or more. Other agents sometimes used in this context include the chemotherapy drugs mitomycin-C and gemcitabine, and the immunotherapy modulator interferon.

The prognosis for invasive and metastatic disease remains poor, though with aggressive chemotherapy regimens, patients can experience complete, though temporary, remissions.

---

1   Dan L. Longo, Anthony S. Fauci, Dennis L. Kasper, Stephen L. Hauser, J. Larry Jameson, and Joseph Loscalzo, eds., *Harrison's Principles of Internal Medicine*, 18th ed. (New York: McGraw Hill, 2012), 790.

Case 1: Patient FZ
A Minimum 19.3-Year Survivor

Patient FZ is an eighty-two-year-old man, a PhD engineer from New Jersey with a history of recurrent bladder cancer.

In terms of relevant family history, Patient FZ's father died of stomach cancer. In terms of his own health history, FZ had never smoked, nor had he been exposed to any toxic chemicals in his work or at home. Other than a two-year history of poor sleep, he had generally been in excellent health when in June 1992 he experienced a single episode of mild hematuria, for which he did not seek medical advice. When in late October 1992 he passed a significant amount of blood, he consulted with his primary care physician, who referred Patient FZ to a local urologist. Cystoscopy performed during the second week of November 1992 revealed a left lateral bladder wall tumor, confirmed by biopsy to be transitional cell carcinoma.

At that point, Patient FZ decided to consult at Memorial Sloan Kettering Cancer Center in New York, where he was first seen during the third week of November 1992. A review of the prior slides from the New Jersey urologist confirmed transitional cell carcinoma of the bladder, grade II/III, indicating a moderately aggressive histology. Repeat cystoscopy at Memorial revealed a single 2 cm papillary tumor on the left bladder wall, which the surgeon excised. Evaluation of the specimen again revealed grade II/III transitional cell carcinoma, but for some reason, the level of invasion could not be assessed.

Postoperatively, because Patient FZ had evidence of only a single lesion, the Memorial urologist did not suggest adjuvant therapy with BCG or chemotherapy. Patient FZ was informed that he needed to be followed closely to track possible recurrence, with cystoscopy recommended every two months initially.

Thereafter, Patient FZ seemed to do well. During the first week of January 1993, he was admitted to Memorial Hospital for a scheduled repeat cystoscopy. A preoperative urine cytology test turned out positive for transitional cell carcinoma, indicating recurrent disease. During the cystoscopy procedure, the urologist found no visible evidence of tumor but, because of the positive urine cytology, performed numerous biopsies "randomly" at various sites including the area of the original tumor.

The pathology report described recurrent disease in the neck of the bladder, not the previous lesion:

> URINARY BLADDER, NECK, BIOPSY:
>
> TRANSITIONAL CELL CARCINOMA INVOLVING VON BRUNN'S NESTS

In addition, postoperative urine cytology was positive for transitional cell carcinoma. At this point, his urologist at Memorial suggested a course of intravesical BCG vaccine treatment, which Patient FZ refused. His urologist, however, insisted he needed follow-up cystoscopy every three months for close surveillance.

Patient FZ, who had an interest in yoga and natural healing, began investigating unconventional approaches to cancer. After learning about our work, he contacted our office in mid-March 1993, and after reviewing his history we accepted him into our practice. Although he did set up the initial two appointments for late March 1993, he canceled, thinking at the time he might have been cured by his surgery.

During the first week of April 1993, repeat cystoscopy at Memorial revealed recurrent tumor, which was resected and found positive for transitional cell carcinoma. At a follow-up cystoscopy in July 1993, his urologist excised another single tumor consistent with transitional cell carcinoma. In September 1993, cystoscopy indicated multiple suspicious areas that were resected and again found to be recurrent transitional cell carcinoma. This time around, Patient FZ experienced a very difficult postoperative course, with difficulty voiding and significant pain. He ended up staying at Memorial for several days for observation, before being released. By this point, he had now experienced six episodes of transitional cell carcinoma, with the most recent indicating his disease had become more aggressive, involving as it did multiple sites.

With his situation worsening, during the third week of October 1993 Patient FZ again contacted our office, wishing to set up the introductory appointments. By that time, I had been in practice for six years and had already dealt with a number of patients we had accepted into the practice who seemed enthusiastic about the treatment but set up appointments only to cancel. Then, they contacted us at some later day in a considerably worsened condition, wishing to start our treatment. We had found such patients usually weren't adequately committed to follow through with the rigorous regimen, so we had instituted a policy to suggest the patient go elsewhere for treatment. In this particular case, Patient FZ strongly argued the case with my staff member responsible for the intake interviews, saying he really thought, as it turned out incorrectly, that he had been cured by surgery. According to my assistant, he appeared to be very determined to pursue our treatment properly, so I agreed to set up the appointments.

When Patient FZ and I first met, during the third week of November 1993, he was still recovering from his most recent hospitalization at Memorial. He reported his energy had been improving, but he still experienced significant urinary difficulties, described as nocturia three to four times, some urgency, and difficulty starting his urinary stream, but no hematuria (blood in the urine). Otherwise, he felt generally well. He did report his Memorial doctors had already broached the issue of BCG treatment, which he was not interested in pursuing.

Though it took some weeks before Patient FZ was fully compliant with the treatment, thereafter Patient FZ proved to be very diligent with the prescribed regimen. He called with an occasional question, and when I saw him next, in mid-April 1994, after he had completed some four months on his nutritional program, he reported that cystoscopy at Memorial two months earlier in February 1994 had, for the first time, been "clean," with no evidence of recurrent cancer. Clinically, he generally felt well, reporting that his urinary symptoms had significantly improved.

Because he lived close to Manhattan, in suburban New Jersey, Patient FZ subsequently returned to my office every three months or so. During these visits, he seemed quite compliant with the therapy and described gradual improvement in his various urinary symptoms. As it turned out, despite my initial reservations he turned out to be very dedicated to the therapy, a low-maintenance patient who followed my instructions and rarely called with any questions.

When I saw him during the first week of December 1994, when he had completed a full year on his treatment, Patient FZ seemed compliant with his regimen and reported feeling "overall better" with "steady" improvement in his general health. Long-standing sleep problems had resolved, and his urination continued to improve. At his last visit to Memorial Hospital in September 1994, cystoscopy once again showed no evidence of recurrent cancer.

During the third week of February 1995, Patient FZ returned to my office for a routine office visit. I learned that he had recently consulted with a local urologist in New Jersey, who some weeks earlier had performed cystoscopy. The urologist could find no evidence of recurrent cancer, only scar tissue from the multiple previous procedures at Memorial Hospital. The physician did suggest some additional surgery to clear out the scars, but because his urination continued to improve, Patient FZ decided against any unnecessary intervention.

In May 1995, screening urine cytology ordered by his local urologist was "Negative for Malignant Cells."

In mid-June 1995, after Patient FZ had completed eighteen months on his therapy, he returned to my office for a routine visit. Apparently compliant with all aspects of the regimen, he reported feeling stronger and better with each passing month. His once-serious urinary symptoms had, by his report, completely resolved. He also continued under the care of his local urologist, whom he was scheduled to see several weeks later.

During his next visit with me, the third week of September 1995, nearly two years after our first meeting together, he reported he had gone camping with his family for two weeks, all the while sticking to his nutritional regimen—including the coffee enemas. By that point, he told me he was feeling very well indeed, with no problems whatsoever, including with his urination.

Three months later, in late December 1995, Patient FZ returned to my office, informing me that his most recent cystoscopy two weeks earlier had been "completely clear." However, I was concerned that now, two years into treatment, Patient FZ admitted his compliance had fallen off. Routinely, he acknowledged missing one to two doses of the all-important pancreas supplement daily, and he said he had been eating more animal protein than the prescribed diet recommended. He had been feeling so well, he explained, it had been easy for him to justify some carelessness with the regimen. I lectured him about the need to remain compliant with the therapy even two years out and, despite the repeat clean cystoscopies, to avoid a recurrence down the road.

When I saw him next, during the last week of February 1996, his compliance had improved considerably, and he generally felt well. He had experienced a bout of gastroenteritis some weeks earlier, which resolved with no residual effects.

I didn't see him again until late June 1996, when he returned to my office for his regularly scheduled visit, now having completed two and a half years on his nutritional program. An ultrasound of the pelvis some two weeks earlier at Mt. Sinai Hospital in New York was "clear." Unfortunately, his compliance had again fallen off somewhat, though not catastrophically. He admitted missing a dose of enzymes a day—not disastrous, but certainly not advisable. He had been in California for two weeks on vacation, during which time his diet, as he said, had been less than ideal.

I gently lectured him about the need for continued vigilance with the supplements and diet despite his recent clean cystoscopies. Clinically he felt fine, with no urinary symptoms—even his weak stream had normalized, and his nocturia was down to once nightly, a significant improvement over the years.

During the second week of September 1996, while walking near his home, Patient FZ experienced a brief episode of chest tightness, associated with shortness of breath and nausea. When we spoke by phone, his symptoms had resolved and he felt well. Nonetheless, I told him he should go to the local emergency room, explaining that chest pain should never be ignored. Despite my instructions, Patient FZ did not go to the hospital, informing me the next day he felt "fine."

When he next returned to my office, in late September 1996, approaching three years on his treatment, his compliance appeared to have improved. Though he reported no further episodes of chest tightness, I insisted he should have a cardiac workup. After much coaxing, he agreed to follow up with his local internist. In terms of his bladder cancer, he reported that he was scheduled to see his local urologist in October 1996.

Fortunately, when a subsequent EKG was within normal limits, his internist felt no further workup was needed. And the planned cystoscopy in January 1997 was again completely clear.

In late November 1996, Patient FZ called with some simple questions. I would not hear from him again for seven years, when in mid-November 2003 he called my office out of the blue—ten years after he had first consulted with me. He spoke at length with my office assistant, explaining he had called to let me know how well he was doing after all these years, and how grateful he was for my past help.

My assistant wrote an extensive note about the conversation:

> He called to express his immense gratitude for the program. He recently celebrated his 11 year anniversary of good health and was overflowing with praise and appreciation for the program which he credits to [sic] saving his life.
>
> He would love to take you to lunch sometimes to express these things personally.

At my instruction, my assistant called him back to express my gratitude for the call and for his kind thoughts about my efforts.

In March 2013, in preparation for this document, I searched the Social Security death index. Patient FZ was not listed, indicating that more than twenty years since his original biopsy diagnosis in November 1992, he was still alive. We have tried to track him down through his old address from our 1993 chart but have been unsuccessful. I hope he is enjoying his life somewhere in some warm tropical climate.

Though bladder cancer can be cured with surgery when localized, frequent recurrences over a short period of time as in the case of Patient FZ predict an aggressive cancer with an increased tendency to invade and spread. After his initial surgery at Memorial Hospital in November 1992, he experienced four recurrences over the next ten months, at different sites from the original tumor. However, after Patient FZ began his nutritional program in December 1993, repeat cystoscopies in subsequent years showed no evidence of recurrent transitional cell cancer.

COLON CANCER

In 2004, 146,940 new cases of colon cancer were reported in the United States, and 56,730 deaths, making the disease the second leading cancer killer.[1] Only tumors of the lung claim more lives. The overall incidence has remained fairly steady over the past thirty years, while the mortality rate has dropped, perhaps due to public awareness campaigns emphasizing early diagnosis and regular colonoscopy in those over fifty, the population most vulnerable to the disease.

Scientists over the years have proposed a number of causative factors, including inherited genetic abnormalities that may play a role in some 25 percent of all cases. Familial syndromes such as polyposis coli, in which afflicted family members can develop literally thousands of colonic polyps, significantly increase the risk for colon malignancies, as does inflammatory bowel disease, particularly ulcerative colitis. Colon cancer develops in up to 30 percent of patients with a history of colitis for more than 25 years.

Much if not most colon cancer has been linked to environmental factors, particularly diet. A number of studies support an association with a high intake of animal fat, presumably due to conversion of saturated fatty acids to carcinogenic compounds in the gut. A correlation between high serum cholesterol, obesity, and colon cancer has also been proposed. However, recent studies suggest that fiber in the diet has little influence on incidence rates despite early positive reports claiming a protective effect.

Clinicians traditionally divide colon cancer into a four-tiered "Dukes" staging system based on the depth of tumor penetration in the bowel wall and named after the researcher who in the 1930s first proposed the schemata. In this hierarchy, Dukes A identifies cancer limited to the superficial layers of the colon with no invasion of underlying tissues. Dukes B indicates the tumor has invaded through the bowel wall but not into regional lymph nodes. Dukes C signifies the disease has spread into local lymph nodes, and Dukes D, the worst, means the disease has metastasized to distant organs such as the liver or lungs. Survival correlates directly with the Dukes stage at the time of diagnosis; more than 90 percent of patients with Dukes A live five years, while only 5 percent, if that many, of those classified as Dukes D last that long.

Studies going back fifteen years confirm that chemotherapy with 5-fluorouracil and leucovorin administered after surgical resection of Dukes C tumors improves five-year survival by about

1   Dennis L. Kasper, Eugene Braunwald, Anthony S. Fauci, Stephen L. Hauser, Dan L. Longo, and J. Larry Jameson, Harrison's Principles of Internal Medicine, 16th ed. (New York: McGraw-Hill, 2005), Robert J. Mayer, 527.

10 percent compared with those undergoing surgery alone. However, aggressive chemotherapy offers little long-term benefit once the disease has spread to distant sites.

In our own practice, we have found that previous aggressive chemotherapy with multiple toxic drugs lessens the chance for success. The patients who have done the best with us, regardless of the extent of their disease, have refused the standard drug approach to pursue our regimen.

Case 1: Patient IL
*A Minimum 15-Year Survivor**

Patient IL is a fifty-seven-year-old man with a family history pertinent because of a brain cancer in his mother, colon cancer in an uncle, and lung cancer in a second uncle.

He himself had generally been in very good health when, beginning in 2000, he noticed a change in his bowel habits, including increased mucus in his stools, chronic indigestion, bloating, and what he described as gas pains. He adopted a whole-foods, vegetarian way of eating, hoping for some relief, but over time his symptoms only worsened.

In mid-2001, he first noticed intermittent bright red blood in his stools. Some months later, in October 2001, he developed symptoms consistent with a bowel obstruction, including severe pain, bloating, abdominal distension, and an inability to move his bowels. When the symptoms resolved after several hours, he chose not to seek medical attention.

Several weeks later, in November 2001, the symptoms returned with a vengeance. He hoped once again to ride out the crisis, but over a three-day period the pain, bloating, and distension worsened to the point that he finally went to the local emergency room. A barium enema revealed an "apple core" lesion in the sigmoid colon indicating a tumor. When a subsequent sigmoidoscopy revealed a complete obstruction, the patient underwent emergency laparotomy, resection of the sigmoid colon along with the tumor, and placement of a temporary colostomy. The surgeon also discovered, as his operative note reported, "palpable nodules in the liver, which I felt to be more cystic than solid, but there were a couple studs that were solid." He removed one of the liver lesions for evaluation.

The pathologist's summary described a large colon tumor but didn't give exact dimensions, though it stated, "The mass locally grossly appears to extend to the underlying adipose tissue," and defined the tumor as "moderately differentiated adenocarcinoma, extending through the bowel wall, and present on the serosal surface." Though cancer had infiltrated two of nine lymph nodes examined, the liver tissue seemed most consistent with a benign hemangioma.

Postoperatively, a CEA (carcinoembryonic antigen) test, a tumor marker for colon cancer, came back elevated at 5.1 (with normal less than 3), an indication of remaining malignant activity. No CEA had been done before surgery, so there were no results for comparison.

IL did subsequently meet with an oncologist, who suspected the tumor had invaded the liver, despite the negative biopsy. He insisted chemotherapy needed to begin quickly, but upon questioning admitted that if the cancer had indeed spread, treatment would do little. IL, who already had a strong interest in alternative medicine, decided to refuse conventional treatment and instead began self-medicating with a variety of nutritional supplements. After learning about our work from a local chiropractor, he chose to proceed with our treatment. He contacted our office in early January 2002, but we suggested he come in only after reversal of his colostomy.

Because the patient had been rushed into surgery in crisis from an obstruction, no preoperative CT scan had been done. Finally, in mid-January, his doctors pushed for a scan, which revealed evidence of multiple metastatic lesions in the liver, as the official report described: "Unfortunately, within the liver there are numerous small hypo-enhancing lesions, some of these are very hypo enhancing to the point where one might consider cysts, but others are more intermediate density. 5 mm thick slices were obtained to increase the sensitivity. The largest of these lesions is only about 1 × 1.5 cm. These are suspicious for metastatic disease."

The radiologist also noted "very minimal subpleural densities seen at the mid left lung field," which he felt "should be rechecked within several months." In his summary, he reported, "I suppose the liver findings increase suspicions of the left lower lobe findings however my feeling is that the lung changes will prove to be benign."

Quite likely, based on the CT findings, cancer had spread into the liver and possibly to the lungs. The negative liver biopsy, the patient was told, might indicate only that the liver contained both benign and malignant nodules, as the CT scan seemed to show.

In late January 2002, the patient returned to surgery for reversal of the colostomy and lysis of adhesions that had formed since the first operation. During the procedure, unfortunately, none of the liver lesions was biopsied.

When IL was first seen in my office, in mid-March 2002, he seemed enthusiastic about the therapy and subsequently followed the regimen faithfully. Today, more than 14.5 years on my treatment, he remains fully compliant and enjoys excellent health.

Over the years that he has been my patient, IL has chosen not to undergo any further CT scans, a decision I have respected. He says that no matter what the scans show, he wouldn't agree to chemotherapy nor would he change his treatment. He doesn't want the radiation exposure, which is significant; the worry; or the expense. So, I have no idea what has happened to the liver, or its lesions; I know only that the patient is alive and well.

Even if we disregard the CT liver findings for a moment, a number of salient signs point toward a dismal prognosis. The literature has reported that patients who initially present with an obstructing lesion have a far worse prognosis than do those who don't, even if the disease is otherwise localized. DeVita has stated in this regard, "The presence of obstruction has been found to reduce the 5-year survival rate to 31%, as compared with 72% for patients without obstruction."[2]

Furthermore, in this patient's case, the fact that the tumor had already invaded through the bowel wall and infiltrated into two lymph nodes signaled future trouble. The CEA level after surgery, though only mildly elevated, nonetheless also warned of a future recurrence—regardless of what may have been going on in the liver. *Harrison's* has reported that a high CEA before surgery, whatever the stage, suggests a poor prognosis: "Regardless of the clinicopathological stage, a preoperative elevation of the plasma carcinoembryonic antigen (CEA) level predicts eventual tumor recurrence."[3]

IL's elevated postoperative CEA served as an even more worrisome prognostic indicator. But finally, if we accept the expert radiologist's conclusion that cancer had infiltrated the liver, the prognosis turns dire. DeVita reported median survivals in the range of 4.2 to 8.7 months for patients diagnosed with metastatic colon cancer receiving aggressive chemotherapy.[4] In a large-scale study, Manfredi et al. reported that one- and five-year survival rates were 34.8 percent and 3.3 percent for synchronous liver metastases (meaning liver metastases occurring at the time of the original diagnosis of colon cancer).[5] These statistics include patients with solitary liver lesions, which can at times be resected along with the primary colon tumor, allowing for long-term survival. In this case, IL, with multiple malignant-appearing tumors on CT scan, not only has far outlived the predicted lifespan but has successfully avoided the toxic treatments his oncologist insisted needed to be done.

*Important Editor's Note:
Dr. Gonzalez died before he was able to update some of these case reports. Therefore, we have updated the survival time for this patient based on his contact with Dr. Gonzalez's widow, Mary Beth Gonzalez in March 2017.

---

2   Vincent T. DeVita, Jr., Samuel Hellman, and Steven A. Rosenberg, eds., *Cancer: Principles and Practice of Oncology*, 6th ed. (Philadelphia: Lippincott William & Wilkins, 2001), 1227.
3   Kasper et al., *Harrison's Principles*, 16th ed., 530.
4   DeVita et al., *Cancer: Principles and Practice*, 6th ed., 1227.
5   Sylvain Manfredi, Côme Lepage, Cyril Hatem, Olivier Coatmeur, Jean Faivre, and Anne-Marie Bouvier, "Epidemiology and Management of Liver Metastases from Colorectal Cancer," *Annals of Surgery* 224, no. 2 (2006): 254–59.

Case 2: Patient II
A Minimum 3.8-Year Survivor

Patient II is an eighty-eight-year-old woman trained in the sciences whose father died from a glioblastoma brain tumor and whose mother survived lymphoma before dying from heart disease. In terms of her past medical history, Patient II had smoked one pack a day for some twenty years, before quitting at age forty-eight. She had undergone a hysterectomy and bilateral salpingo-oophorectomy for uterine fibroids, and bilateral hip replacements because of advanced arthritis. During a period of business stress in the 1990s, she developed chronic fatigue, for which she consulted a variety of local alternative practitioners in the New York City area. She was treated with a variety of nutrients, including intravenous vitamin C for six months. She eventually came under the care of Robert Atkins, MD, the famed diet doctor and nutritional physician, who helped her situation, as she would tell me, significantly.

Patient II had a long history of interest in nutritional and alternative approaches dating back some thirty years and had experimented with diet and supplements even before her bout with chronic fatigue. After her treatment with Dr. Atkins, she followed an organic, whole-foods, largely vegetarian type of diet.

Patient II had been doing well when in early January 2009 she first experienced gradually worsening abdominal discomfort and pain associated with intermittent distension. Initially, she did not seek medical advice, but in mid-January 2009 her condition worsened, with new-onset nausea and emesis. At that point, she consulted a physician at a nearby urgent care facility, who diagnosed only indigestion, for which he prescribed medication for pain and nausea. But when her situation deteriorated significantly over the next twenty-four hours, she contacted her primary care physician, who instructed her to go at once to the emergency room at a local New Jersey hospital. She was found to be "profoundly dehydrated," with a very low potassium at 2.7 (normal 3.3–5.1) and a low sodium level at 129 (normal 135–145).

An x-ray revealed bilateral pleural effusions, and a CT scan of the abdomen showed an "annular obstructing rectosigmoid carcinoma." After being stabilized, the following day Patient II underwent exploratory laparotomy and was found to have an obstructing lesion in the midsigmoid as well as a nodule in the left liver lobe. The surgeon resected both the colon and the liver lesions. The pathology report described the large sigmoid tumor as a "MODERATELY DIFFERENTIATED ADENOCARCINOMA OF THE COLON, 5.5 × 4.4 CM IN DIMENSION," with all eighteen lymph nodes evaluated free of malignancy. However, the liver tissue proved consistent with "METASTATIC ADENOCARCINOMA WITH EXTENSIVE NECROSIS, CONSISTENT WITH COLON PRIMARY."

When she met with her surgeon for a routine postoperative visit, he was not optimistic about her prognosis, stating she might live a year if she were lucky, even with chemotherapy. While still hospitalized, Patient II did meet with an oncologist, who strongly suggested she begin aggressive multiagent chemotherapy immediately. But with her long interest in nutrition and alternative medicine, Patient II decided to refuse the recommended conventional treatment. When she explained her decision to the oncologist, she later reported to me he appeared disappointed with her choice but not hostile to her wish to proceed with an unconventional approach.

After her discharge from the hospital, Patient II spent a week in a rehabilitation center before returning home the third week in February 2009. Subsequently, Patient II consulted with several alternative practitioners before meeting with her surgeon in March 2009 for a routine follow-up visit. Though he respected her decision to proceed with an unconventional treatment, he suggested a consultation with a second oncologist simply so she could explore all options thoroughly. Because the surgeon's recommendation seemed reasonable, several days later Patient II did meet with the oncologist, who discussed the conventional approaches but did not aggressively push for additional treatment. Patient II did bring up the subject of non-traditional cancer therapies, which the oncologist dismissed out of hand as useless.

At that point, although Patient II still chose to decline standard treatment, she agreed to some additional testing, including blood work and a PET scan. A CEA test, a blood marker for colon cancer, came back mildly elevated at 4.18 (normal 0.0–2.5, according to the lab's scale), and the PET scan done mid-April 2009 revealed recurrent disease: "a small abnormal hypermetabolic focus of activity in the left lower lobe to the liver with a maximum SUV of 4.12 (normal less than 2).… A low attenuation nodule is seen in the liver on image 24 of series 8 of the CT scan."

In the impression, the radiologist summed up the findings, stating, "Abnormal hypermetabolism is seen at the site of the left hepatic wedge resection. We are now three months post resection which begins to favor recurrent metastatic disease."

Despite the findings of probable recurrent malignancy, Patient II stood firm in her decision to refuse additional conventional treatment. From her reading—and she has a degree in chemistry—she understood that by the standards of orthodox oncology, chemotherapy, with all its toxic side effects, would not be curative.

In late April 2009, she consulted with a well-known alternative medicine physician, who recommended a variety of supplements and additional blood testing. A repeat CEA came back more significantly elevated than before at 6. Because the rising CEA levels indicated her disease might be worsening, Patient II, who had heard about us from a number of sources, decided to proceed with our regimen.

She passed our screening process, and we met for the first time during the second week of May 2009. During our initial consultation, I found her to be very intelligent, very well informed about her options, and determined to comply with my program exactly as prescribed. She asked about colonoscopy, and I recommended she follow up with Dr. Hiromi Shinya, the surgeon who invented the colonoscopy instrument. When she subsequently underwent the procedure two weeks later, Dr. Shinya noted no suspicious lesions, but only polyps that proved to be benign.

Patient II began her nutritional treatment with great dedication. When seen for a follow-up office visit in August 2009 after completing her first three months of treatment with me, she reported a substantial improvement in her overall energy, stamina, appetite, and well-being. A CEA at that time came back reduced from the prior results at 3.3.

In early October 2009, I suggested CT scan studies of the abdomen and pelvis, which showed "no definite evidence for metastatic disease." The previously noted lesion seemed to have resolved, although repeat CEA testing in early November 2009 showed the level, though still within the normal range, had gone up to 4.3 (normal 0.0–4.7 in this lab).

Patient II continued on her program and continued feeling well. Because she lived in the New York City area, I saw her in my office every three months, and at subsequent visits she reported feeling well, with no difficulties. In March 2010, the CEA was again up, this time to 4.9, now outside the normal range. In response, I increased her dose of enzymes.

When I saw her in the office during the second week of May 2010—a year after she had first consulted with me—she reported continued improvement in her energy, stamina, concentration, and overall well-being. She also said she had been sleeping much better, sounder, and longer. She felt well enough that she had started going to a local gym regularly, pursuing both a cardiovascular and a weightlifting program.

I discussed repeating the CT scans to assess her situation. However, she expressed reservations about the test, based on her understanding of the radiation exposure about which she had been reading. I respected her position but did suggest an ultrasound of the abdomen, for which she had no objection.

In mid-May 2010, she underwent ultrasound testing. The written report of the test stated, "Sonography does not show any hepatic lesion or dilated bile duct."

That month, she also underwent repeat colonoscopy with Dr. Shinya, who found only a single polyp, which was removed and found to be benign.

When I saw her during the second week of August 2010, she described continuing improvement in her overall health. She had continued going to her gym on a daily basis and enjoyed the vigorous exercise.

A CEA test in October 2010 came back right at the border for normal at 4.7. When I saw her some weeks later, during the second week of November 2010, for the first time she reported some serious problems of which I was previously unaware, which were unrelated to her cancer situation. On Election Day, she had tripped on a rug at the polling center and landed hard on her left ribs and shoulder. Later the same day, she had gone to a local salon for a facial and fell on her back when the chair moved from under her.

Both accidents had left her in considerable left shoulder and back pain that was severe enough to keep her from her coffee enemas and that significantly disrupted her sleep. By the time I saw her in the office some nine days later, the pains had improved considerably, though she was clearly uncomfortable. I suggested she add on bromelain, a powerful anti-inflammatory enzyme derived from pineapple with virtually no side effects.

I next saw Patient II in my office during the second week in February. She wasn't doing well, describing continuing pain in both shoulders, both hips, and both arms. Since I had last seen her, the pain had apparently worsened. She still was having difficulty doing the coffee enemas, her appetite was down, and she was losing weight. The constant pain, she admitted, had taken away her desire to eat and her overall motivation. Fortunately, she remained very strict with the supplement regimen, which she knew was the key to my program.

I gave her an order for blood work, and a few days later her CEA was up to 6.2. When I got the results, I called her on the phone and began to question her. As we tried to sort out what might be happening, she offered that for the previous few months she had been sleeping on an electric heating pad, hoping it would help with her pain, and wondered if that might be interfering with her progress. I have seen patients worsen when exposed to new electromagnetic devices, and improve when the source was removed.

Though I told her I couldn't be certain the pad was the culprit, I told her to stop using it in any event. I also suggested it was time to repeat scans, because the CEA was rising. She again expressed her strong reservations about CT or PET testing because of radiation exposure but agreed to an abdominal ultrasound.

In mid-February 2011, she went for the test, which showed no evidence of recurrent disease, as described in the official report: "Negative ultrasound of the abdomen."

That month at my insistence she also consulted with an orthopedist because of persistent right shoulder pain. She explained that since I had seen her in the office in early February 2011, a cyst-like lesion had developed in the area the size of a large orange. Unfortunately, she acknowledged that for several weeks she had not been as compliant with her program, including the supplements; because of her pain, she wasn't sleeping well and her pill schedule was off. And she found it impossible to do the coffee enemas on a regular basis because she could not easily get up and down off the bathroom floor. I suggested she do the enemas while sitting on the toilet—an approach that, though not ideal, had worked with other patients in similar situations.

In early March, she consulted with an orthopedist, who arranged for an MRI of her right shoulder. The test revealed the following:

> Findings most consistent with severe rheumatoid arthritis of the right glenohumeral joint with extensive bone marrow edema … with extensive cartilage loss throughout the joint.

> Very large amount of fluid identified within the subacromial/subdeltoid space comparable with severe bursitis.

The physician strongly suggested that she consider aggressive surgery on the right shoulder, but Patient II was not interested in any aggressive interventions at that point. She instead consulted a chiropractor, who suggested a course of electrostimulation to the involved joint along with gentle body work. She agreed to the plan and began the treatment with him.

In early April 2011, because of Patient II's cancer history, her orthopedist ordered a bone scan to rule out metastatic disease, but fortunately the test showed only abnormal activity consistent with degenerative arthritis. However, a CEA during the second week of April 2011 came back elevated at 10.0, the highest level to date. Some days later, we spoke by phone, during which time she expressed her concern about the rising CEA. She informed me that because of her shoulder pain and ongoing sleep difficulties, she still wasn't as compliant as she needed to be with her nutritional program. She was distracted and very uncomfortable. When I told her the best way to assess her current situation would be a PET/CT, she finally relented, agreeing to proceed with the more aggressive testing.

For some reason, the radiology center where she had been going for her studies arranged for a separate CT done two days before the PET. During the first week of May 2011, the CT scan of the abdomen revealed a recurrent liver tumor: "There is a 3.7 cm mass in the lateral left hepatic lobe consistent with metastasis increased in size compared to 2009. The liver is otherwise unremarkable."

The PET scan then confirmed an active lesion consistent with metastatic colon cancer into the liver: "The mass in the left lobe of the liver described on recent CT scan is hypermetabolic [active] in the range typically associated with malignancy, consistent with hepatic metastasis. No other definitive PET evidence of metastatic disease is seen."

I wasn't surprised by the results, because her disease had initially been aggressive and in recent months her compliance had fallen off. When I called Patient II to discuss the findings, she was disappointed, of course. I feel obligated to review the conventional options with her; because the disease seemed limited to a single liver lesion, I explained surgery might be an option. I also discussed chemotherapy, though she already knew from her extensive reading that that approach, with its significant side effects, would not be helpful long term. Repeat surgery and chemotherapy were out of the question, she said.

She then admitted that in recent months her compliance had actually been worse than she might have indicated to me, but she intended to continue her nutritional program with renewed resolve. Because she had done so well initially when compliance wasn't an issue, she was sure she could get the disease under control. I respected her decision but did suggest that, despite the pain, she needed to be as vigilant as possible with her nutritional program. Otherwise, her situation would only worsen, and we would be facing a potential catastrophe.

Meanwhile, during the second week in May 2011 she consulted with a second orthopedist in her area. She had lost faith with the first physician, whose approach she felt was far too aggressive and simply not practical. The major surgery on the shoulder he suggested would necessarily be followed by a six-month recovery, much of it spent in a rehabilitation center. Even if the surgery was successful, she realized, she would not be able to continue my cancer therapy, with inevitably dire consequences.

The new orthopedist had a completely different take on the situation. After reviewing the previous MRIs, he performed an ultrasound in his office that he felt showed a right rotator cuff tear, the source of her ongoing pain, which apparently had not appeared on the earlier shoulder MRI. In contrast with the first orthopedist, he did not recommend open surgery, which he agreed would be overly complicated and very debilitating. As a more conservative option, he suggested an arthroscopic procedure, but even this, he told Patient II, might require a three-month recovery. Though she liked the man, she realized she could not proceed with any operation that would interfere with her nutritional program.

She did return to my office for a regularly scheduled re-evaluation during the second week in May 2011. Now fully compliant with her regimen, she reported that her biggest ongoing concern was still her right shoulder pain. She asked if I could prescribe a medication with minimal toxicity but some analgesic effect. I suggested tramadol and wrote a prescription for the drug. Thereafter, with chiropractic care and tramadol, her pain became more manageable.

In early June 2011, Patient II once again met with her new orthopedist, who announced he wanted clearance with an oncologist before he proceeded with any procedure. Though Patient II still was against any operation, during the second week in June 2011 she did meet with the recommended oncologist. At the visit, Patient II openly discussed her choice of an alternative treatment for her cancer. The physician did not disparage her therapy with me but emphasized strongly that she most likely had active cancer, though the liver lesion needed to be biopsied for absolute confirmation. As soon as the testing was completed, she needed to start aggressive, multiagent chemotherapy.

After her visit with the oncologist, we spoke at length by phone. We acknowledged that her disease had recently progressed, but during a time when her compliance had fallen off considerably. Furthermore, I was hard pressed to think intensive drug treatment with all its attendant side effects and with no chance of long-term benefit was the most reasonable approach for a woman approaching eighty-eight years of age. However, despite my reservations, I told her that if she chose to go the conventional route, of course I would support her 100 percent. She became almost indignant, as she informed me she had done well on her program when she could follow it as prescribed, she was now again fully compliant, and in any event she would never agree to chemotherapy. End of discussion, she said.

In late June 2011, her local doctor ordered an abdominal ultrasound, which showed a single lesion in the liver as had the CT scan from early May 2011. But this time around, the tumor seemed reduced in size, measuring at 3.2 cm instead of 3.7 cm. I thought the reduction significant, at least an indication that Patient II, now fully compliant, was beginning to respond to her treatment once again. When I spoke to her after receiving the radiology report, she told me that she was feeling much better. In addition, she informed me that after going back and forth on the issue, her current orthopedist had decided against proceeding with surgery because she seemed to be responding to conservative management of her pain.

In mid-July 2011, her CEA was up to 10.5. When we discussed the result, she expressed her determination to stick with her nutritional program, reaffirming that under no circumstance would she agree to chemotherapy.

I didn't see Patient II in my office again until mid-October 2011. At that time, she had completed two and a half years on her nutritional program. Clinically, she seemed to be doing much better: her right shoulder pain had lessened significantly, and otherwise she reported good energy and overall improved well-being.

Several days after her visit with me, her CEA came back elevated once again, this time to 13.1. A repeat ultrasound showed that the liver tumor had progressed, now measuring 5.8 × 3.5 × 4.1 cm, a significant increase in size from the June 2011 test. I called her the day I received the results, to learn that in recent weeks without telling me she had added a variety of supplements to her program, including herbs that I never would have recommended. She was, she explained, trying to make up for lost time. I told her to stop all those extra supplements at once and follow my program only.

I explained that over the years I have seen patients worsen when they begin adding herbs or other nutrients to their program without first discussing the issue with me. Any number of nutritionals can interfere with the efficacy of my therapy, and perhaps the herbs and other nutrients she had added were now neutralizing my therapy. She agreed to be more careful, once again repeating that whatever any test showed, she would never proceed with chemotherapy.

Patient II stopped the extra products and remained vigilant with her prescribed regimen. In mid-November 2011, a month after her previous office visit, we serendipitously had the opportunity to test the validity of my recent suggestions. When she called me because of an episode of hematuria, I suggested she immediately go the emergency room of her local hospital. I thought the problem most likely was a urinary infection, but I didn't want to take any chances.

Because of her cancer history, the doctors at the local ER ordered a CT scan of the abdomen, which showed that the tumor had reduced in size from the October 2011 ultrasound. The report stated, "There is a hypodense lesion in the left lateral segment of the liver in keeping with the patient's known hepatic metastases which contains calcifications and measures approximately 4.5 × 2.3 cm."

Though the lesion had increased from the earlier CT scan from May 2011, it was significantly smaller compared with the October 2011 ultrasound, which indicated a 5.8 × 3.5 × 4.1 cm lesion. With Patient II following my full program as prescribed with nothing added, she appeared to be responding quickly.

The doctors did diagnose a urinary infection, for which they prescribed antibiotics. The bleeding stopped, and she continued on her therapy. When I next saw her for an office visit, during the fourth week of January 2012, she reported feeling well with no further episode of blood in her urine. Her right shoulder pain continued to improve, and the mass-like lesion on the right shoulder, to my surprise, had completely regressed. She was eating better and gaining weight—and not adding any additional products to my therapeutic program.

Two days after the visit, a CEA came back significantly improved at 8.9, down from the previous high of 13.1 in October 2011. Liver function tests were also within the normal range. She was very happy with the results, and more determined than ever to continue her treatment with me.

Though Patient II has been with me only three years, I thought her case very illustrative for a number of reasons. As with so many of my patients, Patient II's course with me has been neither simple nor straightforward. Three months after her January 2009 surgery, a follow-up PET scan in April 2009 showed recurrent disease in the liver. She declined the recommended chemotherapy, instead beginning treatment with me in May 2009.

Initially, she followed her program vigilantly, with a good response. By October 2009, a CT confirmed resolution of the lesion previously noted on the PET scan. In addition, clinically she seemed to be doing very well. But after the two falls, on Election Day 2010 after she had completed some eighteen months on my treatment, her compliance became erratic because of her very difficult situation. The pain affected her sleep, the lack of sleep affected her mood, she had difficulty sticking to the supplement schedule, and for a time she couldn't do the enemas.

These problems persisted for the better part of 2011, though she remained determined to continue only with her nutritional therapy. A May 2011 CT scan had revealed recurrent tumor that by October 2011 had significantly increased in size. During this time, her CEA gradually increased, eventually peaking at 13.1 in October 2011. But as her situation improved along with her compliance, her disease began to regress. The CT scan performed after the episode of hematuria in November 2011 showed significant reduction in the tumor size, and by January 2012 the CEA had dropped substantially, to 8.9.

In this case, response clearly correlated with compliance. When she was able to comply with the therapy fully, her advanced, aggressive disease regressed; when she had difficulty adhering to the prescribed regimen because of unexpected circumstances, the disease took hold. When her compliance improved, so did her disease.

Patients do not live in an ideal, perfect world. Unexpected events seem to be the rule, as they were in the life of Patient II. But I have repeatedly found over the years that if patients can remain disciplined with the treatment, in most cases they pull through despite the difficulties in their lives.

As I have said in other places, I find the diabetes model most appropriate in terms of how I approach cancer. A diabetic, even one with severe disease, can lead a fairly normal life, as long as he or she follows the required diet and complies with the medication prescription. At times, the blood sugar may go out of control; at times, a diabetic patient may end up in the hospital because of some unforeseen stress, such as the flu, that changes the insulin requirements and throws off the blood sugar levels. But with astute management, and good compliance, most often the situation can be brought under control.

Though I have in my practice patients whose success has been fairly straightforward, usually the path is more circuitous, with ups and downs before the disease relents. Determination to follow through with the treatment despite occasional roadblocks and reversals often leads, in my experience, to ultimate victory over malignancy.

Metastatic colorectal cancer is a very aggressive disease, with a five-year survival of less than 5 percent.[6] Although Patient II last contacted me in March 2013 and has not yet reached the five-year mark, her evidence of disease regression and significant clinical improvement at three years portends long-term success.

---

6   Longo et al., *Harrison's Principles*, 18th ed., 772.

Case 3: Patient LR
A Minimum 20-Year Survivor

Patient LR is woman in her sixties originally from the New York area who lived part time in the South, with a history of metastatic colon cancer. No family members had been diagnosed with cancer of any type, and prior to her bout with malignancy, she had generally been in good health. She had never smoked, and though her cholesterol ran on the high side, she had no evidence of heart disease.

In the early summer of 1989, Patient LR first noticed bright red blood in her stool. When the problem persisted and a routine hemoccult test at a health fair at a local hospital indicated blood in the stool, in mid-August 1989 she consulted her primary care physician in Virginia, who ordered a barium enema, which revealed, as described in the radiology report described, a "NORMAL AIR CONTRAST BARIUM EXAMINATION OF THE COLON." With the negative test in hand, Patient LR's physician assured her that the bleeding was most likely due to hemorrhoids and not any serious problem.

Subsequently, Patient LR experienced intermittent bouts of bright red blood in her stool, at least three to four episodes monthly. When she consulted again with her primary physician, he ordered blood work including blood counts, which came back perfectly normal. With no sign of anemia, Patient LR's physician again told her that the bleeding most likely originated in an internal hemorrhoid and required no further tests or treatment.

Over the next three years, the bleeding continued intermittently until June of 1992, when the bouts became more frequent and more copious. In addition, Patient LR experienced difficulty passing stool, associated with a feeling of rectal fullness. She returned to her primary physician, who prescribed hemorrhoid medication, but this time around, Patient LR, suspecting something serious, insisted more testing be done.

In July 1992, Patient LR consulted with a gastroenterologist in Virginia. Blood tests revealed a normal hemoglobin, and a stool culture for pathogenic organisms was unrevealing. But during the second week of August 1992 during colonoscopy, Patient LR was found to have a large annular lesion at 25 cm up the distal sigmoid colon, confirmed by biopsy as "moderately differentiated adenocarcinoma which is probably invasive," as described in the pathology report.

At that point, Patient LR decided to return to New York for further evaluation and treatment. Her New York doctor referred her to a surgeon, who ordered a CT scan of the abdomen and pelvis, completed during the third week of August 1992. Oddly, the test showed nothing in the sigmoid colon, but a lesion in the liver, described in some detail in the radiology report: "The liver is normal apart from a small low-density area adjacent to a vessel most probably representing fat inside the septum. However, a lesion within the liver cannot be entirely ruled out. Suggest further evaluation with ultrasound if clinically indicated."

Two days later, Patient LR underwent the recommended ultrasound, with the report stating,

> There is a 2 cm solid isoechoic lesion with a hyperechoic rim in the right lobe of the liver corresponding to the low attenuation area on CT. It demonstrates increased through transmission in comparison with the surrounding liver parenchyma. Although this is an atypical appearance for a hemangioma [sic]. …
>
> IMPRESSION: SOLID TRANSONIC LESION IN THE LIVER, POSSIBLE HEMANGIOMA. HISTOLOGIC DIAGNOSIS CANNOT BE MADE SONOGRAPHICALLY.

At a follow-up meeting, Patient LR's surgeon explained to her that the findings were of possible liver metastasis. Though the lesion seen on CT scan and ultrasound might be a hemangioma, a purely benign vascular tumor, the radiologist simply couldn't be sure of its true nature. Regardless, she was told that she required immediate surgery to ward off an impending intestinal obstruction from the large sigmoid tumor. The liver abnormality, Patient LR was told, would be localized, evaluated, and hopefully biopsied under intraoperative ultrasound guidance.

During the first week of September 1992, Patient LR underwent exploratory laparotomy and sigmoid colectomy at Maimonides Medical Center in Brooklyn, NY. During the operation, the surgeon examined the liver with an ultrasound probe but could not identify the intrahepatic mass described on both the CT scan and ultrasound, so a biopsy could not be done. Because ultrasound, particularly intraoperatively, is an excellent test for assessing benign hemangiomas, the fact that the lesion could not be located indicated it might be metastatic cancer.

After evaluating the surgical specimen, the pathologist described the large, aggressive-looking tumor: "On sectioning the specimen there is a mass seen which is fungating and ulcerated in the center measuring 5.5 × 5.5 × 1.2 cm."

The cancer clearly had spread locally, as described in the section of the pathology report entitled, "MICROSCOPIC DIAGNOSIS": "Sigmoid colon with an ulcerated infiltrated moderately to poorly differentiated adenocarcinoma; the tumor extends into pericolic fat, lymphatic and vascular permeation by tumor, isolated tumor implants in pericolic fat and metastatic carcinoma in one (1) of fourteen (14) nodes is seen."

After recovering from surgery, Patient LR met with an oncologist who insisted, regardless of the nature of the liver lesion, that she begin aggressive chemotherapy at once. The large size of the primary tumor, its ulcerating appearance, the fact that it had extended through the bowel wall and had spread locally, and the positive lymph node all portended a poor prognosis if not intensively treated.

But Patient LR, already interested in alternative approaches, declined the suggested chemotherapy and instead sought care at the Atkins Center in New York in the autumn of 1991. In the late 1980s and early 1990s, Dr. Atkins, now deceased and long famous for his high-fat approach to dieting, also offered intensive nutritional therapy, including intravenous vitamin C, as an alternative cancer treatment. In late autumn 1992, Patient LR, after learning of our work, decided to discontinue treatment with Dr. Atkins and consult with me.

When I met Patient LR during the first week of January 1993, she had recovered from surgery and generally seemed to be doing well. We discussed the CT scan and ultrasound findings, the possibility of liver metastases, and the pathology report. I brought up the conventional options for her situation, but she made it very clear to me that under no circumstances would she consider chemotherapy.

I ordered standard blood work including a metabolic profile, which revealed elevated liver function tests, with an alkaline phosphatase slightly outside the normal range at 135 (normal less than 125) but with an SGPT, another liver enzyme, significantly elevated at 73 (normal less than 45). These abnormalities represented a significant change from blood work dating from mid-August 1992, before her surgery, when the alk phos and SGPT were both well within the normal range at 102 and 9, respectively. Because the change was dramatic, at least in terms of the SGPT, the results indicated that something new and something serious might be going on in her liver, such as invading cancer. Infectious hepatitis seemed less likely, because she was asymptomatic.

Thereafter, Patient LR proved to be a very determined and compliant patient who took to the therapy without much difficulty. Because she had moved down South once again, I agreed that she needed to return only every six months for an in-office re-evaluation. I was next scheduled to see her in late July 1993, and shortly before the visit she underwent repeat blood testing. This time, the previously elevated liver function tests had completely normalized, with her alk phos falling to 76 and her SGPT dropping to a low 21, both very much within the normal range. And when I saw her in my office, she said her overall health had improved since starting my regimen, with improved energy, stamina, and overall well-being.

Her biggest physical complaint was a mild weight gain of some seven pounds. She also confided to me in some detail that she was separating from her husband of many years, a source of considerable stress for her. I encouraged her to stay on her therapy as prescribed, particularly through the difficult times.

Patient LR did stick faithfully to her nutritional therapy. When I next saw her, in mid-January 1994, after she had completed a year on her regimen, she remained compliant and reported feeling very well, though she was still concerned about some additional weight gain and still acknowledged considerable stress in her life. Blood work done in preparation for the visit was perfectly normal except for a moderately elevated cholesterol. Once again, all the various liver function tests were well within the normal range.

However, in early March 1994, repeat blood testing revealed an elevated alk phos at 123 (normal for this lab less than 117), and the SGPT was again creeping up at 52 (normal less than 46), though it was still lower than the January reading. I made some adjustments to her program at that time. Clinically, she felt fine, and when I brought up the issue of scans she stated she wanted no radiographic studies because she had no intention of changing her treatment, whatever any test would show.

Thereafter, Patient LR continued her program and continued doing well. In preparation for a return office visit scheduled for late July 1994, Patient LR did agree to ultrasound testing of the abdomen, which was done at a radiology facility in New York City. The test revealed that the previously noted liver lesion had actually increased in size, this time reported as 3 cm. The ultrasound report from late August 1992, before her surgery, had described a 2 cm lesion.

In any event, the radiology report of the July 1994 test stated,

> There is a 3 cm. subtle hypoechoic solid mass with a thin echogenic rind in the lateral aspect of the right lobe of the liver. ...
>
> IMPRESSION:
>
> Solid mass in the right lobe of the liver. ... Since there is a history of colon carcinoma, suggest correlation with a CT scan of the liver versus MRI of the liver to exclude metastatic disease versus a hemangioma.

When I saw her in my office shortly after, at a time when she had completed some eighteen months on her nutritional therapy, I discussed the ultrasound and blood test findings with her, indicating to me that we were dealing with a possibly progressing metastatic lesion. When I questioned her about compliance—which to that point had been near perfect—she admitted she had been going through another period of intense personal stress and in consequence hadn't been as vigilant with her program as during the first year of treatment. Apparently, she routinely missed doses of supplements, including the all-important pancreatic enzymes, though she seemed to be sticking to the prescribed, plant-based dietary plan and pursuing the required detoxification routines such as the coffee enemas—which she said helped her well-being "enormously." Despite the stress and the recent compliance lapses, she described her overall health as "very good." Nonetheless, I lectured her about the seriousness of the situation, with a liver lesion that was enlarging and at least one liver function that had worsened. She promised better compliance and, after some pushing on my part, even agreed to a CT scan of the abdomen.

During the first week of September 1994, Patient LR underwent the testing at a new facility in Virginia, where the radiologist apparently did not have in his possession the prior CT scan or ultrasound film for comparison. In any event, the radiologist felt the liver lesion seemed more consistent with a hemangioma, though he seemed ultimately uncertain: "The exam shows, on the unenhanced images of the liver, an area of low density in the right lobe that later shows increased density after IV contrast was given. I favor that this is a hemangioma due to its 'blush' appearance after contrast enhancement. I do not see any lesion in the liver elsewhere."

In addition, the report also described a "somewhat prominent" uncinate process of the pancreas.

It would certainly have been helpful if the radiologist had had the benefit of the prior studies, because certain factors argued, I thought at the time, against this being a hemangioma. Benign hemangiomas of this size do not generally lead to elevated liver function tests, whereas cancerous tumors routinely do. The "blush" described above refers to increased vascularity, a characteristic of hemangiomas but also consistent with a growing tumor in the throes of enhanced angiogenesis. Finally, in the context of Patient LR's history of locally metastatic colon cancer, with the information available to me at the time the possibility and probability of spread into the liver seemed high.

I did suggest a consultation with a liver specialist, but she felt she wasn't going to take any medication or change her therapy whatever the specialist said, and stated rather bluntly that she wanted only to continue with my regimen. I lectured her again about the need for vigilant compliance, and Patient LR returned home with renewed dedication to the therapy. When she subsequently underwent blood testing in late December 1994 in preparation for an office visit with me scheduled for January 1995, the alk phos was up to 154; the GGT, another liver function test, was elevated at 186 (normal less than 51); and the SGPT (now known as ALT) was on the rise, coming in at 84.

When Patient LR returned to my office in January 1995, she reported feeling "very well." The stress in her life seemed to be resolving, her energy was excellent, she denied any symptoms, and she seemed still concerned about her weight, which had been creeping up. I suggested that we have the liver function tests repeated after she returned home to Virginia, this time including a hepatitis screen.

Only days later, Patient LR underwent the blood testing. Since the last report only several weeks earlier, the alk phos was up again to 168, but the GGT had gone down considerably to 144, and the SGPT was within the normal range. Hepatitis B and C antibodies were negative, but the hepatitis A antibody was positive for a past, not current infection, a finding that would not likely explain the current elevated liver function tests. And hepatitis A, the mildest of the various viral hepatitis infections, unlike hepatitis B and C, rarely leads to ongoing, chronic liver damage.

The normal bilirubin level, another measure of liver function, also argued for a past, not current infection. And with active hepatitis, whatever the viral etiology, patients invariably experience a variety of signs and symptoms, including jaundice, fatigue, malaise, weakness, and anorexia, but at the time Patient LR not only was asymptomatic, but reported feeling quite well. After discussing the situation with her, I made some changes to her program, incorporating a milk thistle supplement, an herb I find very useful with liver damage, whatever the cause.

I had requested Patient LR repeat the liver panel again in June 1995, several weeks before another scheduled appointment with me, and this time around the alk phos was 137, the SGPT 122, and the GGT significantly elevated at 261. The LDH, another liver function, was elevated at 671 (normal less than 618 on this lab report), but her bilirubin had stayed within the normal range.

At my instruction, during the first week of July 1995 Patient LR underwent ultrasound testing the morning of her appointment with me. When she arrived in my office later that afternoon, I called the radiologist to discuss the findings. He described a 3 cm lesion in the right lobe of the liver, which he felt, in his candid opinion, based on her history, seemed more consistent with a metastatic, rather than a benign, lesion.

When we discussed the situation, Patient LR seemed as before quite compliant with her nutritional regimen, and despite the elevated liver function tests, she reported feeling quite well, with good energy, stamina, concentration, and appetite. However, she continued under significant ongoing personal stress, which we discussed in some detail. I made adjustments to her supplement program and encouraged ongoing good compliance.

A day later, I received the official written radiology report, which described the liver lesion:

> There is a 3 cm subtle hypoechoic solid mass with a thin echogenic rind in the lateral aspect of the right lobe of the liver. . . .
>
> IMPRESSION:
>
> Solid mass in the right lobe of the liver, as described above. Since there is a history of colon carcinoma, suggest correlation with a CT scan of the liver versus MRI of the liver to exclude metastatic disease versus a hemangioma.

Patient LR continued on her nutritional therapy and continued, at least clinically, doing well. In September 1995, repeat liver function testing showed a mixed picture: the alk phos was slightly up to 146, but the SGPT was down to 80 and the LDH was now in the normal range at 174 (for this lab, less than 250 was considered normal). All her other blood parameters were well within the acceptable range except for her high cholesterol.

In early February 1996—when Patient LR had completed more than three years on her nutritional therapy—blood testing done in preparation for an office visit in the middle of the month showed improvement, with the alk phos down to 134, the SGPT within the normal range at 37, and the LDH within the normal range at 170. Her blood sugar, which tended to run in the mildly elevated range, came in at 138.

When I saw her for her visit in mid-February 1995, she said she continued to feel "very well," with excellent energy, stamina, endurance, and appetite, and her biggest concern remained her weight. Fortunately, the serious stress in her life seemed to be resolving.

However, six months later, when she returned to my office in late August 1996, Patient LR admitted that the stress in her life had again worsened. She and her husband had decided to separate, and she was trying to decide what direction to take with her life, and with all this going on her nutritional program—for the first time since she had been my patient—had suffered. Her compliance with the supplements had fallen off significantly, to perhaps 50 percent of the required doses. She acknowledged that it was easy to justify poor compliance because she felt so well generally, and after three and a half years the routine of the therapy could be difficult. I agreed the program required ongoing discipline and determination but told her that with her history of a large fungating, infiltrating lymph-node-positive tumor, with evidence of possible liver involvement, she needed to adhere to the regimen. She agreed to try harder.

After my visit that day, she went for blood testing, the results of which arrived several days later. Her SGPT and LDH were again normal, the GGTP was 218 but significantly down from previous readings, and the alk phos was at 146, slightly up from the February level.

Thereafter, Patient LR seemed to renew her dedication to the treatment and continued doing well physically. Repeat blood testing in preparation for her next visit in mid-February 1997 revealed a normal bilirubin, LDH, SGOT, and SGPT. Her alk phos was down to 135, mildly outside the lab's normal range of 29–117, though her blood sugar was also again high at 143.

During the visit—now more than four years since she had first started treatment with me—I could sense the serious stress in her life. She and her husband had separated under less than pleasant circumstances, but nonetheless her compliance had evidently improved. Despite her difficult personal situation, she felt generally quite well. I suggested that we proceed with a complete metastatic workup, including chest x-ray, CT scans, and colonoscopy. She was agreeable to the suggestion and over the next month arranged for the testing.

Chest x-ray in late March was completely normal. The CT scan of the abdomen again showed the liver lesion, which this time measured 2 cm, not the 3 cm previously reported:

IMPRESSION:

A 2 CM ENHANCING LESION IS LOCATED WITHIN THE RIGHT LOBE OF THE LIVER. THE ENHANCEMENT CHARACTERISTICS MATCH THE ADJACENT HEPATIC AND PORTAL VEINS. THIS SUGGESTS THAT THIS MAY REPRESENT A VENOUS STRUCTURE SUCH AS A VENUS ANGIOMA OR HEMANGIOMA. FURTHER EVALUATION WITH MRI IS RECOMMENDED....

THERE IS NO ABDOMINAL MASS OR LYMPHADENOPATHY.

The CT scan of the pelvis showed no abnormality.

A week later, Patient LR underwent colonoscopy, which was normal except for a small polyp in the anastomosis of her previous colon surgery. This was excised and proved to be benign.

When she next returned to my office, in late May 1997, she seemed again to be generally compliant with the therapy and reported feeling "great." When we repeated her blood tests in mid-August 1997, the alk phos was at 140, LDH normal at 235, SGOT elevated at 92, and the SGPT significantly up again at 156. She came in for an office visit some two weeks later, in late August 1997, and said, despite the tests, that she was compliant with the treatment and still feeling "fine." She had been exercising regularly and, happily, had lost some ten pounds, which she and I agreed she needed to lose. Once again, she talked at length about the difficult situation with her husband, but I was pleased that she seemed to be getting her life in order. I discussed the possible causes of elevated liver enzymes and suggested we get the tests repeated in two months.

In late October 1997, the alk phos was within the normal range at 114, the SGOT was normal at 212, the SGPT was down to 59, and both the LDH and bilirubin were within the normal range.

In mid-February 1998—after Patient LR had completed more than five years on her treatment with me—her liver function tests were normal except for an elevated alk phos at 168. When I saw her next in the office, in early March 1998, she told me she had moved back in with her husband and that the stress had worsened. She declined my suggestion that she consider counseling to help her with this difficult situation, but fortunately, she seemed compliant with her program and reported feeling well clinically. I suggested she have the colonoscopy repeated, which in mid-March 1998 showed no evidence of recurrent colon cancer, only hemorrhoids and a slightly spastic colon. A liver function panel in early May 1998 was completely normal.

During a visit in late August 1998, now five and a half years after she began treatment, her main concern was her difficult home situation, which we discussed again at length. As before, she declined my suggestion that she consider counseling. Her compliance despite the stress seemed good if not perfect, and physically she felt fine.

In September 1998, Patient LR underwent repeat colonoscopy, which was completely normal. Subsequently, Patient LR continued doing well until mid-November 1998, when she noticed blood in the toilet. Because she was in New York, I suggested she come by the office as soon as possible for an order for urine analysis, and to pick up hemoccult cards to test for stool blood. I also recommended that she make an appointment with her gynecologist.

As it turned out, the urine test was negative for blood, but the Seracult did test positive. Though her recent colonoscopy from early September 1998 had been clear, I felt we needed to repeat the test again in view of recent developments. Though her gynecological workup in mid-December 1998 including a pelvic ultrasound was unremarkable, the colonoscopy had been delayed when her insurance company refused to authorize payment, claiming she didn't need another test so soon after the previous one. I tried to intervene with the insurance bureaucracy but told Patient LR that whatever the outcome in terms of reimbursement, she needed to undergo colonoscopy.

When I saw her in late February 1998—now six years after she had first started with me—she had canceled the colonoscopy twice for various reasons. Though she reported no further bleeding episodes, when I argued how important the test was in view of her history, she agreed to follow up with a gastroenterologist I had recommended with an office in New York. In addition, at my suggestion she agreed to CT testing

Finally, during the second week of March 1999, Patient LR underwent the colonoscopy, which was completely clear, with "no gross evidence of recurrence." A biopsy of the anastomosis site was "unremarkable." When her insurance company now refused to pay for the scheduled CT scan, I decided that with the negative ultrasound and colonoscopy, for now we could delay any further radiological testing.

During her next visit with me, her biggest concern once again was the ongoing severe stress in her marriage. She seemed compliant with her program, and physically she seemed to be doing very well, with no more episodes of bleeding.

In September 1999, hemoccult testing for stool blood was negative, and her liver function tests were negative across the board. Her blood sugar, at 149, was creeping upward, but fortunately her cholesterol was significantly reduced. She had also lost another five pounds, with portion control and exercise.

Despite the terrible continuing stress in her life, Patient LR continued her therapy, and I continued seeing her every six months or so. Her blood work generally was fine with normal liver function tests but a moderately elevated glucose level. In April 2000, an MRI of the pelvis revealed "thickening of the peritoneal reflections in the upper pelvis lower abdomen," a sign of possible recurrent cancer. Three days later, an MRI of the abdomen revealed the same right liver lobe lesion that had been noted before, but this time it was smaller at 1.5 cm, half the size of its appearance in the July 1995 ultrasound, and a third the size of the 2 cm nodule reported in the March 1997 CT scan. The report of the study stated,

IMPRESSION:

1.5 CM RIGHT LOBE LIVER MASS. SUGGEST ULTRASOUND TO CON-FIRM NATURE OF THIS LESION.

This time, the radiologist did not use the term "hemangioma." Because the mass had been regressing as Patient LR followed her nutritional program, I thought the lesion most likely malignant. The pancreatic enzymes we use in our cancer protocols do not affect benign lesions, and from my reading of the literature hemangiomas are not known to gradually regress.

In any event, because of the findings of peritoneal thickening, in late May 2000 Patient LR underwent repeat colonoscopy, which showed no evidence of recurrent disease. At this point, the gastroenterologist thought the MRI findings probably indicated scar tissue from her original surgery. Nonetheless, to complete this round of testing, I ordered a highly specific MRI of the liver, which was completed in mid-May 2000. This time, the radiologist reported not one, not two, but three lesions up to 2.5 cm in diameter, two of which seemed consistent with hemangiomas. But the radiologist, evidently unsure about the nature of the masses, suggested a repeat MRI in three months!

The gastroenterologist suggested a blood test for CEA. In July 2000, this test came back completely negative at 0.8. In my practice, I don't routinely check this marker, which for patients on my therapy can bounce around considerably and has limited usefulness.

When Patient LR returned to my office in early November 2000, she spent considerable time discussing the very difficult situation with her husband. She had left him and was living once again down South, trying to keep away from him. Despite the stress, she had soldiered on, following her nutritional regimen, and overall physically she felt well with no complaints. She had finally found a doctor in her new town who agreed to manage her rising blood sugars, but then shortly after she moved again to another Southern state and could not connect with a suitable doctor to follow her locally. When her blood sugar reached 201 in December 2000, I insisted that she needed an endocrinologist, someone who specializes in diabetes, to supervise her situation.

Repeat CEA testing in January 2001 came back again in the low range of normal. Then in April 2001, Patient LR underwent an abdominal MRI at the same radiology facility where she had gone for the previous set of tests. The radiologist reported that the two large liver lesions were unchanged, but he did not mention the third previously described mass.

During a return office visit in May 2001, eight and a half years after she had started her treatment with me, Patient LR seemed compliant and seemed to be doing very well clinically. Out of her difficult marriage, she finally appeared relaxed about her life. However, she told me that when she had discussed her nutritional cancer therapy with her new internist, he aggressively ridiculed my treatment, an attitude that did not please Patient LR. Fortunately, in December 2001 she found a more suitable physician with an open, more tolerant attitude to LR's unconventional therapy.

During her next appointment, in mid-January 2002, it was clear that Patient LR had remained compliant with her treatment and was exercising regularly and losing weight. Her blood sugars had improved under the watchful eye of her new local specialist, who had started her on an oral hypoglycemic medication.

The January 2002 appointment would be the last time I would see Patient LR, though over the next year she kept in touch on occasion by phone. At one point in February 2003, she called asking if she could still order supplements if she didn't return for the required periodic office visits, and we know that subsequently she did order from the distributor that provided the necessary products for our therapy.

I also know from a relative who happens to be a patient of mine that Patient LR—now more than twenty years since her initial visit in my office—appears to be doing quite well and remains cancer-free. I am always nervous when a patient with a diagnosis of aggressive metastatic cancer discontinues the treatment, even ten years after the diagnosis. Cancer can always come back, but in this case, Patient LR has survived nicely.

Patient LR represents a somewhat complicated course, to say the least. Over the past twenty years, different radiologists have reported different numbers of liver lesions, ranging from one to three, and have provided different explanations as to their likely histology. At times, at least one of the lesions appeared to be more consistent with a metastatic nodule; at other times, the radiologists considered the possibility or likelihood of a hemangioma, a very benign vascular abnormality. Certainly, the possibility of a malignant liver nodule at times seemed strong, arguing for stage IV disease.

If we discount the significance of the liver lesion and assume this to have been benign disease, with a large tumor as originally described and with one of fourteen nodes positive, the website Adjuvant! Online has reported a five-year survival of 49.7 percent—certainly much higher than with stage IV disease, though hardly spectacular, and these numbers include patients treated with aggressive chemotherapy or radiation. Unfortunately, I have been unable to discover any statistics for twenty-year survival of a patient with LR's specific tumor characteristics. Whether the liver lesion was cancerous or not, her long-term disease-free survival treated only with our nutritional regimen after surgery is, I believe, quite remarkable.

Case 4: Patient DO
A Minimum 7.2-Year Survivor

Patient DO is a fifty-year-old woman who has survived more than 7.2 years with a history of Dukes C (or possibly Dukes D) colon cancer metastatic into multiple lymph nodes and possibly into the liver.

Her family history is pertinent because of her paternal grandfather, who died from colorectal cancer, and a paternal aunt who died from stomach cancer. Patient DO herself had a history of peptic ulcer disease first diagnosed at age seventeen, eventually treated effectively with Tagamet and other antacids. More recently, she also had undergone excision of a right breast lesion for what proved to be benign fibrocystic disease.

Patient DO had been in her usual state of good health when in May 2006 she first noticed intermittent bright red blood in her stool. When the problem persisted, she consulted her family physician, who immediately referred her to a gastroenterologist for colonoscopy. However, when the bleeding stopped, Patient DO decided on her own to forgo the recommended evaluation.

She subsequently did well for a year, until May 2007, when she again experienced an episode of bright red blood per rectum. She returned to her primary care physician, who once again strongly suggested a gastrointestinal workup. But when the bleeding stopped, Patient DO chose not to pursue the recommended course of action.

In the spring of 2008, nearly two years after the initial bleeding event, Patient DO noticed a change in her bowel habits, particularly a sense of urgency in the morning associated with some loose stool, but no blood that she could see. These symptoms persisted along with gradually worsening fatigue and generalized malaise. Then in mid-2008, after experiencing copious bloody diarrhea, Patient DO returned to her family doctor, who this time sent her for a CT scan of the abdomen and pelvis. This test revealed abnormalities in the liver, but other than diverticulosis, no colon tumor: "Multiple hypodense lesions are noted in the liver which are too small to characterize. Statistically, they most like represent cysts. … There is scant sigmoid diverticulosis without evidence of diverticulitis."

However, colonoscopy two days later demonstrated a large ulcerated mass in the sigmoid colon that on biopsy proved to be adenocarcinoma. During the last week of July 2008, a CEA blood test, a marker for colon cancer, came back within the normal range at 1.9 (normal 0–3.8).

With cancer confirmed, Patient DO was referred to a surgeon at North Shore University Hospital in Manhasset, Long Island. During the last week in July 2008, she underwent left colon resection for a tumor measuring 3.5 cm in its largest diameter that had penetrated the bowel wall and involved multiple lymph nodes, as summarized in the formal pathology report:

> Final Diagnosis
> Left colon, resection
> -moderately to poorly differentiated adenocarcinoma infiltrating through full thickness of wall and focally extending to pericolonic adipose tissue.
> -metastatic adenocarcinoma to eight out of eighteen lymph nodes...
>
> Histologic grade
> Moderately to poorly differentiated...
>
> Lymphatic (small vessel) invasion
> Present

The poorly differentiated histology, the penetration of the tumor through the bowel wall into surrounding tissue, and the numerous involved lymph nodes all portended a poor prognosis.

After her discharge from North Shore, during the third week of August Patient DO consulted with a North Shore oncologist. During the lengthy session, the oncologist discounted radiation therapy as useful in this case, instead discussing the importance of chemotherapy as the treatment of choice, which she thought essential because of the multiple positive nodes.

Patient DO, who had already begun to investigate alternative approaches to cancer, broached possible nonconventional therapies. The oncologist actually remained quite pleasant and expressed no objection to nutritional or alternative treatments as long as they were only an add-on to chemotherapy, not a primary treatment—as Patient DO would later tell me and as the physician's note explained:

> Impression & Recommendations: ...
>
> Adjuvant chemotherapy—rationale for chemotherapy was discussed. Pt [Patient] was considering alternative means of therapy such as herbs used in Chinese medicine. I told her that chemotherapy is a necessity given the # of positive lymph nodes found at surgery. I explained that alternative medicine can be used in addition to traditional medicine and I would explore this with the pt.
>
> Chemotherapy with FOLFOX was discussed with the patient. ... The patient is going for a second opinion to NYU and Cornell and will let me know of her intentions.

The FOLFOX chemotherapy regimen suggested by the oncologist, often the first-line treatment for patients with aggressive colon cancer, includes the drugs folinic acid, 5-fluourouracil, and oxaliplatin.

Patient DO explained to the oncologist that she would consider the chemotherapy options but first wished to pursue a second opinion before making a final decision about treatment. At that point, the oncologist did order a CEA blood test, which came back within the normal range at 0.4. In addition, the physician did suggest, wherever Patient DO ultimately might choose to continue her medical care, as a next step a PET scan, in which a radioactively labeled glucose is injected intravenously. This marker then concentrates in metabolically active tissues, such as those of cancer, which then light up on the scan.

In this day and age, PET scans, which show metabolic activity and not tumor size, are invariably done in conjunction with a CT. I find the combination PET/CT scans to be quite accurate for picking up small areas of cancer, though infection or inflammatory reactions can show activity and consequently yield false positives. In addition, PET scans can miss very small, possibly malignant lesions.

Patient DO agreed to the plan and underwent PET/CT testing during the first week of September 2008. The PET showed no suspicious activity in the liver but did reveal two positive areas, one in the midabdomen thought secondary to postoperative change, and the second in the right lower abdomen. The radiologist described the findings in his official report:

> LOW GRADE FOCAL METABOLISM ALONG THE BOWEL ANASTOMOSIS WHICH IS LIKELY POST-SURGICAL REACTIVE IN NATURE.
>
> ANTERIOR ABDOMINAL WALL METABOLISM WITH THE MIDLINE PORTION ATTRIBUTABLE TO POST-OPERATIVE CHANGES. THE RIGHT LOWER QUADRANT FOCUS COULD ALSO REPRESENT REACTIVE CHANGES IF LAPAROSCOPY WAS PERFORMED IN THIS AREA. CLINICAL CORRELATION IS SUGGESTED.

Patient DO's surgery was performed on the left side of her abdomen, not the right, but the oncologist nonetheless assumed the findings indicated only postoperative effect.

During mid-September 2008, Patient DO did meet with an oncologist in the Columbia system, who also strongly suggested FOLFOX as the treatment of choice in her situation. By this point, Patient DO, having learned about my work, applied to become a patient in my practice during the third week of September 2008. After reviewing her file, I explained clearly that chemotherapy would be the standard of care option that might offer some statistically significant benefit in terms of disease-free and overall survival. Patient DO, who obviously to me was quite intelligent and had done her homework about treatment options, wrote me back, explaining she understood all this but wished only to begin my regimen.

Patient DO did meet again with her North Shore oncologist, explaining that she would not be pursuing chemotherapy at this time. I subsequently consulted with Patient DO shortly after, during the third week of September, for her initial intake visit. At the time, she had recovered fully from surgery, seemed to have made a very informed decision about her treatment, and was determined to pursue my therapy. She made it clear to me that she had no intention of undergoing chemotherapy ever.

Thereafter, Patient DO proved to be a very vigilant, determined, and compliant patient. In late October 2008, the North Shore oncologist with whom Patient DO had consulted contacted her primary care physician, wondering what treatment she had chosen. The primary care physician in turn contacted Patient DO, who explained she was pursuing an alternative therapy instead of chemotherapy. This information was then relayed back to the oncologist, who was not, apparently, pleased by the turn of events, insisting Patient DO needed to begin chemotherapy as soon as possible. DO stood her ground, feeling only more resolute in her decision to pursue treatment with me, but did agree to a follow-up visit with the oncologist.

During the last week of November 2008, Patient DO did meet as planned with the North Shore oncologist, who ordered blood studies including a CEA blood test, which this time came back elevated over the postsurgical result but still within the normal range at 2.5. Because of the change in the wrong direction, the oncologist strongly recommended a repeat PET scan to assess the situation. When I spoke with Patient DO by phone after her conversation with the oncologist, she seemed somewhat concerned about the CEA results but reluctant to repeat the PET scan because of the radiation exposure involved. I find that in this day and age, particularly with the information available on the Internet, patients, far more than in past years, are very much aware of the potential dangers of PET and CT scans.

DO herself suggested we repeat the CEA at a different lab, to check the trend. I thought the idea most reasonable and sent her an order for the test, which came back during the third week of December at 0.984, a far more reassuring number than the 2.5 reported by her oncologist. At that time, Patient DO faxed me a copy of the blood tests ordered by her oncologist—which I had not yet actually seen—in late December 2008, with an attached note. She expressed in her letter some concern over the blood test results, which showed that two of her liver function tests were outside the normal range. Because of these findings, DO had gone ahead and scheduled the recommended PET scan for the first week of January.

Though I already knew the CEA reading of 2.5 from DO, I hadn't known until I received Patient DO's note with the copy of the lab tests that indeed two important liver function tests, the AST and ALT, were elevated. The AST came in at slightly high at 45 (normal 13–40), the ALT more significantly so at 71 (normal 10–49). These results were actually of more concern to me than the still acceptable CEA, because the AST and ALT reflect with good accuracy liver function. In a situation like this, with a history of metastatic colon cancer in play, these elevated numbers could reflect cancer spreading through the liver.

When we spoke by phone later that evening, I could sense that Patient DO was understandably concerned, because she had been warned that she was making a serious error in judgment by not proceeding with the recommended chemotherapy. I proposed as a first step that we needed to repeat the liver function tests as well as the CEA in two weeks, at the end of December 2008, just to track the trend. She had already scheduled the PET scan, which certainly would give us a fuller picture of what might be going on. I also made some adjustments to her supplement program and told her to discontinue the vitamin A. Though her supplement regimen included only a mild amount of this nutrient, as vitamin A can in even moderate doses affect liver function, I wanted to remove any possible additional stress to her liver.

On December 31, 2009, the CEA came back at 0.0—significantly improved and perfectly negative. However, the AST was up to 50 and the ALT up to 80. When I discussed the results with DO and the need for scanning, she again expressed her concern about the radiation exposure of a PET/CT. She had actually canceled the test scheduled for early January 2009, moving it up to early February. Because she was scheduled shortly to return to my office for a routine three-month follow-up visit, I suggested we could discuss these issues at that time.

Patient DO returned to my office several days later, during the first week of January 2009. She seemed to be extremely compliant with the therapy, despite the fact that she continued to work at a high-stress job in Manhattan. She reported that she generally felt quite well, with good energy, stamina, and sound sleep. In recent months, she had experienced significant night sweats intermittently, but these, she was happy to report, had completely resolved. She again expressed her concern about the upcoming PET scan, which she would rather delay again.

I suggested as a more conservative—and certainly safer—option that we repeat the blood tests in mid-January 2009 to check her liver function, and in addition that she undergo an abdominal ultrasound, which I find to be a good screening test involving no radiation, even if not as comprehensive as PET or CT. She accepted the plan as reasonable, so we proceeded accordingly.

Fortunately, the blood tests from the third week of January 2009 indicated improvement in both the AST and ALT, down to 43 and 66, respectively. Normal ranges for numerous blood tests, including these two parameters, can vary from laboratory to laboratory, and in this case, the results were considered within the normal range for both.

Five days later, I received a copy of the radiologist's report of the ultrasound, which I found quite interesting in showing a perfectly normal liver. The lesions seen on the preoperative CT scan were not visualized on this study:

FINDINGS: The liver is not enlarged. The hepatic parenchyma is homogeneous. No hepatic mass is demonstrated. ...

The gallbladder is unremarkable.

The overall "**IMPRESSION**" was "**Unremarkable examination.**"

When we discussed the results over the phone, Patient DO again brought up the planned PET scan and her reasonable reservations about the test. Because the ultrasound showed nothing and the liver function tests had improved, I told her we could for now delay the PET scan—a recommendation she found very much to her liking.

Repeat blood testing in early April 2009 revealed a CEA as less than 0.4, certainly well within the normal range. The AST came in at 33 and the ALT lower than the previous test result at 60. When I saw her several days later, she reported that she felt fine and that now, six months into her therapy, she had adapted to it quite well. She did explain that in February she had fractured her left wrist while on a ski trip with her family and required a cast for about four weeks. The injury had healed nicely by the time I saw her, with no residual pain or loss of motion.

Two months later, during the second week of June 2009, Patient DO called me to let me know that after a session of intensive yoga, she had experienced back pain, which had been gradually improving. However, in recent days she reported episodes of severe stomach cramping, which had caused some significant "panic," to use her term, because of her history. She had made an appointment with her oncologist, who, I expected, would probably now want the PET scan to be done.

Indeed, when DO met with the oncologist, she did order a PET/CT scan, which was performed during the first week of July 2009. This showed no activity anywhere, as described in the formal report:

> The previously noted activity at the distal colonic anastomosis has resolved. No focal intense activity is noted in this region. The abdominal wall activity has also resolved.
>
> **CONCLUSION:**
>
> **NO EVIDENCE OF METABOLICALLY ACTIVE RESIDUAL/RECURRENT DISEASE.**

I thought it was significant that the radiologist made no mention of any lesions in the liver, even on the CT component of the PET/CT, which had been described in the preoperative CT scan from June 2008.

Several days later, when Patient DO returned to my office for a routine visit, we discussed the findings. Though she remained compliant with the therapy and physically continued feeling well, she had been undergoing a lot of work-related stress. In fact, she was thinking carefully about a new career entirely, away from the high-stress job in Manhattan finance. In any event, she was now a year from her diagnosis, with no evidence of malignancy anywhere.

At the time of DO's next visit, during the first week of October 2009, she had completed more than a year on her nutritional regimen. In preparation for the session, she had gone to a local lab for blood testing, but the results were not yet available at the time we met. Regardless, she remained compliant with her treatment, continued feeling well, and had made major changes in her career path. She would no longer work in the high-stress business world of Manhattan, but instead would be opening an organic café in her suburban town. She talked with great excitement about her plan, in a way in which she had never talked about her finance career.

When I suggested she think about having a repeat colonoscopy, she mentioned virtual colonoscopy, in essence a specialized CT scan that some think has at least the accuracy of the more standard approach. I told her I had no objection to that test and gave her the appropriate order.

Patient DO eventually underwent the "**CT VIRTUAL COLONOGRAPHY**," as it is called, in late December 2009. This test revealed, as discussed in the summary, "No evidence of suspicious colonic lesion." At an office visit a couple of weeks later, in early January 2010, Patient DO reported that she continued feeling quite well and had made great progress with her café, which she planned to open in February.

In March 2010, I ordered another set of blood tests. This time around, the liver function tests were well within the normal range, with the AST at 23 and the ALT at 25. The CEA came in low at 0.5 (normal less than 3.9). When I discussed the results with her, she informed me that her café, now up and running, was already proving to be a great success. I was a little concerned about the long hours involved, but she seemed as always vigilant with her treatment.

Thereafter, I continued seeing Patient DO every three months in the office, and she continued to do well. Her café, open now seven days a week, continued to thrive, and though she seemed quite happy with her new life as a restaurateur, I again warned her not to let the therapy slide.

During the second week of July 2010, Patient DO at my suggestion did undergo another PET/CT, which showed "NO EVIDENCE OF METABOLICALLY ACTIVE REGIONAL NODAL, OR DISTANT METASTATIC DISEASE."

Patient DO and I were both pleased with the findings, to say the least.

When I next saw DO in my office, during the first week of October 2010—more than two years since her first visit with me in 2008—she admitted that her café had become a very consuming, though very successful, effort. She was working up to eleven hours a day, sometimes seven days a week, far more than she had originally intended. As a result, she was missing doses of enzymes, though she seemed quite compliant with the diet and detoxification routines. I explained that with her history, she needed to be always vigilant and never for a second take cancer for granted. She agreed she needed to be more careful.

Despite the stress, DO reported feeling quite well, with excellent energy and endurance. I thought the fact that she could work such long hours with excellent energy was a testament to her good health.

Thereafter, Patient DO tightened up her compliance, continued working hard at her new business, and continued doing very well. In early November 2010, at my suggestion, she underwent blood studies, which showed once again perfectly normal liver function tests and a CEA at 0.6.

During a return office visit, during the first week of April 2011, she reported generally good compliance, despite her very hectic six-day-a week work schedule, up to twelve hours a day.

In late May 2011, a chemistry screen was completely normal, including liver function, and the CEA, although slightly elevated over the previous reading, was also acceptable at 0.8. A PET/CT scan in early July 2011 showed no clear-cut indication of metastatic or recurrent disease, although the test did pick up some "NONSPECIFIC" activity in the anastomosis site of her original surgery and some activity in the right ovary thought to be "PHYSIOLOGIC IN NATURE." In summary, in the "**CONCLUSION**" section, the radiologist wrote, "NO EVIDENCE OF METABOLICALLY ACTIVE REGIONAL, NODAL, OR DISTANT METASTATIC DISEASE."

The radiologist did suggest an ultrasound to assess more clearly the right ovary. I discussed the report with Patient DO, who subsequently underwent ultrasound testing in late July 2011 at her gynecologist's office. The study showed only a benign-appearing right ovarian cyst that as it turned out had been present on prior ultrasounds.

When DO returned for an office visit during the first week of October 2011, I still thought she was working far too hard, but to her great credit her restaurant was a great success, generating considerable interest and following in her hometown. In terms of her regimen, she seemed to be quite compliant. She had no complaints, other than the fact that her work schedule precluded any exercise, which she had long enjoyed.

Repeat blood studies in mid-October 2011 revealed normal liver function and a CEA at 0.7, slightly down from the May 2011 result. During the second week of January 2012, repeat CEA testing showed continued improvement at 0.57.

When she next retuned to my office, at the end of April 2012, she again seemed to be doing well. Other than a brief bout of stomach cramping that improved with antacid treatment, she had no complaints. A PET/CT in early July 2012 again showed "NO CURRENT EVIDENCE OF METABOLICALLY ACTIVE DISEASE." This PET/CT report finding "the previously noted activity in the region of the right adnexa (ovary) has resolved."

Patient DO certainly has done well over the past seven years, with no evidence of recurrent or metastatic disease despite her initial poor-prognosis disease. The previously noted liver lesions seen on the preoperative CT scan from June 2008 have not been evident on subsequent studies.

Of course, we will never know what those liver lesions may have been. If indeed they were evidence of metastatic colon cancer, placing Patient DO in the most advanced Dukes D, or stage IV category for colon cancer, the survival statistics at five years are abysmal, in the range of only 5 percent.

Even if we discount the liver lesions as significant, and consider her at stage Dukes C, indicating metastatic disease only to regional lymph nodes, her projected survival at five years at the time of diagnosis was not great. Certain characteristics of her tumor, such as the poorly differentiated histology, the ulceration of the tumor, and its penetration into regional adipose tissue, portended a poor prognosis, as did the eight positive lymph nodes.

The website Adjuvant! Online, a physician's guide to treatment and prognosis for selected malignancies including colon cancer, projects an overall five-year survival for a woman of DO's age, sex, and tumor characteristics of 22.6 percent without any adjuvant treatment after surgery. So if we consider Patient DO as a Dukes C and ignore the liver lesions, her prognosis at the time of diagnosis was clearly less dismal than that for those patients with Dukes D cancer. Nonetheless, her continued disease-free survival is still unusual and I believe worthy of discussion.

Case 5: Patient MQ
*A 5.2-Year Survivor**

Patient MQ is a sixty-nine-year-old woman from New Jersey with a history of stage IV meta-static colon cancer. Her mother and a maternal aunt both survived breast cancer, but otherwise she reported no additional history of malignant disease in her family.

Prior to developing cancer, Patient MQ had generally been in good health, though she did undergo cholecystectomy for gallstones at age twenty-six. Her current situation dates to late spring of 2006, when she first noted an increase in rectal mucus tinged with blood. She consulted with her primary care physician, who referred her to a gastroenterologist. A colonoscopy shortly after revealed a large partially obstructing sigmoid colon tumor, confirmed by biopsy to be adenocarcinoma.

Patient MQ then met with a surgeon at Morristown Memorial Hospital and, during the third week of July 2006, underwent laparoscopic resection of the large colon tumor, described in the pathology report:

> Colonic adenocarcinoma, moderately to poorly differentiated, measuring 3.5 × 2.5 × 1 cm of the sigmoid colon, invading into pericolic adipose tissue. ...

> Metastatic carcinoma involves two out of nine pericolic lymph nodes.

The surgeon could find no visible evidence of additional metastatic disease

After recovering from surgery, Patient MQ consulted with an oncologist specializing in gastro-intestinal tumors at Morristown Hospital. The oncologist suggested, as a first step, a staging workup, and during the first week of August 2006 a CT scan of the abdomen and pelvis was clear. However, a chest CT revealed a small but concerning 4 mm lesion in the right upper lobe that after review was not thought to be significant. In any event, Patient MQ's oncologist then suggested a six-cycle course of aggressive adjuvant chemotherapy with the drugs oxaliplatin, Leucovorin, and 5-FU, for what was assumed to be Dukes C colon cancer (cancer limited to local lymph node). With drug treatment, Patient MQ was told she had more than a 50 percent chance of remaining disease-free for five years.

Patient MQ agreed to the plan, and during the first week of September, she began chemo-therapy. Initially, she tolerated the treatment well, but with each successive cycle she reacted more strongly, experiencing a host of severe side effects. Her appetite declined, and she lost some forty pounds. In addition, she developed a peripheral neuropathy, associated with numb-ness in her feet, and experienced recurrent dental infections thought to be secondary to the immune-suppressing effect of the drugs. Her muscle tone, which previously had been good, began to weaken.

After completing four cycles of chemotherapy, during a Christmas vacation in Mexico, Patient MQ felt so weak she barely could leave her hotel room. Upon returning home, during the second week of January 2007 she proceeded with the scheduled fifth cycle of chemotherapy. She managed to get through this round but became once again so sick she refused to continue with the last bout of treatment—a decision her oncologist apparently supported.

Subsequently, off all drugs, Patient MQ slowly improved but still experienced a number of ongoing problems, particularly severe pain in her right hip. X-rays of the joint showed no cancer, but instead bone spurs and arthritis. With the passage of time, her energy and appetite did improve, and she began gaining weight.

Patient MQ continued routine follow-up visits with her oncologist, who in September 2007— some eight months after Patient MQ's last dose of chemotherapy—ordered restaging. A CT scan of the abdomen and pelvis during the last week of September 2007 showed "no CT evidence of metastatic disease," but the chest CT demonstrated some slight enlargement in the previously noted right lung nodule, as described in the radiology report: "There is a 5 mm nodule in the right upper lobe which in retrospect previously measured approximately 4 mm. Part of this may be related to differences in technique, however, continued followup evaluation is recommended."

Despite the lung findings, Patient MQ was told she was "disease-free."

Around this time, Patient MQ consulted with a local naturopathic physician, who prescribed a number of Standard Process supplements, including vitamin D, flaxseed oil, cod liver oil, green powder superfoods, curcumin, resveratrol, CoQ10, and others. She changed her diet to a largely organic, whole-foods approach, cutting out refined carbohydrates and "junk food."

On her nutritional regimen, Patient MQ experienced improved good health. It wasn't until October 2008, more than a year and a half after her completion of chemotherapy, that her oncologist—assuming she was cured—arranged for routine follow-up testing. During the third week of October 2008, a CT scan of the abdomen and pelvis revealed as before "no evidence of metastatic disease in the abdomen and pelvis." However, this time around the chest CT revealed two new lesions, one in each lung:

> Impression:
>
> 1.3 cm left upper lobe nodule suspicious for metastatic disease versus primary malig-
> nancy. 4 mm right lower lobe nodule which is new. A small metastatic lesion cannot

be excluded. 5 mm nodular area…into the right major fissure which is unchanged and may be benign.

Patient MQ was told she most likely had metastatic colon cancer in at least two places, for which surgical resection was recommended as the most suitable approach. She subsequently met with a thoracic surgeon at Morristown Hospital, and during the first week of November 2008, she underwent, as described in the Operative Note, "left thorascopy, left upper lobe segmental lung resection, bronchoscopy." The surgeon did not attempt resection of the small right lower lung lesion.

The pathology report described the following:

DIAGNOSIS:

LEFT LUNG, UPPER LOBE, POSTERIOR SEGMENT, WEDGE RESECTION:

METASTATIC COLONIC ADENOCARCINOMA INVOLVING THE LUNG PARENCHYMAS AS A 1.5 CM NODULE.

After recovering from surgery, Patient MQ met with her oncologist, who in an unenthusiastic manner discussed resumption of chemotherapy. He admitted the treatment might give her a "5 percent" advantage in long-term survival as opposed to no additional treatment at the time. When her surgeon seemed even less positive about chemotherapy, Patient MQ decided to decline further treatment, though she did agree to continue close follow-up with both physicians, with scanning to be pursued every three months.

During the first week of February 2009, a CT of the abdomen now revealed possible problems in the abdomen: "There is slightly increased prominence [sic] lymph nodes in the left abdomen…measuring 9 mm in greatest short axis diameter. These are of questionable clinical significance."

The lung scan showed postsurgical change and "a stable 3 mm nodule along the right major fissure."

Her oncologist at that point suggested no treatment, only continued close monitoring. During the first week of May 2009, an abdominal CT scan showed that "the shotty intramesenteric lymph node noted on the prior study is no longer identified." In summary, the radiologist wrote, "THERE IS NOTHING TO SUGGEST INTRAABDOMINAL METASTATIC DISEASE."

The chest CT, however, was a different story: "On the current study, there are several enlarging nodular masses adjacent to the surgical site and more inferiorly. These measure approximately 1.7 × 1.4 cm., and 0.2 × 0.7 cm. ... These are suspicious for recurrence."

Patient MQ herself then requested a PET scan, which measures tumor activity, to define further the CT findings. During the third week of May 2009, this test revealed evidence of recurrent metastatic disease: "Nodular densities are again seen in the left upper lobe in close proximity to the upper portion of the major fissure. A medial nodule measuring 2.2 cm. in diameter is associated with hypermetabolism with a mean standard uptake value of 5.7 consistent with malignancy. The lateral nodule measuring up to 14 mm in diameter and is not associated with hypermetabolism."

After discussing the situation with both her oncologist and her surgeon, during the last week of May 2009 Patient MQ underwent left thoracotomy with "completion upper lobectomy, lymph node dissection, bronchoscopy." The pathology report described the following:

LUNG, LEFT UPPER LOBE, LOBECTOMY:

METASTATIC COLONIC ADENOCARCINOMA MODERATE TO POORLY DIFFERENTIATED, TWO TUMOR NODULES, LARGEST 2 CM. ...

TEN REACTIVE LYMPH NODES NEGATIVE FOR MALIGNANCY.

With her second significant recurrence, this time involving two distinct tumors, Patient MQ decided not to proceed with any additional conventional treatment. She already knew about my work from her colon therapist, who had recommended me highly and thought my approach would be a better option. Patient MQ did meet with her oncologist, who again admitted chemotherapy would offer little chance of cure. With this opinion in mind, Patient MQ contacted my office, and after I reviewed her case I accepted her into my practice.

I first met Patient MQ and her husband in mid-June 2009, some five weeks after her most recent surgery. She reported still feeling weakened from the operation, but that overall her general health was improving steadily. She also made clear to me that she would not pursue chemotherapy under any circumstances, because it had completely failed to keep her in remission. Her decision seemed completely reasonable.

Subsequently, Patient MQ proved to be a very determined and compliant patient. During her initial months on treatment, she would occasionally call with minor questions about the program. When she returned with her husband to my office, during the third week of September 2009, she seemed to have adjusted to the regimen with ease and was doing quite well, complaining only of right shoulder bursitis, a long-standing issue.

Her oncologist wanted to repeat the PET scan at that point, but Patient MQ decided she would wait a bit to minimize unnecessary radiation exposure. Then, during the second week of November 2009, she did undergo repeat PET scanning, which revealed "NO HYPERMETA-BOLIC FOCI TO SUGGEST THE PRESENCE OF RESIDUAL RECURRENT DISEASE AT THIS TIME." She was, understandably, quite pleased with the results, as was I.

When I next met with Patient MQ and her husband, during the second week of December 2009, after she had completed some six months on her regimen, she reported feeling well. I made some minor adjustments in her program, and thereafter she remained quite compliant. In late February 2010, she developed a severe urinary tract infection, treated effectively with antibiotics prescribed by her primary care physician. An ultrasound of the abdomen at the time showed cysts along the upper pole of the left kidney that had been noted on her prior scans, but no other abnormalities, and certainly no evidence of recurrent colon cancer.

When Patient MQ next returned to my office for a routine visit, during the second week of March 2010, she was back to feeling well. Thereafter, she continued on her program, and when I saw her during the second week of June 2010—having completed a year on her nutritional program—her biggest concern was one of her daughters, who had undergone major surgery for a congenital spinal problem. The operation had not gone well, and Patient MQ was very worried about her daughter, though MQ herself remained in excellent health. We talked about the need for a follow-up colonoscopy with her gastroenterologist, but I could tell that she was reluctant to proceed with the test.

Patient MQ continued returning to my office for regularly scheduled visits every three months. A repeat PET scan during the first week of December 2010 again showed "no hypermetabolic foci to suggest the presence of residual/recurrent disease at this time."

Because Patient MQ seemed determinedly compliant with her therapy and clinically appeared to be doing fine, eventually I spaced out her appointments to every six months. Blood studies including liver function tests and the CEA tumor marker remained within the normal range. For example, the CEA during the second week of January 2012 came in at 0.8, well within the normal range of 0.0–3.0.

Currently, Patient MQ is more than six and a half years from her original diagnosis of colon cancer with metastases into two lymph nodes, treated after colon resection with aggressive adjuvant chemotherapy. She is more than four years out from her first recurrence into the left and possibly right lung in October 2008, treated surgically, with a second pulmonary recurrence seven months later, addressed with additional lung surgery in May 2009, during which time two tumors were excised. Since beginning her nutritional program in June 2009, she has remained disease-free while experiencing steadily improving good health.

Despite advances in treatment, the outlook for metastatic stage IV colon cancer remains poor. According to the website UptoDate, with current chemotherapy regimens the median survival has improved from less than a year to 20 months for those diagnosed with stage IV disease, though the five-year survival comes in at less than 10 percent. Patients with isolated hepatic or lung metastasis can at times be cured with surgical resection, if the disease has not spread elsewhere. Kwong and Timmerman, writing in *Cancer: Principles and Practice of Oncology*, reported that in a series of 1,578 patients undergoing surgery with curative intent for presumed localized colon cancer, 8.7 percent subsequently developed lung metastases. Of this group with pulmonary disease, only 11.6 percent were thought candidates for resection of the lung lesions.[7]

In two studies, each tracking more than one hundred patients with pulmonary metastases undergoing surgery, the reported five-year survivals were 31 percent and 37 percent,[8] but these numbers apply to a small subset of patients with colon cancer metastatic to the lungs.

Poor-prognosis indicators include multiple metastases, a high CEA tumor marker, and recurrence within three years.[9] In the case of Patient MQ, routine CEA testing was not done, but she experienced her first definitive evidence of pulmonary recurrence in October 2008, slightly more than two years after her original surgery in July 2006. After undergoing resection of the pulmonary lesion, she developed a recurrence with multiple lesions evident on scans in May 2009, some six months after her first lung surgery. Though she underwent resection of the left malignant tumors, a right lesion was untouched. Clearly, by the standards of conventional oncology, her long-term disease-free survival while she pursued only her nutritional regimen from June 2009 onward is remarkable.

*IMPORTANT EDITOR'S NOTE:
Dr. Gonzalez died before he was able to update some of these case reports. Therefore, we have updated the survival time for this patient based on the patient's office medical file.

According to this patient's medical file, she died in August 2014.

---

7 King F. Kwong and Robert Timmerman, "Metastatic Cancer to the Lung," in *Cancer: Principles and Practice of Oncology*, ed. Vincent T. DeVita, Jr., Theodore S. Lawrence, and Steven A. Rosenberg, 9th ed. (Philadelphia, PA: Lippincott William & Wilkins, 2011), 2170.
8 Ibid.
9 Ibid.

Case 6: Patient ZZ
A Minimum 21-Year Survivor

Patient ZZ is a ninety-four-year-old male who has survived twenty-one years with very poor-prognosis colon cancer.

In terms of family history, Patient ZZ's maternal uncle had died of some type of cancer, primary unknown, and his father had succumbed to brain cancer. ZZ had himself generally been in good health prior to his diagnosis of cancer, with a history pertinent only for ten years of cigarette use and mild osteoarthritis.

He had been in his usual state of good health when, in August 1991, he developed new-onset left abdominal pain/cramping that he initially attributed to gastroenteritis. When the pain persisted and worsened over a period of some six weeks, in October 1991 he consulted with his primary care physician, who prescribed a course of antibiotics for a presumed lingering bacterial colon infection. When the symptoms continued despite treatment, a week later he was referred to a gastroenterologist at The New York Hospital–Cornell for an evaluation. Colonoscopy revealed a large right-ascending colon tumor, found on biopsy to be consistent with adenocarcinoma. A CT scan of the abdomen showed the tumor but no evidence of metastatic disease.

Patient ZZ was then referred to a surgeon and in late October 1991 was admitted to New York Hospital for exploratory laparotomy. As described in the Operative Summary, during the procedure the surgeon found evidence of abnormal local lymph nodes in the region of the tumor but no distant spread: "The primary lesion was palpable in the right colon. In addition, there were enlarged hard mesenteric lymph nodes. Manual exploration of the abdominal cavity revealed no evidence of other masses in the remainder of the abdominal viscera or in the liver."

The pathology report described "a fungating white-yellow mass with ulceration which measures 6 × 6 cm and extends up to 1.5 cm. above the mucosal surface."

The "MICROSCOPIC REPORT" described the following: "RIGHT ILEO-COLECTOMY SPECIMEN SHOWING MODERATELY DIFFERENTIATED COLONIC ADENOCARCINOMA EXTENDING THROUGH THE MUSCULARIS PROPRIA TO THE ADIPOSE TISSUE EXTENSIVE VASCULAR INVASION IS IDENTIFIED.... FOURTEEN OUT OF NINETEEN PERICOLONIC LYMPH NODES ARE POSITIVE FOR TUMOR."

Despite the lack of apparent spread into distant organs, the pathological findings of invasion into the adipose tissue and the fourteen positive lymph nodes portended a very poor prognosis.

After recovering from surgery, Patient ZZ met with an oncologist, who, after explaining the severity of the situation, recommended a course of adjuvant chemotherapy with the standard at the time of 5-fluorouracil and Leucovorin. Patient ZZ, unaware of any other options, agreed to the plan and began chemotherapy in December 1991. However, he experienced severe side effects, particularly extreme weakness and fatigue, anorexia, and a twenty-four-pound weight loss, all of which affected his resolve to continue treatment. In addition, in the spring of 1992 he first learned about my work from a neighbor and patient of mine who had done well under my care. So, after his third cycle of chemotherapy, in April 1992 he decided to discontinue conventional treatment and consult with me.

After Patient ZZ applied to become a patient, I accepted him into my practice, and he was first seen during the third week of May 1992. At the time, he reported he was still recuperating from treatment, and though feeling somewhat stronger in recent weeks, he complained of ongoing weakness and fatigue, as well as insomnia that had developed during his chemotherapy. He said the whole experience had been quite "rough."

The day of his visit, I ordered some blood work, which came back generally within normal limits except for a mildly elevated CEA at 3.3 (normal less than 2.5).

Thereafter, Patient ZZ approached his nutritional regimen with great determination. Though he continued running his high-stress and demanding business, he adjusted well to the treatment. In early August 1992, he called my office several times reporting intermittent bouts of dizziness when getting up from a sitting position. With increased fluid intake, these episodes resolved after a week.

When I next saw him, in late August 1992, after he had completed three months on his therapy, he seemed very compliant and seemed to be doing better. He looked well, reported that his energy and stamina had significantly improved, and said he had no problems at the time.

During the first months on the treatment, Patient ZZ proved to be low maintenance, following the program as prescribed and rarely calling. In preparation for his six-month re-evaluation in late November 1992, I ordered repeat blood work, which this time showed an improved CEA falling into the normal range at 1.8.

When I saw him in the office, he reported that since his last visit his energy had continued to improve, he was sleeping well, his appetite was good, and he had gained some weight.

Only days later, he returned to his surgeon for repeat colonoscopy, which showed only two very small 2 to 3 mm polyps that were excised and found to be benign, described as "HYPERPLAS-TIC COLONIC MUCOSA, INFLAMED. NO TUMOR SEEN."

When Patient ZZ next returned to my office, during the first week of March 1993, after completing some ten months on therapy, he had gotten somewhat careless with the spacing of his enzyme doses throughout the day but otherwise seemed quite compliant. He reported feeling quite well.

In late May 1993, he came in to the office for his one-year re-evaluation. He seemed compliant, reported feeling quite strong, and said his only problem was work-related stress.

Thereafter, I continued seeing Patient ZZ every three months in the office; he remained compliant with the therapy and continued doing well. In late October 1993, two years after his operation, he returned to his surgeon for colonoscopy that this time showed no abnormalities, no polyps, and no evidence of recurrent disease.

Subsequently, Patient ZZ returned to my office every three to four months. In late September 1994, he experienced a single episode of chest pain that proved, on cardiac evaluation by a local cardiologist with an interest in alternative approaches, to be inconsequential. Subsequent colonoscopy in October 1994, three years after his surgery, was completely normal.

When Patient ZZ returned to my office during the second week of September 1995, after completing nearly three and a half years on my therapy, he seemed quite compliant with the prescribed routine, even though he had been traveling considerably in recent months for his business. He reported feeling generally well but had experienced two further episodes of chest pain in the previous weeks, midsternal in location and very brief in duration. He had consulted with his local cardiologist with each bout, but EKGs each time were apparently completely normal. Patient ZZ himself associated the pain with stress. Otherwise, he reported feeling quite well, with good energy, stamina, and concentration.

I made several adjustments to Patient ZZ's nutritional regimen, adding on low-dose niacin, coenzyme Q10—which at the time was first being touted as a remedy for all manner of cardiac dysfunction—and our Heart glandular, consisting of lyophilized beef heart from New Zealand animals. Though I fully realize conventional physicians see little value in the use of such animal organ concentrates, literature going back ninety years asserts their clinical efficacy.

During the second week of November 1995, ZZ called my office to inform me he had recently experienced another episode of chest pain. He had again consulted with the local cardiologist in upstate New York who had been following him. This time, the EKG "showed something," the nature of which hadn't been fully explained to the patient, though he was told it wasn't serious. In response, the physician had prescribed a mass of supplements, which concerned Patient ZZ because he didn't want to take any additional nutrients without first consulting me.

He also expressed some frustration to me about the doctor, who, he said, "didn't explain anything" and didn't address the purpose for the various supplements he had recommended. ZZ asked me if I could refer him to a cardiologist in New York for a second opinion. I suggested a physician in Manhattan who, though conventional, was very familiar with my work and happy to see my patients who might require a cardiology consult.

ZZ did acknowledge that he was under considerable stress at work, which he thought might have contributed to the recent episode of pain. I nonetheless strongly encouraged him to continue to follow up with a cardiologist, whether the local physician or the one I had recommended in Manhattan.

When Patient ZZ returned to my office about a month later, in mid-December 1995, his biggest complaint remained not anything to do with his cancer diagnosis, but the ongoing episodes of chest pain that appeared to be occurring more frequently, and always with exertion. He again described the pain as midsternal and sharp, but lasting only a few seconds. He denied any radiation of the pain to his jaw, arm, or anywhere else. With each episode, he described feeling "winded," but this symptom would also resolve within a few minutes. To me, his symptoms sounded like typical exertional angina.

Since our previous phone conversation, Patient ZZ had decided to continue under the care of his local cardiologist, who had diagnosed a leaky mitral valve and, according to Patient ZZ, angina. The physician had prescribed a variety—about fifteen in fact—of supplements, including a number of homeopathic remedies, which Patient ZZ had been taking. ZZ felt the supplements had done nothing to reduce the frequency or intensity of the chest pain. Fortunately, an EKG the day before his visit with me "looked better," apparently showing no evidence of acute disease or myocardial infarction.

Otherwise, Patient ZZ said that he felt quite well, with good energy and stamina, despite severe ongoing stress at his business. He seemed quite compliant with my regimen, which already provided many of the supplements prescribed by the local cardiologist. I reduced the newly prescribed supplements significantly, eliminating duplications and those products I thought might interfere with my therapy. I also increased the doses of certain nutrients that I had found at that time to be helpful for angina.

Patient ZZ, having given the local doctor a "second chance," remained unhappy with the situation and informed me he would be following up with a more conventional cardiologist near his home for a second opinion. I again adjusted his program somewhat.

I didn't hear from Patient ZZ again until his return visit in early February 1996. He reported that in recent months he had been doing much better, particularly since I had reduced the supplement load prescribed by the cardiologist. With my suggested modifications, Patient ZZ reported that since my visit in December 1995 he had experienced no further episodes of chest pain. And, he told me, his energy, stamina, and importantly his exercise tolerance had all substantially improved. He had also decided not to consult with the second local cardiologist, because he was feeling much better. I however, encouraged him strongly to follow up, explaining once again that chest pain, however minor, should never be taken for granted.

When Patient ZZ returned to my office three months later, in mid-May 1996—now four years since he had started treatment with me—he seemed compliant and said he felt very well as he approached his seventy-eighth birthday. He was working a full day, reported excellent energy, and said his chest pain remained resolved—at least for the time being.

Only five days later, Patient ZZ faxed me a long note explaining that, after our visit, he had experienced a very severe episode of left-sided chest pain at four in the morning that woke him from sleep and kept him awake the rest of the night. The severe pain gradually resolved, though he described some residual chest soreness in the morning. He was able to get in to see his local internist that day, who after an examination suspected the trouble might be stomach related, gastritis or reflux, rather than cardiac in origin. He prescribed cimetidine, currently available over the counter but at that time still a prescription medication.

The physician, to my pleasant surprise, was very supportive of ZZ's treatment with me, assuring him that the medication would not interfere with his nutritional regimen. In fact, cimetidine has long been used by veterinarians to treat certain malignancies in horses. During the 1990s, studies in humans showed an anticancer effect with colon cancer specifically.

But Patient ZZ wouldn't take any medication until I had given my okay. I told him the physician's suggestions were reasonable, and the medication would not interfere with my program. His internist had also given him the name of a cardiologist for follow-up, to rule out any cardiac cause of the pain. Once again, I gave him the contact information for the cardiologist I recommended in Manhattan. Though when we spoke the chest discomfort had completely resolved, I emphasized strongly how important it was to follow up with some cardiologist.

Three months later, during the third week of August 1996—now more than four years after he had begun treatment with me—Patient ZZ and his wife returned to my office for a regularly scheduled visit. He seemed to be quite compliant with the regimen and generally seemed to be doing well, but he reported additional episodes of chest pain, which he clearly related to stress in his life. Though he acknowledged his work could be high pressured, he enjoyed his business, which he had created many years earlier. That, he felt, wasn't really the problem.

Instead, he and his wife talked about his biggest ongoing stress, an adult son who had been, as I learned, a source of great concern because of poor life choices. Whenever this particular family-related stress intensified, the chest pain would come on. The pain could be severe, though it would last only a few seconds and still did not radiate outside the chest. Unfortunately, he had not contacted the cardiologist I had recommended, or the local cardiologist suggested by his internist.

It wasn't until the third week of October 1996 that I received a copy of a fax from Patient ZZ sent originally to his local alternative cardiologist, requesting that his records be sent to the cardiologist in Manhattan I had now recommended several times. I was relieved that he had finally decided to follow up on that suggestion.

Subsequently, during the last week of October 1996, Patient ZZ met with the cardiologist, who within days sent me a lengthy note describing her findings and recommendations. An EKG had shown "atrial premature beats without any other significant abnormality." A stress test demonstrated no evidence of myocardial ischemia. This physician, whom I have long thought superb, believed the arrhythmia to be mild, not requiring any treatment. She had reassured the patient that he had no "significant heart disease."

When I saw Patient ZZ next, in early November 1996, he seemed far more relaxed about his heart because a conventional cardiologist had found no problem requiring treatment. Though the stress with the son continued, Patient ZZ reported feeling quite well.

That day, I ordered routine blood testing, which came back perfectly normal including a PSA at 0.9. His CEA, the colon cancer tumor marker that I had not been routinely testing, was 1.0, the lowest it had been.

When Patient ZZ returned to my office three months early in February 1997, he reported he had recently seen his New York Hospital surgeon. Colonoscopy showed only scar tissue in the area of the 1991 surgery, but no recurrent cancer. The surgeon had suggested a CT of the abdomen, but Patient ZZ expressed his reluctance to proceed with the test because he felt well and wished to avoid unnecessary radiation exposure.

Tragically, about six weeks after the visit with me, a family member called to inform me that one of ZZ's children had died suddenly and unexpectedly, a sad and devastating turn of events for ZZ. I called to express my condolences.

When he returned to my office during the last week of May 1997 for a routine visit—now having completed a full five years of treatment with me—he was still in deep grief because of his recent loss. Through the terrible stress, he had remained compliant with his program, and he found solace in his local church, which had rallied behind his family in their time of terrible need. Not surprisingly, some three weeks earlier he had experienced another episode of chest pain, which, though short lived, was severe enough that he had gone to the ER of his local hospital. A cardiac workup was unrevealing, but additional testing including a chest x-ray indicated ZZ had a case of "walking pneumonia," with no symptoms other than the chest discomfort. He was started on antibiotics but also referred to a local cardiologist with whom he had consulted by the time of his appointment with me. The cardiologist, as had Patient ZZ's internist, believed the problem to be more gastrointestinal in nature and referred him to a local gastroenterologist for endoscopy to rule out ulcer disease.

Several days later, endoscopy showed only a "small hiatal hernia and antral gastritis, but no ulcer." He was prescribed a proton pump inhibitor, which gave some relief. Subsequently, he continued returning to my office regularly and continued doing well. During a return visit to my office during the first week of May 1998—now six years on his therapy—he reported, as he approached age eighty, that he felt quite well and had had no episodes of chest pain for more than a year. His local doctor had started him on atenolol, a mild beta-blocker, which seemed to have helped. He continued working fully at his business, without difficulty.

I continued seeing Patient ZZ regularly. When I saw him in early October 1999, seven and a half years after he had started with me, he lamented that his business, which he loved so much, wasn't doing well because of the changes in technology that were rendering his company obsolete. At age eighty-one, however, he wasn't anxious to give up working and was already looking into other opportunities.

By that point, he hadn't seen his surgeon for several years. In early November 2000, nine years from his surgery, he did return for colonoscopy, which showed no polyps, no tumors, and no evidence of recurrent cancer. When I saw ZZ in my office in mid-January 2001, he remained compliant with his therapy and looked terrific at age eighty-two. He had no complaints, other than some diminished hearing. He reported sadly that he had finally closed his business.

I didn't hear from Patient ZZ for more than a year, when in late January 2003—some ten and a half years after he had begun with me—he sent me a long note, explaining that because he had closed down his business, his financial situation wasn't great. But he continued on the program and continued feeling well at age eighty-four. Though we lost contact after that time, he remains alive at ninety-four years of age, and more than twenty-one years since his surgery in late October 1991.

A number of prognostic indicators predicted for a very poor outcome in the case of Patient ZZ. As a start, his age at the time of diagnosis, at seventy-three, was not in his favor. In terms of his cancer specifically, the large tumor removed at surgery, 6 × 6 cm, was ulcerated and fungating and had broken through the bowel wall into the surrounding tissues, all factors that argued for a terrible prognosis. Then, the fourteen positive lymph nodes certainly argued against long-term survival. Although Patient ZZ did complete an abbreviated three cycles of a proposed minimal six cycles of basic 5-FU chemotherapy, in his situation drug treatment, even with more aggressive contemporary regimens, has not been shown to prolong life.

The website Up-to-date provides an excellent evaluation of prognosis with and without current treatment for various cancers, including colon cancer. Here, physicians can plug in specific characteristics of the patient and the disease in question, such as age, extent of tumor invasion, histological grade, and lymph node involvement. For a patient with ZZ's age and tumor characteristics, the predicted five-year survival without chemotherapy after surgery would be, even today, a mere 5.2 percent, with 88.8 percent of patients dying of cancer. For those receiving a full course of adjuvant chemotherapy, the statistics are identical, with no benefit at all reported; 5.2 percent of patients in this group will survive five years, and 88.8 percent will die of their disease despite aggressive treatment. So Patient ZZ's long-term disease-free survival, now at twenty-one-plus years, is remarkable by the standards of conventional oncology.

KIDNEY (RENAL) CANCER

In the US, 36,000 new cases of kidney cancer were reported in 2004, and 12,500 deaths.[1] Cigarette smoking predisposes one to the disease, with up to 20 to 30 percent of cases linked to the habit. Researchers have suggested associations with obesity, polycystic kidney disease, von Hippel Lindau disease, and certain genetic aberrations. In recent years, though the incidence has been increasing steadily, no clear-cut environmental risk, other than cigarette smoking, has been confirmed.

Renal cell carcinoma, the most common form of kidney cancer, accounts for 90 to 95 percent of all cases. In this type, the disease begins in the epithelial lining cells of the proximal tubules and, if localized, can be cured in well over 50 percent of patients with surgery alone.[2] Once the disease metastasizes, it usually spreads quickly with deadly results. Conventional therapies such as chemotherapy and immune modulation offer little benefit. As *Harrison's* reports bluntly,[3] "Investigational therapy is first-line treatment for metastatic disease as no immune approach or chemotherapeutic agent has shown significant antitumor activity." Interleukin-2, once heralded as a miracle cure in the mid-1980s based on anecdotal evidence, in controlled clinical trials worked no better than placebo.

Some twenty-five hundred cases of cancer of the renal pelvis are diagnosed each year. In its histology, this form resembles transitional cell cancer of the bladder and, if localized, like renal cell, can be cured with surgical resection. When metastatic to distant organs, oncologists treat the disease as they would bladder cancer though with little success. Few patients with metastatic disease survive six months.

---

1   Kasper et al., *Harrison's Principles*, 16th ed., 541.
2   DeVita et al., *Cancer: Principles and Practice*, 6th ed., 1364.
3   Kasper et al., *Harrison's Principles*, 16th ed., 542.

Case 1: Patient DQ
*A 15.5-Year Survivor**
Renal Cell Carcinoma

Patient DQ is an eighty-two-year-old man who had a history pertinent because of celiac disease, gout, and chronic borderline anemia. In October of 1990, his primary physician noted an abdominal mass during a routine yearly physical examination. Subsequent MRI and CT scan studies revealed a 14 cm tumor in the left kidney, with no evidence of metastases. Chest x-ray and bone scan were both clear, and in late October 1990 DQ underwent exploratory laparotomy and left nephrectomy. Pathology studies confirmed renal cell carcinoma, with 1/1 adjacent nodes positive for invasive cancer.

DQ was then referred to a major New York medical center for additional evaluation and treatment. There, in December 1990, he agreed to enter a clinical trial testing alpha interferon, an immune stimulant, against kidney cancer. After repeat chest and abdominal CT scans showed no evidence of residual or recurrent disease, DQ then began an eight-cycle course of intensive interferon, which he completed in August of 1991.

Thereafter, DQ did well until November 1991, when he noticed a lump in the left parietal-occipital region of the skull that rapidly enlarged over a period of several days. In early December, needle aspiration of the mass confirmed "adenocarcinoma, consistent with metastatic renal tubular carcinoma."

A subsequent CT of the head indicated that the tumor had penetrated through the skull into the cranium, as the report stated: "There is a lytic lesion within the left parietal bone with an associated enhancing soft tissue mass, consistent with a metastasis. There is intracranial extension of the enhancing soft tissue, as well as extension into the subcutaneous tissues of the left parietal scalp."

A bone scan revealed "a large focal area of increased radiopharmaceutical uptake with a photopenic center consistent with metastatic disease in the left occipital region of the skull." A CT scan of the chest indicated a "small nodule at the left lung base...which may be an area of fibrosis as described. Two other smaller densities in the middle lobe and the left lower lobe as described of questionable significance." However, these lung findings had not been reported on the chest CT of December 1990.

DQ then began a one-month course of radiation to the skull mass, totaling 4,000 rads and completed in January 1992. Despite the treatment, the tumor regressed only marginally. DQ, having been told he had incurable disease, began looking into alternative approaches, learned of my work, and decided to pursue my protocol. When we first met, in January 1992, only a week after he had finished radiation, DQ reported significantly diminished energy, along with a twenty-pound weight loss occurring during the previous six weeks. On exam, I immediately noticed a lemon-sized mass sticking out of his skull in the left parietal area.

Shortly thereafter, DQ began his nutritional protocol, complied well, and within weeks reported a significant improvement in his energy and well-being, as well as a twenty-pound weight gain. After three months on his nutritional protocol, the previously noted large skull mass completely resolved. A repeat bone scan in June 1993, after DQ had completed some sixteen months of treatment, revealed "no evidence of bony metastatic disease." Not only had the lesion disappeared, but the underlying skull had healed. Today, nearly fifteen years after he first consulted me, DQ remains completely adherent to his treatment, is in excellent health, and is cancer-free.

Several points need mentioning. Renal cell carcinoma, once metastatic, is a very deadly disease: DeVita has reported a median survival of only fifty days for patients with stage IV kidney cancer, despite treatment.[4] This neoplasm resists not only chemotherapy and immunotherapy, but radiation as well. In this case, DQ's doctors suggested radiation not as a potential cure but as palliation, hoping to slow the spread of the tumor into the brain. In any event, the response was negligible. While some radiation oncologists report that at times, the benefit of radiation therapy might continue for up to two months, DQ showed significant response only after his third month on his nutritional program. Furthermore, although his radiologists initially downplayed the new findings on the chest CT in late 1991, in retrospect these lesions may have indicated the beginnings of explosive spread.

*IMPORTANT EDITOR'S NOTE:
Dr. Gonzalez was still editing this case at the time of his death. According to the patient's office file, he died in July 2007.

---

4   DeVita et al., *Cancer: Principles and Practice*, 6th ed., 1369.

Case 2: Patient UB
A Minimum 6.5-Year Survivor
Renal Pelvic Cancer

In July of 1989, Patient UB, at the time a sixty-six-year-old Caribbean woman, first developed hematuria. Cystoscopy revealed only a benign urethrocoele, and a right retrograde pyelogram showed no abnormalities. Subsequent urine cytology in January 1990 was negative, but in May 1991 she consulted her urologist again after noticing blood in her urine. According to the physician's notes, this time, "urine cytology showed atypical cells on 2 occasions and malignant cells in one specimen. Repeat IVP showed a defect in the right renal pelvis."

When repeat cystoscopy in June 1991 revealed a normal bladder mucosa, but significant blood in the right ureter, her urologist suspected she "most likely has a right renal pelvis tumor and have advised her family that she will most likely need nephro-ureterectomy." The patient then agreed to a needle biopsy of the right renal tumor, which showed, according to the patient and her family, renal pelvic cancer—though we do not have the actual pathology report of this test in our possession.

When UB learned of our approach from her daughter who lives in the United States, she canceled surgery despite the urgings of her urologist and decided to proceed with our treatment. During our first session, in July 1991, she reported intermittent right flank pain and urethral burning on urination, but no other symptoms. I urged her to reconsider surgery, which I explained could be curative if the disease proved localized. She adamantly held her course, stating that she had had enough surgery in her life—she had years earlier undergone hysterectomy—and would not allow any more, whether I would accept her as a patient or not. So, with her point well made, we agreed to proceed.

She proved to be a very compliant patient and did well clinically, with rapid resolution of her flank pain and no further episodes of hematuria. On her home island, she studiously avoided contact with all other doctors despite my wish that she consult with them at least on occasion. Because she had no insurance, frequent testing to monitor her progress was simply out of the question—not that she would have agreed to it anyway. But in October 1995, after she had completed four years on our treatment, she did allow an abdominal ultrasound, which revealed a normal right kidney except for a 2.3 cm simple cyst in the pole. Otherwise, the report stated, "No solid tumor mass seen. The left kidney and the remainder of the abdominal organs were normal in appearance."

During the first four years on therapy, UB did return periodically to New York for re-evaluations. After 1995, she could not afford the expense of the trips, so I agreed to follow her by phone.

My last contact with her was in 1998, after she had been on the program for 6.5 years. At that time, she was feeling well, with no complaints.

In this patient, her resolution of signs and symptoms, her lack of disease spread, and her long survival all indicate a good response to treatment, particularly because she refused all orthodox interventions including surgery. Furthermore, ultrasound studies after four years on treatment confirmed that the previously documented renal pelvis tumor had resolved completely. Unfortunately, we never received the actual pathology report of the needle biopsy, so her records are in that sense incomplete. But the patient and family members carefully described the procedure and the results that had been reported to her. And we do have the urologist's discussion of the positive cytology and IVP findings to confirm the diagnosis of cancer. Despite the one missing document, I included her because she did so well following only my nutritional regimen.

Case 3: Patient FR
*A 6.7-Year Survivor**

Patient FR passed away at age sixty-three, having survived nearly seven years with a history of stage IV renal cell carcinoma.

In terms of his family history, FR reported that the only case of cancer he knew of was his mother, who had survived a bout of colon cancer. A former New York City municipal worker, in terms of his own history, he had smoked a pack a day of cigarettes for some sixteen years, before quitting at age thirty. He generally had been otherwise healthy when, in the spring of 1998, he was diagnosed with type II diabetes, managed with diet and oral medications.

His current situation dated to April 1998, just about the time he was being diagnosed with diabetes, when he developed chronic right shoulder pain associated with a gradually enlarging mass. When the pain worsened and the mass continued to enlarge, in July 1998 he consulted his primary care physician, who thought the problem was muscular, suggesting only that he apply ice packs regularly. However, the pain continued to worsen, and when Patient FR consulted with the physician's assistant assigned to monitor his diabetes, he mentioned the worsening pain and the, by that point, clearly evident mass. That same day, FR was sent for an x-ray of the shoulder, which clearly showed a malignant-appearing lesion:

> IMPRESSION:
>
> Lytic lesion distal right clavicle with tumoral appearing paeriosteal new bone suggesting primary bone tumor. Fibrosarcoma. Osteosarcoma or metastatic disease to the clavicle.

At this point, Patient FR was urgently referred to an orthopedist, who saw him within a day. This physician ordered an MRI of the shoulder, which two days later the report revealed the following: "The MRI examination shows a smoothly-marginated enhancing ovoid mass measuring 4 cm in greatest diameter. This appears to destroy the distal clavicle with no involvement of the adjacent AC (acromial) joint."

In the "SUMMARY" section of the report, the radiologist wrote, "It measures slightly in the access [sic] of 4 cm in greatest diameter. This specific etiology of this distal clavicular mass is unclear but in this age group metastasis would be a principle consideration."

A bone scan the following day confirmed the suspicious nature of the lesion: "IMPRESSION Localized area of abnormal activity in the distal right clavicle suggestive of a primary bone neoplasm."

Patient FR was then referred to an oncological orthopedist at the Upstate Medical Center in Syracuse, New York. A biopsy of the lesion during the first week of August 1998 revealed not a primary bone cancer, but "CLEAR CELL NEOPLASM CONSISTENT WITH META-STATIC RENAL CELL (KIDNEY) CARCINOMA." That same day, Patient FR underwent further testing at University Hospital, Syracuse. A bone survey again showed "a destructive lesion of the distal right clavicle." A CT scan of the chest showed the "lytic expansile mass involving the distal right clavicle" but no evidence of lung metastases.

CT scan of the abdomen revealed a right kidney mass "worrisome for malignancy": "A 4 × 4.8 × 4 cm. rounded mass is seen medially in the right kidney which enhances…"

A CT scan of the pelvis was with normal limits.

With the diagnosis now confirmed, Patient FR decided to consult with a urological oncologist at New York University Medical Center, the well-respected Dr. Taneja. Because of the evidence of metastatic stage IV disease, Dr. Taneja suggested a referral to an oncologist at NYU, with whom Patient FR met during the second week of August 1998. The oncologist suggested a number of options including interleukin 2 and interferon, being widely used for kidney cancer at the time, with the hope of shrinking the large shoulder and kidney tumor to allow for more effective surgery afterward. However, the oncologist discouraged the use of either systemic chemotherapy or radiation to the shoulder tumor, neither of which he felt would be helpful with FR's particular type and stage of cancer.

Unsure at that point of how he wished to proceed, several days later, at the Upstate Medical Center, Patient FR met with the chief of urology, who suggested immediate surgery for resection of the kidney tumor. This physician also discussed interleukin-2 and interferon as well. A medical oncologist brought in on the case at Syracuse urged a consultation with a radiation oncologist, who in turn recommended—in contradiction to the NYU oncologist—a course of intensive radiation to the shoulder after proposed shoulder surgery for resection of the clavicle tumor. As Patient FR and his wife would later tell me, they were "completely turned off" by the Syracuse team because their recommendations were so strongly at odds with the thoughtful advice of the NYU group. So, after reviewing his options, Patient FR decided to return to NYU for treatment.

During the fourth week of August 1998, Patient FR was admitted to NYU to begin a course of interleukin-2 and interferon, to be followed by surgery for both the clavicle and kidney tumors. Because of the very toxic nature of interleukin-2, often patients will be admitted for the initiation and treatment and close monitoring. And indeed, shortly after beginning therapy, Patient FR became quite ill with flu-like symptoms, severe nausea, frequent vomiting, malaise, and anorexia associated with a forty-pound weight loss. But over a period of some days, the symptoms lessened, and when he was discharged from the hospital in late August 1998 he was in stable condition, with plans to continue at home with subcutaneous injections three times a week.

Patient FR eventually completed nearly nine weeks of the interleukin-2/interferon treatment. At that point, during the last week of October 1998, Patient FR underwent rescanning at NYU. Unfortunately, the aggressive treatment yielded little benefit. An MRI of the right shoulder showed no reduction in tumor size, and perhaps some growth: "A soft tissue mass measuring 5 × 4 × 4cm in size has replaced the distal end of the right clavicle. … The appearance is compatible with the clinical history of biopsy proven renal cell carcinoma metastasis."

A CT scan of the abdomen and pelvis the same day did show no growth in the right kidney lesion: "There is a 4.5 centimeter enhancing right renal neoplasm visualized at the posterior limb of the mid portion. … The appearance is typical of a primary renal neoplasm however, primary v. metastatic disease cannot be determined."

After the test reports were available, FR met with the NYU oncologist, who suggested it was time to proceed with surgery as quickly as practically possible. So about a month later, during the fourth week of November 1998, Patient FR was admitted to NYU, with plans for resection of the clavicular mass and kidney the same day. The surgery went on as planned, with no complications, though postoperatively FR required a blood transfusion and did develop a pleural effusion treated with chest tube placement. The Discharge Summary described the joint procedures as "RIGHT RADICAL NEPHRECTOMY AND RIGHT CLAVICULAR MASS RESECTION WITHOUT ANY COMPLICATION."

No adjunctive postoperative treatment was suggested, though the NYU oncologist planned to follow FR closely, with repeat scans scheduled for March 1999. However, Patient FR realized that with stage IV kidney cancer, despite the successful surgery, he faced the likelihood of recurrence down the road. So, he and his wife began looking into alternative approaches, learned about my work, applied to become a patient, and were accepted into the practice.

I first met FR during the last week of January 1999, some two months after his surgery. He reported that he still hadn't recovered from his ordeal, describing ongoing fatigue, decreased stamina, and poor sleep.

During the second session the following day, in which I routinely spend two hours reviewing the prescribed protocol, Patient FR and his wife discussed some considerable stress in their lives. But he seemed determined to follow through with his nutritional regimen.

The scheduled bone scan during the second week of March 1999 showed "no scintigraphic evidence for osseous metastatic disease."

I next saw FR in early April 1999, when he had completed nearly three months on his therapy. I was concerned, because his compliance wasn't what it needed to be. Certainly, he was doing much of the program, but not nearly as prescribed. For example, he admitted that he was routinely missing the middle-of-the-night dose of pancreatic enzymes, which we believe is the single most important dose of all the supplements for anticancer effect. He informed me that he had been doing the coffee enemas only once a day, instead of the prescribed twice daily. Some patients initially simply do not realize how important the enemas are, done in the way prescribed, but I learned a long time ago that those patients who cut down on the enemas risk treatment failure.

He also appeared to be "cheating on the diet," not eating all the required foods, and adding foods that he shouldn't be consuming. In great detail, I again reviewed the program, explaining how important it was, with his aggressive type of cancer, to be fully compliant.

However, even cutting corners as he had been, he acknowledged that already he felt the therapy was making a difference in his health. His energy, stamina, endurance, and concentration he described as excellent. He had recently seen his NYU surgeon, who was quite happy with FR's progress. X-rays confirmed good healing, though FR did complain of numbness and tingling in his left arm and leg, due to, the surgeon thought, FR being placed on his left side for hours during surgery.

In early June 1999, Patient FR underwent a routine follow-up radiographic workup at NYU. CT scanning of the chest, abdomen, and pelvis showed no evidence of recurrent or metastatic disease.

When FR returned to my office in early July 1999 for his six-month visit, he reported "feeling great." He said that he had taken my lecture during the April 1999 visit to heart, had tightened up his compliance, and felt his dedication had paid off. The left-sided discomfort had improved substantially, and he had no significant complaints.

During his next visit, in October 1999, again his compliance seemed on target, and again he reported feeling well. The previous August, he had seen both his oncologist and his surgeon, who were both pleased with his recovery from surgery and progress. Repeat radiographic studies had been scheduled for the second week of December 1999.

CT scans of the chest, abdomen, and pelvis during the second week of December 1999, when Patient FR had completed nearly a year on therapy, showed no evidence of metastatic disease. When I saw him in late January 2000, he seemed compliant and reported, as before, feeling very well.

Thereafter, Patient FR continued returning to my office every three months and, for a time, did very well. Repeat scans in June 2000 showed no evidence of recurrent or metastatic disease.

When he returned to my office in late August 2000, after some twenty months on therapy, he acknowledged that once again his compliance had fallen off, this time in terms of the pancreatic enzymes, the most important part of the regimen. Though he seemed to be sticking to the diet and following the various detoxification routines, routinely he was missing two doses of enzymes daily out of a total of six. Once again, I lectured him about the need for complete compliance, to achieve the results we both wanted.

When he returned in late November 2000, his compliance appeared to have improved. Again, he reported feeling quite well and informed me that he was scheduled to return to NYU in December 2000 for appointments with his oncologist and surgeon, as well as radiographic follow-up.

In late December 2000, after FR had completed nearly two years on treatment with me, his repeat CT scans this time showed no evidence of recurrence in his abdomen or pelvis, but new lesions in his right lung as described in the radiology report: "Findings: Study is compared to a prior exam dated 6/—/00. Three parenchymal nodules are now present in the right lung. … This is consistent with metastatic disease."

When I received the report of the study, I immediately checked FR's orders from the distribution company that provides the products needed for our therapy. I was disappointed to learn that he had purchased slightly more than one-half the necessary pancreas enzymes—the main anticancer component of our therapy. With disease as inherently aggressive as stage IV kidney cancer, half compliance with the pancreas simply isn't adequate.

When we spoke by phone later that evening, we discussed options, and he made it clear to me that he wanted only to stay with his nutritional program. As we discussed, interleukin-2—which had recently at the time been shown to be no more active against kidney cancer than placebo—and interferon had done nothing in the weeks before his surgery; in fact, the shoulder tumor had grown. He had already been told chemotherapy and radiation would not be useful for his cancer, so he felt he had no other choice. When we talked about compliance, he promised again to do better.

I always find such situations, as a physician, very difficult. Patient FR and his wife were wonderful people, gracious and enthusiastic about my work, and with great faith in the method. And never do I want to appear to be blaming the patient for program failure. But with aggressive disease, full compliance and great vigilance, as I explained during that phone conversation, is needed.

He informed me that with this new evidence of metastatic disease in the lungs, his surgeon had arranged both an MRI of the brain and a bone scan for early January 2001. Fortunately, both tests revealed no evidence of additional metastatic disease. When the results of these tests were available, Patient FR planned to meet with his NYU oncologist during the first week of January 2001 and scheduled an appointment with me later that day to discuss the situation face to face.

During our session together, FR summed up the meeting with his oncologist, who now recommended various treatments, including more interleukin-2 and more interferon, as well as a bone marrow transplant—though as someone trained to do bone marrow transplants by Dr. Good, I knew then and know now of no evidence that the aggressive and possibly deadly treatment has any effect with stage IV renal cell carcinoma. We discussed the recent *New England Journal of Medicine* article that had shown no benefit above placebo for patients diagnosed with stage IV renal cell carcinoma. FR knew the dismal track record of conventional treatments for his disease, and he repeated what he had said to me before, that he intended only to continue our nutritional therapy.

His NYU oncologist had referred him to an oncologist at the Westchester Medical Center, who was running some type of interluekin-2 clinical trial. I encouraged FR to follow up with the doctor, though he made it clear he would never agree to such a procedure.

When I spoke with Mrs. FR in mid-January 2001, she said she wanted to inform me that the Westchester Medical Center oncologist had never returned their phone calls, and they would not be pursuing that avenue any further. FR, she said, was determined only to stay with my therapy.

FR's NYU urologist had arranged for repeat radiographic studies during the first week of March 2001, when he had completed more than two years on his nutritional program. Fortunately, the CT scan of the chest showed no change:

> Impression:
>
> Lung nodules, suspicious in this clinical setting for metastatic disease. Unchanged however compared to 12-00.

Patient FR returned to my office in late March 2001. He seemed, to my relief, to be again compliant with all aspects of the therapy, particularly with the pancreatic enzymes. He was following the diet as prescribed with no cheating and sticking to the detoxification routine schedule as required. He informed me that he could tell a difference when he was fully compliant: he just felt overall better. During that session, he really had no complaints.

Three months after, in late June 2001, he again returned to my office for a regularly scheduled visit. He told me that he had learned his lesson about compliance; had remained vigilant, it appeared, with all aspects of the therapy; and reported feeling quite well. We discussed repeating the CT scans in September 2001.

In late September 2001, a chest CT scan showed slight enlargement of the lung lesions, reported as "increase in size of the small lung nodules previously identified. … No definite new nodules identified however."

A CT scan of the abdomen showed no evidence of metastatic disease.

A day after the tests, Patient FR returned to my office for a regularly scheduled visit. We talked about the new findings at some length. As a first point, though his compliance had improved, I estimated he still was getting down 80 to 85 percent of the prescribed pancreas dose, not, in my opinion, adequate for a complete response with his aggressive disease. To complicate matters, he and his wife had taken a two-week train ride out West, during which time it was difficult, understandably, to adhere completely to the nutritional regimen. I always become concerned when patients, before their disease is under control, take long trips when they will not have control over their food.

From his perspective, he intended to improve compliance and remained determined to proceed only with his nutritional program. As he said, the much-lauded interleukin-2/interferon regimen had done nothing. Recently, he had met with his NYU oncologist, who repeated what he had said before, that chemotherapy would do "nothing" for metastatic renal cell carcinoma. The physician did suggest an experimental interferon protocol, but FR responded by saying he already had failed an "experimental" interferon protocol.

Clinically, he reported feeling fine, with no respiratory difficulties. His energy he described as "excellent." He kept busy maintaining his impressive organic garden, which brought him great pleasure.

In late November 2001, I received a note from Patient FR informing me that he and his wife intended to consult with an oncologist at Columbia involved with a clinical study testing a new vaccine in patients diagnosed with a variety of malignancies including renal cell carcinoma. He had set up an appointment for the second week of December. Along with his note, FR sent along some information sheets describing the clinical trial in some detail. He made it clear that he intended to continue my therapy but wondered if the vaccine would be a reasonable addition. Of course, I realized that if Patient FR wished to proceed with an experimental therapy on a clinical trial, in fairness to the investigators he would have to give up my treatment.

I did read through the materials, and, as is often the case, the investigators presented considerable esoteric biochemistry that to me was unconvincing as to ultimate effect. I'd been reading about great new "vaccines" for a variety of cancers since medical school, none of which ever turned into anything very beneficial in practice.

When Patient FR, having completed nearly three years on his therapy, and his wife returned to my office during the third week of December 2001, they discussed their visit to Columbia, which from their telling had not been very productive. The physician discussed once again interleukin-2 and interferon, chemotherapy, and the vaccine program. To his disappointment, Patient FR reported that the most enthusiastic recommendation was for interleukin-2 and interferon, which had already failed to slow his disease. He was also aware that chemotherapy did little for his type of cancer, remembering that the well-known NYU oncologist who had first treated him with interleukin-2 and interferon had discouraged the use of chemotherapy in this case, which he thought would be useless. During our conversation, I actually pulled out my most recent addition of *Harrison's Principles of Internal Medicine*, referencing the section of kidney cancer. The authors clearly acknowledged that for metastatic renal cell carcinoma, chemotherapy did little and interleukin-2 and interferon had proved to be a disappointment.

In terms of the vaccine program, only a few patients had been entered and only recently, so there was no data, not even preliminary data, to share. Patient FR said to me that he thought the visit convinced him he wished only to continue with his nutritional therapy, which he credited with keeping him alive for the past three years with stage IV disease.

He also remarked that he had been in touch with his NYU oncologist, who felt there was nothing more he could offer.

After we discussed all this, FR said he actually felt "great," with "excellent" energy, stamina, concentration, sleep, and appetite. He denied any respiratory symptoms of any kind. I also emphasized how important it was for him to remain completely compliant with the treatment, to obtain the results we both wanted.

Several days later, I did receive a lengthy note from the Columbia oncologist, whose reputation I well knew, summarizing the session with Patient FR from December and his suggestions for treatment. I was surprised, as FR had been, that the Columbia physician recommended as his first choice a clinical study combining interferon with Atragen, a vitamin A derivative used primarily with certain forms of leukemia. The note also talked about "chemotherapy options," which from my reading of the literature were dismal for advanced disease.

*IMPORTANT EDITOR'S NOTE:

Dr. Gonzalez died before he was able to update this case report. As stated, Patient FR died at age sixty-three. According to his patient medical files, Patient FR's wife called Dr. Gonzalez in August 2005 to inform him that Patient FR had died. Patient FR had decided to have hip replacement surgery and in preparation for this surgery, Patient FR's surgeons insisted that he stop all of his supplements. During the 4–5 weeks that he waited for his surgery, Patient FR was completely off his nutritional program and according to his wife, the cancer "exploded". The surgeons then decided not to do the operation and recommended radiation instead. Patient FR died within a few days. Patient FR's wife expressed to Dr. Gonzalez "her enormous gratitude for the program and the fact that we gave him nearly seven years of life when no one expected him to live for one year". For most of those years, she said, "the quality of life was superb."

PRIMARY LIVER CANCER (HEPATOCELLULAR CARCINOMA)

The one million cases of hepatocellular carcinoma diagnosed worldwide in 2007 make this malignancy one of the most common internationally, particularly in Africa and Asia. Though relatively rare in the US, nonetheless in 2007 19,160 new cases of the disease were reported, with 16,780 deaths.

Experts have long associated primary liver cancer with the carcinogen aflatoxin B secreted by the Aspergillus mold growing on grains stored at room temperature in tropical climates. Epidemiologists have also linked the malignancy to pesticide exposure, as well as chronic hepatitis B and hepatitis C infection. Regardless of the underlying cause, whether toxic exposure or viral infection, 75 to 85 percent of all patients exhibit underlying cirrhosis at the time of diagnosis.

A variety of staging systems have been proposed in recent years, the most widely accepted being that of Clip and Okuda, graded on a 0–2 range with 2 being the worst, determined according to four distinct criteria. These factors include the number of tumors in the liver (whether single or multiple); the extent of cirrhosis assessed by the Child-Pugh scale; the level of alpha-fetoprotein, a blood tumor marker for the disease; and finally, the presence or absence of portal vein thrombosis.

Hepatocellular carcinoma is quite deadly, with reported mean and median survivals for all stages considered together in the range of three to six months. Though the cancer remains largely resistant to chemotherapy, some new treatment approaches have been somewhat successful in those diagnosed at an early stage. With limited tumor burden, approaches such as hepatic resection, chemoembolization, and the injection of ethanol directly into the tumors have yielded some improved survival but have use only in cases of localized, limited disease. Liver transplantation can, in selected cases, significantly prolong survival, but for the majority of patients the advanced nature of the cancer at the time of diagnosis precludes this aggressive procedure.

The diagnosis of hepatocellular carcinoma does not, in contrast to virtually every other cancer, require a biopsy prior to instituting treatment. Characteristic findings on CT scan and/or MRI, elevated alpha-fetoprotein levels, and a history of hepatitis B or C are sufficient proof of disease.[1]

---

1   DeVita et al., *Cancer: Principles and Practice*, 1164.

Case 1: Patient KN
A Minimum 1-Year Survivor
Resolution of Advanced Liver Cancer

Patient KN is a woman in her fifties with a history of chronic hepatitis C and extensive hepatocellular carcinoma that has regressed on her nutritional therapy. In terms of her family history, three first-degree relatives have been diagnosed with various malignancies, including her father, who died from metastatic prostate cancer.

Patient KN's liver problems first came to light when in the mid-1990s she sought to donate blood as part of a local Red Cross drive. Routine screening revealed hepatitis C, though she had no history of any risk factors such as blood transfusions and was asymptomatic. Initially, the primary physician in charge of her case adopted a conservative watch-and-wait approach, suggesting no treatment. Subsequently, in the late 1990s she came under the care of a hepatologist specializing in hepatitis C, who suggested she begin treatment with interferon and ribavirin, an iron-blocking drug. However, when her HMO insurance refused to cover the costs, the therapy was put on hold.

For a number of years, the hepatologist monitored her status with regular liver function testing, which, specifically in terms of the transaminases, ran in the moderately elevated range of the 70s and 80s (normal less than 40–50). In 2004, when her insurance coverage changed, she did begin a course of interferon and ribavirin. Though her liver function markers improved, she quit the treatment after two months because of serious, debilitating side effects, including a bout of hyperthyroidism attributed to the medication and requiring thyroidectomy.

In 2006, after moving to the southern United States, Patient KN was initially followed by a local gastroenterologist, then later at Duke University in North Carolina, a center for liver transplantation. When she was first seen at Duke, in October 2007, a CT scan of the abdomen revealed mild hepatomegaly and borderline splenomegaly but no focal lesions. Her doctors at Duke suggested no treatment at that point, instead suggesting she be monitored closely over time. During this period, Patient KN, with a long interest in alternative medicine, began taking a number of nutritional and herbal remedies such as alpha-lipoic acid, N-acetyl cysteine, and milk thistle, all proposed as remedies for liver diseases and dysfunction.

And for a time, Patient KN did well, leading essentially a normal life and with her liver function tests remaining moderately elevated, but stable. Her alpha-fetoprotein levels fell and stayed within the normal range until October 2008, when the marker came back significantly elevated at 104 (normal less than 6). Her liver function tests were also higher than they had been previously, with an SGOT of 142 (normal less than 42) and an SGPT at 134 (normal less than

40). A CT scan of the abdomen in early December 2008 again showed a borderline enlarged spleen but no evidence of cancer.

But a repeat alpha-fetoprotein level in December at 303 was higher still than the earlier October test, a warning sign of possible spreading liver cancer. At that point, her doctors at Duke ordered an MRI of the abdomen with and without contrast—a more sensitive test for hepatocellular carcinoma—which revealed multiple tumors in the liver as well as multiple enlarged regional lymph nodes, all described in detail in the radiology report:

> There are multiple early hyperenhancing lesions identified within the left and right lobes of the liver. The largest region of early arterial enhancement is within the right hepatic dome … measuring 1.7 × 2.2 cm. Multiple additional predominantly subcentimeter to 1.5 cm sized hyperenhancing lesions are identified. …

> There are multiple peripancreatic, periportal, periaortic, and paracaval lymph nodes identified. The largest periportal node … measures 1.2 × 2.0 cm.

The summary stated, "MULTIPLE EARLY ARTERIAL ENHANCING LESIONS IDENTIFIED WITHIN THE RIGHT AND LEFT LOBES OF THE LIVER … WORRISOME FOR MULTIFOCAL HEPATOMA. … IN ADDITION, MULTIPLE PERIPANCREATIC, PERIPORTAL, PARACAVAL, AND PERIAORTIC LYMPH NODES, WHICH MAY SUGGEST UNDERLYING REGIONAL METASTATIC LYMPHADENOPATHY."

With the disease essentially confirmed, Patient KN met with the transplant team at Duke. Because of the multiple lesions seen on MRI and the enlarged local lymph nodes, she was ruled ineligible for liver transplantation. The doctors did suggest a biopsy, which the patient refused, though she did agree to a consultation with a staff oncologist. This physician, after explaining what she had been told before, that her extensive disease ruled out transplantation, suggested chemotherapy embolization of the tumors or, as an option, systemic chemotherapy.

According to what the patient later told me, the oncologist seemed to be leaning toward the systemic drug approach as a first-line treatment, because the scans had revealed so many lesions in both lobes of the liver and possible spread into regional lymph nodes. But, when questioned by Patient KN, the oncologist admitted that even with such aggressive treatment the disease ultimately was incurable. He stated that without treatment she might live six to ten months, and with chemotherapy, if she were "lucky," she might live "several extra months."

Patient KN decided to put all decisions on hold, wishing to consider all her options carefully before making any decision. In mid-February 2009, she did agree to a follow-up CT scan, which this time documented numerous liver lesions in both lobes, as described in the radiology report: "Small hyperenhancing focus within the hepatic dome on the arterial phase imaging measures 1.2 × 0.7 cm. … An additional lesion within the dome measures 9 × 6 mm. … A hyperenhancing wedge shaped focus is identified within the periphery of the medial segment of the left hepatic lobe. … A tiny low attenuation focus is seen on the portal venous phase. … Two small low attenuation foci are also identified. … A small lesion measures 5 × 6 mm, the additional lesion measures 5.9 mm."

The summary section stated,

> Small subtle foci within the liver as described above raising the possibility of multifocal HCC [hepatocellular carcinoma][.]
>
> Minimally prominent nodes within the porta hepatis, likely reactive.

An alpha-fetoprotein level at that time came back significantly reduced, interestingly enough, though still elevated at 91 (Patient KN had intensified her nutritional regimen). Her liver function tests, to the surprise of her doctors, had also normalized.

Subsequently, Patient KN learned of my work, decided to proceed with my treatment, and came to the office for the first time during the second week of March 2009. Thereafter, she proved to be a very determined and compliant patient, despite significant stress in her life—including a demanding full-time job she needed to help pay for her supplements. Nonetheless, on her nutritional program, her general health improved rather rapidly, with, as she reported, increased energy, stamina, and overall well-being.

In June 2009, after Patient KN had completed three months on her regimen, a repeat MRI revealed considerable improvement in her disease. The radiologist identified only two small liver lesions, which didn't even register definitely as tumors, and no enlarged lymph nodes: "Minimal hepatic nodularity compatible with early changes of cirrhosis. Mild hypertrophy of the left lobe is also compatible with this diagnosis. Two lesions within segment 8 (measuring 16 and 9 mm in diameter) may represent transient hepatic attenuation differences as they are only seen on early arterial enhancement."

Thereafter, Patient KN continued her therapy and continued to improve clinically. In November 2009, eight months after she began her regimen, she underwent follow-up CT scan testing of the abdomen, which showed no evidence of residual disease, as summarized in the radiology report:

> No acute enteric abnormality. No acute retroperitoneal or intraperitoneal findings. No pathologically enlarged lymph nodes.
>
> IMPRESSION:
> Splenomegaly. No acute findings.

As of early March 2010, one year after beginning her nutritional protocol, Patient KN remains compliant and continues doing well, now planning to return to college.

Patient KN is another fairly straightforward case. When diagnosed fifteen months ago in December 2008, radiographic studies confirmed extensive disease most likely extending beyond the liver. Her doctors predicted a lifespan of some six to ten months, perhaps somewhat longer with aggressive chemotherapy, but she refused the proposed conventional treatments, choosing to begin my regimen. While on her nutritional therapy, she has enjoyed good health clinically, as well as regression of her disease, as described in sequential CT scans.

LUNG CANCER

Devita's has reported that in 2009, approximately 219,440 new cases of lung cancer of all types were diagnosed in the US and 159,390 (28%) total cancer deaths were attributable to lung cancer. Fully 85 percent of all cases occur in current or former smokers, so it remains a largely preventable disease.[1]

Though rates in males have declined in recent years largely due to aggressive antismoking campaigns, incidence in women has increased rapidly. Today, lung cancer is the leading cancer killer in both sexes, surpassing even breast cancer in women. Despite widely promoted early detection campaigns, public awareness of the disease, and advances in treatment approaches, only 14 percent of patients survive five years.

Pathologists divide lung cancer into two major categories, small cell carcinoma and the non-small cell variants, which include squamous carcinoma, adenocarcinoma, large cell carcinoma, and bronchoalveolar carcinoma. Small cell and squamous cell most clearly relate to cigarette smoking, large cell less so. Adenocarcinoma, the most common of the lung cancers, accounts for approximately 40 percent of all cases; large cell, the rarest, affects only 15 percent of patients. Small cell carcinoma responds best to chemotherapy or radiation, the non-small cell carcinomas far less so—though few survive five years in either group. In the conventional medical world, surgical resection of localized disease remains the best chance for long-term survival, whatever the subtype.

---

1   Vincent T. DeVita, Jr., Theodore S. Lawrence, and Steven A. Rosenberg, eds., *Cancer: Principles and Practice*, 9th ed. (Philadelphia, PA: Lippincott William & Wilkins, 2011), Jacob Kaufman, Leora Horn, David Carbone, 789, 799

Case 1: Patient QQ
A Minimum 16.25-Year Survivor*

QQ is a sixty-four-year-old male anthropologist with a long history of recurring febrile episodes, the first dating back to age twenty-three. At the time, he experienced fevers in the range of 104–105°F for a week, associated with swollen joints, malaise, myalgias, arthralgias, and elevated liver function tests. Subsequently, he improved and did well for about a year, until he developed another serious febrile episode. At that point, Patient QQ consulted an American Indian medicine man, who prescribed herbs that seemed to resolve the problem. He experienced two more episodes, at age thirty-three and at fifty-three, in 1999, again treated effectively with herbs.

In early May 2000, while working in Mexico, he developed new-onset urinary symptoms consistent with prostatitis including frequency, urgency, and prostate pain. He relied once again on a mixture of herbal remedies, which seemed to bring the symptoms under control. However, after an airplane trip to the Pacific Northwest, his symptoms recurred, this time with significant prostate and bladder pain that did not respond to herbal interventions.

In mid-June, while back in Mexico, he developed fevers to 101°F with chills, sweats, and digestive symptoms including bloating and left lower abdominal pain. A local urologist prescribed Cipro, which Patient QQ discontinued after two days because of serious side effects. At that point, with his situation deteriorating, he flew back to the Northwest to consult with a naturopathic physician. Blood work revealed elevated liver function tests with an AST of 89 (normal less than 40), an ALT of 94 (normal less than 50), a GGT of 103 (normal less than 65), and an alk phos of 113 (normal less than 110). Urine culture was negative for infection, though QQ's fever persisted to 102°F daily.

The naturopath then prescribed amoxicillin, with some improved urinary symptoms but with ongoing abdominal bloating, lower left abdominal pain, and back pain. At that point, he had become so exhausted he was sleeping twenty hours a day. His physician then switched him to erythromycin, which provoked a severe allergic reaction that improved with discontinuation of the medication.

The patient, whose wife was already a patient of mine, contacted my office, and I suggested an infectious disease consult. Subsequent workup included a negative urine for infection, negative stool test for parasites (done twice), and negative tuberculosis and hepatitis testing. However, repeat blood work on June 27 showed worsening liver function tests, with an LDH of 321 (normal less than 219), AST 94, ALT 95, GGT 1888, and alkaline phosphatase up to 194. The sedimentation rate, an assessment of inflammation, was high at 40 (normal less than 20).

QQ's abdominal symptoms continued, and he remained exhausted, barely able to get out of bed for any prolonged period of time. The patient then consulted with a second physician, who at my suggestion arranged for radiographic studies. A CT scan of the abdomen/pelvis on June 30, 2000 revealed a "mass at the right posterior costophrenic sulcus in the right lower lobe (of the lung)."

The CT of the chest on July 5, 2000 showed the following:

1. Right lower lobe mass, unchanged since the CT scan of the abdomen from June 30, 2000.

2. Multiple, too small to characterize further nodules scattered in the periphery of both lungs.

3. Gastrohepatic ligament adenopathy.

A colonoscopy on July 12, 2000 was negative except for benign polyps.

At that point, Patient QQ, with his long interest in alternative medicine and his familiarity with my treatment, decided to forgo further conventional testing and instead consult with me. When I first met him in my office, in mid-July 2000, he was still quite sick, and he spent most of the first session on the couch in my office. He felt exhausted, though his energy seemed to be improving; he required now "only" eighteen hours a day of sleep instead of twenty, and the fevers, chills, sweats, and abdominal pain had largely resolved.

I suggested that he reconsider biopsy, to obtain tissue diagnosis, but he was not enthusiastic about the idea. All he wanted to do was start my program, and he made it clear to me that he would pursue no therapy other than mine regardless of what any test showed. So, though the diagnosis wasn't certain, I decided to treat him as a cancer patient, with a full dose of enzymes around the clock.

Initially, QQ, as he followed his nutritional regimen diligently, had a rocky course, with episodes of abdominal pain, respiratory distress, fatigue, malaise, bladder pain, etc. But he stuck to his program without missing a beat. By October 2000, only three months after beginning the treatment, he reported to me in a phone conversation that he felt considerably better, with improved energy, stamina, and concentration and a significantly decreased sleep requirement. And repeat blood chemistries in late October showed considerable improvement in his liver function, with both AST and ALT now within the normal range, and alk phos significantly down at 133.

Over the following months, he continued to improve clinically, and by February 2001, his liver function tests were all within the normal range with an alk phos of 95, AST 37, and ALT 40.

A chest x-ray on March 5, 2001 showed no evidence of the large mass and nodules previously noted on the CT scan. The radiology report of the x-ray stated, "Vascularity is normal and lungs are clear."

Patient QQ, who at that point was feeling "great," was understandably quite excited by the finding and continued his program with dedication. When I saw him in my office in January 2001 for his six-month re-evaluation, he reported that the program had "already made an enormous difference in my life." To me, he looked like a different person compared with the very ill patient who could barely get up off the couch in my office. He told me his back pain was "90 percent better," his febrile episodes remained resolved, and his energy, stamina, and concentration had all improved substantially. His various respiratory symptoms had also completely resolved. Overall, he said, "The program has been an extraordinary experience, and I feel it's really helped me enormously."

Since that time, Patient QQ has remained generally compliant with his therapy, except for dietary indiscretions in recent years. His health has generally been good; in May 2009 he developed an episode of pneumonia, which resolved quickly with Cipro. A chest x-ray on August 19, 2009 showed a resolving pneumonia and no evidence of the tumors seen on the CT scans from June 30, 2000. In 2009, he was also diagnosed with sleep apnea and started on a CPAP machine, with mixed results in terms of the soundness of his sleep.

Patient QQ is now eleven years from his diagnosis of metastatic tumors to his lung and abdomen. Though he refused biopsy, subsequent chest x-rays over the years show total regression of the pulmonary masses. He generally feels well, with all his persistent and serious problems present in 2000 having resolved. And over the years, he has been able to pursue his career as a cultural anthropologist with great enthusiasm.

Because Patient QQ experienced such a remarkable turnaround in very serious health problems with resolution of multiple lung tumors on his nutritional program, I decided to include his case history despite the lack of biopsy. I believe his response shows very nicely the power of aggressive nutritional treatment, whatever his original diagnosis may have been.

*IMPORTANT EDITOR'S NOTE:
Dr. Gonzalez died before updating this case report. According to Dr. Gonzalez's office medical files, Patient QQ contacted his office in August 2015 shortly after Dr. Gonzalez's death and last contacted Dr. Linda Isaacs in late October 2016.

Case 2: Patient FV
*A Minimum 8.25-Year Survivor**

Patient FV is a sixty-three-year-old man with a history of myasthenia gravis diagnosed in 1993, which forced him to retire from his high-stress profession. Since then, his myasthenia has waxed and waned, with exacerbations treated with Tensilon.

In June 2003, while playing tennis, he developed significant shortness of breath. At a local emergency room, a chest x-ray showed several pleural-based densities in the left lung, and a CT scan revealed several nodular lesions in the left chest pleura up to 2 cm in diameter. Posterior pleural thickening was also noted, thought to be consistent with mesothelioma. When his symptoms worsened, a second chest x-ray documented a left pleural effusion, subsequently treated with chest tube placement and drainage.

After he recovered from the acute episode, a second CT scan in July demonstrated a collapsed left lung, a persistent left pleural effusion, and numerous large tumors. The official report stated, "The largest pleura bases [sic] mass in the left upper lobe laterally measures 2.976 cm. … The largest mass in the left lower lobe posteriorly measures 5.39 cm. … There are at least 18 pleural based masses present on the left."

FV then underwent bronchoscopy, left video-assisted thoracotomy with pleural biopsies, and pleurodesis. The initial pathology report of the biopsy specimen suggested most likely meso-thelioma, but a review at The Armed Forces Institute of Pathology confirmed not mesotheli-oma, but, as the note described, "Pleura, left, biopsy: Metastatic papillary adenocarcinoma, of pulmonary origin."

His local doctors also sent the pathology slides to Brigham and Women's Hospital in Boston, a research center for mesothelioma, where, in July, the tumor was thought most likely a papillary adenocarcinoma of the lung, staged at IIIB.

In late July 2003, FV decided to consult with Dr. David Sugarbaker, a thoracic surgeon and expert in pleural lesions at Brigham and Women's. At Brigham, CT scans of the abdomen and pelvis were clear. A total-body PET scan confirmed the extensive left pleural lesions but showed no evidence of distant metastatic disease. Because the disease seemed localized to the chest, Dr. Sugarbaker proposed the tumor be treated as if it were a pleural lesion like a mesothelioma with extensive surgery, including removal of the entire left lung, the pericardium, and the left side of the diaphragm.

This debilitating approach seemed excessive, so FV, upon returning home, consulted with an oncologist in the Washington, DC area who believed the situation should be approached initially not with surgery but instead with an aggressive chemotherapy regimen. If the tumors regressed significantly, a less aggressive procedure might be feasible. The oncologist also consulted with three additional thoracic surgeons, including one within the NIH system, who felt the surgical approach suggested in Boston overly aggressive, and that the tumor should be treated as a primary lung cancer, not as a pleural tumor like mesothelioma. All believed chemotherapy should be the initial therapy of choice.

FV then traveled to New York for a consultation with the chief of thoracic surgery at Memorial Sloan Kettering, who concurred that the disease appeared to be lung cancer that had spread to the pleura, not the other way around. She recommended chemotherapy as the first-line treatment, perhaps followed by surgery.

With the debate resolved, in September 2002 FV began a four-cycle course of Gemzar and carboplatin. After he completed his last treatment, in November 2002, a CT scan revealed some slight worsening in the largest tumor, despite the chemotherapy: "The cystic structure in the posterior left upper lung … measuring 4.8 × 6 cm, compared to prior measurements of 4.5 and 5.9 cm. The pleural based lateral left upper lung lesions are also essentially unchanged, measuring 2.6 and 2.9 cm, compared to prior measurements of 2.8 and 2.9. The rest of the pleural-based masses and left basilar pulmonary nodules are unchanged."

Because the disease had progressed, even if slightly, FV began investigating alternative approaches, learned of our work, and consulted with me in mid-December 2003. At the time, he generally felt well and seemed to have recovered from chemotherapy quickly. Thereafter, he began his nutritional regimen with great dedication and superb compliance. When I saw him for a return office visit three months later, in April 2004, he reported feeling "great." Two months later, in June 2004, PET/CT scan testing confirmed improvement in his disease, as he followed only his nutritional regimen. The CT described the following:

> CT-CHEST: Numerous pleural-based masses, and small ones adjacent to the peri-cardial surface are present, similar to the appearance on the CT scan on 11/24/2003. Most of these lesions appear marginally smaller than they previously did, by a few millimeters. The largest lesion, located posteromedially in the mid-chest, again appears largely necrotic. …

> Soft tissue abnormality in the left upper quadrant of the abdomen, anterior to the splenic flexure, appears slightly smaller in overall bulk as compared to the prior study.

Note that the prior radiology reports had not described the lesion in the abdomen, a metastatic focus that would confirm stage IV, not stage III disease. Apparently, the lesion had been evident on prior scans but not described in the official report.

The overall summary of the June PET/CT stated,

> **IMPRESSION:** PET scan shows numerous pleural-based pathologic foci in the left hemithorax, consistent with numerous foci of metastatic neoplasm. A lesion at the anterior aspect of the left upper quadrant of the abdomen, or immediately adjacent diaphragmatic surface is present. …
>
> CT examination of the chest shows minimal decrease in the overall size of the numerous pleural-based masses in the left hemithorax, and in the region located either in the left upper quadrant of the abdomen.

So, while the PET confirmed residual active cancer, the CT scan indicated universal, though slight, reduction in the many tumors with advancing necrosis in the largest remaining tumor.

Since that time, FV has continued his nutrition regimen vigorously and has done extremely well. He has declined all invitations for follow-up CT and PET/CT scanning, stating he wouldn't change his treatment regardless of what the tests show. So, while we don't have clear evidence of additional tumor regression, his continued survival, now at three years since he began his nutritional regimen, and his excellent general health speak for themselves.

His course has had only one complication. In the spring of 2006, FV felt well enough to take a trip to Europe with his wife. Upon arriving abroad, he developed severe headaches requiring hospitalization. After CT scans and MRIs of the head showed nothing, he was eventually diagnosed with a cerebrospinal fluid leak. He returned to the United States, the problem eventually resolved, and once again, FV was back to his usual state of well-being.

In analyzing this case, it's important to keep in mind that although the disease was originally classified as stage IIIB lung cancer, the PET/CT scans in June 2004 clearly showed an abdominal lesion that would indicate stage IV metastatic disease. Though evident on prior scans, this lesion was not mentioned in the formal reports. Also, a CT scan done weeks after FV completed his four cycles of aggressive chemotherapy showed no reduction in any of the tumors, and some enlargement. Only after he had followed his nutritional program some six months did the PET/CT scans document regression in all tumors and the appearance of significant necrosis in the largest.

For patients with stage IV non-small cell lung cancer, studies have shown chemotherapy improves average survival by about one month over supportive care only. Even with the newest, most aggressive chemotherapy regimens, median survival is still only nine to ten months, with, depending on the regimen, a mere 25 to 40 percent of patients living one year. Virtually none survives five years. FV's three-year survival and excellent health are even at this point extraordinary.

*IMPORTANT EDITOR'S NOTE:
Dr. Gonzalez died before updating this case report. According to Patient FV's office medical file, he died in March 2012.

Case 3: Patient RZ
A Minimum .75-Month Survivor

Patient RZ was one of the first patients I treated with a diagnosis of metastatic lung cancer after I opened my practice in late 1987. He had smoked cigarettes heavily for twenty-eight years, before quitting some fifteen years prior to developing cancer. Otherwise, his health had generally been good when, in early 1987, he first developed persistent chest pain and cough. When his symptoms did not resolve, he consulted his local physician. After an x-ray revealed a right lung mass, in March 1987 he underwent bronchoscopy with biopsy confirming adenocarcinoma of the lung. A CT showed two tumors, one in the right apex, the second in the right hilum, though the left lung appeared clear.

Because the disease appeared limited to the right lung, surgery was immediately suggested. RZ initially refused all conventional intervention, but when his symptoms worsened, he agreed to proceed with surgery. In July 1987, he underwent a right pneumonectomy, with the pathology report describing a 2.5 cm lesion, consistent with poorly differentiated adenocarcinoma, extensively invading the hilar lymph nodes. He was staged at III and proceeded postoperatively with a course of radiation to the chest totaling 4,500 rads.

RZ subsequently did well until September 1988, when he developed persistent headaches and olfactory hallucinations described as putrid foul smells. A CT scan of the head in October 1988 revealed multiple tumors located in the temporal, right frontal, and left occipital areas with associated edema.

His doctor prescribed the steroid Decadron to reduce the cerebral swelling, but the symptoms did not improve. In early November 1988, he proceeded with a ten-day course of radiation to the head, ultimately receiving a total of 3,000 rads, with some improvement in his symptoms. In December 1988, a month after completing radiation, a CT scan of the head revealed the situation had worsened despite treatment: "Multiple, bilateral intracerebral ring-enhancing lesions, consistent with metastases. In addition there appears to be an early left cerebellar hemisphere lesion. Many of these were noted on Oct -- 1988. However, several new small areas of abnormality are identified on the present exam, not previously seen."

At this point, with his disease progressing, RZ, who already had been investigating alternative approaches to cancer, came to New York for a consultation with me. He reported severe neurological symptoms, including headaches, that had recently recurred despite Decadron. He thereafter began his nutritional program with initial great enthusiasm, and in January 1989, after he had completed but a month on his nutritional program, a CT scan showed significant improvement: "When compared to the last previous exam of 12 -- 88, there has been diminution both in the size and number of the visualized intracranial lesions. No new areas of abnormality are seen."

According to his oncologist's notes, a bone scan in March 1989 showed clearing of previously noted bone lesions, though I do not have the actual radiology report.

At that point, RZ was symptom-free and strong enough to return to his stressful job. Unfortunately, he felt so well he became careless with his supplement regimen and diet, and by April 1989 was by his own admission less than 50 percent compliant with his overall protocol. Not surprisingly, after his neurological symptoms returned with a vengeance, a CT scan in May 1989 revealed worsening disease: "Increased intracranial edema and size of previously reported intracranial metastases when compared to 3---89."

After a discussion with me about the need for perfect compliance, RZ resumed his full program as prescribed. His symptoms rapidly improved, and a CT scan in July 1989 demonstrated reduction in all his brain tumors: "The three metastatic lesions on the 5---89 CT have decreased in size. No new metastatic lesions are seen."

With the return of his good health, RZ again became careless with his program. I last saw him in September 1989, nine months after our first session, when after several weeks of poor compliance his neurological symptoms had returned. Thereafter, he was lost to follow-up. He had no family that I knew of, and despite my efforts, I could never learn what happened to him.

In this case, the patient's disease, before he had consulted with me, had progressed despite intensive radiation to the brain. After he began his nutritional program, the brain (and apparently the bone) lesions regressed, only to worsen when compliance fell off. When RZ became more adherent to the prescribed regimen, the brain tumors again improved. Ultimately, he lacked the dedication and discipline to stick to the program as required.

Typically there is a median survival of fifteen to eighteen weeks for patients with multiple metastatic brain lesions from non-small cell lung cancer treated with intensive radiation. So, despite his compliance problems, this patient's nine months of survival beat the odds.

And again, despite his lapses, I thought this patient of interest because he remains one of the few I have ever treated with brain metastases from a primary lung neoplasm. Though in recent years occasional patients in this situation have contacted my office seeking information about my therapy, most are so far into the terminal stages of their illness I can't justify trying to treat them.

For better or worse, in this age of aggressive oncology, patients facing this diagnosis invariably get shunted frantically and immediately into multiagent chemotherapy and radiation. Only after months of futile treatment, when the disease explodes and the patients weaken, do they begin looking into alternative options. By then, it is too late. I believe I could help many diagnosed with this terrible condition if, like RZ, they came earlier in their course, but over the last decade this has simply not been the case. And I do not accept patients for treatment whom I believe I can't help.

Case 4: Patient SV
A Minimum 9.9-Year Survivor*

Patient SV is a forty-four-year-old woman who had been in good health when, in 1998, she first noticed the need to repeatedly clear her throat, a symptom she attributed to persistent postnasal drip. By 1999, she had developed a mild nonproductive cough associated with a gradual decline in energy, attributed to the demands of tending to her new baby.

During 1998 and 1999, SV repeatedly consulted her primary care physician because of ongoing respiratory symptoms, but she was reassured she had nothing more serious than a recurrent viral syndrome that warranted no further testing. When the cough and fatigue persisted, she was ultimately referred to an allergist, who thought the symptoms were unrelated to allergies. However, no chest x-ray was suggested.

The cough and associated problems continued into 2000. At one point in 2000 during a family visit, after hearing the cough, the patient's sister, a medical professional, insisted a chest x-ray and TB testing be done. Subsequently, when a TB skin test was negative, SV chose not to follow up with the chest x-ray.

A month later, in October 2000, SV developed a significantly worsening cough associated with a high fever and severe fatigue. She visited her doctor, who, after an exam, announced she once again had a viral infection. When, at end of November 2000, the cough worsened, she requested an x-ray, which her doctor told her showed pneumonia. When the symptoms did not improve after a second course of antibiotics, a repeat chest x-ray revealed a persistent left lung infiltrate. A CT at that point then showed a large lesion in the left lower lung consistent with primary lung cancer.

SV was referred to a pulmonologist for bronchoscopy and biopsy, which confirmed adenocarcinoma of the lung. With the diagnosis finally made, the patient met with a local oncologist, who ordered a full metastatic workup. A CT scan of the abdomen and pelvis showed a porta hepatis mass that was considered insignificant. In January 2001, SV decided to consult with an oncologist and lung cancer specialist at the Mary Hitchcock Medical Center in New Hampshire. At Hitchcock, after a PET scan revealed only the large lung tumor, with no evidence of metastatic disease, the physician recommended surgery for resection of the lesion as soon as possible.

In January 2001, SV then met with the chief of thoracic surgery at Memorial Sloan Kettering in New York. Repeat bronchoscopy at Memorial with transbronchial biopsy confirmed moderately differentiated mucin-secreting adenocarcinoma. Repeat PET scan showed a 5.5 cm lesion in the left lung as well as a 1 cm secondary satellite lesion, but CT scans of the head, abdomen, and pelvis were clear. Subsequently, in February 2001 at Memorial, SV underwent left lower lobectomy with the pathology report describing a tumor 6.2 cm in diameter, consistent with moderately differentiated mucinous adenocarcinoma. Tumor had invaded three of eight lymph nodes evaluated, a very dire prognostic indicator.

According to the patient, the Memorial surgeon warned that neither chemotherapy nor radiation would be very helpful long term and should be held in reserve until the disease recurred, as it most likely soon would. SV decided she nonetheless wished to meet with an oncologist, so she consulted at Memorial with a physician pursuing a vaccine research study designed for patients with stage III lung cancer. At the same time, she began investigating our work, which a friend had discussed with her. The same day she first consulted with me in March 2001 she also visited Memorial Sloan Kettering to discuss both chemotherapy and the vaccine trial. The physician's note from that day clearly expresses the poor prognosis SV faced:

> I had a lengthy discussion with the patient and her husband regarding the situation. The patient already understands that because of her stage, she is at risk for recurrence in the future. We discussed in detail the role of adjuvant chemotherapy and radiation therapy. In one meta-analysis published in 1995, cisplatin based chemotherapy improved the rate of survival by 5% after five years. Radiation typically has been described as improving local control without improvement in survival due to the risk of systemic metastases. One recent trial published in the New England Journal indicated that the addition of chemotherapy with etoposide and cisplatin to adjuvant radiation did not improve survival.

In the same note, though the oncologist clearly admitted that radiation and intensive chemotherapy essentially do little, two sentences later he nonetheless recommended the patient be aggressively treated anyway: "For this patient, who is quite young, I would probably favor aggressive treatment, providing her with some adjuvant chemotherapy with a cisplatin-based regimen. … In addition, I also discussed with her clinical trials."

The vaccine trial, offered as an option to aggressive chemotherapy, turned out to be a preliminary pilot study. Then, after her consultation with me and the Sloan Kettering physician, SV met with her local oncologist, who told her that even with aggressive chemotherapy and radiation, only one in five patients with her specific diagnosis and stage lived beyond a "couple years."

Because little data favored any of the orthodox treatments, SV decided to forgo all conventional approaches and begin our nutritional regimen. When we met for our second session some days later, she handed me a copy of the consent form for the Memorial Sloan Kettering clinical study. I found it informative in that the researchers clearly discussed the aggressive nature of lung cancer and its notorious resistance to standard approaches: "Non-small cell lung cancer is a difficult disease to treat. Even after curative surgery, there is a high likelihood of the cancer returning. Chemotherapy and radiation are sometimes given after surgery to decrease the chance that the cancer will come back; however it is unclear whether this really helps. In this study, we are trying to develop a different approach to treat patients with non-small cell lung cancer after surgery. We are testing a new vaccine designed to boost your immune system against your cancer."

SV then began my therapy with great determination and great dedication. A follow-up CT scan from February 2003 did reveal a 2 to 3 mm nodule in the periphery of the right lung. A follow-up scan in September 2003 showed that "the nodule in the periphery of the right lung posteriorly… remains unchanged and stable." Repeat CT scans in August 2004 reported, "A stable 2–3 mm pulmonary nodule is seen in the right lower lobe. No new nodules are seen." Her most recent scans in October 2005 were completely clear.

Today, more than 5.5 years after first beginning her nutritional therapy, SV remains compliant and in good health with no evidence of recurrent disease. She continues to follow up periodically with her local oncologist, who seems very supportive of the road she has taken.

*IMPORTANT EDITOR'S NOTE:
Dr. Gonzalez died before updating this case report. The last update in Patient SV's office medical file is from February 2011.

Case 5: Patient AI
*A Minimum 7.4-Year Survivor**

Patient AI is a sixty-year-old male with a past medical history significant for elevated cholesterol, hypertension, and emphysema associated with a thirty-five-year history of cigarette smoking, though he quit in 2001. A colonoscopy in 2009 had revealed only a polyp, which proved to be benign.

An engineer and computer expert by training, Patient AI had been generally in good health before developing cancer. Despite a tough work schedule, he exercised regularly and followed up with his annual physical exams at Kaiser. A routine chest x-ray in August 2008 showed "minimal insignificant thickening of pleura at both apices," but otherwise no suspicious lesions. But in August of 2009, he first experienced persistent pain in his right lower flank, the result, he thought, of pushing his exercise routine too hard. Assuming the problem to be trivial, he initially did not seek medical advice.

The pain continued to worsen, and then in October 2009, Patient AI first noticed bright red blood in his stool. He consulted with his primary Kaiser physician, who ordered CT scans of the abdomen and pelvis. The tests completed on October 29, 2009 showed no abnormalities in any of the abdominal or pelvic organs but did pick up a right pleural effusion (fluid in the cavity around the lung). A subsequent CT scan of the chest on November 10, 2009 indicated that "there are now evident multiple right pleural masses ranging in size from 1.5×4.0 cm down to 1.0 cm in the right lower chest with the largest pleural masses measuring 5.0 cm and 2.5 cm in the right pulmonary apex consistent with a Pancoast tumor. ... The 4.0×1.5 cm mass also destroys the adjacent right 7th rib in a permeative fashion consistent with metastatic disease."

Two days later, on November 13, 2009, an enhanced CT scan again confirmed multiple lesions in the right lung along with invasion of the seventh rib. In addition, the study revealed evidence of a left adrenal mass: "The central aspect of the left adrenal gland appears as a convex contour and this is suspicious for a mass that measures 1.0 cm."

On November 25, 2009, a fine needle aspirate of a right pleural-based lesion confirmed squamous cell carcinoma, a type of cancer that can originate in the lung, the head and neck tissues, and the esophagus. At that point, Patient AI's primary care physician suggested Percocet for his persistent pain, referred him to an oncologist, and arranged for a PET scan. This study from December 7, 2009 revealed significant changes from the previous 2008 x-ray:

> There is a hypermetabolic density in the right upper lung involving the pleura laterally and invading the chest wall at the level of the right second (2nd) rib (with possible bony involvement) with a max SUV [activity] of 14.6 measuring 2.9×2.3 cm. There

is another nodular hypermetabolic mass involving the pleura in the right upper lung adjacent to the right fourth (4th) rib (max SUB 11.1 measuring 2.7 × 1.9 cm). There is a conglomerate of at least three (3) pleural-based hypermetabolic densities in the right lower lobe laterally invading the pleura and right lateral eighth (8th) rib. ... An additional similar pleural lesion is noted involving the anterolateral aspect of the right fifth (5th) rib. ...

There is mild focal increased activity in the distal esophagus with a max SUV of 3.7 and mild thickening of the mucosa. There is a right retrocrural node with a max SUV of 10.8 measuring 1.9 cm. There is thickening of left adrenal gland without focal hypermetabolism.

Although the adrenal mass appeared to be inactive, the PET scan did demonstrate extensive metastatic disease.

In the "Impression," the summary of the findings, the radiologist suspected a diagnosis of metastatic lung cancer but raised the possibility of a primary esophageal lesion because of the activity at that site: "A hypermetabolic focus in the distal esophagus is suspicious for esophageal cancer and perhaps the findings in the right lung pleura could be related to metastatic disease. Correlation with endoscopy is suggested."

The appointment with the oncologist went ahead as planned on December 9, 2009. At that point, this physician suggested a bone scan to evaluate the skeletal metastases and referred him to a gastroenterologist for evaluation of the esophageal lesion noted on the PET scan.

The bone scan on December 10, 2009 indicated "findings consistent with osteoblastic metastasis within the right postero lateral eight (8th) rib, correlating to recent PET/CT findings. There is no evidence of osteoblastic metastatic disease elsewhere."

The following day, December 11, 2009, Patient AI underwent endoscopy, which indicated GERD (gastroesophageal reflux disease) but no evidence of esophageal cancer. A head and neck primary was also ruled out.

With the workup completed, Patient AI met again with his oncologist, who explained a working diagnosis of primary lung cancer, with metastasis to the bone. Due to the widespread and aggressive nature of the disease in this case, surgery was not an option, however, and Patient AI's doctor recommended that aggressive chemotherapy with the drugs Taxol and carboplatin begin as soon as possible. However, he also admitted the treatment at best would be only palliative and not curative, and even if Patient AI responded, his life might be extended only several months or so. From his own reading, Patient AI already knew that by the conventional standards his disease was incurable and decided against proceeding with conventional approaches. His physician admitted that without any treatment he might live six months.

The oncologist suggested at least that Patient AI, before ruling out chemotherapy completely, attend a "chemotherapy class" for patients, offered at Kaiser, to get a better understanding of what the treatment involved. Patient AI agreed, but he remained unpersuaded by the class because he understood full well the dire nature of his prognosis even with chemotherapy. At that point, his Kaiser doctors referred him for palliative care as well as to a staff acupuncturist for pain control.

Patient AI then went on a crash course of self-education and reading about alternative approaches. He changed his diet radically, cut out junk food and refined carbohydrates, and began juicing and eating a largely plant-based 100 percent organic diet. He stopped the Zocor and Cozaar he had been taking for his high cholesterol and hypertension.

In late December, through a mutual friend, Patient AI learned about my regimen, and after reviewing our website, he contacted our office expressing his wish to become a patient. Because his attitude seemed so determined, we agreed to take him on as a patient.

I subsequently met with Patient AI for the first time on January 13, 2010. He reported fatigue that had cut into his professional life. From a nonstop schedule, he now could work no more than four hours a day before exhaustion would take over. In addition, the severe right flank pain didn't help the situation. When we discussed his pain, he admitted he hadn't taken the recommended pain medication because he didn't want to ingest any substance that might affect his cognitive abilities, but he intended to continue with the acupuncture treatments, which he found somewhat helpful. I suggested that he start taking the Percocet until the program had a chance to kick in and the pain lessened.

The following day, we reviewed his proposed therapy plan, and a week later he began the full regimen with great determination. He adjusted to the program well, though his pain at times could be unbearable even with Percocet. Then, during the second week of February 2010, he developed diarrhea and severe lower abdominal discomfort after eating several organic plums. He contacted my office, and I suggested he consult with his local Kaiser doctors to rule out diverticulitis. He did consult with his primary care physician, who ordered x-rays of the abdominal cavity, which turned out to be unrevealing. When the pain resolved several days later, no further diagnostic testing was thought necessary for what appeared to be a simple case of food poisoning or gastroenteritis.

After the abdominal pain issue in mid-February 2010, I didn't hear from Patient AI until April 15, 2010, two months later. He explained he hadn't called because he was "doing so well," and that after six weeks on the therapy "the terrible bone pain" from his metastatic disease had completely resolved, to the point that he had discontinued all pain medication. He told me he felt great and looked great. His wife, who was on the other extension with us as we talked, confirmed how well he was doing. In fact, he felt well enough to begin a vigorous exercise program at a local gym.

Patient AI had recently undergone a series of pulmonary function tests, which he said were "perfect." His Kaiser doctors who followed him regularly were, he said, so "amazed" at his progress that they had begun asking him questions about his treatment program with me.

The following month, Patient AI faxed me a note reporting that he had met with his Kaiser oncologist, who asked "many questions about you and your protocol." His blood tests were "great" and his blood pressure at that visit was, off all medication, a perfect 117/77. However, though the severe right flank pain had resolved, he complained of some left shoulder pain that he thought related not to any cancer, but to an old rotator cuff tear on that side.

When the left shoulder pain worsened in June, his Kaiser doctors suggested a PET scan to rule out metastatic disease. Patient AI and I discussed the issue and the risks and benefits of the test, particularly the problems with radiation exposure from such radiographic studies. I suggested an MRI as a first test, because the most likely cause was non-cancer related. His Kaiser doctors agreed to order the study, which during the second week of July revealed no evidence of metastatic spread of his cancer, but only tendonitis and degenerative disease in the shoulder joint, for which his acupuncturist began a course of treatment. I also suggested he start taking bromelain, a natural anti-inflammatory enzyme derived from pineapple, four times a day along with his pancreatic enzyme supplements.

I then saw Patient AI and his wife in my office for his scheduled lengthy six-month follow-up visit on July 21, 2010. He looked, as my note from the session described, "wonderful," and he reported feeling "great." His once-debilitating right rib pain remained resolved, and he told me that within several days of starting the bromelain I had recommended, the left shoulder pain had simply gone away.

He described his energy as "great" and his stamina as "great"; he was sleeping well and could now work a full eight-hour day without difficulty. He reported that a recent cholesterol test at Kaiser was normal. I made some adjustments in his protocol at the time, and once back home, he continued with the same dedication to the therapy as before.

In early September 2010, he experienced several episodes of bright red blood per rectum that proved to be the result of hemorrhoids. When I spoke to him at the time, he reported that otherwise he felt "great."

Patient AI continued doing well throughout the remainder of autumn 2010, past his one-year mark from diagnosis. Then, during the third week of January 2011, he developed severe right back pain in the area of his metastatic rib lesion. He faxed me on January 21, 2011, reporting that the pain was quite severe. When we spoke, I didn't like the sound of what he was telling me and insisted he needed a CT scan as soon as possible. His local Kaiser doctors agreed with me, and that same day he underwent CT studies of the chest and abdomen, his first since his initial working up in the fall of 2009.

The scan demonstrated pulmonary emboli [blood clots] in both lungs, but apparently, to the shock of his doctors, no evidence of the multiple pleural-based tumors noted on the CT from November 10, 2009. The radiology report read, "There are extensive bilateral pulmonary emboli particularly prominent in the right upper lobe branches as well as the left lower lobe branch where there are occlusive changes."

The CT scan of the abdomen did reveal several small lesions in the liver, though the left adrenal mass seen on the enhanced CT scan from November 13, 2009 was not evident: "There are small hypodensities beneath the anterior liver capsule and the dome of the liver suggestive of early metastases. The spleen, gallbladder, pancreas, adrenal glands are normal."

With the diagnosis confirmed, Patient AI was immediately started on Lovenox and Coumadin, injectable and oral anticoagulants, respectively. The following day, ultrasound studies of his lower extremities revealed "an occlusive thrombus involving the right peroneal vein."

After six days in the hospital, Patient AI was eventually discharged on January 28, 2011 on his anticoagulant medication. At that time, his back pain, which I assumed was related to the blood clots rather than any cancer situation, had resolved.

With Patient AI now stabilized, we had a long talk about the recent events. He said his doctors were dumbfounded that the lungs as well as the ribs showed no evidence of cancer whatsoever. Multiple radiologists had reviewed the scans, and there apparently was so much disbelief about the situation they had pulled out the original films from November 2011 to compare and re-evaluate. Indeed, despite their disbelief, the multiple right lung tumors clearly seen in November 2009 were gone. And these had not been small tumors, the largest measuring 5 cm in the widest diameter.

As for the small lesions now noted in the liver, I myself had pulled out the CT of the abdomen from November 29, 2009, as well as the PET scan from December 7, 2009. Neither study indicated any specific abnormalities in the liver at that time, but Patient AI didn't actually start his nutritional regimen under my guidance until late January 2010, some seven weeks after the PET scan. I suspected that during the time lapse between the original CT and PET studies in November and early December 2009 and the time he started his therapy in late January 2010, this aggressive cancer would have continued to spread, perhaps into the liver; after all, he was pursuing no anticancer treatment during that period. We might, I thought, be looking at some remnants of old disease. In my experience, I have never seen multiple large lung tumors resolve, while cancer continued to grow and spread in other regions of the body.

We also discussed the blood clots in some detail. As it turned out, I didn't know the whole story when he had first called complaining of back pain. Just before he developed the backaches in the third week of January 2011, he had driven twelve hours nonstop to visit relatives in the Midwest—a trip he hadn't discussed with me, assuming I would tell him not to do it. After several days with family, he then drove twelve hours back, again nonstop.

I explained that certain cancers such as pancreatic and lung cancer are associated with a significantly increased tendency to clot, but anyone driving two twelve-hour stints without a break within several days was asking for trouble. I told him never to take such a trip again without discussing it with me.

Two days later, on January 30, 2011, Patient AI and I spoke once again. He told me he was back on his full nutritional program, and that he had again spoken with his primary care doctor, who said the disappearing lung tumors not only were "remarkable" but had "caused quite a problem at Kaiser" because no one could dismiss his nutritional therapy as foolishness any longer.

In any event, during the second week of February 2011, Patient AI's primary care physician arranged for an abdominal ultrasound, to re-examine the liver lesions. The doctor's note to Patient AI about the scans reported the following: "Your ultrasound: No abnormal hepatic masses visualized."

The nodules seen on the CT scan from January were apparently gone.

Throughout the spring of 2011, Patient AI and I spoke on several occasions, and each time he reported feeling stronger and better. I next saw him in my office on July 29, 2011, eighteen months after his diagnosis, at which time he reported excellent energy, stamina, and concentration. His various pains remained completely resolved, and he was feeling so well that he had been working ten- to fourteen-hour days without a problem and without any drop in his energy. I told him that because he had been given a terminal prognosis initially, he had to pace himself with his work more reasonably and not try to conquer the world. I also emphasized the need to maintain strict compliance with all aspects of the therapy, regardless of how well he felt.

Patient AI has continued to do very well, as he determinedly follows his prescribed nutritional regimen. Before Christmas 2011, he called asking if he could have a steak, to celebrate his two-year anniversary from diagnosis. Though I am usually pretty strict about cheating at any time, I relented and allowed him one steak—but only one.

Squamous cell carcinoma is one of the more aggressive of lung cancers, with fewer than 5 percent of those diagnosed at stage IV, as in the case of Patient AI, surviving five years. Considering the extent of his disease when initially diagnosed, Patient AI's current survival of 2.5 years is very unusual, particularly because he enjoys such excellent health. On his nutritional program, his debilitating pain has completely resolved, his blood pressure and cholesterol have normalized without drugs, his energy is superb, and he continues his productive, creative life. Furthermore, the regression of all his extensive lung and bone lesions after one year of treatment, and the subsequent resolution of his liver disease, certainly indicates a good response to therapy.

*IMPORTANT EDITOR'S NOTE:
Dr. Gonzalez died before updating this case report. Patient AI attended Dr. Gonzalez's memorial service in June 2016 and has been in contact in early 2017.

Case 6: Patient IG
*An .8-Month Survivor**

Earlier, I discussed the case of RZ, one of my first patients, first seen in 1988, diagnosed with stage IV lung cancer with metastases into the brain, who responded to treatment before discontinuing the therapy. I would now like to discuss a very recent patient, IG, also diagnosed with stage IV lung cancer with multiple metastases to the brain, who has been impeccably compliant and who has responded quickly to his treatment.

In terms of his family history, IG's father, a heavy smoker, died from colon cancer, but no other relatives on either side had been diagnosed with malignant disease.

Patient IG himself never smoked but was exposed to secondhand smoke in his early years from his father, as well as during a previous marriage. His past medical history is pertinent for a bout of mononucleosis in the late 1960s and excision of a testicle in 1975 due to a precancerous, not malignant tumor. Then, in 2006, he was diagnosed with atrial fibrillation and treated with cardioversion. At the same time, after being diagnosed with sleep apnea, he began using a CPAP machine.

In 2007, he underwent cardioversion again for recurrent atrial fibrillation.

His current situation dates to March 2012, when Patient IG developed persistent diarrhea as well as a bad cough. When the symptoms did not improve, he consulted with a local doctor in Florida, where he lives in the wintertime. However, the physician apparently didn't think the symptoms serious enough to warrant any testing.

It wasn't until June 2012 that the diarrhea finally resolved, though the cough persisted. At the time, Patient IG, back home in Pennsylvania, decided to visit his long-time family physician. When liver function blood testing came back elevated, Patient IG's doctor suggested a referral to a gastroenterologist. Despite the lingering cough, a chest x-ray was not done.

Patient IG consulted with the gastroenterologist during the first week of June 2012. Though an ultrasound was done, Patient IG never heard back from the doctor and never learned what the study showed. At one point, Patient IG requested a copy of the ultrasound report, but it was never sent.

At that point, during the second week of June 2012, Patient IG, his cough persisting, returned to his primary care physician. A chest x-ray now revealed "a mass in the right lower lung field worrisome for bronchogenic carcinoma." For further elaboration of the situation, the radiologist recommended a CT scan of the chest.

Several days later, Patient IG underwent the suggested CT testing, which again showed a large mass in the right middle lobe consistent with bronchogenic carcinoma, along with multiple additional lesions, as described in some detail in the formal report:

> Large mass in the right middle lobe measures 3.5 × 2.1 cm. … Findings are concerning for primary bronchogenic carcinoma. … Small nodules scattered throughout the other lobes may indicate metastatic disease.

> Enlarged bilateral hilar, mediastinal, and supraclavicular lymph nodes are suspicious for metastatic disease.

The radiologist in his report identified seven nodules in addition to the main tumor and nine enlarged, suspicious-appearing lymph nodes in the chest.

With CT indicating probable advanced lung cancer, Patient IG was referred to a local pulmonologist whom he had first met during the last week of June 2012. The physician suggested as a next step bronchoscopy, to allow for biopsy of one of the lung lesions. He also advised that because the disease already appeared to be metastatic, an MRI of the head needed to be done, because, as he explained to Patient IG, lung cancer notoriously spreads to the brain.

Four days after the initial meeting, Patient IG proceeded with the bronchoscopy and biopsy of one of the accessible enlarged lymph nodes. In his summary, the pulmonologist described his findings as "diffuse mediastinal lymphadenopathy."

The biopsy results came back the day after the procedure, confirming "adenocarcinoma" consistent with a lung primary. That same day, Patient IG underwent the MRI of the head, which revealed multiple lesions in the brain, as described in the report: "There are 2 subcentimeter enhancing lesions within the right frontal lobe with a possible small third lesion. With the patient's history the findings are compatible with small cell metastatic disease."

After discussing the initial biopsy results with Patient IG, the pulmonologist recommended a total-body PET scan, which was done during the first week of July 2012. This test revealed metabolic activity consistent with malignant tumor within the right middle lobe, the site of the largest lesion, but also additional suspicious lesions in both lungs, in the right and left hilar areas, and right and left mediastinum, as discussed in the radiology report: "Focal uptake within 3.5 × 2.1 cm mass in the right middle lobe consistent with metabolically active cancer in this region. Focal uptake within a 1.8 cm right supraclavicular node, multiple ipsilateral [same side] and contralateral mediastinal nodes and bilateral hilar nodes consistent with metabolically active tumor in these areas. Focal uptake in 7 mm nodule right upper lobe image 82 suspicious for metabolically active metastatic disease."

Patient IG, told the cancer was inoperable, was then referred to a medical oncologist in Allentown, Pennsylvania, with whom he met during the second week of July 2012. This physician discussed chemotherapy, targeted therapies, and the need for radiation to the brain. In addition, the oncologist wanted the pathology specimens to be sent to a specialty laboratory for further evaluation, to determine if targeted therapies might be of use. However, as it turned out, the specimens were not suited for such an evaluation, so the oncologist suggested a second bronchoscopy be done to obtain more tumor tissue.

That same day, Patient IG met with a radiation oncologist, who suggested the gamma knife approach to the brain, requiring only a single session and not the many weeks—often five or six—usually recommended with traditional radiation. In the gamma knife treatment, a multitude of gamma rays is targeted specially onto the tumor sites, in a way that concentrates the effect while minimizing damage to surrounding tissue. This was subsequently completed in one session during the third week of July 2012, with minimal side effects to the patient.

During this period, Patient IG also met with a certified nutritionist, who recommended a whole-foods, plant-based diet with juicing, coffee enemas, and multiple supplements, including homeopathic remedies, vitamin C, resveratrol, coenzyme Q10, and others.

During the third week of July 2012, Patient IG underwent a second bronchoscopy with biopsy. Subsequent evaluation indicated the cancer cells lacked the specific genetic marker that would have made them vulnerable to available targeted therapies. At that point, the patient met again with his medical oncologist, who strongly recommended traditional chemotherapy with the drugs Taxol, carboplatin, and Alimta. He was told bluntly and honestly that even this aggressive treatment might prolong his life by some months but would not ultimately be curative. Nonetheless, Patient IG, realizing his limited options, went so far as to meet with an oncology nurse to discuss the side effects of the proposed regimen, which were quite significant, and, to the patient, quite onerous. Meanwhile, as he arranged to begin chemotherapy, he continued on his nutritional program.

During the first week of August 7, 2012, Patient IG and his wife met with an associate of his oncologist assigned to conduct "chemotherapy teaching." However, the information as presented about the limited benefit and significant risks only made Patient IG's concerns about chemotherapy for his situation worse. He was reluctant enough to proceed as planned that he began to look into alternative approaches, learned about my office, and applied to become a patient. After reviewing his file, I accepted him as a patient into my practice, with his first appointment scheduled for the very end of August 2012.

Meanwhile, the radiation oncologist had ordered a repeat MRI of the brain, to assess any effect of treatment. This was done during the third week of August 2012, and it revealed that the lesions had increased in size: "Again identified are 4 focal enhancing lesions in the right superior frontal lobe. The lesions appear slightly larger in size with increase in surrounding edema when compared to prior examinations."

Several days later, IG underwent a repeat CT scan of the chest, which again revealed extensive metastatic disease: "Lung centered windows again demonstrate masslike consolidative density within the right middle lobe…measuring approximately 4.0 × 2.7 cm. The findings are compatible with the patient's known primary malignancy with some associated postobstructive atelectasis [collapse]. Enlarged right hilar lymph nodes encase the right mainstem bronchus and bronchus intermedius. Lung centered windows also demonstrate scattered tiny bilateral pulmonary nodules suspicious for metastatic disease."

In addition, the scan also indicated a large pulmonary embolus (blood clot) within the left pulmonary artery. When Patient IG's primary care physician reviewed the scan report, he sent Patient IG off to the local emergency room for management of the embolus, a potentially life-threatening situation, thought to have originated from his legs. Ultrasound confirmed multiple deep venous thrombi (blood clots) in each leg.

Patient IG was hospitalized and started on aggressive anticoagulation with IV heparin, before he was switched to daily subcutaneous Lovenox. He was told that for long-term protection he most likely would do best with a venous filter placed in his vena cava, to prevent further embolization into the pulmonary vasculature.

Meanwhile, Patient IG decided to refuse the recommended chemotherapy, instead choosing to proceed only with my treatment. When we met as planned for our first lengthy session in late August 2012, he seemed stabilized from his recent hospitalization. Our second visit, during which time I planned to review in great detail the proposed treatment, was scheduled for some five days later, during the first week of September 2012.

When he returned for that appointment with his wife, Patient IG informed me that the previous evening he had experienced what he described as a "grand mal seizure," from which he quickly recovered. Regardless, when he came to, his wife wanted him to go to the hospital with her, but he refused—apparently because he didn't want to miss his appointment with me. From his description to me, the episode sounded more like a complex type seizure rather than a grand mal. At the time of our meeting together, he seemed to have completely recovered, reporting no residual neurologic or cognitive deficits of any type.

As it turned out, the following day he did have a previously scheduled appointment with a neurologist whom he had not met, and who would be monitoring his postradiation condition. I discussed with him that his episode the previous evening must be taken seriously and might indicate some progression of his brain disease. He expressed his unwillingness to go to the hospital because he was asymptomatic, though I insisted he must call 911 should he experience another episode before his appointment with the neurologist. As a precaution, I gave him a prescription for Decadron, a steroid preparation that reduces brain swelling. I also started him on nattokinase, an enzyme derived from soy that dissolves blood clots quite effectively.

We then spent two hours together reviewing the nutritional protocol, but I must admit, with recent developments I realized that he was a very sick patient, with possible rapidly advancing disease. I discussed bluntly the seriousness of the situation, which he and his wife fully understood. But they also expressed their strong wish to proceed with my therapy, explaining he felt realistically he had no other option.

The following day, the meeting with the neurologist went ahead as planned. Subsequently I received a faxed report of the EEG (electroencephalogram study of the brain) that had been done, which was read as completely normal. When Patient IG called me about the visit, he reported that the neurologist felt he had experienced a focal seizure related to his brain tumors and had started him on Keppra, an anticonvulsant. The medication left him very sedated and spacey, with difficulty concentrating, but a nurse in the neurologist's office with whom he had spoken about the situation explained that with Keppra, often the symptoms lessen with time. Patient IG also seemed to be diving into his nutritional regimen, with complete dedication.

In the days that followed our second visit together, Patient IG called several times, with various questions about the regimen, and to report on his situation, which seemed to be improving. Then, during the third week of September 2012, Patient IG's local doctors repeated the CT scan of the chest to assess the pulmonary emboli. This showed the following: "Interval resolution of pulmonary emboli on the left. No significant change in appearance of mediastinal and hilar lymphadenopathy since the prior examination. Lymphadenopathy has decreased since the examination dated 06/20/12. There is now complete atelectasis [collapse] of the right middle lobe which obscures previously seen mass."

I thought that the scan revealed some initial response to my therapy, even after just two-plus weeks.

Patient IG discussed the findings with his pulmonologist, who suggested, as a next step, a repeat bronchoscopy to investigate the cause of the right lung collapse. He also brought up laser treatment that could be performed during the procedure to open up the collapsed bronchi and hopefully reinflate the middle right lobe. When we discussed these recommendations, I told Patient IG to go ahead with the bronchoscopy and proposed laser therapy, which in no way would interfere with my therapy. However, Patient IG eventually decided not proceed with the treatment, because he wanted only to continue his nutritional regimen.

Bilateral ultrasound studies of both legs during the first week of October 2012 showed that previously noted thrombi had completely resolved. At that point, with the blood clot issue under control, Patient IG and his wife journeyed by train to Florida, where they usually wintered. There, he had arranged for another group of doctors, including a pulmonologist, to follow him.

Shortly after arriving in Florida, during the third week of October 2012, Patient IG underwent repeat MRI scanning of the brain. This showed some improvement, after some six weeks on his nutritional regimen: "There are intracranial lesions consistent with metastases noted. Previously noted largest lesion is again identified. This lesion measures 16 mm and is slightly smaller than previous [sic] where it measured 17 mm in size. The vasogenic edema has improved. … In the right frontal region a peripherally enhancing 5 mm lesion appears stable. An additional right frontal lesion has decreased in size. … A more posterior right frontal previously 2 mm lesion is no longer identified."

Because the tumors had initially increased in size after the gamma knife radiation, I thought the improvement most likely was due to his nutritional regimen—particularly because the recent CT of the chest had also showed some tumor regression (and the lungs had not been radiated).

In early November 2012, Patient IG's doctors in Florida arranged for a total-body PET scan. I personally thought, in terms of so much radiation exposure in such a short interval, that he was being over scanned, particularly because no beneficial conventional options really existed for him. Nonetheless, Patient IG and I were both pleased with the results, compared with the PET study of early July 2012, nearly two months before he began treatment with me. The scan showed some significant improvement in areas, but also several new areas of disease:

IMPRESSION:

1. Findings suggest moderate improvement in previously noted diffuse metastatic mediastinal and bilateral hilar lymphadenopathy, as well as the area of increased density in the right middle lobe as compared to the patient's prior study … but with increased glucose metabolic activity still seen in multiple small metastatic mediastinal lymph nodes.

2. There appears to be interval increase in the number of metastatic supraclavicular lymph nodes which now appear to be bilateral, but all measuring less than 1 cm in size, as compared to the prior study. A few bony metastatic lesions are also now suggested … which were not present on the prior examination.

I suspected that the bony lesions had developed in the two-month period between the previous PET scan of early July, and when Patient IG began his nutritional regimen in early September 2012. In my experience, it would be very unusual to see significant tumor improvement in one area and worsening and new cancer development in others. When Patient IG and I discussed the report, he suspected the "new" lesions probably had developed before he began treatment with me. In any event, he made it clear to me he intended only to continue his nutrition therapy.

An MRI of the brain during the third week of November 2012 showed stabilization of the multiple metastatic lesions:

IMPRESSION:

THREE RIGHT FRONTAL LESIONS ARE AGAIN EVIDENT, NOT SIGNIFICANTLY CHANGED FROM OCTOBER. THE LARGEST MEASURING APPROXIMATELY 1.5 CM AND THE SMALLER TWO BETWEEN 4.5 MM. A FOURTH LESION IS AGAIN NOT APPARENT.

FAINTER FOCUS SEEN IN THE POSTERIOR RIGHT PARIETAL LOBE IS AGAIN EVIDENT, AND STABLE.

I thought, and Patient IG concurred when we talked, that with aggressive metastatic lung cancer, stabilization of brain metastases (after some shrinkage) is at least a partial victory. Plus, as he explained, he was feeling better and stronger, with improvement in his energy, stamina, and concentration. He had adjusted to the Keppra and fortunately had experienced no further neurologic episodes of any kind. His cognition had improved, he felt optimistic about his future, and he remained vigilantly compliant with his therapy. He has proven to be a very determined patient, despite his daunting odds.

Patient RZ, one of my early patients from 1988 and also diagnosed with lung cancer, experienced considerable reduction in his brain metastases on his nutritional program before he abandoned his therapy and was lost to follow-up. I decided to include Patient IG, who twenty-four years later has experienced some improvement, both in his lungs and brain, on his nutritional regimen. His case illustrates that many years after I began my practice, compliant patients continue to respond.

Experts consider the histologic type of cancer diagnosed in this case, adenocarcinoma, to be one of the most aggressive and treatment resistant of the lung malignancies. Adenocarcinoma falls in the category of "non-small cell carcinoma of the lung" to distinguish it from "small cell" lung cancer, which responds more favorably to standard treatment.

Schrump et al., writing in *Cancer: Principles and Practice of Oncology*, reported a mere four-month median survival in patients such as IG diagnosed with non-small cell lung cancer with multiple metastatic lesions to the brain, treated with radiotherapy.[2] So Patient IG, seven

---

2 Schrump et al., *Cancer: Principles and Practice of Oncology*, Chapter 75: "Non-small cell lung cancer", 9th Edition, 844.

months from diagnosis, has already beaten the odds. And his performance status, which usually declines quickly in such cases and serves as a good marker of eventual prognosis, continues to improve dramatically.

*IMPORTANT EDITOR'S NOTE:
Dr. Gonzalez died before updating this case report. According to the office medical files, Patient IG died in May 2013 after not being able to continue his nutritional protocol for several weeks.

MESOTHELIOMA

A relatively rare cancer, mesothelioma arises from the pleural, pericardial, or peritoneal tissues that respectively line the lungs, heart, and abdominal cavity. More than 70 percent of all mesotheliomas originate in the pleural sac.

Scientists have long associated this malignancy with exposure to asbestos, a mixture of mineral silicates that very efficiently insulates against heat and electrical current. According to the website UpToDate.com, approximately 70 percent of cases are linked to the material used extensively in industry up until the 1970s. During World War II, long before the connection with cancer had been established, thousands of American shipbuilders experienced exposure to asbestos in their work, leaving them vulnerable to this cancer. Even brief exposure of less than two years and secondhand exposure can set off the late development of this neoplasm.

Mesothelioma percolates slowly, with a latency period of twenty to forty years from the time of exposure to the diagnosis of the disease. It is estimated that up to eight million Americans currently alive have experienced workplace exposure to asbestos over the past half century according to UpToDate.com. With exposure, rates of many cancers skyrocket, not just mesothelioma. Sherman et al. reported that the "average asbestos worker has a 50 percent chance of dying from a malignancy, compared to around 18 percent for the average American. The vast majority of cancers in asbestos workers involve the lung, either primary lung carcinoma or mesothelioma."

Approximately thirty-three hundred cases of mesothelioma are diagnosed yearly in the US, though the incidence seems to have peaked. Recent declines in incidence seem related to a significant reduction in industrial uses of asbestos.

By the time of diagnosis, most often the disease has spread to the point that surgical cure is no longer an option. Resistant to radiation, chemotherapy, and immunotherapy, this cancer is among the deadliest, with a median survival between six and eighteen months even with aggressive treatment.

Over the years that I have been in practice, I have seen only one patient with mesothelioma, whose course on my therapy was most unusual.

Case 1: Patient RG
A 7-Year Survivor

In his initial meeting with me in late February 1992, Patient RG reported a significant family history of cancer. His mother died with pancreatic cancer, a first cousin died from melanoma, another first cousin at the time was battling brain cancer, a maternal uncle died from lung cancer, and a maternal aunt died from breast cancer. Another maternal uncle had been diagnosed with renal cell carcinoma. One of Patient RG's sisters had been diagnosed with thyroid cancer, and a second sister had undergone surgery for multiple benign ovarian tumors.

In terms of his past medical history, Patient RG had survived three heart attacks and had been diagnosed with hypertension and insulin-dependent diabetes. A farmer at the time I met him, he had never smoked but reported significant exposure to asbestos when he worked in construction. His cancer situation dates to November 1991, when he first experienced significant hip pain. He went for an evaluation at the local VA hospital in Chicago, where a hip x-ray showed no significant pathology but a routine chest x-ray in late December 1991 revealed a right pleural effusion.

A CT scan of the abdomen was "of poor quality and cannot be interpreted." A bone scan documented abnormalities consistent with metastatic disease at the T6–8 level of the thoracic spine. Subsequently, the pleural fluid was drained, but cytology studies were described as negative for malignancy. At that point, Patient RG was, for some reason, referred to a psychiatrist after describing significant stress in his life.

On his own, in early January 1992 Patient RG decided to seek a second opinion for his lung problems at the Mayo Clinic in Rochester, Minnesota. There, he underwent a full radiographic evaluation. A CT scan of the chest on January 10, 1992 revealed a "right pleural effusion." A CT of the abdomen and pelvis indicated splenomegaly but no definite evidence of metastatic disease. A bone scan the same date demonstrated a suspicious area in a right rib initially thought to be benign in character: "a single focus of increased uptake in the right 8th rib posterolaterally. This is likely post-traumatic in spite of the negative right rib view of 1-8-92."

Then, on January 14, 1992, he underwent thoracoscopy with a biopsy of the pleura that confirmed "malignant melanoma, right pleura." Two days later, a CT scan of the brain was read as essentially normal.

At that point, Patient RG's doctors told him his disease was inoperable and referred him to a Mayo oncologist, who suggested a course of both chemotherapy and radiation. When questioned by Patient RG, the physician admitted neither would be curative and that his disease was terminal. In their discussions, Patient RG learned about a Phase I (preliminary) clinical trial currently up and running at the National Cancer Institute investigating the value of surgical debulking of visible tumor along with photodynamic therapy for malignancies specifically of the pleural space, such as mesothelioma.

In this regimen, the patient first was to receive an intravenous bolus of a drug, Photofrin, that researchers proposed cancer cells selectively absorb. One or two days later, the patient then would proceed to chest surgery with removal of all visible tumor. With the chest still open, the surgeon would shine a red light beam onto all surfaces, in theory activating the Photofrin and killing any remaining cancer cells. The photodynamic treatment was therefore a one-time event, not a many-month course of treatment as is common with chemotherapy. The study, under the direction of Dr. Harvey Pass of the NCI in Bethesda, was entitled "Surgery and Intrapleural Photodynamic Therapy for Pleural Malignancies" and had been accruing patients for about a year and a half at that time.

Before contacting the NCI, after leaving Mayo Patient RG decided to consult with experts at the Dana-Farber Cancer Institute in Boston, a Harvard teaching and research center. There, in the third week of January 1992 the doctors suggested aggressive surgery, but the procedure would have been so debilitating that Patient RG refused to proceed with that option. At that point, the Harvard doctors recommended as an option that he consider the same NCI clinical study previously mentioned by the Mayo oncologist.

After contacting the NCI and forwarding the Mayo records of his case to Dr. Pass's group, Patient RG learned that on preliminary review he appeared suitable for the clinical study. Subsequently, he flew to Washington for an initial evaluation in late January 1992. At the time, a chest x-ray showed evidence of some vague abnormalities: "A density is seen in the area of the right costophrenic angle, presumably pleural reaction, possibly a small right pleural effusion. … A vague nodular density is also present in the area of the right costophrenic angle but never clearly seen."

After meeting with the various doctors involved in the clinical trial, he was scheduled for a more intensive intake evaluation, including cardiac studies to assess his suitability for surgery in early March 1992. Surgery was tentatively proposed—assuming the cardiology team gave their approval—at that time.

The information given Patient RG during this visit to the NCI described in some detail the nature of this clinical study:

> Your doctors have explained to you that you have cancer involving the chest cavity, either on the lining of the lung or on the inside of the chest muscles and ribs that surround the lung. This is particularly difficult to treat even with chemotherapy and

radiation therapy. At this time there is no indication that your cancer has spread outside this chest cavity to any other parts of the body.…

Present therapy for these problems is not considered curative. Conventional chemotherapy is usually unable to cure patients of cancers that involve the chest cavity and this is also true of radiation therapy which would also require giving a substantial dose of this treatment to the lung itself. In cases where the cancer is not localized in one place in the chest cavity, surgery itself has a low chance for cure. You are therefore being considered for a treatment which is experimental and may also not result in cure of your tumor. This experimental therapy involves removing as much of the cancer from your chest cavity as possible with surgery and then treatment of any areas of cancer that are left with a technique called photodynamic therapy. This experimental cancer treatment involves the administration of a drug (Photofrin II) that concentrates in tumor cells and that can be activated by red light to destroy cancer cells. This study's primary… [sic] is to determine whether this treatment can be delivered safely to patients who have removal of their cancer from the chest by an operation.

While Patient RG prepared to return to Bethesda, a local doctor of his interested in alternative approaches knew about our work and suggested he also consider my treatment. He subsequently contacted my office, and after I reviewed his records, I though him suitable for my regimen even if he proceeded with the NCI protocol, because the experimental approach involved surgery and a single session of photodynamic treatment, but neither chemotherapy nor radiation.

I first met with Patient RG in late February 1992, only days before his scheduled return visit to the NCI. He reported generally feeling well, except for a mild persistent cough. His diabetes seemed under control, and he described no cardiac symptoms. He seemed very determined to follow my treatment regimen but described considerable financial stress, as well as stress involving battles with various government regulatory agencies over alleged pollution on his property.

Then, in early March 1992, Patient RG returned to Bethesda for his cardiology workup and planned surgery. When his doctors decided to delay treatment until late April 1992, he returned home and began his prescribed nutritional program with great dedication.

In retrospect, I am somewhat perplexed why Patient RG had been deemed eligible for this clinical trial, because the written documents in my possession required the disease be localized to the chest. The bone scan from December 1991 at the local VA indicated metastatic disease in the thoracic spine, as clearly documented in the NCI admission note from March 1, 1992: "He had a bone scan done, which apparently was positive with increased activity with 6–8 on the right side."

Evidence of distant metastatic disease precluded admission to the NCI program, as the previously mentioned first paragraph from the official protocol reads. Though the NCI admission note referenced this scan finding, I can find no discussion in the copious records from the NCI that this issue was ever discussed as a possible reason for exclusion. Nonetheless, in late April 1992 Patient RG again traveled down to Bethesda for the planned treatment despite the earlier bone scan findings. Then, after receiving the bolus of Photofrin II, on April 23, 1992 he underwent thoracotomy, pleurectomy, and photodynamic therapy. As planned, during the procedure the surgeon removed all visible tumor.

The subsequent pathology report dated May 1, 1991 described "Malignant Mesothelioma" in the pleura as well as in two pleural nodules that had been excised during surgery. A "diaphragm nodule #1" was found consistent with a metastatic mesothelioma deposit, and the "inferior pleura" was also infiltrated with the malignancy.

After recovering from the procedure, Patient RG was eventually discharged from the NCI hospital on May 2, 1992, with plans for him to return periodically for re-evaluation of his status. Meanwhile, once home, he dove into his nutritional therapy once again with great dedication.

In June 1992, he visited the NCI for postsurgical rescanning of the chest, abdomen, and pelvis. The official radiology report stated, "No significant adenopathy is seen in the chest, no nodules or masses are identified. … No focal lesions are seen in the liver or spleen. The pancreas, gallbladder, adrenals, and kidneys look unremarkable."

Due to financial constraints, Patient RG could not travel to New York for his August 1992 six-month follow-up appointment and re-evaluation with us. However, he did return to the NCI for routine testing in September 1992, when a bone scan revealed multiple suspicious lesions, as described in the official report: "There is a small focus in the left temporal skull, suggest correlation with X-rays of the skull. In addition, there is increased activity in two foci one in the 7th and the other in the 6th rib posterolaterally on the right. There is increased activity in the right 3rd rib anterolateral. There is a focus of soft tissue activity adjacent to the right 6th rib anteriorly, suggest correlation with X-rays of the check. Many of these findings may be related to surgery."

A CT scan of the abdomen revealed "scattered tiny low density areas in the liver, too small to characterize." These findings had not been described in the report of the June 1992 scans.

At that point, Patient RG's physicians adopted a conservative approach, and after returning home, he continued his nutritional program. When he returned to Bethesda in late March 1993, on repeat bone scanning the previously noted skull lesion was not observed, and the other abnormalities remained unchanged. Due to the stability of the findings, the radiologist now assumed they must represent postsurgical effect: "The current scan continues to show increased tracer uptake in approximately the right 6ᵗʰ, 7ᵗʰ, and 8ᵗʰ ribs posteriorly. This finding was present on the previous scan and is unchanged and likely related to previous thoracotomy. … The previous scan showed a focal abnormality near the junction of the left parietotemporal bone. This abnormality is no longer seen."

The CT scans of the chest and abdomen revealed,

> Small shotty nodes are seen in the axillary regions bilaterally without significant change. … There is no evidence of significant adenopathy in the chest.
>
> No definite hepatic lesion is identified.

This time around, the earlier documented liver lesions were not apparent.

Subsequently, as Patient RG continued his nutritional therapy, we continued to be in touch by phone, and he reported feeling well. I would tinker with his protocol as I thought necessary, sending him the proposed alterations by mail.

When he returned to the NCI in January 1994, he again underwent a full radiographic workup. In the bone scan report, the radiologist did not mention the abnormalities in the sixth and seventh rib but did describe the skull lesion originally observed on the September 1992 scan. He seemed to feel the lesion had simply been missed in March 1993. Regardless, clearly overall the scan showed no worsening since September 1992 and most likely indicated improvement.

The CT scan of the chest revealed no significant pathology: "No parenchymal masses, infiltrates, or pleural effusions are seen. The bilateral axillary and precarinal densities are too small to characterize by CT criteria and remain unchanged."

The report of the abdominal CT did not mention the previously noted liver lesions: "There are no focal hepatic, splenic, pancreatic, adrenal, or renal lesions."

Back home, he continued his nutritional treatment, and though he felt well, his follow-up testing at the NCI in July 1994 did show some changes. The report of the chest CT described the following: "There is a 1.2 cm nodule at the right lung base (image 315) which was not present on the study of 4 January 1994. In view of the patient's history, this is very worrisome for a metastatic deposit."

The abdominal CT revealed "areas of heterogeneity in the liver. But these could conceivably represent opacified vascular structures."

Apparently, Patient RG's doctors at the NCI did not think the findings significant and told him, according to what he would later say to me, that for now they considered him "cured." He and I kept in touch by phone, though I had not seen him in person since his original consultation with me in February 1992, two and a half years earlier.

In late August 1994, he called my office to give me an update on his status. When he very honestly reported a period of significant noncompliance with the supplements, I encouraged him to resume the program fully. He did tell me that of some forty patients entered in the NCI clinical trial, he was the only survivor, though I had no independent verification of the claim at that time.

Patient RG did not return to the NCI follow-up in six months as had been recommended. However, in July 1995—a year after the questionable findings noted on the chest CT—he did rescanning at the local Chicago VA. Though I do not have a copy of the official reading, I learned from the NIH records of "a CT scan of the chest in July 1995 at a VA hospital which revealed a small right lower lung nodule." At that point, he contacted his NCI doctors, who arranged for a return trip to Bethesda in early September 1995 for further testing. The report of the chest CT stated, "There is a nodule measuring 11 mm along the right hemidiaphragm. This has increased by approximately 1 or 2 mm since the prior study from 7-5-94, but did not appear to be present on the earlier scans. Given the patient's history of known malignancy, this is suspicious for a recurrence."

The abdominal CT scan was essentially unrevealing, with again no evidence of the previously noted "tiny" liver lesions.

After reviewing all the reports, his NCI team suggested he undergo surgery, because based on the radiographic evidence the recurrence seemed limited to only one lesion that could easily be resected. Unfortunately, he did not contact me at this time to let me know what was going on. He later told me he felt somewhat guilty, because he had not yet resumed his supplement program. Regardless, his NCI doctors scheduled surgery for late November 1995.

Subsequently, in mid-November 1995 he underwent right thoracotomy for what was intended to be a simple resection of a single lesion. However, during the procedure the surgeon noted multiple lung lesions, none of which was resected, as described in the operative note:

> The patient had presented with a solitary lung nodule in the setting of having had me-sothelioma of the right chest treated with PDT [photodynamic therapy] four years ago. This solitary lung nodule was in the right lower lobe just above the diaphragm. … After entering the right chest and mobilizing the right lung, it was obvious that there were multiple small nodules along the diaphragm as well as along the chest wall. The lesion that had been on CT scan in the right lower lobe of the lung could be seen on the

113

under surface of the right lower lobe and there was another nodule just next to this one. … The second nodule was biopsied and sent off for frozen which came back consistent with mesothelioma. The lung nodule that had been seen on CT scan was left in place in order to be evaluable as an area of evaluable disease for future chemotherapy.

The final pathology report confirmed malignant mesothelioma.

After recovering from surgery, Patient RG was discharged from the NCI hospital in late November, with plans to contact Dr. Pass for further discussion of experimental chemotherapy. However, Patient RG had already been told by multiple doctors that chemotherapy had proven ineffective for his disease—the very reason he had agreed to participate in an NCI clinical study of photodynamic therapy in the first place. Though he kept in touch with the NCI, Patient RG decided to refuse chemotherapy and instead resume my full program. He contacted my office and made an appointment for a return visit in January 1996—almost four years after his original appointments with me in February 1992.

When I met with him, he was very happy to be back and anxious to restart his nutritional regimen. He admitted that his noncompliance wasn't strictly financial; his doctors in Bethesda had been so enthusiastic about his condition that he got "cocky" to the point that he became careless with the supplements. He repeated what he had told me before, that of all the mesothelioma patients entered into the study, he was the only survivor!

We had a long discussion about the seriousness of his situation and the need for vigilant compliance. He seemed to understand fully the gravity of his situation and left my office with newfound dedication. In my mind, his course to date only proved the effectiveness of the therapy: while he remained compliant, his disease remained quiescent or even improved. But within months of discontinuing the supplements, his disease had recurred aggressively.

Shortly after his trip to New York, in mid-March 1996 he underwent an evaluation locally at the Chicago VA. A bone scan revealed lesions in the right sixth and seventh ribs consistent with metastatic disease, and a chest CT indicated moderate pleural thickening. At that point, Patient RG continued his program with great determination, we continued to be in touch via telephone, and he continued to report he felt fine.

In early October 1996, repeat scans at the Chicago VA confirmed considerable improvement in the earlier described lesions in the bone and pleura. The report of the bone scan stated, "There was evidence of improvement of bone metastasis at the right sixth and the seventh ribs as compared to the previous bone scan on 3/13/96."

The report of the chest CT documented a "mild decrease in the pleural thickening in the right base. No other significant change."

Patient RG did keep in touch with his NCI doctors. In mid-January 1997—nearly five years after his first visit with me—he reported to me that he had been told the clinical study he had entered had been officially canceled and that all mesothelioma patients had died—with the exception of him.

Patient RG couldn't afford to return to New York regularly as I normally suggest, but we kept in contact periodically by phone. Throughout 1997, he appeared to be very compliant with his program. In late 1997, he vacationed in Florida, where CT scans at the West Palm Beach VA showed no evidence of disease. But in 1998, his financial situation deteriorated as his legal battles with the government intensified. I thought it tragic that he was the only mesothelioma survivor in a federally funded clinical trial, while at the same time another branch of the same government seemed determined to put him in the grave. We offered to treat him for free and even subsidized his supplement costs with a grant from a foundation set up with donations from our grateful friends and patients. Nonetheless, by mid-1998, as he later admitted to me, his compliance had again fallen off

Patient RG spent most of 1998 in Florida. In late fall, after developing severe pain in his right chest, he returned to the West Palm Beach VA, where on exam his doctors detected a mass in the right lobe of his thyroid. This finding, coupled with his chest symptoms, prompted a CT of the neck and chest in late December 1998. This time around, the scan revealed changes suspicious for recurrent disease:

> There are some enlarged lymph nodes within the mediastinum, pretrachea, precarinal. This is a new finding. There are some subcentimeter nodules with the right upper lobe, numbering at least three, which is a new finding. There are some pulmonary nodules or focal areas of pleural thickening involving the base of the right hemithorax … these do appear somewhat enlarged when compared to previous study.…
>
> Concern mass right lobe thyroid gland.

He was begun on pain medicine, and he then contacted Dr. Pass at the NCI, who suggested exploratory chest surgery to debulk visible tumor. Without my input, Patient RG agreed to the plan, scheduling a return to Bethesda for mid-February 1999.

In early January 1999, some seven years after our first meeting together, Patient RG called my office. I hadn't heard from him in about a year, and my repeated attempts to contact him at his home in the Midwest had proven unsuccessful. He hadn't told me he was living more or less permanently in Florida, nor had he provided my office with his new contact information. I was happy to hear from him, though I was concerned about the new radiographic findings. He admitted that he had once again "got a little bit confident" and had been off the supplements for "some time" even though we had been willing to underwrite the costs. I was saddened to hear that his legal battles with the government had only worsened over the past year, leaving him disconsolate and broke from the ongoing legal fees.

He relayed the gist of his recent conversations with his NCI doctors and their wish to proceed with surgery. He told me his doctors felt he had done so extraordinarily well that they wanted to remain aggressive with him. According to what Patient RG told me in that conversation, they confirmed that in the final accounting of the clinical trial, of the sixty-two total patients entered including those with non-mesothelioma pleural cancer, he remained the only survivor. I told him that news should encourage him to resume his full program, reminding him of how well he had done in past years.

I was not, however, very enthusiastic about the prospects of the surgery proposed by his NCI physicians. First, when he underwent surgery in 1996, the surgeon had found the cancer too extensive for resection. What would change now, from a surgical perspective? And as far as I was concerned, he had done well in the past as long as he followed his full nutritional regimen, and I assumed he would do well once again once compliant. Patient RG explained that he fully intended to resume my therapy, but that he felt it would be in his best interest to undergo the suggested operation at the NCI. I told him I would support him in his decision but nudged him again to resume the full nutritional program and, this time, stay compliant.

After our conversation, I actually called the NCI to check up on the status of the clinical study. I learned from an NCI information specialist that just as Patient RG had told me, the study had indeed been shut down because all of the patients entered into the trial had died except for one. I was told the results had not been published, the research group had been disbanded, and no publication would be forthcoming.

Subsequently, in preparation for Patient RG's trip to the NCI, an ultrasound of the neck at the VA in mid-January 1999 confirmed two nodules within the right lobe of the thyroid "measuring 3.3 × 2.0 × 21. cm and 1.5 × 1.3 × 1.3 cm, respectively." A biopsy confirmed thyroid cancer, thought to be related to radiation exposure as a child.

During the second week of February 1999, a week before the planned surgery, I called Patient RG to check on his progress. He reported that he was once again back on the full program for a number of weeks and already could feel the difference. He described significantly improved energy, and the chest pain that had been so severe in December had completely resolved, to the point that he was off all pain medication. He felt hopeful again and said, "The program worked before, and I know it will work again."

My note documenting the conversation reported, "His energy, stamina and endurance have already improved. His breathing is better. He said he can tell the difference within weeks.

I suspect he is going to do very well as he has done before. He sounded very strong and very upbeat."

But when I didn't hear from him after surgery, in late February 1999, I called his home and his wife answered the phone. She relayed a terrible message. During the operation in Bethesda, he developed bleeding, the source of which could not be effectively determined. Eventually, the hemorrhage seemed to stabilize, so that the procedure was concluded and he was sent to the recovery room.

But, when the bleeding resumed shortly after, he was taken back to the operating room. Tragically, during this second exploratory procedure he suddenly experienced cardiac arrest and died on the table—nearly seven years to the day of our first meeting in February 1992. It was a sad end for a very courageous patient, who tried as best he could to fight a terrible disease, and who for the most part faced the enormous obstacles in his life with a sense of hopefulness.

Twelve years later, as I write this in February 2011, I still remember well Patient RG, our first meeting, and his faith that I could help him survive the daunting odds that had been given him. I remember so well his telling me of his trials and tribulations against a relentless government bureaucracy determined to "crush him" as he once said, for something he didn't appear to have done.

Though his course was complicated, with periods of worsening disease and periods of improvement, his story is most informative. When he complied he did well, and his disease remained controlled. When his compliance fell off, usually within some six months the disease recurred. When he resumed his program as he did after a period of poor compliance in 1996, the disease regressed, documented at that time with successive bone and CT scans.

Though he ultimately wasn't cured, he did experience years of good-quality life, succumbing at the end because of a surgical procedure gone bad. And his seven-year survival for such a deadly disease is remarkable, especially as he far outlived all the other subjects in an NCI study that had to be shut down because of poor results. I do wish he had been more consistently compliant, and of course I wish he had declined the last surgery, which I thought unnecessary.

Over the years, I've thought about him quite a bit, his heroic battles, his sense of humor, and his candor when he would admit he had "goofed up" with the program. He certainly wasn't a perfect patient, but even with his compliance lapses he still managed to enjoy many years of good-quality life that his conventional doctors hadn't expected. I still miss him, as a patient and as the friend he became over the years, as we both worked together trying to give him the life he so deserved.

OVARIAN CANCER

In 2009, 21,550 women developed ovarian cancer in the United States, and 14,600 died from the disease, making it the leading cause of gynecological cancer deaths in women.[1] Ovarian cancer tends to occur in family clusters, with some 5 percent of all cases linked to inherited genetic aberrations, particularly mutations in the BRCA1 and BRCA2 genes—mutations long associated with breast cancer as well. The protein products of two these alleles normally serve as tumor suppressors, so irregularities in the DNA encourage carcinogenic transformation.

The disease has also been linked to infertility, use of fertility-enhancing drugs such as Clomid, and nulliparity. Each pregnancy reduces the risk, as does breastfeeding. Regular use of oral contraceptives actually lessens the risk of ovarian malignancy, while hormone replacement therapy doesn't influence incidence either way, despite earlier concerns.

Ninety percent of women diagnosed with strictly localized disease survive five years, many of them cured by surgery alone. Once the disease spreads, ovarian cancer can be very aggressive, with fewer than 5 percent of stage IV patients living five years despite aggressive treatment.[2] Chemotherapy regimens that include one of the taxane derivatives, given along with platinum agents such as carboplatin, cut the recurrence rate for localized tumors and marginally improve survival for those patients with advanced disease.

1 DeVita et al., *Cancer: Principles and Practice*, Chapter 104: "Ovarian Cancer…", 9th ed.1368
2 Ibid.

Case 1: Patient AL
A 20.25-Year Survivor

Patient AL, prior to developing cancer, had a long history of neuromuscular symptoms dating to 1979, when she first developed a mass in her left calf, associated with muscle pain, atrophy, and numbness. In the intervening years, as the symptoms worsened, she consulted numerous physicians at numerous centers. Though multiple muscle biopsies had all been unrevealing, she was nonetheless treated empirically and unsuccessfully with a variety of drugs including prednisone.

In 1985, she sought another evaluation at the Mayo Clinic, where a muscle biopsy confirmed polymyositis. After she was also diagnosed with motor and sensory neuropathy, type II, AL began another course of prednisone but with little improvement, followed by six months on Imuran. The latter drug did nothing for her disease but did lead to weight gain, insomnia, and anxiety.

As her symptoms worsened, AL, who knew of my work from a family member, decided to seek treatment with me for her neuromuscular problems. When she first came to my office, in 1989, she had been off all medications for some three years, during which time her symptoms of weakness, nerve pain, and numbness continued to progress. When I first saw her, she had no gynecological problems other than the history of a hysterectomy for uterine fibroids.

I designed a protocol to treat this patient's muscle and neurological problems, without the high doses of enzymes we use against cancer. Subsequently, AL complied well with her program, and when I saw her for a return visit in August 1989, she reported her condition that had worsened without respite over the previous ten years had improved significantly. She described a "20 percent" overall gain in motor strength and calf thickness, a marker her previous doctors had used to track her decline. The proximal muscle weakness in both legs had reversed to the point that she could stand from a sitting position for the first time in years. However, on exam I detected a small pelvic mass and told her she needed to follow up with a gynecological evaluation upon returning home.

Some weeks later, in early fall, an ultrasound revealed a 7 × 8 cm cystic lesion posterior to the bladder. Then, in early November 1989, at the Moffitt Cancer Center in Tampa, she underwent exploratory laparotomy and was found to have extensive malignant disease throughout her pelvis and abdomen. Her surgeon proceeded with bilateral oophorectomy, omentectomy, and extensive lymphadenectomy of pelvic, periaortic, and precaval lymph nodes. The pathology report described "omentum diffusely infiltrated by papillary serous carcinoma of ovarian origin," as well as tumor in both ovaries that involved both fallopian tubes. Cancer had infiltrated into all 21 of 21 nodes evaluated, and peritoneal washings were positive for "metastatic adenocarcinoma consistent with ovarian primary."

After surgery, AL met with an oncologist, who strongly recommended intensive chemotherapy, but she decided to refuse all conventional treatment, instead choosing to begin the cancer version of my therapy. At that point, I redesigned her regimen to include high doses of pancreatic enzymes throughout the day.

In December 1989, her oncologist wrote a summary note to me, which accompanied the records of her recent hospitalization. In his letter, he stated, "She is diagnosed as having a Stage IIIC Grade I papillary serous cystadenocarcinoma of the ovary. I have recommended that she receive chemotherapy. She would be a candidate for GOG Protocol 104 intravenous Cisplatinum and Cyclophosphamide versus intraperitoneal Cisplatinum and Cyclophosphamide. Mrs.----unfortunately did not wish to pursue the idea of chemotherapy."

She thereafter followed her program diligently for six years. By the mid-1990s, her muscle weakness began to progress once again, making return trips to New York difficult, though she continued on the regimen and we worked together by phone. In recent years, when we spoke on the phone, she always expressed her enormous gratitude for the treatment and the benefit she had derived from it. We last spoke in early 2009, when she reported her biggest problem was her ongoing neuromuscular weakness in her legs, requiring that she use a walker for ambulation. She suddenly passed away in the spring of 2009 from pneumonia, at age eighty-seven. At the time, she was cancer-free, over twenty years from her diagnosis of extensive ovarian malignancy.

DeVita has reported, regarding ovarian cancer patients such as this, that "patients with stage III disease have a 5-year survival rate of approximately 15–20% that is dependent in large part on the volume of disease present in the upper abdomen."[3]

In this patient's case, the disease did extend into the upper abdomen at the time of diagnosis. Furthermore, these survival statistics refer to patients treated with aggressive chemotherapy, which AL refused, choosing to follow only my protocol. Her prolonged disease-free survival can be attributed only to her nutritional program.

---

3   DeVita et al., *Cancer: Principles and Practice*, 9th ed. 1375

Case 2: Patient QR
*A Minimum 24-Year Survivor**

Patient QR, a nurse, had a long history of colitis but otherwise had generally been in good health when, in January 1992, she herself detected a mass in the left pelvic area, associated with some abdominal distension. She consulted her gynecologist, who on exam detected a large pelvic mass consistent with an ovarian neoplasm. After an ultrasound in late January 1992 revealed a 12 to 14 cm pelvic mass, the patient underwent CT scanning. This revealed

> AT LEAST TWO SUBCENTIMETER LESIONS IN THE HEPATIC DOME TOO SMALL TO ACCURATELY CHARACTERIZE....

> SCANS OF THE PELVIS ARE REMARKABLE FOR THE PRESENCE OF A LARGE MIDLINE PREDOMINANTLY CYSTIC MASS WITH SOME AREAS OF SOFT TISSUE NOTED.

In early February, the patient was admitted to New York University Medical Center in Manhattan and underwent a total abdominal hysterectomy and bilateral oophorectomy. The pathology report described "serous cystadenocarcinoma, moderately to well differentiated," grade 2 of 3, indicating a moderately aggressive histology, with the large tumor measured at "10 × 8 × 4 cm." The day after surgery, CA 125—a tumor marker for ovarian cancer—came back elevated at 91.

Postsurgery, Patient QR met with a gynecological oncologist, who explained that because of the size of the tumor and the possibility of liver metastases, she required immediate and aggressive chemotherapy with carboplatin and Cytoxan. Her oncologist also recommended she be considered for the addition of experimental growth factor treatment. However, Patient QR, as she later explained to me, who as a nurse had seen too many patients die "miserable deaths" from cancer despite chemotherapy, would not agree to a toxic conventional approach to her disease. According to Patient QR, her oncologist was not pleased, warning that her disease would reoccur and inevitably prove deadly. But through friends, Patient QR already knew of my work and had decided to proceed with me.

I met Patient QR in mid-February 1992, only a few days after her discharge from NYU. She thereafter proved to be a very determined, compliant, and enthusiastic patient. Her course over the years has been complicated only by Lyme disease in mid-1992 that responded quickly to antibiotics, and periodic exacerbations of her colitis. But generally, she has enjoyed excellent health, with no return of her cancer, despite the dire predictions of her gynecological oncologist. An ultrasound of the abdomen and pelvis in August 1996 was completely clear, with no evidence of recurrent disease or the previously described liver lesions. An ultrasound the following year was also clear. And throughout the years, her CA 125 has fallen within the normal range, except for a single slightly elevated result of 37.1 (normal less than 35) in June 1997.

In late June 1997, Patient QR developed persistent, though mild, hematuria (blood in the urine), which her local doctor diagnosed as resulting from a kidney stone. A CT scan of the abdomen and pelvis on June 29, 2009 showed "minute calcifications in both of the kidneys," presumably contributing to the bleeding. The report of the test described the "liver and spleen to be normal," once again without the evidence of the two hepatic lesions noted in the preoperative scan from January 1992, 17.5 years earlier.

Patient QR, now retired, continues to enjoy a full and productive life, surrounded by friends, family, and nature, in the retirement community in which she lives. And certainly, by the standards of conventional oncology, her long-term, disease-free survival is most remarkable. At the time of diagnosis, her tumor was huge, and CT studies indicated suspicious liver lesions, which on her nutritional regimen completely resolved. Her oncologist insisted that without aggressive chemotherapy, she had little chance of prolonged survival.

*IMPORTANT EDITOR'S NOTE:
Dr. Gonzalez died before he updated this case report. According to Patient QR's office medical file, she contacted Dr. Gonzalez in July 2015 and her last contact with the office was in late January 2016.

Case 3: Patient JR
A Minimum 22.6-Year Survivor

Patient JR is a fifty-seven-year-old woman whose father developed both rectal and primary liver cancer, and whose mother survived breast cancer before dying of pancreatic cancer. She herself had a history of gynecological problems dating back to 1981, when at age thirty-one she was first diagnosed with bilateral ovarian cysts. Over the years, her gynecologist followed her with sequential ultrasounds and recommended surgery when she developed persistent severe pelvic pain. JR refused his suggestion, instead deciding to treat herself with alternative approaches, including several visits to the Hippocrates Institute, a live-in facility offering a raw vegetarian approach to various diseases. She believed her nutritional interventions did help her overall health, though the cysts did not regress.

In March 1993, during a period of extreme personal stress, the patient herself felt that the cysts had enlarged. An ultrasound at Johns Hopkins Hospital revealed

> a large approximately 14 × 10 × 12 cm mass in the mid line pelvis... Multiple foci of hyper-echogenicity are noted. ... Therefore, this mass likely arises from the left ovary. ...

> Within the right ovary, there are two hypoechoic regions and a focus of calcification. ... The largest hypoechoic region measures approximately 1.5 × 1.6 × 1.5 cm.

At that point, her gynecologist insisted she undergo exploratory surgery, but JR instead returned to the Hippocrates Institute for a several-week stay. Despite the aggressive dietary intervention, the mass continued to grow.

In mid-October 1993, JR returned to her gynecologist, with the large pelvic mass clearly evident. Another ultrasound revealed that the mass had grown considerably since March, now measuring "20 × 22 × 15 cm." The radiology report stated, "This has moderately increased in size since the last examination. ... A normal right ovary is identified."

JR then proceeded with surgery at Johns Hopkins Hospital after her physician agreed to remove only the mass and the associated ovary, not the uterus or right ovary. During the procedure, she was found to have a huge tumor that had penetrated into the rectosigmoid area of the colon. Though the surgeon did preserve the uterus and right ovary, his resection was quite extensive, as documented in the Discharge Summary: "The patient... underwent surgery on November --- 1993, undergoing an exploratory laparotomy ... resection of ureterosacral tumors, resection of left parametria, omentectomy, resection of rectosigmoid, left common iliac node dissection and para-aortic lymph node dissection."

The pathology report described an enormous tumor, measuring "17 × 12 × 7 cm," consistent with "adenocarcinoma probably serous," though the tumor was finally classified as a clear cell subtype of ovarian adenocarcinoma. The lymph nodes appeared free of cancer, as did the right ovary. Because the disease appeared to be largely limited to the left ovarian mass, big as it was, and though the tumor had penetrated the colon, she was assumed to have "localized" stage I cancer.

Postoperatively, JR met with an oncologist at Johns Hopkins, who strongly recommended chemotherapy. She initially agreed to the treatment, but after her discharge from Hopkins— with plans to return to start therapy—she then consulted with a second oncologist at George Washington University Medical Center, who was less insistent about the need for immediate treatment. JR therefore decided to refuse conventional approaches, though she did agree to return for routine surveillance. A CA 125, a blood marker for ovarian cancer, was 16.1 at the time, within normal limits.

After learning of my therapy, she first came to my office in January 1994 and subsequently followed her nutritional therapy faithfully. When she returned for her first follow-up visit in April 1994, three months after she had begun treatment with me, she reported feeling "better than I have in years," with significant improvement in her energy, stamina, and well-being. Shortly after that session, she experienced mild mid-cycle bleeding and consulted her local gynecologist, who felt a mass in the pelvis on exam.

JR detailed the interaction with her oncologist in a note to me in late April: "I continue to feel great. What is so frustrating, though, is going to the doctor and being told something might be wrong when I am feeling the best I have in years. I think that on some level, Dr---- [the oncologist] hopes that something will be wrong so that he can prove to me that my program will not work."

Despite the concern, an ultrasound in May showed no lesions on the ovary and no fibroids, and a follow-up exam with her gynecological oncologist was normal. Subsequent CA 125 tests all fell within the normal range.

JR continued doing well until mid-December 1995, nearly two years after she had started her nutritional program, when she developed sudden-onset abdominal pain associated with nausea and vomiting. When the CA 125 came back elevated at 52 (normal less than 36), her oncologist immediately suggested radiographic studies. Before any testing could be done, her symptoms became so severe that she went to the local emergency room, where an intestinal obstruction was ruled out. After intravenous hydration, she improved and went home, with a diagnosis of gastroenteritis. A repeat CA 125 in December came within the normal range at 22, and a CT scan showed a right ovarian cystic area, but nothing suspicious.

Since that time, JR has diligently followed her nutritional program and is in excellent health. Her CA 125 has been within the normal range, the most recent level from 2005 coming in at 7. She excels at a stressful job that requires considerable travel and nonetheless manages her nutritional program efficiently and effectively. Today, more than twenty-three years after she began with me, she has no evidence of cancer and has been able to avoid the intensive chemotherapy her doctors at Johns Hopkins aggressively pushed so long ago. Her long-term disease-free survival to me is certainly intriguing.

In fact, the two patients I have discussed with a history of ovarian cancer—AL and JR—both refused the chemotherapy that was strongly suggested after the initial surgery documented extensive disease. I find that patients with a diagnosis of ovarian cancer who have received, before consulting with me, multiagent chemotherapy tend to have a more difficult course, with many ups and downs.

Case 4: Patient BL
A Minimum 21-Year Survivor

Patient BL is a seventy-nine-year-old white female, with a family history significant because of her father, who died of some type of "bone cancer," and her mother, who survived colon cancer.

In terms of her own health, Patient BL had smoked two packs a day of cigarettes for some twenty years, having quit in 1972. Prior to developing cancer, she generally had been in good health, with bouts in the past of an irregular heart rhythm, chronic lower back pain, and a history of thyroid nodules.

Patient BL had been in her usual state of good health when, in late January 1987, she first developed left flank pain radiating down into the left lower abdomen. She consulted her primary care physician, who ordered a barium enema, revealing diverticulosis, and an intravenous pyelogram that was unremarkable. At that point, Patient BL was referred to a gastroenterologist who, suspecting diverticulitis, prescribed a course of antibiotics, with resolution of the patient's discomfort.

Patient BL did well until mid-March 1987, when she developed intermittent lower abdominal pain that gradually worsened in frequency and intensity over a period of two weeks. With the symptoms progressing, during the first week of April 1987 she decided to return to her primary care physician, who this time detected a "diffuse mass palpable in the lower abdomen," according to his notes. He referred Patient BL for a pelvic ultrasound, which several days later revealed a large tumor in the pelvis, described in the radiology report: "A large septated cystic but partially solid mass is identified filling the posterior cul-de-sac. It measures 10.3 cm in length × 7.1 cm in height. It would appear to originate from one of the ovaries, most probably the left."

Patient BL was then referred to a gynecological surgeon, who recommended exploratory laparotomy to determine the nature of the mass. Most likely, she was told, she would require hysterectomy.

During the second week of April 1987, Patient BL was admitted to Humana Hospital Hoffman Estates for the planned surgery. During the procedure, Patient BL was found to have widespread disease extending from the left ovary "with extensive metastases into the omentum, parietal peritoneum," as described in the operative note. With evidence of extensive cancer, during the operation the gynecologist called in a general surgeon for assistance for what was proving to be a difficult situation.

This surgeon's operative findings clearly documented the amount of cancer present: "I have been called intraoperatively to assist and help Dr.---- perform his exploratory laparotomy. ... Omentum and sigmoid colon wrapped up around the left ovarian tumor. Left ovarian tumor was literally covering the whole pelvis completely and also the peripheral organs. She has free ascites and omentum was as omental cake [cancer] from hepatic flexure to splenic flexure. Diaphragmatic area has small gritty tumor nodules and gutters has tumor nodules. Small bowel also was adhesive to this ovarian cancer."

The surgeon then completed a total abdominal hysterectomy, oophorectomy, omentectomy, appendectomy, and "general intraperitoneal tumor debulking." Because of the extent of cancer, the surgeon was unable to resect all obvious tumor.

The formal pathology report available three days after surgery clearly documented the large amount of cancer present:

A. OVARY CONTAINING AN INFILTRATING MODERATELY WELL DIFFERENTIATED PAPILLARY CYSTADENOCARCINOMA.

B. TISSUE CONSISTENT WITH ORIGIN FROM SEROSA OF SIGMOID COLON CONTAINING A METASTATIC OVARIOUS SEROUS CYSTADENOCARCINOMA.

C. TUMOR CONSISTENT WITH ORIGIN FROM CUL-DE-SAC CONTAINING METASTATIC OVARIAN SEROUS CYSTADENOCARCINOMA.

D. MODERATELY WELL DIFFERENTIATED PAPILLARY SEROUS CYSTADENOCARCINOMA OF LEFT OVARY W/EXTENSION TO LEFT FALLOPIAN TUBE AND METASTASIS TO SEROSAL SURFACE OF UTERUS.

E. TISSUE CONSISTENT WITH ORIGIN FROM SEROSA AND PELVIC BRIM, RESPECTIVELY, BOTH CONTAINING METASTATIC OVARIAN CYSTADENOCARCINOMA.

F. ...

G. TISSUE CONSISTENT WITH ORIGIN FROM RIGHT URETER SHOWING A METASTATIC OVARIAN SEROUS CYSTADENOCARCINOMA

H. TISSUE CONSISTENT WITH OMENTAL ORIGIN SHOWING A METASTATIC OVARIAN SEROUS CYSTADENOCARCINOMA

I. ...

J. APPENDIX CONTAINING METASTATIC OVARIAN SEROUS CYSTADENOCARCINOMA

At this point, Patient BL was told she had at least stage III, and probably stage IV, disease that required aggressive adjuvant chemotherapy, because all the existing cancer had not been removed at surgery. But after her discharge from the hospital, she decided she would travel to the University of Wisconsin for a second opinion.

During the first week of May 1987, Patient BL met with a Wisconsin oncologist, who suggested a chest x-ray and an abdominal CT scan be done. The CT showed no residual tumor, but the chest x-ray revealed a left pleural effusion. As a result, during the first week of May 1987 she was admitted to the University of Wisconsin Hospital for thoracentesis. Subsequent evaluation of the pleural fluid revealed the presence of malignant cells, confirming stage IV disease.

After her discharge from the hospital, Patient BL planned to begin an eight-cycle course of chemotherapy with the three drugs Cytoxan, carboplatin, and cisplatin, this being the days before Taxol and the Taxol derivatives. During the first week of June 1987, Patient BL re-entered the University of Wisconsin Hospital to begin the planned treatment.

Over the next five months, though Patient BL tolerated the treatment poorly with multiple side effects, she eventually completed the scheduled regimen in late November 1987 with plans for a "second look" laparotomy, as was commonly done at the time, to search for residual cancer. So in early January 1988 she returned to the University of Wisconsin Hospital and underwent the exploratory operation. She was found to have extensive adhesions along the bowel wall, with evidence of "multiple gritty, 1 mm nodularities noted in the pelvic peritoneum." The surgeon biopsied multiples areas, but the pathologist found no evidence of residual malignancy.

Several days after her discharge from the hospital, when Patient BL returned to the Oncology Clinic for a routine follow-up visit, she was told the good news about the surgery, and that clearly the chemotherapy had been a great success. Thereafter, she returned every six months for routine follow-up evaluations at the Oncology Clinic at Wisconsin. She seemed to be doing quite well, as documented in a note from the second week of January 1989 written by her oncologist, a year after her "second-look" surgery: "Patient BL was seen in clinic today. She is a woman with stage IV ovarian carcinoma on the basis of pleural effusion who has an excellent response to eight courses of chemotherapy with carbo-platinum cis-platinum and cytoxan [sic]. She had a second look laparotomy which was found to be normal."

Subsequently, Patient BL continued doing well and continued returning to the Oncology Clinic at Wisconsin every six months. However, during a routine follow-up visit in January 1991, her physician detected a left-sided abdominal mass suspicious for recurrent disease. A barium enema revealed a near-obstructing large annular lesion in the transverse colon, as described in the radiology report: "There is an annular lesion involving the distal transverse colon just at the splenic flexure area. This measures 10 cm in length, mucosa is not totally destroyed but is markedly irregular. … I feel strongly that this is neoplastic rather than inflammatory."

The lesion was also noted on a CT scan from the same day: "Annular lesion distal transverse colon. This most likely is a neoplasm although I could not definitely exclude inflammatory process."

Subsequently, colonoscopy showed "an apparently extrinsic compression in the region of the proximal descending colon."

At the very end of January 1991, Patient BL was readmitted to the University of Wisconsin Hospital for exploratory laparotomy and colon resection. The day of her admission, she underwent the procedure, with "extended left hemicolectomy from the mid transverse colon onto the upper sigmoid colon," as reported in the Discharge Summary of the hospitalization. The note also described the histology of this large tumor: "Pathological analysis of the specimen, however, showed the mass to be a serous cystadenocarcinoma consistent with metastases from the patient's previous primary ovarian tumor. The tumor, itself, was noted to involve the wall of the colon, pericolonic adipose tissue and 12 of 13 pericolonic lymph nodes."

After recovering from surgery, during mid-February Patient BL decided to consult with Michael Williams, MD, PhD, a Harvard-trained oncologist with a PhD in immunology who has long worked for the Cancer Treatment Centers of America and who at the time headed his own cancer consulting service based in Chicago. I know Dr. Williams, as he attended a lecture I gave at a cancer conference in Washington, DC many years ago. During the question session at the end of my talk, Dr. Williams seemed quite angry and borderline confrontational in his questioning about my therapy, an approach I thought quite odd.

In any event, BL's husband spoke by phone with Dr. Williams about his wife's situation. Apparently, Dr. Williams recommended high-dose chemotherapy with bone marrow transplant—though no evidence to my knowledge existed then or exists today that such an aggressive, toxic, potentially deadly approach has any benefit in the treatment of women with recurrent, metastatic ovarian cancer. Nonetheless, Patient BL and her husband decided they would follow up with Dr. Williams after a visit to their University of Wisconsin oncologist scheduled for the last week of February.

In his note from the session, the Wisconsin oncologist documented his discussion with the patient and her husband, emphasizing the seriousness of the situation and the need to reinstitute aggressive chemotherapy:

> I discussed the possibilities with both Mr. and Mrs. [Patient BL]. The options are a) no treatment at this time; the likelihood of subsequent recurrence is close to 100% but treatment could be delayed until recurrence recurs; b) intraperitoneal therapy with VP-16 and carboplat, a total of six cycles which would be based on the Howell data following adequate debulking of recurrent lesions. ... Her husband has consulted by

phone a cancer consulting service in Chicago. This is staffed by Dr. Williams. ... His recommendation over the phone was consideration for high dose chemotherapy with bone marrow transplant. The [BLs] are going to Chicago and consult with Dr. Williams.

After a brief vacation, Patient BL did meet with Dr. Williams but she thought the suggested treatment far too aggressive and risky. In addition, by that point she had already begun investigating alternative approaches to cancer, had learned about our work, and had decided she would decline all further conventional treatment and instead pursue my treatment.

I first met Patient BL during the second week of April 1991. Although during our first session together she seemed very determined to follow the program, upon returning home, she initially found the regimen difficult. She experienced some gastric distress I thought related to her recent surgery, but after I adjusted the supplement protocol she seemed to tolerate the supplements better. Eventually, she adjusted nicely to the program, appeared to be complying appropriately, and in subsequent phone conversations reported feeling quite well despite the seriousness of her prognosis.

Although I normally require patients, wherever they may live in the world, to return to New York at least every six months during the first years of treatment, because of Patient BL's financial situation I agreed to do a phone consultation with her in January 1992 instead of the normal in-office visit. She appeared to be compliant with her program, and though she complained about the rigors of the regimen and the expense, she seemed grateful for a nontoxic approach to her situation.

Thereafter, Patient BL periodically kept in touch with me by mail and by phone, though I would never see her in my office again. In early January 1993, after she had completed more than eighteen months on the therapy, she sent a note to me, wishing me a "Happy New Year" and reporting on her status: "I'm still feeling great and am hoping getting better every day."

Seven months later, in late August 1993, she sent me another lengthy letter reporting on her status: "I am still feeling fine and doing lots of square dancing and bike riding as well as swimming. Hope my good health continues. I am already many many months past when doctors from U. of Wisc. guaranteed me 99.99% the cancer could come back. Of course I still worry but keep busy and hope for the best."

When I spoke to her on the phone in early November 1993, when she had completed more than two and a half years on the therapy, she told me she was following her regimen, remained cancer-free, and was "doing well." I wasn't pleased that she hadn't returned to the office since the initial consultation, but because she appeared to be thriving, and because her finances were still not great, I didn't make an issue of the visits.

However, that phone conversation proved to be my last direct contact with Patient BL. I had no record of any further communication from or about her until I received a letter in mid-July 2001 written not by BL herself, but by the husband of a prospective patient with a diagnosis of very advanced ovarian cancer, who had been referred to my office by Patient BL. Patient BL, who at that point was ten and a half years out from her January 1991 colon resection for recurrent metastatic ovarian cancer, had spoken glowingly about my treatment and recommended it highly.

I have long provided, on my website, instructions to prospective patients, outlining the information they need to send me to help me in my evaluation of their situation. In her letter, the writer followed the suggested outline: "How we heard about the office: Patient Referral: About 1989 [sic—it was 1991] you treated [Patient BL] for advanced ovarian cancer after her doctors gave up on her after she had numerous chemo, radiation [sic], and surgical procedures. By 1991 she was cancer free and is alive and cancer free today. Mr. and Mrs. [Patient BL] strongly recommended that we contact Dr. Gonzalez as soon as possible since ---- has a similar condition although ... is in better condition than [Patient BL] was when she saw Dr. Gonzalez."

In preparation for this book, in mid-2012, I attempted to track Patient BL down. She had moved but was still alive and apparently remains cancer-free, more than twenty-five years since her original diagnosis of stage IV ovarian cancer and more than twenty-one years since her aggressive recurrence.

Certainly, Patient BL's twenty-one years of disease-free survival since first consulting with me is unusual. She was diagnosed with stage IV disease in May 1987 at the University of Wisconsin based on positive cytology of pleural fluid. Then, after eight cycles of intensive chemotherapy with Cytoxan, carboplatin, and cisplatin, in January 1991 she underwent colon resection for aggressive recurrent metastatic disease, with twelve lymph nodes positive for cancer. Told she had a near "100 percent" chance of a recurrence, she nonetheless refused the various chemotherapy options presented, including bone marrow transplantation, instead choosing to begin treatment with me.

According to Cannnistra, Gershenson, and Recht, writing in *Cancer: Principles and Practice of Oncology* (9th ed.), the five-year survival for stage IV ovarian cancer is less than 10 percent.[4] With Patient BL's extensive recurrence in 1991 occurring after eight cycles of intensive chemotherapy, her five-year prognosis would inevitably have been much worse, close to zero. Once the disease returned, the chances in this case of twenty-plus years of survival would have been from my reading of the literature virtually nonexistent.

---

4   Stephen A. Cannistra, David M. Gershenson, and Abram Recht, "Ovarian Cancer, Fallopian Tube Carcinoma, and Peritoneal Carcinoma," in *Cancer: Principles and Practice of Oncology*, ed. Vincent T. DeVita, Jr., Theodore S. Lawrence, and Steven A. Rosenberg, 9th ed. (Philadelphia, PA: Lippincott William & Wilkins, 2011), 1375.

Case 5: Patient DN
A Minimum 6.8-Year Survivor*

Patient DN is a fifty-nine-year-old woman from New England with a history of stage IV ovarian cancer who has survived ten years from her original diagnosis, and seven years since developing recurrent disease after aggressive chemotherapy.

DN's family history is pertinent because of five first-degree relatives who succumbed to cancer. Her father, a smoker, died of lung cancer in his early sixties. DN's maternal grandfather died from liver cancer. Two maternal second cousins died from cancer, one with prostate and one with brain malignancy. A maternal first cousin died with metastatic breast cancer.

Patient DN had battled a number of health problems before developing cancer. She was diagnosed with juvenile rheumatoid arthritis at age five and has a long history of anemia with a hemoglobin that runs generally in the 10.5 range. Though she has consulted a number of hematologists over the years, the etiology remains undetermined. Apparently, chronic anemia, like cancer, runs in the family, having affected both her mother and a sister. DN also experienced three serious major motor vehicle accidents, each leading to severe whiplash treated with physical therapy and chiropractic.

DN had been on the birth control pill for a number of years, as well as injections of Depo-Provera, a synthetic progesterone prescribed also for birth control.

While on Depo-Provera, beginning in 2002 and throughout 2003, Patient DN experienced a gradual decline in her general health and well-being, particularly progressively worsening fatigue and malaise. She also noted what she perceived as a persistently bloated abdomen and pelvis. In early 2003, she consulted with her gynecologist, who dismissed her concerns as inconsequential, telling her there was "nothing wrong." But when her symptoms, particularly the bloating, continued to worsen during the spring of 2003, she returned to her gynecologist. However, a pelvic exam was unrevealing. Again, she was told "not to worry."

When the bloating and abdominal distension worsened, in June 2003 she was finally sent for a pelvic ultrasound, which showed a large tumor replacing the left ovary. A subsequent CT scan of the abdomen and pelvis confirmed a 13 cm tumor consistent with a left ovarian primary. At that point, Patient DN was referred to a gynecological oncologist.

Then, at Hartford Hospital during the last week of July 2003, Patient DN underwent exploratory laparotomy, total abdominal hysterectomy, bilateral oophorectomy, omentectomy, resection of tumor nodules in the pelvis, and removal of all visible tumor.

The pathology report described the following:

LEFT ADNEXA, RESECTION: ENDOMETROID ADENOCARCINOMA, FIGO GRADE II, NUCLEAR GRADE II-III; TUMOR SIZE 13 CM, FOCAL MICROSCOPIC AREAS OF PAPILLARY SEROUS CARCINOMA (5–10% OF TOTAL TUMOR MASS)….

OMENTUM, CUL-DE-SAC, LEFT PELVIC SIDEWALL, RIGHT UTEROSACRAL NODULE: METASTATIC ENDOMETROID ADENOCARCINOMA.

Based on the pathology findings, Patient DN was assigned stage IIIB. During subsequent meetings with her oncologist, he suggested aggressive chemotherapy with carboplatin and Taxol, but he warned that even with treatment, based on the extent of her disease she most likely would not live beyond five years. Despite her physician's negative ultimate prognosis, Patient DN agreed to the plan, beginning chemotherapy in late August 2003, some four weeks after surgery.

Eventually, Patient DN completed a full six cycles of treatment as originally recommended, finishing in December 2003. Her course wasn't easy; at one point, she had to be hospitalized when the PICC line inserted into her chest for administration of chemotherapy became infected.

After finishing chemotherapy, her oncologist recommended she consider a clinical trial involving a vaccine that would be made from her tumor and then injected subcutaneously. Apparently, twenty to thirty patients would be entered into the study. After agreeing to this plan, Patient DN proceeded with the vaccine treatment.

During this time, she was also tested for mutations in BRCA1 and BRCA2 (breast cancer susceptibility genes) associated with familial clusters of both breast and ovarian cancer. Both tests proved negative, despite the strong family history of cancer.

Thereafter, DN was followed very closely by her oncologist, with office exams and CT scans scheduled initially every three months for the first two years. Beginning in 2006, the scans and visit were reduced to every six months, when all tests came back negative for recurrent disease.

Patient DN did well for some three years after her original diagnosis, until September 2006. At that time, she began experiencing gradually worsening fatigue and malaise, as she had before her diagnosis in 2003. A regularly scheduled CT scan of the abdomen and pelvis revealed a single mass in the left lobe of the liver measuring 1 cm in size in its largest dimension. The CA 125 blood tumor marker, developed specifically for ovarian cancer, came back in the normal range at 12 (normal less than 35).

Patient DN was then sent for a liver biopsy, which showed no evidence of cancer. According to what Patient DN would later tell me, the interventional radiologist apparently missed the tumor, hitting normal liver instead. After this unrevealing procedure, an MRI confirmed the CT scan findings of a single suspicious lesion, though it seemed to have grown somewhat.

At that point, Patient DN herself insisted that a PET scan be done. Initially, her doctors refused her suggestion, but as her fatigue and malaise continued to worsen, DN repeatedly argued the case. Finally, in December 2006, three months after the September 2006 scans, her doctors arranged for the PET study, which revealed that the tumor had nearly doubled in size, measuring 1.5 × 0.5 × 1.3 cm, though there was no evidence of additional metastatic disease.

Just about that time, her original gynecological oncologist, with whom she had a very good relationship, moved out of the state where she lived, leaving her in the care of a physician whom DN found very unpleasant. After thinking about her options, she decided to consult with a surgeon at the University of Connecticut Health Center, who suggested left lobe hepatectomy, to remove the lesion. She agreed to the plan, and on December 21, 2006, Patient DN underwent exploratory laparotomy, biopsy of segment IV of the liver, resection of the evident nodule in segment III, and cholecystectomy (removal of the gallbladder).

The pathology report described metastatic adenocarcinoma in the segment IV biopsy, as well as in the nodule from segment III:

> Liver, segment IV, biopsy:
>
> Metastatic adenocarcinoma, consistent with known ovarian primary. …
>
> Liver nodule, segment III, excisional biopsy:
>
> Metastatic adenocarcinoma, consistent with known ovarian primary; [sic] extending to the hepatic capsular surface.

After recovering from surgery, Patient DN consulted with the medical oncologist who had supervised her chemotherapy treatment in 2003, to discuss further options. But before deciding on a course of action, in mid-January 2007 Patient DN traveled to MD Anderson Cancer Center in Houston, for a second opinion. There, the consulting gynecological oncologist suggested six rounds of carboplatin and Taxotere, which he discussed with her local Connecticut medical oncologist.

Shortly after returning home, DN began the recommended chemotherapy, which this time around she tolerated only with great difficulty. She struggled with low platelet counts and worsening anemia requiring marrow stem cell stimulants such as Epogen. During this period of drug treatment, she also began to look into nutrition and alternative medicine approaches. She came under the care of a local acupuncturist, who helped with the side effects, such as nausea, from the chemotherapy. Based on her reading, she changed her diet significantly, cutting out junk food, refined carbohydrates, soda, etc., while switching to a largely plant-based, organic, whole-foods diet. She also began consuming a number of supplements, including vitamin C and ginger.

Patient DN completed her second course of chemotherapy in mid-2007, thereafter continuing her whole-foods diet and supplement regimen.

At that time, she learned that out of the thirty or so patients entered into the vaccine trial from late 2003, all had experienced a recurrence, and nearly all had already died. From what she was able to learn, she thought she was actually the only survivor.

Subsequently, Patient DN returned regularly to her medical gynecologist for follow-up evaluations. Yearly CT scans showed no evidence of recurrent disease—a fortunate and unusual situation, she realized, given the aggressive nature of her disease.

In late 2009, Patient DN first read about my work in Suzanne Somers's best-selling book *Knockout*, which contained a lengthy chapter about me and my protocol. At that point, DN decided to contact my office, wishing to begin my treatment. From her note summarizing her medical history, I could sense that she was a very determined woman anxious to fight what she realized was a very poor-prognosis situation. I was impressed that through all her treatment beginning in 2003, she had continued working in a supervisory position for the state where she lived. She was also active in her church and her community and seemed to be living her life as normally as possible.

DN passed my screening process, and we first met during the first week of January 2010, some six and a half years from her initial diagnosis in July 2003, and some three years from her diagnosis of recurrent disease in the liver in December 2006. Her most recent radiographic evaluation from May 2009, including a bone scan and CT scans of the chest, abdomen, and pelvis, had shown no evidence of recurrent or metastatic disease. As we discussed her history, she emphasized that she realized, despite the most recent clear scans, she had a poor prognosis with a likelihood of recurrence. She knew, as she told me, that she had already beaten the odds, having been told by her medical oncologist in 2003 that she most likely would not live beyond five years.

Thereafter, Patient DN proved to be a very vigilant, determined, and compliant patient, despite her very high-stress job. To her great credit, she was quickly able to work the program, despite its rigors, into her schedule.

In mid-January 2010, some two weeks after beginning treatment with me, DN underwent regularly scheduled restaging ordered by her medical oncologist. CT scans of the chest, abdomen, and pelvis were again clear. When we spoke about the results, she seemed indeed very pleased.

In early March 2010, while at work, DN experienced a nasty fall, landing on her side and hitting her head hard. Afterward, she developed severe back and neck pain, to the point that she went on short-term disability. I recommended she consult with Dr. Angelo Colavita, a chiropractor with offices in Clifton, New Jersey, who had been trained in the "atlas orthogonal" methods of Dr. Roy Sweat in Atlanta. She subsequently met with Dr. Colavita in early April 2010, days before a scheduled office visit with me.

When I saw her during the first week of April 2010, she had completed three months on her nutritional therapy and appeared to be very compliant. In fact, she had stayed on her supplements throughout her recent difficulties, though for two weeks she had been unable to do the enemas because of her severe back and rib pain. By the time I saw her, she was already feeling better, reporting that the atlas treatment had indeed helped considerably. She was still not feeling up to par, but her energy, stamina, and sleep had been improving. Prior to the fall, she told me, she actually had been feeling quite well on the treatment.

In mid-March 2010, DN had also consulted with a new gynecological oncologist. Her exam was unrevealing, and a CA 125 test came in the low normal range at 6. But, as DN reminded me, throughout her years of fighting ovarian cancer this blood marker had never really tracked the state of her disease accurately.

When she next returned to my office in mid-July 2010, she had completed six months on her therapy, seemed very compliant, and reported that she generally was doing well, though she described ongoing back pain resulting from the March fall. DN had been back to see Dr. Colavita several times since our last visit and thought the treatment had helped. She was feeling well enough that she had gone back to work, but unfortunately the stress there, with her many responsibilities, heavy workload, and interoffice politics, had increased. As before, she managed adeptly to work her program into the day, no matter how stressful it might be.

Despite the stress, DN reported good energy, stamina, and concentration, and other than the back pain, no major or minor symptoms. She also reported that a long history of dry eyes that had required Restasis for treatment had resolved on the nutritional regimen. She had consulted her ophthalmologist recently, who suggested she no longer needed the medication.

She was scheduled to return to her medical oncologist and gynecologist in late July 2010 for routine follow-up. During the fourth week of July 2010, CT scans of the abdomen and pelvis showed no evidence of recurrent disease.

In July 2010, DN contacted my office complaining of symptoms consistent with a urinary tract infection. She had consulted a local physician, who arranged for a urinary culture and started her on an antibiotic. Initially the symptoms had improved, but then more recently they had worsened. She continued on the antibiotic but then experienced a severe allergic reaction, with edema and redness in her hands.

When she called my office to discuss her symptoms, I told her to stop the antibiotic immediately, suggesting instead she begin d-mannose, a sugar that has a powerful effect against the common gram-negative bacteria associated with urinary infections. The d-mannose worked quickly, and her symptoms finally resolved. When we subsequently discussed the situation, I suggested she continue on the d-mannose indefinitely to avoid a recurring problem.

When Patient DN returned to my office for a routine office visit during the second week of October 2010, she had continued on the d-mannose with no more urinary symptoms reported. She also seemed generally compliant with the program. However, she admitted that the stress at her workplace had worsened significantly. She was working long hours, in a difficult situation. Nonetheless, her energy remained quite good, so good in fact that she remarked that her work colleagues were amazed at her stamina during very long days.

A recent hemoglobin came in at 13.7, the highest, she told me, it had been since she was twelve years old. She believed that my nutritional program had done what multiple hematologists over the years had been unable to do: fix her chronic anemia.

When I next saw Patient DN, during the third week of January 2011, she had completed slightly more than a year on her nutritional program. She remained compliant with all aspects of the therapy, though the stress at work had not abated. Fortunately, she had experienced no further recurrences of her urinary infection, but she had developed chronic pain in her right arm and elbow, thought to be related to her long hours at her workplace computer. On the advice of her office, she had consulted with a rheumatologist, who had made the formal diagnosis of tendonitis. Otherwise, she seemed to be doing quite well and continued following up with both her medical and gynecological oncologists.

We discussed the value of bone density testing, which she hadn't done since 2004. During the first week of March 2011, she underwent the study, which revealed osteoporosis. When we discussed the findings over the phone, I made several adjustments to her program, increasing the vitamin D and adding on strontium—which I find helpful in such situations. We also discussed the usefulness of vitamin K2—her suggestion actually—which I knew in multiple studies has shown great effectiveness in removing calcium from soft tissues and depositing it where it belongs in the bones.

I didn't hear from DN again until she returned to my office during the second week of May 2011. She admitted she'd been under considerable additional stress, with a death in the family. In addition, her house had recently been broken into and robbed. Though she wasn't home at the time, the situation had left her understandably shaken.

Though she remained compliant with the supplements and detoxification routines, she acknowledged that with all this recent severe stress in her life, her dietary compliance had fallen off, to the point that she was indulging in sugary foods, as she said, "all the junk" that she had with great determination been avoiding. I appreciated her honesty, as well as her resolution to return to full dietary compliance.

DN had recently seen both her medical and her gynecological oncologist. A pelvic exam had been unrevealing, and the CA 125 marker came back at 6.6, well within the normal range.

She did describe some recent fatigue, which she attributed to the combination of work and home stress. Fortunately, she had continued on the d-mannose, which kept her urinary infections completely at bay.

When DN returned for an office visit during the second week of August 2011, she had completed some nineteen months on her nutritional therapy. She reported the stress continued, but she had with diligence tightened up her dietary compliance. She seemed to be doing generally well despite the stress, with improved energy since our last visit together. She informed me that the following week she was due to see her oncologist, who would repeat the CA 125 tumor marker.

We next spoke by phone during the fourth week of August 2011, when she called to report on the recent visit with her oncologist. Her CA 125 had come back somewhat elevated from the previous reading, at 9.6. Although the test was well within the normal range, she was concerned because at the time she had developed liver metastases in 2006, the level had been up only to 12, still normal, but higher than previous readings.

I suggested she consider repeat scanning, either CT or PET, to assess the situation more accurately. She herself would prefer a PET scan, she said, but only if her insurance would agree to pay for the test. Regardless, she agreed to follow up on that issue and get back to me. I also suggested she have her oncologist repeat the CA 125, to determine if we were witnessing an upward trend.

Fortunately, when her oncologist repeated the test some three weeks later, it had dropped from 9.6 to 8.9. Though admittedly a slight drop, at least the marker was now moving in the right direction, a finding reassuring to both DN and myself.

Perhaps the slight bump in the CA 125 meant nothing, or perhaps, as it had before in DN's case, it did indicate some increased cancer activity. Whatever the fluctuation did mean, after all my years in practice I remain always amazed at how significantly stress can influence the progress, even the outcome, of a cancer patient.

Thereafter, DN continued returning to my office every three months and continued doing well, with her usual good compliance. Though the stress in her life had not really abated, particularly at work, she seemed to be handling a series of difficult situations very well. I felt growing admiration for DN, who worked long hours at a stressful job while managing stresses in her family, at the same time diligently following my complex nutritional program.

In February 2012—after DN had completed more than two years on her nutritional program— her CA 125 came back, after the previous drop, elevated at 9.7. Understandably, she was again concerned because minimal variations in the wrong direction had, in the past, indicated worsening disease. I suggested again, if for no other reason than to assuage her anxiety about the situation, to proceed with scanning. I offered to write the order for a CT or PET if her oncologist was unwilling to do so.

Her physician, however, did agree to restaging, and during the third week of March 2012 DN underwent CT scans of the abdomen and pelvis, which revealed no evidence of recurrent or metastatic disease. When we discussed the findings by phone, we were both quite happy with the results.

DN returned to my office in early June 2012. She seemed very compliant with all aspects of the therapy and reported that she was feeling quite well. Her energy had improved in recent months, though her sleep was somewhat erratic—a situation she attributed to the ongoing tensions at her workplace. She reported some new-onset GERD and symptoms that, upon questioning, I suspected indicated a hiatal hernia. I recommended a simple treatment that usually works well.

For reflux, GERD, or hiatal hernia symptoms, I suggest patients make an ice pack out of ice cubes wrapped in a cloth, then placed beneath the sternum (breastbone) for ten minutes before each meal, three times a day for two weeks straight. Usually, after two weeks, the situation and symptoms will resolve.

Shortly after our visit, during the second week of June 2012, a repeat CA 125 came back significantly down from 9.7, at 8.0—a level that left her feeling once again relieved and reassured.

At that point, her medical oncologist reduced the frequency of her visits to once a year, with her next visit scheduled for January 2013. For now, she would still follow up with her gynecological oncologist every six months for pelvic exams.

When DN returned to my office, during the first week of September 2012, once again she seemed determinedly compliant, and she informed me she was doing very well—though as per usual, the work-related stress, which seemed quite serious, continued without a break. In my note from that visit, I remarked how much I admired DN, for fighting so vigilantly against her serious illness, remaining compliant with my difficult therapy while working full time at a very demanding and difficult job.

When I next saw DN, during the last week of April 2013, she seemed to be doing very well, now having completed more than three years on her nutritional program. She was also coming up to seven years from her diagnosis of liver metastases. Her medical oncologist, during her last visit with him, felt she was doing so well that she no longer needed to return, and her gynecologic oncologist had decided to extend her return visits to just once a year—a sign that he too felt she was doing exceptionally well.

I believe DN's long-term survival, now ten years from diagnosis, seven years from her recurrence, and five and a half years on my program, to be quite remarkable. When initially diagnosed in 2003, she was found to have a huge 13 cm primary ovarian tumor as well as aggressive and extensive disease involving the omentum, cul-de-sac, and left pelvic sidewall. Although the surgeon tried to remove all obvious tumor, with such profuse spread the chances that residual unseen cancer remained were great. Her medical oncologist at the time gave her little chance of surviving beyond five years even with intensive chemotherapy.

After a course of treatment with carboplatin and Taxol, as well as an experimental vaccine, DN actually did well for some three years, until the CT scan in September 2006 showed a single lesion in the liver. After surgery and resection of the tumor, confirmed to be metastatic ovarian cancer, she completed another course of chemotherapy with carboplatin and Taxotere.

According to the website UpToDate, the median survival for women with relapsed ovarian cancer after initial chemotherapy, treated the second time with carboplatin and Taxotere, is twenty-nine months. I could not find a specific breakdown for patients experiencing a recurrence in the liver who underwent surgery before pursuing the second course of chemotherapy.

I did find an article entitled "Hepatic Resection for Noncolorectal Nonendocrine Liver Metastases,"[5] which discussed the outcome for patients treated surgically for liver metastases originating from a variety of primary sites, including ovarian. The authors reported a 50 percent five-year survival for women diagnosed with metastatic ovarian cancer to the liver undergoing surgical resection. But this article does not break down the ovarian cohort according to the original pathology or extent of the initial disease, which in DN's case already portended a poor prognosis. In her situation, the recurrence in the liver three years after completing aggressive chemotherapy only confirmed the likelihood of a poor outcome. Furthermore, it appears that she very well may be the only survivor of the thirty patients entered into the vaccine clinical trial.

---

5   *Annals of Surgery*, Oct 2006, Adam et al, PMC1856551

I believe her ten-year survival from her original diagnosis in 2003, and her seven-year survival from her recurrence in 2006, make her story compelling, particularly in view of her gradually improving health on her nutritional program.

*IMPORTANT EDITOR'S NOTE:

According to Dr. Linda Isaacs' office, Patient DN continues to do well on her nutritional program and last communicated with the office in October 2016.

PROSTATE CANCER

For 2007, *Harrison's* reported 218,890 new cases of prostate cancer in the US, with 27,050 deaths.[1] Though in younger men this malignancy can be quite aggressive, in the elderly it often follows a more indolent course. Among men in the eighth decade of life succumbing to non-cancer-related illness, autopsy studies have revealed evidence of previously undiagnosed prostate malignancy in more than 70 percent of cases.

Traditionally, researchers have claimed that the disease requires testosterone for its formation, growth, and spread—hence, the common use of various testosterone-modifying agents that work either indirectly through the pituitary (leuprolide, for example), or by directly blocking the testosterone receptor (flutamide). However, androgen end products from steroid metabolism such as estradiol or dihydrotestosterone may be the real culprits, rather than testosterone itself.

The use of prostate-specific antigen (PSA) as a screening tool continues to spawn debate, with randomized studies failing to confirm any benefit for routine testing. Furthermore, the traditional view of PSA as a "prostate-specific" protein, synthesized only in normal prostate epithelial cells and prostate cancer cells and useful for disease monitoring, may not be accurate. A study entitled "Antiangiogenic Activity of Prostate-Specific Antigen" appearing in the October 6, 1999 issue of the *Journal of the National Cancer Institute*[2] reported that high levels of PSA appear not only in males diagnosed with prostate cancer, but in those with lung cancer as well and even in women with breast cancer—and women, of course, have no prostate.

To further confuse the picture, those women undergoing treatment for breast malignancy with the highest levels of PSA did the best: "PSA is neither prostate specific nor made exclusively by prostate epithelium. PSA has been found in patients with breast, lung, and uterine cancers. Circulating serum concentrations of PSA have been documented in healthy women and in women with benign and malignant breast disease. … In one study of particular interest, patients with breast tumors with high levels of PSA had a better prognosis than those patients whose tumors had lower PSA levels."[3]

In a series of laboratory experiments, these same investigators discovered that PSA may actually function as an antiangiogenic agent, released to slow the growth and spread of cancer. In our

---

1   Anthony S. Fauci, Eugene Braunwald, Dennis L. Kasper, Stephen L. Hauser, Dan L. Longo, J. Larry Jameson, and Joseph Loscalzo, eds., *Harrison's Principles of Internal Medicine*, 17th ed. (New York, NY: McGraw-Hill, 2008), 594.

2   Anne H. Fortier, Barbara J. Nelson, Davida K. Grella, and John W. Holaday, "Antiangiogenic Activity of Prostate-Specific Antigen," *Journal of the National Cancer Institute* 91 (1999): 1635–1640.

3   Ibid. 1635

practice, Dr. Isaacs and I find little value in sequential PSA readings for those of our patients diagnosed with prostate cancer, most of whom have advanced disease. I have been following patients for years with PSA levels in the hundreds who seem to be doing very well despite the allegedly ominous lab results.

Early-stage prostate cancer can be successfully treated any number of ways, including prostatectomy, external beam radiation, brachytherapy (the insertion of radiation seeds into the prostate), hyperthermia, and hypothermia—and for nonaggressive histology in elderly males, even surveillance only with no intervention. Once metastatic, however, the disease ultimately resists all treatment. Though testosterone blockade remains the cornerstone of therapy for advanced prostate cancer, it is not curative, and the side effects—including fatigue, gynecomastia, hot flashes, loss of libido, and accelerated osteoporosis—are many. Chemotherapy in recent clinical trials prolongs life, but only minimally.

Case 1: Patient KU
A 20.4-Year Survivor*

Patient KU is an eighty-year-old man who has been following his nutritional program now for twenty years, with a diagnosis of aggressive-histology prostate cancer.

Prior to developing cancer, Patient KU had been treated for mild hypertension and hypothyroidism. Otherwise, Patient KU had generally been in good health when, in December 1989, he experienced new-onset painful urination associated with a weak urinary stream, urgency, and urinary frequency. He consulted with a local urologist in Houston, who, suspecting prostatitis, prescribed an antibiotic.

When a PSA test, relatively new to the world at the time, came back elevated at 8.9, in January 1990 Patient KU underwent a transurethral resection of the prostate. Evaluation of the tissue specimens confirmed a well-differentiated adenocarcinoma, Gleason's score 2–3. When a bone scan in late January 1990 was clear, Patient KU's urologist suggested a prostatectomy, which he explained could be curative for his apparently localized disease. However, Patient KU, determined to avoid any surgery, refused the procedure.

At the end of January 1990, as he considered his options, Patient KU and his wife traveled to a health spa in New England, where an on-staff physician referred him for a second opinion to Beth Israel Hospital in Boston, a Harvard teaching institution. There, in early February 1990, the patient met with Dr. William DeWolf, a staff urologist, who, after a repeat PSA came back within the normal range, suggested a conservative "watch-and-wait" approach because Patient KU's cancer appeared to be very localized.

For follow-up care in Texas, Dr. DeWolf suggested Patient KU consult with Dr. Peter Scardino, a well-known urologist in Houston at the time. Subsequently, in March 1990, under Dr. Scardino's supervision, Patient KU underwent a repeat evaluation, with an ultrasound showing a suspicious lesion in the left base of the prostate. A repeat bone scan as well as a CT scan of the pelvis showed no evidence of metastatic disease, and a third PSA test came back within normal limits.

Dr. Scardino, concerned nonetheless by the ultrasound findings, did recommend rebiopsy of the prostate to confirm the extent of the disease. Patient KU agreed to the plan, but this time biopsy studies indicated the disease to be far more advanced than previously thought, as discussed in a letter written in early April 1990 by Dr. Scardino to Dr. DeWolf:

> Unfortunately, I found considerably more cancer than was present on his initial biopsy. Both in the right middle and right apex of the prostate, a Gleason 3+3=6 adenocarci-

noma was identified, and in the left middle and left apex, mild interductal dysplasia was seen.

As result of these findings, I recommended that he proceed with treatment. Needless to say, he is quite confused and upset by all of this and wants to give it some thought. He will return in 3 months to talk about it further.

He and his wife and I today discussed in detail the probable natural history of this lesion and the alternative forms of treatment including various forms of radiotherapy and a radical prostatectomy. I discussed the risk of impotence and incontinence with each one, and I think they understand the issues quite well, but are determined to think it out at home before coming back.

Shortly after, Patient KU and his wife decided to consult with a local alternative physician in Houston, Dr. John Trowbridge, who in turn referred him to me in New York. I first met with Patient KU in late May 1990, at which time he reported feeling quite well, with only minimal urinary symptoms, including nocturia once a night. He reported that he had lost twenty pounds after changing from the typical steak-and-potatoes American diet to a more whole-foods, plant-based way of eating.

Over the next twenty years, Patient KU proved to be a very compliant, determined, enthusiastic patient, grateful for the chance to avoid the debilitating treatments recommended by his Houston urologist (who is now, incidentally, chief of surgery at Memorial Sloan Kettering). During this time, Patient KU—long retired—and his wife have moved around somewhat, living for a while in Mexico and now firmly enjoying life in Florida. I have continued to see him yearly in my New York office for routine follow-up, but during the 1990s and early 2000s he declined to consult with a urologist locally. Because he wouldn't agree to their treatments anyway, he didn't see the point, and I couldn't really disagree, as he felt so well. I also didn't push PSA testing, because I had already reached the conclusion that the marker was of limited value for monitoring patients on my therapy.

Patient KU remained largely symptom-free until the spring of 2004, when he experienced an episode of dizziness while playing tennis. Though he had been compliant with his supplement regimen to that point, he had strayed from his prescribed diet somewhat, gradually adding more forbidden foods such as white sugar and refined carbohydrates. He consulted with a local cardiologist, who performed an extensive evaluation including EKG and a stress test, which revealed no significant abnormalities.

However, after a subsequent episode of syncope, angiography revealed considerable coronary atherosclerosis, for which Patient KU underwent stent placement. In addition, his cardiologist prescribed a beta-blocker and a calcium channel blocker for newly diagnosed atrial fibrillation.

At the urging of his local cardiologist, in 2005 he did agree to meet with a urologist and undergo PSA testing, which came back mildly elevated at 5. Patient KU expressed his dismay that the urologist seemed indifferent to his long survival since his original diagnosis of cancer—fifteen years at that point—and expressed absolutely no interest in his nutritional program.

Two years later, in mid-2007, his PSA level had risen somewhat to 8.8. Patient KU's urologist offered the usual caveats, explaining once again the standard treatments—prostatectomy, radiation, and hormonal blockade—all of which Patient KU refused.

Patient KU continued doing well until April 2009, when he experienced groin pain after a particularly hard game of tennis, associated with some slight hematuria. Although Patient KU assumed he had only traumatized his kidneys, his urologist voiced his concern about recurrent, metastatic cancer. A PSA level came back significantly elevated at 92, and a repeat test was even higher at 104. The physician then recommended CT scans of the abdomen and pelvis, which in early May 2009 revealed nothing except an enlarged prostate, thought to be normal for the patient's age. The summary on the official report read,

> Liver, spleen, adrenal glands, kidneys and pancreas intact. No free fluid or bulky lymphadenopathy … bladder is slightly thick walled, though decompressed. Prostate is enlarged with median lobe hypertrophy. Multilevel DDD (degenerative disc disease, or arthritis) no blastic bone lesions.
>
> Impression:
>
> No acute abnormality.

A bone scan ten days later indicated activity only in the lower pelvis, thought to be consistent with artifact of the testing, not cancer, and follow-up x-rays of the pelvis were completely normal. Patient KU did undergo cystoscopy, which revealed a normal bladder, with washings showing no evidence of malignant cells. Though a urine culture was negative, the urologist nonetheless prescribed a two-week course of antibiotics on the off chance that the elevated PSA reflected prostatitis.

Subsequently, Patient KU resumed his usual activities, with no further episodes of hematuria. When in November 2009 the PSA had risen to 476, I explained that in my experience with my particular therapy, I had never found this test to be of much use for monitoring a patient's progress. Because he had no intention of changing treatments, Patient KU continued as before on his nutritional program and continued feeling well.

In mid-December 2009, Patient KU developed significant, acute onset pain in his buttocks that persisted over a several-week period. He consulted with an orthopedist; x-rays of the lumbar spine were completely negative with no evidence of metastatic cancer or any other problem. At that point, with the tests unrevealing, the orthopedist assumed the culprit most likely was structural trauma from years of vigorous tennis playing.

Over the next few weeks, the pain in the buttocks resolved, but then Patient KU experienced severe discomfort in the right foot. This eventually cleared, only to be followed by new pains in the right knee, right groin, and, some days later, left groin. Patient KU consulted with a physical therapist, who suspected sciatica and lumbar disc disease.

In mid-January 2010, with the problem persisting, Patient KU called me about the situation, expressing his understandable concern about his symptoms. He realized we needed to consider possible metastatic cancer in his bones even after all these years, and even after the completely negative radiographic studies from mid-2009. I suggested an MRI, which in late January 2010 revealed no cancer whatsoever, but rather disc herniation at the L4–L5 area, I suspect the result of his decades of tennis playing. Relieved that the problem wasn't related to his prostate malignancy, Patient KU is currently pursuing conservative treatment for his disc disease at an excellent local spine center. So, after twenty years on his nutritional therapy, repeat CT scans, bone scans, x-rays, and an MRI of the lumbar spine show no evidence of residual or metastatic disease.

Although, at the time of his diagnosis in early 1990, Patient KU's cancer seemed limited to the prostate, clearly, as his second set of biopsies in Houston confirmed, the cancer had evolved rather quickly into an aggressive form invading multiple areas in both lobes of the prostate—an ominous sign. He refused the recommended standard treatments, including prostatectomy and radiation, choosing only to pursue our nutritional regimen. Overall, he has had a good life these past twenty years despite some recent ups and down.

I have frequently observed very high PSA levels in our patients diagnosed with prostate cancer who by radiographic studies show no evidence of active or metastatic disease. I suspect that the antigen may, as some believe, reflect more the body's attempt to keep the cancer under control, rather than worsening tumor load.

*IMPORTANT EDITOR'S NOTE:
Dr. Gonzalez died before updating this case report. According to the last record in Patient KU's office medical file, he died in October 2010.

Case 2: Patient QC
*A Minimum 24.8-Year Survivor**

Patient QC is an eighty-three-year-old optometrist with a history of prostate cancer who has followed his nutritional program now for over twenty years.

With a long-term interest in nutritional and alternative medicine, Patient QC had generally been in good health when in 1989 he suddenly fainted for the first time in his life. His local physician referred him to a neurologist, who, diagnosing orthostatic hypotension, suggested only that Patient QC increase his salt intake. Even with this dietary change, Patient QC still experienced frequent bouts of dizziness, lightheadedness, and weakness, particularly when standing from a sitting position, though he didn't faint again. On repeated testing by his local physician, his blood pressure appeared to be chronically low.

Because of the persistent and annoying symptoms, in 1991 Patient QC decided to begin the macrobiotic diet, a largely cooked-foods vegetarian approach heavy on beans and grains that garnered some popularity in the 1980s. He also began consuming a number of nutritional supplements recommended in the writings of the German physician Dr. Hans Nieper.

When Patient QC's symptoms of orthostatic dizziness and weakness failed to resolve despite the various dietary modifications and supplements, he finally decided to seek out another opinion at the Mayo Clinic branch in Jacksonville, Florida. There, in September 1991, Patient QC underwent an extensive evaluation, complete with blood pressure studies, which ruled out orthostatic hypotension. The Mayo doctors proposed a twenty-four-hour Holter monitor to check for a cardiac rhythm abnormality—a potential cause of persistent weakness—but the test was completely normal. However, routine blood analysis revealed previously undiagnosed low thyroid function, thought to be the probable source of his symptoms and for which his doctors prescribed thyroid hormone replacement.

But, in addition to the abnormal thyroid markers, a routine PSA came back significantly elevated at 9.1. After sigmoidoscopy and an ultrasound of the pelvis were both within normal limits, he underwent prostate biopsy in late September 1991, which revealed, as described in the pathology report, "Grade II adenocarcinoma, acinar type (needle biopsy left base and left mid prostate)." When a subsequent chest x-ray and bone scan showed no evidence of metastatic disease, the Mayo doctors suggested he undergo prostatectomy for his presumed localized malignancy. Though they told him the procedure could be curative, Patient QC wasn't anxious to undergo any surgery at that point—particularly when a urologist friend argued against the intervention. Ultimately, Patient QC declined the recommended treatment, instead beginning an intensive nutritional/lifestyle regimen including a plant-based diet, a variety of supplements, and coffee enemas prescribed by a local chiropractor.

In early 1992, after reading about my work in a magazine article, Patient QC decided to consult with me. When first seen in mid-March 1992, he reported feeling generally quite well, with his chronic dizziness having resolved. He also denied symptoms of hematuria, nocturia, urgency, or urinary frequency. At the time, he was taking multiple nutritional supplements but no prescription medications.

Thereafter, Patient QC proved to be a very determined and enthusiastic patient, complying well with the nutritional program I prescribed and periodically continuing his follow-up care at Mayo. There, during a subsequent visit in late October 1993, after Patient QC had completed eighteen months on his nutritional therapy, his PSA level had fallen to 5.9. Patient QC explained in some detail the treatment program he followed under my direction to the Mayo urologist, who to his credit made no disparaging remarks.

In subsequent years, Patient QC has remained asymptomatic, with his PSA staying for the most part in the 5 range; for example, in March 1996—four years after Patient QC began treatment with me—his PSA came in at 5.2.

In 1998, Patient QC developed acute-onset severe arthritic-type pains in his hands and in multiple joints consistent with rheumatoid arthritis. I adjusted his supplement program accordingly—we have a protocol for the disease—and within six months, the pain completely resolved, never to return again.

In March 1999, seven years after he had begun his treatment, Patient QC returned to his urologist for routine follow-up. PSA at the time came in at 5.7, and when the urologist detected no gross abnormalities on rectal prostate exam, he encouraged Patient QC to continue his nutritional regimen. During a subsequent consultation with me in New York, Patient QC reported feeling "quite wonderful" with excellent concentration, energy, and stamina—and with his dizziness, weakness, and arthritis long in the past.

Patient QC continues to return to New York every six months for a routine re-evaluation, and he continues doing very well clinically. His PSAs recently have run slightly higher than in past years, in the 6.4–8.4 range, levels that I find of little concern. When in 2008 he experienced mild urinary symptoms, he underwent a microwave ablation to shrink his somewhat enlarged prostate. The therapy went well, with resolution of his symptoms, and when last seen in my office in September 2009 he felt very well and, as he had before, expressed his gratitude for the therapy.

Patient QC's history is rather straightforward. After a biopsy in September 1991 at the local Mayo Clinic facility in Florida confirmed moderately aggressive prostate cancer, he declined the recommended surgery, instead beginning a nutritional regimen under the direction of a local practitioner, which he followed until he consulted with me in March 1992. Since then, he has followed his program with great diligence and remains in good health now more than eighteen years after his diagnosis.

*IMPORTANT EDITOR'S NOTE:

Dr. Gonzalez died before updating this case report. According to Patient QC's office medical files, his last office visit with Dr. Gonzalez was in August 2014 and Patient QC last met with Dr. Linda Isaacs in late January 2017.

Case 3: Patient SL
A Minimum 12.9-Year Survivor*

Patient SL is a retired educator from Long Island, currently in his seventies, with a history of recurrent, metastatic prostate carcinoma, alive more than nine years after beginning his nutritional regimen.

Prior to developing cancer, Patient SL had been in good health with no history of major or minor health problems. In fact, he hadn't seen a physician since his college days when, in May 2000, at his wife's urging, he agreed to consult her internist for a general evaluation. His physical examination, including a rectal, was unrevealing, but in late May 2000 a PSA screening test came back significantly elevated at 12.8. He was referred to a local urologist, with whom he met during the second week of June 2000. Needle biopsy of the prostate confirmed adenocarcinoma, Gleason's 6 (3 + 3). A CT scan of the pelvis in late June 2000 demonstrated thickening of the gallbladder but a normal-sized prostate, normal seminal vesicles, and normal bladder, with no evidence of metastatic disease.

In early July 2000, Patient SL sought a second opinion with Dr. Michael Doroller, a urologist at The Mount Sinai Hospital in Manhattan. There, a review of the previous biopsy slides confirmed a Gleason's 6 (3 + 3) adenocarcinoma involving 10 percent of the involved tissue. With the diagnosis certain, Dr. Doroller suggested a standard radical prostatectomy, but Patient SL decided to confer with another urologist at Mount Sinai, who utilized a less invasive approach to prostate surgery. However, Patient SL and his wife, after considering the options presented, decided to go elsewhere for treatment.

In late July 2000, Patient SL met with Dr. Herbert Lepor at New York University Medical Center, who also suggested radical prostatectomy. Subsequently, during the first week of August 2000, Patient SL underwent the recommended surgery at NYU.

Evaluation of the prostate tissue indicated the disease to be more advanced than initially thought, now classified as a moderately differentiated adenocarcinoma, Gleason's stage 7 (3 + 4), with tumor occupying 30 percent—and not 10 percent as previously thought—of the prostate. The largest focus of cancer measured, as described in the pathology report, "2.4 cm × 0.9 cm," extending beyond the prostate capsule, a sign of spreading disease. The pathologist also indicated the presence of lymphatic and perineural invasion, also evidence of an aggressive malignancy. At a postoperative follow-up visit, Dr. Lepor recommended no additional treatment despite the findings because the surgical margins appeared to be clear of disease.

Two months after surgery, in mid-October 2000 a routine PSA test came back elevated at 3.7. Dr. Lepor decided to repeat the test in two months before jumping to conclusions, but the

PSA in December 2000 was even higher at 5.53. At this point, Dr. Lepor informed Patient SL that the cancer had recurred, and because his prostate had already been removed, the rising PSA most likely indicated metastatic disease. And once metastatic, Dr. Lepor explained, prostate cancer was inevitably incurable, ultimately resistant to all standard treatments, though hormone-blocking therapies might control the malignancy for a time.

Nonetheless, Dr. Lepor did suggest a course of Lupron Depot—usually administered intramuscularly every three months—a recommendation to which Patient SL, in a state of shock as he would later explain to me, agreed. He received his first—and what would be his only—Lupron injection that day. Overall, as Patient SL reported to me, that session with Dr. Lepor was a "devastating experience." And because the standard therapies were not curative, after considering his situation he decided he would not return for further treatment with Dr. Lepor.

At that point, Patient SL, who knew about my work from family members following my nutritional regimen, decided to consult with me. I first met with him during the third week of January 2001, at which time he made it clear to me he had no intention of continuing Lupron or any other standard drug treatment. He explained that Dr. Lepor—a world's expert in the disease—told him bluntly that even with such treatment, he might live three to five years if he were lucky, certainly no longer.

Subsequently, Patient SL proved to be a very compliant, determined, and vigilant patient, grateful that I would provide an alternative to the usual therapies that had been previously proposed. Though he was set on following only my treatment regimen, I did encourage him to consult with a urologist somewhere, either locally on Long Island or in Manhattan. During early spring 2001, he met with a urological oncologist at Memorial Sloan Kettering, as well as with two specialists in prostate cancer at Long Island Jewish Hospital in Nassau County. All recommended that he resume Lupron as a first-line therapy—and all agreed ultimately that this drug, as well as any of the other available testosterone blockers, would not cure his recurrent disease. All agreed, as well, that he would be lucky to live five years.

With the dismal prognosis confirmed, Patient SL declined the treatment offered, firmly intending to continue only with our regimen, but he did agree to undergo a staging workup during the second week of May 2001. At that time, CT scans revealed two hepatic cysts, but no evidence of recurrent disease in the prostate bed or elsewhere in the pelvis and abdomen. However, a bone scan documented possible metastases: "**IMPRESSION:** Abnormal activity is seen near the anterior ends of the right 7th, 8th and 9th ribs. This may be due to rib fractures or due to skeletal metastases. Radiographs of the right ribs are recommended for correlation."

When we discussed the findings, Patient SL repeated what he had said before, that he would not proceed with standard treatments under any circumstances and would continue his nutritional regimen.

Over the years, as Patient SL has followed his therapy vigilantly, he has remained very active physically. He undertook major remodeling of a house he and his wife own, he jogs regularly, he works out at his local gym, and he routinely has bicycled long distances three to four times weekly. Periodically, I rechecked his PSA, but only with the promise that I would not share the results with him.

In May 2003, more than two years after he had first consulted with me, the level was 18.41 (normal less than 5.0). I suggested he undergo a new set of CT scans to assess his status. He declined my recommendation, stating that he wouldn't change his treatment whatever the tests revealed. I didn't press the issue, as his logic seemed eminently reasonable.

Over the years, Patient SL has returned to my office every three months for routine follow-up and has continued doing well, reporting excellent endurance, energy, and stamina and normal urinary function. He maintains his vigorous activity and exercise routine without missing a beat. And periodically I order comprehensive blood analysis, including, on occasion, a PSA. In July 2005, after Patient SL had completed four and a half years of treatment with me, his PSA came back at 22.47.

In the spring of 2007, while working on his house, he fell off a ladder, hitting his head, an injury requiring seventeen stitches to his forehead. He recovered uneventfully, but in late August 2007, he fell off his bike while riding at a high speed, again hitting his head, but this time around he needed no sutures. He recovered as before uneventfully, with no residual neurological deficits.

By August 2008, seven and a half years after beginning his nutritional regimen, his PSA had risen to 220, though again he declined radiographic staging. He had already beaten the odds, he explained, and he repeated what he had said before: he wasn't about to change his program, whatever any test showed. And clinically he felt great, reporting no urinary symptoms or bone pain.

Patient SL continued doing well when, in early October 2009, he fell at home at night, hitting his head, his third head trauma within two years. He didn't think the injury serious enough to warrant calling for an ambulance, or even calling me. I didn't learn about the accident until Patient SL returned to my office in early November 2009 for a routine visit, at which time he mentioned the incident. He reported no residual effects of the fall, and on exam, his neurological function seemed completely normal.

In early January 2010—nine years after his first consultation with me—his wife noticed that his right pupil was bigger than his left. A local ophthalmologist subsequently diagnosed Horner's syndrome, suggesting any number of causes including brain metastases from his cancer. Though referred to a neuro-ophthalmologist, Patient SL chose instead to discuss the situation with a family friend, a neurologist, who, concerned about metastatic cancer, ordered an MRI of the brain, as well as CT scans of the chest, abdomen, and pelvis.

The brain MRI revealed only mild ischemic change typical for someone of Patient SL's age, but no evidence of metastatic disease, as described in the radiology report: "IMPRESSION: Mild chronic microvascular ischemic changes. No evidence of acute ischemic insult. Mucosal inflammatory changes in the paranasal sinuses. Otherwise normal … MRI of the brain."

The CT scans also indicated no metastatic disease in the lymph nodes or internal organs. The radiologist did describe "patchy sclerosis" in the bones without specifying the location or the number of bones involved. Though the report suggested the sclerosis might indicate "metastatic disease," it also stated, "The visualized bones do not show any lytic or blastic lesion," the characteristic findings for metastatic prostate cancer to bone.

The neurologist friend of the family called the radiologist for a more precise evaluation of the findings. Apparently, the "patchy sclerosis" involved only two small areas, the T4 vertebral body and the right femur, which I believe reflected areas of bone healing, not new disease. Sclerosis signifies a thickening of the bone, occurring at times in response to bone disease or healing of damaged bone. In my experience over the years, I have seen sclerosis in patients with a prior history of bony metastases that over time resolve, leaving a thickened area equivalent to a scar. Certainly, other than the Horner's syndrome, which I attributed to his various head traumas including his recent fall at home, Patient SL reported his usual excellent health and high activity level.

Patient SL initially agreed to consult with a local urologist after undergoing the radiographic studies but then canceled the appointment because the scans indicated no metastatic disease to his brain, the primary concern, or essentially anywhere else, and he wasn't about to change his therapy anyway. When I saw him in mid-February 2010, he had resumed his vigorous exercise program and reported feeling "great," with no bone pain whatsoever despite his jogging and weightlifting routine. Today, more than nine years since his diagnosis of recurrent prostate cancer after radical prostatectomy, he continues enjoying his active, symptom-free life.

*IMPORTANT EDITOR'S NOTE:
Dr. Gonzalez died before updating this case report. According to Patient SL's office medical files, he last contacted Dr. Gonzalez in November 2013.

Case 4: Patient LZ
*A Minimum 11.4-Year Survivor**

Patient LZ is a sixty-two-year-old male physician-inventor with a history of localized prostate cancer. Though he was initially trained as a physician, after completing his training he embarked on a successful career as an inventor and businessman.

Prior to developing cancer, Patient LZ had had a long history of recurrent Epstein-Barr infections and severe chronic fatigue. His first bout in 1982 left him fatigued for a time, though eventually he did recover. But in 1995, he experienced a recurrence of the mononucleosis with very high Epstein-Barr tiers. After the acute infection regressed, he developed severe, chronic, unrelenting fatigue, "exhaustion," decreased mental acuity, brain fogginess and spaciness, and all the symptoms that would be consistent with chronic fatigue syndrome.

He could no longer function at his highly stressful, intellectually demanding job as a designer of computer technologies. Several physicians he consulted confirmed a diagnosis of chronic fatigue but could offer no suggestions for treatment. With no other options, he began investigating nutritional approaches to his disease, changed his diet, and began taking a number of supplements and herbal remedies, with gradual, though not complete, improvement in his symptoms.

In addition, Patient LZ had a long history of recurrent kidney stones, first diagnosed when he was in his twenties, and always affecting the left kidney system. In his mid-twenties, he finally underwent surgery, with findings of an atretic left ureter requiring dilatation and hydronephrosis. Because of his compromised renal system, he experienced recurrent infections, requiring hospitalization on six separate occasions. In the summer of 2004, he underwent lithotripsy twice for multiple recurrent and large stones, but the procedure proved only partially successful.

In 2001, when his first PSA test came back borderline elevated at 4, his urologist at the time suggested a prostate biopsy, which came back negative for cancer. Nonetheless, his urologist felt the PSA needed to be monitored closely, every six months, and over a period of several years the level gradually increased. In March 2005, when the PSA reached the 6.0 range, the urologist recommended another biopsy, which was performed on March 4, 2005. The pathology revealed a single microscopic focus of prostate adenocarcinoma and focal high-grade prostatic intraepithelial neoplasia, considered a premalignant change. The left lobe biopsy showed atypical cells and again focal high-grade intraepithelial neoplasia.

The slides were then sent to University Hospital in Cleveland for further review. There, the pathologist reported again in the right lobe biopsy a "single microscopic focus of prostate adenocarcinoma" as well as "focal high grade prostatic intraepithelial neoplasia." The left lobe biopsy slides indicated as before atypia and "focal high grade prostatic intraepithelial neoplasia."

His urologist then discussed repeating the biopsy in three months for final confirmation of the extent of disease. He also discussed with Patient LZ the various therapeutic options, including cryosurgery, prostatectomy, and radiation. However, Patient LZ decided at that point not to continue with further diagnostic tests, because he would not agree—though highly trained in conventional medicine—to proceed with standard treatment. He had actually been following my work and research efforts for some years, and with the diagnosis of cancer now confirmed, he decided he would proceed with my treatment.

I first met Patient LZ and his wife in mid-April 2005. At the time, he reported a number of urinary symptoms including urgency, frequency, and nocturia three to four times nightly, but no hematuria. He also described ongoing problems with fatigue, malaise, an ongoing need for ten to twelve hours of sleep a night, and poor stamina, but improved concentration since his previous bout of mononucleosis. He seemed very determined to pursue our treatment and was insistent that he would not submit to the conventional approaches.

Patient LZ subsequently proved to be a very determined, compliant, enthusiastic, and grateful patient. By July 2005, his PSA had dropped nicely to 3.99, and he reported some improvement in his energy, stamina, and concentration and a significantly decreased need for sleep. Since that time, he has remained compliant with his program, as his health has gradually improved. His PSA has varied somewhat over the years, reaching a high of 7 in early 2010, then gradually dropping again down to 5.6 in early January 2011. His urinary symptoms had at that point improved considerably, with nocturia reduced to once a night, along with decreased urgency and frequency during the day.

He has in recent years experienced intermittent high blood pressure, which we are attempting to manage nutritionally. He reported an 80 to 85 percent improvement in his once-debilitating chronic fatigue symptoms: he now requires only eight hours of sleep per night and wakes rested, able to concentrate on his various demanding scientific projects. And persistent migraine headaches have become a thing of the past.

Though he has no interest in standard radiographic testing, over the past six years his clinical status, both his urinary and his chronic fatigue symptoms, have steadily and impressively improved. He has successfully avoided the debilitating conventional treatments initially suggested for his prostate cancer, and now, in early 2011, he continues his nutritional therapy, grateful for his good health.

*IMPORTANT EDITOR'S NOTE:
Dr. Gonzalez died before updating this case report. According to Patient LZ's office medical file, he contacted the office in October 2015, after Dr. Gonzalez's death in July 2015, and spoke with Dr. Isaacs. Patient LZ last contacted Dr. Isaacs in September 2016.

Case 5: Patient OD
*A Minimum 8.8-Year Survivor**

Patient OD is a seventy-eight-year-old man who has survived five years with a history of prostate cancer. In terms of his family history, a maternal uncle had died with colon cancer, and his sister had undergone surgery for uterine cancer.

Patient OD had smoked one and a half packs of cigarettes daily for some thirty years, before finally quitting in 1978, and prior to developing cancer he had a number of health issues. In 1974, he was diagnosed with rheumatoid arthritis, so severe that he was unable to walk. He was hospitalized at New York University Medical Center, where the experts wanted him to start taking Ecotrin (aspirin), twenty-eight tablets a day. After his release from the hospital, he tried the recommended treatment but with disastrous results. After several days, the side effects were so severe that he discontinued the medication and decided to look elsewhere for help.

Serendipitously, a good friend gave him a book discussing a dietary approach to arthritis, which he read avidly. Quickly, he changed his eating habits from the typical American diet to a whole-foods, organic, plant-based regimen, and within six months, the pain had completely resolved. From that point on, he had little faith in conventional medicine, because he had had better results with suggestions from a book than from the experts at a major teaching hospital.

In 1977, when his then-wife developed extensive stage IV cancer with no useful conventional options available, after discussing the situation they decided to consult with Dr. Kelley, who was living in Winthrop, Washington, at the time. His wife, who never underwent conventional treatment, dutifully followed the rigorous Kelley regimen, with total resolution of her cancer. She is still alive today.

Not long after his wife had been successfully treated for her cancer, in 1979 Patient OD himself began experiencing chronic severe digestive problems, associated with the development of a large mass in the right lower quadrant of his abdomen. Though his primary care physician referred him to a surgeon, Patient OD decided to refuse any conventional evaluation or treatment, because he was already witnessing his wife's tremendous progress as she followed the Kelley therapy. So, Patient OD consulted with Dr. Kelley, who, based on his evaluation, suspected Patient OD had a case of advanced colon cancer. Under the direction of a dentist colleague of Dr. Kelley's in Chicago, Dr. Harris Kimbrough, Patient OD then began the nutritional regimen.

In addition to prescribing a diet and supplement regimen, Dr. Kimbrough designed a mandibular equilibration device, a dental apparatus that the patient inserts beneath the tongue, and that gradually pushes the teeth, and in turn, the skull bones, into proper alignment. Dr. Kelley had helped develop this instrument when he was working as an orthodontist in the late 1950s. It worked simply and well for misaligned teeth as an alternative to standard orthodontia, but Dr. Kelley believed the apparatus provided far greater benefit than just attractive-looking teeth. Dr. Kelley felt that dental, jaw, and skull misalignment contributed to the development of cancer and other serious illnesses, due to pressure on the brain and brainstem. The brain and nervous system, after all, control everything in our bodies, and when they are under stress, nothing can work well.

The mandibular equilibration device re-established a normal tooth and skull architecture with release of pressure on the brain and its nerves. In turn, many systemic problems would resolve. In any event, with these various nutritional and structural interventions, Patient OD gradually improved, with resolution of his large abdominal mass within six months.

In 2003, Patient OD had been diagnosed with hypertension, subsequently well controlled with beta-blockers and calcium channel blockers. At times, he would experience bouts of palpitations associated with lightheadedness that tended to be minimal when he was adequately hydrated. Halter monitor studies had been unrevealing.

He also had a history of what was diagnosed as benign prostatic hypertrophy, dating back to about 2000, with symptoms including nocturia, urinary frequency, and urgency.

Although Patient OD didn't tend to turn to conventional medical doctors, as his urinary symptoms worsened in the spring of 2007 he decided to consult with an internist in upstate New York who combined conventional and alternative medicine approaches. On rectal exam, the prostate was enlarged and hard, and a PSA on May 11, 2007 came back elevated at 11.16 (normal less than 4).

This was the first PSA reading for Patient OD, so there was no prior test with which to compare. Regardless, the elevated level, Patient OD was told, warranted an immediate referral for a biopsy.

Despite his reservations about conventional medicine, in mid-June 2007 Patient OD did consult with a urologist. A repeat PSA at the time came back higher than the first reading at 13.7—not a good sign. Then, on August 9, 2007, Patient OD underwent a transrectal prostate biopsy, which confirmed adenocarcinoma of the right lateral base with a Gleason score of 6, involving 20 percent of the biopsy specimen. At that point, the urologist suggested a full metastatic workup.

With his long-standing interest in the Kelley approach to cancer, Patient OD was familiar with my work, and he contacted my office on August 24, 2007 in the middle of his ongoing evaluation, explaining his wish to proceed with my treatment. In his note, he summarized his prior experience with Kelley's regimen:

> I am well acquainted with what is involved with your treatment method: I did The Kelley Program in 1979–1982 for the successful treatment of colon cancer under the care of Dr. Harris M. Kimbrough, who was a colleague of and worked closely with Dr. Kelley. I had been cancer-free until now. …

> I wish to treat this cancer as I did the colon cancer. I know of the commitment and hard work involved. I don't wish to consider mainstream allopathic methods.

As I was assessing his case, he did continue with the recommended testing; a repeat PSA on August 27, 2007 came back the same as the previous reading at 13.7, and on August 28, 2007, he underwent an abdominal CT scan. The report of the study stated, "The prostate is markedly enlarged, measuring at least 6.7 × 6.2 × 7 cm. There is posterior indentation of urinary bladder. Diffuse thickening of urinary bladder is probably secondary to chronic outlet obstruction."

In addition, the radiologist described "several subcentimeter low attenuation lesions within the liver, differential diagnosis includes hemangiomas or metastasis," and suggested a multiphasic MRI of the abdomen to help evaluate these abnormalities more precisely.

Meanwhile, Patient OD's urologist strongly recommended hormonal treatment as well as a consultation with a radiation oncologist, which happened on August 29, 2007. This physician agreed with the urologist's plan, outlining a course of hormonal therapy to be followed by intensive external beam radiation therapy: "From the available information, patient is in the intermediate risk group with a PSA of >10ng/ml. I have reviewed his CT of the pelvis which shows markedly enlarged prostate gland (6.7 × 6.2 × 7.0 cms—median lobe projecting into the bladder). In view of the above findings and his urinary symptomatology (signs of prostatism) I have recommended a course of neoadjuvant hormonal therapy for a period of three months to be followed by definitive external beam radiation therapy."

The radiation oncologist also ordered a bone scan, done on August 21, 2007, which revealed no evidence of skeletal metastatic disease. Then, on September 7, 2007, the MRI of the abdomen indicated most likely not metastatic cancer into the liver, but benign hemangiomas. With all the testing now completed, Patient OD decided to refuse all conventional treatment and follow my treatment program.

I first met Patient OD on September 19, 2007. I found him to be extremely intelligent, gracious, and absolutely determined to deal with his latest health challenge the same way he had done the first time around. I reviewed with him the standard approaches, primarily hormonal blockade followed by radiation as discussed by his previous physicians, but he made it clear to me he had no intention of following that approach.

He thereafter proved to be a very determined and vigilant patient, though I had to adjust his enzyme dosing several times during the first months of treatment. He was extremely sensitive to our pancreas product, which he found quite strong, and on the usual standard dose we recommend he developed severe flu-like symptoms, to me a sign the enzymes were doing what they are supposed to do. Frequently, though not always, during the first months on therapy our cancer patients develop various symptoms, most commonly fatigue, malaise, aches, pains, even low-grade fevers, chills, and night sweats. We assume these symptoms are an immune response to the dead tumor wastes that begin circulating in the bloodstream once the patient begins the regimen. In Patient OD's case, the symptoms were significant enough that I reduced his dose repeatedly. On the revised schedule, he tolerated the program better and seemed to respond appropriately.

A repeat PSA on December 8, 2007, some three months after he had begun his therapy, had dropped considerably to 8. Though I was happy with the result, I advised Patient OD when we spoke about the number that in my experience the PSA can bounce all over, with significant and dramatic rises and falls as patients proceed with their enzyme treatment. I believe that often the PSA can shoot up when tumor dies and the protein antigen is released from dying cancer cells. I also agree with the finding in the NCI published studies from 1999 showing that PSA may actually be an indicator of the body's fight against cancer, rather than a simple marker of tumor growth as is generally preached.

When Patient OD returned to my office in mid-January for a three-month follow-up appointment, he seemed to be feeling fine and following his regimen. His urinary symptoms of frequency, urgency, and nocturia persisted but did seem to be improving.

When I saw him next, in mid-April 2008, after he had completed more than six months on treatment, his biggest complaint as before related to his ongoing urinary problems. I had already prescribed the natural supplements that often help with the symptoms of an enlarged prostate, such as saw palmetto and the trace mineral zinc. But because he seemed no better, I did discuss the usual medications, such as Proscar, which he made clear to me he had no intention of using. I then suggested he consult with his urologist for a possible transurethral resection of the prostate (TURP) in which the prostate tissue encroaching on the urethra gets essentially reamed out. He declined the suggestion, wishing only to continue with his nutritional program.

Thereafter, I continued seeing Patient OD every three months, and he continued doing well. However, during a return visit on January 15, 2009, I learned that without my knowledge he had been off the enzymes for some three months, because of some significant side effects that would come on after each dose of enzymes. Even on the modified regimen, Patient OD described very significant fatigue, so severe he would have to go to bed during the day. On his own, he decided to discontinue the pancreatic supplement, with subsequent resolution of his symptoms.

OD, of course, well understood the Kelley approach, having been through the treatment before, and realized that most patients will feel worse before they feel better. The reasons for this, I believe, are really quite simple: First of all, as the normal body tissues begin repairing and rebuilding, now provided with all this intense good nutrition, all manner of stored toxic debris gets released into the bloodstream, such as heavy metals and pesticides, for example, that have been stored in our cells for years. These wastes are filtered in the liver and ultimately excreted, but the amount can at times exceed the liver's detoxification systems, with resultant symptoms. In addition, as cancerous tumors break down under the assault of the enzymes, enormous amounts of debris get released into the bloodstream from the dying cancer cells, before being filtered again in the liver. Of course, cancer cells are very abnormal, and they synthesize and excrete many molecules that are foreign and toxic to normal healthy tissues. If you break a tumor down too fast—as any conventional oncologist knows—patients get sick, at times very sick in the syndrome of tumor lysis.

On my program, in most patients, the rebuilding process proceeds rapidly, and tumors break down steadily, so that the liver gets somewhat overloaded, and patients become symptomatic. Usually, I can control the situation nicely by having patients cycle on and off the supplements, and with the various detoxification routines we prescribe such as the coffee enemas. Admittedly, Patient OD's response to the enzymes seemed far stronger than I normally observe, but I certainly wasn't happy he had decided to stop them completely.

Not surprisingly, his most recent PSA done before his visit had jumped up to 11.6. We discussed our options, including a further reduction in his enzyme dose. To me, the level of symptoms indicated that he simply responded more intensively to the pancreas product than do most of our patients, and probably could do fine on a minimal dose. As we talked, he said he realized he needed to resume the enzymes, to keep his cancer in check, so I suggested a reduced dose, and he agreed to try again.

When Patient OD returned to my office in mid-April 2009, when he had completely some eighteen months on treatment, he seemed to be tolerating the supplements and pancreas much better, with far milder flu-like symptoms. Fortunately, he reported that his urinary symptoms, though persistent, had actually improved since our previous visit together three months earlier. We talked about retesting his PSA level, but since his last visit with me he had, at my suggestion, done considerable reading on the subject, and he felt the test was not particularly useful.

More importantly, he told me, he didn't really care what the level was because he wasn't going to proceed with standard approaches under any circumstances and wished only to continue with our treatment. He made it clear to me that he just didn't want the PSA tested again.

When I saw Patient OD three months later, in mid-July 2009, clinically he was doing very well, and he was pursuing full time his landscape business, which was always busiest in the summer. He was able to work long days at physically demanding work with excellent energy, stamina, and endurance. And when I saw him again in early October 2009, with two years of treatment under his belt, he seemed to be tolerating his current supplement and enzyme regimen well, and he said he felt overall "great" now at age seventy-five.

Thereafter, he continued dutifully on his therapy. In the spring of 2011, he developed persistent palpitations associated with an irregular heart rhythm. His local physician diagnosed atrial fibrillation, for which I suggested an herbal remedy consisting of, among others, hawthorn and cayenne, both heart tonics. He reported to me some months later that the preparation had helped enormously, and that both the irregular heart rate and the palpitations were under control.

Patient OD, now seventy-eight years old, has completed five years on his program with me. He generally feels quite well and functions at a high level, still running his business and pursuing his various hobbies. Over the years, his urinary symptoms, though not completely resolved, have improved.

Though not yet an exceptionally long-term survivor, I have included Patient OD as a case for a number of reasons that make his story, at least to me, interesting. First of all, he has been able to avoid the debilitating treatments proposed by both his urologist and his radiation oncologist. The combination of hormonal blockade followed by radiation initially suggested provokes a variety of potentially serious side effects, ranging from impotence and feminization, to interstitial cystitis (inflammation of the bladder) and chronic irritable bowel brought on by radiation damage to the intestines.

In addition, I thought his case interesting because his wife, diagnosed with terminal cancer, had been cured by the Kelley regimen in the 1970s. Then, when in 1979 Patient OD developed a large mass in his abdomen, he rejected all conventional interventions including biopsy and surgery, to proceed with the Kelley program. Within six months, the tumor—or whatever it might have been—was gone. Though I don't have confirmation that it was a cancerous lesion, I have gotten to know Patient OD very well over the years and have always found him to be an accurate and reliable historian. I have also met Patient OD's ex-wife, who accompanied him on an early office visit, and who confirmed the story about her proven terminal cancer, her cure with Kelley's regimen, and her husband's abdominal tumor that went away also with the Kelley treatment. Certainly, it's an interesting story.

In any event, when, thirty years later, Patient OD developed biopsy-proven prostate cancer, he didn't think twice before contacting me. After all the appropriate standard testing had been completed and the conventional options discussed, without hesitation he chose to seek treatment with me.

Someone like this is my idea of an ideal patient. He knew what he wanted to do when the diagnosis was confirmed, he took responsibility for his decision to proceed with an alternative treatment, he didn't think twice about his choice, and he didn't spend time second-guessing or going on the Internet looking always for "something better." He didn't have doubts because I'm not accepted by the conventional medical world, or that, horror of horrors, I am considered controversial. Though his initial course on the program wasn't simple—I had to adjust his pancreatic enzyme dose repeatedly before I found a schedule that worked for him—he remained dedicated to staying with the treatment and working with me. And he's done great.

*IMPORTANT EDITOR'S NOTE:
Dr. Gonzalez died before updating this case report. According to Patient OD's office medical files, his last office appointment with Dr. Gonzalez was in April 2015. Patient OD met with Dr. Linda Isaacs in July 2016.

Case 6: Patient DB
A 9.9-Year Survivor

Patient DB passed away at age eighty-two after surviving almost ten years on his nutritional program with a history of prostate cancer recurring after intensive radiotherapy.

Patient DB's family had a significant history of aggressive cancer: a grandfather had died from metastatic prostate cancer, an aunt and a first cousin had both died from progressive breast cancer, and another first cousin died with lung cancer. In early 1992, Patient DB himself had undergone surgery at Memorial Sloan Kettering Cancer Center for removal of a sarcoma from his left thigh. Because the tumor seemed to be purely localized, his Memorial doctors suggested no additional adjuvant therapy after resection.

Otherwise, after a major heart attack in 1986, Patient DB had been followed closely by a cardiologist. His blood pressure ran on the high side, and he also experienced intermittent vertigo, treated with Meclizine.

In the fall of 1992, he underwent his first PSA test, which came back significantly elevated at 21 (normal less than 4), though he had experienced minimal urinary symptoms to that point. On digital rectal exam, his prostate seemed enlarged, so his internist referred him to a local urologist. Subsequently, on December 9, 1992, Patient DB underwent ultrasound-guided biopsy of the prostate. Biopsy of the right lobe revealed "foci of well differentiated prostatic adenocarcinoma, Grade I, II (Gleason's) stage A1." The left lobe specimen, however, showed no evidence of malignancy, and Patient DB was thought to have very early-stage, purely localized disease.

After discussing the options with his urologist, Patient DB then agreed to proceed with seven weeks of external beam radiation to the prostate, which he completed in March 1993. After the therapy, his PSA dropped to the normal range (though not zero) and remained there until June of 1995, when a routine check showed the PSA had risen to 4.1 from the previous level of 2.5. He met with his urologist, who explained that based on the rapidly rising PSA the disease had recurred and now required aggressive treatment. A variety of options were discussed with Patient DB, including prostatectomy (removal of the prostate) or cryoablation (freezing of the gland) if the disease was still localized, followed by hormonal blockade. However, Patient DB was advised that even with such treatment, he was in a difficult position because his cancer had resurfaced after intensive radiation and, regardless of additional therapies, most likely would quickly spread and ultimately prove refractory. He was told he might live a couple of years, perhaps, if he were lucky, five years.

The urologist suggested that, before any treatment begin, Patient DB undergo a thorough diagnostic workup. A bone scan showed several ambiguous positive "gray areas" that might or might not indicate metastatic disease, though a biopsy of the prostate in October 1995 was clear. Because of the biopsy findings, at that point Patient DB's urologist assumed that the disease had spread beyond the prostate, perhaps into regional pelvic lymph nodes. Patient DB was told he most likely had metastatic disease, for which hormonal blockade would be the appropriate treatment.

So, he subsequently began monthly injections of Lupron and daily oral doses of flutamide, both designed to block testosterone synthesis. With the treatment, he quickly developed the usual side effects—hot flashes, gynecomastia (breast enlargement), diminished sex drive, and weight gain of some twenty pounds over a period of only several months. To help ameliorate the hot flashes, his urologist prescribed daily doses of Megace, a synthetic progesterone, which proved only marginally effective.

During the early months of 1996, Patient DB first heard about my work from one of my patients also being followed by his urologist. Aware of the limitations of conventional approaches to recurrent prostate cancer, and with his urologist's blessing, he decided to contact my office. I approved him for our practice, and I first met with him and his wife on March 11, 1996. Though he was anxious about his situation, he seemed determined to pursue my therapy diligently and expressed his intention to discontinue the hormonal blockade after he started his nutritional regimen because of the ongoing side effects.

At the time of his first appointment with me, he reported a number of prostate-related symptoms, including urinary frequency, some urgency, and nocturia two to three times a night. He was on a number of prescription medications; in addition to the Lupron, flutamide, and Megace for his prostate disease, for years he had been on Procardia for high blood pressure, Zocor for high cholesterol, a baby aspirin, Tagamet and Librax for indigestion, and Antivert for chronic vertigo.

After beginning treatment with me, Patient DB initially continued the hormonal blocking regimen. When I saw him three months later, in early July 1996, he reported feeling well and again expressed his wish to stop all conventional treatment—which he knew would not be curative—and proceed only with my program. At the time, his PSA had dropped to 0.1. After discussing the risks and benefits of the hormone approach, I left the decision about continuing testosterone blockers up to him. Unlike chemotherapy, we have not found that drugs like Lupron or flutamide significantly interfere with my therapy.

About a month after this visit, with his urologist's approval, Patient DB discontinued the hormonal treatment. His urologist was willing to watch Patient DB as he followed my treatment plan, with the conventional options always available should the disease begin to advance.

When I next saw Patient DB in my office, on October 1, 1996, after he had completed six months on his therapy, he reported feeling much better off the hormone blockers. His hot flashes had improved significantly, though unfortunately not completely. Nonetheless, he seemed at the time to be very determined and very compliant with my regimen, to which he had adjusted with minimal difficulty. A PSA ten days later again came in at 0.1.

When Patient DB returned to my office the first week of January 1997, he was recovering from a mild flu-like illness but otherwise felt fine. His urologist had retested his PSA, which remained at 0.1.

However, a PSA on February 7, 1997 came back at 3.25, significantly elevated from prior readings. Such an increase, in the conventional world, usually indicates spreading disease, though on my therapy, as I warn patients, the level can rise and fall over the years. In any event, I spoke with his urologist, who seemed willing to monitor Patient DB closely on my program without pushing for resumption of conventional treatment at this point. Then, six weeks later, the PSA was 3.25, the exact same level as the February reading.

When Patient DB returned to my office in late April 1997—more than a year after beginning treatment with me—he reported that his urologist had suddenly become anxious about the situation and suggested a consultation with a colleague at Columbia to consider experimental chemotherapy. Patient DB seemed somewhat surprised, and annoyed, by the suggestion. He told me that he had made it clear to his urologist he would have no part of chemotherapy ever, would not go to Columbia even for a preliminary discussion about options, and would only continue his nutritional program. I respected his strong stance but urged him to continue following up with his local urologist, who seemed reasonable and whom I assume was acting only out of true concern.

So Patient DB pursued his nutritional treatment with great diligence. When a repeat PSA in late May 1997 was elevated to 4.45, outside the normal range, Patient DB and I talked about the results at some length over the phone. He quite strongly explained to me that he would not change treatments regardless of a lab value, and that he already knew conventional approaches were not curative for recurrent metastatic prostate cancer. After all, that is why his urologist had suggested he consider aggressive experimental chemotherapy: the standard approaches ultimately fail in his situation.

I appreciated his position and explained that we often find with our patients diagnosed with prostate cancer that the PSA level will bounce around somewhat, even into the hundreds in those who clinically appear to be doing well. Though the NCI studies reporting PSA might actually be an antiangiogenic molecule the body synthesizes to fight cancer hadn't yet been published, I already suspected that, at least with enzyme therapy, the test really didn't have much prognostic value.

Patient DB subsequently returned for a visit on July 30, 1997, after completing sixteen months on his nutritional program. He felt fine overall, though he reported ongoing, though improved hot flashes, and persistent symptoms of urinary frequency and nocturia. I suspected the symptoms might be not the result of growing cancer but a side effect of the seven weeks of radiation completed back in 1993.

His urologist had recommended a bone scan as well as a repeat PSA, but Patient DB had refused both tests. I asked him why he had declined even the PSA, and he was very straightforward about the issue. First of all, he had already been told that standard treatments would not be curative. Second, whatever the PSA level might be, he would not change his treatment, so there was no point in continuing to monitor the test.

He also explained that when he had been diagnosed with his recurrence in 1995, he had been told that he might not live a year, and here he was, feeling great with minimal symptoms well beyond a year after he had started with me. I couldn't argue with his logic, though I encouraged him to keep up a good relationship with his urologist and suggested he might reconsider his stance on regular PSA testing, however limited in value the test might be. He said that if I wanted him to get the test done, he would do it.

So, in late October 1997, the PSA was up slightly to 5.11. When he returned to my office in mid-November 1997, he seemed quite compliant with his program and reported feeling well. He had an appointment with his urologist scheduled in several weeks, but he explained that he intended to cancel. Patient DB told me he felt completely "stressed out" every time he visited or spoke with his urologist, who inevitably had a story of "gloom and doom" about the situation, and who was becoming more strident about the need to consider hormonal or experimental approaches. Despite his understandable discomfort, I encouraged him to keep the appointment, because the urologist had been at least somewhat supportive of Patient DB's decision to proceed with my therapy. But by the end of the session, I wasn't completely sure my reasoning had prevailed.

At the next office visit, in mid-February 1998—as he approached two years on his nutritional program—Patient DB reported he was feeling very well, with minimal symptoms. Even his urinary frequency had improved. I was disappointed to learn that he had not kept the appointment with his urologist.

When he returned three months later, in late May 1998, Patient DB had developed a rash and described some recent bouts of dizziness. When I examined him, I thought the skin problem appeared to be a classic drug reaction. In addition, his blood pressure was low, in the 95–100/60 range, a result, I assumed, of his antihypertensive medications. I told him I thought his new symptoms, particularly the dizziness, might be related to the medications prescribed by his cardiologist and suggested it was time to start reducing the list.

First of all, he was taking both Prilosec—at the time a prescription item—and Tagamet, drugs that each reduce hydrochloric acid production in the stomach. I advised him to stop both, to see whether the reflux for which the two had been prescribed was still a significant problem for him. If the symptoms returned, he could always resume the drugs. In addition, I suggested he leave off the Antivert, the antivertigo drug he had been taking for years.

Over the next several weeks, it seemed that our experiment with drug reduction had worked out fairly well. His rash quickly resolved, and off the two acid blockers his reflux was only minimal. Off the Antivert, he reported no return of his previous severe vertigo. At that point, I recommended he change to low-dose atenolol, a mild beta-blocker that I find is far better tolerated than the Procardia he had been taking. His wife, a retired nurse, would monitor his blood pressure on a daily basis, so if it started to climb, we could always increase the dose. Fortunately, his pressure returned to a normal range of about 120/80.

When he returned to my office, in mid-August 1998, he seemed as always very compliant with his treatment regimen and reported feeling much better on his reduced medication regimen, with no rash and with normal blood pressure readings. His urinary symptoms were minimal, and a PSA—which he allowed me to order—done a day after his visit came back at 4.1, lower than the previous reading of 5.1.

At a subsequent visit in mid-November 1998, he reported feeling "great" on the reduced medication schedule. His symptoms, other than nocturia several times nightly and the ongoing hot flashes, were minimal. When seen next in late February 1999—having completed three years on his therapy with me—he again seemed to be doing very well, though a PSA in early April 1999 was elevated, at 6.8. His blood pressure, he reported when we spoke by phone, had also been recently gradually rising, to the 150/80 range, a change that concerned him. After discussing the issue, we agreed to change back to low-dose Procardia.

In May 1999, a PSA ordered by his internist came back at 7.1, and by September 1999 it had risen to 9.32. When we talked about the result by phone, he said he was concerned particularly because he was feeling fine, now having completed three and a half years with me. He did tell me his internist had sent a copy of the PSA test to his urologist, whom he had not seen in some time. The doctor had called, urging him to come in for a visit. I told him I had of course no objection to his following up with the urologist, though he expressed his unwillingness to do so. He saw no point in the visit, because under no circumstances would he resume conventional therapy for his cancer. In any event, I made several adjustments to his supplement program.

When he returned to my office during the second week of November 1999, he said that, now having reached age seventy-six, he felt "great," his blood pressure was nicely controlled, and his urinary symptoms remained minimal. His biggest complaint was his hot flashes.

In late May 2000, after four years on his nutritional regimen, his PSA jumped up to 18.58. When we talked about this finding, I suggested he consider returning to his urologist—a recommendation he rejected outright. He explained that he had already completed four years of therapy with me, having outlived the grim prognosis given when his disease recurred in 1995; he felt great, and he wanted only to continue his treatment regimen under my direction, period.

When I saw him in August 2000, he reported that his nocturia had worsened somewhat, to the point that he was getting up to urinate two to three times each night. In addition, his hot flashes oddly had recently worsened: he expressed his annoyance that he had ever agreed to proceed with Lupron and flutamide back in 1996 when his disease recurred, and he felt he was still paying the price for his decision.

He seemed to be compliant as always with his program, and I again suggested he consider returning to his urologist to discuss options, not for cancer therapy but to help alleviate his urinary frequency. I thought an old-fashioned transurethral resection of the prostate (TURP) might give him relief and allow him to sleep more soundly through the night. He didn't seem enthusiastic about the idea at all, but in any event, I increased his dose of saw palmetto, which subsequently did help reduce his urinary symptoms. And as it turned out, he did not at that time return to his urologist.

When he visited with me in early November 2000, Patient DB talked openly about considerable family stress involving one of his adult children who had entered his life in the previous few months. The incident he described had been a source of great dismay and anxiety, though fortunately the situation seemed to be resolving. With the stress, his blood pressure had been erratic, and he had been consulting with his cardiologist regularly, who had adjusted his antihypertensive medications. Otherwise, he seemed to be doing generally well, with improvement once again in his urinary symptoms. When I suggested we repeat the PSA test, he answered that he saw no point in the test, because it created anxiety and, whatever the level, would not alter his choice of treatments.

When he returned for his next visit, in mid-March 2001, his biggest complaint remained the nocturia, generally two to three or more episodes nightly. Fortunately, most often he returned to sleep afterward, and he reported that his energy overall was excellent.

When I again saw him, in early August 2001, he again complained about the nocturia but as usual seemed otherwise to be doing fine. But then, several weeks later, in late August 2001, he called to inform me he had recently developed some intermittent urinary incontinence, a late effect, he probably correctly assumed, from the radiation treatment in 1992. He had been warned at the time that radiation to the prostate could cause many problems that often began many years after the completion of treatment. In any event, he had finally relented before contacting me, having arranged a consultation with his urologist, whom he hadn't seen in some four years.

In late September 2001, Patient DB kept his appointment with his urologist, who performed a pelvic ultrasound that showed an enlarged prostate and thickened bladder wall. The urologist had recommended cystoscopy and biopsy of the bladder as well as of the prostate. Though I again suspected the thickened bladder wall was a postradiation effect, I nonetheless advised that he follow through so we could assess the situation more definitively. So in late October 2001, Patient DB did undergo cystoscopy, TURP, and tissue sampling, which this time around confirmed "invasive poorly differentiated prostatic carcinoma, Gleason's score 5+4+9/10, seen in approximately 35% of the tissue submitted." However, the bladder biopsy was negative.

When Patient DB returned to my office, during the third week of November 2001, he was somewhat annoyed because his urinary incontinence had worsened significantly since the TURP. His urologist had warned him that the problem might persist for another few weeks but should eventually subside. He had also been informed that the PSA had come back at 9.0.

We talked about the biopsy findings, which didn't seem to concern him all that much. From my perspective, I explained that the radiation he had undergone in 1992 had left the entire area damaged and vulnerable to localized recurrence of cancer, but I thought it unlikely the disease had spread elsewhere because he had been so compliant with the therapy. In my own experience with patients following my regimen, cancer can at times recur or persist in compromised tissues, such as those previously radiated, but rarely did the disease metastasize outside of the region in question. Just to be on the safe side, I recommended he undergo CT scan testing, and this time he agreed to follow through. But he did remark, as he had many times before, that whatever the scans showed he would not change his treatment.

Though I gave him an order for the scan, he initially decided to hold off proceeding with any testing. But during the first week of February 2002, six years after he had started treatment with me, he developed cellulitis in his left leg where he had undergone resection of the sarcoma in 1991. He was hospitalized for some ten days for aggressive intravenous antibiotic therapy, with gradual resolution of the problem. He called me several times from the hospital to keep me informed of his progress and at one point told me quite happily that a CT scan of the abdomen and pelvis showed "nothing."

Meanwhile, his local urologist had been kept abreast of the recent developments. Several days after Patient DB was discharged from the hospital, the urologist called me, explaining he wanted to order a bone scan. I agreed that the test under the circumstances would be appropriate, but later that day, when I spoke with Patient DB by phone, he said he had done enough testing and wouldn't agree to it. Once again, he said he wasn't going to change his therapy regardless of what any test showed, so he saw no point in exposing himself to unnecessary radiation. He would never agree to chemotherapy, and his brief experience with hormonal blockade had left him so "miserable" he would never submit himself to that again. I accepted his position and did not push the bone scan issue.

I eventually received the reports of the various tests performed while Patient DB had been hospitalized for treatment of his cellulitis. A chest x-ray was completely normal. The report of the CT abdominal and pelvic CT scans did, as Patient DB had informed me, show nothing indicating recurrent or metastatic disease, only a few small benign-appearing kidney cysts and a "partially distended bladder... suggestive of inflammatory changes around the prostate." I suspected the scan was simply revealing persistent radiation-induced damage. The test assuredly indicated no evidence of cancer spreading into the lymph nodes, bone, or abdominal organs.

When I saw Patient DB during the second week of March 2002, he seemed as always compliant with his program and seemed again to be doing well, having recovered completely from the bout of cellulitis. Fortunately, his urinary symptoms had improved since the October 2001 TURP.

But, as spring of 2002 progressed, Patient DB reported to me that his urinary symptoms, particularly urinary frequency at night, had worsened since our visit. He now felt the recent TURP ultimately had done very little to relieve his symptoms. Finally, at my suggestion, in early May 2002 he returned to his urologist, who prescribed imipramine, an antidepressant that sometimes can help with urinary symptoms. With my blessing, he tried the medication but stopped after several weeks when he experienced no change but side effects such as dry mouth and erratic blood pressure. At that point, I adjusted his supplements once again.

When we next spoke, during the first week of June 2002, he told me he had "given up" on his urologist, whom he said kept calling and pressuring him to have additional testing and interventions. Patient DB felt the urologist was more anxious about the cancer than he himself was. But when in September 2002 his symptoms of urinary obstruction worsened, he went to the emergency room of his local hospital, where he was taught to self-catheterize himself, a solution that would prove enormously helpful. Subsequently, his situation improved, but then in late October 2002 he was hospitalized for ten days after he fell and fractured his left kneecap. He required surgery and placement of a metal plate to stabilize the joint, with the intention of removing the plate at some later date.

His leg had then been placed in a cast, which the doctors said would be needed for some two months during his recuperation. During this time, Patient DB had been unable to continue his program, though he was clearly anxious to get started again. With some anxiety, he explained to me that he didn't see how he could possibly do the coffee enemas, as he was unable to get up from the floor. I suggested as an interim compromise that the enemas be done while sitting on the toilet—not an ideal solution, but one that has worked for other patients in similar circumstances.

When he returned for a visit in late February 2003—now having completed seven years on his nutritional program—he was feeling fine except for the urinary problems that persisted, despite my adjustments to his protocol. Though I recommended he reconsider a consultation with his urologist, Patient DB essentially said "no way." The physician, as well intentioned as he might have been, only made Patient DB nervous and stressed, and his suggestions, however reasonable—like the TURP in October 2001—ultimately had proved not helpful. Patient DB also strongly vetoed any further PSA testing, repeating to me what he had said many times before: he wasn't going to change his therapy regardless of the test, so there was no point in doing it. Frankly, I agreed with his argument and didn't push the issue.

In June 2003, he underwent surgery to remove the plate in his left kneecap, a procedure that went off without a hitch. While hospitalized, he did consult with a new urologist sent in by his surgeon. Patient DB, who liked this new doctor quite a bit, agreed to see him for follow-up surveillance. Apparently, this physician appreciated how well he had done over the years on his unconventional treatment and wasn't pushing him to change to a more conventional approach.

In early August 2003, as planned and with my blessing, Patient DB met with the urologist, who unfortunately seemed to have a changed attitude, now insisting that Patient DB begin hormonal therapy as soon as possible. Not surprisingly, Patient DB strongly refused the suggestion. When I saw him a few days later for a regularly scheduled appointment, he repeated he would never ever again proceed with any conventional therapy for his cancer, ever. As he said, he felt "great" and felt my various nutritional interventions had helped his prostate symptoms significantly. And by this point, he had long outlived the one- to five-year prognosis offered by his urologist when his disease had recurred in 1995.

He just couldn't understand why the urologists just couldn't leave well enough alone and insisted on bringing up other treatments, which hadn't worked in the first place and couldn't succeed long term in his particular situation. I accepted his position but did encourage him to continue seeing the new urologist, because I felt Patient DB needed someone locally on board in case he ended up unable to urinate again.

During the second week of February 2004—now eight years after he had begun treatment with me—Patient DB called me, explaining he was very annoyed, having met with the urologist the day before because his urinary symptoms had worsened somewhat. The doctor, Patient DB said, seemed quite anxious and announced that advancing cancer was the cause of his urinary symptoms, and that he undoubtedly "had cancer everywhere." I didn't understand the fear tactics, and I asked if the physician had any tests in his hands to confirm the allegation of widespread disease. Patient DB retorted with great annoyance, "No, nothing." By that point, I had come to know Patient DB quite well and always found him to be a precise and accurate historian, never prone to exaggeration, so I accepted his account of the meeting.

As we discussed the situation, Patient DB said that he believed the physician was trying to "scare" him into standard testing and standard treatment, an approach that made no sense to him because the urologists had made it clear that any such intervention would not prolong his life significantly. Why, he asked, would he give up a nontoxic treatment that was working, had extended his life, and had improved the quality of his life, for an approach that wouldn't work as well and came with a load of terrible side effects? He reminded me at that point that he was still experiencing bouts of hot flashes from his first brief "run-in," as he said, with Lupron and flutamide. At this point, he was only going to continue his nutritional program and wished that the conventional doctors would respect his decision. When I then suggested perhaps a CT scan and PSA might be advisable, he shook his head negatively, without saying a word.

Thereafter, he continued his program. When I next saw him, during the third week of March 2004—eight years after he had started with me—he reported, as he approached eighty-one years old, feeling generally very well, with his urinary situation if not ideal, at least stable for the moment.

At his next visit, during the third week of October 2004, he reported that his urologist had recently placed a Foley catheter and bag to drain urine, to deal with his worsening urinary symptoms. The setup helped his situation and was to be changed on a monthly basis. Otherwise, Patient DB remained vigilant with his nutritional program and seemed to be doing well.

In early December 2004, at a subsequent appointment, his urologist suggested a TURP, which might eliminate the need for ongoing catheterization. I agreed with the recommendation, and during the second week of December 2004, Patient DB underwent the procedure.

The pathology report of the resected prostate tissue described the following: "Invasive prostate cancer. Gleason's 5+4+9/10 seen in all of the tissue fragments submitted."

After the biopsy findings were available, his urologist called, once again urging him to begin hormonal blockade as soon as possible, and Patient DB once again declined the suggestion. When he called to report the recent turn of events, I told him to continue taking his enzymes and not worry about what the urologist had said. The urologist proved to be quite persistent: in early January 2005, Patient DB called me, sounding once again very upset, informing me that on the previous day he had met with the urologist for a catheter change, who again brought up the urgent need for intensive hormonal therapy. This time, Patient DB told the doctor he had already done the supposed "right things"—aggressive radiation, which had damaged him considerably and ultimately did nothing, and hormonal blockade, which his urologist at the time admitted would not be curative but which nine years later still left him with significant side effects. He told me he just wanted "the urologist to leave me alone!" Though I appreciated his dedication to my treatment, I urged him to continue to follow up with the urologist, whose help we did need.

In late January 2005, I actually spoke with the urologist, who did seem very respectful, and who began the conversation by saying he was amazed at how well Patient DB had done, now nearly nine years from his diagnosis of recurrent disease after radiation. He then informed me that DB had finally agreed to a bone scan, just to convince the urologist that he didn't have cancer "everywhere." As the doctor explained to me, to his surprise the scan was completely negative.

In terms of Patient DB's urinary obstructive symptoms, the physician thought that the problem really was indeed postradiation effect, with considerable damage to his ureters leading to fibrosis and blocked outflow from the kidneys. He had suggested to DB a course of depot Zoladex, an injectable hormonal blocker given every three months, and daily oral Casodex, a second hormone blocker, in the hopes of relieving some of the strain on the kidneys. I told him I would be in favor of a trial of the drugs and thought it interesting to hear from a urologist that the problem was not "cancer everywhere" but radiation damage from years earlier.

So with my approval, in early February 2005 Patient DB began the Zoladex and Casodex, with the near immediate onset of terrible side effects including worsening hot flashes and severe fatigue. When Patient DB and I did a lengthy phone consultation in late April—at age eighty-two, it was just too difficult for him to travel into New York for visits—he said he would not continue the hormones beyond three months. It just wasn't worth it, and the urinary symptoms hadn't improved.

Unfortunately, in mid-August 2005, Patient DB experienced a severe heart attack, requiring prolonged hospitalization and discontinuation of his nutritional therapy. He then developed severe congestive heart failure, a potentially deadly situation in which the heart cannot pump effectively. As a result of this and the resulting compromised systemic blood flow coupled with his postradiation urinary obstruction, his kidneys had begun to fail, to the point that his doctors were talking about dialysis—which he was fortunately able to avoid. After his discharge from the hospital, he then lapsed into a persistent severe depression—not unusual after a cardiac event—gave up, and stopped his program, an extraordinary turn of events for a patient who had been so dedicated to his regimen.

I didn't learn about any of this until mid-October 2005, two months after his heart attack, and after he had been off his treatment for two months. Though Patient DB usually kept in touch with me by phone whenever he had a problem, he said he had been so despondent he didn't have the motivation to call, to let me know what had happened. He said he spent a lot of time just "looking out the window." But all this had now passed; he realized he wanted to live, and he was anxious to resume his full nutritional program. I immediately adjusted his protocol, incorporating supplements such as Coenzyme Q10 and hawthorn berry extract, both with a long history of helping with heart failure and its related problems.

Despite his enthusiasm, the next few weeks proved very difficult for him. In late November 2005, he suffered a serious stroke, was hospitalized, and was then sent to a rehabilitation center, where apparently he experienced a second stroke that wasn't initially properly diagnosed. His wife finally was able to bring him home in mid-December 2005, at which point he tried to resume his nutritional program, with mixed success. Finally, on February 5, 2006—one month shy of his tenth anniversary with me—he died as a result of his heart and kidney failure, both complicated by the neurological damage from the stroke.

His wife wanted me to know, when we spoke by phone, that it wasn't cancer that killed him but his weakened heart. According to Mrs. DB, at the time of his death his cardiologist, who had been with him for many years, said that his heart was pumping at only 10 percent of its capacity, and his kidneys were working at about 15 percent efficiency. She then expressed her enormous gratitude for all that I, and my therapy, had done for her husband, giving them many unexpected years of good-quality life together.

As with so many of my patients with poor-prognosis cancer, Patient DB's course was neither simple nor straightforward. As a start, when he first arrived in my office in March 1996 with a diagnosis of prostate cancer, he had previously undergone surgery for resection of a left thigh sarcoma. He also had a history of serious coronary artery disease, had survived a major heart attack, took multiple medications for poorly controlled hypertension, and had other problems such as chronic vertigo.

After his diagnosis of prostate cancer in 1992, he completed seven weeks of intensive external beam radiation to his pelvis. Today, some twenty years later, oncologists have become more precise with their use of radiation, employing seed implants and more targeted interventions that limit collateral damage. Back then, the shotgun approach was still the standard of care, unfortunately leading to all manner of severe side effects including impotence, chronic interstitial cystitis (inflammation in the bladder), irritable bowel-type syndromes, and, as in this case, fibrosis of the ureters with accompanying compromise in kidney function.

Radiation also damages the target organ, eliciting a fibrosis response that can affect circulation and function of remaining normal tissue. Importantly, radiation is in and of itself carcinogenic, a most serious downside to the treatment, frequently resulting in the development of secondary cancers. These radiation-induced malignancies, often occurring years after the initial treatment, tend to be very aggressive and generally resistant to standard therapies. The eighteenth edition of *Harrison's* reported an incidence of such second cancers of 1 to 2 percent a year beginning after ten years in patients who received radiation, culminating in a whopping 25 percent after 25 years. The authors of this section, using young women treated for Hodgkin's disease as an example, stated that such patients have a 29 percent risk of developing breast cancer by age fifty-five.[4] These are not insignificant numbers, nor risks. I wonder if Patient DB's residual disease in the prostate, as documented by biopsies in 2001 and 2004, might not have been radiation induced.

Though he did have evidence of persistent cancer based on these two biopsies, the disease never progressed outside the previously irradiated prostate bed. I have found over the years that patients such as this, having undergone a course of radiation before beginning treatment with me, can develop recurrent or new cancers in the treated tissue but remain free of additional ominous spread.

Dr. Kelley once told me when I was investigating his practice that he would rather treat a patient who had two years of chemotherapy than two weeks of radiation, a statement I initially, in my naiveté, found perplexing. He explained that the damage of radiation is more significant than that of chemotherapy and can persist for decades, as the data currently confirms. The treatment ironically creates protected areas where cancer can recur, or where new, secondary cancers can begin forming. He suspected that the blood supply in radiated organs was so compromised that his enzymes could not easily penetrate to reach malignant cells. As I knew from my review of his records, he certainly could succeed with previously radiated patients, but the course was invariably more difficult and more complicated, with many ups, downs, and side-ways detours. I have found the same to be true in my own practice.

When Patient DB's PSA rose to 4.1 in June 1995 from its previous, normal level of 2.5, his urologist explained that prostate cancer recurring after intensive radiation usually ultimately proves fatal, and even with treatment, he might live a couple of years, five years at most. When the biopsy at the time came back negative, the urologist assumed the disease had already spread outside the prostate, making the situation even more dire. Patient DB did then begin a course of Lupron and flutamide, which he discontinued shortly after starting treatment with me

4 Longo et al., *Harrison's Principles*, 18th ed., 842.

in March 1996. For the next nearly ten years, he would proceed almost exclusively with my regimen, though he did undergo two TURPs for relief of his urinary symptoms, in October 2001 and in December 2004, each of which confirmed recurrent, though apparently localized, prostate cancer. CT studies in February 2002 and a bone scan in January 2005 showed no evidence of metastatic disease.

Patient DB did agree to a brief three-month course of Lupron and Casodex in February 2005, in the hope of relieving his urinary obstruction, but he quickly discontinued the drugs when the side effects became unbearable. Thereafter, he continued with only my treatment until his heart attack in August 2005.

In my opinion, the website for the National Cancer Institute provides the best capsule discussion of the survival statistics for patients in DB's situation, technically considered "Recurrent Prostate Cancer" after initial treatment. The relevant section states, "An occasional patient can be salvaged with prostatectomy after a local recurrence following definite radiation therapy: however, only about 10% of patients treated initially with radiation therapy will have local relapse only. In these patients, prolonged disease control is often possible with hormonal therapy, with median cancer-specific survival of 6 years after local failure."

I would like to make a couple of points about this paragraph. Here, the author is talking about the use of continuous hormonal blockade treatment employed indefinitely after postradiation recurrence. Of course, Patient DB stopped hormonal treatment when he began my regimen in 1996.

Second, in recent years, I have noted the widespread use of the term "cancer-specific survival," which excludes from consideration those patients diagnosed with cancer who may have died of nonmalignant causes such as heart disease or stroke. Such data manipulation tends to make the survival statistics for cancer patients look better than they really are, because noncancer deaths are excluded. However reasonable it might seem to cancer statisticians, this interesting technique discounts those patients who may have died as a direct result of treatment. For example, in the case of patients treated for prostate cancer, though some may think hormonal blockade less toxic than chemotherapy, it does come with multiple significant side effects, as summarized on the NCI site: "In a population-based study within the Veterans Administration system, LHRH agonists [such as Lupron] were associated with an increased risk of diabetes as well as cardiovascular disease, including coronary heart disease, myocardial infarction, sudden death, and stroke."

However, patients diagnosed with prostate cancer who died directly as a result of such side effects will not be counted as cancer deaths in the survival statistics.

In any event, I wonder if perhaps the three-month course of Zoladex and Casodex prescribed by his urologist in early 2005 may not, in this patient with a history of severe coronary artery disease and a prior heart attack, have contributed to his second major heart attack in August 2005, followed by his debilitating stroke.

In summary, for most of the almost ten years Patient DB followed his nutritional program, he experienced a good quality of life, marred primarily by the side effects from his previous radiation therapy and bouts of hormonal blockade. These treatments left him with chronic urinary obstruction and severe persistent hot flashes, without curing his disease. However, on his nutritional program he remained free of metastases, right up until the time he died.

Case 7: Patient NT
*A Minimum 20.75-Year Survivor**

Patient NT is a seventy-three-year-old man with a history of twice-recurrent prostate cancer, with evidence of metastases into bone.

In terms of his family history, a maternal aunt died with leukemia in her thirties, and a paternal grandfather died with some type of cancer, primary unknown. A maternal cousin succumbed to prostate cancer, and a second maternal cousin died with cancer, again, primary unknown.

Prior to his cancer diagnosis, Patient NT had generally been in good health with past allergies to pollens and environmental chemicals. In 1994, his first PSA came back within the normal range at 3.2, but a second reading a year later was significantly elevated at 7.5. At that point, his primary care physician referred him to a urologist, who noted a normal-sized prostate on exam. However, after five out of six biopsy specimens were positive for prostate adenocarcinoma, Patient NT underwent a radical prostatectomy. After the procedure, his PSA went down to the hoped-for 0.0, but Patient NT was told that based on the aggressive histology of his malignancy, his disease most likely would recur. Nonetheless, his urologist suggested no additional adjuvant treatment, either radiation or hormonal therapy, suggesting instead to reserve such interventions for a later time when the disease returned—as, Patient NT was told, it inevitably would.

Subsequently, as his physicians adhered to a "watch-and-wait" approach, Patient NT did well, with yearly PSA testing initially coming in at 0.0, indicating no active disease. But in the spring of 2001, when Patient NT was experiencing a particularly stressful period in his personal life, the PSA rose to 0.5. Though it was only a minor elevation over previous readings, urologists believe any increase above 0.0 after radical prostatectomy indicates recurrent disease. Patient NT discussed options with his urologist, including radiation to the prostate bed and systemic hormonal blockade, but instead of proceeding, he began investigating alternative approaches to cancer. Eventually, in December 2001, Patient NT decided to consult with Dr. Stanislaw Burzynski of Houston, who provides a broad-spectrum approach to malignancy, including use of "anti-neoplastins," which purportedly reverse genetic anomalies in cancer cells.

At the Burzynski Clinic, Patient NT met with a number of staff members, including a nutritionist who gave some basic dietary advice. When Patient NT realized he could not afford the ongoing costs of the Burzynski treatment, he decided not to proceed, though he did follow the nutritional advice offered, changing his eating approach to a whole-foods, plant-based diet. He also incorporated some of the tenets of the Hallelujah approach, a biblically oriented program that recommends for all cancer patients a raw-foods, whole-foods, plant-based diet, including frequent doses of freshly made vegetable juice.

With his various dietary interventions, by May 2002 his PSA was down to 0.12, though not to the desired 0.0. It seemed to Patient NT that his self-designed dietary approach might be having an effect, but on this purely vegan diet his weight had dropped forty pounds, from 168 to 128. Then, in February 2002, he developed a severe flu-like illness and lost another sixteen pounds, which he could ill afford.

In late May 2002, Patient NT, suspecting he needed a more organized, more scientifically based approach in his battle with cancer, first visited the Cancer Treatment Centers of America (CTCA) branch hospital in Tulsa, Oklahoma. This hospital system provides state-of-the-art conventional treatment, along with "complementary" and alternative interventions such as dietary and nutritional supplement support, mind-body techniques, and acupuncture.

Patient NT stayed in Tulsa for four days and underwent a battery of tests. His PSA there was elevated up again to 0.28, though a bone scan in late May 2002 was "within normal limits."

After these initial tests were completed, Patient NT met with a radiation oncologist, who, suspecting the disease was still only localized, discussed radiation to the prostate bed as the most reasonable approach. In addition, Patient NT met with a staff nutritionist, who recommended a number of supplements.

Patient NT, wishing proof of active disease before agreeing to proceed with radiation, then underwent an ultrasound-guided needle biopsy of the prostate bed on June 4, 2002. Of six tissue samples evaluated, the pathology report described "adenocarcinoma, grade II (Gleason's grade 3,3;6/10)" in the left superior prostate bed, although the other five specimens appeared to be free of malignant tissue.

A chest x-ray the following day, on June 5, 2002, showed essentially a "negative chest" with some "minimal evidence of healed granulomatous disease," an indication, most likely, of a prior infection. With recurrent disease confirmed, Patient NT agreed to a course of "salvage external beam radiation" to the prostate bed and pelvis at the CTCA, scheduled to begin July 25, 2002. In addition, the staff naturopathic physician prescribed a variety of supplements, including a probiotic, enzymes, zinc, calcium, an "immune tea," selenium, quercetin (an antioxidant), glutamine, carnitine, and several others that Patient NT subsequently dutifully took.

The day he returned to begin therapy, his PSA was up to 0.42. Through the remainder of July and August and into early September 2002, Patient NT completed thirty-three days of radiation, totaling 6280 cGy. However, when the PSA stayed in the 0.5 range despite treatment, the oncologist in charge at CTCA told Patient NT the disease most likely had spread outside the prostate bed and would at this point be incurable. The physician discussed hormonal blockade but suggested this approach be reserved for a later time when the disease became more widely and more obviously metastatic—as it inevitably would.

During his stay, Patient NT also met with the assigned naturopathic physician. Apparently, he had been losing weight on a low-protein, low-fat plant-based diet he had adopted, so to help with caloric intake the physician recommended Patient NT incorporate high doses of soy protein into his regimen. As an aside, in my practice I never recommend soy products or derivatives in any form, which we believe not only block thyroid function, but also inactivate pancreatic proteolytic enzymes—the very type of enzyme I use in my cancer protocols.

Thereafter, Patient NT returned to CTCA in Tulsa every three to six months for routine follow-up. In mid-December 2002, the PSA was down slightly to 0.28, but even this low level indicated to the oncologist persistent cancer. With radiation treatment, his doctors had hoped the number would fall to 0.0, as it had after the initial prostatectomy in 1995. Despite the elevated PSA, the oncologist still suggested a continued "watchful waiting" approach rather than instituting aggressive hormonal treatment. He did prescribe the drug Proscar and the herb saw palmetto, both of which act by blocking the conversion of testosterone to dihydrotestosterone, thought to be a culprit in resistant prostate cancer.

In mid-March 2003, when Patient NT returned to CTCA for his regular six-month visit, his PSA was 0.22, slightly down from the previous reading on Proscar and his various nutritional interventions, but not to the hoped-for zero. When he then returned to CTCA three months later in late May 2003, his PSA was up slightly but insignificantly to 0.25. The oncologist who had been supervising the case again advised Patient NT that the disease most likely was outside the prostate area but that hormonal blockade should still be reserved for the future.

Patient NT's oncologist described the conversation in his note from the day:

> I told him that his PSA can take up to 5 or more years to reach a nadir value after radiation therapy. Alternatively, he may have disease outside the prostate bed and this is what is causing the current rise in PSA. Whether he has persistent local disease in the future or whether he has additional recurrence, the treatment will be the same, hormone therapy. There is no benefit to starting his hormone therapy at the current time rather than waiting awhile. Therefore, I told him that I do not abdicate [sic] any further tests until his PSA goes above 1.0 in the future.

During his visit to Tulsa, Patient NT met with his assigned naturopathic physician, who recommended some changes in his supplement regimen.

Patient NT was next seen at CTCA in early January 2004, when his PSA was up to 0.37. Despite the worsening test results, his urologist suggested deferring radiologic studies until the PSA reached 1. In his note from the session, Patient NT's physician wrote, "At some point in the future, we will likely need to start him on hormone therapy. This is merely a question of at what point."

When he returned to CTCA in early May 2004, Patient NT's PSA came in at 0.38, still at a level, the oncologist thought, that did not warrant aggressive treatment. It was suggested that NT, for the time being at least, continue on this supplement regimen.

In conversations with his naturopathic physician during that visit, Patient NT first learned of my work and my use of high-dose pancreatic enzyme to treat advanced cancer. With his physician's approval, Patient NT decided to incorporate enzymes into his nutritional regimen, though he had not at that point contacted my office. Note that the naturopath had also suggested he continue a very high-calorie diet to ward off weight loss.

When seen again at CTCA in late November 2004, his PSA was down slightly to 0.32. His oncologist summed up the situation in his note:

> He had a radical prostatectomy. He then had a non-zero PSA and underwent salvage external beam radiation in July and August 2002.... This seemed to have no effect upon his PSA, hence his recurrence is felt to be outside the prostate area likely.

> He has made some great improvements with his diet and metabolic rate. Apparently, with the addition of pancreatic enzymes via one of Dr. Gonzalez's protocols, he has succeeded in lowering his metabolic rate and lowering his caloric intake down to 3000 calories or so per day.

During the spring of 2005, Patient NT read one of the popular books on "metabolic typing," an offshoot of Dr. Kelley's pioneering work. Based on the self-help quiz in the book, he had decided to adopt a "carnivore" meat-based diet—which we find totally unsuited for patients diagnosed with prostate cancer. In addition, at that time Patient NT first developed persistent low back and knee pain. During his next visit to the CTCA in June 2005, his PSA was up to 0.50, and he discussed the chronic pain with his oncologist, who then referred him to an orthopedist. Routine blood testing revealed a low white count at 3.5 (normal 4–12.0), and slightly low hemoglobin at 12.7 (normal 13.2–16.4), indicating anemia.

Subsequently, the back pain gradually improved, though when he returned to CTCA in September 2005, his white count and hemoglobin both remained low at 3.6 and 12.7, respectively. His oncologist did not think the low counts were related directly to the prostate cancer but did suggest the tests be repeated in a month or so to track any trend that might be developing. However, Patient NT did not undergo retesting until May 2006, when his white count and hemoglobin had normalized. The PSA, however, was up once again, this time to 0.56.

About that time, Patient NT—who had known about my work now for two years—decided to apply to become a patient. After I accepted him into my practice, we first met during the second week of July 2006. At the time, he generally felt well but seemed concerned, understandably, about his situation. He knew, and his oncologist had made the point repeatedly, that prostate cancer recurring after prostatectomy, and then again after intensive radiation therapy, tends invariably to be very aggressive and ultimately incurable with standard treatments such as hormonal blockade. Patient NT, believing he needed to be more aggressive with his nutritional approach, thought my therapy would be most suitable for his situation. During our first session together, he certainly appeared to be very determined, and I suspected he would take to the therapy without difficulty. He also planned, with my encouragement, to continue his routine follow-up appointments at CTCA.

Thereafter, Patient NT proved to be a very diligent patient, compliant with all aspects of the treatment. A repeat PSA in October 2006, after Patient NT had completed three months on his therapy, came back at 0.6, slightly elevated from the previous reading. When we talked about the results, he seemed pleased that the rate of increase seemed to have slowed, but I warned him that on our program, the PSA levels often bounce around, and at times go up when prostate tumors die, when the antigen is released in the bloodstream from disintegrating cancer cells.

Though normally we require patients such as NT who live some distance from the office to return every six months, in early November 2006, after he had completed only four months on his therapy, he returned for an interim office visit. He seemed very vigilant with all aspects of the therapy and reported feeling "great" with a "significant difference" for the better in his general health. I made some minor adjustments in his program, and he returned home.

In mid-February 2007, after completing some seven months on his therapy with me, Patient NT returned to CTCA, where his oncologist decided to proceed with a more intensive workup. His PSA was down slightly to 0.55, and a total-body PET scan on February 14, 2007 showed no evidence of residual or metastatic disease, as described in the official summary: "No focal areas of elevated glucose metabolism to suggest PET avid neoplasm."

In his note from the day's session, the oncologist mentioned that Patient NT had consulted with me in New York and stated, "Certainly, it is encouraging to see his PSA stabilize."

Two weeks later, in late February 2007, Patient NT returned to New York for a six-month re-evaluation. When he described his recent visit to CTCA, he reported that his oncologist there was quite pleased with the way he was doing. And Patient NT confirmed that his nutritional therapy had already made "an enormous difference" in his overall health. His energy, stamina, concentration, and even his sleep had all improved considerably, and his chronic arthritis was far less problematic.

When next seen at CTCA in October 2007, Patient NT's PSA was slightly up to 0.64. Nonetheless, Patient NT later reported to me that his doctors were very pleased with his progress and his improved health on my therapy. When I saw him during the second week of November 2007, he explained he felt "wonderful."

He continued doing well until early February 2008, when he experienced an attack of what he described to me as gout in his feet. He also developed swelling and terrible pain in his right upper extremity, to the point that his right arm was "not functional." His local doctor ordered some blood chemistry tests including uric acid, all of which came back completely normal, though his PSA was somewhat elevated over prior readings at 0.9.

That spring, however, his health began to deteriorate. When he experienced severely worsening fatigue and malaise associated with fevers and a persistent cough, he was diagnosed with pneumonia and treated effectively with antibiotics. For about a month, during the worst of his symptoms, he could not adhere to his nutritional program. Overall, he was off his program for a full month, a turn of events I found very troubling in a patient who previously had been so compliant. From my long-distance perspective, clearly something was systemically wrong.

Eventually he was diagnosed with a large abscess in an old root canal tooth that required intensive dental treatment that dragged on until mid-May 2008. Finally, with the tooth infection resolved, his various systemic health problems resolved, and he was able to resume his full nutritional therapy.

Shortly after this episode, during the third week of May 2008, Patient NT returned to CTCA, where his PSA was slightly down to 0.7. However, a bone scan revealed new evidence of possible metastatic disease: "There are focal areas of increased activity involving a lateral rib anteriorly bilaterally query trauma, correlate with plain film."

Although he had no recent history of injury to his ribs, when CT scans of the chest, abdomen, and pelvis showed no suspicious lesions, the bone scan finding was considered mostly likely insignificant.

When I saw him some weeks later, during the first week of June 2008, he had turned the corner for the better. Fortunately, his dentist had been able to save the tooth, and his systemic infection had completely cleared. Patient NT was back on his full regimen, and he was feeling once again well.

A PSA at the CTCA in late 2008 came back slightly elevated at 1.0, but the oncologist was not particularly concerned about the rise. When he returned to New York during the second week of December 2008 for a six-month follow-up visit, he appeared fully compliant with all aspects of his nutritional regimen and reported feeling "better than I have in years."

During his next visit at the CTCA, in early July 2009, when he had completed three years of treatment with me, his PSA was up to 1.22. His oncologist, generally pleased with Patient NT's clinical progress, wrote a thoughtful note summarizing the situation to that point:

> The patient is being followed for his prostate cancer. He was initially diagnosed in 1995 and was treated with a radical prostatectomy. He had a biochemical recurrence. The PSA went up to 0.5 in 2002… He underwent a prostate bed biopsy in 2002. This was positive for bilateral Gleason 6, recurrent carcinoma. He underwent prostate bed radiation from July through September 2002, but this seemed to have no impact at all on his PSA strangely, and hence this recurrence. It is believed to be also systemic.…
>
> We discussed the strategies and goals of treatment. I recommended doing scans every 12 months at this point. Once the scans show metastatic disease or once the PSA starts to rise rapidly or hit a certain predefined threshold such as 5.1, I would recommend starting hormone therapy. In the meantime, he will continue with an aggressive diet and supplement program.

Several days after his visit to Tulsa, Patient NT returned to New York. Although he remained compliant with his nutritional program and seemed physically to be feeling quite well, he arrived with a host of concerns, including the possibility of mercury contamination in his water supply. I didn't understand why this should now become an issue, but he showed me pages of documents related to the minerals in the local water in the county in which he lived. He was also troubled that a factory opening up some twelve miles from his house might become a source of airborne pollution. I tried to reassure him, telling him that his aggressive nutritional and detoxification program was intended to keep him healthy whatever the outside influences might be.

He was also dismayed that his oncologist at CTCA would shortly be leaving the hospital to enter private practice and Patient NT had not yet arranged for a suitable physician to follow him in Tulsa. Fortunately, eventually another oncologist was assigned to his case at the CTCA, allowing him to continue his follow-up.

Thereafter, Patient NT continued doing well. During the last week of March 2010, he underwent a complete restaging metastatic workup. CT scans of the chest, abdomen, and pelvis were, fortunately, all clear, but a bone scan revealed a suspicious area in the left pelvis, though the previously noted rib lesion had improved: "There is a linear area of increased activity involving the left public symphysis, recommend follow up: this is new from the previous study. The rib activity on the previous study had improved."

When his PSA came back elevated to 1.53, his CTCA physician didn't panic, only suggesting that the bone scan be repeated in five or six months. After all, the rib lesion of earlier concern had significantly improved, and Patient NT seemed clinically to be doing so well. With all this in mind, Patient NT was advised only, interestingly enough, to continue his treatment with me.

Several days after his CTCA consultation, during his March 2010 visit with me, Patient NT seemed compliant with his therapy and again reported feeling very well. He was less concerned about mercury contamination or pollution; this time around, he appeared to be mainly troubled by a recent late winter storm in his area that had knocked out his extensive organic garden, which had been flourishing to that point.

When Patient NT returned to Tulsa in early August 2010, a repeat bone scan showed no evidence of metastatic disease, as described in the radiology report: "The previous area of increased activity involving the left inferior pubic ramus is resolved. No definite evidence of metastatic disease is identified."

Though his PSA had climbed to 1.97, with the improved bone scan his CTCA oncologist suggested he simply continue his treatment with me. Several days later, in mid-August 2010, during his visit with me in New York, Patient NT reported good compliance and good health, with excellent energy, concentration, and normal urination.

At the CTCA in mid-March 2011, his various doctors in Tulsa were pleased when Patient NT's PSA dropped to 1.78. When I saw him shortly after in New York for his regularly scheduled six-month return visit, he was approaching five years of treatment with me. He reported that during his recent trip to Tulsa, his doctors there admitted that no one at CTCA had expected him to live five years when his PSA began rising after both prostatectomy and radiation to the prostate bed. Overall, they were very impressed with how well he had done, and continued to do, under my care. From my perspective, I found the situation quite refreshing, working together cooperatively with a team of conventional physicians who didn't mock, belittle, or denigrate my therapy, who weren't insistent on standard treatments that they knew couldn't cure, and who were willing to acknowledge a response to an alternative therapy.

In late fall 2011, of his own accord and without my knowledge beforehand, Patient NT underwent an extensive allergy evaluation using the ALCAT test, a type of blood test analysis. He was found allergic to many foods that in my estimation he actually seemed to tolerate without difficulty. Nonetheless, the ALCAT report advised that he follow a rotation diet, in which a particular food can only be eaten every four or more days, with all tolerated foods rotated in this way. Patient NT began adjusting his diet according to the tests and recommendations—not something I would have ever suggested. Unfortunately, when he returned to CTCA in mid-October 2011, his PSA had jumped to 2.52, though his doctors were not particularly concerned, nor did they recommend any conventional treatment.

When I saw NT ten days later, in late October 2011, he explained his recent investigation of alleged allergies, his new elimination and rotation diet, and his belief that all his health problems, perhaps even his cancer, resulted from such food intolerances. I responded by stating that in my experience over the years such diets are a nightmare to follow, create enormous anxiety on the part of the patient who must create elaborate dietary plans, and rarely if ever lead to a positive outcome. When I questioned him, he admitted that the laboratory findings and recommended eating plan had created a whole new level of stress in his life, which he didn't, from my perspective, need. From my vantage point, I wished that NT would simply continue following the nutritional program and diet I had prescribed, a therapy that had served him so well for more than five years at that point, and not look for new areas of trouble.

Nonetheless, despite his various concerns such as heavy metals and now allergies, currently, in mid-2012, now more than six years since his first visit with me, Patient NT continues doing well. Fortunately, he follows the prescribed supplement and detoxification program, and hopefully, in time, he will realize how well he did on the diet I suggested.

Patient NT is a rather straightforward case. During the early years of his disease, he followed the standard plan of action as recommended by his conventional physicians. After an elevated PSA in 1995 and a positive biopsy for aggressive adenocarcinoma, NT underwent a radical prostatectomy. He thereafter did well for six years, until his PSA began rising in 2001. A biopsy confirmed recurrent cancer in June 2002, after which he received a course of aggressive radiation to the prostate bed. When his PSA subsequently began rising once again, he refused standard treatment, instead choosing to begin my nutritional regimen in July 2006.

Over the past six years, he generally has been compliant and has done well clinically. A suspicious lesion that appeared on a May 2008 bone scan subsequently regressed, and a left pelvis lesion consistent with metastatic disease first noted in a March 2010 bone scan has also resolved. Both the rib and the pelvic lesion appeared during periods when the patient was experiencing unusual personal stress that subsequently resolved. I have seen this scenario play out many times before, in patients who are doing well, then seem to worsen at a time of stress, then continue improving when the stress lessens.

Prostate cancer recurring after prostatectomy, then after radiation, is an aggressive disease that usually kills within five years, particularly with evidence of bone metastases. In this case, the bony lesions in the ribs and pelvis seen on successive bone scans resolved in time, and though the PSA has increased somewhat to its most recent level of 2.52, he continues to do well clinically. He has already outlived the five-year prognosis given him when his PSA began rising after radiation therapy given for his first recurrence.

*IMPORTANT EDITOR'S NOTE:
Dr. Gonzalez died before updating this case report. According to Patient NT's office medical files, he last communicated with Dr. Isaacs in May 2016.

Case 8: Patient IU
A Minimum 2.1-Year Survivor*

Patient IU, a PhD psychologist, has experienced regression of localized prostate cancer after some two years on his therapy. Though he is not yet a long-term survivor, I thought his success with the therapy interesting enough to warrant inclusion.

Regarding his family history, Patient IU's son had been treated effectively for very localized thyroid cancer. Otherwise, no other relatives had been diagnosed with malignant disease. IU himself had a long history of labile hypertension, first diagnosed in 1996 and managed with a variety of medications over the years. More recently, his blood pressure had become more erratic after he and his wife had experienced some difficulties with a professional venture and clinic they had been managing.

Patient IU also had been diagnosed with gastroesophageal reflux disease (GERD) in 1996, initially treated with proton pump inhibitors, that could at times be quite discomforting. In 2006, a colonoscopy revealed only polyps that proved to be benign. A repeat colonoscopy in 2009 showed recurrent polyps, all benign, and endoscopy confirmed esophagitis despite the medication that had been prescribed. His chronic reflux and esophageal symptoms improved when he changed his diet to a more plant-based, whole-foods type of program.

In terms of his prostate cancer, Patient IU's first routine PSA screening in January 2006 came in at borderline normal at 3.8 (normal less than 4), but a repeat test some twenty-three months later, in November 2007, was actually lower than the initial reading, at 3.1. During this period, he had experienced no urinary-type symptoms whatsoever. Then, in September 2008, another routine PSA was this time elevated at 5.5. He was asymptomatic at the time, but a month later he developed sudden-onset urinary urgency, associated with nocturia (urination at night) up to five times nightly. He consulted with his primary care physician, who diagnosed prostatitis and benign prostatic hypertrophy, for which he prescribed Flomax, which blocks the effects of testosterone on the gland. On the medication, the symptoms improved significantly, with his nocturia lessening to once a night, and this was associated with a stronger urinary flow. After Patient IU completed a month on Flomax, his PSA came down to 4.7—although not normal, lower than the previous reading.

Although Patient IU's symptoms appeared to be improving, his internist decided to refer him to a urologist for further evaluation. He was first seen in late February 2009, at which time his prostate was found to be two and a half times normal size. The urologist diagnosed "presumptive low grade chronic prostatitis," for which he prescribed a month-long course of the antibiotic Bactrim. Blood studies that day showed that the PSA was up again, this time to 5.8, but Patient IU, with an interest in alternative approaches, chose not to begin the course of antibiotics.

In April 2009, the urologist called Patient IU to find out how he had fared on the treatment. When the doctor learned Patient IU had never taken the Bactrim, he urged him to begin the drug as soon as possible. Patient IU then relented, eventually completing the four-week regimen as originally prescribed. In late May 2009, a PSA reading came back somewhat lower than the previous elevated test, but still high at 4.51.

In early June 2009, Patient IU returned to his urologist for a follow-up evaluation. When on exam the prostate still appeared to be grossly enlarged with no apparent improvement, the urologist suggested a prostate biopsy, subsequently completed on June 24, 2009. Of six core samples, only the right apex was found positive for cancer, described as adenocarcinoma (ungraded), Gleason's 3 + 3 + 6.

At that point, the urologist recommended a complete metastatic workup. A chest x-ray on July 15, 2009 revealed a "Subtle irregular linear density in the right upper lobe" thought to be most likely due to previous infection. An x-ray of the abdomen on July 20, 2009 showed "mild fullness of the right renal pelvis." A bone scan the same day indicated "no signs of osseous meta-static disease," but a CT scan of the abdomen revealed vague fullness, as described in the official report: "There are a few mesenteric lymph nodes with a subcentimeter short axis diameter the largest measuring 0.8 × 1.2 cm in the left mid abdomen with other smaller in size. These are all located in the region where there is slight increased vague density of the mesenteric fat."

The pelvic CT showed that "the prostate is enlarged measuring approximately 5.6 cm AP × 5.0 cm transverse × 7.5 cm cephalocaudal prominent bullae impressing into the bladder floor."

With the disease confirmed and all the testing completed, on August 21, 2009 Patient IU returned to his urologist to discuss treatment options. Radiation and prostatectomy were discussed. After the session, Patient IU decided to seek out a second opinion at the Virginia Mason Clinic in Seattle. In September 2009, he met with a surgeon, who did not suggest prostatectomy but instead radiation. The radiation oncologist with whom Patient IU subsequently consulted suggested a clinical trial in which patients would be randomized to "watchful waiting," that is, no initial treatment, or to radiation. After thinking about this option, Patient IU decided he did not wish to enter the clinical study because he would not agree to receive radiation should he be assigned to that group.

In mid-October 2009, Patient IU returned to his urologist after his symptoms of urinary frequency and nocturia worsened significantly. When cystoscopy showed no acute pathology, the urologist diagnosed an exacerbation of prostatitis, for which he recommended a course of the antibiotic Cipro, with subsequent resolution of the acute-onset symptoms. At the time, the urologist also prescribed Flomax and Avodart and suggested the biopsy should be repeated by early 2010.

Patient IU already knew about my therapy from his neighbors, a husband and wife who had both been following my regimen with great benefit to their health. After speaking with them about his situation, he contacted my office with great enthusiasm for my approach, and I accepted him as a patient.

I first met Patient IU and his wife the first week of February 2010. At the time, he had decided not to return to his urologist for the recommended biopsy, and he had not followed up at Virginia Mason. He explained that having witnessed the serious health problems of his neighbors resolve on my therapy, the only treatment he wanted was our nutritional regimen.

During our first session together, he reported feeling generally "great," other than some ongoing prostate problems such as urgency and frequency, though his symptoms had improved on his current medication regimen. When I discussed the standard options that had been presented to him, including "watchful waiting," surgery, and radiation to the prostate, he made it clear to me he would do no aggressive intervention.

After returning home, Patient IU began his program with great determination. Over the next few months, he called occasionally with minor problems, such as an attack of sinusitis. When I saw him in August 2010, after he had completed some six months on his nutritional program, Patient IU was working full time and generally feeling quite well except for ongoing problems with urinary frequency, urgency, and nocturia, which disrupted his sleep. He had continued on the Flomax and Avodart, and I had already prescribed supplements such as zinc and saw palmetto that often help relieve symptoms associated with an enlarged prostate.

IU reported that the previous months had been, professionally, quite stressful, though he hoped the worst was over. During the meeting, he also explained that he had no intention of returning to his urologist, whose manner, apparently, had been at times less than pleasant—a complaint I hadn't heard before. I suspected some problem had erupted between them, the details of which I did not pursue, though I encouraged him to find a urologist for local follow-up care.

In the subsequent months, IU proved to be a very pleasant patient in our practice, who followed the program as prescribed without complaints and always with gratitude that we made the treatment available. When I saw him in February 2011, after he had completed a full year on the therapy, he appeared to be compliant and seemed generally to be feeling well. He reported "terrific" energy and stamina and substantially improved memory and concentration. Nocturia remained a problem, but when I suggested he consider a consultation with a urologist, he declined, stating he intended only to follow my therapy.

IU informed me that he had discontinued a number of his prescription medications, including Flomax and Avodart, which in the final analysis he felt had done little, and his internist had changed his blood pressure medications several times. IU reported, as he had before, that he and his wife, who worked with him, had been through another stressful period as they had not received a hoped-for federal grant.

Thereafter, Patient IU continued doing well. When I saw him in September 2011, after he had completed eighteen months of treatment with me, he said he was generally doing well and happily informed me that his long-standing problem of esophageal reflux was "99 percent better." He also relayed an interesting, though not surprising, observation about his nocturia. We have all our patients, whatever the underlying medical problem, cycle on and off the prescribed supplements, usually twenty or twenty-five days on, five days off. In Patient IU's case, because he had most likely early-stage disease, I had recommended a twenty on, five off routine.

In recent months, Patient IU realized that on the five-day breaks, his nocturia improved considerably, with his sleep disrupted maybe once nightly. On the other hand, while on the supplements he was up repeatedly, probably, we both agreed, because of the amount of water he was drinking with the multiple daily doses of enzymes and other supplements I had prescribed. Overall, his urinary stream was much stronger, so I suspected that his prostate was healing as I had hoped it would do. As a practical solution, I suggested he try to ingest the supplements with as little water as practically possible, or instead take the pills with organic applesauce, which seems to lubricate the esophagus, making pill swallowing easier and eliminating the need for excessive water intake. Thereafter, when he incorporated my recommendations, the symptoms improved substantially.

I didn't hear from Patient IU until the first week of March 2012, when he faxed my office a long note accompanied by the results of some recent tests, including a report of a prostate biopsy from some ten days earlier. I hadn't been aware he had been scheduled for a biopsy, but his note certainly told an interesting story of what led up to the procedure.

IU explained that in December 2011 he had changed his insurance to a local well-known HMO carrier, Group Health, with its own clinics and hospitals. When, in January 2012, he punctured his foot on a nail, he went to the assigned emergency room, his first visit to that facility, where the superficial wound was treated. Because Patient IU had just recently changed insurance to Group Health, after tending to the immediate problem the conscientious emergency room doctor did a rather thorough history, learning in the process of the prostate cancer diagnosis. Not shy at all about his situation, Patient IU then explained in some detail that he had chosen an alternative course of treatment with me, which apparently did not please the well-meaning physician, who strongly suggested a referral to a urologist and a biopsy to assess that status of his disease.

As Patient IU wrote me, "When I revealed to this MD that I was being treated for cancer with you, he asked me when my last biopsy was performed. I told him that it was around three years back. Again, I explained to him that I was following your treatment, but he didn't want to listen and discounted the possibilities of getting better. So, he scheduled an appointment with an urologist for me."

In any event, a PSA test at the time came back at 4.6, virtually unchanged from the reading from nearly three years earlier.

Although Patient IU had mixed feelings about meeting with the urologist, he did reluctantly go to the appointment scheduled for the last week in February 2012. As Patient IU wrote, "On 2/24/12 I went to see a Group Health Urologist…. Again, I gave him plenty information about the kind of treatment I have been following for the past 2½ years. However, he discounted your interventions and flatly told me that he did not believe that that kind of treatment worked, but he respected my decision."

Patient IU did agree to the biopsy that same day, hoping to prove his conventional doctors wrong about the therapy. And as it turned out, the pathology report described "no evidence of malignancy" in either the right or the left prostate lobes. Patient IU, who had received a copy of the biopsy evaluation from Group Health, told me the good news and said he would be meeting with the urologist the following day: "However, my joy is not only to receive such wonderful news, but to see the face of this Dr. tomorrow, and what [he] has to say after denying the possibility of being free of disease by following your treatment. As a matter of fact, when I saw him before, he asked me to go home and start to think about radiation, as he told me this was the most effective way to fix me!"

Patient IU concluded his note to me by saying, "Finally [my wife], my kids and I want to thank you for the wonderful work you do, and we are looking forward to seeing you in May."

Patient IU has been following his regimen now for less than three years, so admittedly he is not yet a long-term survivor, and when diagnosed he had no evidence of advanced or metastatic disease. Nonetheless, I thought his case instructive and certainly worthy of inclusion for a number of reasons. Most notably, to the surprise of his doctors at Group Health his prostate cancer seemed to have resolved after two years on the unconventional therapy they insisted could not possibly be effective. And despite the suggestions and warnings of his various doctors, both when he was first diagnosed and more recently, he has been able to avoid radiation and surgery. His body remains intact, and as he has pursued his treatment with me, his general health—his energy, stamina, concentration, and memory—have substantially improved.

For a number of reasons, in my mind IU is an example of an ideal patient. From our first meeting, it was clear to me he had full faith in the treatment and in me; he subsequently didn't endlessly second-guess his decision to consult me and didn't spend one minute on the Internet reading about his illness or the various options available, either conventional or alternative. Very self-reliant, IU has never once complained about the rigors of the regimen, has followed and continues to follow his therapy as prescribed, and didn't waver when his conventional doctors recently criticized his choice of treatment. Whenever we talk, he remains full of gratitude for his improving health, and that I make the treatment available to those who want it.

I am not running a cult out of my office, nor am I looking for cult followers, and Patient IU is hardly the type of person prone to "blind faith." He and his wife are both highly educated psychologists pursuing extremely creative and insightful work in their field. But patients like IU who take full responsibility for the decision and trust their choice always seem to do the best.

*IMPORTANT EDITOR'S NOTE:
Dr. Gonzalez died before updating this case report. According to Patient IU's office medical file, his last official contact with Dr. Gonzalez was in March 2012, at which time he was rejoicing at being "cancer-free."

Case 9: Patient FI
A Minimum 18-Year Survivor

Patient FI is a sixty-seven-year-old man from the New York area with a history of prostate cancer.

Other than a brother who died from colon cancer, FI is unaware of any other family history of malignant disease. In terms of his own medical history, he had generally been in good health prior to developing prostate cancer, with a long-standing and serious interest in bodybuilding and nutrition. Beginning in the mid-1980s, FI began consulting with a local Long Island nutritionist, who prescribed a whole-foods type of diet and a variety of nutritional supplements.

In the early 1990s, Patient FI experienced several severe motorcycle accidents, including one in 1993 when he ended up unconscious and in intensive care for a week. When he regained consciousness, his doctors informed him that most likely he would never walk again—a prediction that would prove false.

Nonetheless, his rehabilitation was difficult to say the least. Over a three-year period in the mid-1990s he underwent eight surgeries on his legs and hands as well as a hip replacement because of injuries sustained during his various accidents.

For many years afterward, Patient FI experienced chronic groin and pelvis pain, attributed to chronic prostate inflammation despite the lack of urinary symptoms such as dribbling, frequency, hematuria, or urgency. For this problem, his nutritionist prescribed a variety of herbs and supplements, which offered only temporary relief.

Because of his ongoing pelvic discomfort, in July 1997 at his primary care physician's suggestion FI underwent his first PSA testing, which came back significantly elevated at 55.5 (normal 0–4). A repeat PSA in mid-August 1997 came back again elevated at 50.4. At that point, FI was referred to a local urologist, with whom he consulted in late August 1997. FI was given a prescription for antibiotics for presumed prostatitis but was also informed he needed a biopsy as soon as possible.

Several days later, Patient FI consulted with a urological oncologist, who also agreed that a biopsy was necessary, and soon, because of the high PSA. So, during the second week of September 1997, Patient FI underwent ultrasound-guided biopsy of the prostate, which confirmed adenocarcinoma in multiple biopsies. The lengthy pathology findings were succinctly summed up in the urologist's note: "Pathology report showed moderately differentiated adenocarcinoma, Gleason's score 7, involving the right apex, left apex, and left base of the prostate."

A CT of the abdomen and pelvis in late September 1997 demonstrated a kidney cyst, but no evidence of metastatic disease. The prostate itself was described as "normal." A bone scan the same day showed only arthritic changes in the right ankle and evidence of the hip replacement, but again, no indication of metastatic disease.

Shortly after, with the disease now confirmed, Patient FI met with his urological oncologist to discuss the conventional options: hormonal blockade, prostatectomy, and radiation. The urologist favored a course of the testosterone blockers Lupron and Casodex to bring the PSA down, to be followed by total prostatectomy and then radiation to the prostate bed. Reluctant to begin such an aggressive course of treatment, Patient FI sought out a second opinion at Stony Brook University Hospital. All options were again discussed, including hormonal blockade, radical prostatectomy, radiation, and, in addition this time around, radiation implants. This second urological oncologist recommended most strongly a course of hormonal therapy, followed by external beam radiation and then insertion of prostate implants. It was hoped that with this aggressive approach combining hormonal blockade and radiation, surgery might not be needed for the apparently localized disease.

Patient FI then met with a second urological oncologist at Stony Brook, who favored starting Lupron and Casodex hormonal blockade at once, but holding off on radiation until the PSA was more under control. To FI, this approach seemed the most conservative, so, hoping to save his prostate, in October 1997 Patient FI began Casodex and Lupron Depot, usually administered intramuscularly every three months.

By early December 1997, only two months after his first injection of Lupron, Patient FI's PSA had dropped to 8.2. However, FI already felt displeased with the serious side effects of the treatment, which included sexual dysfunction—an inevitable side effect of blocking testosterone—muscle weakness, and insomnia. He did agree to a second injection in early 1998, but after that time, he felt so poorly he refused any further conventional treatment—to the great consternation of his urologist.

Instead, Patient FI began a largely self-designed nutritional approach including Laetrile, shark cartilage—being promoted at the time as an anticancer agent—and a variety of other supplements. He also shifted to a very strict whole-foods vegetarian diet, but when his energy began to fail quickly and he began to lose weight, he added some animal protein to his plan.

During the summer of 1998, Patient FI consulted with a well-known alternative practitioner in the New York area, who recommended, based on blood typing, a diet with considerable fatty red meat. At the time, "The Blood Type Diet" approach was the rage among alternative practitioners.

This physician also recommended a variety of intravenous nutrients such as vitamin C, but Patient FI decided not to follow up with the plan, choosing instead to continue his own nutritional approach, in collaboration with his long-time nutritionist on Long Island. At one point, he did consult with a second nutritionist, who prescribed a variety of herbs including saw palmetto.

Patient FI would never resume any conventional treatment. In early February 1999, some sixteen months after his original workup, Patient FI's urological oncologist contacted him, concerned that he had not followed up for more than a year: "I had a long discussion with you previously about the options available for treatment for your prostate cancer and had recommended a form of therapy over one year ago. To this date we have no record of sending your papers to any other urologist or any other facility and I would appreciate if you would notify our office by mail that you did receive therapy for your prostate cancer."

By that point, FI had learned about my work, applied to become a patient, and had been accepted into my practice.

Before his visit, during the last week of February 1999, routine blood testing showed that the PSA had bounced up considerably from the low of 8.4 to 65.4, a rate of increase usually indicative of rapidly growing disease.

I first met Patient FI during the second week of March 1999. At the time, he reported he generally felt well, with some mild urinary symptoms including slight burning on urination and occasional urgency. He was still recovering from his bout with a vegetarian diet, which had left him, as he explained, feeling quite weak.

Thereafter, Patient FI began his therapy with some determination. During the first months on therapy, he called occasionally with questions as he adjusted to the regimen. In late April 1999, he developed a case of severe gastroenteritis, which resolved after several days.

When I saw him next for a three-month follow-up visit in mid-June 1999, he seemed to be compliant but complained of ongoing reflux, occurring both when he was on his supplements and during the five-day breaks. During our first visits together, FI hadn't mentioned an apparent long history of gastrointestinal problems going back many years, evaluated by more than one gastroenterologist. The symptoms had been quiescent until recently, when, as he explained, he was going through a stressful time in his personal life. Otherwise, he seemed to be doing well with the program.

In subsequent weeks, Patient FI called several times because of his ongoing problems with reflux, which at times could make swallowing the many supplements difficult. But he seemed determined to do the program as prescribed.

In preparation for his next office visit, scheduled for late September 1999, Patient FI under-went PSA testing, which did come back once again significantly elevated at 86.0, more than

20 points higher than the February 1999 reading. However, I often find that initially PSA will rise on the therapy, sometimes to quite high levels in patients who ultimately do well.

When Patient FI, his girlfriend, and I next met together, during the third week of September 1999, six months after our first meeting, he seemed generally compliant with all aspects of the program. Physically, he reported some serious but long-standing arthritic pain in various joints, the end result, as he said, of his multiple accidents, multiple injuries, and eight surgeries. His digestive problems had improved, and otherwise he felt well, with good energy and fairly normal urination. He did acknowledge ongoing stress related to his relationship with his girlfriend, a situation we discussed at some length with both of them present.

In early December 1999, Patient FI called my office complaining of worsening heartburn, particularly at night when he lay down to go to sleep. His local holistic practitioner had performed some electrodermal testing based on acupuncture medians, which apparently revealed an increased need for hydrochloric acid. I often find that heartburn resolves when patients increase their mealtime hydrochloric acid, contrary to the approach of conventional physicians who in such situations want to block HCL production. So, we agreed cautiously to increase the dose of HCL with meals and track progress closely.

A couple of weeks later, FI returned to my office for a routine visit. He seemed as before compliant with the regimen but again complained of ongoing digestive problems, primarily reflux at night. As we talked about the situation at some length, I made it clear that it was critical we proceed with a formal workup including endoscopy to rule out ulcer or any other treatable pathology. Because he was in an HMO at the time, in order to get insurance coverage he would have to go through his primary care physician for a referral.

I didn't hear from FI again until he returned for his one-year re-evaluation, scheduled for the last week of March 2000. He seemed to be compliant with his regimen and looked very well. He explained that after our last visit in December 1999, instead of pursuing a conventional gastroenterology workup as I had suggested, he consulted with a chiropractor he had known for some years who performed a diaphragm maneuver for a hiatal hernia. After the treatment, FI informed me his reflux and pain had improved substantially. Fortunately, he was now able to tolerate the prescribed supplements without discomfort.

During the visit, we talked about repeating the PSA. However, always inquisitive, FI, who had been reading extensively about the subject, had come across the articles about PSA that at the time had only recently been published in the *Journal of the National Cancer Institute*. The authors had conclusively demonstrated that PSA may be synthesized in normal tissue, even in nonprostate tissue in women, and that higher levels may indicate the body's response to cancer, rather than growing cancer itself. Though I suggested he have the test done anyway, he declined, stating he wasn't about to change his therapy anyway regardless of what the PSA level might be. At my suggestion, he did agree to CT scanning of the abdomen and pelvis.

During the second week of April 2000, CT scanning showed no evidence of local or distant disease, in the abdominal and pelvis organs, lymph nodes, and visualized bony structures. Though the prostate was described as "enlarged," the radiologist reported no suspicious lesions in the gland itself.

When FI returned to my office during the first week of July 2000, at the time sixteen months since our first meeting, he seemed compliant with his regimen. His symptoms fortunately remained under control, and overall he seemed to be doing very well. His biggest complaints revolved around the various stresses in his life, including concern over his ongoing and rocky relationship with his girlfriend.

He did agree this time around to PSA testing, which in mid-September 2000 came back at 93.0, seven points higher than the previous reading from September 1999, a full twelve months earlier. Based on my experience with patients on my therapy, I thought the slight increase in a year fairly inconsequential, particularly because FI felt so well.

When I saw Patient FI next, during the second week of October 2000, after he had completed eighteen months on his nutritional program, he seemed compliant and reported he was feeling overall quite well. This time he came to my office alone, without his girlfriend, with whom, he explained, he had broken up some weeks earlier. He said the breakup had been the best for them both, and interestingly enough, he reported, since then his digestive problems had completely resolved. He expressed his belief that his recent symptoms related strictly to stress over his difficult relationship.

In mid-January 2001, Patient FI returned to my office. I was somewhat concerned about his compliance with the supplement regimen, though he seemed to be vigilant with most other aspects of the program. Generally, he was doing well, with his biggest complaint related to his right shoulder, which he had injured while doing some work around his house.

During the second week of February 2001, I received a summary note from FI's orthopedist, with whom he had consulted over recently worsening knee and shoulder pain. The orthopedist, concerned about a possible rotator cuff tear in the shoulder and a meniscal tear in the knee, had ordered MRI studies.

During the third week of April 2001, Patient FI returned for an office visit, now two years after our first meeting. His biggest concern remained his persistent shoulder pain. As it turned out, the MRIs ordered by his orthopedist had shown severe degenerative changes and arthritis, in both the shoulder and the knee, for which surgery had been recommended.

At this orthopedist's suggestion, he had begun a course of physical therapy and exercises, which seemed to be helping somewhat. Otherwise, he reported feeling quite well, with no urinary symptoms whatsoever. He was also quite agreeable to my suggestion that we repeat CT scan studies of the abdomen and pelvis.

CT scans of the abdomen during the first week of May 2001 appeared to be essentially normal. The radiologist reported no evidence of metastatic disease anywhere, nor any abnormalities in the prostate itself.

During the first week of June 2001, Patient FI underwent repair of what proved to be a torn rotator cuff. FI's postoperative course proved to be quite difficult, with severe pain lasting for three weeks before only gradually resolving. When I next saw him, during the first week of August 2001, he had improved considerably, though he still reported some minor shoulder pain. He seemed compliant with his nutritional regimen and, other than the pain, reported feeling quite well. Now, nearly two and a half years on treatment, he made it clear to me he would proceed with no therapy other than mine, whatever any test might show.

Though scheduled to return to my office in November 2001, he called my office, asking if we could do a consultation by phone instead. This was shortly after 9/11, and many of my local patients were quite nervous about coming into the city, with frequent news reports suggesting new attacks might be imminent. I agreed to the suggestion, and when we talked, he seemed to be compliant with his therapy, appeared to be doing well, and had largely recovered from his surgery.

A PSA in late December 2001 came back elevated at 120. When we talked about the results, FI again made it clear to me he felt well, had no urinary symptoms, and intended only to continue on my therapy whatever the PSA result might be.

In January 2002, Patient FI's primary care physician ordered an upper GI series, when his reflux symptoms and pain recurred. These tests showed only mild gastroesophageal reflux disease (GERD) and a "mild hiatal hernia."

When I next saw him, in mid-February 2002, he had completed nearly three years on his nutritional program. He was as determined and dedicated as ever, and when I discussed the most recent PSA reading of 120, he agreed to undergo repeat CT and bone scanning.

The bone scan from mid-March 2002 showed evidence of the hip replacement as well as ankle arthritis as noted before, but no suspicious lesions. The radiology report stated, "IMPRES-SION: No significant interval change from prior bone scan study dated 9/--/97."

The CT scan also showed no suspicious findings, including in the prostate: "IMPRESSION: CT of the abdomen and pelvis including bone windows fails to reveal any acute abnormality. Degenerative changes of the left SI joint and lumbar spine are seen."

I was quite pleased with the findings, as was Patient FI.

Over the next three years, FI would return to my office regularly. During a visit in May 2004, when he had completed more than five years on his therapy, he complained now of foot pain, but otherwise he seemed to be compliant and appeared to be doing very well.

Shortly after that visit, in June 2004, repeat CT scanning of the abdomen pelvis showed no evidence of metastatic disease. The radiologist described "central prostate calcifications," which I often find in areas of healing cancer: "There are central prostate calcifications. There is no pelvic adenopathy or ascites. The seminal vesicles and bladder are grossly unremarkable.... There are no blastic or lytic osseous lesions."

However, the PSA came back elevated at 200.6, the highest reading to date.

When we discussed the results over the phone, I explained that the normal CT findings, including a normal prostate, were all very good news. We also discussed the confusion in the literature about the meaning of PSA readings. Out of due diligence, I suggested he might consult with a urologist, a recommendation he politely declined, saying he would not again do conventional therapy, particularly because he felt very well.

I wouldn't hear from FI for well over a year. In October 2005, more than six and a half years after he had begun treatment with me, I received results of some new blood tests ordered by his primary care physician. PSA had come back at 266.77. A month later, in mid-November 2005, his physician faxed me office reports of abdominal and pelvic CT scans done that month. The prostate was described as "mildly enlarged," but the radiologist indicated "THERE IS NO EVIDENCE OF METASTATIC DISEASE."

When Patient FI came to my office for a re-evaluation during the first week of December 2005, despite his long absence of more than a year he seemed compliant, looked well, and reported feeling fine except for pain in his "normal" nonreplacement hip. He had consulted with his orthopedist, who suggested a replacement in this hip, though the situation was not thought to be urgent. Some of FI's other joint pains had actually improved over the previous year, and I was happy to learn that his reflux had not been a problem.

We discussed his rising PSA in the context of essentially normal CT scans. He responded by saying he felt well, had no urinary symptoms, the CT scans showed no evidence of spreading disease even in the pelvis, and he would not change his therapy regardless. He spoke with great firmness about his decision and his choice of treatment.

After that visit, I didn't hear from FI for some time. I called his house several times and left messages but did not hear back. I wouldn't in fact hear from him until February 2013, more than seven years after his last visit to my office and our last contact. He called my office and spoke at some length with my office assistant. She informed me after the call that he was living out in the Midwest now, was doing well, and wished to return for a re-evaluation. He was, by all accounts, doing fine, fourteen years from his first office visit with me.

FI's case provides an instructive case history for a number of reasons. First of all, his long-term survival with no evidence of metastatic disease, now more than fifteen years from his first evidence of prostate cancer in August 1997, is, at least to me, impressive. Other than a short-term course of Casodex and the two injections of Lupron Depot in the six months after his diagnosis—which left him feeling miserable—he has been able to avoid the suggested further use of hormone blockers, radiation, radiation implants, and possible surgery, which were thought necessary to save his life. He has been able to avoid prolonged hormone treatment, radiation of any type, and surgery. His prostate remains intact and he appears to be in good health, without any of the significant damage the recommended treatments would invariably have caused, ranging from radiation enteritis and cystitis to impotence.

FI's story also illustrates the difficulties, at least on my treatment, of relying on PSA to determine outcomes, particularly the spread of prostate cancer or ultimate survival. I have treated many patients over the years whose PSA went up to what any conventional urologist might consider catastrophic levels, who nonetheless show no evidence of worsening disease on radiographic studies, even after many years of significantly elevated PSA. I have come to believe that, after considerable experience with such patients, on our particular therapy, a rising PSA can reflect, as the *Journal of the National Cancer Institute* articles have argued, the body's response against the cancer, rather than a disaster in the making.

Though I wish FI had kept up his return visits, I think of him as an instructive success story, a patient who refused the aggressive and complex treatments his conventional doctors insisted were necessary for survival, but who had the convictions and confidence to ignore their railings and forge his own path. I admire FI enormously, as a man who never doubted his choice of treatment, never looked back, and never second-guessed his decision. I find that patients with convictions as firm as FI's usually do the best, lacking the anxiety, doubt, fear, and second-guessing that can torment patients psychologically and compromise their therapeutic response biologically. Anxiety, doubt, fear, and second-guessing in my experience never lead to healing, ever. And, FI was also grateful that I provide this treatment to those, like himself, who want it, a quality I often find in my successful patients.

Case 10: Patient EP
A Minimum 19.6-Year Survivor*

Patient EP is a seventy-year-old army veteran with a history of treatment-resistant recurrent prostate cancer, now eighteen years on his nutritional program.

Patient EP reported no family history of cancer on either side. In terms of his own past, he generally had been in good health prior to his cancer diagnosis. His current situation dates to November 1992, when, during an annual physical exam, a routine PSA check, his first test, came back elevated at 8 (normal less than 4). EP was referred to a urologist, with whom he met during the fourth week of November 1992. A pelvic ultrasound at the time revealed an enlarged prostate gland weighing 52.7 grams, with a suspicious-appearing "0.87 cm hypoechoic nodule involving the peripheral zone of the midportion of the gland just to the left of the midline."

Because of possible malignancy, the urologist proceeded with three biopsies of the suspect region, all of which contained cancer, Gleason's score 3 + 2. The formal pathology report stated, "MICRO: All of the cores are involved by a moderately well differentiated adenocarcinoma."

A bone scan several days later indicated no evidence of metastatic disease. A "recheck" PSA came back slightly higher than the initial test, at 8.5.

With cancer confirmed, Patient EP met with his urologist to discuss options. The physician favored a radical prostatectomy and "bilobe pelvic lymph node dissection," a plan that seemed appropriate to Patient EP.

During the second week of December 1992, Patient EP was admitted to Boulder Community Hospital for surgery. The initial evaluation of the specimens indicated no evidence of metastatic disease in the lymph nodes, but the slides of the prostate itself were sent to the University of Colorado. There, the final pathology showed the cancer had penetrated into the prostate capsule and appeared at the surgical margin, though the seminal vesicles were clear of disease:

> Adenocarcinoma, Gleason's Grade 3-3.
>
> Tumor involving left posterior quadrant in basal half with small amount of tumor extending to right posterior quadrant.
>
> Tumor involving capsular connective tissue and present at inked margin in left posterior quadrant.

Postsurgery, despite the positive margins, no further adjuvant radiation or hormonal therapy was suggested.

Thereafter, Patient EP was followed closely with PSA testing every three months. A repeat PSA in mid-March 1993, three months after surgery, came back at 0.2. Although low, the PSA reading was of some concern because after radical prostatectomy, the level should be undetectable, that is, zero. At times, in some men cured by surgery the PSA will be slightly elevated due to regeneration of residual prostate tissue. Of course, in 1992, PSA was still a fairly new test, and the details of the significance of postsurgical PSA levels above zero had not been completely worked out. In 2013, some twenty-one years later, according to the Prostate Cancer Foundation (PCF) website, experts generally now consider any reading greater than 0.2 rising on two separate occasions more than two weeks apart as indicative of a recurrence.

In any event, based on 1993 science, Patient EP's urologist decided to pursue a conservative approach, suggesting no immediate additional treatment but instead continued monitoring of the PSA. By late March 1994, a year later, the PSA had risen to 0.6. At that point, Patient EP's urologist suggested that the test be repeated in August 1994, when it came back elevated once again, at 0.8. In November 1994, the PSA was at the same level as in August, at 0.8. Nonetheless, the steady rise over a number of months indicated recurrent disease, so Patient EP was referred to a radiation oncologist, with whom he met in late November 1994.

This physician went into some detail about the risks and benefits of radiation, as documented in his thorough note: "Results of post-prostatectomy irradiation appear to vary significantly, with little effect on the overall course of disease in patients with seminal vesicle invasion. As his seminal vesicles were negative and the capsular penetration/positive margin area appears focal, especially with a Gleason sum less than 7, I would recommend treatment for me, as some studies show 60–78% four-year freedom from failure (following serum PSA)."

Ultimately, the radiation oncologist suggested a six- to seven-week course of treatment totaling 6,400–6,500 cGy.

During the first week of December 1994, Patient EP began radiation, eventually completing the recommended course in the third week of January 1995. He tolerated the therapy with only minimal side effects.

A repeat PSA in late May 1995, four months after EP had completed radiation, came back elevated at 0.4. Two months later, in late July 1995, the level was up to 0.5, and a month later it was up to 0.8. At this point, in August 1995, Patient EP underwent CT scan studies of the abdomen and pelvis, which showed no evidence of obvious recurrent or metastatic disease, though a microscopic recurrence was considered likely. With PSA evidence of recurrent disease by the rising PSA despite the negative radiographic studies, Patient EP began investigating alternative approaches to cancer, learned about my work, and applied to become a patient. I accepted him into my practice, and we first met in my office during mid-October 1995.

At the time, Patient EP, who was working full time in the computer industry, reported that overall he felt well, with no serious complaints. He described his urination as normal.

Subsequently, Patient EP proved to be a very determined, disciplined, and compliant patient. When he returned in mid-May 1996 for a six-month follow-up visit, he reported feeling "great." He had continued working long hours at his job but seemed able to work the program into his schedule. His energy, stamina, and concentration all, he said, were good.

His PSA some weeks previously in early April 1996 had dropped slightly to 0.7. Though not a substantial fall, we were both pleased that the upward direction had reversed.

I didn't hear from EP again until early September 1996, when he sent me a fax reporting some persistent pelvic pain that concerned his local physician, enough so that a bone scan had been ordered. In addition, EP's white count had dropped to 3.0 (normal 4.0–10.0), another source of concern, prompting talk of a referral to a hematologist. However, the PSA had dropped to 0.0—the first time at that level since he had begun being tested in November 1992.

When I spoke to him over the phone, I explained that I doubted that the pelvic pain indicated recurrent cancer because the PSA had been dropping and had now reached 0.0. EP agreed with my line of reasoning, adding that he didn't wish to undergo any further radiographic studies unless necessary, to avoid further radiation exposure. I also explained that I thought the low white count to be a late-onset effect of the radiation therapy. I made some adjustments in his supplement program, and I suggested we repeat the blood counts in five weeks. Subsequently, during the third week of October 1996, the white count had gone up to 3.7, though his PSA had risen slightly to 0.1.

When EP and his wife returned to my office in early November 1996, now more than a year after he had begun treatment with me, he seemed compliant with the program, reported feeling well, and had no complaints.

I didn't hear from EP until late February 1997, when he faxed me a note reporting that a recent PSA ordered by his urologist had come back again at 0.1. He wrote, "The local doctors think this is great."

During his next visit to my office, in late April 1997, after eighteen months on his therapy, Patient EP had no complaints and reported feeling well.

In early October 1997, in preparation for a return visit to my office, repeat blood testing showed a PSA back to 0.0 and a white count within the normal range at 5.5. When I saw him about a week later, he admitted that he was overworked and overstressed at work but remained compliant with his program. He said he felt well despite the stress, with no complaints other than some worsening nocturia, two to three times a night. But the pelvic pain had long resolved.

Thereafter, Patient EP returned to New York every six months for his regularly scheduled visits, remained compliant, and continued doing well. A PSA in September 1998, nearly three years after he began his nutritional treatment, came back at 0.1.

During the third week of December 1998, EP faxed me a note, reporting that he had recently experienced an odd episode of disordered thinking and behavior, witnessed by his wife at home. He had kept repeating himself over and over, not making much sense as he talked. He was taken to the local emergency room, where a CT scan of his head was perfectly fine. Over a period of hours, his mentation normalized and he had no recollection of the event. He reported some loss of memory for very recent events but no other signs or symptoms.

After a thorough workup, he was told he had experienced an episode of "transient global amnesia," a self-limited and usually brief episode of disordered cognition and lost memory around the event. His local doctors had explained the symptoms, as frightening as they might appear, did not reflect brain disease or damage, but more resembled a transitory migraine headache. Patients sometimes will have several subsequent events but often never experience any further difficulty.

I didn't hear from EP until early April 1999, when he faxed me a brief note with some questions about the regimen. Someone in the prostate cancer support group he had been attending for some time warned that "recent evidence" indicated flaxseed oil can stimulate prostate cancer cells to grow. This concerned EP because I had included a small amount, a teaspoon daily, of flaxseed oil, which I often recommend for my cancer patients as a good source of the essential omega-3 fatty acid alpha-linolenic acid.

In the decades that I have been studying nutrition, and in the twenty-six years that I have been in practice, I have heard that just about every food can cause, or prevent, or help treat, cancer. In terms of flaxseed oil specifically, the "evidence" being discussed related to tests on prostate cancer cell lines. On the other hand, the late Dr. Budwig in Germany developed a cancer protocol in which she prescribed up to six to eight tablespoons of flaxseed oil daily, mixed with cottage cheese, which she claimed helped activate the anticancer nutrients in flax. Though I never fully accepted the efficacy claims Budwig's proponents have made regarding this simple approach, I have never believed, based on my review of the literature and my experience in practice, that flaxseed oil causes prostate cancer to grow in human beings. I reassured EP, reminding him that on my therapy, his PSA, which had previously been steadily rising, had rather quickly gone down to the undetectable range.

In late September 1999—after completing four years on treatment—EP returned with his wife to New York. He seemed compliant, looked well, and reported continuing good health. He and his wife had recently moved in the same Colorado town, downsizing to a smaller home, and the change had been somewhat stressful. But he remained on his treatment throughout. His most recent PSA had come back at 0.1, which again pleased his local Colorado doctors.

After that visit, I agreed that EP could return once a year to New York, to cut down on expenses, though I insisted we needed to keep in touch by phone or fax. He next visited during the second week of October 2000, when he again reported feeling quite well, with no complaints. A PSA test several weeks earlier had come back somewhat lower than previous readings, at 0.04.

A year later, because of the 9/11 attack in New York, I agreed to do a phone consultation with EP during the second week of October 2001. In preparation, EP's local doctor had ordered standard blood work but did not request a PSA be done for some reason. Regardless, as before, now six years on treatment, EP reported that clinically he was doing quite well. He had retired from his full-time job but had continued working as a consultant. Overall, he was enjoying his retirement.

During the third week of September 2002, in preparation for EP's mid-October 2002 visit to New York, the PSA was described as less than 0.1, essentially undetectable.

During our meeting, EP and his wife explained that they had recently moved out of Colorado, which they thought was getting too crowded, to the Southwest, a change they described as a new adventure for them. They seemed happy with the move, to an area notable for wide-open spaces.

EP, now seven years on therapy, appeared to be doing very well. He described some minor leg cramping after prolonged hiking but otherwise said he felt "great."

In late 2003, EP developed intermittent cramping lower abdominal pain that he himself thought might be due to postradiation damage. He had read that often such problems don't develop until years after the actual treatment. Regardless, to be on the safe side, his local doctor had ordered CT scans of the abdomen and pelvis.

The abdominal scan did pick up a "4–5 mm" nodule in the left lung that was too small to characterize. Otherwise, the scans showed no evidence of recurrent or metastatic disease, only postradiation effects including sigmoid wall thickening. Some postoperative changes, due to his 1992 prostatectomy, were also described.

His local physician wasn't concerned about the lung lesion and agreed that the radiation from 1994 probably explained the abdominal discomfort. Nonetheless, EP was referred to a local gastroenterologist who, after a lengthy consultation, agreed the problem was most likely due to radiation effect. No further testing was thought necessary, because a colonoscopy only a year earlier had been clear.

In November 2004, Patient EP experienced a severe attack of gout, confirmed by a blood test showing an elevated uric acid level. The episode was effectively treated with the drug allopurinol, prescribed by his local physician. I encouraged him to eat cherries daily and add a celery root supplement to his regimen, both of which in my experience help with elevated uric acid.

Subsequently, EP continued returning to New York on a yearly basis. His PSA in September 2005 came back at 0.1; a year later, in September 2006, again in preparation for a trip to New York, it was lower at 0.07. In August 2007, the PSA was lower again at 0.04.

During EP's visit to my office during the third week of October 2008, he reported some sinus problems, which I thought were related to the geographic area in which they were living, noted for the high incidence of pollens in the air and resultant allergies. He also had been experiencing some arthritic pains in his hands, for which his local doctor had suggested eliminating the gluten grains from his diet, a suggestion I thought reasonable. Otherwise, as always, EP seemed compliant, and he told me he was doing very well.

In August 2010, the PSA came back somewhat higher than previous readings, at 0.114, but neither EP nor I was terribly concerned. Then, some thirteen months later, in September 2011, the PSA was 0.156. At this point, he was somewhat worried about the trend, and I in turn suggested he increase his daily pancreatic enzyme dose.

In December 2011, EP and his wife moved to an agricultural area of Colorado, quite distant from their original residence in the Boulder area. They hoped that their new home, situated right in the middle of miles of farmland, would be an idyllic retreat. Unfortunately, as they learned, the area was heavily sprayed on a regular basis from May to September, at least once a day, and sometimes twice daily, with very toxic pesticides. The planes would come right over their house, releasing the toxic brew. Because daily pesticide exposure of this magnitude was not part of their plan, they eventually moved to a rural town with no nearby spraying.

In early 2012, when EP's PSA went up to 0.19, I suggested that he again increase his pancreatic enzyme dose. I wasn't surprised by the result, because I have found over the years that significant exposure to toxic chemicals, and the stress of moving, can affect progress.

In preparation for a return visit in mid-October 2012, seventeen years after he first began treatment with me, EP's PSA had dropped, though slightly, from the previous reading, to 0.18. When we discussed the results by phone, he seemed more relaxed about the change in the right direction. And he reported that he continued feeling very well, with no significant complaints.

I believe EP's long-term survival, now twenty-one years since his original diagnosis in November 1992, to be most unusual. Although radiographic studies never showed evidence of overt recurrent or metastatic disease, his rising PSA after his initial prostatectomy in December 1992, and his rapidly rising PSA after radiation therapy in late 1994 to early 1995, would be considered an indication of aggressive, active prostate cancer. The UpToDate website has provided a very comprehensive discussion of just this issue, entitled "Rising Serum PSA Following Local Therapy for Prostate Cancer: Definition, Natural History, and Risk Stratification."

The authors reported that after radical prostatectomy, the PSA level should go to 0.0 and any level above this indicates "residual prostatic tissue, which presumably represents locoregional or systemic cancer." The guidelines of the American Urological Association, the preeminent professional organization of urologists, defines a biochemical recurrence as a PSA level greater or equal to 0.2 on at least two consecutive readings.

In this case, the post-prostatectomy PSA in March 1993 of 0.2 indicated residual or systemic disease. Furthermore, the "doubling time" of PSA posttreatment also reflects the aggressive nature of the disease: the more quickly the level doubles, the more aggressive the cancer and the worse the prognosis. By March 1994, Patient EP's PSA, though still low, had tripled over the initial postsurgery reading, to 0.6, before eventually rising to 0.8 in November 1994.

By that point, EP's urologist, convinced that the disease hadn't been cured by surgery and was spreading, referred him for radiation therapy. But his first postradiation PSA four months after the treatment, in May 1995, came back still elevated at 0.4. Two months later, it was up slightly to 0.5, again indicating "biochemical" recurrence. A month later, in August 1995, it was up to 0.8, a doubling over the May 1995 value. A doubling of PSA within three months such as this represents a poor prognostic indicator.

Once EP began his nutritional program, his PSA began dropping, reaching 0.0 for the first time in September 1996, after he had been pursuing his nutritional therapy for nearly a year. At that time, he was on no other treatment but mine.

True, in August 2010 EP's PSA came back somewhat higher than previous readings at 0.114, but it was still far lower than the postsurgery, postradiation levels. The PSA would reach 0.19 in early 2012, when I once again increased his pancreatic enzyme dose. By October 2012, the upward trend had reversed, when the PSA came in slightly lower at 0.18. During the period of PSA increase from 2010 to early 2012, EP and his wife were experiencing considerable stress in their life, moving from their adopted home state in the Southwest back to their original home state of Colorado, only to find themselves exposed to a daily barrage of toxic pesticides. Now having moved again to a nonagricultural area, and with the toxic exposure out of their lives,

EP's PSA has again begun to decline. In my experience, stress and unusual exposure to toxic chemicals can interfere with the efficacy of my therapy. The combination can be catastrophic.

I have been unable to find specific survival statistics for patients such as EP, whose PSA never went to zero after radical prostatectomy, and whose PSA in fact doubled within three months after he completed five weeks of intensive post-prostatectomy radiation. Regardless, EP's long-term survival, twenty-one years from his original biopsy proving prostate cancer in November 1992, and eighteen years from his first visit with me in mid-October 1995, is certainly gratifying.

One final comment: over the years, Patient EP has been a wonderful patient in my practice, determined, dedicated to the treatment, compliant, and grateful that I make the therapy available to patients such as himself. He, and his wife, have been unfazed through periods when I have been under aggressive attack by my conventional colleagues. He never doubted the utility of my approach or my motivation in providing it. Patients with such an attitude, I find, always do the best regardless of their underlying disease and conventional prognosis.

*IMPORTANT EDITOR'S NOTE:
Dr. Gonzalez died before updating this case report. According to Patient EP's office medical file, he last contacted Dr. Gonzalez in April 2015.

SALIVARY GLAND CANCER

In the year 2009, 48,010 cases of head and neck cancer were diagnosed in the US,[1] with some 2,000–2,500 cases of salivary gland tumors specifically, of which three-fourths are benign, one-fourth malignant. Most of these lesions develop in one of the two parotid glands, the main salivary glands located in the posterior cheek region on either side. Tumors can form, although far less commonly, in the minor salivary glands dispersed throughout the mouth and tongue surface. Approximately 50 percent of tumors arising in a minor salivary gland tend to be malignant, more so than for lesions originating in one of the parotids.[2]

Radiation exposure increases the risk of salivary gland tumors. Japanese survivors of the nuclear bombs dropped on Hiroshima and Nagasaki were noted to have an increased incidence in such lesions. More recently, it has been noted that patients receiving radiation treatment to the head and neck for Hodgkin's disease or for other purposes also show a significantly higher incidence. Smoking, and certain viral infections, particularly HIV, correlate with an increased risk of salivary tumors according to the website UpToDate.

For localized malignant disease, surgery remains the mainstay of treatment. Mendenhall et al., writing in *Cancer: Principles and Practice of Oncology*,[33] described a series of 434 localized cancerous tumors originating in a minor salivary gland, of which 90 percent were treated surgically (presumably the other 10 percent received radiation). The five, ten, and fifteen-year survival for the group came in at 44 percent, 32 percent, and 21 percent, so the eventual mortality, even for localized disease, is significant.

Once the disease is metastatic, systemic chemotherapy offers little benefit. The website UpToDate describes the goal of treatment as palliative, that is, easing of "disease-related symptoms."

---

1   DeVita et al., *Cancer: Principles and Practice*, 9th ed., 7290.
2   Ibid., 777
3   Ibid., 778

Case 1: Patient HC
A 7.2-Year Survivor*

Patient HC is a European-born woman in her late seventies, a successful artist in New York, with a history of stage IV adenocarcinoma of a minor salivary gland, now six years from her diagnosis. Her family history is pertinent because of her father, who died at an advanced age with prostate cancer, and a maternal aunt who died from breast cancer, also at an advanced age.

Patient HC, who never smoked, has long been interested in alternative medicine and healthy eating habits, going back to the 1960s when she adopted a whole-foods, organic diet. For whatever health problem she might face, she always preferred alternative approaches, rather than standard conventional medicine.

In terms of her precancer health, she had a long history of irritable bowel-type symptoms, associated with chronic severe constipation, which she kept under control for years with her dietary approach.

In 1999, Patient HC first developed severe, chronic, persistent abdominal pain. She consulted a number of physicians, all of whom attributed her symptoms to her chronic constipation. Finally, the pain worsened to the point that she was admitted to a local hospital in New York and underwent exploratory surgery. She was found to have peritonitis, not due to a ruptured appendix, but rather the result of a colonic abscess. Postsurgery, she was treated aggressively with intravenous antibiotics, and though she eventually recovered after a lengthy hospitalization, since that time her constipation and irritable symptoms have been more pronounced.

In addition, since childhood she has experienced chronic eczema, for which she consulted a number of physicians over the years, who inevitably prescribed some form of steroid lotion. Such treatment, however, provided only temporary relief.

In 2002, when her skin problems worsened, she sought treatment with an alternative-type physician in New York, who diagnosed Candida and prescribed a variety of nutritional supplements. With the treatment, her skin only worsened, and eventually she consulted with a conventional dermatologist. A skin biopsy revealed cutaneous lupus, a variant of the more systemic and often debilitating autoimmune disease. She was then begun on a course of Plaquenil, originally developed as an antimalarial, with subsequent clearing of her skin. But after she discontinued the medication, the skin lesions returned. Because of her wish to avoid pharmaceuticals, subsequently Patient HC would take a Plaquenil every few days, a routine that seemed to afford some benefit.

Her intermittent Plaquenil approach kept the situation to some degree in check until 2006, when the skin rapidly worsened. She developed diffuse wheal-like lesions over her entire body, associated with significant itching and burning. A rheumatologist she consulted discounted lupus as the diagnosis and recommended she consult with a celiac expert at Columbia University's Celiac Center in Manhattan. Extensive blood testing was not definitive, indicating only the possibility of celiac. Nonetheless, Patient HC decided to exclude all gluten grains from her diet, but with no improvement in her symptoms.

She was then referred to an allergist, who after extensive testing found Patient HC reactive to wheat, corn, and sugar among other foods, as well as multiple medications, dust, dust mites, and molds. Unfortunately, though she subsequently avoided the offending foods and created a more nonallergenic living situation, her skin failed to improve.

In terms of her cancer history, in 1987 Patient HC first noticed a nodule at the juncture of her soft and hard palate, about the size of a big almond. She treated herself with a variety of herbal gargles and salt water, which did, she think, slow the growth of the lesion. It didn't regress but on the other hand didn't continuing growing. In the late 1980s, she did undergo a needle biopsy, which was unrevealing.

In 1999, while living in Europe, the lesion opened up, prompting consultation with a surgeon. A biopsy at the time was again negative for malignancy. After the procedure, the lesion didn't heal properly, remaining somewhat ulcerated. Once again, Patient HC resorted to a variety of herbal remedies that seemed to help in terms of the open sore, but the nodule did not regress.

In 2006, while in New York, Patient HC noticed the lesion seemed to be growing once again. She consulted with an oral surgeon in Manhattan, and this time a biopsy revealed "adenocarcinoma, of minor salivary gland origin." With cancer now confirmed, HC was referred to Dr. Jay Boyle, a head and neck surgeon at the Memorial Sloan Kettering Cancer Center in New York, where she was first seen in late July 2006. At the time, on exam she was found to have enlarged right cervical lymph nodes.

A review of the biopsy slides by a Memorial pathologist indicated possibly a benign tumor or cancer, as described in the pathology report: "WE FAVOR THIS TUMOR AS BEING A CELLULAR PLEOMORPHIC ADENOMA. HOWEVER, A LOW GRADE SALIVARY GLAND CARCINOMA CANNOT BE RULED OUT IN THIS BIOPSY."

During the second week of August 2006 at Memorial, Patient HC underwent a fine needle aspiration of an enlarged right neck lymph node that proved to be "NON-DIAGNOSTIC." A week later, an MRI of the nasal cavity and neck revealed the lesion on the palate, as well as additional areas of concern in the neck:

There is an apparent mass arising within the right anterior lateral aspect of the soft palate measuring at least 1.6 cm × 1.2 cm in maximal diameter....

There is associated right neck...adenopathy with a dominant 2.5 cm × 2.2 lymph node.

A 1 cm oblong lesion is identified within the superficial lobe of the right parotid gland. This lesion is indeterminate.

To help define further the extent of disease, Dr. Boyle recommended a PET scan, which Patient HC declined. He then insisted that Patient HC required extensive surgery, because the disease seemed to be spreading into the neck lymphatics, but this too Patient HC refused.

Instead, in August 2006 Patient HC consulted with a lay nutritionist in New York, Ruth Sackman (now deceased), who prescribed a regimen of raw plant foods, juices, and a variety of supplements from the company Standard Process, based in Wisconsin. However, after she began the treatment in earnest, Patient HC's skin quickly worsened, with wheals forming diffusely throughout her skin, which began to peel, crack, and bleed. The pain and itching kept Patient HC from sleep. Ms. Sackman suggested Patient HC switch to more cooked food, but with this adjustment the skin only continued to worsen. On her own, Patient HC then underwent the AMAS test, a blood marker for cancer that came back positive.

During the first week of September 2006, Patient HC did return to Dr. Boyle for a follow-up visit. In his note from that date, he described the situation:

Level II lymph node, it remains 2 ½ cm firm and suspicious. The needle biopsy however is non-diagnostic. The MRI scan was performed but the patient refused gadolinium. She also refused the PET scan. I advised her in no uncertain terms that I have a high degree of suspicion that she has a minor salivary gland tumor, which is probably malignant and probably metastatic to the right upper neck.

She understands my high degree of suspicion of malignancy and the possibility that this could threaten her life. She will consider her options against medical advice. She knows that I will support her in her decision making. She knows with great certainty what my advice is for this lesion.

With her symptoms worsening, in September 2006 Patient HC quit Ms. Sackman's therapy and consulted, by phone, a practitioner who designs aggressive nutritional programs, again relying primarily on Standard Process supplements. But Patient HC, unconvinced about the suggestions, never ordered any of the prescribed products.

For several months, beginning in September 2006, Patient HC really pursued no treatment other than her self-designed whole-foods, organic, low-animal-product diet. However, to her great dismay she realized the palate lesion seemed to be growing, and rather rapidly.

In late fall, Patient HC learned of a Dr. Salvatore Caruana, a head and neck surgeon affiliated with Beth Israel Hospital and the NY Eye and Ear Infirmary, both in Manhattan. She consulted with Dr. Caruana in early December 2006, at which time she agreed to proceed with more intensive scanning. A PET scan during the first week of December 2006 revealed not only the palate lesion, but also multiple areas of suspicious activity in the right neck as well as two potentially troublesome areas in the right lower lung:

> Abnormal hypermetabolic activity is seen involving the right oral cavity … mean SUV range 4.2–4.9 [note; normal generally considered less than 2] The corresponding anatomic images demonstrate a subtle soft tissue involving the lateral aspect of the right soft palate without appreciable hardpalate involvement … this lesion measures 2.0 (anteriorposterior) × 0.8 (transverse) cm.

> There is hypermetabolic right neck nodal disease with mean SUV range 4.2–4.3….

> The corresponding anatomic images … demonstrate a conglomerate centrally necrotic right level IIa lymph node which measures 2.1 (transverse) × 2.4 (anteriorposterior) × 3.2 (craniocaudad) cm.…

> Three are right level IIb hypermetabolic lymph nodes with mean SUV range 2.0–3.…

> There is a hypermetabolic right level III lymph node.…

> In the right lung base … there is a solid appearing 1.5 × 1.0 cm soft tissue nodule which on the corresponding functional images, is not hypermetabolic. This lesion however is indeterminate.

> A more subtle ground glass opacity is seen lateral to the more solid nodule … measuring 4 mm in size.

A CT scan two days later confirmed the lesions reported on the PET study.

In a subsequent meeting, Dr. Caruana strongly recommended extensive head and neck surgery to remove the primary soft palate lesions as well as the suspicious-appearing right neck lymph nodes. The procedure was then scheduled for early January 2007. A chest x-ray during the first week in January 2007, done in preparation for surgery, revealed a left lung lesion, as described in the report, but no mention was made of the two areas in the right lung seen on the PET scan from December 2006: "Superimposed … is a poorly marginated focus of increased parenchymal density in the anterior aspect of the left upper lobe measuring approximately 1 cm in dimension."

214

This new finding did not preclude the scheduled surgery, which went ahead as planned several days later at the New York Eye and Ear Infirmary. The procedure involved, as planned, excision of the palate lesion and right neck lymph node dissection. The final pathology indicated intermediate-grade disease involving eleven lymph nodes at all levels of the right neck:

Hard palate mass, excision:

Invasive adenocarcinoma, not otherwise specified, 2.7 × 1.6 × 0.7 cm in depth, grade II of III. . . .

In toto: 11 of 40 lymph nodes are positive for metastatic carcinoma.

The findings were presented to the tumor board at the infirmary. Unanimously, the group agreed that radiation to the neck was now indicated, and Patient HC was referred to a radiology oncologist at Beth Israel, with whom she consulted in March 2007. Initially, she agreed to the treatment, but because of her ongoing skin condition she couldn't tolerate the mask that she would need to wear as part of the procedure. The oncologist suggested she consult with a rheumatologist to get the cutaneous lupus under control, so she might proceed with the proposed radiation.

Instead, Patient HC decided to consult with a second radiation oncologist at the now-defunct St. Vincent's Hospital, who discussed in detail the serious side effects of the treatment including loss of the use of her tongue, loss of salivation, and possibly even diminished speech. He admitted the required radiation would be very debilitating—a scenario that had not been fully explained by the first radiation oncologist. After thinking about the situation, Patient HC decided that at her age the side effects weren't worth any potential benefits, so she ultimately refused the treatment.

She did then meet with a physician at the Memorial Sloan Kettering Complementary Medicine Division, who suggested a course of chemotherapy and recommended a consultation with a Memorial oncologist, an expert in head and neck tumors. Patient HC did meet with this physician, who honestly told her chemotherapy would offer her no benefit and suggested only that she return to her previous radiation oncologist.

At that point, Patient HC learned about my work from an employee at a local health food store who recommended me. After investigating my approach, she applied to become a patient, and I ultimately accepted her into my practice.

I first met with Patient HC at the end of April 2007. I knew of her from her reputation as an artist, and from our first meeting together I found her extremely intelligent, clearly dedicated to alternative approaches to health care, and determined to follow through with my therapy. At the time of our visit, she had obvious right supraclavicular adenopathy, with a single larger node 3 cm in diameter, hard and fixed, and multiple smaller satellite nodules. In addition, her skin appeared to be quite inflamed from what had been diagnosed as cutaneous lupus.

Initially, when Patient HC first began her supplement program in early May 2007, she experienced difficulty swallowing the large number of pills, so we worked over the phone, seeking to find a routine she could better tolerate. She was very committed to the therapy, so the problem with the capsules left her somewhat frustrated. I reassured her that we would find an acceptable dose that she could tolerate.

I suspected that her swallowing difficulties may have been related to her lupus. Though she had been diagnosed—with some debate among her previous treating doctors—with cutaneous and not systemic lupus, autoimmune diseases in my experience can affect the esophagus.

With each new patient, I design our dietary and supplement protocols based on my long experience with many patients and many different forms of cancer. Most of the time, though not always, patients tolerate the initial prescription well with only minor difficulty, but an occasional patient—such as HC—experiences far more persistent problems. In HC's case, she found the pancreas capsules I prescribe away from meals as the main anticancer supplement difficult to swallow, and provoking a burning sensation in her esophagus. In such situations, I lower the daily dose of pancreas until patients can swallow the supplement without excessive discomfort. I have learned over the years that patients can still respond to a lower than ideal dose, but progress tends to be slower than for those who ingest the full recommended amount of capsules.

During the third week of May 2007, Patient HC reported to me that her skin—which had appeared quite inflamed when I first examined her in April—had gotten worse. She also described persistent heartburn after taking the pancreas enzymes away from meals, but not after ingesting the supplements we prescribe with meals. Her energy and stamina were also down.

None of these symptoms to me was unexpected. I often find, as I have discussed elsewhere, that patients commonly report a flare-up of symptoms as the treatment kicks into gear, in a type of Herxheimer reaction. First, as the normal tissues begin repairing and rebuilding in response to the therapy, toxic waste such as stored pesticides, toxic metals, hydrocarbons, etc., are released into the bloodstream, ultimately to end up at the liver and kidney, before processing and excretion. In addition, as the proteolytic enzymes attack areas of cancer, significant amounts of debris from dying malignant cells circulate, adding to the burden of toxic waste in the bloodstream, awaiting sequestering and removal in both the liver and the kidney. The rapid and often significant release of such irritating substances into the systemic circulation can provoke a host of symptoms, often eczema in patients with no previous skin problems, but especially in those with a prior history of skin lesions, such as Patient HC. The skin, after all, among its other functions, is a major detoxification organ, with a large surface area, that assists the liver and kidneys in the excretion of noxious wastes.

In the first months on the therapy, patients routinely report malaise, at times a profound fatigue, along with muscle aches and pains, joint pains, headaches, skin eruptions—and intermittent swallowing difficulties. Such symptoms do frequently mean only that the therapy is doing what it is supposed to do, and the patient is reacting as expected.

I did make some further adjustments to her therapy, reducing supplements that might be irritating to her esophagus and stomach. I also switched her to the lamb pancreas product, which I use as a milder alternative for those who have problems tolerating our preferred pork supplement. Though I think the pork has a better effect, lamb does work, if not as strongly.

During May 2007, Patient HC continued contacting me on a regular basis by fax, which she found the most efficient way to communicate with my office. During the first week of June, Patient HC reported her current situation, which she found quite dismal: "I am absolutely miserable today. My skin on my face and neck and hands hurt, and is painfull [sic]. It is swollen, inflamed, irritated, scally [sic], itchy. My eyes are red."

In her note, she requested to come by the office briefly so I could examine her skin and assess the situation. When I saw her that day, indeed her skin seemed more reddened and scaly, but I explained that in my experience initially on the program such worsening is to be expected. If I were correct, and this was a normal reaction to the treatment, the symptoms should at some point peak and then begin improving.

By mid-June 2007, the skin had calmed somewhat, but she experienced again a worsening of her esophagitis reaction to the pancreatic enzymes even though she had switched to lamb and I had reduced the total daily dose. After discussing the situation at length with her, I suggested she proceed on an every-other-day routine with the supplements, until she had completed a total of fifteen days on the pills, then break for five days. I recommend that all my patients, whatever their underlying problem or illness, periodically cycle off all supplements for five days, a course Dr. Kelley found worked best some forty-five years ago as he refined his therapy. Usually, I suggest patients take the supplements for anywhere from twenty to thirty days—the exact number of days depending on the disease extent—then break for five.

For those rare patients who report ongoing difficulties swallowing the supplements even after I have reduced the daily dose and changed to lamb, I have found resorting to an every-other-day approach can make a huge difference. So Patient HC proceeded accordingly, and during the fourth week of June 2007 she reported, in a fax sent while she was on her five-day break of supplements,

OVERALL I FELL [sic] GOOD AND IT IS GREAT TO BE OFF THE PILLS....

I trust in your knowledge and advice. Much thanks for your time.

Thereafter, she continued with the therapy with far less difficulty.

When I saw her for a routinely scheduled office visit during the third week of August 2007, she was tolerating the every-other-day supplement regimen, though by day ten she would feel washed out, then better on the five-day break. Her skin, both by her statements and my exam, had improved considerably, and overall she said, other than the malaise at the end of her pill cycle, she felt "great" with excellent energy. She was working long hours at her artwork with superb stamina and concentration.

During the second week of September 2007, after several weeks of calm, her skin had flared up once again. When we discussed the situation, she informed me she had decided to consult with the dermatologist who had previously monitored her skin condition. I thought her suggestion a good idea, to get a more conventional opinion about her situation. She wondered if she might not have psoriasis rather than cutaneous lupus. When I questioned her, it turned out she had been consuming large amounts of nightshade vegetables, which include eggplant, peppers, potatoes, and tomatoes. These vegetables, it is well known, contain a substance, solanine, that in sensitive people can provoke arthritis and psoriasis. I suggested she exclude all these vegetables from her diet.

During the second week of September 2007, Patient HC consulted with her dermatologist, who diagnosed not psoriasis or cutaneous lupus but atopic dermatitis, to me a vague technical term for skin irritation. He did perform a biopsy, and he agreed with me that she should stop all nightshades, including tomatoes—which she admitted to me in another faxed note she had been eating on a "RAMPAGE OF RAW ORGANIC IN SEASON TOMATOES, LIKE 5 A DAY." The physician also suggested she exclude citrus, a frequent culprit in atopic dermatitis, and minimize hand washing to prevent removal of the oils that protect the skin.

In subsequent months, Patient HC's skin eruptions would wax and wane, a pattern I often see during the first months of therapy in those patients with a history of skin difficulties.

In late September 2007, Patient HC first complained of pain and discomfort in her neck, worse when she was on her supplements. Then, during the second week of October 2007, when she faxed me yet again complaining that her skin had worsened, I suggested she come by the office so I could take a look. When I saw her the day of the fax, she explained she had been using a natural-type cream with minimal effect. And on exam, her skin was diffusely inflamed red, scaly, and excoriated from scratching. The eczema involved most of her body—all four extremities, her trunk, and her face. I suggested a homeopathic remedy and recommended she try Florasone cream, an herbal "cortisone" anti-inflammatory.

Meanwhile, the dermatologist had informed Patient HC that the skin biopsy came back showing nothing of diagnostic significance. It wasn't until late October 2007 that I finally received a copy of the formal pathology report, which described "ECZEMATOUS AND DELAYED DERMAL HYPERSENSITIVITY REACTION" consistent with a "TYPE IV [delayed] IMMUNE RESPONSE TO A CIRCULATING AND/OR DISTANT CUTANEOUS ANTIGEN." Essentially, she was reacting to something, but what that something might have been we didn't know.

During a phone conversation the first week of November 2007, HC reported that basically, after all her ups and downs, she was feeling "really well" and her skin had actually improved somewhat with our various interventions. At times, the eczema would regress for a few days, before flaring up. The fact that she reported significant improvement led me to believe that we might be dealing with the usual symptomatic worsening patients experience during the initial months on the therapy.

Some weeks later, she sent me a fax to report on her progress. Along with her note, she sent me a notice announcing various showings of her work in New York, Paris, and other locations in the US and Europe. She was working hard at her career and receiving considerable international recognition.

Patient HC returned to my office during the third week of November 2007, having completed some seven months on her nutritional program. She generally felt well, described her energy as "excellent," and said her skin had improved considerably; in fact, it appeared nearly normal. She was quite pleased about her work, which recently had been featured in a documentary.

I was, however, concerned about her compliance. She had been sticking to the diet "religiously," and she followed the various detoxification routines as prescribed. But she had been regularly missing doses of pancreatic enzymes, the main anticancer supplement in our program. She explained she had been feeling quite well, felt more confident about her progress, and had been traveling regularly for work-related trips. It had become easy, and habitual, to miss doses of the pancreas product. From what she told me, I suspected she was missing perhaps 50 percent of her enzyme doses, and she was already following a modified regimen. I emphasized that because I had already reduced her enzyme intake, she had to be strictly compliant.

On exam, as before, I detected the enlarged lymph node mass in the supraclavicular area of the right neck, which I thought was slightly larger than during her previous visit with me. We discussed options such as surgery, which she immediately rejected, promising instead to be more compliant with the treatment I had prescribed.

She did report ongoing neck and shoulder pain, which I now suspected might be the result of a significant misalignment of her spine requiring some form of structural therapy. For this, I recommended she consult with my friend Dr. Roy Sweat in Atlanta, Georgia, the developer of the atlas orthogonal approach to chiropractic, the system of chiropractic I most wholeheartedly recommend. Dr. Sweat, now eighty-six years old, believes that the atlas bone, the first bone of the cervical spine, functions as the key to spinal and nervous system integrity, and he adjusts only the atlas.

The seven cervical spine bones are essentially circular discs, through which the upper spine passes. In this regard, the atlas bone, the highest of the cervical bones, does sit in a most pivotal position, right underneath the skull. It was named after the Greek god who held the Earth up on his shoulders—as the atlas bone holds up the skull.

Normally, the atlas—and the other cervical vertebral bodies—should be parallel to the ground and perpendicular to the spine. Any misalignment of the atlas out of this neutral position creates a number of problems. First, the atlas nestles in the lower portion of the brain stem, from which the spinal cord forms. This brain area directly regulates essential physiologic functions such as respiration and cardiovascular and endocrine activity. Pressure here can precipitate serious symptoms, ranging from dizziness, fatigue, and headaches, to tachycardia and endocrine disruption.

In addition, two critically important arteries, the vertebral arteries, course through holes on either side of the cervical spine bones. These arteries bring oxygen and nutrients to the back third of the brain, including the upper portions of the brain stem. Should the atlas move out of its ideal position, these arteries can be torqued, reducing blood supply and in turn the supply of oxygen and nutrients to the back of the brain.

The atlas can be pushed out of its ideal position for any number of reasons, such as whiplash or other types of head trauma. Once out of place, the atlas does not spontaneously return back to its neutral position.

Before treating any patient, Dr. Sweat performs an extensive neurologic and trauma history. Then, relying on specialized x-rays and mathematical equations he has developed over the years, he measures the precise angles of misalignment of the atlas.

In terms of his treatment, he doesn't use his hands, as do most chiropractors, but a very sophisticated instrument he developed working in conjunction with mathematicians and engineers. The instrument has a small stylus that he can move into the proper position based on his calculations from the x-rays. He then presses a button, which automatically sends the appropriate pressure-force through the stylus to the atlas. Because the technique is so mathematically precise, the pressure applied is barely noticeable by the patient, but the effect can be extraordinary. It is a very accurate, effective, and completely nontraumatic method of adjusting.

With the atlas in place, the abnormal pressure on the brainstem resolves and the vertebral arteries open up. In addition, as I have myself have observed in posttreatment x-rays, within minutes the rest of the cervical bones pop back into their normal position, along with the rest of the thoracic and lumbar vertebrae. This simple adjustment often results in long-lasting benefit without the need for frequent and repeated treatments. And usually the benefits can be felt immediately.

When I was in research, working under Dr. Good in the mid-1980s, I had the time to spend two rather extraordinary weeks in Dr. Sweat's office watching him work. I remember a patient I met in his office, whom Dr. Sweat had been treating for some time after he experienced terrible whiplash in a motor vehicle accident that totaled his pickup truck. This trauma left him with severe and chronic neurological dysfunction, including persistent headaches, and in addition, he had developed diffuse psoriasis. After Dr. Sweat had treated him a number of times, the patient reported to me that all his neurological symptoms had rather quickly improved, and to his surprise, his psoriasis had also completely resolved.

By the time I met the man, he was in very good shape, coming back to the office for a routine follow-up visit. Photographs of his skin taken by Dr. Sweat when the patient first began treatment showed extensive and obvious inflamed psoriasis. When I examined the patient the day we met, his skin was perfectly clear, as it apparently had been for many months. Dr. Sweat remarked to me that over the years he had witnessed many patients show such improvement in seemingly non-neurological problems after the atlas adjustment. To me, this made sense; after all, the nervous system ultimately controls all physiological processes, and when the cervical spine was out of its preferred alignment, the nerves could not function efficiently.

In mid-November 2007, at my recommendation Patient HC traveled to Atlanta to consult with Dr. Sweat, who found her cervical spine to be grossly misaligned, perhaps the reason for ongoing severe shoulder and neck pain. After the adjustment, she went back to her hotel and slept restfully for several hours. When she awoke, her chronic neck and back symptoms had improved significantly. Later, after she returned to New York, she spoke enthusiastically about her experience and about Dr. Sweat, whom she thought was indeed a "genius."

When I next saw Patient HC, in mid-March 2008, she had completed some eleven months on her nutritional program. She generally felt well and continued working hard at her art, and her skin remained considerably improved. As before, I was concerned about her compliance, though she seemed more diligent than during her last visit, in November 2007. But she still followed a very reduced program of pancreatic enzymes, some six capsules six times in twenty-four hours, far fewer than the sixteen we recommend for each dose, six doses daily for patients with solid tumors.

On exam, her skin, particularly her face, appeared clear except for some scaly areas on her extremities.

Thereafter, she did increase her dose of pancreatic enzymes, which she tolerated well, though her eczema seemed to flare up somewhat. By the last week of April 2008, the situation had worsened to the point that she made another appointment with her dermatologist, a specialist in autoimmune-type conditions. When she met with him during the first week of May 2008, he diagnosed only eczema, not cutaneous lupus, for which he prescribed a steroid cream.

When Patient HC returned to my office for a visit during the fourth week of June 2008, her skin had suddenly improved substantially. In fact, it appeared to me completely clear, with no inflammation or redness, and no scaling. She herself described her skin as "perfect" and informed me that the itching, which at times in the past had kept her from sleeping, had completely resolved. With a smile, she reminded me that when she first started her therapy I had advised her that often it takes a year for skin problems to resolve, after periods of waxing and waning, worsening and improvement. She was, then, right on schedule.

In addition, she reported excellent energy, stamina, and concentration and said that at this point she really had no problems. She also appeared to have resolved the swallowing difficulty with the supplements, by opening the capsules and drinking the powder down with water—or for the mealtime pills, with juice—a laborious solution, but one that seemed to be working. Though she was still on a reduced dose of pancreatic enzymes, she could get the powder down every day without the need to alternate with a day off.

During the subsequent months, she didn't fax me as she had been doing, so I assumed she must be doing well. During a routine office visit in the second week of October 2008, she seemed to be doing well, and her skin remained clear. She had been able to stick to the supplement program more determinedly, as long as she opened the capsules and took them down with liquid. She remained on a reduced dose of pancreatic enzymes—the equivalent of nine capsules, six times in twenty-four hours, away from meals. Though this was still fewer than the ideal of fourteen to sixteen pancreas capsules each dose I normally prescribe for my patients with solid tumors, she herself seemed willing to work toward a higher intake.

In mid-April 2009, approximately two weeks before a scheduled visit with me, Patient HC had consulted with an otolaryngologist (ear, nose, and throat) specialist after developing some discharge from her right ear, which turned out to be related only to excessive buildup of earwax. This physician found no evidence of recurrent disease inside the mouth.

In late April 2009, after two years on her program, Patient HC returned for her office visit and reported that she was able to get down each day the equivalent of ten pancreas capsules with each dose, six times daily. She had been alternating the mealtime pills, which she found more difficult to swallow, but the system seemed to be working. Her right neck adenopathy seemed perhaps slightly bigger, but certainly not significantly, and I detected no other enlarged lymph nodes on the left side of her neck.

During her next visit, in July 2009, she was doing well and working ten to twelve hours a day at her artwork. Her skin appeared clear, the lymph nodes on the right side of the neck were unchanged, and she was excited about an upcoming trip to France, where her work was to be showcased at a major exhibit. Because she maintained an apartment in France, she would be able to continue her nutritional program without difficulty, and she hoped for a very successful, productive trip.

I next saw Patient HC during the third week in October 2009, after she had returned from her sojourn abroad. The trip had been a success, and as promised, she had stayed on her nutritional program without missing a beat. She informed me she would shortly be returning to France, again to present her work, so evidently her art was going very well indeed.

Her skin remained very clear, and her biggest complaint related to a recurring problem with mouth sores while she was away in Europe. I suggested she avoid, at least for the time being, all nuts, which have significant amounts of the amino acid arginine, which, as valuable as it can be, can provoke outbreaks of the herpes virus, the culprit with most mouth sores. I also prescribed monolaurin, a coconut oil derivative containing lauric acid, which in my experience with patients effectively kills all forms of the herpes virus. With these adjustments, the problem seemed to improve. On exam, the right neck adenopathy appeared unchanged.

I didn't hear from Patient HC again until the fourth week of November 2009, when she called my office from France, sounding very upset. She had planned to leave for New York the day she called but had taken a very bad fall, fracturing her right shoulder (humeral head) in the process. The French doctors caring for her felt she didn't require surgery but had put her in a cast, which left her pretty much immobile and unable to travel. Unfortunately, she would be forced to stay in France another two months, until early in 2010, to allow for full recuperation under the supervision of her doctors there. I gave her some tips on how to manage the program with her arm in a cast.

Patient HC next contacted me by fax in late January 2010, after she had finally returned from Europe. She was out of the cast, but by the tone of her note I could tell the ordeal of the fall and the long recuperation had taken a toll on her. When we spoke by phone, she told me she had developed terrible diarrhea while in France, to the point that she had to cut back on the supplements. Though she had improved somewhat, she admitted she wasn't feeling well, and that the right adenopathy seemed to have worsened in recent weeks. I explained that with all the stress in her life since the fall, and the recent compliance issues, I wasn't at all surprised by what she was telling me. Fortunately, the diarrhea had resolved, to the point that she was back on her regimen.

When I saw her in my office during the first week of February 2010, she explained she had been in a cast for a month and had actually been off the coffee enemas during that time. And she admitted that with the cast and the diarrhea, during that period she might have ingested 50 percent of her supplements—and she was already on a reduced regimen. She really had been feeling "awful," and her energy had been terrible. But she was now on the mend, and dutiful patient that she was (and is), now back in New York she was again following her nutritional protocol as prescribed.

She also was continuing with the physical therapy program that had been started while she was in France. The treatment seemed to be helping. Despite the enormous stress of the past few months, her energy and stamina had come back to the point that she was working twelve to fourteen hours a day.

I was amazed at how clear her skin looked, and the adenopathy, despite her concerns, seemed to be about the same, with the main node and the smaller satellite nodes around it.

When we next met, in mid-May 2010, she seemed completely back to normal, her shoulder had healed nicely, and she was complying well. On exam, her skin was clear, but the right neck adenopathy seemed slightly bigger, though only minimally, than during her previous visit with me. When we discussed the issue, she made it clear to me that she wanted no standard testing done at that point, no CT or PET scans. She also informed me that she was returning to Europe for a three-month stay, to attend exhibitions of her work at various galleries and partake in other functions in honor of her work.

After a successful trip to Europe—this time with no injuries—she returned to my office in late August 2010, three years and three months from our first visit together. I was concerned because her three months in France had been a whirlwind of gallery exhibitions, special dinners, and other events, and not surprisingly her compliance with the diet had been less than perfect. She had remained on her adjusted supplement regimen, taking her six doses of enzymes every day for fifteen days before cycling off for five days. The mealtime pills that I normally prescribe as three times a day, every day during the supplement cycle, she was getting down every other day, and only once a day. She felt she simply couldn't tolerate any more of these particular supplements. I encouraged her to at least try to stay on the pills for a full twenty days before breaking off.

Generally, she had been feeling fine, with excellent energy, and her skin remained clear. In mid-July, while in France, she had decided to undergo a neck CT scan. Patient HC handed me a copy of the report, in French, which she translated. Apparently, the scan showed the multiple lymph nodes evident in the right supraclavicular area, the largest measuring 1.7 cm, actually less than I had estimated from my own previous measurements. Patient HC had discussed the scan results with the radiologist, who thought most of the nodes by appearance were likely reactive, not cancerous.

When we next met, during the third week of December 2010, she reported that she had been sticking to the supplements for twenty days as I had suggested but felt quite fatigued by the end of the cycle. Then, on the five-day break, her energy quickly improved. Overall, she felt fine.

We talked about the right conglomerate of lymph nodes, which visually, and on exam, seemed about the same, a mass of nodes totaling 3 to 4 cm in widest diameter. I did discuss further scanning, but she was reluctant because of the radiation exposure. I also brought up surgery, to clean out the nodes, but she was adamantly against any aggressive intervention. She felt surgery would be debilitating without much benefit. And at that point, she had completed more than three and a half years on her nutritional program, generally felt "great" to use her term, and wanted only to continue on her therapy with me.

During the second week of January 2011, she sent a very troubling fax. Several days earlier, right after New Year's, she had developed a blister on her forehead, cracking sores in the corner of her mouth, and pain on swallowing. A couple of days later, she noticed extensive redness in her left eye, associated with blurred vision and photophobia. In our conversation, she herself brought up shingles and the dangers of ocular viral infection—my own concern as well, based on what she was telling me. I explained that with visual problems such as this, as much as she wanted to avoid conventional medicine, one can't procrastinate, and I insisted she go to the emergency room at New York Hospital–Cornell.

When we spoke again two days later, it turned out Patient HC had followed my instructions, had gone to the ER after our phone conversation, and had been seen quickly by an ophthalmologist. She had been diagnosed with uveitis, a potentially serious inflammatory condition of the eye at times associated with autoimmune disease such as Reiter syndrome. The possibility of a secondary herpes zoster (shingles) infection was also thought likely. The physician had started her on steroid drops that evening but no antivirals because her first symptoms went back a week or so, and these medications are effective only if begun during the first three days after obvious infection. In any event, Patient HC informed me that the steroids had already reduced the inflammation some 50 percent. She had been back to the ophthalmologist the day after her emergency room visit. He was pleased with her progress and would be following her closely.

Follow-up blood studies confirmed a moderately elevated C-reactive protein and erythrocyte sedimentation rate, both markers of inflammation. The HLA-B27 genetic test for autoimmunity, however, was negative, as were other autoimmune markers with one exception. When seen at Cornell during the third week of January 2011, she had improved considerably, and in our subsequent conversations, she expressed her enormous gratitude that I had insisted she go to the emergency room when she first informed me of her symptoms. She also said the care at Cornell had been "superb."

When I saw her next, in late March 2011—after she had completed nearly four years on her nutritional regimen—she generally seemed compliant with her adjusted protocol and was doing well. Her left eye was about "90 percent" back to normal, though not completely. Ultimately, her ophthalmologist at Cornell believed the uveitis had developed as a result of herpes zoster. He would for now continue to follow her regularly.

She continued hard at work with her art, putting in long hours each day in her studio. Her energy was excellent, and stamina excellent—and her skin remained virtually completely clear.

In early May 2011, Patient HC faxed me a note reporting on her latest visit to the ophthalmologist. Apparently, her doctor was concerned because the uveitis, though substantially improved, had not completely resolved. The doctor was referring HC to a uveitis specialist, whom HC met in mid-May 2011. This ophthalmologist, based on HC's history, was concerned about lupus as the underlying problem setting off the uveitis. So, as a next step, she was being referred to an ophthalmologist who specializes in autoimmune-related eye problems.

I wouldn't hear from Patient HC again until the last week of June 2011, when she returned to my office for a regularly scheduled visit. At the time, she told me a most interesting story. She had visited with a physician in Atlanta who performs a sophisticated energy analysis, using an instrument that measures acupuncture meridians. He had pinpointed the cause of her uveitis as decay under a crown on the left side of her mouth. Upon returning to New York, she had consulted with her dentist, who agreed to take off the allegedly problematic tooth, and he did find decay under the crown. The tooth had been cleaned up and a new restoration put in place. To HC's great satisfaction, the uveitis had completely resolved.

As instructed, she had also consulted with the ophthalmologist who specializes in autoimmune disease. He believed indeed that lupus was the underlying source of the problem, but with the decay issue corrected, all her symptoms had resolved. And her sedimentation rate, which I ordered, came back perfectly normal.

Patient HC also remained compliant with her nutritional program, and in the months that followed, she continued doing well until mid-January 2012, when she called my office with several serious complaints. She had developed an upper respiratory infection, associated with fevers, chills, and a productive cough. In addition, she described her intestines as "stuck," meaning she felt terribly constipated, along with severe abdominal pain. She hadn't moved her bowels for several days and could barely eat. The intestinal problems began after she had gone with friends to a local restaurant and eaten shellfish, and she wondered if she might have food poisoning, a reasonable possibility based on her symptoms. I told her to start ingesting bentonite clay liquid, a quarter cup three times daily, a remarkably useful treatment for any type of gastroenteritis or food poisoning.

When she seemed to worsen the day after the phone call, I asked her to come to the office so I could examine her. Her respiratory symptoms, including her cough, seemed to be improving, but she reported worsening nausea, chronic abdominal pain, and anorexia. She hadn't moved her bowels for four days, and she felt so weak she had even stopped the coffee enemas. I was concerned about dehydration, so after examining her, I suggested she go right from my office to the emergency room at Cornell New York Hospital.

She complied with my instructions, and in the emergency room an abdominal x-ray showed no intestinal obstruction, but her serum sodium level came back quite low at 122 (normal 135–146). For this, she was treated with normal saline intravenously and oral fluid restriction. Aware of her cancer history, and with her recent respiratory difficulty, the emergency room doctors ordered a chest x-ray, which showed no pneumonia but "a round mass measuring approximately 3.7 × 3.7 cm … in the right posterior lower lobe [lung]." After being told of the findings, Patient HC was informed she needed a CT scan for further elaboration of the mass. This study revealed "a lobulated 4.2 cm × 3.9 cm size altered lobulated mass in the posterior basal segment of the right lower lobe corresponding to the abnormality seen on the recent chest radiograph. … There are at least two 2 mm nodules in the left upper lobe. … A 6 mm nodule is noted in the superior segment of the right lower lobe."

We spoke several times while she was in the emergency room. I reminded her that the PET scan from early December 2006, some four months before she started treatment with me, had demonstrated a right lower lung mass 1.5 × 1.0 cm in diameter, so the lesion on the chest x-ray, though bigger, wasn't new. I also expressed my belief that at this point, we needed to get more aggressive with her supplement program, particularly her pancreatic enzymes.

With the test results in, her physicians ultimately attributed her low sodium to cancer-related SIADH, the inappropriate secretion of antidiuretic hormone (ADH). This hormone, normally secreted by the posterior pituitary, helps regulate salt and fluid balance in the body and is often secreted excessively by certain cancers, including lung cancer. In excess, it can lead to water retention and dilution of the blood sodium. This can be a serious situation, because if the sodium level drops too low and too fast, fluid then can leak out of the blood vessels into the brain, potentially leading to seizures. The usual treatment, intravenous sodium chloride and oral water restriction, usually reverses the dilutive effect of SIADH on the blood.

Though her physicians argued strongly that she needed to be admitted for further evaluation and biopsy of her neck or lung, after her sodium improved Patient HC checked herself out of the emergency room without having been formally admitted.

When we spoke the following day, I had already received the records from the Cornell emergency room. We discussed the findings in detail and the wish of the Cornell physicians to biopsy at least the neck mass, if not the larger right lung lesion as well. As we talked about the situation, she made it clear to me, as she had before, that she had no intention of proceeding with a biopsy, because she would not ever agree to standard treatments and wished only to continue on my therapy. As Patient HC reminded me, she had been eating organically for some forty years and believed in alternative approaches, specifically my treatment.

We agreed that although the reduced supplement regimen I had designed had held her cancer in reasonable check for nearly five years, clearly we needed to get more aggressive. I told her to push the enzymes to sixteen capsules each dose, and to try to stay on the pills for twenty-five days before cycling off for five days. She was quite willing to try her best to comply with my suggestions.

I was happy to learn that her bronchitis-type symptoms had resolved, as had her stomach discomfort. She was feeling much better and seemed as determined as ever to remain on her nutritional program. From our conversation, I suspected that Patient HC had developed low sodium because she hadn't eaten or taken in much fluid for the four days prior to her trip to the ER, not necessarily because of overproduction of ADH by her cancer cells.

However, over the following days she experienced worsening weakness and fatigue, which concerned her and me greatly. When her symptoms failed to improve, I suggested she return to the Cornell ER. There, when her sodium came back again low in the ER at 124, she agreed to be admitted to New York Hospital, where she was assigned a hospital physician in charge of the case. With fluid restriction and IV normal saline, her sodium quickly improved.

A PET/CT scan performed several days after her admission revealed the following:

> The level 4 lymph node on the right just deep to the sternocleidomastoid muscle measures 1.4 × 1.0, max SUV 3.0 [borderline positive]. A rounded right supraclavicular lymph node measures 2 cm, max UV 8.5 [highly positive]....

> Patient's known right lower lobe mass is FDG avid with a max SUV of 9.0. Maximum dimensions are on the order of 4 cm.... Three additional small nodules described on

comparison chest CT are not well identified on this partial exploratory study [meaning the CT scan] but no additional FDG avid foci are seen to correlate with these regions.

After discussing the findings with the staff physicians and with me, Patient HC agreed to a biopsy of the right supraclavicular lymph node mass. This was done, and after six days, before the final pathology results came back, when her sodium remained stabilized and her symptoms resolved, she was discharged from the hospital. During this period in the hospital, to her credit, she remained as compliant with her supplement regimen as possible.

We spoke several times in the days after her discharge. She had resumed her full regimen, including the higher dose of pancreatic enzymes, which she seemed to tolerate, though she continued on fluid restriction. I instructed her to salt her food heavily as well. She was somewhat depressed about recent events but firm in her determination to avoid standard treatment, which she understood from the Cornell team, based on the findings of stage IV disease, would not be curative. I had nothing but admiration for her courage and the strength of her convictions.

In the hospital records that Cornell faxed to me during that time, I noted that the physician in charge of the case had indicated that the patient had a greater than 50 percent chance of dying within the next year.

A repeat sodium in early February 2012 came back completely normal at 138, so that crisis seemed finally to be resolving. And when her ADH levels drawn at Cornell came back completely normal, cancer-related SIADH apparently was not the cause of her low sodium. I suspected the problem had resulted, as I initially thought, from her food poisoning, unintended fast, and dehydration, and, as it turned out, it would not be a problem again.

Patient HC contacted me during that time to inform me that she had heard from her doctor at Cornell, who had reported the preliminary results of the neck biopsy as "adenocarcinoma," possibly of ovarian or colon origin, but clearly not originating from a lung primary. However, the final pathology report sent to me several days later indicated that the primary was neither ovarian nor gastrointestinal: "This immunohistochemical pattern is not specific, however, a lung, GYN [gynecologic] renal or GI primary is not favored."

When we discussed the results, she again made it clear that she would continue only with my therapy and was grateful for the generally excellent quality of life she had enjoyed during the five years on my treatment plan. She also informed me that she continued to tolerate the higher dose of enzymes and the longer pill cycle without difficulty.

Patient HC returned to my office after all the results were back in early February 2012. She brought a close friend into the session, who obviously strongly supported HC's choice of our alternative therapy. As Dr. Gerson wrote some fifty-plus years ago, supportive family and friends can often make the difference between treatment success or treatment failure.

Patient HC looked well despite her recent difficulties. During her crisis and hospitalization, her skin had flared up somewhat but already had improved significantly by the time I saw her. She described no residual symptoms from either her earlier upper respiratory infection or the gastroenteritis. At one point, when we discussed the results of the recent tests, she got somewhat teary eyed and asked if I thought she was going to die soon. I expressed my true feelings, that she had already done remarkably well with advanced disease over the years, and though she clearly had significant disease remaining, if she could ramp up her enzyme dose I believed she would continue on as before, productive and enjoying her life.

Thereafter, she continued on her therapy and continued doing well. When she next returned to my office, in mid-April 2012, she was feeling well and working long hours, up to ten hours a day, at her art, which seemed to be going quite well. One of her pieces had been selected to be part of the permanent collection of a museum honoring the 9/11 tragedy. Her face was clear, she was long off fluid restriction, and her sodium levels had remained well within the normal range. Her lymph node mass in the right supraclavicular area remained unchanged.

Since then, I have continued seeing HC every three months, and she continues in good health. We have not repeated any radiographic studies; first of all, she is completely asymptomatic and is well aware of the risk of radiation exposure from CT and PET scans, which she would prefer to avoid. She feels fine and says she would not change her therapy, whatever a test might show. And her life is going well, as her work continues to receive wide international acclaim.

Patient HC has completed five and a half years on her nutritional program, remains in excellent health now in her late seventies, and continues fully compliant with her nutritional program. Though clearly residual cancer remains in her right neck, the nodes there are stable on exam.

I suspect that, at the time of diagnosis, Patient HC's disease was already at stage IV. The eleven positive lymph nodes at the time of the initial surgery in January 2007 indicated considerable local spread, and the original PET scan from December 2006 showed evidence of a right lower lung mass that would later be documented as consistent with malignant disease in the PET scan from January 2012.

Though her disease hasn't completely regressed, it clearly seems under control. Though frequently tumors do regress, in some patients they simply remain stable for many, many years. And as long as they do not continue to spread, I find patients can lead normal, productive, high-quality lives.

I suspect in this case that Patient HC's intolerance of a full dose of supplements, particularly the pancreatic product, impeded her progress to some degree. She certainly seems to be doing better, now that she follows a more intensive protocol. But nonetheless, even on the reduced dose of enzymes I had prescribed, for many years her disease remained unchanged. And along the way, her serious skin problem, whatever it may ultimately have been, has largely resolved, except for occasional flare-ups that seemed more related to stress.

Because salivary cancer is relatively rare, there are few studies evaluating the effectiveness of standard treatment for those with metastatic disease, such as HC had. One randomized trial reported in the website UpToDate compared the drugs vinorelbine administered along with cisplatin versus vinorelbine alone in patients with metastatic disease. For those receiving the two-drug protocol, survival beyond one year increased from 5 percent to 38 percent—so clearly, once metastatic, even with those receiving chemotherapy, salivary cancer is quite deadly. And Patient HC had been diagnosed originally, and again more recently, with the more aggressive adenocarcinoma form. With this information in mind, her long-term survival and generally excellent good quality of life are impressive.

I find patients like HC an encouragement to me as a physician. Her courage and determination in the face of terrible illness serve as an example to me, and for all of us. She has never for a second wavered in her choice of treatment, works with me to find solutions for whatever problem she might face, and, through thick and thin, continues bringing great art into the world.

*IMPORTANT EDITOR'S NOTE:
Dr. Gonzalez died before updating this case report. According to the office medical files, patient HC died in June 2014.

THYROID CANCER

Thyroid cancer affects approximately 9 in 100,000, or some 27,000 Americans yearly,[1] afflicting approximately twice as many women as men. Most thyroid cancers develop in the follicular cells that produce thyroid hormone, but some form in the C cells of the thyroid, responsible for synthesizing calcitonin, a peptide that drives calcium into bone.

Scientists have linked thyroid cancer to radiation exposure, both from medical purposes and from environmental contamination such as occurred in World War II after the nuclear bomb explosions in Japan at Nagasaki and Hiroshima, and in Chernobyl after the nuclear power plant explosion in 1986. In such cases, genetic aberrations induced by ionizing radiation seem to be the cause.

Right up through the 1950s, physicians in the US—mistakenly assuming radiation to be safe—recommended radiation, in addition to cancer treatment, for any number of nonserious conditions ranging from acne, to an enlarged thymus, to enlarged or infected tonsils and adenoids. Such cavalier misuse of radiation fell into disfavor as researchers discovered, to their alarm, its carcinogenicity, but not before many millions of children, adolescents, and adults had been exposed to medical radiation for trivial indications. Many of those treated were children, whom we now realize are more susceptible to the damaging effects of radiation than adults are, and who now as they age continue to develop any of the various forms of thyroid cancer.

Iodine deficiency has also been associated with thyroid cancer, particularly the follicular variant. In areas of iodine-insufficient soils, repletion of iodine, in the form of iodized salt or as supplement iodine, has led to reduction in thyroid cancer incidence.

Pathologists divide thyroid cancer into four basic types: papillary, follicular, anaplastic, and medullary. The first three develop from the follicular, thyroid-hormone-producing cells of the gland.

Papillary, the most common form, tends to be very indolent, with the great majority of patients diagnosed at an early stage, when surgery is curative. Most patients presenting with this type live normal life spans. Follicular thyroid cancer, prevalent in iodine-deficient areas of the world, has a poorer prognosis than papillary carcinoma, though most patients are nonetheless diagnosed early and cured of their disease. Patients diagnosed with the Hürthle cell variant of follicular carcinoma, however, have overall a much poorer outcome. The ten-year survival for non-Hürthle cell follicular carcinoma has been reported as 75 percent; that of patients diagnosed with the Hürthle cell variant runs only 41 percent.

---

1 Longo et al., *Harrison's Principles*, 18th ed., 2934.

Anaplastic thyroid carcinoma typically follows a much more aggressive course than either papillary or follicular carcinoma, with most patients dying within six months of diagnosis regardless of treatment used.[2] Medullary carcinoma of the thyroid, arising in the calcitonin-secreting cells of the thyroid, comprises only 5 percent of all thyroid cancers.[3] This variant, which tends to be aggressive, often occurs in familial clusters along with other endocrine tumors of the pituitary and pancreas.

Located in the anterior neck area, the thyroid gland is easily accessible on physical exam, so consequently most often the disease is discovered early and palpated as a distinctive hard nodule or mass. For those diagnosed with either papillary or follicular carcinoma of the thyroid, surgery remains the mainstay of treatment, allowing for cure in the majority of patients. In cases in which not all thyroid tissues can be removed due to technical considerations, or if the disease has spread to local lymph nodes or beyond, radioactive iodine remains a mainstay of treatment. Thyroid cells, whether normal or cancerous, selectively tend to take up the iodine, leading to apoptosis or cell death. The papillary and follicular variants often remain responsive to thyroid stimulating hormone, a peptide released by the anterior pituitary that stimulates the synthesis and release of thyroid hormone. The use of supplemental thyroid hormone reduces this pituitary output, in turn keeping residual papillary or follicular cancer under control.

Anaplastic carcinoma of the thyroid does not respond to radioactive iodine, thyroid suppression, or chemotherapy. For patients diagnosed with medullary carcinoma, surgery for localized disease is the main treatment. Because this cancer does not develop from the thyroid-hormone-producing cells, it does not take up or concentrate iodine selectively, and so the treatment has no effect.

---

2   Ibid., 2938.
3   Ibid.

Case 1: Patient KL
A Minimum 27-Year Survivor

Patient KL is a sixty-eight-year-old man, an optometrist by profession and entrepreneur from the New York City area, with a history of the aggressive Hürthle cell variant of follicular carcinoma, now 26.5 years from his original diagnosis of locally metastatic disease.

Patient KL reports no family history of cancer. In terms of his own medical history, he had smoked cigarettes, approximately one pack a day for fifteen years, quitting in 1975. Importantly, at age five he underwent radiation treatment of a nodule in his right neck that failed to respond to a course of antibiotics. As an adult, he had a history of multiple benign thyroid nodules, several of which were removed. Otherwise, he experienced a torn meniscus in his knee, the result of a football injury in high school.

His cancer situation dates from mid-January 1990, when he first noted a "lump" in his throat. He consulted with his primary care physician, who detected an enlarged thyroid. A subsequent thyroid ultrasound revealed that both lobes of the thyroid were enlarged, each demonstrating "abnormal echo patterns, with several nodules present." In the "IMPRESSION" section of the report, the radiologist described the nodules: "IMPRESSION: ENLARGED THYROID, PARTICULARLY THE LEFT LOBE, WITH SOLID NODULES IN BOTH—THE NODULE ON THE LEFT MEASURES 4.5 C 2.8 CM."

Note that lesions larger than 4 cm carry a worse prognosis than smaller lesions do.

In any event, Patient KL was asymptomatic at the time. A chest x-ray was clear, and thyroid function tests were within the normal range. During the fourth week of January 1990, a fine needle aspiration of the left thyroid nodule, performed at a local New Jersey hospital, revealed only benign tissue.

At that point, Patient KL decided to seek a second opinion with a thyroid surgeon at Columbia Presbyterian Medical Center, Dr. Carl Feind, who felt the lesion as detected on ultrasound seemed suspicious for cancer regardless of the biopsy findings. After Dr. Feind suggested that both the left and right lobe nodules be removed, during the last week of February 1990, at Columbia, Patient KL underwent resection of most of his thyroid.

A frozen section biopsy revealed a "follicular lesion? Hürthle cell type, of thyroid." The final pathology report indicated not all the tumor had been removed, with disease extending to the surgical margins: "Focally the tumor is seen on the inked line of excision." In addition, the "DIAGNOSIS" section of the report further described extensive disease, involving one local lymph node: "Carcinoma, well differentiated, mixed papillary and follicular type, multifocal, of thyroid with metastasis to 1 cervical lymph node (partial thyroidectomy)."

Because of the extensive disease, the fact that not all tumor had been removed at surgery, and the presence of metastasis in the one examined lymph node, postoperatively Dr. Feind strongly recommended adjuvant treatment with radioactive iodine. Initially, the patient, thinking he had no other options, agreed to the plan, though with misgivings because of his wish to avoid exposure to more radiation; after all, his doctors had already told him that most likely the external beam radiation treatment he had received at age five had, decades later, precipitated his cancer situation. But, as KL would later tell me, Dr. Feind told him that without the therapy, his cancer would explode, so despite his reluctance the therapy was scheduled for April 1990.

Though I had been in practice less than three years at the time, the patient learned about my treatment through friends and became convinced that this was the way to go. He applied to become a patient and was accepted into the practice. During the last week of March 1990, KL, accompanied by his supportive wife, came to my office for his initial consultation. At the time we met, he had recovered nicely from surgery and reported generally feeling quite well. Because of his cancer situation, he had backed off considerably from his work as an optometrist, as well as from his business ventures. He said he wanted to concentrate on mastering my program and getting well. I thought this approach quite appropriate, considering his situation.

He explained, as we talked, that he planned to cancel his appointment for the radioactive iodine treatment. I was surprised that none of his other physicians prescribed thyroid medication, even though most of the gland had been removed. So in addition to his nutritional program, I recommended Armour Thyroid, a nonsynthetic form derived from the pig thyroid, at a moderately high dose to keep his TSH somewhat suppressed.

After KL wrote to his surgeon to cancel the planned radioactive iodine treatment, Dr. Feind, apparently concerned about KL's decision, sent him a note: "I received your letter regarding further treatment of your thyroid condition. I would be most interested in speaking with your current physician regarding the course of treatment he plans and to give him the needed details he may need regarding your past treatment. Please call the office and let my secretary know his name and address."

However, Patient KL, realizing Dr. Feind most likely would not be open to an alternative approach, simply did not respond.

Patient KL proved—and has proven all these years—to be a very vigilant, determined, and compliant patient with all aspects of his nutritional regimen. I next saw him in early July 1990 for a routine office visit, after he had completed three months on his treatment plan. He reported feeling "great," informing me that his energy and stamina had significantly improved since starting treatment with me. He denied any symptoms and had but a few minor questions regarding some details of his therapy.

Thereafter, I continued seeing Patient KL in my office every three months; he remained very compliant with his therapy and continued doing well. When I saw him in mid-April 1991, when he had completed a year on his treatment, he reported he had been in two significant car accidents within a six-week period but had recovered with no residual neurological problems.

At times during his office visits throughout 1991, Patient KL reported some business-related stress but generally seemed to be doing quite well physically. He remained a very determined, very compliant, and increasingly grateful patient, as time passed with no evidence of worsening cancer. Every six months, I ordered routine blood work including thyroid function tests, all of which came back within the normal range.

When KL returned to my office during the third week of April 1992, he had completed two years on therapy, and he reported that he felt, as he had said to me before, "great."

In October 1993, some two and a half years after Patient KL had begun treatment with me, routine blood chemistries showed a calcium level of 10.6, which at that time was still considered within the normal range (8.5–10.6), though borderline. However, this reading was still considerably higher than previous tests, which often came back in the mid-9 range. In retrospect, this was the first sign that perhaps something was amiss with one of KL's parathyroids.

We have four such glands located in the thyroid gland itself, with two in the right lobe and two in the left. These glands release parathyroid hormone, normally in times of dietary calcium shortage or vitamin D deficiency (normal calcium absorption from the gut requires adequate vitamin D). Often during thyroid surgery, all four parathyroids will be removed, with one of them then implanted into the arm. In KL's case, I couldn't be sure, based on the official pathology report, how many of the parathyroids had been left in the neck in the residual thyroid tissue.

In my experience, radiation exposure—as in KL's case—often predates primary hyperparathyroidism, in which one of the four glands becomes spontaneously overactive, releasing unneeded large amounts of the hormone. In this case, calcium levels, as the mineral is released from bone, begin to rise, often at first gradually and imperceptibly. Symptoms of hyperparathyroidism can be quite insidious, with patients initially experiencing only vague aches and pains, followed often by mood changes, particularly depression and fatigue. Fortunately, in cases of primary hyperparathyroidism, usually only one of the four glands becomes overactive, and nearly all of these remain benign. Surgery to remove the offending gland is simple and usually effective.

Because in those days a calcium of 10.6 was considered normal, I didn't think a referral to an endocrinologist, or back to his original Columbia surgeon, necessary. Plus, KL felt "great," as he kept telling me, even during his October 1992 office visit, with none of those symptoms usually associated with an overactive parathyroid. And repeat blood chemistries in mid-January 1993 showed the calcium level had dropped to a more acceptable 10.0.

In early April 1993, after KL had completed three years on his nutritional program, the calcium level bounced up again to 10.5 (normal 8.5–10.6), still technically within the normal range, but once again borderline.

When I saw KL in my office during the third week of April 1993, he reported feeling "stronger, better, and more energetic" with each passing month on his nutritional therapy. He used the term "wonderful" to describe his overall state of health and said he had no problems whatsoever. He looked well and remained compliant with all aspects of the treatment.

Blood work from late July 1993 came back fine, though the calcium remained right at the higher limit of normal at 10.6. When he returned to my office for a routine visit during the second week of August 1993, he had completed more than three years on therapy, seemed ideally compliant, and reported to me he felt as before "great." For the first time since he had been my patient, he was talking about resuming a full workload. He felt well, no longer feared cancer, and was, as he said, "anxious to get back to work."

By January 1994, as KL approached four years on treatment, his calcium level was well within the normal range at 9.9.

Over the following years, KL continued returning to my office for his regularly scheduled visits and continued doing well. His calcium tended to run in the low 10 range, at times borderline high, but in those days, again, not high enough to warrant concern for hyperparathyroidism.

At an office visit during the second week of February 1999, as he approached nine years on his nutritional regimen, KL reminded me that when he first had been diagnosed, his surgeon at Columbia had warned him that without radioactive iodine treatment, his cancer, because of the Hürthle cell pathology and lymph node metastasis, would "explode." At that time, KL expressed his enormous gratitude for the therapy, which had allowed him to avoid any toxic conventional approaches. As he told me, he couldn't be happier with his choice of an alternative therapy.

When I saw KL in my office during the last week of June 2000, we celebrated his ten-plus-year anniversary on his therapy with me. He as always remained compliant, said he felt "great," and along with his wife expressed his sincere gratitude for the therapy we offered. He said the treatment was to him "a gift that changed my life and probably saved my life."

Two weeks later, KL's primary care physician, whom he had been seeing periodically over the years, decided to order parathyroid hormone (PTH) blood levels after routine chemistry screening revealed an abnormally high calcium for the first time, at 11.3. Prior to that, for years KL's calcium had been holding within the normal range, in the low 10s. Nonetheless, the PTH levels from mid-July 2000 were well within the acceptable range at 47 (normal 10.0–65). This PTH level was surprising, because with a high blood calcium one would expect a high PTH. Dietary and supplemental calcium in my experience would not explain a high calcium level like this, and in any event KL's regimen included only very minimal amounts of the mineral. High vitamin D intake can lead to overabsorption of calcium and high blood levels, but I had recommended only very modest doses.

When KL and I talked about the recent high calcium, he informed me that his primary care physician had referred him to an endocrinologist to help sort out the somewhat perplexing findings. I agreed that we now needed the input of an expert. Subsequently, during the first week of August 2000, KL met with an endocrinologist in the Columbia system. After his appointment, KL sent me a note explaining what had transpired. Despite the normal PTH, the endocrinologist believed the high calcium probably represented "primary hyperparathy-roidism," that is, spontaneously overactivity of one of his remaining glands.

The physician, a woman, had explained to KL that in nearly all cases the overactive gland is a benign lesion, so he need not worry about a second cancer developing. Furthermore, she explained that surgery was the treatment of choice, in fact, the only treatment. To complete her evaluation, she had ordered bone density studies, because in primary hyperparathyroidism the excess hormone can leach enough calcium out of the bones to bring on osteoporosis. She had also ordered a twenty-four-hour urine collection for calcium and repeat blood tests. KL explained in his note that he had already undergone an ultrasound of the neck, which had revealed no abnormalities.

In his note, KL expressed his concern over more surgery on his neck, which he felt had already been compromised by the thyroidectomy in 1990. When we spoke later that day, I explained that parathyroid surgery, in experienced hands, is usually quick and effective, and that he shouldn't worry too much about it. I also recommended that he consider, if primary hyperpara-thyroidism proved to be the issue, a trip to Tampa, Florida, to the Norman Parathyroid Center. Many in the field consider the center's founder, Dr. James Norman, who pioneered minimally invasive parathyroid surgery in the 1990s, the pre-eminent world expert in parathyroid disease. Prior to Dr. Norman, parathyroid surgery could be a complicated, long procedure.

At his clinic, Dr. Norman and his associates have developed simple testing procedures to determine precisely which of the four glands needs treatment, followed by a simple surgical procedure that takes about seventeen minutes. I had already sent several patients with clear evidence of primary hyperparathyroidism to Dr. Norman, with superb results. No one in my opinion then and today knows more about the disease, or how to treat it, than Dr. Norman.

During the last week of August 2000, after KL consulted with his Columbia endocrinologist again, we spoke by phone. A repeat ultrasound that day had shown residual right thyroid tissue and a left thyroid "density" consistent with a parathyroid adenoma, the typical benign lesion of the gland. An ultrasound of the kidneys showed no kidney stones, often present in patients with hyperparathyroidism, as calcium gets drawn out of the bones and deposited in soft tissues where it doesn't belong. Interestingly enough, a repeat blood calcium showed some improvement, from 11.3 to 10.8, though the level was still elevated. Although the calcium had dropped, oddly enough the parathyroid hormone level had risen significantly to 104 (normal less than 54), more than doubling since the July 2000 reading.

The bone density studies demonstrated bone loss only in the back, in a region damaged from his football days, but no osteoporosis. Then, after reviewing all the tests, the endocrinologist told KL that because he was asymptomatic, she did not recommend surgery at this time, but only close monitoring of calcium and PTH levels every three months. She also suggested a CT of the neck, about which KL had mixed feelings because of the known risks of additional radiation exposure from the scan. During our conversation, he made a point of telling me that despite the recent findings, he overall felt "great" on my treatment.

As a side comment, though pancreatic enzymes aggressively attack malignant tumors, they do not work as effectively against benign lesions, which, in their fundamental molecular biology makeup, more closely resemble normal tissue.

Several days later, I received the records from his endocrinologist, including the ultrasound report dated August 10, 2000, which clearly showed an abnormal parathyroid gland:

> IMPRESSION:
>
> Status post subtotal thyroidectomy with residual tissue in the right thyroid bed
>
> Solid hypervascular 13 mm structure in the left thyroid bed is compatible with a parathyroid adenoma [benign lesion]

Blood work from that visit included calcium at 10.8, a TSH reading in the suppressed range at less than 0.01, and a vitamin D level well within normal at 55 (normal at that time on this lab was 15–60).

At that point, the endocrinologist suggested a CT scan of the neck as well as lowering the Armour Thyroid dose, from seven grains daily to four grains. Though indeed in a hyperthyroid state thyroid hormone, like PTH, will draw calcium out of the bone, I thought, based on the ultrasound findings of at least one and most likely two adenoma, the problem was most likely hyperparathyroidism, not suppressive levels of thyroid hormone (routinely used as an adjuvant treatment for thyroid cancer).

The CT scan of the neck performed during the first week of October 2000 revealed the following:

> RIGHT THYROID ... residual right thyroid tissue and postoperative fibrosis. ...
>
> LEFT THYROID: Previous left thyroidectomy. No evidence for residual left thyroid tissue or recurrent neoplasm with the left thyroid gland. ...
>
> PARATHYROID: There are 4 probably enlarged parathyroid glands.

The CT scan of the chest showed no evidence of recurrent or metastatic thyroid cancer.

A follow-up dedicated ultrasound of the neck and thyroid revealed two nodules in the left thyroid bed, along with two enlarged right parathyroid glands:

> THYROID/PARATHYROID SONOGRAM shows no evidence for residual left thyroid lobe tissue, following left thyroidectomy. ... There is a 1.0 × 0.5 × 0.5 cm heterogeneous echogenic/echopoor structure in the upper medial right thyroid bed, containing a 0.6 cm upper and a 0.3 lower hypoechoic moderately vascular nodules. These are presumably hyperplastic nodules within residual right thyroid parenchyma. There is no convincing sonographic evidence of recurrent or metastatic thyroid carcinoma.
>
> There are two upper parathyroid adenomas, measuring 1.6 × 0.6 × 0.8 cm ... on the left, and 0.9 × 0.4 × 0.6 cm ... on the right. ... There are also probably two lower hyperplastic parathyroid glands ... on the left. Since these are not vascular on Doppler, it is conceivable that they may represent hyperplastic lower cervical lymph nodes.

During the second week of October 2000, shortly after the testing was completed, Patient KL and his wife returned to my office for a regularly scheduled visit. The formal report of the CT from earlier in the month was not yet available, but we discussed the ultrasound findings. KL also informed me that bone density studies showed no bone loss except in the lumbar spine, which he again attributed to football injuries.

He reported that his endocrinologist had suggested a cautious, watch-and-wait approach, with regular follow-up testing of calcium and PTH levels. During the visit, we discussed surgery, which I still thought was his most reasonable option. In any event, he was scheduled to see his endocrinologist the following week. All his doctors including me agreed that the radiation he received as a child explained not only the thyroid cancer, but also the hyperactive parathyroid adenomas.

In terms of his clinical status, KL reported feeling fine, with excellent energy, stamina, and concentration. He denied any of the symptoms often associated with hyperthyroidism, or too much thyroid hormone, such as anxiety, insomnia, and tremor.

I didn't hear from KL until late October 2000, because he and his wife had taken a brief vacation. As planned, he had met with his endocrinologist after our visit together in early October 2000. She felt he didn't yet need surgery despite the quite high PTH levels, suggesting instead continued monitoring, along with the lowered dose of Armour at four grains daily. When we chatted, KL reported that he felt "terrific." I was pleased that he felt so well, because primary hyperparathyroidism can be associated with a myriad of symptoms, including fatigue and depression. I still thought surgery made sense but felt I would defer to the endocrine expert.

During the second week of January 2001, at a time when KL had completed nearly eleven years on his nutritional program, follow-up blood testing by his endocrinologist revealed the calcium had again risen to 11.0 (normal 8.5–10.5), and the parathyroid hormone level remained elevated at 94 (normal 11–54). I wasn't happy with the results, nor the "watch-and-wait approach," because untreated hyperparathyroidism can be so problematic. Fortunately, his endocrinologist did agree to refer for a special dye study of the parathyroids, the "sestamibi" test, which involves injecting a radioactive dye, sestamibi, that overactive parathyroid glands preferentially concentrate. This not only allows for the diagnosis of primary hyperparathyroidism, but also helps the surgeon pinpoint the problematic gland.

When KL and his wife next returned to my office, during the first week of March 2001, he generally felt well, but his recent calcium ordered by his endocrinologist was high at 11, and the PTH was still significantly elevated at 94. He reported that the sestamibi assay was scheduled for the third week of March 2001.

Subsequently, the test confirmed a diagnosis of primary hyperparathyroidism, with two hyper-active glands identified. The report described "bilateral parathyroid adenomas in the neck." His calcium was up to 11.4, the PTH still high at 84, though somewhat lower than the prior test.

When we spoke by phone about the findings, both KL and his wife expressed their dissatis-faction with their endocrinologist for a number of reasons, indicating their intention to find a new specialist. Neither felt the current physician was moving fast enough, in the face of such clear evidence of primary hyperparathyroidism. And, to their irritation, she kept focusing on the natural Armour Thyroid as the source of the problem, wishing to switch KL to the synthetic Synthroid. Though I am well aware that endocrinologists almost universally prefer preparations like Synthroid, which provides only the inactive T4 form of thyroid hormone, I have always opted for a more natural form such as the Armour product, containing both T4 and the active T3.

KL and his wife next returned to my office during the fourth week of June 2001. As usual, he seemed vigilantly compliant with all aspects of the program and reported feeling "great." For the moment, despite his misgivings, he had decided to continue with the same endocrinologist who had been following him. Recent blood testing showed a calcium level that, though somewhat lower than several recent readings, was still high at 10.6. The physician had once again reduced his Armour, this time to 2.5 grains, and continued to argue that Synthroid was a better preparation than Armour, allegedly because it was being manufactured under more strictly "controlled" conditions as a synthetic pharmaceutical. As I discussed the issue with KL and his wife, I found that argument rather odd, because just recently at the time the FDA had issued an alert that its own extensive laboratory testing had revealed that often the Synthroid tablets did not provide what was claimed on the label. The FDA warned that if the manufacturer couldn't resolve the problem, Synthroid might be removed from the prescription marketplace.

During the third week of August 2001, KL called me to discuss some recent problems. Since his Armour dose had been reduced to 2.5 grains (150 mg), he had experienced gradually worsening fatigue and an overall drop in his stamina, his motivation, and even his sex drive. He thought, and I agreed, that the culprit was the lowered dose of Armour. Because he was due to see his endocrinologist the following week, I suggested we talk after his visit with her. I also recommended that in addition to the usual blood work his endocrinologist usually ordered, he request testosterone levels be checked.

Two weeks later, I received the results of the blood testing ordered, not by his endocrinologist, but by his primary care physician. Testosterone levels were well within the normal range, so I suspected that the problem was more likely the lowered dose of thyroid. Though an overly high dose of supplemental thyroid hormone can push up the calcium, it made no sense to blame the Armour dose for the problem because repeated PTH testing had been so high and the sestamibi test had already confirmed primary hyperparathyroidism.

When I next met with KL and his wife, during the last week of September 2001, he had continued on the lower dose of Armour. Not surprisingly, his energy and sex drive remained low, and to make matters worse KL, previously lean and trim, recently had been gaining weight though he hadn't changed his diet. All of these symptoms began after his endocrinologist reduced his Armour dose from four grains daily to two and a half grains. Because he just wasn't feeling well, I suggested that he increase his dose to three grains daily.

At least he had, at the suggestion of his endocrinologist, met with a head and neck surgeon, who thought excision of the overactive glands in KL's case would be difficult because of the prior surgery. So for now, his endocrinologist argued for a continued conservative approach.

When KL's symptoms didn't improve on three grains of Armour, I upped the dose to four grains, and at that level, his energy, stamina, concentration, and sex drive all improved very quickly, within a matter of weeks. And he reported none of the symptoms normally associated with excessive thyroid supplementation.

In early April 2002—when KL had completed twelve years on his therapy with me—he called my office to inform me his calcium level was up to 11.4. To his annoyance, his endocrinologist had also suggested reducing the Armour to three and a half grains daily.

KL had also consulted, for a second opinion, with a very well-respected thyroid surgeon at Cornell, Dr. Thomas Fahey, who agreed it was time to remove the two overactive parathyroids. Dr. Fahey, who felt he could remove the two thyroids with minimally invasive surgery, also agreed with me that KL's prior radiation exposure at age five probably led to both the thyroid cancer and the parathyroid adenomas.

When I saw KL next in my office only days later, during the second week of April 2002, he reported he had been going through considerable personal stress. He and his wife, after many years of marriage, had separated, though they were trying to resolve their difficulties. I was concerned for both of them, because I had come to know both KL and his wife well over the past twelve years.

Despite his personal stress, KL remained compliant with his treatment, which he credited with keeping him cancer-free all these years. He reported that he actually felt quite well, with good energy, stamina, and concentration, much better since I had suggested upping the Armour dose. He told me that he had decided, before submitting to parathyroid surgery, to seek out a third opinion, which he had scheduled for later in April.

After the appointment with the surgeon, KL called, telling me this physician completely agreed with Dr. Fahey that the overactive parathyroid gland needed to come out. KL, now resigned to surgery, was mulling over which surgeon to use. In late May 2002, he called to let me know surgery had finally been scheduled for mid-June 2002, with Dr. Fahey.

The day after the procedure, KL's wife called to let me know everything had gone very well. The overactive parathyroids had been removed, along with some residual thyroid tissue and some adjacent lymph nodes, all of which, to their relief, were negative for cancer. The one normal parathyroid, as per the usual protocol, had been implanted into his left wrist.

KL had met with a new endocrinologist, who insisted he change from Armour to Synthroid, so once again I faced the endless synthetic versus natural argument. I told him I had no objection, at least for the time being, for him to try the Synthroid. As I told him, we could always switch back should he not feel as well on the synthetic drug.

Two days later, KL himself called, letting me know he was doing well, and that his first post-operative blood testing showed that both his calcium and parathyroid hormone had dropped to the normal range.

In September 2002, KL's primary care physician ordered routine blood studies, which this time around again showed a calcium level well within the normal range at 9.7. At the time, KL continued on Synthroid and seemed to be doing well on the drug.

When I next saw KL and his wife, during the second week of November 2002, he remained compliant with his therapy, felt well, and had recovered without a hitch from his surgery. Recent calcium levels were perfectly normal once again. Under the direction of his latest endocrinologist, he continued on Synthroid, but he reported that he didn't feel as well on the synthetic as he had on the Armour. Despite the opinions of conventional endocrinologists who seem to despise Armour, I have often heard patients with the same complaint, that they didn't feel well on Synthroid and related drugs. After talking about the situation, I agreed to switch him back to Armour at a dose of two grains daily.

I didn't hear from him again until he returned to my office during the last week of February 2003, when he had completed nearly thirteen years on his nutritional program. As per usual, he seemed extremely compliant with all aspects of his therapy and reported that within a week of switching back to Armour he felt much better, with improved energy, motivation, concentration, and even sex drive.

In April 2003, his endocrinologist ordered repeat blood testing, showing a calcium level at 9.2, well within the normal range. Both parathyroid hormone and vitamin D levels also fell in the acceptable range. When I spoke to him by phone after I received the results, he reported that he was continuing to feel "great."

During the first week of June 2003, KL returned with his wife—they were reconciled—to my office. He remarked how well he felt on the Armour, and how annoyed he was with his various conventional endocrinologists, all of whom insisted he needed to be on Synthroid.

Thereafter, I continued seeing KL every three months in my office, he remained compliant with his program, and he continued doing well. However, throughout 2004, he first began experiencing symptoms associated with prostatitis, such as urinary frequency, some urgency, and the need to get up to urinate repeatedly through the night. His PSA had been and remained in the normal range. I recommended he start taking saw palmetto, the herb frequently used for any type of persistent benign prostate problem and referred him to a urologist for an evaluation and follow-up. Subsequently, after a thorough exam and a pelvic ultrasound, the urologist diagnosed low-grade persistent inflammation in the prostate, but nothing more serious. On saw palmetto and Flomax prescribed by his urologist, his symptoms improved considerably.

In late December 2006, KL's PSA shot up to 7.2 (normal less than 4), nearly a doubling of the previous result. The urologist suspected "low-grade prostate congestion and/or inflammation" as he wrote in his notes, for which he prescribed a course of the antibiotic Levaquin. When the urologist rechecked the PSA in early June 2007, it had dropped to a perfectly normal 2.08.

In December 2007, routine blood testing revealed that his calcium was creeping up, though at 10.0 (normal 8.5–10.4) it still remained within the acceptable range. However, his parathyroid hormone level was quite high this time around, at 209 (normal 7–53). I told him, as a first step, we needed to recheck both the calcium and the PTH levels. When the tests were redone only days later, the calcium and parathyroid levels were both within the normal range. I began to suspect the high reading was simply a fluke, for whatever reason.

In late March 2008—after completing eighteen years on his nutritional program—KL called, concerned about an article he had read linking intake of flaxseed oil with prostate cancer. I was already familiar with the article, and the alleged science behind it, which I found faulty. KL had been on low-dose flaxseed oil and ground flaxseed since beginning treatment with me, as were most of my cancer patients, including those diagnosed with prostate cancer, and I had only found it helpful. Flaxseed oil provides a fair amount of the polyunsaturated essential omega-3 fatty acid alpha linolenic acid (ALA), which can turn rancid if not refrigerated or provided without accessory antioxidant nutrients such as vitamin E.

True, I have found that patients who have been taking excessively large doses, up to six to eight tablespoons daily as recommended by the late Dr. Joanna Budwig of Germany, often do end up with serious problems. Such high doses of ALA can lead to an imbalance with the other fatty acids, even leading to a deficiency of the essential omega-6 linoleic acid. I had one patient in my practice who without my approval began ingesting six to eight tablespoons of flaxseed oil daily. He developed serious neuropathies that resolved when he cut out the flaxseed oil. I suspected he had created a linoleic acid deficiency, which can provoke serious neurological symptoms including neuropathies. In any event, I reassured KL that the moderate levels of flaxseed oil he had been consuming should not be a problem.

During the second week of July 2008, routine blood testing ordered by KL's primary care physician revealed an extraordinarily elevated PTH level at 504, a level higher than I had ever heard reported. His calcium, however, was within the normal range at 10.0, so the high PTH levels made no sense. When the blood was rechecked only ten days later, the PTH was completely normal at 26—one-twentieth of the previous high level! The situation was perplexing to his endocrinologist, as well as to me.

A repeat PTH in mid-December 2008 was again considerably elevated at 560. Neither his endocrinologist nor I had any idea what was going on. I referred him, as I had when he was first diagnosed with primary hyperparathyroidism, to Dr. Norman's group in Tampa, Florida. If anyone could resolve this odd set of findings, it would be them.

Patient KL dutifully, as per my instructions, contacted Dr. Norman's office and spoke to one of the nurse assistants, who informed KL that about 1 to 3 percent of their patients require repeat surgery for a newly hyperactive parathyroid. KL might, the doctor explained, fall into that category. The physician on the case did suggest that KL gather all his records together and send them on to Dr. Norman's office for review.

Repeat PTH levels at the end of December 2008 came back perfectly normal again, at 34.9, and the calcium level had actually dropped to a very respectable 9.7. The situation, at least to me, remained perplexing until his endocrinologist resolved the issue. At KL's original surgery, one presumably normal parathyroid gland had been implanted into KL's left arm. If the nurse or technician drew blood from the left antecubital fossa (at the elbow bend), this blood would be downstream from the active parathyroid gland in the forearm, so not surprisingly the level would be high. But this high level reflected an artifact of the procedure, not an indication of a serious problem.

As it turned out, whenever the nurse drew blood from the right arm without an implanted parathyroid gland, the PTH levels fell within the normal range. Problem solved simply enough, and the endocrinologist ordered his nurse to draw all future blood from the right arm.

To test this hypothesis, in mid-January 2009 KL's endocrinologist instructed his nurse to draw blood from both the right and left arm for PTH sampling. To everyone's further confusion, the alleged blood from the right arm came back high at 237, and the blood from the alleged left arm with the implanted parathyroid gland came within the normal range. As it turned out, the nurse may have gotten the tubes mixed up. I urged him to have the dual test done again, this time with meticulous attention paid to which blood came from which arm.

During the third week of January 2009, KL spoke directly with Dr. Norman, who after reviewing all the records said definitively that KL did not have residual primary hyperparathyroidism, and that in the recent testing someone had gotten the tubes mixed up. As the endocrinologist had concluded, Dr. Norman insisted that from this point forward, all blood samples should be drawn from the right arm.

KL's New York endocrinologist did have his nurse repeat the dual arm blood draw, this time carefully labeling the tubes. As expected, the PTH level from the right arm, the arm without the active parathyroid, came back completely normal, but the level from drawn the left arm, with the active implanted parathyroid gland, was over 500. So this problem that had been dragging on for many months was simply a function of inconsistent blood drawing technique.

During the second week of February 2009, I received a thoughtful note from Dr. Norman's physician associate. Apparently, Dr. Norman and his colleagues, who have seen just about everything that can be seen related to the parathyroid gland, remarked that they had witnessed this type of confusion before, brought on by blood draws in the arm with the implanted parathyroid. The physician concluded,

> Hopefully, this can help to clarify any confusion and to help in the interpretation of any future results.

> Of course, our hope is that this letter finds you doing well and that your good relationship with KL continues to prosper, as he clearly holds you in high regard.

During this period, KL had been consulting with an orthopedist because of persistent knee problems, most likely the result of his football-playing past. I told him to add chicken collagen Type II to his program, a supplement he reported, several weeks later, helped significantly.

During the third week of October 2009, the orthopedist, to be safe, ordered a bone scan to rule out metastatic thyroid cancer, which can often settle into bone. However, the test came back negative, with "no evidence of metastatic disease." KL did show evidence, however, of degenerative arthritis. A subsequent MRI of the spine indicated some type of lesion in the L4–L5 area, thought to be a benign hemangioma.

Since then, I have continued seeing KL every three months in my office, he has remained vigilantly compliant with all aspects of his nutritional program after twenty-three years, and he has not had another problem with either his thyroid cancer or his primary hyperparathyroidism. His recurrent prostatitis recently seems under control. As for his knee arthritis, he eventually underwent a procedure developed in Germany, involving removal of a patient's blood, then mixing it with an anti-inflammatory substance of some sort, then reinjecting the blood into the affected joint. Many athletes have undergone the expensive procedure, with anecdotal reports of great success. After thinking about the risks and benefits, in March 2013 he underwent the therapy, with a total of five injections. He subsequently reported some, though not complete, improvement in his bilateral arthritic knee pain.

Today, more than twenty-three years since he first began treatment with me, KL continues doing well. To any objective mind, this patient's long-term, cancer-free survival certainly is remarkable, in view of the numerous poor prognostic indicators at the time of his surgery in February 1990. First of all, patients diagnosed at age forty or greater have an overall worse prognosis than those under forty according to the website UpToDate. KL was forty-four at the time of diagnosis. Furthermore, his large tumor, at 4.5 cm in diameter, also correlates with an ultimate poor prognosis. The Hürthle cell histology particularly portends for a poor prognosis; as mentioned in the introduction to this section, patients with non-Hürthle follicular carcinoma have a ten-year survival of 75 percent, compared with 41 percent of those with the Hürthle cell variant—a significant difference.

Most importantly, his surgeon could not excise all tumor, as the pathology report clearly indicated, so he had obvious residual cancer when he first came to see me. And finally, the positive lymph node further confirmed a poor prognosis.

KL's conventional physicians all warned he would end up in serious trouble if he refused the recommended radioactive iodine therapy, but refuse it he did without a second thought or regret.

A CT scan of the chest from 2000 as part of his workup for primary hyperparathyroidism showed no evidence of recurrent or metastatic disease, and to this day he shows no evidence of cancer.

Both his original thyroid cancer and his primary hyperparathyroidism, as his conventional surgeons agreed, most likely developed as a result of radiation exposure at age five. Since his surgery in June 2002, the hyperparathyroidism has remained resolved.

During our twenty-three years working together, KL has been an ideal patient. Once he learned about my work, for whatever reason something about the therapy resonated with him. He never looked back, never second-guessed his decision to proceed with an alternative approach, and never regretted his decision to refuse conventional treatment. Through career and personal stress, he has always remained compliant with his nutritional regimen, which he feels has saved his life and given him the gift of good health.

Case 2: Patient IZ
A Minimum 7.5-Year Survivor*

Patient IZ is an eighty-two-year-old retired business executive from the New York area who has survived more than eleven years with a history of recurrent metastatic poor-prognosis Hürthle cell variant of thyroid cancer.

He reports a fairly extensive family history of cancer. His mother died from a gynecological malignancy; his father died from colon cancer; a paternal aunt and a paternal uncle both died of some type of cancer, primary unknown in each case to the patient. His paternal grandfather died from prostate cancer, and the patient's son has survived Hodgkin's disease.

Patient IZ did smoke cigarettes, one pack a day for some twenty-five years, before he quit at forty-four years of age. He has no history of known radiation exposure.

In 1992, he was diagnosed with prostate cancer and treated successfully with prostatectomy, with no adjuvant radiation considered necessary. In addition, he has a history of hypertension for many years treated with a variety of medications.

His current situation dates to February 2002, when his wife noticed a distinct swelling in his right neck. Vacationing in Florida at the time, IZ consulted a local physician, who thought the swelling was due to a benign cyst. Upon returning to New York, IZ consulted with his primary care physician, who referred him to an endocrinologist. A subsequent CT scan from the last week of March 2002 demonstrated a significant right thyroid mass, described in the official report: "Approximately 4.5 × 4.5 × 3.0 cm homogeneous soft tissue mass largely replacing and expanding the right thyroid lobe.... The lesion extensively compresses the common carotid artery and internal jugular vein."

However, no pathological adenopathy was noted. At that point, Patient IZ was referred to Dr. James Hurley, an endocrinologist at New York Hospital–Cornell in Manhattan. During the second week of April 2002, Patient IZ met with Dr. Hurley, who after reviewing the CT scan believed the mass represented a malignant process and referred IZ to Dr. Thomas Fahey, a well-known thyroid surgeon at Cornell, for needle biopsy of the mass. However, Dr. Fahey, during his initial consultation with IZ several days later, recommended that the suspicious-appearing mass needed to be taken out quickly. So, during the fourth week of April 2002, Patient IZ underwent a total thyroidectomy at New York Hospital. The pathology report described a large, aggressive tumor of Hürthle cell histology, a very aggressive form, extending beyond the thyroid and into the localized vasculature and two adjacent lymph nodes:

> Hürthle cell (oncocystic) carcinoma, widely invasive
> Tumor measures 4 cm in diameter and is located in the right lobe.

Presence of extensive capsular invasion

Presence of vascular invasion

Presence of extrathyroidal extension

Tumor is adherent to perithyroidal skeletal muscle and a single unremarkable parathyroid gland

Tumor is less than 1 mm from inked margins....

Two perithyroidal lymph nodes positive for metastatic carcinoma (2/2)

Postsurgery, IZ met with the endocrinologist, Dr. Hurley, who prescribed the thyroid replacement drug Cytomel. In addition, he was scheduled for both a PET scan and a thyroid scintigraphy to rule out residual cancer.

The scintigraphy scan during the last week of May 2002 showed clear evidence of metastatic disease. The PET scan further confirmed metastatic disease:

Findings: The coincidence images demonstrate foci of increased uptake in the right paratracheal and right hilar region....

IMPRESSION:

Abnormal F-18 FDG scintigraphy.

1. Right paratracheal, right hilar lymph nodes, most consistent with metastatic disease.

A CT scan during the second week of June 2002 revealed the active nodes seen on the previous PET.

With the testing completed, in mid-June 2002 Patient IZ underwent the planned radioisotope iodine treatment, administered at New York Hospital.

Dr. Hurley's note from late June 2002 summarized the findings of the various scans: "The PET scan performed at New York hospital on the --- of May showed focal accumulation of radiotracer in the right paratracheal and right hilar regions, consistent with metastases to lymph nodes. CT scanning of the chest ... showed tiny right paratracheal nodes just below the sternal notch."

At that point, IZ was begun on thyroid suppression therapy with Levoxyl. However, as the patient would later tell him, Dr. Hurley was not very hopeful about his long-term prognosis, because the Hürthle cell variant of thyroid cancer is notoriously resistant to radioactive iodine. And, Dr. Hurley explained, other than radioactive iodine there were no truly beneficial treatments that could be offered for his disease.

At that point, Patient IZ began looking into alternative approaches to cancer, reading just about every book he could find. He learned about the pioneering mind-body work of Dr. Carl Simonton, now deceased, and even went to California to spend a week at Dr. Simonton's retreat in September 2002. IZ would later tell me that he found the experience very helpful, in terms of dealing with his serious situation.

Back in New York, Patient IZ also consulted with another well-known alternative practitioner of mind-body approaches, Dr. Tula Forlani, who has also passed on. IZ consulted with Dr. Forlani on a regular basis for some three months, an experience he also found very useful.

During this period, Patient IZ also began an intensive supplement program that he essentially designed on his own. He experimented with a variety of diets, including the rather odd—at least from my perspective—"non-nutritional diet" in which patients indulge in white sugar, white flour, etc., in an attempt to provide a nutrient-deficient diet that would starve the cancer. After a couple of months, however, IZ gave up this approach, at that point consulting with an alternative practitioner in Connecticut, who added on a variety of supplements to IZ's self-prescribed program.

As Patient IZ continued experimenting with diet and supplements, he gradually lost faith in conventional medicine, and after a visit during the third week of September 2002, he discontinued the recommended follow-up visits. During that session, Dr. Hurley reported in his note that he had raised the dose of Levoxyl because the TSH was not at that point suppressed, and IZ complained of "persistent symptoms of fatigue and lack of energy."

Over the following years, IZ did not consult with any endocrinologist (Dr. Hurley retired in 2005) for his thyroid cancer, or a urologist for his distant prostate cancer, though his primary care physician did continue to prescribe Levoxyl, both as a replacement for his absent thyroid and for suppression of residual cancer. Despite the lack of oncologic follow-up, Patient IZ seemed to be doing remarkably well, as he continued to lead his normal, very active life, while taking a huge number of supplements based on his own readings.

Then, during the first week of April 2009, seven years after his diagnosis of metastatic thyroid cancer, IZ noticed a swollen lymph node in his right neck. Through his reading, IZ had at that point learned about an endocrinologist at Columbia, and he consulted with him. Blood work indicated thyroid suppression, but not complete. An ultrasound of the neck at Columbia during the final week of April 2009 revealed the following:

> No residual thyroid tissue appreciated.
>
> A lymph node in the right surgical fossa inferiorly measures 1.8 × 0.4 × 0.8 cm. A smaller right mid fossa lymph node measures 0.8 × 0.4 × 0.5 cm.

The largest left mid fossa lymph nodes measures 0.9 × 0.3 × 0.5 cm.

Ultrasound-guided biopsy of the enlarged nodes, however, was "NON-DIAGNOSTIC," showing only blood and a few lymphocytes.

At that point, Patient IZ decided to seek out a second opinion with Dr. Tuttle, an endocrinologist at Memorial Sloan Kettering. Dr. Tuttle recommended a PET scan, which was done in late May 2009 and showed the following:

FINDINGS:

A 2.1 × 2.2 upper paratracheal mass and a 1.2 × 1.1 cm slightly superior and lateral nodule are both hypermetabolic with a SUV max up to 20.1.

SUV activity levels above 3 indicate cancer, levels above 10 usually significant cancer, and levels in the 20 range indicate very active, aggressive disease.

In the summary section, the radiologist wrote,

IMPRESSION:

Hypermetabolic right paratracheal nodule and mass consistent with metastasis.

With this evidence of metastatic disease, Patient IZ was referred to a head and neck surgeon, Dr. Shaha, at Memorial Sloan Kettering. He also began looking intently for alternative approaches to cancer, learned of our work, applied to become a patient, and was accepted into our practice. IZ scheduled his initial appointment with us for the third week of June 2009, a week after his scheduled appointment with Dr. Shaha.

During the initial consultation, Dr. Shaha pushed aggressively for surgery but at the same time warned that the procedure would be very aggressive, requiring that he explore deeply into the neck region. The right recurrent laryngeal nerve, which controls speech, might be damaged, leading to paralysis of the larynx.

When IZ next met with me, as we reviewed his history, he explained that Dr. Shaha wanted him to undergo yet another CT scan of the neck, but IZ was becoming increasingly concerned about the radiation exposure from these repeated PETs and CTs. He was thinking of canceling the radiology appointment. IZ also made it clear to me that he was very reluctant even to consider surgery, considering how damaging it might be, with the possibility of cure remote in any event.

Nonetheless, IZ also informed me that he had set up an appointment the same day as his appointment with me with his original Cornell surgeon from 2002, Dr. Fahey, for a second opinion. I encouraged him to keep the appointment.

At the time we first met, IZ described his general health, despite the evidence of recurrent disease, as "great." He had been eating organically for years and following a low-animal-fat diet, while taking large amounts of supplements he had prescribed for himself.

The following day, IZ came to my office to review with me his prescribed therapy regimen. He informed me that he had indeed met with Dr. Fahey, who proposed a surgical approach less aggressive than that suggested by Dr. Shaha at Memorial Hospital. IZ was going to reconsider surgery, he said, but at the same time he was quite determined to begin my nutritional treatment.

During the days that followed, IZ called my office a number of times to review his options again. He was again feeling very reluctant at his age to undergo aggressive surgery, when the chances of cure would not be good and the possibility of significant damage high. Dr. Fahey had arranged for both ultrasound and CT testing, about which IZ again felt quite conflicted. I told him to think about the situation calmly and go with his gut.

Patient IZ also experienced a difficult course, during the initial weeks on the program, reporting extreme fatigue, malaise, muscle aches, and pains. When I discussed these issues with him by phone, I reassured him, explaining that nearly all my patients have a host of flu-like symptoms during the first weeks and months of the regimen, as the various body tissues repair and rebuild and stored toxic waste gets released into the bloodstream, for eventual filtering and excretion through the liver.

During the third week of July 2009, after IZ had completed just a month on his treatment, he underwent ultrasound testing at Memorial, which showed a reduction in the superclavicular node, from 1.8 cm in its widest dimension to 1.2 cm. After the test, Patient IZ met with both Dr. Shaha and Dr. Fahey, who both now suggested a conservative "watch-and-wait" approach. IZ himself lauded my program, saying there could be no other reasonable explanation for the shrinkage in tumor size. IZ continued on his nutritional therapy but also did finally schedule surgery at Memorial for August 2009. However, after reviewing all of IZ's records, Dr. Shaha called off the procedure, informing IZ the cancer was "inoperable."

In early September 2009, IZ called my office, greatly concerned that his blood pressure, which he measured at home regularly, had suddenly shot up to the 180–190 range (systolic). At the time, his most recent TSH was low at 0.03, so I suspected his primary care physician—now managing his thyroid replacement treatment—needed to lower the dose. I explained to IZ that excess thyroid hormone will raise blood pressure.

In addition, IZ's blood sugar was high, at 138. That marker had been trending upward, though this was the highest it had been. I made some adjustments in his program, while encouraging him to follow up with his primary care physician.

IZ returned to my office during the third week of September 2009 for a routine office visit, having completed three months on his nutritional program. At the time, he seemed quite compliant with his nutritional program. In addition, his internist has prescribed Actos for his high blood sugars, as well as Aldactazide and Zestril for his hypertension. He remained on Levoxyl 200 mcg, which he took now for six days, leaving the drug off the seventh day of the week.

His most recent blood sugar had improved to 114, with a hemoglobin A1C, a marker for diabetes, slightly elevated at 6.8 (normal less than 5.8). Clinically, IZ seemed to be doing well, but he complained of somewhat worse peripheral artery disease and lower extremity pain, particularly when he had been sitting for a prolonged period of time. On the other hand, he had been playing vigorous tennis twice a week with no difficulty. I suggested he add on a mixed vitamin E 400 IU in addition to the vitamin E on his original protocol. Studies going back to the 1940s and the Shute brothers in London, Ontario, have demonstrated the efficacy of vitamin E at high doses in patients experiencing leg pain from compromised circulation.

IZ reported that he had seen Dr. Fahey, his Cornell surgeon, some six weeks prior to his visit with me. An ultrasound in early September 2009 indicated an enlarged lowered right supraclavicular (neck) lymph node measuring 2.2 × 0.8 × 0.4 cm, as well as a 1.3 × 0.6 × 0.5 mid-left cervical chain node. The previously noted mid-right node had increased slightly from the prior study, from 1.2 to 1.4 cm in its widest dimension. Dr. Fahey proposed continued surveillance with no surgery at present, but he did suggest a CT scan of the chest and neck be repeated in six months.

In early November 2009, IZ faxed me a note complaining that he had been experiencing some significant fatigue while on his supplement cycle that worsened as days passed. During his previous five-day break, he had felt "great." When I discussed the issue with him, I suspected that he was responding unusually strongly to the pancreas product, so I reduced the dose from sixteen each time to twelve. With that change, some days later he reported his fatigue had indeed improved. As I warn all patients, during the initial months of treatment, as the body repairs and rebuilds, they will get tired, sometimes very tired. All the body's energy seems to go into the regenerative process, leaving little for the routine activities of day-to-day living.

In a conversation one time discussing the issue of symptoms on the treatment, Kelley used the analogy of a baby. A baby will sleep eighteen hours or more a day, waking essentially only to eat. During these early months of life, the infant is rapidly growing its body and refining the various organ systems—a process, Dr. Kelley said, that requires considerable energy, leaving the baby tired and prone to sleep. On his program, he said, patients were regrowing their bodies, an energy-consuming process, for sure. In the case of IZ, however, I suspected that I could lessen his fatigue and slow the process down somewhat so that he could function at least more normally. And, indeed, that is what seemed to happen.

Toward the end of November 2009, IZ faxed me a note in which he complained of some abdominal pain after eating. After discussing the situation with him by phone, I reduced his pancreas dose and made some other slight adjustments to his therapy. In any event, his primary care physician had referred him to a gastroenterologist for endoscopy and colonoscopy, scheduled for the end of November 2009.

As it turned out, IZ had no stomach or duodenal ulcer and no colonic polyps, but diverticulosis, which the gastroenterologist thought might be the source of his erratic postprandial pain. I suggested that he eat more cooked food rather than raw, and stay off the supplements until the pain resolved. Several days later, in early December 2009, when IZ and I spoke by phone he informed me that with my suggestions, the abdominal pain had resolved.

When I next saw IZ for a routine visit during the second week of December 2009, he had completed six months on his therapy, had resumed his full supplement program, and seemed to be doing well.

He was pleased that the colonoscopy had revealed no polyps. He reported that five polyps had been noted and removed during his first colonoscopy at age sixty-three. Subsequently, he underwent colonoscopy every several years, and each time the gastroenterologist removed multiple polyps, which fortunately were benign. This was the first time the colonoscopy showed no polyps, a finding he attributed to my therapy.

In mid-December 2009, routine blood work showed a sugar high at 140 (normal less than 100), cholesterol at 173, and a low TSH at 0.11, an indication he needed less thyroid hormone. In response, his internist had reduced his Levoxyl by one-half, to 100 mcg three times a week.

During the first week of January 2010, repeat ultrasound showed no evidence of the large lower right cervical node, the left cervical node, or the mid-right enlarged node. However, the radiologist did describe a 1.3 cm nodular focus in the right thyroid bed and a 0.9 cm focus in the left thyroid bed.

When I discussed the results with IZ, he seemed perplexed about the findings of small lesions in the thyroid bed but no evidence of the previously described three enlarged left nodes, two on the right, one on the left. I assume that with his nutritional program, we had seen some improvement, and perhaps the thyroid nodules as described were artifact. I explained, as the radiologist had suggested in his formal report, that a CT or PET scan would give us more definitive data, but IZ explained that, as far as he was concerned, he had had enough radiation exposure from various tests. However, IZ told me he intended to contact the radiologist himself, to get some kind of explanation about the thyroid bed nodules.

Several days later, IZ called, to relay his discussion with the radiologist. As far as this physician was concerned, the thyroid bed nodules most likely indicated scarring with inflammation.

IZ next returned to my office during the third week of March 2010, when he had completed nine months on his nutritional therapy. He reported that after reading about the potential dangers of Actos, he had discontinued the medication and chose—without discussing the change with me—to adopt a very low-fat, high-complex-carbohydrate diet that was being promoted by an anti-fat nutritional fanatic. Unfortunately, IZ had incorporated large doses of soy in its various forms into his diet, as recommended by this physician in his writing. I explained, as I had explained to him when I had first reviewed his prescribed protocol, that soy not only blocks the action of thyroid hormone, but inactivates the proteolytic enzymes such as trypsin that I use in my therapy.

When I suggested we have the ultrasound of the neck repeated, he said that he was reluctant to return to any of his previous doctors. However, in late May 2010, he did return to his prior radiologist for the study. This time around, the physician reported,

> IMPRESSION: Status post total thyroidectomy. Two nodules in the right thyroid bed consistent with recurrent tumor. The larger 1.2 cm upper nodule is not appreciably changed since previous study; 8 mm lower thyroid bed nodule is new.
>
> Previously noted nodule in the left thyroid bed is not appreciated currently.
>
> 2.4 cm right supraclavicular presumed nodal metastasis is slightly enlarged compared with 2008 study.

When we discussed the findings by phone, IZ expressed his confusion, insisting he had not undergone ultrasound testing in 2008, but I explained the physician probably had meant 2009, during the period of his recurrence.

I did call the radiologist to clarify the situation. He explained that he was comparing an ultrasound to a previous CT scan, which I understood could not provide an exact comparison. He recommended a CT or PET scan to obtain more accurate information. However, when I discussed the suggestion with IZ later that day by phone, he made it clear to me he had no intention of proceeding with studies involving radiation exposure.

During the second week of June 2010, IZ had contacted my office complaining of a new symptom related to the supplements, lightheadedness after each dose of pancreas. When I discussed the issue with him by phone, I suggested that perhaps he had developed an allergy to the pork product and should switch to the lamb. In my experience, the lamb pancreas supplements do not work as well as the pork, because the pork pancreas in its physiology and biochemistry is most like the human gland of all the commercially available sources. The lamb pancreas is assuredly less similar to the human than is the pig—lambs are pure vegetarian; pigs, like us, are omnivores—but our supplier does keep a supply of lamb pancreas on hand for those who have significant pork allergies. It does work against cancer, but not quite as well as the pork.

I discussed all these issues with IZ, and he ordered a supply of lamb. However, some ten days later, he faxed me a note saying he had developed a dull frontal headache after beginning the lamb that would recur with each dose. I suggested that he cut his dose down to four capsules each dose, instead of the twelve he had been taking.

When IZ next returned to my office for a routine follow-up visit during the fourth week of June 2010, he had completed a year on his nutritional program. He seemed at the time quite compliant with all aspects of the therapy, particularly with the reduced dose of lamb pancreas, reporting that he felt overall "great." He appeared to be tolerating the reduced dose of enzymes just fine. Sometimes, as in this case, it takes time and work to reach a therapeutic dose that works and can be tolerated by the patient.

We again discussed at some length the recent conflicting ultrasound report, with some improvement, some worsening, and some stabilization. I expressed the radiologist's opinion that only a CT or PET could give us exact information about the extent of his recurrent disease, but IZ explained that he had been fighting thyroid cancer now for eight years primarily his own way, and he would continue to do it his own way—and that path did not include further radiation exposure. I respected his position, of course, feeling I would behave no differently if I were in his position.

Only days later, at the beginning of July 2010, IZ called my office, complaining this time that he felt sick even with the very low dose of lamb pancreas. We had a long talk, in which I expressed my concern that if he could not tolerate the minimal doses of lamb pancreas product, my program would not be effective. I hesitantly brought up options, which he rejected outright: he had already exhausted the conventional treatments including radioactive iodine, and he would not consider another alternative approach, which he believed would not offer the efficacy of my treatment. Because he seemed so determined to stay with me, I recommended he switch back to the pork product, at a very minimal dose to start. After all, he had been ingesting the pork at a fairly high dosage for many months before problems set in.

In my experience over the years, though most patients tolerate the full therapeutic dose of pancreas without difficulty, I have encountered several like IZ that have, at periods of time, difficulty tolerating even moderate doses of either the lamb or the pork. As I learned from Dr. Kelley years ago, the practitioner must listen to the patient carefully, not approach him or her with a preconceived notion of what needs to be done. In IZ's case, I suspected his intolerance wasn't necessarily a "bad" omen, but perhaps a reflection that he utilized the enzymes very effectively, hence requiring a minimal, rather than a maximum, dose. Furthermore, he explained that he felt truly "great" during his five-day break off all supplements, a sign to me that his baseline health was actually quite good and that his symptoms were in response to the aggressive repair and rebuilding the program invariably sparks. In any event, he remained determined to try again and switched back to the pork pancreas.

During the third week of July 2010, IZ contacted my office, and we spoke at length. He reported that recently he had been feeling sick even on his five-day break, now suspecting the problem wasn't the pancreas at all, but his blood sugars that were running too high, in the 140–150 range (normal less than 100), not catastrophic but certainly too elevated. He had stopped the Actos and felt reluctant to try another medication, because the side effects and long-term problems seemed so daunting. He had consulted with an endocrinologist specializing in diabetes in Manhattan but had little faith in that physician and would not, he told me, return to him.

True, I had prescribed a number of supplements, such as alpha lipoic acid, chromium, magnesium, and others that help with blood sugar regulation, but I explained, as I had told him before, that I am not a diabetologist. I felt he needed an expert guiding that particular problem. In any event, I increased the dose of chromium, made some other adjustments, and encouraged IZ to think about consulting with a conventional expert in diabetes.

During the second week of September 2010, IZ faxed me a long note, explaining that the program was going easier and easier, and the symptoms were fewer and less intense: "Progress report: the protocol continues to get easier, faster and more 'streamline'—I'm finally getting used to it, and have kinks and conflicts worked out of the scheduling. In the last few weeks I've been experiencing days with low energy after lunch, during the early afternoon, and sometimes on into the evening. Taking an afternoon nap (which historically I haven't done) often helps raise my energy. The lower energy is often accompanied by aching around my eyes (similar to having a fever or the flu)."

IZ's note nicely summed up the classic symptoms reported during the earlier stages of the therapy: fatigue, usually worse during the mid-afternoon; various aches and pains; and a "flu-like" feeling. Dr. Kelley once explained that between 2:00 and 4:00 a.m. and 2:00 and 4:00 p.m., in the mid-afternoon, due to normal circadian patterns, the body's repair processes rev up intensely, often provoking a sensation of exhaustion. Dr. Kelley recommended that all his patients, at least during the first couple of years on the program, take an afternoon nap. "The body heals best at rest," he was fond of saying, and I agree wholeheartedly with the statement.

IZ had been a high-power business executive, a CEO of a major corporation, always blessed with great drive, energy, and stamina, so it was difficult to accept rest as part of his life. But patients such as IZ learn over time how to manage their program most efficiently, and usually that management involves taking an afternoon nap.

Routine blood work that I ordered in late September showed a blood sugar of 147 (on this lab, for a Patient IZ's age the normal range was 65–139) so I assured him he really wasn't that far off course. All other parameters, including the TSH and other thyroid tests, were within the normal range, with the TSH at the very low limit of normal—where I wanted it, for suppression of any thyroid cancer cells lurking around. His thyroglobulin level, another marker used to track thyroid cancer, was within the normal range (less than 20).

IZ returned to my office for a routine visit during the first week of October 2010, when he had completed some sixteen months on his nutritional program. To my relief, he was tolerating the supplements, including the pork pancreas product, with no difficulty. He had gradually increased each dose to ten capsules, which caused no digestive or other effects. He seemed compliant with the diet as well, and with the various detoxification procedures. He also continued on Actos, though he remained nervous about the drug based on what he had read.

He looked well and said he felt well. He was back to exercising vigorously, which he thought would help his diabetes. He reported that in the morning when he first checked his sugars, the level was generally high, in the 150 range. Then, after taking a long walk with his dogs, the sugar level when retested would be in the normal range at 118. In addition, he was back to playing vigorous tennis four times weekly and was swimming regularly in his own pool.

He reported that his symptoms of peripheral artery disease, which had been quite severe in the past, had also improved remarkably. Before he had started treatment with me, he said, he couldn't walk fifty feet without experiencing severe leg pain. This problem had, over time, completely resolved, a situation he described as "miraculous." Overall, he described his energy as "excellent" and his stamina as "excellent" as well. So after his initial rough start, he had adjusted and adapted nicely to the treatment and already was seeing benefit.

A week later, he contacted my office after reading about metformin in *Life Extension Magazine*. I myself have been a member of *Life Extension* for many years and find the monthly magazine informative. Indeed, I had read the same article, in which the author praises metformin, an older-generation medication used to treat type II diabetes (non-insulin-dependent diabetes). In more modern terminology, the drug seems to help fight insulin resistance, in which target cells become insensitive to insulin. Metformin appears to increase the efficiency of the hormone in its job of driving sugar out of the bloodstream and into the cells, where it can be used for energy. In recent years, a number of researchers have also proposed an anticancer effect for the drug as well. As pharmaceuticals go, metformin has a good safety profile, with few significant side effects in patients.

Though I explained to IZ that I would be happier if he were under the care of a diabetologist, I agreed to write the prescription, because he was so anxious to get off the Actos.

Fortunately, in late October 2010, IZ did, at my insistence, follow up with the diabetologist he had seen in the past. Blood work done this time around showed a glucose level slightly elevated on this scale at 114 (normal less than 105). His hemoglobin A1C was down to 6.0, a nice drop from the previous level. The physician, apparently pleased with how well IZ seemed to be doing, recommended that for now he only stay on Actos and not change medication.

In early November 2010, IZ contacted my office, wishing to speak with me. When we spoke by phone later than evening, he reported that he was ready to have another ultrasound done, though as before he would not agree to either a CT or a PET scan. I wrote the order.

*IMPORTANT EDITOR'S NOTE:
Dr. Gonzalez died in July 2015 before updating this case report. Patient IZ contacted Dr. Isaacs' office in January 2017.

UTERINE (ENDOMETRIAL) CANCER

In 2010, 43,470 new cases of cancer of the uterine lining were reported, along with 7,950 deaths.[1] Fortunately, in about 75 percent of all cases, the disease is diagnosed at an early stage when surgery can be curative. For decades, radiation to the pelvis has been routinely recommended as adjunctive postsurgical treatment for localized endometrial cancer. However, the data from the two large controlled clinical trials completed to address the effect of radiation, published in 1980[2] and 2000[3] respectively, shows overall no survival advantage compared with surgery alone. In certain subgroups, the authors reported patients receiving radiation actually have shortened survival times.

Once metastatic, uterine cancer resists chemotherapy and usually kills quickly, with a median survival reported in the range of six to eight months, and a five-year survival rate at 5 percent or less. Hormonal blockade with the synthetic progesterone, Megace, or similar drugs can offer temporary benefit in some 20 percent of patients with widespread disease, but the responses usually are short lived.

1. Case 1: Patient JK
2. A Minimum 16-Year Survivor

Patient JK is a sixty-two-year-old woman who had been in good health when, in the fall of 1990, she required hospitalization for two episodes of deep venous thrombosis. She was placed on Coumadin but shortly thereafter suffered an episode of severe vaginal hemorrhage. When the bleeding persisted, in December 1990 she underwent a D&C, which revealed endometrial carcinoma. After a CT scan in January 1991 showed extensive abdominal and pelvic lymphadenopathy, she underwent a total abdominal hysterectomy with bilateral salpingo-oophorectomy.

The pathology report described endometrial adenocarcinoma with areas of squamous differentiation, high nuclear grade (FIGO grade III), and papillary serous carcinoma, one of the most lethal of uterine malignancies. The tumor had spread to the left ovary, obliterating the fimbriated end of the left fallopian tube. Biopsies of the peritoneal cul-de-sac as well as the rectal serosa confirmed metastatic disease, and, due to the extent of metastasis, her doctors warned her of a very poor prognosis.

1 Longo et al, "Gynecologic Malignancies", *Harrison's* 18th Edition, (2012), 814.
2 J. Aalders, V. Abeler, P. Kolstad, and M. Onsrud, "Postoperative External Irradiation and Prognostic Parameters in Stage I Endometrial Carcinoma: Clinical and Histopathologic Study of 540 Patients," *Obstetrics and Gynecology* 56 (1980): 419–27.
3 Katherine Y. Look, "Who Benefits from Radiotherapy in Treatment of Endometrial Cancer and at What Price?," *Lancet* 355 (2000): 1381–82.

Postoperatively, JK met with a radiation oncologist, who insisted treatment begin at once. Before agreeing to any therapy, JK decided to consult with a second oncologist in a Southern tertiary care center. Once again, radiation was aggressively pushed as essential to delay spread of her aggressive disease.

However, JK decided to refuse all orthodox treatments, instead choosing to medicate herself with a variety of nutritional supplements, including high-dose vitamin C and red clover tea.

An abdominal MRI in March 1991 showed a "decrease in degree of periaortic lymphadenopathy with persistent evidence of matted lymph nodes." Pelvic MRI documented a "decrease in the degree of diffuse pelvic lymphadenopathy although there is persistent evidence of pelvic mass lesion most notable in the left hemi-pelvis. There is evidence of surgical defect presumably from previous hysterectomy." So, with surgery, there had been improvement, though clearly extensive disease remained.

About that time, after learning of our work, JK decided to pursue my therapy. When first evaluated in my office in April 1991, she reported persistent fatigue, a substantial recent weight loss of fifteen pounds, "terrible night sweats," and poor sleep.

JK subsequently followed her regimen with great determination. Seven months later, in December 1991, repeat MRIs showed no change in the periaortic lymphadenopathy as compared with the study of March 1991, but significant regression of the pelvic adenopathy and the pelvic mass in the left hemipelvis. The official report stated, "Compared to the study of 3---91, there is continued improvement with near complete resolution of previously seen pelvic lymphadenopathy. Currently, there is no appreciable residual mass lesion present within the left hemipelvis."

Thereafter, JK continued her nutritional program diligently, with reported improvement in her general health. MRI studies of the abdomen and pelvis in January 1993, after she had completed some twenty months on therapy, indicated that the previously noted extensive disease had completely resolved. The pelvic scan revealed that "there is no identified pelvic lymphadenopathy." The official report of the abdominal MRI stated, "There is no evidence of significant periaortic or periportal lymphadenopathy."

MRI studies completed fourteen months later, in March 1994, confirmed that "there is no distinct evidence of metastatic or recurrent disease."

JK followed her regimen faithfully until early 1997, when I last had formal contact with her. At that time, six years from her diagnosis of metastatic aggressive histology endometrial cancer, she remained disease-free and generally in good health. She subsequently continued her therapy in a reduced way and, at last report, now nearly sixteen years from diagnosis, is alive and apparently doing well.

This case is straightforward: the patient was diagnosed with extensive, aggressive histology uterine cancer, including papillary serous, one of the most deadly subtypes. The surgeon could not excise all the visible cancer, as MRI studies after surgery documented. She then experienced complete regression of her advanced disease while following her nutritional program and remains alive sixteen years later.

Case 2: Patient EK
A 10.75-Year Survivor*

In terms of her family history, Patient EK's maternal grandmother had died as a consequence of breast cancer, but no other relatives had been diagnosed with malignant disease.

Patient EK never smoked and had a long-standing interest in nutrition and alternative medicine approaches dating back to her mid-twenties. For many years, she had listened to the controversial nutritionist Carlton Fredericks, author of a number of best-selling books, on the radio. For decades, she had eaten well, following a whole-foods type of diet while avoiding the classic American junk food, refined food way of eating.

In 1999, Patient EK developed unexplained right hydronephrosis, enlargement of the kidney usually brought on by some form of obstruction of the urinary tract, though in her case thought to be secondary to an atrophic right ureter. She eventually underwent surgical correction of the problem, though her right kidney function never returned.

Patient EK also had a long history of hypothyroidism, treated with thyroid replacement medication.

She had otherwise been in good health when in October 2003 she first experienced symptoms consistent with a urinary infection, primarily a sensation of pressure in the pelvis along with increased urinary urgency and frequency, but no fevers, chills, or sweats. When the symptoms did not clear after several days, she consulted her primary care physician, who in turn prescribed a course of antibiotics. Despite some improvement, she still felt considerable pelvic discomfort.

Five days after completing the antibiotics, Patient EK developed severe unrelenting pelvic pain radiating into the right kidney. At one point, she doubled over in pain, which she would later describe as "excruciating."

Patient EK then decided to contact a urologist in her area who had previously treated family members. When she met with the physician in early November 2003, he told her he did not think the problem related to her atrophic nonfunctional right kidney, but he nonetheless ordered a pelvic ultrasound, which revealed on the right side a "large adnexal (ovary) mass measuring 11.6 × 7.2 × 8.2 cm." Though the lesion seemed consistent with an ovarian primary, the same day a CA 125 test, a marker for this specific malignancy, came back within the normal range at 23.0.

Patient EK was then referred to a gynecological oncologist, who performed a pelvic exam and PAP smear, both of which were unrevealing. But a CT scan several days later, in mid-November 2003, showed a large pelvic tumor, as documented in the radiology report: "Evaluation of the pelvis shows the presence of an approximately 8 to 9 cm cystic mass noted in the mid-line deep within the pelvis. There is a soft tissue component noted measuring approximately 3 cm, within the superior most aspect of this cystic pelvic mass."

In the summary section, the radiologist reported, "The possibility of a malignant neoplastic process cannot be excluded." In addition to the atrophic right kidney, the radiologist also described "a 0.5 cm area of low attenuation noted with the anterior aspect of the right lobe of the liver, too small to fully characterize by CT criteria. Correlation with ultrasonography of the liver is recommended."

The earlier ultrasound had evaluated only the pelvis, not the upper abdomen, but nonetheless, the recommended test was not pursued. Instead, during the third week of November 2003, Patient EK underwent exploratory laparotomy, total abdominal hysterectomy, and bilateral oophorectomy for what appeared to be an endometrial (uterine) rather than an ovarian tumor. Frozen section evaluation during surgery confirmed an endometrial carcinoma, but unfortunately the surgeon did not biopsy the liver lesion noted on the CT scan.

The pathology report of the surgical specimen described fairly extensive disease, though a single examined lymph node was free of cancer: "A 3CM DOMINANT PAPILLARY FOCUS OF MODERATELY TO POORLY DIFFERENTIATED ADENOCARCINOMA HIGH GRADE…SHOWING A FOCUS OF INVASION TO JUST WITHIN THE INNER HALF OF THE MYOMETRIUM…AS WELL AS FOCAL INVASION INTO SUPERFICIAL MYOMETRIAL LYMPHATICS. SMALLER PAPILLARY FOCI OF SIMILAR ADENOCARCINOMA ARE PRESENT ELSEWHERE ON THE UTERINE WALL AND MULTIPLE FOCI OF ENDOMETRIAL INTRAEPITHELIAL CARCINOMA ARE PRESENT AS WELL."

In the "Comment" section summarizing the findings, the pathologist noted, "THE HIGH-GRADE APPEARANCE ITSELF AS WELL AS THE OCCURRENCE OF INTRO-EPITHELIAL CARCINOMA AND A WEAK TO NEGATIVE ESTROGEN AND PROGESTERONE RECEPTORS ARE FEATURES OF PAPILLARY SEROUS CARCINOMA AS WELL."

This finding was quite significant, as papillary serous carcinoma is one of the most aggressive, if not the most aggressive, form of uterine cancer, notoriously resistant to both chemotherapy and radiation.

Patient EK recovered from surgery uneventfully, and after her discharge from the hospital she was referred to an oncologist, whom she met during the second week of December 2003. The physician explained to Patient EK that she faced a very serious situation, because of the size of the tumor and the poor-prognosis nature of her specific cancer. He therefore strongly recommended adjuvant treatment with six weeks of pelvic radiation followed by intensive chemotherapy with the drugs Taxol and carboplatin.

However, Patient EK, already interested in alternative medicine, had learned about my approach from a close friend who had been following my regimen with great success since 1990, after a diagnosis of serious recurrent, metastatic cancer. So, after discussing the situation with her husband, she decided she would forgo any of the recommended conventional treatments and instead pursue my therapy. She contacted my office and passed the initial screening, and we then set up appointments after she sent us a letter acknowledging that she was aware that radiation and chemotherapy were the standard approaches to her situation but she of her own accord declined both treatments.

During my first meeting with Patient EK, in early December 2003, I found her and her husband to both be extremely intelligent, gracious, and convinced that my treatment represented the best approach in her situation. I felt it my duty, as per usual, to discuss the standard treatments while commenting that papillary serous endometrial carcinoma was considered resistant to both radiation and chemotherapy.

In terms of radiation specifically, I discussed the two large controlled studies reported in the literature evaluating its effectiveness with endometrial carcinoma limited to the uterus. In the first of these, published in 1980, Aalders described reduced local recurrence with pelvic radiation but an increased rate of metastasis and no overall improvement in survival.[4] In a *Lancet* article appearing in 2000, the author again reported no improvement in survival with the use of radiation in women with poor-prognosis localized endometrial cancer.[5]

The Morrow study published in 1991, the classic large-scale controlled trial of chemotherapy used as adjuvant treatment for poor-prognosis endometrial cancer, showed an actual worsened survival with women receiving treatment as opposed to those who only underwent surgery.[6]

Based on the available scientific literature, Patient EK did not understand why the oncologist she had consulted recommended both radiation and chemotherapy. With her histological diagnosis particularly, and with the possibility of liver metastases, I agreed that it would not be irrational for her to seek out an alternative method.

During that first session, Patient EK shared with me that she had been under extreme stress, caring for her two sickly parents, both in their mid-nineties, and an adult child who had not been in good health either. But she was very determined to follow my regimen properly.

4   Aalders et al., "Postoperative External Irradiation."
5   Look, "Who Benefits from Radiotherapy."
6   C. P. Morrow et al., "Relationship between Surgical-Pathological Risk Factors and Outcome in Clinical Stage I and II Carcinoma of the Endometrium: A Gynecologic Oncology Group Study," *Gynecologic Oncology* 40 (1991): 55–65.

Initially, Patient EK's course on the therapy was somewhat difficult. When she had difficulty tolerating the pork-derived pancreas product I use with our cancer protocols, I switched her to a lamb enzyme. Though not as effective in our opinion as the pork supplement, the lamb pancreas does work well. In any event, after several additional adjustments, Patient EK was able to tolerate the therapy without difficulty and thereafter proved to be vigilant, determined, and compliant. When I next saw her for an office visit toward the end of April 2004, after she had completed some four months of treatment, she reported feeling "great" with "superb" energy. After only several months, she could feel a substantial improvement in her overall health.

Several weeks later, during the second week of May 2004, her gynecological oncologist ordered a CT scan of the abdomen and pelvis, which revealed the following:

> Arising from the liver are several oval low attenuation lesions of varying sizes ranging up to approximately 1.5 × 0.8 cm, and most of these are likely cysts. The smaller of these are too small to characterize. There is some fullness of both adrenal glands without focal mass. The left kidney appears normal. The right kidney is hydronephrotic and shows marked cortical volume loss….

> Imaging at the level of the GE [gastro-esophageal] junction shows a mass-like soft tissue abnormality in association with the GE junction. While likely related to the GE junction it is unusually prominent and cannot be differentiated from a mass in this location and either an esophagram or endoscopy should be performed.

Several days later, Patient EK met with her gynecologist to discuss the findings. As a side note, Dr. Parvis Pour of the University of Nebraska Medical Center had just published his findings in the peer-reviewed journal *Pancreas* showing substantial efficacy of our enzyme product in a mouse model of aggressive pancreatic cancer. Patient EK, who had learned of the publication, brought a copy with her to the visit, but she was disappointed, as she later told me, when the gynecologist seemed completely uninterested. Quite the contrary, the physician expressed her extreme disappointment that Patient EK would not reconsider her decision to refuse both radiation and chemotherapy. She also arranged for a consultation with a gastroenterologist to assess the lesion in the GE juncture.

When I subsequently received a copy of the CT scan report, I discussed with Patient EK that the radiologist seemed to be describing more lesions in the liver this time than reported in the CT scan from November 2003. I was concerned enough that some of these might represent metastatic disease that I adjusted her supplements accordingly.

In late June 2004, Patient EK consulted with a gastroenterologist and underwent endoscopy, which fortunately showed no esophageal tumor but only a hiatal hernia. When I saw her again in late July 2004, she reported she felt "terrific," with superb energy, stamina, concentration, etc. Although the stress in her life continued, she was generally quite compliant with the pre-scribed regimen.

Subsequently, I continued seeing Patient EK in my office every three months, and she continued doing very well. When I saw her in January 2005, after she had completed some thirteen months on treatment, she again reported feeling great; in fact, she said with each passing month, her overall well-being improved. I had also switched her from her synthetic thyroid medication to our nonprescription glandular, and she found with the change her energy not only had improved, but her long-standing cold sensitivity, which had persisted for years despite her use of standard thyroid medication, had finally resolved.

In addition to her visits with me, Patient EK also continued her regularly scheduled follow-up with her gynecological oncologist. In March 2005—after Patient EK had completed some sixteen months on her nutritional program—the gynecologist ordered a CT scan of the abdomen and pelvis, which was performed at the end of the month. This time around, the scan revealed fewer and smaller liver lesions, with only three described in the summary: "CT scan shows three small hypodense lesions in the right lobe of the liver. These are felt to be cysts. However, a metastatic lesion cannot be excluded."

I suspected, and told Patient EK my opinion, that because the liver lesions appeared to be reduced in number and size, at least some of them had been most likely metastatic cancer in nature, because the enzymes have no effect against benign tumors or cysts. When I saw her in my office during the third week of April 2005, she had just seen her gynecologist, who acknowledged the liver lesions were regressing.

Several days after our visit, Patient EK and her husband moved to a new home in northern Connecticut. The move proved to be stressful, and for several weeks Patient EK was less than ideally compliant with her nutritional therapy. But she and her husband were quite pleased with their new home, which had sufficient land for a large garden.

When I next saw Patient EK, in mid-July 2005, she was very laudatory about her nutritional program, which she said had "changed my life" and had provided unexpected benefits. As an example, she reported her seasonal allergies that had plagued her for many years had virtually resolved, despite a high pollen count that spring and summer. She also informed me that she had seen her gynecologist two weeks earlier, who, according to Patient EK, had "finally given up" trying to convince her she needed to proceed with radiation and chemotherapy.

During a subsequent visit to my office, during the third week of October 2005, her biggest concern was her father, who was now in his late nineties, and who had recently been diagnosed with terminal metastatic cancer. He was in hospice, and, unfortunately, her mother, also in her late nineties, was not doing well either. Her father eventually passed away in December 2005, her mother in March 2006. Through all the stress in her life, Patient EK continued on her program, continued her regular visits with me—which I had by that point cut back to every six months—and continued doing extremely well.

In July 2007, she was referred to a urologist after an episode of severe flank pain associated with the passage of "sand and sludge" in her urine. A CT scan of the abdomen and pelvis revealed "nonobstructing left renal calculi" and, as before, "multiple" liver cysts but this time no suspicious lesions. For her stones, I suggested a very effective treatment I first learned from a Dr. David Williams newsletter, four ounces of reconstituted lemon juice in twenty-eight ounces of water, two quarts daily for two weeks. With the treatment, the stones passed, and the pain resolved.

When I saw Patient EK in mid-December 2008, after she had completed five years on her therapy with me, she again reported feeling generally "great." She seemed generally quite compliant with her regimen and really had no complaints other than her concern for her intermittently ill child. A week earlier, she had seen her gynecologist, who, with the passage of time and Patient EK's good health, seemed more accepting of my therapy.

In late May 2009, Patient EK was bitten by a deer tick, which are very endemic in her part of Connecticut. Though she didn't develop the classic "bull's eye" rash characteristic of Lyme disease, she did experience a flu-like illness with low-grade fevers, chills, malaise, arthralgias, and myalgias. An astute emergency room doctor at her local hospital diagnosed borreliosis, a tick-borne illness often accompanying Lyme disease. After starting on antibiotics, she improved rapidly.

In 2010, Patient EK came under the care of a cardiologist after an episode of chest pain that proved, after a full workup, to be insignificant. Then, in July 2012, she underwent lancing of a rectal abscess that had developed while she was vacationing in the Caribbean. This healed nicely after the procedure, and when she returned to my office in December 2011—after eight years on her nutritional program—she reported she was again feeling well. As she had before, she expressed her gratitude for the program.

She had only recently seen her gynecologist for routine follow-up, and this time around the physician, quite pleased with her progress after eight years, told her to "keep doing what you're doing." In addition, Patient EK informed me that her rectal surgeon had expressed some enthusiasm for my therapy, after hearing about her long-term disease-free survival under my care. During her last office visit, in June 2012, Patient EK—at the time eight and a half years on her treatment with me—reported again feeling "wonderful." Her biggest concerns were her children and their various difficulties with health and life. But she herself was doing "great," still following her program.

For a number of reasons, when she was diagnosed, Patient EK's prognosis for long-term disease-free survival was certainly very poor. The initial CT scan from November 2003 revealed an "8 to 9 cm" mass in the mid-pelvis, quite large for a primary endometrial tumor. After her hysterectomy, the pathologist described extensive disease throughout the endometrium, the inner lining of the uterus, extending up to 50 percent of the underlying muscular layers—another poor prognostic indicator. Perhaps most importantly, the actual type of uterine malignancy diagnosed in this case, papillary serous carcinoma, is a relatively rare but very aggressive form of the disease. According to the website UpToDate, "At the time of presentation, approximately 60 to 70 percent of women with USC [uterine serous carcinoma, identical to papillary serous] will have disease spread outside of the uterus."

Although the initial abdominal CT scan indicated the presence of several benign cysts, in addition the radiologist mentioned another lesion that could not be characterized. A subsequent CT in March 2005 reported some regression in the nodules and specifically raised the issue that one of these might represent "a metastatic lesion." Because none of these liver areas was biopsied, we do not know for certain what they might actually have been, but based on their appearance over time, it is quite possible that at the time of diagnosis Patient EK had a combination of benign and malignant liver tumors. Regardless, the size and histology of the primary endometrial tumor portended a very poor prognosis, so poor the gynecological oncologist with whom Patient EK consulted after her surgery insisted she begin a course of intensive pelvic radiation to be followed by aggressive chemotherapy, treatments she refused, instead choosing to begin my regimen. Despite the initial dire predictions of her oncologist, on treatment with me she has remained free of her cancer, and now nine years from diagnosis Patient EK enjoys excellent health and continues following her unconventional therapy.

*IMPORTANT EDITOR'S NOTE:
Dr. Gonzalez died before he updated this case report. According to her patient file, Patient EK died in September 2014.

PART II:

Parasympathetic-Dominant Cancers

LEUKEMIA

The leukemias are cancers of the white blood cells, the cells designed to protect us from bacterial, fungal, and viral infection and to regulate inflammation, a necessary part of tissue repair. Neutrophils specifically are those phagocytes that predominantly scavenge bacterial invaders, while lymphocytes protect us against fungal and viral pathogens, as well as cancer, and synthesize antibodies, proteins that serve to identify and mark foreign microorganisms, making them easy targets for the neutrophils.

Cancer can occur in either of these cell lines, and over the years, researchers have identified a variety of different forms of the disease, based not only on the specific type of white cell involved, but also on the degree of inherent aggressiveness. As a general rule, the more immature the cancerous cells, in terms of their molecular biology, appearance, and behavior, the more deadly; the more similar to mature white cells, the more indolent the course.

The myelocytic leukemias affect the neutrophils, while the lymphocytic leukemias develop in the lymphocytes. Acute myelocytic (AML) leukemia and acute lymphocytic (ALL) are among the most aggressive of cancers; before the advent of effective chemotherapy regimens, the lifespan for patients with each of these illnesses was often measured in weeks. On the other hand, chronic myelogenous leukemia is far less aggressive; in the past, even untreated patients could often live three or more years. Today, with targeted therapies such as Gleevec, which dismantles a critical enzyme system in leukemia cells, patients are living long and productive lives.

According to *Harrison's*, in 2010 14,990 cases of chronic lymphocytic leukemia, or as it is currently called, B-cell chronic lymphoid leukemia, were diagnosed in the US.[1] To date, the cause remains, in conventional oncology, unknown, though interestingly the disease appears to be quite rare in Asia—an indication perhaps of some type of genetic or environmental influence. This malignancy can evolve very slowly; up to 75 percent of patients live five years, and up to half live ten years, but most frequently the cancer ultimately turns aggressive and at that point incurable, despite use of aggressive chemotherapy. For patients diagnosed with a more aggressive subtype, the median survival drops precipitously to one and a half years.

Overall, leukemia, whatever the type, is generally a disease of adults, particularly in the case of the chronic leukemias, both CML and ALL. Acute lymphocytic leukemia can target children, but fortunately this particular disease does respond to aggressive multiagent chemotherapy in more than 50 percent of cases. This success with childhood ALL represents one of the few outstanding victories in the conventional oncology war against aggressive cancer.

---

1 Longo et al., *Harrison's Principles*, 18th ed., 919.

In the following discussion, I describe two patients diagnosed with a poor-prognosis form of chronic lymphocytic leukemia, both of whom have experienced significant regression of their disease and enjoyed generally healthy lives while pursuing my treatment only.

I also describe a woman presenting with hairy cell leukemia, a rare malignancy of the B lymphocytes considered a subclass of chronic lymphocytic leukemia. However, unlike patients with classic CLL, those diagnosed with the hairy cell form usually have a low white count instead of high. As with CLL, patients often present with anemia and low platelets (pancytopenia). The designation "hairy cell" refers to the appearance of the lymphocytes under the microscope.

Like the other chronic lymphocytic malignancies, hairy cell leukemia can be very indolent in nature or, in certain cases, more aggressive. This cancer does respond to a variety of chemotherapy agents such as cladribine and pentostatin, as well as immune modulators such as Rituxan, technically a monoclonal antibody, and many patients experiencing a remission with drug treatment live ten or more years. My patient, who has now survived nearly twenty years, has experienced excellent health on her nutritional program while avoiding the need for any conventional interventions.

___

Case 1: Patient BH
A 22.3-Year Survivor*

Patient BH is an eighty-eight-year-old male, a World War II combat veteran and Ivy League–educated engineer and businessman who had followed the Kelley regimen in the early 1980s for general preventive reasons. When he first consulted with me in early July 1992, he had not been diagnosed with leukemia, but he sought to resume an intensive nutritional program because of ongoing urinary symptoms. For some three years, he had experienced gradually worsening urinary frequency, urgency, and nocturia (urination at night) and a feeling of incomplete bladder emptying. In December 1989, he experienced a three-day episode of hematuria (blood in the urine), which resolved with no treatment. He subsequently did well until July 1, 1992, when he again noticed blood in his urine over a twenty-four-hour period.

He had been followed closely over the years at the local VA, where he received all his medical care. An initial PSA reading in July 1991, a year before he consulted with me, was significantly elevated at 14 (normal less than 4), but a needle biopsy of the prostate at the time revealed only inflammation, not cancer. A repeat PSA in January 1992 was even more elevated, at 22.7. A repeat test in February 1992 came back somewhat lower but still high at 15.7. Further studies, including a second biopsy and CT scans, were suggested but refused by the patient. Instead of pursuing the conventional diagnostic route, he began following a self-designed nutritional program including pumpkin seeds and saw palmetto, an herb that blocks the enzyme 5-alpha reductase implicated in prostate enlargement and prostate cancer. With these supplements, his urinary symptoms improved substantially.

In addition to his prostate problems, he had a long history of hypertension and macular degeneration, which he hoped my program might stabilize, if not cause to regress.

Several weeks before his initial visit with me, his primary care physician had ordered a complete blood panel. His hemoglobin was perfectly fine at 15.6, indicating no anemia, and his white blood count fell within the high normal range at 9.90 (normal 4.10–10.9). However, the differential, a breakdown of the individual white cell subtypes, showed an elevated number of lymphocytes at 5969 (normal 1049–3581). According to some old laboratory tests he had sent to me, it appeared his lymphocyte count had been gradually increasing since 1989.

As I reviewed his records the day we first met, in July 1992, I suggested we repeat the PSA, which this time came back elevated once again at 15.6.

Because his urologist suspected the abnormal results indicated not cancer but only chronic prostatitis, I initially designed a preventive nutritional regimen for Patient BH without the large doses of pancreatic enzymes we reserve for those with a diagnosis of malignant disease.

When I first met Patient BH and his wife, I found them both to be very charming, very interested in nutrition, and very determined. I suspected he would prove to be a very compliant patient, and most likely a pleasure in the practice. And he subsequently followed his prescribed regimen with great dedication.

I didn't see Patient BH back in the office until some six months later, on January 28, 1993, when he returned for a re-evaluation. Blood studies from ten days prior to the visit were essentially unremarkable except for a PSA reading of 19.6, once again on the rise. In addition, his white count was now elevated at 11.8 (normal 3.8–10.8), with a lymphocyte percentage at 69 percent (normal 18–47).

At the session, he reported significant improvement in many symptoms since beginning his therapy with me. His nocturia, urinary urgency, and frequency during the day had basically resolved. He did describe considerable stress in his business, which he talked about at length. I made some minor adjustments to his program and planned to see him in another six months.

In April 1993, a repeat PSA ordered by his primary physician at my suggestion came back somewhat lower than previous tests, at 15.4.

Prior to our next scheduled visit, on September 20, 1993, Patient BH went for blood studies. His PSA was up a little at 17.4 but was still more or less in the same range it had been. I was more concerned about his white count, which now had reached 13.1 and seemed to be following a steady upward trajectory. His lymphocyte percentage came in elevated at 63 percent, and I wondered if he might be heading toward CLL. I discussed the findings with him, suggesting a consultation with an oncologist. He asked me if his situation would warrant treatment in the conventional world, and I explained that even if this turned out to be CLL, watchful waiting would be the most likely recommended course of action in any event. He said he would defer any such consultation for now and simply follow the white count with me.

I was also concerned because Patient BH had been traveling abroad frequently since I had last seen him for various overseas work projects, and unfortunately his compliance had fallen off. His wife also remarked that he was consuming increasing amounts of sweets. I gave my usual lecture about the need for vigilant compliance in order to achieve the results we both wanted, he promised to do better, and we agreed to continue following his PSA and white counts regularly.

When repeated three months later in mid-December 1993, the PSA was slightly lower again, at 15.0. Then, prior to Patient BH's next office visit on March 1994, his PSA was up slightly to 17.2, but his white count, though still elevated, had dropped somewhat to 12.8. His platelets—small subcellular units needed for normal blood clotting—had dropped slightly outside the normal range for the first time to 124 (normal 130–400). Often, as any of the leukemias advance, the growing numbers of white cells can crowd out the platelet precursors in the bone marrow, leading to a low count. However, the level was only slightly outside of the normal range and hardly indicative of any pending immediate problem. I suggested he add on a supplement "Bone Marrow," consisting of beef bone marrow, which we find very effectively helps elevate low platelet counts.

When Patient BH and I met together on March 22, 1994, he reported feeling "fine" in all areas, with no urinary difficulties whatsoever. He described great energy, was trying to cut out sweets (though he still admitted to some cheating), and otherwise seemed quite compliant with his prescribed regimen. His blood pressure, which he monitored regularly at home, had improved significantly. We talked about his elevated white count and low platelets, but when I explained in response to his questions that he was not in danger, he again declined a referral to an oncologist.

When his VA doctor repeated the blood work in June 1994, his white count came in at 12.9, and his platelets were now at a normal level at 154. When repeated on October 18, 1994, the white count was up slightly to 13.9 and the platelets were now well within the normal range at 213. The PSA came in at 17.7. When I saw him for a visit the following week, in late October 1994—now more than two years since his first visit—he reported feeling very well, with no urinary or other problems.

Blood studies in late February 1995 indicated a white count at 14,000, platelet count at 168,000, and PSA at 16.9. When he came in for an office visit on March 7, 1995, he seemed quite compliant with the supplements and detoxification routines, but once again he admitted to dietary indiscretions, essentially, a sweet addiction. But he felt well and had no complaints.

I didn't see Patient BH again until November 20, 1995, some nine months later, and more than three years after he had started treatment with me. At the time, he appeared to be compliant with most aspects of the regimen but admitted to ongoing dietary cheating, sometimes significant, with sweets, cookies, cakes, etc. He also described stress with his work and stress in his personal life, which he discussed at length.

He hadn't gone to the VA for his usual blood work before the visit, but in mid-December his primary care doctor did order a PSA, which came back higher at 19.0. We didn't repeat the blood counts until March 1996, when his white cell level came back at 12.9 and platelets borderline normal at 132. Two weeks later, when he returned to my office for a visit, he reported that he continued to feel well and continued to cheat with his diet but otherwise adhered to the regimen. I still did not feel the need to change him over to a full cancer program, because his white count seemed to have stabilized only slightly outside the normal range.

Six months later, in September 1996, he returned for another office visit and again reported feeling fine. A day later, he went to the VA for blood testing. At this time, his white count had actually fallen to the normal range at 10.0, his hemoglobin remained perfectly normal, and his platelets were well within the normal range at 168.

He continued doing well when, in early December 1996, some three months after our previous office visit together, he experienced a two-day period of hematuria. At my suggestion, he consulted with his urologist, who arranged for an intravenous pyelogram (IVP), a dye study of kidney function. The test revealed a rather large bladder tumor at least 2 cm in diameter consistent with a primary bladder cancer. I spoke to his urologist, who intended as a next test a cystoscopy, insertion of a tube directly into the bladder that allows for both visual inspection as well as biopsy of any abnormal tissue. In preparation for the test, a complete blood count indicated a white count at 16.6, the highest level to date.

In late January 1997, Patient BH underwent cystoscopy, which revealed no bladder tumor but a significantly enlarged prostate lobe that had confounded the IVP. His urologist, concerned about possible cancer, performed a prostate biopsy in late January 1997; fortunately, no cancer was evident in the specimen, only benign changes. I subsequently spoke with the urologist, who admitted that he was surprised that multiple biopsies showed no malignancy. He did suggest that, because the median (middle) prostate lobe was so big, Patient BH undergo a transurethral resection of the prostate (TURP), to prevent future obstruction of the urethra.

In preparation for the procedure, a post-void residual test of bladder function showed Patient BH was not retaining urine despite the enlarged prostate—a finding that further perplexed his urologist. I suspect our various nutritional interventions had kept the urine flow going, so that Patient BH experienced minimal symptoms. Consequently, Patient BH, with the consent of his urologist, chose to defer the TURP until such time as his urinary symptoms worsened. In a letter to me, Patient BH's urologist reported that his urine flow was "impressive, given the size of his prostatic obstruction." He suggested that Patient BH begin both Proscar and Hytrin for his enlarged prostate. When I subsequently discussed the recommendations with Patient BH, he agreed to give the medication a try.

A PSA on February 19, 1997 was significantly elevated at 31.5, a result I attributed to the various procedures and the biopsies that had disrupted the prostate. When I saw Patient BH on April 1, 1997, he reported feeling fine, with nocturia no more than once a night if that much, but otherwise no symptoms of urinary obstruction. At that point, I decided to include two doses of pancreatic enzymes away from meals, to deal with the presumptive CLL and help ward off any future prostate cancer.

A PSA that day arranged at the VA was, at 12.2, nearly 20 points down from the high reading in February 1997. In July 1997, a repeat PSA was even lower at 12.0.

On September 26, 1997—more than five years after he had started treatment with me—Patient BH's white count came in at 15,400, platelets normal at 151,000. When I saw him for an office visit on October 7, 1997, we discussed the white count, which, although lower than the February 1997 reading, had been running consistently elevated. I discussed the possibilities, including CLL, but mentioned that even if this were the case, with his white count fairly stabilized a "watch-and-wait" approach remained appropriate. However, I again suggested a consultation with an oncologist-hematologist would be indicated, if his white count again started rising. After all, I explained, if the diagnosis of CLL were confirmed, I would switch him to a full cancer program.

In December 1997, the WBC had dropped to 11.0, but when, a month later, in January 1998, it had risen to 14.1, I referred him to an oncologist friend who is quite happy to work with my patients without being critical of their choice of an alternative treatment approach. Patient BH agreed to meet with the physician, and during the spring of 1998 he underwent a full hematologic evaluation.

Studies of Patient BH's peripheral blood confirmed CLL, as documented in the pathologist's report:

> The study shows the presence of a monotypic B-Cell population....

> In summary, the immunophenotypic findings are those of chronic lymphocytic leukemia (CLL).

A CT scan of the chest on April 24, 1998 was unrevealing. A CT scan of the abdomen and pelvis that same month demonstrated a "markedly enlarged" prostate gland measuring 8 × 8 cm and a 2 cm mass on the left adrenal gland, "most likely representing an adenoma," a benign tumor. There was, however, no evidence of enlarged lymph nodes or an enlarged spleen as is often seen in advanced CLL.

My oncologist friend wrote me on May 13, 1998, summarizing the findings and stating his opinion about the case: "Since he does not have any cytopenia or lymphadenopathy [enlarged nodes] he does not require any treatment at this point."

When I met with Patient BH in July 1998, his white count was at 13.4, but his PSA had jumped on medication to 34.0—a substantial increase. He felt fine, however, and reported no urinary symptoms. At this time, with the diagnosis of CLL confirmed, I recommended Patient BH increase his enzymes to five doses during the day away from meals, not quite at the level we recommend for overt aggressive leukemia.

When he returned three months later, in late October 1998, he reported that he and his wife had just returned from a five-week tour of the US via Amtrak. He seemed to have complied fairly well with his supplement program during this time. Though he tried to stick to the prescribed diet, certainly the food wasn't organic and the cramped conditions prevented him from continuing the various detoxification routines I had prescribed, including the coffee enemas.

For the first time he also reported some new-onset fatigue, which he attributed to the Hytrin prescribed by his urologist. Although effective against prostatic hypertrophy, the drug has long been used to treat hypertension. In his case, he suspected his lowered blood pressure left him feeling tired, certainly a real possibility. Patient BH said he wished to stop the drug for two weeks, a suggestion I thought perfectly reasonable. Subsequently, off the Hytrin he did feel somewhat better, but he then decided to resume the medication when his blood pressure began to rise.

Blood studies performed in December 1998 before a scheduled January 1999 office visit with me showed a white count at 16,000 and a platelet count at 139,000. He reported no new symptoms, and when I saw him again in late April 1999, his biggest concern was his fluctuating blood pressure. He had undergone a complete medical workup at the local VA, including an EKG and chest x-ray, both of which were "fine." However, his PSA had gone up to 38.

His physicians had suggested a new medication for his blood pressure as well as a consultation with a VA oncologist to deal with the CLL and the rising PSA. After reading about the side effects of the recommended drug, he told me he wasn't anxious to switch from Hytrin. However, he was open to the oncology consult, just to have someone locally involved with his care. We also discussed several herbal interventions for the prostate, which he incorporated into this program.

Blood studies ordered by his VA primary physician in March 1999 showed a white count up to 21,000, the highest it had been. At that point, he arranged for the oncology consultation at the VA, which he pursued prior to our next visit, on July 29, 1999. This time, his white count was down to 17,000 and his PSA had dropped to 23, a significant change in the right direction from the previous reading of 38.

A CT scan of the chest on July 13, 1999 was as before unremarkable, but this time around, the CT scan of the abdomen and pelvis revealed an enlarged spleen, a sign the organ was sequestering extra white cells. As before, the prostate was grossly enlarged but approximately the same size compared with the studies done in April 1998, more than a year earlier.

When I saw him in early November 1999, his white count was at 17,000 and his PSA had fallen again to 20.07. He felt well, and no one at the VA was urging any treatment for his leukemia. His blood pressure, which he continued to check regularly, had been more nicely controlled after I had suggested adding the amino acid taurine, shown to reduce hypertension, to his protocol.

Throughout 2000, Patient BH and I were in frequent contact by phone, and I continued seeing him in the office on a regular basis. In addition, he regularly followed up with his VA hematologist, who now arranged for blood testing. That year, his white count began to climb, reaching 23,000 in September 2000. I increased his dose of enzymes substantially, to the full therapeutic range we use when treating leukemia—six doses during the day away from meals, and a seventh dose in the middle of the night (to keep enzyme blood levels constant). Subsequently, the white count when measured in March 2001 had dropped to 13,500, but his platelets were down to 94,000. A platelet count below 100,000 signals a poor prognosis for those diagnosed with CLL. By May 2001, his white count was up again, this time to 26,400, but his platelets had improved to 133,000.

In late October 2001, after an episode of hematuria, Patient BH was admitted to the VA for an evaluation. The attending urologist suggested a TURP, and this time around we all agreed that this was the appropriate course of action. Unfortunately, after the procedure the bleeding only worsened, to the point that his hemoglobin dropped to 8.8. Fortunately, after I suggested he add on high doses of the bioflavonoid rutin—which nicely controls hemorrhage—the problem resolved and he was able to avoid a transfusion.

He was discharged from the VA in early November 2001, but two weeks later his left leg, which had been injured during his WWII service, swelled considerably. His physician diagnosed a blood clot in the venous drainage system of the leg, an issue that brought him back to the hospital to begin the anticoagulation drug Lovenox. He also underwent placement of a Greenfield screen in the groin to block any emboli, pieces of the clot, from reaching the lungs—a potentially deadly outcome if not prevented. The screen went in without difficulty, but the Lovenox prompted another episode of urinary bleeding, which continued after he left the hospital. When the problem didn't resolve in late November 2001, his doctors discontinued the medication.

Unfortunately, with his hospitalizations and recuperation from the hospitalizations, he had been off his supplement program, with the exception of iron and the rutin. When I saw him in my office in mid-December 2001, he admitted that after some nine years on his nutritional program, even months before his hospitalization for the TURP he had gotten quite careless with his regimen for the first time. He said that before his recent difficulties, he had been feeling so well it was easy to make excuses for not following the program properly. I lectured him gently about the need for ongoing vigilant compliance not only for his prostate issues, but also because of his diagnosis of leukemia. He understood, said he had learned his lesson, and promised to do better.

On my exam that day, his left leg was swollen from the toes to the knee, but he reported it had actually improved in recent days. I suggested he continue close follow-up with his local doctors, raised his dose of iron, and also instructed him that once back home he eat liver daily for the next few weeks—an old Dr. Kelley trick for anemia. The iron and liver worked wonderfully, and within weeks his hemoglobin, though still low, had improved substantially.

By January 2002, he was back on his full regimen, though he continued to cheat with sweets, as his wife alerted me during one of our phone conversations. Nonetheless, his white count improved to 11,900, the lowest it had been in many years, and his PSA at that time was down to 12. However, his left leg remained swollen, so on January 31, 2002, he underwent a CT scan of the pelvis, to rule out lymphatic blockage of the venous or lymphatic outflow. The test showed no lymphadenopathy but did reveal a 4 cm mass in the bladder, described as a "soft tissue density," which seemed similar to the mass first noted some five years earlier during the IVP in December 1996. Nonetheless, his VA doctor suggested a referral back to the urologist.

Patient BH and I talked on February 8, 2002 about the developing situation. His left leg was still swollen, and in addition to the urology consult, his primary VA doctor wanted him to follow up with a vascular surgeon. When he asked my opinion, I referred him to a cardiologist and urologist in Manhattan to whom I had referred patients for many years. Subsequently, during the first week of March 2002, Patient BH met with the cardiologist, who after a thorough evaluation suggested only conservative management of the leg swelling. She also suggested a calcium channel blocker for his blood pressure, which was significantly elevated during her evaluation of him at 200/95. I concurred with her recommendation, and Patient BH began the medication.

In late March 2002, Patient BH met with the urologist, who, after reviewing the CT scans from January, suspected the lesion most likely represented a malignant lesion, perhaps a primary bladder cancer. However, during a subsequent exploratory cystoscopy and biopsy on April 19, 2002, on visual inspection the mass appeared to be a dead tumor, as described in the doctor's note to me: "He has a large necrotic area in the right side of his bladder. I am assuming that this is a tumor."

As we awaited the official pathology report, the physician arranged for an in-hospital second cystoscopic procedure at Lenox Hill Hospital on May 9, 2002 with the intent of removing the lesion, whatever it might be. Several days later, I heard from Patient BH, who said the tumor "was basically a piece of necrotic tissue with a fungal growth around it." It proved to be too big to resect via cystoscopy, so the urologist suggested a direct approach through the pelvic wall and a slit in the bladder. I expressed my opinion that this mass, which might actually have been the source of his previous episodes of hematuria, should come out.

So during the second week of July 2002, again at Lenox Hill Hospital, Patient BH underwent surgery for removal of the tumor via a suprapubic incision. As it turned out, the mass was bigger than previously thought at more than 6 cm in diameter, and completely free-floating with no attachment to the bladder wall. And it was completely dead, as described in the official pathology report:

Infarcted tissue, consistent with hyperplastic prostate, with bacterial colonies.

NOTE: Viable [living] tissue is not identified

According to Patient BH, his doctors were quite perplexed by the findings. I suspected we were dealing with a once-cancerous prostate tumor that had invaded through the bladder walls years earlier and had subsequently died when I placed Patient BH on a more intensive enzyme program in early 1997.

Meanwhile, routine preoperative blood testing on July 2, 2002 revealed a white count of 21,700 and a platelet count at 139,000.

Thereafter, I continued seeing Patient BH in my office every three months, and clinically, he continued doing well. In early January 2003, his white count rose to 37,800, and his platelet count dropped to 125,000, though his hemoglobin was within the normal range. When we talked about the results during a phone conversation, he said he felt fine but admitted that over the holidays he had cheated considerably. Unfortunately, he planned to be traveling for several weeks again, so I suspected his compliance would not be ideal. He had scheduled an office visit for January 29, 2003, after his trip, so we agreed to repeat the blood count at that time.

Unfortunately, he had come home to what he described as a disaster. While he was traveling, the pipes in his house had first frozen and then burst. During a subsequent thaw, the broken pipes had leaked water all through his house, forcing him and his wife into a hotel while repair crews tried to get the situation under control.

With all this going on, before his visit with me he returned to his urologist for a routine follow-up cystoscopy, which revealed a normal bladder, urethra, and prostate. Blood studies on February 2, 2003 showed the white count, now at 40,700, was inching up, and the platelets, at 111,000, were moving downward. When we talked, he told me he was feeling fine and wanted only to continue on his nutritional regimen. When we repeated the test six weeks later, on March 25, 2003, the white count and platelets had both stabilized at 40,500 and 112,000, respectively.

Throughout the first half of 2003, Patient BH and his wife continued living in a hotel as the repair work on his extensively damaged home continued. The whole situation, he told me during a phone conversation, was extremely stressful, and though he was able to follow the supplement regimen and do the enemas in the hotel bathroom, he had less control over his diet. He was doing the best he could.

When we repeated the white count on May 29, 2003, it had risen to 50,300, though the platelets had dropped only slightly to 109,000. Because he was living with such significant and ongoing stress, I decided to increase his enzyme dose again, and a white count in July 2003 had gone down slightly to 49,700. When his urologist repeated the PSA in early August 2003, it came back at 5.64, the lowest reading in many years, and certainly the lowest level since he had started with me in July 1992, more than eleven years earlier.

However, the white count continued climbing, reaching 70,600 in mid-December 2003. When we discussed the results, he told me he felt well and had no intention of changing treatments. Then, when we repeated the test in late January 2004, the white count had fallen to 52,200 and the platelets had gone up to 123,000.

His VA oncologist, who respected fully Patient BH's choice of an alternative treatment, suggested a restaging set of scans, to learn if there had been any change since the last set of CT studies from July 1999, four and a half years earlier.

A CT of the abdomen showed the same splenomegaly but no evidence of new disease. The official report described "no change compared to 7/13/99 study."

The CT scan of the pelvis indicated a "markedly enlarged prostate. Compared to 7/13/99, [sic] study no change is noted."

We were both pleased that the scans demonstrated no adenopathy and no change in the prostate in the years since the last testing had been completed.

Throughout 2004, Patient BH's white count began climbing. When it reached 97,700 in September 2004, his internist urged him to consider chemotherapy. I modified the enzyme dosing but also suggested he meet with his oncologist. Patient BH responded by insisting he would never agree to chemotherapy unless his life was at stake.

In October 2004, his VA oncologist proceeded with a bone marrow biopsy, which confirmed what we already knew: "Morphologic findings consistent with marrow involvement by chronic lymphocytic leukemia of B cell lineage."

During a subsequent phone conversation with me, his oncologist suggested Patient BH now start chemotherapy with chlorambucil, to knock the white count down. When later that day I discussed the situation and the recommendations with Patient BH, he made it clear to me he would not begin chemotherapy now, or at any other time. He knew from his review of the literature that while the treatment might lower his white count, it was never curative, came with a host of side effects, and might actually select for a more aggressive form of his disease—arguments that I believed to be valid. Then, when a repeat white count ordered by this oncologist dropped to 89,000, we all agreed that Patient BH, at least for now, would continue only his nutritional program.

Throughout 2005, Patient BH appeared be doing well clinically, as he pursued his program generally appropriately except for ongoing dietary indiscretions. After I increased his enzyme dose, his white count dropped to 45,500 on May 3, 2005—though it then bounced up to 75,320 in August. Regardless, his oncologist no longer mentioned chemotherapy, as Patient

BH, now eighty-one years old, seemed to be asymptomatic on his nutritional regimen after some thirteen years as my patient.

Though he felt well, in October 2005 I referred Patient BH for Doppler ultrasound studies of his leg as well as his prostate, just for a follow-up check of both areas. The leg was fine with no evidence of any residual clot, and to my surprise, the prostate appeared only slightly enlarged, with no evidence of tumor and with completely normal blood flow. Now at 5.0 × 5.2 × 2.9 cm, it had reduced considerably compared with the prior two CT scans in 1999 and 2004.

When we checked his blood on November 19, 2005, Patient BH's white count had reached 124,800, the hemoglobin was down to 9.7, and platelets were normal at 183,000. By January 2006, the white count was down to 107,000.

During late 2005 and early 2006, Patient BH experienced new-onset digestive problems, particularly pain that began after a course of antibiotics prescribed for an upper respiratory infection. When the pain persisted, in January 2006 he underwent endoscopy at the VA, which revealed gastritis but not overt ulcer disease. However, biopsies confirmed a MALToma (mucosa-associated lymphoid tissue), a type of B-cell lymphoma associated with the bacteria Helicobacter pylon a causative agent in ulcer disease. Usually, a course of antibiotics to eliminate the infectious bacterium reverses this problem, so when the gastroenterologist suggested antimicrobial treatment, I agreed with the plan.

Subsequently, Patient BH's digestive problems resolved nicely. But, though the stomach lining appeared significantly improved on repeat endoscopy in April 2006, a biopsy indicated some residual MALToma. A CT scan of the upper abdomen on April 17, 2006 showed the left adrenal lesion as before, and a "massively enlarged spleen," unchanged from prior studies, but no enlarged lymph nodes. A pelvic CT scan revealed an enlarged prostate at 5.6 × 5.9 cm in size, with some protrusion into the bladder.

His white count reached 159,500 on July 6, 2006, but when his oncologist repeated the test on August 1, 2006, it was down to 140,250, a significant drop. Subsequently, on November 26, 2007, he underwent repeat staging workup. A CT scan of the abdomen showed no change from the previous scans, with the same left adrenal mass evident, along with the enlarged spleen, but no indication of residual MALToma within the stomach.

When we met again for an office visit on February 2, 2007, he told me his gastroenterologist and his oncologist wanted him to consider starting chemotherapy not for his CLL, but for his MALToma—even though the scans had been clear. He was not interested in pursuing such treatment, and we both agreed that before even considering aggressive conventional treatment, endoscopy should be repeated.

On March 28, 2007, Patient BH did undergo endoscopy, which, according to the notes of the gastroenterologist, revealed the following: "Multiple abnormalities were identified in the stomach. … On the greater curvature, at the junction between the antrum and the body, there is a diffuse area of erythema [redness] with nodularity which measures 4.0 × 6.0 cm."

The physician biopsied several of the abnormal areas in the stomach proper, as well as an enlarged node adjacent to the stomach and an enlarged mediastinal lymph node.

The stomach lesions proved to be completely benign, consistent with inflammation but with no evidence of MALToma or H. pylori. The mediastinal biopsy, however, confirmed "chronic Lymphocytic Leukemia Small Lymphocytic Lymphoma."

Patient BH reported to me that his white count performed at the VA had come back at 190,000, which would be his highest level. After I reviewed all the results, we talked about the situation, and he again expressed his wish never to proceed with chemotherapy—particularly for the MALToma, which seemed to have resolved. Because of the rising white count, I once again increased his dose of enzymes, while urging him to be vigilantly compliant with all aspects of the prescribed treatment. When the white count was repeated on June 30, 2007, it had dropped to 142,900, nearly 50,000 points lower. His VA oncologist repeated the test two weeks later, and on July 14, 2007, the white count had dropped still further to 120,400 on the higher enzyme dose.

Over the next twelve months, Patient BH avoided chemotherapy and continued doing very well clinically. His white count fluctuated for a time in the 120,000–140,000 range and then dropped to 109,000 by June 2008. By March 2009, it was down to 82,360—more than 100,000 points lower than the high of 190,000 in the spring of 2007. Over the following year, his white count stayed in that range.

In March 2010, shortly before he was to turn eighty-six years old, he underwent repeat TURP because of worsening urinary symptoms. The procedure went without complications, and his symptoms improved.

He continued doing well, with his white count stabilizing in the 60,000 range, until mid-April 2011, when he developed a bad case of shingles involving his right back and flank. He experienced excruciating pain, malaise, and severe fatigue. I prescribed a course of Valtrex for seven days, as well as the coconut oil extract monolaurin, shown to have an antiviral effect. I also added on capsules of lysine, an amino acid that specifically targets any form of herpes virus, the causative agent in shingles.

Unfortunately, he was so ill that for a period of several weeks he discontinued his supplement program and the coffee enemas. His appetite was down, and he lost some fifteen or so pounds.

In the midst of all this, his white count went up to 103,200. Fortunately, eventually his symptoms slowly resolved and he resumed his full nutritional program. By July 2011, he was feeling much improved, and when I ordered blood counts in October 2011, his white count had dropped to 56,300.

When seen on October 17, 2011, he had only residual evidence of his once-flagrant shingles, and he seemed back on course with his supplements and the rest of the therapy. He reported good energy and resolution of his urinary symptoms, and said to me that he was again doing "well."

In the spring of 2012, as he approaches eighty-eight years of age, he has completed nearly twenty years on his nutritional program. His white count has gradually fallen, registering 49,900 on January 13, 2012, then 44,700 in mid-February 2012. His hemoglobin has improved from prior levels to 10.8, and his platelets came in at 110,000. Clinically, he remains active with no complaints.

I have included Patient BH's history in some detail because it illustrates a number of points about my therapy, and the reasons why patients who persevere most often do well. Certainly, his course over the past twenty years has hardly been simple or straightforward, complicated at times by erratic dietary compliance. But his determination has never wavered, nor has his belief that in working with me we could overcome his various health problems.

When Patient BH first consulted with me, in June 1992, his main concern was his significantly elevated PSA. Though a biopsy had been negative, he knew a continued high level warned of possible cancer brewing. But because he did not have a formal diagnosis of malignancy at that time, I chose not to prescribe a high-dose enzyme program. Our therapy is not covered by insurance, the expense can be significant for a full cancer regimen, and if he didn't have proven cancer I did not want to treat him as if he did.

His white count was in the high normal range at 9,900 (normal less than 10,800), though the differential indicated a lymphocytosis—a harbinger of future trouble. By January 1993, his white count was elevated but only slightly at 11,800, an indication of a developing chronic lymphocytic leukemia. Because the disease can be indolent, the situation at that time did not in my opinion warrant my full cancer therapy. And over the next three years, his white count hovered in the 12,000–14,000 range and, in fact, dropped to normal at 10,000 in September 1996—more than four years after he had begun treatment with me.

Only when his white count began increasing steadily did I suggest a modified enzyme program in April 1997, at about one-third the daily dose I would normally prescribe for active cancer. It wasn't until January 1998 that I referred him for a formal hematology consult that would confirm CLL. With the diagnosis now certain, I modified his program to include the full enzyme dose I recommend for chronic leukemia.

Throughout all this time, clinically he continued generally doing well, even when his white count did increase to a high of 190,000 in the spring of 2007. At that time, he was also diagnosed with the MALToma, the B-cell lymphoma of the stomach lining. In response, I increased his dose of pancreatic enzymes substantially, and since then, he has gradually improved, with his most recent white count in February 2012 at 44,700, the lowest level in many years. Both repeat CT studies and endoscopy have confirmed resolution of his MALToma.

Meanwhile, his PSA over the years has gradually fallen to 5.64 in August of 2003 after reaching a peak of 38 (normal less than 4) in April 1999. He has undergone two TURP procedures to relieve symptoms of urinary obstruction, in October 2001 and in March 2010. In addition, a dead "tumor" was removed from his bladder in July 2002.

Over the years, Patient BH has successfully avoided any conventional chemotherapy, initially suggested by his VA oncologist in October 2004. He has enjoyed his life fully, traveling frequently both in the US and abroad, and enjoying visiting his children scattered around the country as well as his grandchildren. At eighty-eight years old, he certainly is grateful for the good health he has generally enjoyed.

Although oncologists consider CLL a rather indolent cancer, the situation is really far more complex. As with most cancers, certain characteristics portend for a good prognosis, others for a rapidly progressive disease and usually quick death.

For those patients with evidence only of lymphocytosis (high lymphocyte count) in the peripheral blood and bone marrow, my experience is that the median survival runs about ten years. Often, these patients do not initially require treatment, but commonly the disease evolves to a more aggressive form warranting chemotherapy. However, even in those patients who initially respond, the disease invariably proves resistant to treatment.

A hemoglobin less than 10 and a platelet count less than 100,000 are indicators of a poor prognosis, with median survivals measured in the range of one and a half years only, despite aggressive treatment.

When I first met Patient BH, in June 1992, his disease was in an incipient state. It wasn't until six months later that his white count came back elevated at 11.8. In April 1997, I suggested he add on two extra doses of pancreatic enzymes, and in the spring of 1998 I referred him to an oncologist for a formal evaluation, which confirmed CLL. His disease seems to have peaked in March 2007, when his white count rose to 190,000 and a mediastinal lymph node biopsy confirmed cancer in the chest. During this time, I adjusted his program extensively, and eventually his counts began to improve.

Patient BH's course illustrates my fundamental approach to cancer, not only chronic leukemias, but all cancers. Traditionally, oncologists and conventional researchers have approached malignancy as a deadly invidious invader that needed to be destroyed completely down to the very last cell, to avoid horrible and deadly outcomes. My mentor Dr. Kelley, as eccentric as he could be, had a different take. He insisted that practitioners needed to approach cancer as a potentially chronic disease that can be managed nicely for many years, even if the cancer is not completely obliterated.

He used the analogy of diabetes, which, if untreated, can be quickly deadly. But with proper management, diabetics can lead normal lives, as long as they follow their prescribed diet and take the required medication. Cancer, Kelley insisted, is no different, and with proper nutritional intervention, it can be controlled effectively for years. In my practice, I have patients now in their nineties who started with me many years ago, who continue to do well, and who danced at my wedding to my wonderful wife, Mary Beth, in 2001. As long as they adhere to their protocol, they do well, even if I would hesitate to call them completely "cured."

This case also demonstrates that managing a cancer patient with my therapy is never a simple process: ups and downs over the years are inevitable, at times requiring adjustment to the regimen. In the case of Patient BH, I changed his therapy as I thought necessary, to adjust to the evolving evidence of disease progression.

Today, twenty years after Patient BH began treatment with me, his leukemia has improved substantially by the standard blood tests, his MALToma seems to have resolved, and his prostate disease—whatever it may actually have been—has become a nonissue, with his PSA nearly in the normal range.

*IMPORTANT EDITOR'S NOTE:
Dr. Gonzalez died before he was able to update this case. According to his office patient files, Patient BH died in November 2014.

Case 2: Patient AR
A Minimum 18-Year Survivor*

Patient AR is a woman in her seventies with a family history pertinent because of a father with prostate cancer and an aunt who developed breast cancer at an advanced age. In terms of her own past, she had smoked briefly when younger and had been diagnosed with osteopenia, which was treated with hormone replacement therapy, and thyroiditis, which was treated with steroids.

She had generally been feeling quite well when, in mid-August 1998, she first noticed multiple small and larger bruises on her body and developed cold feet. She consulted her primary care physician, who ordered routine blood tests. A chemistry screen on August 12, 1998 was unremarkable except for a mildly elevated calcium at 10.6. The hemoglobin and platelets were within the normal range, but the white count was significantly elevated at 88,600 with a lymphocytosis of 87.6 percent (normal 15–45). The peripheral smear was "consistent with chronic lymphocytic leukemia."

Patient AR was immediately referred to a hematologist, with whom she consulted only two days after the blood tests revealed a high white count. Repeat blood studies performed in the hematologist's office revealed a white count somewhat down from the prior reading at 48,600, but still significantly elevated. He discussed with Patient AR the implications of her disease and suggested chemotherapy would be needed when the white count hit 100,000:

> I had a long discussion with Mr. and Mrs. [Patient AR] and thoroughly reviewed chronic lymphatic leukemia and the implications of this diagnosis. I reviewed the natural history of this disease and explained that, although very treatable, this disease is not at present curable. I discussed the high likelihood of chemotherapy in the very near future with the absolute magnitude of this patient's count and suggested that we repeat a count in a couple weeks to see if she were stable or the count was rising. I discussed oral chemotherapy in the form of an alkylator with steroids....
>
> We also discussed several experimental approaches to the treatment of chronic leukemia to include bone marrow transplantation.

A week later, Patient AR traveled to MD Anderson Hospital in Houston for a second opinion. There, repeat blood studies and a bone marrow biopsy confirmed a B-cell lambda form of CLL. The MD Anderson oncologist felt Patient AR did not at that time require chemotherapy, though he suggested she return for testing in Houston yearly and follow up regularly with her local oncologist.

Meanwhile, she remembered a radio interview with me from the mid-1990s and decided to contact our office. We accepted her as a patient, with plans for her to travel to New York in mid-September 1998.

On September 1, 1998, the white count came back at 79,800, and another reading from September 11 was up to 82,300. In addition, this time the calcium level was within normal limits at 10.0.

I first met with Patient AR in the fourth week of September 1998. From the outset, I placed her on a full enzyme program, and she subsequently followed her prescribed regimen with great diligence and dedication. In the months after her visit, she kept in touch by phone with any questions she had and continued monthly follow-up visits with her local oncologist. By late November 1998, the white count was down to 57,800.

On a repeat chemistry screen in late February 1998, her calcium had jumped to 11.9, a significant rise. I suggested the test be repeated along with a parathyroid hormone (PTH) level, a hormone secreted by the four parathyroid glands in the neck. This hormone draws calcium out of the bones to keep the blood levels of this mineral ion constant, but in the case of hyperparathyroidism, when one or more of the four glands release an excessive amount, too much calcium leaches out of the bones and the blood levels rise. This can be a significant concern because, if untreated, even mild hyperparathyroidism can initiate and accelerate osteoporosis. In the most extreme case, very high calcium blood levels can lead to kidney failure, coma, and even death. The usual treatment is surgical removal of the abnormal parathyroid gland or glands.

The repeat calcium on March 29, 1999 came back normal at 9.7, though the PTH level was just over the upper limit of normal at 66 (normal 10–65). Though the blood calcium had normalized, her oncologist felt a referral to an endocrinologist for a parathyroid evaluation was indicated. This was arranged for May 1999, after an appointment scheduled with me for the last week in April. However, her primary care physician repeated the calcium and PTH levels the third week in April; though the calcium was fine at 9.0, the PTH level had increased to 230.

This picture can indicate a vitamin D deficiency; this hormone-like vitamin is needed to assist with the absorption of calcium during digestion. Without adequate blood levels, calcium absorption falls, and the parathyroid glands begin releasing PTH in high amounts to keep the blood calcium levels in a safe range. I did include vitamin D in her regimen, but in modest doses. A subsequent vitamin D level was at the lower limit of normal, and I increased the dose slightly.

At our visit together in late April 1999, Patient AR seemed very compliant with all aspects of the therapy and reported excellent energy, stamina, endurance, and overall health. She had informed her oncologist that she had chosen to consult with me and follow my treatment regimen, and he seemed quite happy to follow her without initiating conventional treatment. In fact, Patient AR told me, he was quite pleased her white count had dropped so significantly as she pursued my therapy.

Back home, the endocrinology evaluation continued. Parathyroid imaging indicated two possible parathyroid adenomas, benign growths typically associated with hyperparathyroidism. But when all the testing was completed by June 1999, the endocrinologist diagnosed "mild hyperparathyroidism" that in his opinion warranted only careful monitoring of her calcium levels, but no treatment. Meanwhile, her white count suddenly rose to 85,000, an increase that concerned her and me. I decided not to make any adjustments with her supplements but wait until the next results were available in a month.

In late August 1999, Patient AR returned to MD Anderson for a yearly visit. Her white count was 82,600, in the same range as the original reading in August 1998 of 88,600. She reported to me that although her white count remained significantly elevated, her MD Anderson doctor was actually quite pleased that her disease seemed quite stable. In addition, a repeat calcium level came back within the normal range at 9.7.

Patient AR returned to New York for a visit with me the first week of October 1999. She again seemed very determined to follow my program properly and reported feeling well other than a flu-like syndrome after her visit to Texas that eventually resolved with a course of antibiotics.

Three weeks after she returned home, her local oncologist repeated the blood studies; her white count this time around had dropped to 64,000, but her calcium was up again to 10.6.

Thereafter, she continued her regular visits with her local oncologist and periodically with the endocrinologist. By the spring of 2000, her white count was up slightly to 86,600, though her calcium had dropped to the normal range at 10.2. When I saw her in April 2000, she reported feeling fine.

In late August 2000, when she returned to MD Anderson for her yearly visit, her white count had risen to its highest level, at 106,100, and her calcium was up again to 10.7. However, her Texas oncologist felt, based on the extensive blood studies he had ordered, that she was still fairly stable and not in need of conventional treatment. After her visit there, we had a long phone conversation about the situation: I suggested she remove all calcium from her supplement program and increase her daily enzyme dose, suggestions with which she was happy to comply.

By September 2000, her white count had dropped to 95,000, and her calcium was well within the normal range at 8.9. When I saw her in October 2000, after she had completed more than two years of treatment with me, she reported feeling "superb" with high energy and endurance. She said that she really could feel the difference the program was making in her overall health status.

Subsequently, her white count stabilized, coming in at 99,000 in January 2001. She continued seeing her local oncologist regularly and returned to New York for consultation with me every six months. In August 2001, she was seen again at MD Anderson. At that time, her white count was up to 116,000. During the months preceding that visit, she had been under considerable stress, with a very sick son with a variety of severe medical problems, and a husband whose health was also deteriorating.

We kept in touch by phone, and because of the severe stress in her life, I agreed to do a lengthy phone consultation with her in early October 2001. A week before the session, her local oncologist did repeat the white count, which this time had dropped to 102,000. Though still too high, at least the trend had reversed for the better. By December 2001, it was down to 97,600, but then in late March 2002 it rose again to 123,800. Throughout the first half of 2002, the white count peaked at 124,000 in March, before dropping to 110,000 by July 2002.

Patient AR continued doing well clinically, though the stress in her life reached a peak in late December 2002 when her chronically ill son passed away. She stayed with her therapy through this terrible period, and in mid-February 2003 she returned to MD Anderson. When her white count at the time came back at 112,200, her Texas oncologist once again felt there was no need to institute therapy because she felt well and the counts had basically stayed in the same range. In addition, her calcium remained at a normal level.

She continued to return to New York every six months for a visit with me. In addition, she consulted with her local oncologist every six months and at MD Anderson yearly. In February 2004, her white count was in the same range as it had been, at 110,100, and a bone marrow biopsy confirmed B-cell chronic lymphocytic leukemia, with a positive CD 28 marker, characteristic of the malignancy. Once again, her Texas physician recommended no therapy.

Though her calcium level remained within the normal range, a repeat bone density in July 2004 indicated her bone density had progressed from simple osteopenia to early osteoporosis. At that point, I increased her vitamin D level.

The summer of August 2004, she moved to a new city and consulted with a new oncologist who was willing to follow her regularly. Her white count came back considerably lower at that time at 75,600. Her physician concurred with the MD Anderson team that no conventional therapy was indicated.

In December 2004, I received a note from Patient AR, informing me that after passing all the requirements for her doctorate, she had formally received the degree and could now officially call herself "Dr." She wished me and my staff a happy holiday season, then wrote, "I'm feeling great (thanks to you) but I also thought I'd let you know I'm finally official (note the letterhead)!"

Throughout 2005, Patient AR continued returning to New York for her six-month appointments. She also followed up with her local oncologist every six months and with her specialist at MD Anderson yearly. In January 2005, her white count came in at 75,000; in October 2005, it went up slightly to 86,700. Then in January 2006, it was down slightly at 81,000.

In subsequent years, she continued doing well, with her white count falling in the 70,000–80,000 range. Though we still met every six months, after a visit to MD Anderson in 2007, she decided to forgo any more trips to Texas. She felt well and believed that her local oncologist and I could monitor her progress well enough.

In January 2009, when her white count rose to 89,000, her oncologist expressed some concern. But she had just returned home from a trip abroad and reported feeling not well. I made some minor adjustments to her protocol at the time, and by April 2009 it was down again to 82,800.

A year later, in January 2010, she slipped on ice and fractured her T11 vertebral body. An orthopedist insisted surgery was necessary, but she read the literature about the procedure, which wasn't all that positive, and, after discussing the situation with me, chose only conservative management with physical therapy—and my intensive nutritional regimen. She recovered nicely, with no residual pain or disability.

A white count taken on March 29, 2010 came back reduced at 57,700, and in February 2012 the level was down again, this time to 51,470—its lowest level since she has been on my protocol.

For years, Patient AR's white count stabilized in the 80,000–100,000 range. It peaked in March 2002 at 124,000, before gradually dropping to its present level of 51,470, a fall of some 72,000, while pursuing no treatment but mine. Currently, she continues on her nutritional therapy, continues doing well, and continues returning to New York every six months. She has moved again, to a Southern city, and fortunately has found a sympathetic oncologist who is willing to follow her on a regular basis without pushing any standard treatment approaches.

Now, having passed seventy years of age, she enjoys excellent health and enjoys her life. Her calcium incidentally has fallen within the normal range in recent years, though her osteoporosis has progressed somewhat. I am planning another evaluation for hyperparathyroidism, which might explain her ongoing though very gradual bone thinning while following my nutritional program.

Though CLL can follow an indolent course, invariably the disease progresses with a rise in white count, sometimes gradually, and sometimes more acutely. In AR's case, when her levels peaked in 2002 I adjusted her program accordingly, with good results. I doubt her white count will ever reach the normal range, but I suspect she will continue to enjoy good health and lead a normal life.

This case also illustrates a valuable lesson about our treatment approach. Patients who trust in what I do, even when the situation appears to be worsening, most commonly pull through nicely. Even when her white count reached its high of 124,000, Patient AR didn't panic and didn't start doubting the treatment, but only wondered what I might do differently to get the count to move in the right direction. When I suggested a change in enzyme dose, she complied, never thinking about dropping the therapy or beginning chemotherapy despite the suggestions to consider conventional options expressed by her worried oncologist.

*IMPORTANT EDITOR'S NOTE:
According to her patient medical file, Patient AR contacted Dr. Gonzalez's office after his death in July 2015. She last met with Dr. Isaacs in October 2016.

Case 3: Patient QF
A Minimum 16-Year Survivor*

Patient QF is an eighty-year-old man with a diagnosis of chronic lymphocytic leukemia. There has been a fair amount of cancer in his family: his maternal grandfather died at a young age from a sarcoma, a maternal uncle died with stomach cancer, and his mother survived colon cancer. His older sister had died from chronic lymphocytic leukemia seven years after her diagnosis in the mid-1990s, while being treated with aggressive chemotherapy. With a long interest in nutrition and alternative approaches, Patient QF had tried to interest his sister in less conventional approaches, but to no avail. He would later report to me her death had been "miserable."

In terms of his own past medical history, Patient QF had survived a case of rheumatic fever at age nine that left him with a slight heart murmur but no serious disability. At age twenty-two, after being discharged from the service during the Korean War, he was diagnosed with a very mild case of tuberculosis that did not warrant any treatment.

In addition, he described a long history of easy bruising going back decades, which his doctors thought was insignificant. In July 1999, the situation worsened: he developed severe spontaneous bruising on his trunk as well as all extremities that was far worse than he had previously experienced. In addition, he experienced significant night sweats, persistent fatigue, and bilateral leg cramps at night.

Patient QF consulted with his internist, who was affiliated with the Cleveland Clinic. His exam was unremarkable, but routine blood testing revealed a significantly elevated white count at 27,000 (normal 4,000–11,000), a borderline hemoglobin at 12.8 (normal 13.5–17.5), and low platelets at 116,000 (normal 150,000–400,000). At that point, his physician, after advising Patient QF that he most likely had developed CLL, referred him to a hematologist at the Cleveland Clinic.

When he was first seen there, during the third week of July 1999, on exam the hematologist noted enlarged lymph nodes in the neck and in both axillary regions and told Patient QF he most likely had poor-prognosis stage III or IV CLL, as recorded in the note from the session: "This probably represents chronic lymphocytic leukemia. I will try to confirm this diagnosis by immunophenotyping the peripheral blood today. Assuming the diagnosis is correct, he would be classified as stage V [sic] given his anemia and thrombocytopenia."

Repeat blood studies showed some improvement in the white count, with a drop to 24,230, a normal hemoglobin at 13.5, and improved platelets at 129,000. Flow cytometry studies confirmed CLL, and with the new blood work in hand, the hematologist thought QF's disease was most likely stage II or III, not stage IV. A bone marrow biopsy was thought unnecessary at this time, as was any aggressive treatment. However, the well-meaning hematologist told him that at some point his disease would advance, at which point chemotherapy would be needed but would nonetheless not be curative. Even with treatment, the specialist explained, he would be fortunate if he lived seven years—actually the lifespan of his sister after her diagnosis with the same disease.

Patient QF decided to seek out a second opinion at University Hospital in Cleveland, where the hematologist, after his evaluation, agreed with the diagnosis of CLL, that a bone marrow biopsy wasn't needed, and that treatment should be delayed until the disease progressed. When Patient QF, based on his own reading, subsequently changed his diet to an organic, whole-foods approach, the night sweats resolved.

Patient QF continued looking into alternative approaches to his disease, learned about my work, passed the initial screening, and was first seen in my office during the third week of August 1999. During that visit, he admitted he had been under considerable stress during his first marriage, stress that he felt might have been a root cause of his current problem. Fortunately, his second wife was stable, steady, and very supportive in every way.

Thereafter, Patient QF followed his nutritional protocol with great determination. In mid-October 1999, three months after his consultation with me, he went back to the Cleveland Clinic, at which time his white count came in at 25,820 and platelets at 143,000. When we talked by phone, clinically he seemed to be doing well. His biggest problem was a long-standing issue with constipation; I made several suggestions, which he followed with some improvement.

When he returned to the Cleveland Clinic during the second week of January 2000, his white count was 24,750 and platelets were 132,000, more or less in the same range as in October 1999.

When I met with him for his six-month follow-up visit in mid-February 2000, he seemed to be complying with his regimen diligently and generally felt well, with his only real problem his ongoing severe constipation. He had found the enemas very difficult—an unusual occurrence in my experience—but he was determined to try to make them work. A recent colonoscopy at the Cleveland Clinic had been unremarkable, and I suggested he follow up with his gastroenterologist.

In April 2000, he underwent a barium enema at the Cleveland Clinic, which showed no abnormalities. His white count at the time was in the same range as before, at 24,150, and his platelets were up to 146,000, only slightly below the lower limit of normal. During the second week of July 2000, a month before he was due to return to New York for his one-year visit with me, his white count was slightly up to 29,470, his platelets down to 120,000, and his hemoglobin at 12.8.

In early August 2000, just before his trip to see me, he developed a "rash" on his arm that was diagnosed as a mild case of shingles. He was started on antiviral medication with rapid improvement. When he returned to New York one week later, the shingles had already regressed, and he was generally doing well. He wondered if his ongoing constipation might be a combination of allergies and anxiety, both, I thought, reasonable possibilities. Subsequently, he pursued allergy testing and desensitization with a local chiropractor trained in the NAET technique, and, along with some relaxation techniques, the chronic constipation and intestinal discomfort lessened.

Patient QF also continued his regular three-month visits at the Cleveland Clinic and his six-month consultations with me in New York. Clinically he continued doing very well, particularly since the constipation had been more effectively controlled. His white count throughout 2001 hovered in the 29,000 range; platelets ranged from a high of 113,000 in July 2001 to a low of 97,000 in October 2001. When I saw him in February 2002, he seemed to be doing very well, but subsequently, in early April 2002, his white count jumped to 43,160, the highest it had been, though the platelets had improved to 106,000. On exam at the Cleveland Clinic, the lymphadenopathy remained stable, and the spleen appeared to be normal in size, so his hematologist wasn't particularly concerned.

Throughout the remainder of 2002, QF's white counts remained very stable, but in October 2002 his platelet count fell to 83,000, a drop that concerned his hematologist, who now suggested a bone marrow biopsy be done. For the first time in more than three years, he also advised that chemotherapy might now be indicated. Patient QF called me to discuss the situation; he remained adamantly against chemotherapy, mentioning during our conversation how horribly his sister had done with conventional approaches to the same disease. I said that I certainly would support his decision. In terms of the low platelets, I suggested he increase his dose of a supplement, Bone Marrow, and have the blood counts repeated in three months so we could track the trend. He thought my suggestions reasonable and continued his nutritional therapy.

During the fourth week of October 2002, Patient QF consulted with a chiropractor because of chronic low back pain. An x-ray at this doctor's office revealed what appeared to be an abdominal aortic aneurysm, never before noted and of great concern to Patient QF because he had read how deadly these can be if they should unexpectedly burst. When we discussed this new finding, I suggested he undergo CT scanning to assess the size. I told him that, often, such abnormalities can be watched over time; if the aneurysm didn't change, or remained below a certain critical size—usually 5–6 cm in diameter—surgery wouldn't be necessary. I also assured him that should he at some point require an operation, as a patient at the Cleveland Clinic he was already under care at a world-class center renowned for its cardiovascular program.

Subsequently, a CT in early November 2002 confirmed a 3.1 cm aortic aneurysm, which in the opinion of the Clinic experts did not require surgery. He was told that their surgeons didn't operate until an aneurysm reached 5 cm in diameter. Meanwhile, with the supplement changes I had advised, his platelet count had increased to 111,000.

When he returned to New York in February 2003, he seemed to be doing well. With the NAET system of allergy desensitization, he felt he had reached a new level of well-being, though unfortunately his constipation continued to be an intermittent problem. He had tried a senna-cascara herbal laxative I recommend, with some benefit, but then overdid the dose and developed loose stool. I told him to be reasonable with the supplement.

Throughout 2003, Patient QF's white count varied slightly in the 40,000 range, reaching a high of 47,520 in August 2003 with a platelet count of 96,000. When I saw him for a return visit in mid-August 2003, despite the high white count he reported continued improvement in his various problems. He was continuing the intensive NAET allergy treatments, which had helped, he said, enormously, and with proper dosing, the senna-cascara formulation I had recommended seemed to be resolving his constipation.

In January 2004, his white count reached a low of 25,530, though his platelets were still below 100,000, at 92,000. Then, in August 2004, he called wondering whether psychological or spiritual counseling might be helpful for him. I already knew he was a devout Christian and asked him why he had brought up the issue now that he had been on my therapy for some five years. He explained in some more detail the difficulties in his past life. His first wife had been an alcoholic, and Patient QF had spent years taking her to various detox centers, rehab centers, AA groups, and psychiatrists specializing in substance abuse, all to no avail.

It was, he explained, for his own sanity that he finally left the marriage—in retrospect, the only sensible decision he could have made. To complicate the issue, several sons, with whom he had broken off contact years earlier, were unrepentant alcoholics. I knew he had a wonderful and kindly relationship with his current wife, who always accompanied Patient QF on his visits to New York. She seemed devoted to him, and a partner in his therapy with me, helping ensure he followed his prescribed regimen diligently.

But now, as he thought and prayed about his past life, understandably he felt remorse and sadness, particularly over the situation with his three sons. He wondered if that psychological stress could affect his healing. I told him I absolutely believed that to be the case, but I also knew he had done the work to move on from the past.

The conventional medical world, particularly the oncology world, still, even in this day and age of 2012, approaches patients as if they were two-dimensional laboratory rats with no mind, for whom disease is strictly and only a biochemical issue. After twenty-five years in the trenches with very sick patients, let me assure you this is not the case.

When I was a medical student beginning my investigation of Dr. Kelley's therapy and practice, I very much believed, as did my professors, that physical disease, even psychological disease, was strictly and only a biochemical/physiological condition, and with appropriate intervention—either pharmaceuticals or nutritionals, as in Dr. Kelley's case—the disease, whatever it might be, would go away, and in turn people would be healthy and happy. But I learned early on that Dr. Kelley, whatever he would eventually become, whatever bitterness and resentments ultimately undermined his own mental health, was more complex in his approach to patients, always looking for psychological and spiritual issues in each of their lives. At one point, somewhat confused, I asked him, "What percentage of disease in your mind is purely physical-biochemical, purely psychological, and purely spiritual?"

"That's easy," he answered with a wry smile. "It is 100 percent biochemical-nutritional, in every single patient."

Then he waited a few seconds, as I naively nodded my approval, before continuing. "It's also 100 percent psychological, and 100 percent spiritual, in every single patient. There is no line of demarcation, and someday you will come to realize the truth of this."

I was, I admit, somewhat perplexed, and indeed it would take some years in practice before I would come to realize just how truthful his statement was. I would also eventually appreciate another truth Dr. Kelley tried to teach me. At one point in our relationship, he remarked that often, not always, but most often, as patients follow their therapy, get through the most pressing danger facing them in terms of their illness, and begin improving, they begin analyzing their past, their past choices in their lives, their relationships, their careers, and their future. Usually, they begin to ask more spiritual questions, about God and their place in the world. I have seen this over and over again, as in the case of Patient QF. Usually, such self-assessment, as difficult as it might be, ultimately only helps with healing on all levels—the physical, psychological, and spiritual.

Too often, patients arrive in my office thinking that I can provide some wonderful nutritional program that in and of itself magically will transform their bodies and eliminate their disease, whatever it might be. I wish healing were that simple, but most assuredly it is not. The nutritional foundation I provide is just that, a foundation, on which to build the real tough work of healing. In the final analysis, as Kelley told me thirty years ago, the psychological and spiritual should follow, for healing to proceed as powerfully as it should. Yes, I have patients who never ask greater questions about their lives, never look inside or higher up, and do well. But I will say with some certainty that those patients who evolve psychologically and spiritually as they follow their nutritional regimen tend to do better as a group and tend to do better faster.

I do find that leukemia patients in general tend to be very easygoing in terms of personality style, very compassionate toward others, and usually not driven by resentment or anger. Sometimes, they have trouble standing up for themselves, and not infrequently they find themselves in unhappy or even abusive types of relationships, often with a drug or alcohol user. And it can be difficult for them to extract themselves from such situations. But ultimately, they most often find their way, ending up quite happy in their jobs and lives.

In any event, throughout 2003 and 2004 Patient QF continued his regular visits with his Cleveland Clinic oncologist-hematologist and with me in New York. His white count varied somewhat from the low of 25,530 in January 2004 to a high of 48,760 in August of that year.

Throughout the first half of 2005, his white count remained for the most part in the mid-40,000 range, once dropping below 40,000. His platelets varied considerably, from 99,000 to a high of 140,000 in May 2005.

Prior to a visit with me in August 2005, he sent me a long note, discussing some simple issues and a more complicated problem with another one of his adult children. When I saw him in my office, he elaborated somewhat. He and his daughter had had a tentative relationship over the years that recently had essentially fallen apart for reasons that seemed not of QF's doing. For whatever reason, like his sons, she had broken off contact with Patient QF. The loss pained him for many reasons, particularly because his relationship with his daughter's children, his grandchildren, had been so good. He missed them in his life.

When we talked about the situation, his thoughtful wife added that Patient QF's grief was so severe over the situation that she was afraid "he might die of sadness." Much of the trouble, she thought, was the first wife, who had worked hard to turn all of Patient QF's children, including the alcoholic sons, against him—not an unusual scenario when alcohol rules family relationships. Though I have come to learn the hard fact that such devastating stress and deep-rooted loss can undermine progress against cancer, Patient QF remained vigilant with his program, whatever was going on in his life, and his white count fortunately had remained fairly stable. He remarked that he knew his "life depends on sticking with the treatment." Clinically, his biggest problem at that point was leg cramps, which had bothered him from time to time but which recently seemed to have taken a turn for the worse. I suggested he follow up with his doctors at the Cleveland Clinic and get a referral for a vascular workup.

In September 2005, QF underwent a thorough evaluation, which showed only mild atherosclerosis in the leg, not significant enough to elicit the pain he described. He thought perhaps allergies might be the issue, so he continued with his NAET treatment. In addition, in the months that followed he tried a variety of nutritional and herbal products designed especially for leg cramps.

Throughout 2006, his white count varied minimally, from a low of 46,860 in February to a high of 49,390 in May. His platelets had also stabilized somewhat, ranging from 88,000 in February to 101,000 in November.

I saw him for a return visit in early August 2006, at which time he reported feeling quite well. He told me, smiling, that he felt he had reached a major milestone for a number of reasons: when first diagnosed at the Cleveland Clinic in the summer of 1999, his doctors had given him perhaps seven years to live, even with aggressive chemotherapy, the same lifespan as his sister. Well, he pointed out, he had now completed seven years on his program with me and had outlived the dire prognostications, and his white count, although not normal, was stabilized. He generally felt great at seventy-four years of age and thanked me for all that he felt the therapy had done for him.

On exam, I noted two pea-sized nodules, one on his right occipital area, the other behind his right ear. He had been aware of these lesions, which he said hadn't changed, for some months now. I suggested he point them out to his Cleveland Clinic hematologist, whom he was scheduled to see in February 2007.

After his visit at the Cleveland Clinic, he sent me copies of his blood tests, which this time showed a white count up slightly to 50,590 and platelets down to 88,000. On exam, for the first time his physician had detected an enlarged spleen as well as enlarged lymph nodes in the back of his neck, in the back of the ear, and in the groin. But because his white count seemed stabilized, he was not pushing chemotherapy at this time.

When Patient QF returned for his regularly scheduled six-month visit with me in early February 2007, we spent much of our one and a half hours together talking about the recent stress with his daughter, who fortunately was moving away. He felt the physical distance between them would certainly be best for him, so he wouldn't have the constant reminder of their estrangement. In addition, a psychologist with whom he had consulted suggested some simple exercises to help minimize stress.

In May 2007, QF's white count went up to 56,150, the highest level to date, and his platelets came in at 102,000. Subsequently, in August 2007 after a visit to the Cleveland Clinic hematologist, QF informed me that for the first time his doctor there was talking about removing the spleen, which he felt was increasing in size. As a first step to assess the situation, the physician had recommended a CT scan of the abdomen, which was scheduled for early September 2007.

Patient QF and I talked over the phone about the proposed surgery, often done in patients with leukemia to lessen discomfort and prevent possible rupture, a possible risk with even minor trauma as the spleen enlarges. Also, the organ can begin sequestering platelets, so its removal can frequently raise the levels of these blood elements. But because Patient QF didn't report any discomfort, I suggested the operation be delayed.

During the second week in August 2007, only days after his visit to his hematologist, Patient QF returned to New York for a visit with me. He seemed to be doing much better in terms of the stress in his life, and physically, as before, he felt well. When I examined Patient QF, I felt the previously noted lymph nodes on his forehead and behind the ear had resolved, but new ones in the supraclavicular area (above the clavicle) on the right side had popped up. I agreed that the spleen was certainly enlarged, about three to four fingerbreadths below the lower right rib cage.

In early September 2007, the day he received the results of the CT scan, Patient QF faxed me a long note describing the findings as relayed by his hematologist. The spleen indeed was enlarged, measuring 21 cm in widest diameter (normal 11–13 cm). The study also detected "lesions" within the spleen of varying size, which indicated to the hematologist the CLL might be converting to a more aggressive lymphoma. Because of these abnormalities, the hematologist more seriously recommended a consultation with the surgeon to consider splenectomy.

In addition, the CT scan showed that the abdominal aortic aneurysm had increased in size from its previous 3.1 × 3.3 cm to 4.3 × 4.2 cm. This was still less than the 5.5 cm diameter at which point surgery would be indicated.

When I received a copy of the actual radiology report several days later, it confirmed what Patient QF had relayed to me over the phone. From what I read, it appeared that the spleen had been largely replaced by lesions, and enlarged lymph nodes were noted along the small bowel mesentery.

In November 2007, Patient QF did meet with a surgeon at the Cleveland Clinic, who apparently was "amazed" at his eight-year survival since diagnosis without conventional treatment and his overall good health. The physician described the procedure, which because of the spleen's size could not be done through a laparoscopic approach. In any event, the surgeon didn't think an operation was indicated at this time.

The white count in November 2007 came in at 57,480 and the platelets at 95,000. By February 2008, the white count had risen to 64,910, and the platelets were at 85,000. In March 2008, the count dropped slightly, but it then jumped up in early May 2008 to 71,450, with the platelets at 86,000. Fortunately, a repeat study in early June 2008, a month later, showed a white count down significantly to 56,420, though the platelets had dropped again, this time to

79,000—not a good sign, because low platelets represent a bad prognostic indicator in those diagnosed with CLL.

In mid-August 2008, about a week before he was scheduled to return to New York, his white count jumped up to 72,140, and his platelets dropped to 75,000. When I saw him in the office, we discussed the situation. He made it clear to me he would never do chemotherapy and would rather die doing my therapy than suffer through the misery of drug treatment—which he reminded me he had witnessed firsthand when his sister had been treated for the same disease. I understood his position, made some changes in his supplement program, and increased his enzyme dose. Several weeks later, the white count had dropped to 66,190, and the platelets were up to 91,000—a reversal of the previous worsening trend.

During the third week of December 2008, QF contacted my office to let me know he had been to the emergency room at the Cleveland Clinic after losing control of his right arm and right fingers, symptoms that resolved after about twenty minutes. He was nonetheless hospitalized a day and underwent a full neurological workup. An MRI showed minimal changes thought perhaps to be resulting from small emboli in the middle carotid artery, but nothing thought to be terribly significant or worrisome. Doppler ultrasound studies of his carotids showed no significant occlusion, and an ultrasound of the abdomen showed that the aneurysm had increased in size again, to 4.9 cm in its widest dimension. His white count at the time of his hospitalization came in at 67,000, and his platelets were up to 108,000. After all this, he was ultimately diagnosed with a transient ischemic attack (TIA) and sent home.

Meanwhile, his various Cleveland Clinic doctors, after discussing the situation, felt it was time to consider surgery to correct the aneurysm. Unfortunately, they explained, the surgery would be difficult because access to the aorta would be complicated by the enlarged spleen. And there was a great chance the spleen might be damaged during surgery, a potentially catastrophic possibility. Because the spleen is a highly vascular organ, even a minor nick could provoke uncontrollable hemorrhage. So the abdominal surgeon and a vascular surgeon had consulted together and put together a plan to remove the spleen at the time of the aneurysm surgery—a safer approach than trying to work around the spleen. All agreed this was the best way to proceed, and they suggested July 2009 as the target date for the operation.

When Patient QF and I talked about the options over the phone after his visit to the Clinic, he made it clear to me he didn't like the idea of major surgery to remove the spleen and correct the aneurysm. I understood of course his reluctance, but I suggested he seriously consider his doctor's proposal, because at this point his enlarging aneurysm became more likely to rupture. The actor John Ritter and Jon Larson, the composer of the Broadway hit *Rent*, had both died suddenly of previously undiagnosed aneurysms. As to the spleen, if the surgeon couldn't access the aorta without removing the organ, so be it. We might not have any choice.

In February 2009, QF's white count hit its highest level to date at 81,850, though the platelets remained stable at 100,000. When we talked about the results, Patient QF reiterated his determination to stay on my program. By May 2009, his white count was down to 55,870, but his platelets had dropped to 68,000. Although technically blood will still clot even when the patients fall to the 20,000 range, such readings in a patient with CLL usually indicate a turn for the worse, even though the white count had improved by some 24,000 points.

When he came to New York for his scheduled March 2009 visit, we talked about the surgery, which at this point was his major concern. Otherwise, he had experienced some recurrent sinus infections but had recovered nicely from his TIA with no residual neurologic deficits.

During a subsequent visit at the Cleveland Clinic during the second week of August 2009, his white count was holding steady at 57,500, but his platelets had dropped again to 62,000. However, on exam, the spleen seemed to be somewhat smaller than during his previous visit. Nonetheless, his hematologist, who expressed his serious concern about the falling platelets, suggested beginning chemotherapy with an aggressive multiagent protocol consisting of the drugs fludarabine, Cytoxan, and Rituxan (a monoclonal antibody).

When QF returned to my office a week later, we discussed the meeting with the hematologist. Again, Patient QF repeated he would never do chemotherapy under any circumstances, and though he had relayed his intentions to the Cleveland Clinic doctors, to their credit they were willing to continue following him regularly. In addition, surgery, for now, had been on hold. I made several suggestions in terms of his supplement protocol, and Patient QF continued his therapy with me. Interestingly, he reported that the chronic leg pains had virtually resolved.

In September 2009, QF's white count came in at 57,370, virtually the same as the August reading, but the platelets had dropped once more, this time to 50,000. When we talked about the situation, I learned that some time ago he had stopped taking a sesame oil product I recommend for low platelets. I assumed he had continued the supplement, but I now suggested he add it on as soon as he returned home. By January 2010, although the white count was up somewhat to 69,670, the platelets fortunately were up as well to 60,000, reversing the previous downward spiral. I hoped the sesame oil derivative was working.

In February 2010, several weeks before Patient QF was scheduled for a visit with me, his white count was lower at 61,790, and his platelets down again to 50,000. His hematologist again broached the subject of chemotherapy, but gently, because Patient QF had fully informed him repeatedly over the years of his sister's disastrous experience with conventional treatment of CLL and his reluctance to ever consider that approach. In any event, on exam at the time, the spleen had enlarged.

When Patient QF returned to New York in March 2010, we discussed his various issues. He admitted the previous six months had been quite stressful. He had undergone three eye surgeries for excessive tearing, including placement of small tubes to drain the fluid into his sinuses. The tubes repeatedly had gotten blocked, and he was scheduled for a fourth surgery. Otherwise, he reported he felt "great" overall.

In July 2010, a repeat abdominal ultrasound at the Cleveland Clinic showed the aneurysm had increased in size to 5.4 cm—just under their level for surgery at 5.5. But a CT scan showed the aneurysm to be at 5.7 cm. He met with the surgeons again, who talked about the two-step operation, first removal of the spleen, and then correction of the aneurysm. After we talked about the situation, he finally decided to proceed with the surgery, now scheduled for the third week in August 2010, as much as he would have liked to avoid it.

Prior to the operation, in early August 2010 QF ended up in the emergency room at the Cleveland Clinic after experiencing difficulty signing his name and pronouncing words, and feeling a sensation of thickness on his tongue. The symptoms, attributed to a TIA, resolved quickly with no residual deficits. At that time, the white count dropped to 42,420, and the platelets dropped again to 39,000. I began to suspect his enlarged spleen was sequestering platelets as quickly as his bone marrow could make them.

Patient QF returned to New York in mid-August, for a six-month visit. He seemed to be doing well, and we spent much of the time talking about the surgery planned for the end of August. In terms of his neurological status, he had no residual symptoms from his recent TIA.

Patient QF did finally undergo the planned surgery at the end of August 2010. The procedure, both removal of the spleen and correction of the aneurysm, went, as his wife said, "without a hitch." Postoperatively, he was stable and doing well. A month later, his white count was down to 38,950, and his platelets were for the first time up to the normal range at 190,000. When the blood work was repeated in mid-November 2010, his white count was at 43,320, and his platelets were holding in the normal range at 192,000.

His only complication had been a terrible itching, scaly, red inflamed eczema over his entire body, thought to be the result of a reaction to Coumadin or Lovenox, both of which had been prescribed to prevent clotting in the immediate postoperative period. In addition, a number of lymph nodes in his neck had suddenly swelled up. When the drugs were discontinued, the rash gradually improved, and the lymph nodes began to regress.

By late January 2011, the white count was down to 28,320, and the platelets, although lower, were still fairly high at 147,000. When I saw him in March 2011, he seemed to have recovered from his operation—and his drug-induced exfoliative dermatitis.

After his visit to me in March 2011, Patient QF experienced an attack of gout affecting his left middle toe, complicated, it was thought, by reduced circulation into the foot. The problem actually had begun after he had stubbed his toe in September 2010, but it seemed to worsen in the early months of 2011. The toe swelled, turned red, and was quite painful. The situation became so serious that when he consulted with his Cleveland Clinic doctors they talked about amputation of the toe. I suggested a number of natural remedies including ingesting a half pound of dark cherries daily along with capsules of celery root, both of which seemed to help somewhat. On these supplements, his uric acid level gradually improved from a high level of 10.1 (normal 3–8) to 8.

Patient QF kept me posted about the situation regularly by phone. When I next saw him, in August 2011, he reported that he had consulted with two podiatrists associated with the Cleveland Clinic, both of whom suggested strongly that the affected toe needed to come off. We talked about the issue and agreed that because the pain and swelling had improved significantly, the toe for now should stay in place.

In mid-October 2011, Patient QF sent me a fax informing me that during a recent visit his podiatrist had backed off his earlier suggestion that the toe be amputated, instead suggesting a "wait-and-see" approach.

In terms of his leukemia, a blood test in late December 2011 showed a white count at 30,510, a hemoglobin at 10.4 (normal 13–17), and a platelet count of 114,000. In the spring of 2012, he seemed once again to be doing very well: his gouty toe had essentially returned to normal, his leg cramps seemed controlled, and at age eighty he remained active and involved with life and with his church.

I do not claim that my nutritional therapy "cured" Patient QF, but he is an informative case history for a number of reasons. When he was first diagnosed in July 1999 at the Cleveland Clinic, the experts there told him his disease was aggressive and mostly likely at stage IV. With additional testing, the doctors thought his disease was somewhat less aggressive, probably at stage III—but still quite serious, though they thought chemotherapy should be held in reserve for a time when the disease progressed. Subsequently, when his white count rose and his platelets count dropped below 100,000, his oncologist-hematologist strongly advised he begin chemotherapy, though Patient QF with great determination has repeatedly refused conventional treatment, choosing only to follow his nutritional regimen.

Now, thirteen years since diagnosis and at age eighty, his choice seems to have served him well. His sister, diagnosed with the same illness some years earlier, chose the conventional route and died a "miserable death," to use QF's words, while pursuing aggressive chemotherapy—which not only worsened her quality of life but also failed to halt the progression of her disease.

Though QF has had some detours along the way, with episodes of peripheral artery disease that ultimately improved, and gout that also improved, in general he has done very well indeed. I suspect that he will remain a very determined patient and will continue doing well clinically with occasional manageable setbacks.

As discussed previously, the most significant indicators of a poor prognosis for patients diagnosed with CLL are lymphocytosis and a platelet count below 100,000. According to *Harrison's*, such patients can expect an average survival of only one and a half years.[2] From the time of his diagnosis in July 1999, Patient QF has been well until today, thirteen years later, though his blood counts certainly indicate a lymphocytosis. And, at various times, his platelets have dropped below 100,000. So clearly, the major prognostic indicators suggested a short life span, not the thirteen years he has enjoyed to date.

*IMPORTANT EDITOR'S NOTE:
Dr. Gonzalez died before updating this case report. Patient QF last contacted Dr. Gonzalez's office in late August 2015.

---

2   Longo et al., *Harrison's Principles*, 18th ed., 924.

Case 4: Patient FG
A Minimum 22.6-Year Survivor*
Hairy Cell Leukemia

Patient FG is a seventy-year-old female whose mother died of a bone-marrow-related malignancy but who has no other family history of cancer. Her own history was pertinent because of uterine fibroids and ovarian cysts treated surgically with a hysterectomy and single oophorectomy, and fibrocystic breast disease that her doctors monitored closely.

In April 1992, Patient FG, with a history of sinusitis, developed a severe sinus infection that was treated with antibiotics. When the problem persisted, she was referred to an ear, nose, and throat specialist, who, after examining her, scheduled a septoplasty, correction of a deviated septum, for late spring 1992. However, routine preoperative blood studies on June 24, 1992 revealed a low white count at 2,000 (normal 4,000–10,800) and a mildly low platelet count at 138,000 (normal 150,000–450,000).

At that point, the surgery was canceled and Patient FG was referred to a hematologist, who first met with her during the last week of June 1992. The physician reported in his note that during the initial consultation Patient FG was quite upset, fearing the worst because her mother had died of a blood-related cancer. Her physical exam, however, was normal, with no evident splenomegaly. In-office blood studies indicated a white count of 2,300 and a platelet count of 108,000. An evaluation of a blood smear showed the typical B cells of hairy cell leukemia.

Flow cytometry indicated a decreased lymphocyte count and a decreased T4/T8 lymphocyte ratio at 0.6. Serum protein electrophoresis (to evaluate possible multiple myeloma) was unrevealing. Bone marrow biopsy yielded findings consistent with hairy cell leukemia, and special staining studies of peripheral blood confirmed the TRAP-positive cells again consistent with hairy cell leukemia.

With the studies completed, the patient returned for a follow-up consultation with the hematologist during the second week of July 1992. He explained that, at that time, she required no treatment, and that patients with this particular form of cancer can often live for years without therapy. He did discuss with her the standard interventions available at the time should they become necessary, including splenectomy, the immune stimulant interferon, pentostatin, and cladribine, which had just been found effective in clinical trials.

During the first week of August 1992, her hematologist repeated the blood studies, which again showed a low white count at 2,400, along with a depressed platelet count at 104,000. He suggested no therapy but routine follow-up tests and office visits, initially every three months, to monitor her progress.

At that point, Patient FG began investigating alternative approaches to cancer, learned about my therapy, applied to become a patient, and was first seen in my office during the first week of October 1992. At the time, she reported feeling "well," with no symptoms attributable to her disease. Two days later, she returned to review the treatment plan, which she approached with a fair amount of enthusiasm.

Thereafter, Patient FG proved to be a very vigilant and determined patient, compliant with all aspects of the regimen. She had even taken a leave of absence from her work as a teacher, so she might adjust more easily to her situation and to my regimen, which she incorporated into her life with minimal difficulty.

Repeat blood studies in late December 1992 showed a white count somewhat improved at 2,800 and a platelet count still low at 127,000.

When I saw Patient FG for a six-month follow-up appointment during the first week of April 1993, she seemed to be following the treatment to the letter and reported feeling very well. She was still on her leave of absence, but with my program mastered, she talked about returning to work full time.

Her white count in late June 1993 was 2,900, and her platelet count was still low at 116,000. In August 1993, she reapplied for a three-month renewed sick leave, so she could concentrate on her therapy. Though she felt significantly stronger on the treatment, she reported to me that some days she felt very fatigued, a very common side effect during the first year on our regimen.

A repeat white count in September 1993 came back at 2,700, with platelets at 103,000. When I saw her for her second follow-up visit several weeks later, in early October 1993—after she had completed a year on treatment—she reported bouts of fatigue but in general felt continuing improvement in her energy and stamina.

In November 1993, she decided to reapply for an extension of her sick leave. In a note to me explaining the situation, she reported, "The progress I am making on the diet and supplement program is encouraging. I am feeling stronger and less fatigued."

By December 1993, her white count was up to 3,100, the highest it had been since the first reported low test in June 1992, but the platelets were still low at 110,000.

In February 1994, she decided to reapply for an extension of her sick leave until August 1994, so she could continue concentrating fully on her treatment and healing. As before, she seemed compliant with all aspects of my therapy and very determined to get well.

In late June 1994, her white count was again down, this time to 2,500, and the platelets had dropped to their lowest level, at 89,000. When repeated in December 1994, the white count came back at 2,500 again, but the platelets were up to 109,000.

I continued seeing Patient FG in my office every six months for routine follow-up reevaluations, and she continued doing well. She had returned to work in August 1994 and seemed able to manage her teaching responsibilities along with the rigors of my therapy.

Throughout 1995 and 1996, her white count hovered in the low to mid-2,000 range, and her platelets remained slightly above 100,000. Her oncologist, with whom she also consulted every six months, felt she was quite stable and did not require conventional treatment. Then, in July 1997—after Patient FG had completed nearly five years on my therapy—her counts finally began to rise to the normal range. Her white count at the time was 3,900, the highest in five years, and her platelets, though still low, had improved to 125,000 from the 100,000 range. She felt great, was enjoying teaching, and felt grateful for the good health my program had provided her.

By June of 1998, her white count finally reached the normal range at 4,300 (normal 4,000–11,000), and her platelets were well within the normal range at 276,000. Her oncologist was perplexed but happy for her, and she continued diligently on my treatment plan.

Since that time, now fourteen years ago, Patient FG has continued my therapy, remains very compliant and determined, and continues doing well. Her white count and platelets for the most part remain well within the normal range, with occasional mild dips. I still see her every six months routinely, as does her hematologist. Her most recent blood studies from the second week of August 2011 showed her white count and platelets perfectly normal at 4,900 and 169,000, respectively.

Over the years, her primary care physician has been concerned about a high cholesterol in the range of 250–280. With certain nutritional modifications, we have been able to keep it down in the lower 200s, a level I find acceptable for my leukemia patients, who, in my experience, actually do best with a cholesterol level that most doctors would consider elevated. But these patients we believe need the nutritional benefits of cholesterol, including its free radical scavenging ability.

During the two decades I have been following Patient FG, her fibrocystic breast disease has remained fairly stable, as documented by routine mammography and ultrasound testing. Her bone density, originally categorized as osteopenic, has actually increased over the years as she follows her nutritional program.

Although hairy cell leukemia is a relatively indolent malignancy, over time it usually evolves into a more aggressive form, and 90 percent of patients do eventually require chemotherapy. Perhaps more would need treatment if the disease struck generally those at a younger age. In any event, since her diagnosis in the spring of 1992, Patient FG has avoided all conventional interventions and has enjoyed what must be technically called a long-term—apparently permanent—remission of her disease over a twenty-year period while following my treatment. In addition, she has experienced gradual improvement in her general health as she has gotten older, including improvement in her osteopenia, and not worsening as is usually the case.

I would like to make a couple of points about this case history. First of all, Patient FG's white count and platelets both stayed low for much of the first five years as she followed her treatment plan, before finally rising to and staying within the normal range. As I tell patients, my therapy is not a quick fix, but a long-term proposition involving repair and rebuilding of all tissues and organs. Such a process invariably takes time, and this treatment is not for the impatient. It takes decades to create a cancer, and it is going to take some years' time to reverse the situation effectively. I do not mean to imply that the program doesn't start working from day one, because it certainly does, but I estimate that it takes two to four years to reconstruct most of the body, and four to seven years to complete the job, in just about everybody. With each patient, I first aim for stabilization, followed by the slow, gradual process of rebuilding a damaged body.

Also, I believe this patient made the right decision when she delayed her return to work for some two years after she first started treatment with me. As I always say to patients, the body heals best at rest, whatever the underlying problem, and heals slowest when stress chronically complicates the picture. Certainly, I have patients who for financial or other reasons must continue working while on their nutritional program, but I do find patients improve faster if they can take some time off from work activities.

*IMPORTANT EDITOR'S NOTE:
Dr. Gonzalez died before updating this case report. According to the office patient files, Patient FG last contacted the office in April 2015.

NON-HODGKIN'S LYMPHOMA

Traditionally, researchers have differentiated Hodgkin's disease from the non-Hodgkin's lymphomas, though both are malignancies of the lymphocyte cells of the immune system. For 2017, the American Cancer Society's website, www.cancer.org, predicted 72,240 new cases of non-Hodgkin's lymphoma, and 20,140 deaths. This umbrella term actually includes well over a dozen different types that range from the very indolent to very aggressive, potentially deadly disease.

Case 1: Patient IL
*A Minimum 24-Year Survivor**

Patient IL is a sixty-four-year-old woman from the Southwest who in the fall of 1987 first developed vague abdominal discomfort. When the pain persisted, in January 1988 her physician referred her for a CT scan, which revealed several large abdominal tumors. In January 1988, she underwent exploratory surgery, hysterectomy, and bilateral salpingo-oophorectomy, with resection of two large masses attached at the mesentery together measuring 9 × 8 × 8 cm in diameter. The pathology report described the lesions as consistent with diffuse mixed lymphoma, mixed small and large cleaved cell type, a very aggressive form of the disease.

IL then completed six months of chemotherapy with MACOP-B, an intensive regimen consisting of five different chemotherapy drugs and the steroid prednisone. Repeat CT scans in August 1988, at the completion of treatment, were negative, and her doctors assumed her to be in remission. Subsequent scans were clear until May of 1991, when a CT picked up two nodules in the lungs, the largest in the lingula measuring 1.6 cm, the smaller in the left lower lobe measuring 0.6 cm. In addition, the report described "small periaortic lymphadenopathy at the level of the kidneys," which had been noted on prior scans. A chest CT in July 1991 revealed a 2.5 × 2 cm mass in the left hilar area, an abnormality of the lingula, and a left lower lobe mass:

1. Left hilar mass and posterior left lower lobe nodule.

2. Progressing mass and associated atelectasis or infiltrate in the lingula.

Although her doctors discussed resuming chemotherapy, IL, as she says, had "had enough." After learning of our work from a friend, she then decided to pursue our program.

When I first saw IL in my office, in September 1991, she generally felt well, and she thereafter proved to be a very compliant patient. Six months after beginning her regimen, in March 1992, a repeat CT scan of the chest demonstrated a small pleural-based density associated with the anterior left cardiac margin, approximately 1 × 1.5 cm in size, that had significantly regressed since the scans of 1991. And the additional lesions previously described were not evident. An abdominal CT scan revealed "slightly prominent nodes on the para-aortic area measuring up to 1 cm in diameter" but no other worrisome lesions.

In September 1992, after Patient IL had been on her program a full year, CT studies of the abdomen and pelvis were clear, but the chest CT showed a "3.5 cm × 2 cm density in the left mid lung and lower lung field which, according to the previous dictation, has increased in size significantly and, therefore, must be considered an active lesion."

When I discussed the findings with IL, she seemed determined to continue with her nutritional program only, expressing no interest in pursuing any other treatment. After I made some adjustments in her protocol, she decided to forgo future CT scan studies. She said not only did they create enormous anxiety, but she had no intention of changing treatment whatever the tests showed.

Over the next decade, IL continued her regimen, with excellent compliance. She generally enjoyed good health, despite some ongoing problems I related to her earlier chemotherapy, such as a persistent irregular heart rhythm and episodic respiratory symptoms, including shortness of breath with exertion. One of the drugs in the MACOP-B regimen, daunorubicin, has long been associated with heart damage in a significant number of patients, and bleomycin often provokes pulmonary fibrosis, sometimes years after treatment. In January 2004, she did undergo both cardiac and pulmonary evaluations, which revealed no significant underlying disease. A chest x-ray at that time—her first radiographic study since the CT scan of 1992—showed a "small left apical pneumothorax. Chest x-ray is otherwise radiographically normal." The previously described masses seen on CT were gone, and I related the area of collapse to bleomycin use years earlier.

IL today, now on her nutritional regimen more than fifteen years, continues in good health with apparent total resolution of her once-aggressive disease. She enjoys her life and is grateful that she has lived to see her children grow, marry, and raise their own children.

The diffuse and diffuse mixed types represent particularly aggressive forms of lymphoma that frequently come back after even the most aggressive of chemotherapy regimens. *Harrison's* has reported that the disease recurs in nearly 50 percent of treated patients with this diagnosis, and of these, fewer than 10 percent will respond to additional chemotherapy. Certainly, this patient faced a grim future, once the CT scan studies in 1991 confirmed new disease.

*IMPORTANT EDITOR'S NOTE:
Dr. Gonzalez died before updating this case report. According to Patient IL's office medical records, she contacted the office in late September 2015.

Case 2: Patient LL—Dr. Linda Isaacs' Patient
*A Minimum 21-Year Survivor**

Patient LL is a fifty-four-year-old man who previously had been in good health when, in July 1995, he developed severe chronic indigestion, abdominal pain, and constipation. His symptoms did not improve despite a variety of medications and dietary changes. After he developed swelling of the left testicle in September 1995, he was referred to a urologist, who ordered a CT scan of the abdomen and pelvis. The test, done in October 1995, revealed "extensive retroperitoneal adenopathy including retrocrural, periaortic, mesenteric and paracaval adenopathy. The nodes measure up to 5 cm in diameter individually and in conglomerate measure nearly 15 cm in transverse diameter and 8–10 cm AP."

An excisional biopsy of an enlarged cervical lymph node revealed nodular non-Hodgkin's lymphoma (mixed lymphocytic/histiocytic type).

After the diagnosis, he received no orthodox treatment, instead choosing to follow our regimen. He was first seen by Dr. Isaacs in November 1995, and as he subsequently followed his nutritional regimen, he experienced a gradual improvement in his overall health. For a number of years, he avoided all testing, until May 2001, when a CT of the abdomen and pelvis showed "resolution of previously noted adenopathy. The study at this time is essentially unremarkable."

This patient's course has been very simple and straightforward. He was diagnosed initially with extensive stage IV moderately aggressive histology disease, refused all standard treatments, followed his nutritional program appropriately, and enjoyed complete regression of his cancer and long-term survival. He is now eleven years from diagnosis, still in good health.

*IMPORTANT ADDENDUM FROM DR. LINDA ISAACS:

As of August 2016, this patient is alive, well, and active and has no evidence of lymphoma. He is now nearly **21 years** from diagnosis.

Case 3: Patient DC
*A Minimum 18.9-Year Survivor**

Patient DC is a sixty-three-year old woman who in 1992 first noticed a robin's-egg-sized lesion in the right lower abdominal wall. She consulted her primary care physician, who, suspecting a benign lipoma, suggested no testing be done.

Over the next three years, as the nodule remained stable, DC continued in good health, with no symptoms other than a single episode of night sweats and occasional pruritis. At one point, when she was found to be mildly anemic, her physician prescribed iron supplements.

In the fall of 1994, her gynecologist, after a routine exam, suggested a diagnostic evaluation of the abdominal wall lesion. A CT scan revealed a solid mass on the right lower abdominal wall, but no other abnormalities. Then, in November 1994, the nodule was excised and described in the pathology report as 4.5 × 4.0 × 1.8 cm, consistent with "malignant lymphoma, diffuse, small lymphocytic type (well differentiated lymphocytic lymphoma) of abdominal wall."

After referral to an oncologist, a subsequent bone marrow biopsy was clear, but she was again found to be anemic, with a hemoglobin of 11.8. In January 1995, she underwent repeat CT studies, which revealed new nodularity in the left pelvis side wall and in the cul-de-sac, thought most likely to represent new pelvic malignant lymphadenopathy.

The hospital tumor board then discussed the case and recommended a conservative approach initially, with regular follow-up CT scans to assess disease progression. A bone scan in October 1995 was negative. CT scans in January 1996 demonstrated two lesions within the right lobe of the liver, the largest measuring 2.0 cm in diameter, that were thought to have been present on the prior exams. In addition, the radiologist noted "redemonstration of a large, inhomogeneous central pelvic mass with prominence in both adnexal regions," as well as "thickening of and some inhomogeneity to the appearance of the left piriformis muscle when compared to the right."

Though her physicians still recommended a conservative approach, DC began investigating alternative approaches, learned of my work, and in April 1996 first consulted with me. When first seen, she reported no significant symptoms.

DC proved to be a determined and compliant patient, whom I don't think has missed a dose of supplements in the 10.5 years she has been my patient. Periodically, I have recommended CT scans, which generally have showed no change in the pelvis lesions. Her most recent scan in May 2006 revealed the same "two small low density lesions within the liver … unchanged and measuring up to 1 cm." In terms of the pelvic mass, the report stated, "There is large lymphadenopathy contiguous with the left piriformis muscle, unchanged in size measuring 9 cm in length × 4.5 cm. in width. Again noted are areas of linear enhancement. … There is a 4.5 cm. in length × 2.7 cm in width soft tissue mass in the proximal aspect of the left thigh which is slightly decreased in size."

The diffuse forms are among the more aggressive of the lymphomas, usually calling for aggressive chemotherapy. In this particular case, the consulting oncologists opted for a conservative approach, holding chemotherapy in reserve for a time when the disease would inevitably progress. However, during the 10.5 years DC has followed her nutritional program, the disease has remained generally stable, with some recent regression.

In many of our patients, regardless of the cancer type, tumors resolve, as in the case of Patient LL already described. At other times, as with Patient DC, the tumors can remain stabilized for years. I have never been able to offer a reasonable scientific explanation why this should be so, why sometimes large tumors regress remarkably, and at other times in other patients the tumors don't grow or spread, but don't disappear either.

*IMPORTANT EDITOR'S NOTE:
Dr. Gonzalez died before updating this case report. According to the office medical files, Patient DC last contacted Dr. Gonzalez in late January 2015.

Case 4: Patient DK
A Minimum 10.3-Year Survivor*

Patient DK is a forty-eight-year-old woman who prior to developing cancer had a long history of lower back pain treated conservatively with acupuncture, massage, yoga, and swimming, modalities that offered some relief. In 1993, when her pain worsened, she underwent laminectomy of the L2–L3 disc. Postoperatively, her back pain, although reduced, did not resolve completely. In November 1993, she underwent an MRI of the lumbar spine, which showed L5–S1 disc bulging, and some degeneration in several other lumbar discs. In addition, the radiologist noted left para-aortic adenopathy. The patient then consulted with an oncologist at New York Hospital–Cornell, who recommended a CT scan, which, in December 1993, confirmed enlarged left para-aortic lymph nodes, though the patient was not informed of the findings.

Because she didn't hear from her oncologist, DK assumed "everything must be fine." Thereafter, she did well until mid-1998, when she developed gradually worsening fatigue, associated with recurrent upper respiratory infections. In the fall of 1998, she consulted her primary care physician, who detected a right parotid mass as well as cervical lymphadenopathy. Initially, her internist was not concerned, assuming the enlarged nodes related to her most recent bout of the "flu." But, when the adenopathy failed to regress, DK consulted the oncologist she had seen years earlier at New York Hospital.

The physician referred her for an MRI of the neck in March 1999, which revealed two 1 cm lesions in the right parotid gland as well as enlarged upper cervical nodes. A CT scan of the chest in April 1999 demonstrated abnormal hilar nodes, the largest measuring 17 × 12 mm. CT scan of the abdomen revealed "a chain of enlarged nodes (2–3 cm) in the left paraaortic region from the level of left renal hilar vessels ... extending into the proximal left common iliac chain. Largest node at L3 level measures 3×2 cm."

A biopsy of the parotid lesion then confirmed malignancy "consistent with a B cell (non-Hodgkin's) lymphoma." A bone marrow biopsy was clear. ,

With the diagnosis established, the oncologist recommended a "watch-and-wait" approach, holding off chemotherapy for a time when the disease worsened. DK then sought a second opinion at Memorial Sloan Kettering, where the slides were reviewed and the diagnosis confirmed. The Memorial oncologist suggested two options: the conservative, no immediate treatment approach, or a course of aggressive chemotherapy.

DK then met with a third oncologist, a lymphoma specialist at New York Hospital, who recommended no treatment initially, but that the scans be repeated in October 1999 to assess disease status.

DK, with a long interest in alternative medicine, knew about my work and decided to consult with me. When we first met in June 1999, she had obvious cervical adenopathy. Thereafter, she followed her nutritional regimen initially with great determination and good compliance. Follow-up CT scans in March 2000, when she had been on her therapy only nine months, showed substantial improvement. The report for the CT scan of the neck stated, "Appearance of regression in intraparotid nodes on the right."

The CT of the chest showed "interval complete regression in adenopathy. There is no evidence for active lymphoma."

The CT scan of the abdomen indicated "interval virtually complete regression in adenopathy. There is no evidence of active lymphoma."

The CT scan of the pelvis revealed "interval complete regression in adenopathy. There is no evidence for active lymphoma."

As DK continued her nutritional therapy, she experienced a gradual improvement in her overall energy and well-being. When in mid-2001 she went through a period of severe personal and professional stress, her compliance with therapy fell off somewhat. On exam, I could see clearly that the neck disease had worsened. CT scans in October 2001, nineteen months after the documented disease regression, showed little change in the chest, abdomen, and pelvis but increased "pathological adenopathy in the right neck."

After I lectured her about the need for diligent compliance, for a time she seemed more determined, but the stress continued unabated and her compliance varied. At times, she might have been doing 50 percent of the therapy, and a CT of the neck scan in January 2002 revealed continued progression in the adenopathy. The report of the abdominal and pelvic CT scans described "mixed behavior of nodes with periaortic nodes slightly less prominent and hyperplastic nodes in the small bowel mesentery more prominent.... Interval appearance of focal splenic lesions."

This time, we talked about the need for complete compliance with all aspects of the regimen, regardless of the difficulties in her life. Fortunately, her oncologist did not insist that chemo-therapy begin at once, as she had previously responded so well to my treatment. DK renewed her dedication to the regimen, with repeat CT scans in January 2003 confirming the benefit. The neck CT showed "substantial decrease in the extensive adenopathy in the right neck."

The abdominal CT scan indicated "interval disappearance of small splenic lesions and slight decrease in sight of spleen. … No pathologic adenopathy is seen in the abdomen or pelvis."

Thereafter, she followed the therapy as prescribed and continued doing well. A neck CT in March 2004 revealed "complete regression in pathologic and borderline sized neck nodes."

The CT scans of the abdomen and pelvis were completely clear, as the official report described: "There is no other interval change and no evidence for active lymphoma in abdomen and pelvis."

Unfortunately, her stress level subsequently increased markedly, and after a long-term relationship dissolved, for a number of months she went off her program completely. Her energy worsened, and her sleep became disturbed. Predictably, a CT scan of the neck in February 2006 showed "new and progressive adenopathy along the right jugular chain and posterior triangle." CT scans of the chest, abdomen, and pelvis showed recurrent disease.

She is now again on her program, determined once again to get well, and clinically the enlarged neck nodes are regressing. She feels stronger, more energetic, and more positive.

Though DK has not followed a straight and narrow path, her course does say much about my treatment. When she complied fully, her extensive disease regressed completely. When her compliance fell off, the disease recurred, and it again regressed when she resumed her full protocol. Over the years, her disease status has correlated precisely with her compliance.

Patients, including mine, do not lead perfect lives. Often, they must deal with many life stresses above and beyond their cancer, stresses that can influence mood, motivation, and dedication to treatment. But DK, despite her lapses, has generally done very well over the past 7.5 years on her nutritional program, has successfully avoided all chemotherapy and radiation, and currently feels strong and healthy.

*IMPORTANT EDITOR'S NOTE:
Dr. Gonzalez died before updating this case report. According to the last note in Patient DK's office medical file, she contacted the office in November 2008.

Case 5: Patient LR
A Minimum 20.2-Year Survivor*

Patient LR is a sixty-year-old woman with a history of an insulinoma, diagnosed in 1977, treated effectively with partial pancreatectomy. Her doctors recommended neither chemotherapy nor radiation after surgery, and thereafter she did well until December 1993, when she first noticed swollen lymph nodes under her chin. When the swelling did not regress, in January 1994 she consulted her internist, who suspected the problem related to infected gums. She was referred to a periodontist, who performed gum debridement, but when the lymph nodes enlarged further in February 1994, she returned to her internist, who prescribed penicillin, without effect.

About that time, she first developed significant night sweats that persisted for a week, as well as abdominal pain. Her physician referred her for an ultrasound, which revealed a large 7 cm cystic mass in the tail of the pancreas, which a CT scan confirmed. The radiologist thought the lesion consistent with a benign pseudocyst, and when a needle biopsy proved inconclusive, her doctors recommended no further testing.

Because of the persistent enlarged lymph nodes in her jaw, in April 1994 LR consulted an ENT specialist, who did not initially suggest biopsy, but in June, LR noted new inguinal adenopathy. At this point, the patient's internist prescribed a course of Cipro for what was now thought to be cat scratch fever, which antigen testing did confirm. Although the nodularity persisted even after she completed a course of rifampin, her primary physician remained unconcerned. When the adenopathy progressed throughout September, LR again returned to her doctor, who again told her "not to worry." In one of the physician's notes from the time, he described her as "borderline hysterical."

Finally, LR decided to consult the surgeon who years earlier had resected the insulinoma. In October 1994, this physician—somewhat more disturbed by the adenopathy—removed a nodal mass from the posterior neck–right shoulder junction that proved to be "follicular lymphoma, predominantly small cleaved cell type (nodular poorly differentiated lymphoma)." Experts at the Pathology Laboratory of the National Institutes of Health reviewed the slides and confirmed the diagnosis.

In late October, a CT scan of the chest revealed "marked lymphadenopathy in multiple mediastinal, left hila [sic], retrocrural and axillary areas … consistent with the clinical diagnosis of lymphoma."

An abdominal CT scan showed that "there is extensive adenopathy in the abdomen and pelvis, with lymph nodes ranging up to 3×4.4 cm and 4.6×6 cm." A gallium scan documented extensive uptake in the mediastinum and abdomen.

Shortly thereafter, in November 1994, LR began chemotherapy with CHOP, a standard lymphoma protocol, at a local academic medical center. In late December, after she had completed three cycles of the proposed course, CT scans demonstrated improvement, but not resolution, in both the chest and abdomen, reported as "interval decrease in size of adenopathy within the right paratracheal group, subcarina, left axillary and retrocrural nodes." In the abdomen, the radiologist noted, "lymphadenopathy has decreased by more than 50% since exam of 10---94 consistent with partial response to chemotherapy."

In March 1995, after LR had completed the full six cycles of the regimen, CT scans indicated some continued response to therapy, but definitely not complete remission. The chest CT showed "slight continued improvement in right paratracheal lymph node disease with stability of disease elsewhere." The abdominal CT revealed that, "when compared to previous examination, the lymphadenopathy appears stable except for an apparent worsening in the region of the root of the mesentery."

With chemotherapy completed but her disease not in remission, LR began investigating alternative approaches, learned of my work, and first consulted with me in April 1995. Her exam was unrevealing, except for multiple palpable right cervical lymph nodes.

She thereafter began her program with great determination. In November 1995, restaging with CT scans of the chest, abdomen, and pelvis confirmed significant improvement: "No significant mediastinal or hilar adenopathy is identified. The lungs are clear without evidence for masses. … Retrocrural adenopathy seen on the previous examination is now not identified. Small periaortic and mesenteric lymph nodes are identified which have decreased in size since the previous examination. "

CT studies in February 1996 showed no evidence of recurrent disease, as did subsequent scans over a period of two years. Throughout this time, she was noted to have, on exam, several small right cervical nodes. In May 1998, the oncologist who followed her along with me suggested a biopsy of one of the neck nodes, which did reveal residual lymphoma, described as "follicular, mixed small cleaved and large cell type." At that point, the oncologist recommended, along with my therapy, a course of Rituxan, a monoclonal antibody treatment designed specifically to attack lymphoma cells. I felt the treatment unnecessary because she had already responded so well to my regimen, but the oncologist was persuasive, and I did not push the case.

So, in the spring and early summer, she completed four cycles of the drug, which she tolerated with minimal difficulties. On exam, her cervical nodes had regressed completely. CT scan studies of the chest, abdomen, and pelvis in September 1998 reported "no evidence of recurrence." CT scan of the neck showed "multiple small subcentimeter lymph nodes bilaterally which have decreased in size and number since the previous study."

Since 1998, LR has done exceptionally well, now twelve years from her original diagnosis of stage IV lymphoma, and 11.5 years from her first visit with me. She has enjoyed generally excellent health with no recurrence of her once widespread disease. The most recent PET/CT scan in April 2006 documented that "there is no PET/CT scan evidence of recurrent or metastatic disease."

Her course is unusual, in terms of both the long-term survival and the near-total resolution of the disease as documented by CT scans after only six months on her nutritional therapy. In 1998, before she completed a course of Rituxan, scans of the chest, abdomen, and pelvis had been clear. I suspect her neck nodes eventually would have resolved without Rituxan. Studies do show that 35–50 percent of patients with follicular lymphoma who relapse after chemotherapy will have some response to the drug, though the duration of effect is variable with few long-term remissions. In any event, in this case the disease had nearly completely resolved before her oncologist urged in 1998 that she proceed with Rituxan, at the time a fairly new, and highly promoted, drug.

*IMPORTANT EDITOR'S NOTE:
Dr. Gonzalez died before updating this case report. According to the office medical file, Patient LR last contacted Dr. Gonzalez in June 2015, a month before his death, and was in contact with Dr. Isaacs' office in late October 2016.

Case 6: Patient BQ
A Minimum 7.9-Year Survivor*

Patient BQ is a thirty-plus-year-old woman with a diagnosis of Burkitt lymphoma, unresponsive to chemotherapy.

In terms of her family history, at least seven of Patient BQ's close relatives had been diagnosed with cancer, including her father with prostate cancer, a sister with cervical and skin cancer, a grandfather who died of leukemia, a grandmother who died from colon cancer, an uncle who died of lung cancer at a young age, a first cousin who died of colon cancer, and another first cousin with metastatic colon cancer.

Prior to developing cancer, Patient BQ had a long history of allergies, first diagnosed when she was ten years old, and treated with a whole-foods-type organic diet as well as a variety of nutritional supplements. The dietary and nutritional approach helped, according to the patient, enormously, and thereafter she generally did well. Throughout her twenties, she remained careful with her diet and health habits and pursued athletic and outdoor activities with great dedication.

Patient BQ had been in her usual state of good health when, in March 2008, she first experienced persistent low back pain associated with onset of drenching night sweats, diminished appetite, and weight loss of ten pounds over a several-month period. During this time, she consulted her family physician, who generally seemed unconcerned, though at one point he prescribed Valtrex when the patient herself suggested her symptoms might be due to shingles (herpes zoster), but the symptoms continued to worsen throughout the late spring and early summer of 2008.

After developing a large mass described as "one-half the size of a football" in her lower back, Patient BQ was referred to a local oncologist in Lacey, Washington, who ordered a metastatic workup. A CT scan in mid-August 2008 revealed an anterior mediastinal mass 7.1 × 10.8 × 10.1 cm, compressing both the main pulmonary artery and aorta, and a mass adjacent to the spinal cord 5.7 × 7.4 × 7.4 cm, invading the posterior chest wall and thought to be the cause of her back pain.

Two days later, a bone marrow biopsy was negative, but a CT-guided fine needle aspiration of the anterior mediastinal mass confirmed a B-cell lymphoma, positive for the CD20 antigen, the presence of which distinguishes certain lymphomas. Further molecular biology studies revealed a rearrangement of the c-Myc gene, which regulates cell division and a translocation of the 8:14 chromosomes. Both of these abnormalities help differentiate Burkitt lymphoma from the many other subtypes of the disease.

Burkitt lymphoma tends to be rapidly progressive, requiring immediate therapeutic intervention. By the time Patient BQ was admitted to Providence St. Peter's Hospital in Lacey, Washington, only several days after her biopsy in mid-August 2008, her respiratory status had already been compromised. A PET/CT at the time revealed a 15 cm anterior mediastinal mass, an 11 cm right paraspinal mass, a 2.5 × 3.6 left ovarian mass, and a 1.8 cm mass within the small bowel.

Patient BQ began treatment with the Magrath protocol designed for patients with Burkitt lymphoma, consisting of two (CODOX-M regimen A/IVAC regimen B) very intensive forms of multiagent chemotherapy that alternate one with the other. In this case, her physicians also opted to add on Rituxan, technically a monoclonal antibody, an immune therapy that targets the CD20 antigen present on the membranes of certain lymphoma cells.

In August 2008, Patient BQ began treatment with Magrath A, with the drugs cyclophosphamide, doxorubicin, vincristine, methotrexate, and leucovorin rescue. Beginning day one of treatment, she also received Rituxan. In addition, she underwent intrathecal (into the spinal canal) treatment with the drug Ara-C (cytosine arabinoside), to help eliminate any cancerous cells within the central nervous system.

After the first cycle of chemotherapy, Patient BQ's oncologist switched her to the Magrath regimen B (IVAC), with ifosfamide with mesna rescue, etoposide, and Ara-C, which she completed in early November 2008. At that time, she also consulted with Dr. Paul O'Donnell, a lymphoma expert, at the Seattle Cancer Care Alliance (SCCA) at the Fred Hutchinson Cancer Research Center in Seattle to discuss treatment options, including stem cell transplant to ensure long-term remission. Dr. O'Donnell recommended that she begin harvesting stem cells, for a transplant after she entered complete remission. However, after attempts to collect bone marrow stem cells from Patient BQ apparently failed, she returned to St. Peter's Hospital to complete another two cycles of chemotherapy.

A PET scan in mid-November 2008 documented a significant response to treatment described in the radiology report:

> Complete or near complete metabolic response in the anterior mediastinal mass with marked anatomic reduction in tumor size....

> Complete metabolic response in the right lower chest lesion with near anatomic resolution.

> Complete metabolic response and anatomic resolution of mass in the left ovarian region and left lower quadrant bowel.

Patient BQ then returned to SCCA to complete the successful harvesting of her stem cells. In December 2008, in preparation for the planned stem cell transplant, the slides from St. Peter's were reviewed at SCCA, confirming the diagnosis of Burkitt lymphoma. CT scan studies from mid-December 2008 showed that

> within the anterior mediastinum adjacent to the ascending aorta and main pulmonary [sic] is a heterogeneously appearing mass with calcifications measuring 5.5 × 3.0 × 2.6 cm which has not significant changed compared to the November 11 examination. . . .

> The previously identified right paraspinal mass with atelectasis has decreased in size to 4 × 8 mm and now is only a small area of pleural or extrapleural thickening with a small amount of adjacent right lower lobe atelectasis.

Patient BQ eventually completed the full six cycles of Magrath A and B in early January 2009 with a sense of satisfaction and great hope, expecting to be in remission and believing stem cell transplant would give her ultimate cure.

Unfortunately, a restaging workup beginning in late January 2009 showed Patient BQ had failed to enter remission, despite the aggressive chemotherapy. CT scan studies of the chest, abdomen, and pelvis in late January indicated that the anterior mediastinal mass, though somewhat reduced in size, had not completely regressed, nor had pleural thickening and nodularity in the right lung base. A PET/CT performed the same day revealed increased activity in the mediastinum and pleura, consistent with residual malignancy: "Heterogeneously increased activity with max SUV of 4.5 is associated with 28 × 51 mm anterior mediastinal mass. . . . There is increased metabolic activity with a max SUV of 3.6 associated with foci of right basal pleural nodularity and thickening."

Though the tumor had decreased in size in comparison with a PET from August 2008, it had increased in size when compared with an outside PET performed in November 2008, as described in the official report: "As compared to previous PET from August 08, significant reduction in size of the mediastinal mass is noted, however, as compared to 11/--/08 outside PET, there is mild interval progression."

With that bad news, several days later, in early February, Patient BQ returned to SCCA for a meeting with a stem cell transplant expert, who bluntly stated that because she had not achieved a full remission, her chances of a successful outcome with transplant were no more than 20 percent, with a significant possibility of death from the arduous treatment. According to Patient BQ, the oncologist did not at all push for further chemotherapy or the stem cell transplant, because the odds were so stacked against her, though when asked about the prognosis, she admitted that without any further conventional treatment, she might have only six months to live. Patient BQ, who already knew about my work from someone I had successfully treated, suggested an alternative approach, an idea the oncologist thought to be reasonable.

The official note from that session stated, "Therefore our interpretation is that the patient's disease is progressing under a debulking chemotherapy she received during the last few months."

After discussing the issue with her parents, Patient BQ decided against proceeding with any further chemotherapy, instead choosing to begin my treatment.

When I first met with Patient BQ, during the second week of February, she reported good energy, but drenching night sweats—a bad sign—requiring change of bed clothes four or five times. She also described chronic low-grade fevers, headaches, and a persistent neuropathy, a side effect from her chemotherapy.

Thereafter, despite her dire situation, Patient BQ proceeded on her nutritional therapy with great determination, great dedication, and great enthusiasm. With all she had been through at her age, I marveled at her positive outlook—she understood fully the severity of her situation but would do everything she could, she said, to "beat the odds." And within weeks of beginning the regimen, she reported a significant change in her health for the better. She began riding a bicycle daily and said she felt "like a million bucks."

CT scan studies performed March 31, 2009—after BQ had completed some six weeks on her nutritional therapy—showed a significant reduction in her tumors of approximately "50%," according to her oncologist, compared with the CT scan from mid-December 2008. The radiology report stated,

> There has been decrease in the size of the anterior mediastinal mass which now measures 3.7 × 2 cm in transverse diameter, compared to 5.6 × 3 cm previously. There are more prominent calcifications due to treated lymphoma. There is somewhat less prominent, mild soft tissue fullness in the right paraspinal region at the T11 and T12 levels, without definite focal mass seen in this region.
>
> No significant mediastinal adenopathy or other masses are seen.

These findings were particularly significant because the radiologist compared the March 2009 scans with those from mid-December 2008, not the PET/CT performed in January 2009, at which time the tumors had grown—so the response was even more significant than the report might indicate.

Then, a chest x-ray ordered by her oncologist during the third week of June 2009 showed apparently near-total resolution of the mediastinal mass compared with an x-ray from early January 2009:

Impression:

Decreased mild residual fullness of the left hilum and left AP window region.

No acute cardiopulmonary process.

For Patient BQ, battles still lie ahead, some because of the damage to her caused by the intensive chemotherapy. She runs a low white count, for example, one downside of marrow damage caused by the drugs. Nonetheless, her response has been rapid and substantial, particularly for her situation with Burkitt lymphoma that failed to go into remission despite intensive full-court chemotherapy. And in addition to the objective radiographic findings, her clinical status continues to improve.

I have never been able to understand why in some patients, such as BQ, tumors resolve rapidly, while in others, they may stabilize for years, or even initially grow until stabilizing. But no matter to me, as long as the patients survive their deadly disease.

*IMPORTANT EDITOR'S NOTE:
Dr. Gonzalez died before updating this case report. According to Patient BQ's office medical files, she last contacted Dr. Gonzalez in June 2015. She last contacted Dr. Linda Isaacs in January 2017.

MELANOMA

Melanoma originates in melanin-synthesizing cells located in various pigmented areas of the body. Melanin gives color to the skin and provides protection against sun damage, and though we generally associate melanoma with the body surfaces, the disease can begin in the retina of the eye and even, rarely, in the nasal sinuses.

Excessive sun exposure, especially a history of blistering sunburn in childhood, predisposes one to the disease, particularly in those with light skin, red hair, and blue eyes. A large number of moles also increases the risk, with 30 percent of melanomas developing in pre-existing nevi. Any change in a mole's size, shape, or color (particularly to blue or purple) or bleeding from a nevus should alert the patient and physician to a possible problem.

According to *Harrison's*, in 2004, approximately 54,200 new cases were reported in the US, with 8,200 deaths.[1] Melanoma has attracted much attention in the research community because of its rapidly increasing incidence in the United States, with a 300 percent rise in the number of cases over the past forty years. Scientists speculate that the dramatic change may correlate with increased recreational sun exposure, perhaps coupled with the shrinking of the ozone layer, which in times past may have more effectively reduced penetration of mutagenic ultraviolet light rays.

If diagnosed early, melanoma can be cured with surgery in most cases. Once metastatic, the disease has a dismal prognosis, as *Harrison's* has reported: "Melanoma can metastasize to any organ, the brain being a particularly common site. Metastatic melanoma is generally incurable, with survival in patients with visceral metastases generally <1 year. Thus, the goal of treatment is usually palliative. Patients with soft tissue and nodal metastases fare better than those with liver and brain metastases."[2]

Chemotherapy, immunotherapy, and vaccine therapy have been heralded to some degree in recent years, but none has proven effective to date once the disease has recurred and spread.

---

1 Longo et al., *Harrison's Principles*, 18th ed. 723.
2 Ibid. 729.

Case 1: Patient UT
A Minimum 27-Year Survivor*

Patient UT is a seventy-seven-year-old male professor with a history of recurrent malignant melanoma who has remained cancer-free since beginning his nutritional program twenty-two years ago. In terms of his family history, his father had died from a heart attack shortly after surgery for brain cancer, and a sister died at a fairly young age, also from brain cancer.

Prior to his diagnosis, Patient UT had generally been in good physical health, with no prior serious medical problems. In early May 1987, he first became aware of a small growth in the back of his lower neck that seemed irritated. He consulted his internist, who immediately referred Patient UT to a dermatologist. Three days later, the physician removed the nodule, which proved to be malignant melanoma, with a maximal thickness of 1.7 mm and evidence of cancer extending beyond the resection margin.

The pathologist described the lesion as "at least level IV of invasion in Clark's classification," an indication of a potentially aggressive cancer. Because the margins were not clear, the patient was referred to Dr. Daniel Roses, a surgeon at New York University Medical Center, where Patient UT was first seen in early June. There, a review of the pathology slides confirmed "malignant melanoma" described as "thick."

Dr. Roses suggested a metastatic workup to rule out metastatic disease. Should the cancer appear to be localized, he then strongly recommended further surgery, a wide local excision and cervical (neck) lymph node dissection, to remove any residual local cancer.

A chest x-ray and liver-spleen scan the second week of June 1987 showed no evidence of metastatic disease. Blood studies were for the most part within normal limits except for a mildly low white count at 4,000 (normal 4,800–10,800). Several days later, Patient UT underwent "wide and deep" re-excision of the previous surgery site and removal of ten lymph nodes from the right posterior cervical region…The pathology report from the procedure described melanoma in two sections: "Two…of 18 additional sections reveal residual melanoma in the deep reticular dermis, at a depth of 4 mm beneath the skin surface at the edge of the scar from the previous biopsy."

The ten lymph nodes examined were free of any additional malignancy, so the NYU physicians were optimistic that the disease had been surgically cured. No additional adjuvant treatment—chemotherapy, radiation, or immunotherapy—was recommended.

Thereafter, Patient UT returned for follow-up visits with Dr. Roses every three months, and initially he seemed to be doing well. A year after his surgery, in early June 1988, a CT scan of the chest was clear of metastatic disease. But in early March 1989, during another routine examination, Dr. Roses discovered an enlarged right supraclavicular lymph node, which he biopsied via fine needle aspiration. An evaluation of the lymph node sample confirmed recurrent malignant melanoma.

Dr. Roses then ordered extensive testing to rule out distant metastatic disease. A chest x-ray and CT scans of the brain, chest, abdomen, and pelvis were all unremarkable. Routine blood studies were mostly within normal limits except for his white count, which had dropped from the previous level to 2,800. Then, in mid-March 1989, at NYU Medical Center, Patient UT underwent right posterior cervical lymph node dissection. Of seventeen axillary nodes examined, one was positive for metastatic melanoma.

With evidence of recurrent and metastatic disease into the lymph node chain, this time around Dr. Roses explained the situation was not so rosy, the prognosis not so good. He suggested Patient UT consider an NIH vaccine clinical trial for patients with poor-prognosis melanoma that was up and running at NYU under the direction of one of their well-known melanoma researchers. In this study, a vaccine would be made out of the patient's own melanoma tissue, with the hope that with its application the immune system would mount an aggressive response to eliminate any residual disease. Because no chemotherapy or radiation was involved, Patient UT agreed to enroll, receiving his first vaccine treatment in May 1989 with a plan to repeat the process every six months.

In addition, Patient UT continued following up with Dr. Roses on a regular basis. In early November 1989, repeated CT scans of the head, chest, abdomen, and pelvis were all unremarkable. This being the days before physicians worried about radiation exposure from scans, just two months later, in January 1990, Patient UT underwent yet more CT scans of the head, abdomen, and pelvis, all of which were clear of recurrent or metastatic disease. In addition, his white count had normalized at 4,900.

Patient UT continued his vaccine treatment, and in mid-May 1990, CT scans of the head, chest, abdomen, and pelvis were again normal. Despite the reassuring news from his doctors, Patient UT didn't feel comfortable with his situation. He realized his prognosis remained quite guarded with his history of recurrent disease into a lymph node after a wide excision of the original site, and the vaccine treatment was strictly experimental with no proof it might benefit patients in his situation. So Patient UT began looking into alternative approaches, learned about our work, and decided to apply to become a patient. He seemed suitable to us, and we first met in late June 1990. I found him to be very engaging and very determined to follow my therapy to the letter.

Because Patient UT lived in the New York metropolitan area, initially he returned for follow-up visits every six weeks. When I saw him in mid-August and then in late September 1990, he seemed very compliant with all aspects of the prescribed program, which he managed to work into his schedule of teaching and writing at the university where he worked. He reported, as most patients do during the initial months of the program, some ups and downs, particularly fatigue, but overall he felt his health had definitely improved since beginning his treatment with me. The vaccine clinical trial, he reported, had also come to a close; apparently, the results were so disappointing, the NIH had actually shut the study down.

Patient UT also continued his regular visits to his surgeon, who in January 1991 ordered a CT scan of the head and chest, both of which were, again, unrevealing. When I saw him several days later, he again seemed very compliant with his nutritional regimen and reported generally feeling well.

At this point, I was seeing Patient UT in my office every three months instead of every six weeks, and he continued his regular visits with his surgeon. In July 1991, a year after he had first consulted me, a metastatic workup including CT scans of the head, chest, abdomen, and pelvis indicated no evidence of recurrent disease. Clinically, he seemed to be doing very well as he dutifully followed his nutritional program.

Thereafter, Patient UT continued returning for a visit with me every three months, continued his treatment program, and continued doing well. CT scans in August 1992 revealed for the first time a "tiny lesion" in the left lobe of the liver. His surgeon didn't think the findings significant and suggested only that Patient UT continue undergoing rescanning on a regular basis to track the abnormality.

Patient UT subsequently did well until early 1993, when he developed bouts of severe nausea associated with new-onset constipation. He was concerned because, for the first time since he had started treatment with me, he found it difficult to get his supplements down. When the problem did not resolve, I became concerned enough about possible recurrent melanoma that in early March 1993 I ordered an ultrasound of the abdomen and pelvis, which revealed an enlarged bladder, presumed bladder outlet obstruction, and a mildly enlarged prostate—perhaps the source of the trouble. Fortunately, there was no evidence of tumor anywhere, including in the liver.

Blood studies showed, for the first time, significantly elevated creatinine and blood urea nitrogen (BUN), both markers of kidney function and indicating something was wrong with the urinary system. The situation was perplexing because Patient UT had not previously reported any symptoms referable to an enlarged prostate such as urinary frequency, urgency, weak urinary stream, dribbling, or repeated awakenings at night with the need to urinate. At that point,

I quickly referred him to a urologist I had been working with since I had started in practice six years earlier. After an evaluation of Patient UT, the urologist performed a suprapubic cystoscopy, in which a catheter is inserted into the bladder through the skin to drain urine directly into a bag. This was thought to be the quickest way to get the situation under control.

Patient UT was diagnosed with "silent prostatitis," in which a mildly enlarged gland blocks urine flow in the absence of any significant symptoms. Subsequently, in late March 1993, he underwent transurethral resection of the prostate (TURP) to open up the urethral pathway through the prostate, and at the same time the suprapubic catheter was removed. After the procedure, the urologist admitted that the prostate was barely enlarged at all—explaining why no one had picked up on the situation earlier. Fortunately, when I saw him for an office visit during the first week of April 1993, only days after the procedure, he reported feeling much better, with good energy, and that the chronic nausea had resolved. His kidney function tests had also improved dramatically and quickly after surgery, though not completely into the normal range. Though he had been off all his supplements for some six weeks because of his nausea and surgery, shortly after his visit with me he resumed his full nutritional program.

By July 1993, when I saw Patient UT for an office visit, he was feeling quite well and his creatinine and BUN had improved once more, to nearly the normal range. By this point, he had stopped returning to his NYU surgeon, so in December 1993, I arranged for a repeat metastatic workup. A CT of the brain and chest were as before unremarkable, but the abdominal study revealed two liver lesions, which apparently had been present on the August 1992 scans though the earlier report had described only one abnormality.

The radiologist wrote, summarizing the findings, "The CT scan of the Chest, Abdomen and Pelvis demonstrates two tiny low densities with the liver which were seen in August of 1992 and have not changed. No definite evidence of metastatic disease or lymphadenopathy is seen."

I wasn't sure of the significance of these findings, which had not been described prior to August 1992, but to be on the safe side I increased Patient UT's daily dose of pancreatic enzymes.

In early January 1994, Patient UT was seen by his urologist, who was quite pleased with his progress, as documented in a letter to me: "He has done very well since his surgery. He voids well without any complaints, and his urinalysis is entirely normal. … A repeat bladder sonogram shows nearly complete emptying of his bladder with a prostate volume less than 30 grams (normal)."

His creatinine and BUN remained elevated, but at this point only slightly outside the normal range.

Patient UT continued returning to my office for routine follow-up every three months. He appeared to be pursuing his treatment with diligence and continued doing well. Though he was teaching a full load of courses, both undergraduate and graduate, he was handling the workload and my therapy without difficulty.

In December 1994, I ordered MRI scans of the brain, chest, and abdomen, hoping to reduce his yearly radiation exposure. By that point, I had already read literature from Europe suggesting that CT scans might not be as safe as previously claimed, with radiation exposure equaling at times that of 1,000 chest x-rays. MRIs on the other hand involve no radiation whatsoever.

The chest MRI revealed a previously undescribed "probable 1.0 node" adjacent to the superior vena cava at borderline size for significance. The abdominal MRI indicated the same two liver lesions as previously described, which appeared unchanged from the prior CT of December 1993.

Throughout 1995, Patient UT continued doing well. When at the end of the year we discussed restaging studies, he and I decided to go with CT scans this time around, which I hadn't ordered for two years. The radiologist compared the studies with the prior MRIs of December 1994. The chest nodule appeared smaller than in the MRI of December 1994, and the two liver lesions were no longer evident, as described in the radiology report:

> A 6 mm node is noted adjacent to the superior vena cava … which is decreased in size compared to 12/--/94. . . .

> No definite evidence of metastatic disease to the liver or spleen is identified.

In the years that followed, Patient UT remained vigilant with his nutritional regimen and returned to my office every three months. He would undergo yearly CT scans, which revealed no evidence of recurrent or metastatic disease. At times, the radiologist could detect a single tiny lesion in the dome of the liver as before, but this had not changed from its first appearance.

In mid-2001, when Patient UT's BUN and creatinine jumped up a bit, his urologist suggested a referral to a nephrologist at New York Hospital–Cornell. After a thorough evaluation, the physician diagnosed, as recorded in his note to the urologist, "chronic obstructive nephropathy which seems stable." He suggested no treatment, nor did he feel follow-up visits with him were needed at this time.

Patient UT continued his regular visits with the urologist, to assess his prostate function. In May 2002, his PSA went up from a previous borderline normal level of 4.07 to 5.29, an increase that was of concern to the urologist, who strongly suggested a biopsy. After he talked about the situation with me, we decided first to proceed with a prostate Doppler ultrasound, a sophisticated study that can fairly accurately assess blood flow into tissues. In a cancer situation, the Doppler can pick up enhanced angiogenesis, characteristic of malignant change.

In early June, the Doppler study showed only mild inflammation at the tip of the gland, but no suspicious legions or areas of increased blood flow. After discussing the findings with me, Patient UT decided against biopsy. I made some changes in his protocol, adding saw palmetto and some extra zinc, both of which I have found helpful with prostate enlargement and inflammation.

Three months later, in early September 2002, when he experienced a single episode of hematuria, at my suggestion he returned for a visit with the urologist. When urine cytology came back as unremarkable, the physician suspected the hematuria reflected only ongoing inflammation in the prostate.

In January 2003, Patient UT was due for his yearly CT scan evaluation. He had read about PET scans, which were becoming more widely used at the time, and he asked me if that study would be a more accurate assessment for his situation. The PET involves intravenous injection of a radioactive glucose "dye" that is taken up by cancer cells more selectively and more readily than by normal tissues. When the patient is then scanned, the equipment will pick up areas in which the dye concentrates, such as in a cancerous tissue.

I explained that, in my opinion, a PET would be more useful than a set of plain CT scans, though again, he would be exposing himself to a considerable amount of radiation. After thinking about the options, he chose the PET scan, which was done in early January 2003. The report of the study stated, "No evidence of metabolically active disease identified."

In early February 2003, the PSA had improved slightly to 4.92, and the free PSA came in at 20 percent—a good prognostic indicator. The higher the percentage for free PSA, the lower the probability of a cancerous situation.

In June 2002, repeat blood chemistries indicated a BUN of 43 and a creatinine at 1.8—both elevated, but at the levels they had been for several years.

A Doppler ultrasound in late July 2003 showed "increased midgland inflammation," but once again, no suspicious nodules or areas of increased vascularity. I tinkered with his supplements somewhat, and in late February 2004, some seven months later, a repeat ultrasound showed improvement, described simply as "decreased midgland inflammation." He was essentially asymptomatic and had reported no further hematuria since the single episode in September 2002.

In April 2004, he underwent PET scanning, which showed as before "no evidence of metabolically active disease."

By March 2005, the ultrasound showed not only that the prostate was smaller but also that the earlier noted areas of inflammation had completely resolved. As before, no discrete nodules were noted, but for the first time the radiologist detected a small 7 mm focus of increased vascularity at the left base of the gland. This finding was confirmed on a subsequent MRI of the prostate, which showed a left base lesion extending into the left seminal vesicle associated with an irregular prostatic capsule—sometimes an indication of invasive cancer. I discussed the results with Patient UT, recommending as well that he get in to see his urologist as quickly as possible.

I arranged to have the scans sent to the urologist, who, after reviewing the ultrasound and MRI, wrote a strong letter to Patient UT insisting that a biopsy was now necessary:

> The evidence is now that there is most likely a malignancy within your prostate, particularly seen on the MRI study of your prostate.
>
> A biopsy of the prostate is now absolutely necessary.

We also talked about proceeding with another PET scan, as a year had already passed since the last study. Meanwhile, in late March 2005 he met with the urologist, who performed a very thorough rectal exam and could find no evidence of abnormal nodularity, contrary to the ultrasound and MRI findings. In addition, a PSA came back significantly lower than the previous reading at 4.0, with 27 percent as free PSA—a very good indication. When the lab work came back, in a note to Patient UT the urologist wrote:

> It has always been my feeling that your PSA fluctuations are due to chronic prostatitis.... However, [the radiologist's] most recent report to us indicates that he now believes that you may have a malignancy within your prostate which is invading the left vesicles.
>
> Digital rectal examination did not bear this out. Your prostate is a perfectly smooth, elastic gland. I feel no tissue densities and no irregularities.... Furthermore, you have 27% of your total PSA in the free or non-protein form.... An abnormal prostate containing carcinoma will usually cause a significant drop in this free PSA ratio to 10% or less.

After all this, the PET scan in late March 2005 showed "no evidence of hypermetabolic disease in the head, neck, chest, abdomen and pelvis and lower extremities." So the prostate crisis seemed to have passed uneventfully.

In October 2005, Patient UT returned to the urologist for routine follow-up. A PSA at the time was 4.0, identical to the previous reading, but the free level had gone up to 32 percent—yet another good sign. And when the ultrasound was repeated in late October 2005, it showed "left base vascular focus decreased.... Invasion into left seminal vesicle decreased."

When we next repeated the PET scan, in late April 2006, it showed "normal whole body PET/CT scan; no evidence of recurrent neoplasm." And a Doppler ultrasound in early June 2006 indicated the previously noted lesions had completely resolved, described simply in the report as "no vascular foci."

Throughout the remainder of 2006, Patient UT continued on his nutrition program, visited both his urologist and me regularly, and continued doing well. A PET scan in March 2007 was again completely normal. However, in the spring of 2007, he developed persistent indigestion and abdominal pain that not only interfered with eating, but also made it difficult for him to get his supplements down. When at the same time a right inguinal hernia became quite painful, I suspected this might be the source of his digestive problems. Patient UT was very concerned, understandably, because he had been such a compliant patient for some seventeen years.

I referred Patient UT to a gastroenterologist I know, who agreed that the hernia might be the source of the trouble. At that point, I recommended Patient UT consult with a surgeon at NYU, and in early June 2007 he underwent repair of the hernia. He recovered from the procedure without complication, with subsequent complete resolution of his pain and eating difficulties.

Thereafter, Patient UT continued doing well. A PET/CT in April 2008 was fine. However, when in late 2008 he developed significant and persistent pain in his right groin, UT returned to his NYU surgeon, who thought the repair simply wasn't holding up. Though a second operation to correct the situation was certainly one option, the physician suggested holding off on any invasive procedures until the situation worsened further. When we talked later after the consultation with the surgeon, Patient UT asked about acupuncture to help healing in the groin and perhaps reduce the pain. I thought the suggestion a good one and referred him to an acupuncturist I have known for many years. Subsequently, with regular acupuncture care, the pain lessened considerably, and Patient UT was able to avoid another operation.

A PET/CT in April 2009 was once again "negative...with no evidence of hypermetabolic recurrent neoplasm."

In late August 2009, Patient UT experienced recurrent hematuria, the first episode in seven years. His urologist ordered an ultrasound of the pelvis, which revealed a 1.8 cm lesion in the right bladder base, "suspicious for a neoplastic lesion." However, during subsequent cystoscopy, the urologist did not identify the supposed "nodule" seen on the ultrasound. In a letter to me, the urologist suspected the radiologist was observing folds of bladder muscle, not a cancerous lesion. And urine cytology was negative for cancerous cells. Though his PSA was up a bit at 4.6, the free level came in at 38 percent, a finding arguing against prostate cancer. As the urologist wrote, "Nothing needs to be done at this time."

To control the bleeding, I suggested Patient UT add rutin, a bioflavonoid nutrient, to his program three times daily. This worked quickly, and Patient UT experienced no further episodes of hematuria.

In early 2010, a renal scan ordered by Patient UT's urologist indicated an asymmetry in kidney function, prompting a return visit to his nephrologist, whom he hadn't seen in some nine years. After another evaluation, the physician reported that after all this time, "[Patient UT's] renal function appears to be stable or actually improving."

A PET/CT scan in May 2010 again showed "no evidence of recurrent or metastatic disease." PET/CT a year later, in June 2011, similarly was unrevealing.

Most recently, his PSA has been running in the 5.0 range, with a very high free level, so his urologist remains unconcerned. In July 2011, his BUN came in at 45 (normal 8–27) and creatinine at 1.49 (normal 0.76–1.27), both similar to previous readings over the past ten years.

Patient UT has now completed twenty-two years on his nutritional program with a history of recurrent, locally metastatic melanoma. I believe his very prolonged disease-free survival while following his nutritional program to be remarkable for a number of reasons. When initially diagnosed in the spring of 1987, after the original lesion was removed by a dermatologist, Patient UT underwent "wide and deep" re-excision of the original biopsy site with residual melanoma detected in the sample. However, the disease appeared localized with no evidence of spread in the ten lymph nodes evaluated. But within two years, the disease had recurred in a right neck lymph node.

In patients diagnosed with melanoma, recurrence after wide local excision is a sign of a very poor prognosis. Slingluff et al., writing in *Cancer: Principles and Practice of Oncology*, reported only a 9–11 percent five-year survival in those patients experiencing a "local" recurrence after wide excision.[3] Furthermore, Patient UT's recurrence wasn't in the skin or original surgical site, but rather some distance away in a regional lymph node, a finding in and of itself associated with a poor prognosis.

---

3   Craig L. Slingluff Jr., Keith Flaherty, Steven A. Rosenberg, and Paul W. Read, "Cutaneous Melanoma," in *Cancer: Principles and Practice of Oncology*, ed. Vincent T. DeVita, Jr., Theodore S. Lawrence, and Steven A. Rosenberg, 9th ed. (Philadelphia, PA: Lippincott William & Wilkins, 2011), 1663.

Patient UT's case is interesting for yet another reason. At the suggestion of his surgeon, Patient UT did agree to enter an NIH vaccine trial. For about a year, Patient UT proceeded with the experimental treatment while also following my nutritional regimen. Eventually, he dropped out of the study to continue only my therapy when he began to suspect the results for the vaccine weren't very favorable. In fact, I have learned that the data apparently was never published, after the NIH shut the trial down because patients were simply not responding.

I have been told that ultimately, there were only two long-term survivors out of some sixty or so patients entered into the trial—and both turned out to be my patients. During the 1980s and 1990s, oncologists had placed great hope in creating a melanoma vaccine that might be effective even against advanced disease, but the optimism has long ago waned. In the discussion of such interventions, the newest edition of *Harrison's*, from 2011, has reported gloomily that "none of these approaches have met with much clinical success."[4]

Admittedly, there have been a number of ups and down over the years, particularly Patient UT's chronic "silent" prostatitis, which led to some compromise in his kidney function. Even this has improved over the years, and his PSA and kidney function blood tests have been stabilized for a decade. His very conservative nephrologist, with whom he consults regularly every nine years, admits his kidney function has actually improved over time. Clinically, he continues doing well with no current problems. At age seventy-seven, he teaches full time and remains a very active and vital gentleman.

Patient UT to me represents an ideal patient. He began with me in the spring of 1990, when I hadn't even been in practice for three years, and long before I would develop any sort of reputation in the alternative medical world. But from the moment he entered my office, I remember so well that he trusted me, trusted the treatment, and believed I would do everything possible to help him overcome his situation.

Since that time, he has been fully compliant with his program, except for those two brief periods when he couldn't get the supplements down, first because of the bladder obstruction, the second time because of his hernia. Once these problems were corrected, he resumed his program with full dedication. I don't think, again, other than these two episodes, that he has missed more than ten pills in twenty-two years. And he still has faith that I will always do the best I can do for him. With such faith and such trust, healing is much, much easier.

*IMPORTANT EDITOR'S NOTE:
Dr. Gonzalez died before updating this case report. According to Patient UT's office medical file, he contacted the office in June 2015. He met with Dr. Isaacs in February 2017.

---

4   Longo et al., *Harrison's Principles*, 18th ed., 729.

Case 2: Patient VL
A 16-Year Survivor

Patient VL, a research scientist, had been in good health when, in the spring of 1983, he first developed persistent left-sided sinus congestion. Over the next year, his doctors prescribed a variety of medications, including steroids, with little effect. An ENT physician diagnosed a deviated septum, so when VL's symptoms persisted, he underwent surgery in September 1984 for septal repair. Incidental biopsy of a large nasal polyp revealed, unexpectedly, malignant melanoma of the sinuses. A CT scan after surgery documented a residual soft tissue mass in the right anterior ethmoid sinus, with destruction of the intrasinus wall.

The patient was then referred to Memorial Sloan Kettering for further evaluation. In November 1984, at Memorial, VL returned to surgery for a left medial maxillectomy, with wide resection of the cribriform plate, resection of both ethmoids and frontal sinus, scraping of the mucosa of the sphenoid sinuses, and resection of the contents of the left maxillary antrum. The nasal septum and right superior turbinate were removed en bloc, and the floor of the anterior cranial fossa was reconstructed with a pericranial flap. The pathology report documented "residual malignant melanoma of the left ethmoid sinus mucosa with involvement of superior nasal septum. Tumor erodes underlying bone. … All margins of resection are free of tumor residual disease, with apparently clean margins."

Postoperatively, the Memorial surgeon did not recommend radiation, which he felt would only cause tissue damage and interfere with healing of the reconstruction.

VL subsequently did well for a time. In late 1986, routine blood chemistries revealed an elevated LDH, a possible harbinger of recurrent cancer, but his local doctors pursued no additional investigations at that point. But in the late spring of 1987, VL developed persistent abdominal pain associated with bloating and indigestion. When his symptoms worsened, in July 1987 he returned to Memorial for a full metastatic workup: a biopsy of the ethmoid sinus was negative for cancer, as was a CT scan of the head. However, an abdominal CT in July 1987 revealed a large abdominal mass, consistent with metastatic disease.

In September 1987, he underwent exploratory laparotomy and was found to have massive adenopathy that collectively measured 12–14 cm in diameter positioned in the distal small bowel mesentery and invading several loops of small bowel. Tumor seeding was identified throughout the pelvis, and the large tumor mass had ruptured, forming a contained cavity adjacent to the terminal ileum. The surgeon resected the involved small bowel with primary anastomosis and debulked as much cancer as possible, but much remained.

The pathology report described "metastatic melanoma involving mucosa, submucosa and muscularis of a segment of small bowel. Melanoma also involves three mesenteric lymph nodes."

In a note to the patient's local oncologist, the Memorial surgeon discussed the extensive abdominal cancer he had encountered, and his prediction of a poor prognosis:

> As you know, a percutaneously guided aspiration revealed cells compatible with malignant melanoma, and at surgery, it was clear that the patient's problem was due to massive adenopathy in the distal small bowel mesentery invading several adjacent loops of bowel and rupturing. ... The involved loops of bowel were resected with primary anastomosis, but the pelvis had seedlings of tumor adjacent to the major mass. ... For that reason and the fact that the tumor had ruptured and subsequently become contained by the adjacent mesentery, it was felt appropriate only to "debulk" the mass. ... There is minimal gross disease left in the patient's abdomen, but since seedlings had occurred and tumor had ruptured prior to surgery, the likelihood of diffuse melanomatosis is high....

> While in hospital the patient was seen by Dr. ---- who is in charge of our various melanoma research protocols including Interleukin-2, immunotherapy, etc. Dr ---- reviewed what is available at our Institution and the results of standard and experimental therapy here and elsewhere. ... I think he needs to digest what has been told to him, share it with his wife and discuss these options with his internists at home. He has a very poor prognosis, a tragedy in someone so young, courageous and knowledgeable. I only wish we had more concrete options to present to him. His training as a scientist allows him to understand our investigative protocols but also to realize that they are, indeed, investigation only.

With his options dismal, after recovering from his surgery VL began to consider alternative approaches. He learned of the late Dr. Robert Atkins, who in the late 1980s sought to branch out from his diet work and began offering his own nutritional approach to diseases such as cancer (he eventually would abandon the effort to concentrate again on obesity).

In November 1987, VL began therapy at the Atkins Center in New York City. Initially, his disease seemed stable, with a CT scan in January 1988 showing no overt evidence of recurrence. However, over the following months, VL developed an enlarging mass in his lower abdomen, visible on repeat CT scan in May 1988 and described as a "recurrent 4.5 × 3.5 cm soft tissue mass in the region of the aortic bifurcation consistent with recurrent melanoma." At that point, VL consulted with his Memorial surgeon, who, after reviewing the CT scan, argued against further surgery, which, he said, would be very debilitating and noncurative. He told VL that he might, if he were lucky, live six months.

VL had learned of my research study of Kelley and had heard I had recently begun seeing patients in New York. After discontinuing treatment with Dr. Atkins, he consulted with me in May 1988. On exam, he had obvious inguinal adenopathy as well as a hard, easily palpable large midpelvic mass. Thereafter, VL began his nutritional regimen, which he followed faithfully.

A baseline abdominal CT study in July 1988—shortly after our first meeting—documented worsening disease since the prior scan. Not only had the mass grown slightly to 5 × 3.5 cm, but now the radiologist noted new adenopathy: "There has been a definite change since the study of 5----88 with left retroperitoneal and probably left lower mesenteric adenopathy now being present. Additionally, the mass described previously in the low left retroperitoneum has undergone slight further enlargement."

The tumors described in May and July were solid tumors, through and through, with no areas of necrosis. A follow-up CT scan in September 1988, when VL had completed four months on his regimen, showed slight increase in the size of the main tumor (4.5 × 6 cm) but improvement in the adenopathy, as the official report stated: "The previously described left periaortic adenopathy and mesenteric adenopathy is not as evident on this current study."

A CT scan three months later, in December 1988—six months after VL had begun his protocol—showed considerable improvement, with stabilization of the large mass and resolution of previously described adenopathy: "A lower left retroperitoneal prominent mass, described on earlier scan is again identified. ... It measures roughly 4.5 cm in AP diameter and roughly 5 cm. in width. This indicates little change in the size of this mass since the previous study. Left retroperitoneal adenopathy below the level of the renal hila, appreciated on the study of 7---88, is not clearly seen at this time. ... No mesenteric adenopathy is indicated on the current study."

During this time, VL felt well, in fact so well that he was able to resume his executive and scientific work full time. The next CT scan in June 1989 indicated that the "mass in the left periaortic retroperitoneal soft tissue is unchanged in size and appearance. ... Mass unchanged since 12/22/88."

In late 1989, after he had completed some nineteen months on treatment, VL wrote his surgeon at Memorial to inform him of his good health and apparent progress. The physician wrote back, saying, "Your letter of December --- 1989 arrived during the Christmas season and carried with it much good cheer! I was thrilled to hear that your disease is stable and has bothered you no further since we last spoke in September of 1988. ... It is wonderful to know that you have done so well despite a rather frightening situation which we encountered during your operation in September of 1987."

In November 1990, VL's internist ordered an MRI of the pelvis, which revealed that the previously solid mass had evolved into a more necrotic lesion: "This study is suspicious for a LEFT SIDED PELVIC MASS which may be necrotic."

Over the next two years, VL remained extremely compliant with his nutritional therapy, enjoyed excellent health, and actually won an award for perfect attendance at his workplace. However, in the summer of 1992, after four years on his nutritional regimen, he became noncompliant with the prescribed diet, though he followed the supplement and detoxification protocols diligently. We have found over the years that for ultimate success, adherence to all aspects of the therapy is absolutely essential. A patient who disregards the dietary recommendations is, in our experience, asking for trouble.

For our melanoma patients, we always prescribe a diet that emphasizes red meat, with the fat, preferably more than once a day. We forbid certain commonly enjoyed vegetables, such as leafy greens, and allow fruit only once a day, and never citrus. Such recommendations countered most expert recommendations emphasizing "low fat" and "no meat" that dominated the orthodox and alternative world during the 1990s, particularly in regard to cancer. In this case, after VL's daughter adopted a completely vegetarian way of eating, VL decided, without telling me, to switch himself to a similar diet in the summer of 1992, contrary to what I had prescribed.

By late fall 1992, his local oncologist felt, on physical exam, that the pelvic lesion had grown for the first time in years. An abdominal CT scan in December 1992 revealed a 7.0 cm soft tissue mass in the pelvis, containing areas of necrosis and calcification. The radiologist also noted a second 2.0 cm nodule, also showing areas of calcification, in the right abdomen at the umbilical level.

After a number of conversations with me, VL and I decided he should return to Memorial for surgery, because the mass was beginning to cause symptoms. His former physician, astonished VL was still alive nearly five years after his previous recurrence, agreed, after CT scans of the brain and chest were clear, to operate. In late January 1993 at Memorial, VL underwent "exploratory laparotomy, resection of tumor from mesentery/pelvis and right iliac vein and artery." The tumors, the patient was later told, came out very easily, as if they had been encapsulated.

The pathology report from Memorial described mostly dead tumor, with the large main pelvic lesion described as "an 8 × 6 × 5.5 cm mass of predominantly necrotic tumor tissue. The tumor is grossly present at the surgical margin." The pathologist identified some residual viable cancer, described as "high grade malignant neoplasm consistent with metastatic malignant melanoma.... Tumor is present at surgical margin."

In an additional resected nodule, no viable cancer cells were found: "Mesenteric nodule excision: Necrotic tissue suggestive of a metastatic neoplasm largely replacing a fibrotic lymph node; cannot identify viable tumor cells."

A second node examined also appeared cancer-free. Overall, although some cancer remained, much of the original tumor evident in the spring of 1988 had died, now replaced by scar tissue.

According to the patient, while he was still recovering from the procedure, his surgeon met with him and discouraged him from consulting with any of the Memorial melanoma "experts." He suggested that he only continue his nutritional program—advice given, VL said, "off the record."

After recovering from his ordeal, and after several more lectures from me about the need for total compliance, VL resumed his full program—including the high red meat diet. He said he had learned his lesson. During the following eight years, he remained faithful to the treatment, enjoyed great health, retired from his job, and began a consulting firm. He also repeatedly expressed gratitude for the program, gratitude for the years of life the therapy had given him.

Unfortunately, beginning in 2001, after he had been on the therapy for thirteen years, I noticed a distinct change in attitude. He began to grouse about the program, about the "expense," though money didn't seem to be a problem for him. He complained about the supplement protocol, which required he take enzymes throughout the day. He repeatedly urged me to cut down the number of pills on his regimen, to make his life "easier." I was reluctant to do so with his melanoma history, and in view of the fact that residual tumor remained after his 1993 surgery. Regardless of how well he had done, he was always at risk for recurrent disease.

Eventually I relented and reduced the number of enzyme capsules to what I considered a minimal dose. I later learned that VL decided without telling me to lower the dose still further, mistakenly thinking he was cured, that cancer could never be a problem again.

Despite the compliance lapses, VL did very well until late November 2003, when he developed chronic digestive problems, diminished appetite, and a seven-pound weight loss. In mid-January 2004, he consulted his local physician, who, on exam, detected new inguinal adenopathy. When I saw VL two days later in my office, in addition to the enlarged groin nodes I could now feel a new small mass in the midabdomen. A CT scan the next day—his first scan in twelve years—showed "INTERVAL DEVELOPMENT OF EXTENSIVE UPPER ABDOMINAL, PORTA HEPATIS, AND SUPERIOR RETROPERITONEAL ADENOPATHY. MULTIPLE SPLENIC MASSES. SEVERAL TINY LOW DENSITY HEPATIC LESIONS ARE ALSO SEEN, NOT IDENTIFIED ON PREVIOUS EXAMINATION."

The disease had taken off. I immediately raised the dose of pancreas significantly, and VL agreed to do whatever he needed to do to fight back against the recurrent cancer. Unfortunately, his abdominal disease had progressed so far he had trouble eating, and in February both his local oncologist and I agreed surgical debulking might be helpful. VL called Memorial, only to learn his former surgeon—who had done the abdominal procedures in 1987 and 1993—had retired. He consulted with the younger replacement, who felt the main abdominal mass was inoperable but strongly suggested he meet with a Memorial oncologist to discuss chemotherapy. VL, who well knew chemotherapy offered little benefit for his disease, declined the invitation. In early March, he did consult with an abdominal surgeon at Columbia, who concurred that surgery would not be feasible. But at Columbia the patient was aggressively encouraged to consider an interleukin-2 clinical trial, though the drug had proven to be a consistent failure for more than fifteen years.

VL did decide, despite my warnings, to consult with the interleukin-2 expert, who helped convince him to enter the study, to "shrink the tumors." In a later conversation with me, VL told me that, feeling at the time somewhat desperate, he had agreed to proceed with interleukin just "temporarily," to get him in better shape so he could follow my program more religiously. Ethically, I could not tell him to refuse the treatment.

So in mid-March, VL went into the hospital for his first series of eight interleukin-2 treatments, and during that time he could not follow my program at all. To my surprise, his doctors never expressed any interest in his sixteen-year survival with metastatic disease under my care, refused to speak to me about what they were doing, and, when VL began to crash on the drugs, didn't seem anxious even to talk with him.

After finishing the first course of treatment, VL went home to bed. After regaining some strength over a period of several weeks, he chose to re-enter the hospital for another round of interleukin. This time, the drug left VL far more debilitated, with severe anemia and weakness, and once home, he was unable to leave his bed for days. Not only was he exhausted and ano-rectic, but the bill for two weeks of treatment, he said, exceeded $200,000. By that point, VL decided to refuse all further conventional treatment, but he was so debilitated he could not resume my therapy.

A CT scan done in early May 2004 showed not only an increase in the size of the previously noted tumors despite interleukin, but new lesions in the liver as well. The treatment had done nothing but make the situation worse. A local oncologist suggested chemotherapy; his friends began suggesting a variety of odd treatments including a special immunotherapy available only in Argentina. I urged him to rest, to regain his strength, and to try to restart his nutritional program, which had beaten back his disease in the past. Instead, VL flew to California to consult with a well-known melanoma expert and surgeon at the John Wayne Cancer Center, hoping this physician might be able to resect the tumor. But after several meetings, VL was told surgery would not be possible.

VL returned home, only further tired from the trip. He remained anemic, exhausted, and debilitated. He was angry he had ever allowed himself to be talked into the course of interleukin. In mid-June, we had a long conversation about the situation, reported in my office notes: "He is very upset about the interleukin experience. ... He said he wrote to Dr. ---- but never heard a word. No one has followed up. He said it is as if they do not care after spending a couple hundred thousand dollars on two sessions. ... They just do not care how he feels."

A week later, not having resumed his nutritional treatment, VL finally died at age seventy-three, sixteen years after he had begun treatment with me in 1988, when his predicted life expectancy was only months. Certainly, his long survival is extraordinary, as is his significant reduction of disease during his first years on the therapy, when he followed his prescribed regimen diligently. In the fall of 1992, when he decided to adopt a diet completely unsuited for his metabolism (by our standards), his disease progressed. When his compliance improved after surgical debulking, he remained disease-free for eleven years, despite the aggressive nature of his cancer.

After his compliance flagged, he ultimately suffered an explosive recurrence in early 2004 and was unable to resume his full program. Well-meaning friends, his own fears, and the power of orthodoxy ultimately led him to an ineffective course of interleukin that left him considerably weakened and with his disease worsened. Nonetheless, though he ultimately died, he had many productive and very happy years. We do miss him.

Case 3: Patient QM
A Minimum 25.3-Year Survivor*

Patient QM is a seventy-two-year-old Englishman who had been in excellent health when in July 1990 a pre-existing mole on his left ear suddenly enlarged and turned black. When the lesion continued to grow, in January 1991 QM went to his local physician, who immediately referred him to a surgeon. He then underwent excision of the lesion, which proved to be melanoma, Clark level IV, with a 1.9 mm depth.

In late January 1991, QM returned to surgery for a neck dissection, superficial parotidectomy, and excision of the left ear in toto. The pathology report described residual melanoma in the original site to a depth of 1.2 mm, but the lymph nodes and parotid were free of cancer. His doctors warned the disease might recur but recommended no additional treatment.

In June of 1991, just five months after his major surgery, QM developed two nodules in the left mastoid area adjacent to the previous surgical incision, as well as a nodule in the skin of the right axilla. In late June, he consulted his surgeon, who removed the lesions:

> At a recent follow up visit in June I noted that he had a couple of little nodules under the skin of the mastoid area on the left adjacent to the ear resection and he also showed me another little clump of nodules in and under the skin of the right upper arm. I excised all these under local anaesthetic and histology of that has confirmed that all three are malignant melanoma....

> I have put [QM] and his wife fully in the picture about the fact that his melanoma appears to have spread by the bloodstream and may turn up at other distant sites in the future.

After the surgery, QM underwent a full metastatic workup. A chest x-ray was clear, as were CT scans of the head, chest, and abdomen. However, QM's doctors advised him that his disease would recur and prove terminal, most likely within a year. No further treatment with either chemotherapy or radiation was thought warranted, due to its ineffectiveness.

QM began investigating alternatives, learned of my work, and first came to my office in September 1991. At that time, he felt well and had a normal physical examination except for evidence of his extensive head and neck surgery. He thereafter proved to be a very compliant patient, and on treatment, he felt well and continued his demanding career. When seen in March 1993, after completing eighteen months on his nutritional regimen, he felt fatigued from overwork and frequent air travel but otherwise appeared well.

When I saw him nineteen months later, in October 1994, after three years on the regimen, he reported increasing stiffness in his neck and symptoms consistent with optical migraines occurring one to two times a month. When his headaches worsened upon returning home to England, he consulted with a London neurosurgeon. A CT scan of the brain revealed a 4.5 × 2 × 2 cm mass in the right occipital area of the brain. Because the tumor appeared easily accessible, the surgeon strongly recommended resection, and after QM and I discussed the situation by phone, I agreed he should proceed with surgery, the sooner the better.

So, in mid-December 1994, QM underwent craniotomy and excision for what proved to be an encapsulated melanoma tumor. The pathology report stated, "Sections show a discrete tumor mass bounded by gliotic brain. Tumor extends to margin of excision in some sites. There are conspicuous lymphocytic collections around the tumor. The tumor consists of sheets of poorly differentiated cells. A few contain granules of melanin. There are areas of necrosis."

He had no further conventional treatment and resumed his program as soon as he returned home from the hospital. Initially, he felt quite well, with his neurological symptoms resolved, but by February 1995, just two months later, he had once again developed persistent head-aches. A CT scan and MRI of the brain confirmed that a tumor had regrown in exactly the same location as the prior lesion. His surgeon felt that once again the tumor could be easily resected, so after multiple phone consultations with me, in early March 1995 he underwent repeat craniotomy and excision of the mass. The pathology confirmed "recurrent metastatic amelanotic melanoma." The report elaborated, "The appearance resemble those of the previous biopsy, but now inflammation is less obvious and there is much more necrosis."

His local doctors suggested two doses of localized stereotactic radiation, to eliminate any lurking malignant cells in the tumor bed, and I concurred with the recommended treatment. QM tolerated the radiation well and subsequently continued on his nutritional program, which I adjusted to take into account the recent series of events. After that, he experienced no further recurrence, and today, nearly twelve years from his last surgery, he remains compliant with his full regimen, now fifteen years since he first consulted with me. He is in excellent health and continues his productive professional life.

Although a CT scan of the brain in July 1991 showed no tumor, QM didn't start his nutritional program until early October, a full three months later. Given the nature of his disease and its tendency to spread and kill quickly, it is possible the brain lesion first grew in the interim before he started treatment with me. During that three-month period, he was on no therapy whatsoever, and it is also possible that once he began treatment, tumor growth slowed. In my experience, it would be unusual to see, in a fully compliant patient, new tumor forming.

In late 1994, QM traveled considerably, and perhaps this physical stress, not an inconsequential variable, weakened him enough to allow the tumor to grow despite his good compliance. But then, within two months of the first brain surgery, the tumor recurred in the same exact location. We do find that in areas of prior surgery, blood circulation, and with it the enzyme supply, can be compromised due to fibrosis and scar formation. In such protected areas, sometimes tumors can reform, though rarely do they spread beyond the scarified boundaries. The fact that in the nearly twelve years since his second surgery QM has remained completely cancer-free indicates something unusual was going on in that particular area of the brain in 1994. I admit that what I propose here falls into the realm of conjecture, but it's important to keep in mind that metastatic melanoma usually kills within months, regardless of the conventional therapy, such as radiation, that might be employed.

DeVita has reported that "metastatic melanoma has a median survival of only 6 to 9 months and current systemic therapy has been shown to induce complete durable responses in only a small minority of patients."[5]

The DeVita chapter on melanoma has a section devoted to brain metastases specifically. In this case, the author wrote of the dismal prognosis even when the disease is treated aggressively: "A series of patients with symptomatic solitary intracranial lesions showed a median survival after craniotomy of only 10 months."[6]

Radiation offers little additional survival benefit to surgery.

Finally, I want to remark about this patient's attitude toward me, and the program. When he developed evidence of recurrence in December 1994, he didn't immediately assume the program had "failed," and that I didn't know what I was doing. Quite the contrary: he understood he had terrible disease, and he knew his survival even at that time was unusual. Though perplexed by the recurrence, he listened carefully to my hypothesis that perhaps this tumor was not new. When the disease recurred two months later, he again assumed that the therapy would eventually gain control of the situation, as it apparently has over the past twelve years. At no point did he ever lose faith in the treatment, or in me, and within days of each of his two brain surgeries, he resumed his full program with only greater devotion.

*IMPORTANT EDITOR'S NOTE:
Dr. Gonzalez died before updating this case report. Patient QM was in contact with Dr. Gonzalez's widow, Mary Beth, in August 2016. He last communicated with Dr. Isaacs in January 2017.

---

5   DeVita et al., *Cancer: Principles and Practice*, 9th ed.1672.
6   Ibid. 1687.

Case 4: Patient IJ
A Minimum 26-Year Survivor*

Patient IJ is a sixty-eight-year-old man with a history of significant sun exposure when younger, including summer stints as a lifeguard. He first developed skin cancer in 1987, thought to be secondary to excessive sun damage. Over the following year, his dermatologist removed twelve basal and squamous cell carcinomas from his chest, back, and face. Then, during a routine follow-up exam in 1988, IJ was found to have a suspicious lesion in his scalp above his left ear. This was removed in September 1988 and was described as a "malignant melanoma, near left ear, measuring at least 1.3 mm in greatest thickness." A chest CT at the time showed no evidence of metastatic disease.

Shortly after surgery, in the fall of 1988, IJ detected a new lesion anterior to his left ear. Initially, his surgeon and dermatologist were unconcerned, but when the lesion continued to grow, he was admitted for evaluation to a New York City hospital in August 1989. After CT scan studies of the brain, chest, and abdomen were negative for metastasis, IJ underwent left superficial parotidectomy and left radical neck dissection. The pathology report described "metastatic malignant melanoma to intraparotid gland lymph node," but no other areas appeared infiltrated with cancer.

However, a postoperative CT of the neck showed a new subcutaneous lesion in the back of his head, in the occipital area. At this point, IJ, aware of his dismal prognosis with recurrent melanoma, began investigating alternative approaches to cancer, learned of our work, and first consulted with me in November 1989. During my initial examination, I detected a small 0.5 cm nodule in the scalp of the right occipital area, as well as many areas of sun damage on his chest and back.

Subsequently, IJ proved to be a very determined, compliant patient. By March of 1990, when he came to the office for a routine visit, the occipital lesion had completely regressed. Thereafter, as he continued his program diligently, he reported an overall improvement in his general health and returned to work after a medical leave to resume leadership of a successful business.

Over the next two years, his dermatologist removed several small pre-existing superficial basal and squamous cell carcinomas in sun-damaged areas, but his melanoma did not recur. After 1992, he developed no more skin cancers while following his nutritional regimen.

IJ continued on therapy fully for some five-plus years, before his compliance fell off during mid-1994. In July 1996, after an eighteen-month absence, he returned to the office and reported he had adhered to the prescribed diet and continued the detox procedures, including the coffee enemas, but had gradually dropped off the supplement protocol. He felt "great" and admitted he had gotten careless because his diagnosis of recurrent melanoma seemed so far in the past.

After that visit, I periodically heard from him by phone, but I didn't see him in the office again until May 2001. He told me that after following the full regimen for another year or two after the 1996 visit, he had gradually drifted away from the supplements once again. In early 2001, he had developed a nodule on his left shoulder, which had been excised in March 2001 and found to be not melanoma, but a cutaneous leiomyosarcoma. After experts at the Armed Forces Institute of Pathology confirmed the diagnosis, IJ had undergone a wide excision of the original area, but no additional cancer was detected.

He also reported that after stopping the supplements, he had once again developed a number of squamous cell carcinomas of the skin after being cancer-free for years. But after our May 2001 visit, IJ resumed his full nutritional program, which he followed faithfully for more than a year, before again slacking off the supplement regimen. However, neither his melanoma nor his sarcoma has recurred; he recently reported to my office staff that he was in "great shape," cancer-free since his last bout in 2001.

Clearly, this patient's course has been unusual. He had a history of poor prognosis, recurrent melanoma with, at the time he first consulted me, evidence of a suspicious new lesion in his skull. This nodule regressed quickly and completely on our therapy. During his first two years on the regimen, a number of basal and squamous cell carcinomas were removed, but these I suspect had been festering for years. Eventually, as long as he followed his program fully, no new malignant skin lesions developed.

IJ ran into trouble after his compliance fell off in the late 1990s, when once again squamous cell cancers, but no melanoma lesions, began forming. After he developed cutaneous leiomyosarcoma in 2001, he resumed his protocol and remains today, seventeen years from our first meeting, cancer-free.

*IMPORTANT EDITOR'S NOTE:
Dr. Gonzalez died before updating this case report. According to Patient IJ's office medical file, his last contact with Dr. Gonzalez was in January 2011; however, in 2016, Patient IJ submitted a written tribute to Dr. Gonzalez after his July 2015 death.

Case 5: Patient RS—Dr. Linda Isaacs' Patient
A Minimum 14.75-Year Survivor*

Patient RS is a fifty-year-old man with a history of widely metastatic melanoma, alive more than eleven years since his original diagnosis, and more than eight years since his recurrence.

He had previously been in good health when, in early 1998, Patient RS's wife noticed a new pigmented lesion in his right flank that bled when irritated. A local dermatologist removed the lesion, found to be consistent with malignant melanoma. Subsequently, at Massachusetts General Hospital in Boston, Patient RS underwent wide local excision, sentinel node mapping, and biopsy of a deep right axillary node. The pathologist reported no residual melanoma in the original site or in the four lymph nodes examined. Because the disease seemed localized, no additional therapy was recommended at that time.

Thereafter, Patient RS was re-examined every six months at the University of Pennsylvania. He did well until routine chest x-ray in February of 2001 revealed a 2.5 cm mass in the hilum of the left lung. A CT scan of the lung confirmed the suspicious lesion, though abdominal and bone scans were clear. However, an MRI of the brain demonstrated a 1 cm mass in the right prefrontal gyrus, consistent with a metastasis.

Patient RS decided to return to Massachusetts General Hospital for further evaluation and treatment planning. There, the doctors suggested an aggressive approach beginning with thoracotomy (chest surgery) and resection of the lung tumor, coupled with stereotactic radiation to the brain. In late April 2001, Patient RS underwent left thoracotomy and left lingulectomy, with the tumor subsequently found to be a 2.4 cm metastatic melanoma.

In late May 2001, after a repeat MRI at Massachusetts General once again documented the right brain lesion, Patient RS underwent the planned stereotactic radiation. But then, a follow-up CT scan of the chest in late June 2001 at Massachusetts General Hospital revealed possible recurrent disease in the chest, as described in the radiology report: "Left upper lobe mass located superior to the resection margin. Uncertain etiology, but could represent recurrent tumor or surgery related hematoma."

Patient RS then consulted at Johns Hopkins in Baltimore, where a PET scan in early July 2001 demonstrated activity in the lung consistent with recurrent metastatic disease: "This study demonstrates abnormal activity in the left hilum which is suspicious for malignant disease and clinical correlation is highly recommended.... No other abnormality noted within the abdomen, pelvis, or lower extremities. Also, brain images revealed no significant abnormality."

An MRI of the brain a month later, in August 2001, was clear, and repeat CT scans indicated the left chest hilar lesion to be stable, reported as 2.2 × 2.3 cm, but considered again a metastatic nodule.

At that time, Patient RS met with a medical oncologist, who explained that no therapy had been proven significantly useful against metastatic melanoma, and consequently his disease would most likely—if not inevitably—prove fatal. Nonetheless, the physician did suggest a one-year course of granulocyte-macrophage colony-stimulating factor (GM-CSF), an immune cell stimulant considered still an experimental treatment for melanoma, which by some anecdotal evidence prolongs survival from the disease, though it is not curative. With no other options evident at the time, in August Patient RS agreed to the treatment and completed his first two weeks of GM-CSF injections. When he asked about his chances of long-term survival, his oncologist—as the patient later told Dr. Isaacs—stated bluntly he didn't expect him to live a year.

Looking for more hopeful options, Patient RS then contacted the National Cancer Institute in Washington, but he was told they felt he had been treated properly, and they made no further suggestions. Patient RS then began investigating alternative approaches, learned of our work, and, in early September 2001, began treatment with Dr. Isaacs. At the time of his first visit, he reported feeling well despite his situation, and he subsequently began his program with great diligence and determination. At the same time, he continued the GM-CSF protocol under the direction of his oncologist.

A repeat metastatic workup at Massachusetts General in April 2002, after Patient RS had completed six months on his nutritional region, showed no change in the lung lesions. However, an abdominal CT scan showed a lesion in the spleen not previously detected. Because his doctors believed he was already receiving the best of possible available experimental treatments, GM-CSF, they chose a "watch-and-wait" approach.

Five months later, in early September 2002, when he completed the proposed one-year course of GM-CSF, he underwent further radiographic testing. An MRI of the brain showed no evidence of recurrent disease. On CT scanning, the lungs appeared clear, but the lesion in the spleen had clearly grown, as documented in the radiology report: "There is a 2.2 cm low attenuation lesion within the anterior aspect of the spleen which is increase [sic] in size compared to prior exam. It is unclear whether this enhances. Regardless, interval growth implies metastatic disease."

A PET scan two weeks later, in mid-September 2002, again indicated possible recurrent disease, but this time in the lung as well as the spleen: "A linear focus of subtly increased FDG [radioactive dye] uptake is noted within the left lung hilum. This focus of hypermetabolism appears to correspond to a small loculated pleural fluid collection in the left major fissure adjacent to the left hilum as noted on the previous CT of the chest. Although the intensity of uptake is very mild, its appearance on FDG-PET imaging is concerning for metastatic disease."

Also noted on previous CT of the chest, abdomen, and pelvis was an interval increase in the size of a rounded soft tissue attenuation focus in the spleen, believed to be consistent with a metastasis. A very subtle focus of FDG uptake was noted in the left upper abdomen on the current PET examination; however, this appeared to represent focal accumulation of radiotracer within the bowel rather than the spleen.

Because he felt well and had completed his regimen of experimental treatment, at that point, his Massachusetts General doctors adopted a conservative approach, suggesting no additional treatment, but only regular rescanning. In terms of the treatment, Dr. Linda Isaacs increased the enzyme dose, and thereafter Patient RS continued only on his nutritional program and continued feeling well. When he underwent retesting in late March 2003, an MRI of the brain remained clear, and a total-body PET scan revealed significant improvement in the previously noted lung activity and absent activity in the right upper abdomen:

> There has been significant decrease in tracer activity in the left hilum, but is still mildly increased. The mediastinum is otherwise within normal limits. There is no evidence for a mass or lymphadenopathy in mediastinum, axilla, and supraclavicular region. The lungs are unremarkable.

> No abnormal tracer activity is identified in visualized abdomen, including the liver, spleen, kidneys, and adrenal glands. The imaged pelvis appears grossly unremarkable.

The patient's wife sent copies of the scan, along with a note addressed to Dr. Isaacs dated late April 2003.

> It has been almost one year since [Patient RS]'s last appointment with you and I am happy to report that he continues to feel wonderful and his scans continue to show no new disease....

> He continues to follow all of your instructions and we feel his good health can certainly be attributed to this.

Six months later, in September 2003—as Patient RS pursued only his nutritional therapy— repeat MRI again showed no evidence of recurrent disease in the brain. But the PET scan at that time showed possible worsening of the chest lesion:

> There is faint increased abnormal FDG uptake in the region of the left hilum; this is slightly increased from the prior examination and is clearly visible. However, the amount of uptake is still decreased from the scan dated 9/--/02. Despite this

increased uptake, the level of uptake is nonspecific and may represent inflammation or malignancy....

There is no abnormal uptake in the spleen. Otherwise, no other abnormal increased FDG uptake in the chest, abdomen, pelvis or legs is identified.

Again, his oncologist suggested no additional therapy, recommending the scans again be repeated in six months. At that point, Dr. Isaacs doubled Patient RS's enzyme dose.

This change in the protocol seemed to work well; repeat scanning in mid-March 2004, after Patient RS had completed nearly three years on his nutritional regimen, showed significant improvement. As before, an MRI of the brain remained clear of recurrent disease, but this time CT scans of the chest and abdomen showed complete resolution of the previously described lesions in the lung and spleen:

Parenchymal abdominal organs are unremarkable. In particular, a cystic appearing lesion anteriorly in the spleen seen on the previous study has resolved....

CT of the chest was done according to standard departmental protocol with intravenous contrast. Comparison is made with the prior study from 9/--/02. There is no hilar or mediastinal adenopathy and the Airways [sic] are patent. ... The lungs show no evidence of nodules or masses.

Since then, Patient RS has continued faithfully on his nutritional program and has continued doing well, with repeat scans remaining clear. He was last seen in our office in early March 2010, after completing nearly nine years on his nutritional regimen. He said he felt great with no complaints and was working full time, and he expressed his gratitude for the treatment. Since then, he has continued on his regimen and remains cancer-free, now eight years since his diagnosis of widely metastatic melanoma.

This patient's very unusual and fortunate course isn't that difficult to evaluate. After his disease recurred in early 2001 with evidence of metastases to both the brain and the lung, he faced a dire prognosis. He did initially undergo resection of his lung lesion and stereotactic radiation to the brain tumor. However, though surgical removal of a single metastatic focus in the brain (or elsewhere) can occasionally yield long-term survival, I have found no evidence that treatment of disease metastatic to two separate sites ever cures. The National Cancer Institute website reported, as of July 2009,

Isolated metastases to the lung, gastrointestinal tract, bone, or occasionally the brain, may be palliated by resection with occasional long-term survival. Radiation therapy may provide symptomatic relief for metastases to brain, bones and viscera.

Advanced melanoma is refractory to most standard systemic therapy, and all newly diagnosed patients should be considered candidates for clinical trials.

After his chest surgery and the stereotactic radiation to the brain, Patient RS did pursue a one-year course of GM-CSF concurrently with his nutritional regimen. However, even as of 2010, this immune modifier is still considered experimental and is still undergoing clinical trials. The National Cancer Institute's website section on treatment of advanced melanoma doesn't even mention this approach as an option, even in a clinical trial setting. The University of Pennsylvania's Medical Center website section of melanoma as reported by Keith T. Flaherty, MD (Assistant Professor of Medicine – Hematology/Oncology), on July 4, 2009, "GM-CSF as adjuvant therapy continues to be investigated in clinical trials, with no clear signal yet as to whether or not it helps to prevent recurrences of melanoma. … In conclusion, right now, the jury remains out on GM-CSF."

Regardless, his disease recurred and continued to progress both in the chest and the spleen as sequential CT and PET scans documented, even after a year of his GM-CSF. Only after he dropped this experimental treatment and continued only on his nutritional therapy did both the chest and splenic lesions completely resolve.

We usually discourage patients from trying to combine our treatment with any conventional therapy, because often the two approaches will cancel each other out, consequently interfering with the efficacy of our regimen. In this patient's case, his disease completely regressed only when he discontinued the GM-CSF.

*IMPORTANT ADDENDUM FROM DR. LINDA ISAACS:
This patient as of June 2016 is working full time with no evidence of recurrence, representing a minimum **14.75-year** survival. He ran a half-marathon in the spring of 2016.

Case 6: Patient IQ
A 5.2-Year Survivor*

Patient IQ's past medical history prior to developing cancer is pertinent because of concussion due to an injury in 2001, which resulted in persistent petit-mal-type seizure activity, not formally diagnosed until a year after the incident, in 2002, when he underwent extensive neurological testing. At the time, the patient's physician prescribed Depakote for the seizures, which left him feeling "like a zombie." After Patient IQ struggled with the medication for a year, the neurologist switched him to Lamictal, which helped control his symptoms significantly.

In terms of his cancer history, Patient IQ underwent excision of a basal cell carcinoma from the left neck area in 2000. He subsequently seemed cancer-free until the spring of 2004, when his wife noticed three lesions, one on the right scalp, one on the left scalp, and one on the skin of the left cheek. Initially, Patient IQ did not seek medical attention, because he assumed the lesions represented, at worst, unaggressive basal cell carcinomas. Finally, in August 2004, he consulted his primary care physician, who scraped all three lesions. The right scalp and left cheek lesions both proved to be basal cell carcinomas, and the left scalp lesion was initially classified as benign keratosis.

Although Patient IQ was referred to a dermatologist for further excision as needed, he failed to follow up immediately, assuming he was "fine." Some months later, in November 2004, he did consult with the dermatologist, who performed a wider excision in the area of the two basal cell lesions, and a repeat scraping of the "benign" scalp keratosis, which this time, to everyone's surprise, turned out to be a malignant melanoma with evidence of ulceration, Clark level IV (deep) at 1.3 mm. Several days later, the dermatologist did a punch biopsy, which confirmed melanoma, but this time Clark level V at 3.6 mm.

In late November 2004, the patient consulted with an oncologic surgeon at Polyclinic in Seattle, who suggested more extensive surgery with wider margins in the scalp with skin grafting, to be followed by systemic treatment with interleukin-2, or perhaps even an experimental protocol. Patient IQ agreed to the surgery, which was scheduled for December 3, 2004. In preparation, on December 2, 2004, Patient IQ underwent a metastatic workup including CT scanning of the chest, abdomen, and pelvis. The scan of the test revealed a 2–3 mm nodule in the left lung fissure consistent with a lymph node and not thought to be evidence of metastatic spread. Other than a small right kidney cyst, no other abnormalities were noted.

Patient IQ proceeded with the surgery, with a skin graft from the left neck. No residual melanoma was identified in the original site, and two sentinel nodes removed from the neck were negative for cancer.

At a routine follow-up visit in mid-December, the surgeon admitted that no residual or metastatic cancer had been identified, but because of the depth of invasion the cancer most likely would recur. He discussed adjuvant treatment and referred the patient to two oncologists, Dr. Henry Li at Polyclinic and Dr. John Thompson, an interleukin expert, at the University of Washington.

In mid-December, Patient IQ met with Dr. Li, who discussed both interferon and interleukin, but he decided not to proceed with additional treatment at that time. Instead, Patient IQ decided to seek a second opinion with an oncologist, Dr. Nicholas Chen at the Seattle Cancer Treatment and Wellness Center. Patient IQ met with Dr. Chen in January 2005, who suggested, as had Dr. Li, a one-year course of interferon. Patient IQ decided to proceed with the treatment, but he quit after only six weeks because of debilitating side effects. Dr. Li suggested he continue interferon at a lower dose, but after another two weeks and terrible symptoms, Patient IQ quit interferon for good.

He did agree to a course of Leukine, an immune stimulant, which he pursued for only two weeks before quitting, again because of side effects. At that point, he consulted with a local naturopath supposedly knowledgeable about nutritional approaches to cancer, but the proposed intervention again left Patient IQ so ill he quickly discontinued treatment.

In mid-April 2005, Patient IQ noticed a nodule anterior to the left ear lobe, about the size of a pea. He consulted Dr. Chen, who, suspecting recurrent melanoma, immediately referred him back to his surgeon. A needle biopsy on April 22, 2005 confirmed, "The malignant cells are consistent with the patient's history of melanoma."

Then, on April 25, 2005, the patient underwent a PET/CT, which revealed clear evidence of metastatic disease in the neck and liver, as described in the radiology report:

> IMPRESSION:
>
> 1. Hypermetabolic 1 cm, nodule in the left preauricular [ear] far demonstrates maximum SUV of 11.8 compatible with malignancy. Hypermetabolic left intraparotid lymphadenopathy is also consistent with malignancy. Subtle hypermetabolism in a mildly enlarged left level II lymph node is also concerning for malignant nodal involvement....
>
> 2. Single hypermetabolic focus in the left lobe of the liver is consistent with metastasis.

An MRI of the head done two days later showed no evidence of metastatic disease in the brain but did reveal an 8 mm focus in the left mandible condyle consistent with metastatic disease.

Patient IQ then decided to consult with Dr. John Thompson, an interleukin expert at the University of Washington, who said the drug might at best offer a 7 percent chance of response, but no cure. Dr. Thompson apparently painted a bleak picture of the treatment, which would be debilitating and potentially dangerous and would require for its administration a stay in the university's intensive care unit. Dr. Thompson told Patient IQ he might have six to twelve months to live, with or without the therapy, and suggested he start thinking about hospice care.

About that time, after learning about my approach through a friend of his wife's, he decided to proceed with me. I saw him for the first time May 16, 2005, at which time he admitted he was still in shock over the terminal nature of his recurrent disease.

Thereafter, the patient followed his nutritional program with determination and diligence. Though he seemed to improve clinically, a repeat PET scan study in November 2005, after Patient IQ had completed six months on treatment, showed a mixed picture, with some improvement and some worsening of his disease:

IMPRESSION:

1. Interim decrease in radiotracer accumulations with the left preauricular soft tissue nodule, which may be slightly smaller in size.

2. Definite interim increase in size and degree of hypermetabolism associated with enlarged left intraparotid lymph nodes, consistent with progression of metastatic nodal involvement. Slight interim increase in size of a left level II lymph node is suspicious for nodal tumor involvement....

3. Definite interim increase in size and radiotracer accumulation of a solitary left hepatic lobe lesion, compatible with progression of hepatic metastasis.

In our experience, during the first six to twelve months of our treatment, scans often show a mixed picture, with some improvement and some worsening. Management of patients on this therapy requires vigilance, with appropriate adjustment of enzyme dosing when needed. In this case, I increased the daily enzyme intake.

Thereafter, clinically, he continued doing well. In May 2006, after the patient had completed a year on therapy, a repeat PET/CT scan again revealed a mixed picture:

Neck:

1. There has been mild progression of the left preauricular tumor which is larger on the current exam and does demonstrate more radiotracer accumulation.

2. One of the left intraparotid lymph nodes is grossly unchanged in size from prior exam. The lymph node remains hypermetabolic, and may even be more hypermeta-

bolic on the current exam. ... In addition, there has been an increase in size of one of the left intraparotid lymph nodes.

3. Although the left level 2 cervical lymph nodes are not hypermetabolic, this has increased in size and is suspicious.

Abdomen:

1. The left hepatic liver metastasis is unchanged in size. The amount of radiotracer accumulation is probably unchanged. This does remain hypermetabolic indicating viable tumor.

2. Increase in size of the peripancreatic lymph nodes as well as new hypermetabolic within the lymph node consistent with tumor progression.

Despite the findings, the disease certainly hadn't exploded throughout his body as had been expected. He felt well and had already outlived the dire predictions of Dr. Thompson at the University of Washington. When we discussed the situation by phone, the patient made it clear to me he had no intention of changing treatments, so I once again changed his enzyme dosing.

We waited some eighteen months before repeating the scans, because the patient himself was growing wary of the radiation exposure involved. Finally, in mid-December 2006, after two and a half years on the regimen, he did undergo PET/CT scanning, which this time revealed considerable improvement:

IMPRESSION:

1. The hypermetabolic lesion in the left lobe of the liver identified previously has apparently resolved. No new liver lesion.

2. Stable size and degree of hypermetabolism within the enlarged peripancreatic-porta hepatic lymph node... .

3. Suspect a modest improvement in nodal disease in the left neck. Two nodes within the left parotid gland have decreased mildly in size, and show a mildly lesser degree of hypermetabolism. Although the preauricular lymph nodes have not changed in size, it also appears mildly less hypermetabolic.

Thereafter, Patient IQ continued on his treatment and for a time, because he felt well, decided to defer any radiographic studies. The biggest problem he faced was management of his postconcussion cognitive and mood problems, requiring several adjustments of his medication, which produced ongoing severe side effects. In late 2008, after a period of medication changes, his left parotid tumor—which had remained quiescent for nearly two years—seemed to grow.

At that point, in mid-November 2008, he agreed to undergo PET/CT testing, which once again revealed no evidence of metastatic disease in the chest or abdomen. However, the parotid tumor, which appeared to be largely necrotic, had grown somewhat. I adjusted his regimen, and the lesion seemed to stabilize. Then, in the spring of 2009, he experienced blunt trauma to the left parotid, right on the tumor itself, which seemed to grow slightly for a time afterward, as confirmed by an MRI of the brain in mid-May 2009. Currently, more than four years since he first consulted with me in May 2005, he is doing well clinically with stabilization once again of the left cheek mass.

*IMPORTANT EDITOR'S NOTE:
Dr. Gonzalez died before updating this case report. According to Patient IQ's office medical file, he died in July 2010.

Case 7: Patient JL
A Minimum 9-Year Survivor*

Patient JL has a long-term interest in alternative and nutritional medicine, dating back some forty years. Prior to developing cancer, she had consulted a well-known alternative practitioner in New York for treatment of chronic fatigue, food allergies, and hypoglycemia, with apparent initial improvement in symptoms. After her physician retired in the early 1980s, her symptoms flared up once again. This time around, her problems persisted despite treatment prescribed by a number of unconventional physicians. She followed an anti-Candida diet and was treated for parasites, food allergies, and inadequate digestion, with only minor success.

In terms of her cancer history, in 2003, a plastic surgeon in New York excised a small lesion from the patient's right thigh in 2003, found to be consistent with malignant melanoma. The disease was thought to be localized, and no additional treatment was recommended at the time.

Patient JL subsequently did well until the spring of 2006, when she first noticed a small translucent new lesion on the skin of her left shoulder, about the size of a pencil eraser. Initially, she assumed, because of the pale color, that the lesion was benign, so she did not consult with her dermatologist. However, in late June 2006, Patient JL returned to her dermatologist at Columbia-Presbyterian for a routine follow-up examination. A biopsy of the lesion confirmed a Clark level III malignant melanoma. Because of the depth of invasion, the dermatologist warned JL that the disease might be in her regional lymph nodes, and she was referred to a surgeon at Memorial Sloan Kettering, Dr. Daniel Coit.

In early August 2006, Patient JL first consulted with Dr. Coit, who suggested a wide local excision. A week later at Memorial, Patient JL underwent the procedure, along with sentinel sampling in the left axillary region. The pathology report described residual melanoma to a depth of 2 mm in the shoulder tissue and a single axillary lymph node involved with cancer—a very ominous prognostic indicator.

In early September 2006, Patient JL proceeded with a staging workup: a total-body PET scan revealed increased activity in the neck and left axilla. A CT scan documented the following:

> There is a cluster of small nodules in the left upper lobe [of the lung] and a small 3 mm nodule in the right middle lobe.

> There are tiny low density liver lesions. ... In addition there is a focal area of increased density in the subcutaneous fat of the right body wall of the level of the pelvis. Attention to this area at the time of followup examination is recommended.

Then in late September at Memorial Hospital, Patient JL underwent further axillary dissection, but all twelve excised lymph nodes were clear of cancer. After surgery, Patient JL met with an oncologist, who discussed a clinical trial evaluating a new melanoma vaccine but also admitted that this approach had so far failed to yield any encouraging results. Then, after noticing a lesion in the left supraclavicular region on exam, the oncologist referred her back to Dr. Coit, with whom she consulted in late November 2006. After a fine needle aspiration of the neck nodule confirmed metastatic malignant melanoma, Patient JL claims she was told she had "stage IV disease."

A repeat PET/CT in early December 2006 revealed the following:

1. New left supraclavicular nodes consistent with melanoma

2. Focal uptake in left axilla consistent with a local recurrence

In mid-December 2006, Patient JL returned to surgery yet again, this time for a modified neck dissection. "Metastatic malignant melanoma" was identified in "one out of twenty lymph nodes."

With evidence of multiple recurrences, rapid spread, and evident metastatic disease, Patient JL began investigating alternative approaches to cancer, learned of my work, and first met with me in mid-January 2007. At the time, she made it clear to me she would never consider chemotherapy, radiation, vaccine therapy, immunotherapy, and particularly clinical trials that she knew had yielded no real promising results to date. On exam, I detected a 2 cm left anterior cervical node, suspicious for metastatic disease.

Patient JL immediately began her nutritional therapy, which she followed very diligently and enthusiastically. In addition, I encouraged her to follow up with Dr. Coit, the Memorial surgeon. In early February 2007, Dr. Coit excised the anterior cervical mass, which proved to be infiltrated with "metastatic malignant melanoma involving one lymph node." At this point, four different procedures after the initial biopsy in June 2006 had confirmed metastatic melanoma, including involvement of lymph nodes in the left axilla and on three separate occasions in the neck, all within an eight-month period of time.

Thereafter, Patient JL continued her nutritional program with great determination. A repeat CT scan series in late March 2007, after JL had completed two months on her therapy, showed "unremarkable liver, spleen, pancreas, adrenal glands." The earlier-described liver and pelvic lesions apparently had resolved. However, the CT scan of the chest did reveal "new small subpleural opacity on the left upper lobe and new patch opacity in the right lower lobe, probably represents atelectasis and/or a mild inflammatory process. Follow-up CT is suggested."

A CT scan of the neck indicated only postsurgical change.

On her therapy, Patient JL generally did well, though her course was complicated by a bout of esophageal herpes, which resolved with both nutritional and pharmaceutical intervention. Repeat CT scans in late July 2007, after she had completed six months on therapy, documented continued improvement, revealing again an "unremarkable liver, spleen, pancreas." In addition, the report described improvement in the lung lesions: "Decrease in the previously new patchy opacities in the left upper lobe and right lower lobe since 3/--/07."

Her most recent scans from early January 2009 again showed no suspicious lesions in the neck, abdomen, or pelvis, and continued improvement in the lung: "Decreased left lower lobe pleural based nodular opacities."

Currently, Patient JL, in her eighties, remains very active as an artist and sculptor, recently the recipient of a grant to help support her work. She remains disease-free, now two and a half years since she first began her nutritional program.

Although her survival at this point isn't exceptional, I think even the most skeptical of critics would have to take notice of this patient's course on treatment. Prior to beginning our therapy, she had biopsy evidence of four recurrences and metastatic disease within an eight-month period, with evidence of possible lung, liver, and pelvis metastases. Since beginning her program, her disease has remained completely quiescent, the previously noted liver lesions have apparently resolved, and her lung lesions continue to improve. Plus, she enjoys generally excellent health.

*IMPORTANT EDITOR'S NOTE:
Dr. Gonzalez died before updating this case report. According to Patient JL's office medical file, she last contacted Dr. Gonzalez in late January 2015. Patient JL last communicated with Dr. Isaacs in the end of December 2016.

Case 8: Patient EH
A Minimum 6.4-Year Survivor*

Patient EH is a forty-two-year-old woman from the United Kingdom with a history of stage IV melanoma.

Patient EH reports no family history of cancer. She herself had been in excellent health with no prior major or minor medical problems when first diagnosed with melanoma.

Her current situation dates to December 2006, when while on vacation in Europe with her husband, they both noticed that a long-standing nevus on her right abdominal wall seemed to have increased in size and turned "crusty." Initially, neither she nor her husband thought much about the change, but while shopping with her for clothes in the spring of 2007, her mother noticed the lesion, which she thought looked suspicious. That May, she consulted with her primary care physician in Scotland, who happens to be a dermatologist. He agreed that the mole, now ulcerated, required treatment.

He excised the nevus, which proved to be a melanoma, some 4 mm deep. Subsequently, Patient EH underwent wide local excision at the original site with sentinel node sampling. No residual cancer remained either in the skin or in the three lymph nodes examined. Her physicians, believing her to be cured of what seemed to be purely local disease, suggested no additional adjuvant treatment at the time.

Thereafter, Patient EH continued follow-up care with her dermatologist/primary care physician every three months. She seemed to be doing well, with no sign of recurrent disease for some two and a half years, until January 2010, when she developed chronic abdominal discomfort and pain that worsened over a period of some weeks. Initially, she did not return to her physician, but when the pain persisted, she consulted with him. Her doctor was concerned enough by her symptoms that he ordered a CT scan of the abdomen, which the radiologist reported was completely clear. When the pain ultimately resolved some weeks later, both EH and her doctor assumed the symptoms had nothing to do with her original cancer diagnosis.

But in mid-June 2010, while lying in bed, Patient EH felt a mass in her left abdomen. She returned to her physician, who ordered a CT scan of the chest, abdomen, and pelvis. Though the chest scan was described as clear (this assessment would later change), the abdominal CT revealed extensive disease, as described in the formal report, including a tumor that apparently had been present, though smaller and not reported, on the May 2010 scan: "A 6.5 × 4.3 × 3.7 cm soft tissue mass lesion is demonstrated with the left upper quadrant. With retrospect this is present on the previous CT scan although not as large. This is a progressively enlarging mass. A number of small soft tissue nodules are demonstrated in relation to this mass and appearances are highly suspicious of recurrent melanoma. The upper abdominal organs are otherwise unremarkable."

With recurrent disease evident, Patient EH was referred to an oncologist in the British National Health Service. After reviewing the two sets of scans, the physician determined that the disease was too extensive to allow for surgery with curative intent, and instead suggested she enter a clinical trial with ipilimumab (Yervoy), a monoclonal antibody "targeted therapy" designed for patients with metastatic, inoperable melanoma.

Though Patient EH and her husband were willing to consider the clinical trial, they were not yet willing to give up on the surgical option. From a search on the Internet, they learned about a surgeon in Holland, Dr. Eggemyt, known to operate when other surgeons would not. After contacting his office, Patient EH and her husband traveled to Holland to meet with Dr. Eggemyt. After reviewing the case, he felt surgery was indeed an option, though he seemed convinced that there must be a surgeon in Scotland who would be willing to operate.

After returning to Scotland, Patient EH and her husband continued their search and learned of a melanoma expert in Israel, whom they contacted. This physician, after reviewing the scans, suggested she undergo chemotherapy to shrink the tumors before proceeding with surgery. Patient EH found this approach daunting and unacceptable, and she and her husband continued searching for a surgeon in Scotland who would be willing to operate without requiring drug treatment first.

Meanwhile, EH and her husband kept in touch with the oncologist, still considering the clinical study as a possible option. As part of the initial evaluation for the trial, she was required to undergo PET testing, which was done during the first week of August 2010. The official radiology report described extensive disease:

> Two FDG avid mass lesions are confirmed in the abdomen. The larger mass is in the left upper quadrant and measures approximately 6 × 5 cm in diameter with multiple smaller surrounding nodes identified. This lesion extends posteriorly and is closely related to the left psoas complex/left ureter....

> The second more inferiorly placed mass in the left side of the abdomen appears to involve a small bowel loop medial to the mid descending colon and measures 3.5 × 3.3 in diameter....

> There is paraspinal muscle uptake to the left of the C6/7 spinous processes. Although this is less intense that the abdominal [sic] and may be benign in aetiology, correlation with MRI... is recommended.

> Diffuse bony uptake is noted without any focal spots. Appearances are probably benign.

A follow-up MRI of the cervical spine several days later showed no suspicious lesions, and endoscopy and colonoscopy were also clear.

While this testing was in progress, Patient EH and her husband succeeded in locating a surgeon in Glasgow willing to operate, though he admitted the procedure would be difficult. He proposed an initial laparoscopic approach to first identify the extent of disease and the possibility of resection. With this plan in mind, only days later, during the second week of August 2010, Patient EH underwent surgery. After the initial laparoscopy, the surgeon proceeded with a full laparotomy, tumor resection, and small bowel resection. The operative note described the findings at surgery: "The abdominal cavity was inspected and the small bowel tumor was identified which was associated with significant lymphadenopathy."

Evaluation of the operative specimens confirmed widely metastatic malignant melanoma, including involvement of lymph nodes, though the surgeon was hopeful he had removed all visible disease.

Postsurgery, EH underwent repeat scanning. MRI of the brain, CT scans of the chest and abdomen, and total-body PET scan were all clear of any evident residual or metastatic disease. At that point, Patient EH's oncologist informed her that although all visible disease had been removed and the scans were clear, because of the extent and nature of her cancer, the chances of recurrence were very high. However, she was also informed that because of the debulking procedure, she no longer qualified for the ipilimumab clinical trial. He also, according to Patient EH, did not push chemotherapy as a particularly useful option, suggesting just "watchful waiting" with implication of treatment when the disease recurred.

Patient EH then consulted with a private oncologist outside of the NHS system, who recommended regular follow-up visits and repeat CT scans in December 2010. In addition, Patient EH and her husband began looking at alternative approaches; she learned about our work, applied to become a patient, and was accepted into our practice.

I first met Patient EH and her husband during the last week of September 2010, some six weeks after her surgery. Having recovered nicely from the procedure, she reported to me that she generally felt quite well. She denied any serious or even minor symptoms and approached my treatment with great interest and enthusiasm. Both she and her husband were clearly very intelligent people who understood the seriousness of recurrent, metastatic melanoma. The whole situation, she admitted, had been quite devastating, but she was optimistic about her chances with my therapy.

Shortly after her appointment and her return to Scotland, Patient EH's husband sent me a long and thoughtful fax, thanking me for the time I had spent with them over two days, and reporting,

She is absolutely committed to your program and I have no doubt that she will complete 100% of your suggestions. Hopefully this will present her with the long term solution you indicated.

Having done a lot of research on Melanoma I find it amazing that your program has not been more widely adopted. Why do you think this is?

Thereafter, Patient EH and her husband kept in touch regularly by phone, by fax, and by letter. She seemed to be following her prescribed treatment plan with great diligence, with, as her husband reported, "100%" compliance. A follow-up visit with her oncologist in October went well, and CT scans done at the time were apparently clear. In early December 2010, after EH had completed three months on her therapy, her husband sent me a note informing me that "[Patient EH] is doing very well with your treatments and we are very grateful for all of your support."

EH subsequently did well. In early February 2011, her husband faxed me a note, concerned that she had experienced several episodes of rectal bleeding. I encouraged them to follow up quickly with their local doctors, a suggestion they followed. Her oncologist didn't suspect a serious problem but nonetheless arranged for a colonoscopy that was scheduled for the last week of February 2011. As it turned out, this showed no evidence of cancer, but only a minor rectal fissure.

Patient EH had scheduled her first six-month follow-up appointment with me for the last week of March 2011. A week prior to the visit, her oncologist had arranged for CT scanning of the chest, abdomen, and pelvis, which this time around revealed a 2.0 mm lesion in the liver, not detected on the prior scans. The day EH got the news from her oncologist, we spoke by phone, only days before her planned visit with me. I didn't yet have a copy of the CT scan report, but she described what her oncologist had told her. Though the finding had left her understandably concerned, her physician, believing the lesion too small to biopsy at this time, recommended only that the scans be repeated in two months, an approach I thought quite reasonable.

The following day, EH's husband faxed me a copy of the radiologist's findings, which to my surprise now included mention of several pulmonary lesions that apparently had been present on the previous CT though not described in the formal report:

> There are several small pulmonary nodules. Nodules measure up to 4 mm on long window settings and are unchanged from the previous CT [from October 11, 2010].

> Previous small bowel resection and small bowel anastomosis are noted. There is no definite local recurrence [in the abdomen]. Again, small mesenteric nodes measuring up to 10 mm are noted. ... There is a new ill-defined 0.7 cm hypodense lesion in the posterior segment right lobe liver.

I suspected that the lung lesions might indicate further metastatic disease that in retrospect would have been present during EH's first visit to my office in September 2010.

When EH, her husband, and I subsequently met together in New York, we discussed at length the recent CT scan findings. As a start, EH expressed her concern about the radiation exposure from repeated CT scans. She'd already gone through three "total body" scans and wondered if an MRI of the abdomen would be an acceptable alternative during a planned re-evaluation in May 2011. By this time, the truth about the radiation exposure from CT scans and their potential carcinogenicity—which has been a big secret kept for some eighteen years—was out in the media, leaving patients like EH understandably worried.

I explained that indeed, for the abdomen and pelvis, an MRI would be appropriate, but not for the lungs. MRIs are very motion sensitive, even to slight movement such as breathing, which distorts the final pictures. In any event, I suggested she discuss all these issues with her oncologist.

I also explained my opinion that quite possibly, the very small liver lesion had been present but not detected on previous CT scans. As useful as a CT scan can be, the test works by sequential x-ray images of the body, taken in "slices." If a small lesion sits between two successive slices, it can be missed. I also told EH that whatever the lung lesions might be, these hadn't changed since the prior CT scan, to me a good sign. Regardless, when EH expressed her continued determination to stay on her nutritional therapy, I encouraged her to take each day one at a time, enjoying her life and her children.

Other than her concern about the CT findings, EH generally felt very well. The rectal bleeding fortunately had stopped, and she reported the findings of the recent colonoscopy. Otherwise, she described very good energy and stamina, both of which she said had improved considerably on her nutritional program. She told me that in February 2011 she and her husband had gone on a ski trip in France with their children, which they all enjoyed immensely.

I made some changes in her supplement protocol, and she returned home to Scotland, with continued dedication to her treatment.

During the second week of May 2011, Patient EH, despite her reservations about radiation exposure, did undergo repeat CT scans of the chest, abdomen, and pelvis. The summary of the scans read,

> Impression:
>
> 1) unchanged 0/7 cm hypodense lesion within segment 6 of liver. This can be further assessed at next follow-up.

2) deep bilateral small indeterminate pulmonary nodules are unchanged.

At that point, EH's Scottish oncologist suggested an MRI of the abdomen, to evaluate more closely the liver lesion. This study, done several days later, indicated to the radiologist that the liver lesion mostly likely represented a "simple tiny cyst."

In early August 2011, while I was out of town for a lecture, Patient EH contacted my office, complaining of weakness and inability to focus her eyes after a coffee enema. The symptoms had lasted only about twenty seconds. Later that day, Dr. Isaacs, covering for me, contacted the patient, who by the time of the call seemed to have completely recovered without any residual deficits. Dr. Isaacs thought the problem might have been a vasovagal episode, in which the vagus nerve suddenly fires strongly, in turn dropping the blood pressure acutely, to the point that patients can faint. Such events, often associated with stress, are usually short lived and generally do not indicate any significant neurological pathology.

Several days later, after I had returned to New York, Patient EH's husband again faxed my office, alerting us that his wife had experienced an episode of lightheadedness associated with near syncope, lasting only thirty seconds. When I spoke to her, again the event sounded vasovagal in nature, though I instructed her to contact her local doctors for an assessment. I was somewhat concerned, because melanoma notoriously can spread to the brain. In any event, as it turned out she was due to see her oncologist for a regularly scheduled appointment in several days.

During the third week of August 2011, I spoke with EH at length. Her oncologist, who like myself was concerned about the "spells," had ordered an MRI of the brain, which had shown a 3 cm lesion in the right frontal lobe. This tumor appeared to be operable, so her oncologist had arranged an appointment with a Glasgow neurosurgeon. The oncologist also advised her that, assuming EH proceeded with surgery, she should expect to undergo a single dose of stereotactic radiation after the operation. EH made it clear to me that, after surgery, she intended to resume her nutritional program.

I made several suggestions, including upping the daily enzyme dose, and pushed the cycle of supplements to twenty-five days on, five days off. During this time, Patient EH, her husband, and I were in contact on a daily basis, by fax and phone. Understandably, they both wanted my opinion, which they appeared to respect, about what might be going on.

Indeed, an MRI after her abdominal surgery, during the second week of August 2010, had shown no evidence of metastases to the brain. However, I wasn't to meet EH for another six weeks, during the last week of September 2010. Melanoma can be a very aggressive disease that spreads rapidly, and certainly the extent of EH's abdominal metastases indicated we were dealing with a difficult situation. Furthermore, when later reviewed, CT scans of the chest from that time indicated possible disease in both lungs. As I thought about the situation, it certainly was plausible to me that the cancer had already spread to the brain between the clear August 2010 MRI and the time EH actually had begun her enzyme protocol in early October 2010, some two weeks after our meeting in late September.

I explained to EH and her husband that possibly we weren't looking at program failure, but disease that might have been brewing at the time she first walked into my office. Perhaps, the enzymes, as they do, had provoked an inflammatory response around a pre-existing tumor, provoking, as they do, swelling that in turn led to her recent symptoms. I had been through a similar situation some sixteen years earlier with a patient diagnosed initially with metastatic melanoma, who underwent brain surgery some two years after beginning treatment with me when he developed new-onset neurological symptoms. After surgery and a course of stereotactic radiation, he resumed his nutritional program, never experienced another recurrence, and today remains in excellent health. In any event, it would be unlikely, in my experience, for melanoma to spread like this in a patient as compliant as EH. Even if this were a new tumor, a change in enzyme dosing most likely, I thought, would bring the situation back under control.

In one of our phone conversations, I did say I would understand completely if EH wanted to stop my treatment and go in a different direction. But both she and her husband, acknowledging they understood there really weren't any conventional beneficial treatments for her condition, made it clear to me that after the proposed surgery, she would continue her program with the same dedication as before, incorporating the recommended changes in enzyme dosing. Though of course concerned about the situation, they both still had great faith in the treatment. In fact, in one of his faxes to me, her husband wrote, "Thank you for your invaluable and ongoing assistance."

Treating aggressive cancer with any therapy, conventional or alternative, including mine, is never simple and never straightforward, and it always involves, at least initially, ups and downs that require vigilant management and at times program adjustment. I have witnessed many times that patients whose faith in the treatment doesn't waver during the difficult times usually come out fine.

During the last week of August 2011—after she had completed eleven months on her therapy—EH underwent the planned brain surgery with excision of the single lesion. Apparently, the operation had gone very well, as her husband informed me in a fax:

> Dr. Gonzalez,
>
> I am glad to say that EH's operation last week was successful and they managed to remove the tumor. Not sure if it is relevant but the surgeon said that the tumor "just popped out."

EH is keen to get back on your program as soon as she can. She is home now, but feeling tired.

From what the husband told me about his discussion with the surgeon when we talked the day I received his fax, the tumor seemed to have been completely encapsulated, not penetrating at all into the surrounding brain tissue—something we find happens with the enzyme therapy, as the body works to wall off a malignant mass. In such cases, the tumor lacks the projections growing into adjacent brain tissue usually seen with aggressive tumors, allowing for easy and complete resection.

In early September 2011, I received a copy of the formal pathology report, which described a tumor with the "appearance of melanoma" based on immunocytochemistry testing, with necrosis (dead tumor) "readily identified." After reading the report, I suspected EH, with her enzyme regimen, was fighting the tumor hard, killing some, encapsulating the rest.

The stereotactic radiation was scheduled for the third week of September 2011. EH was reluctant to proceed with this additional treatment, concerned as she was about the side effects to her brain. I reassured her, explaining that the new technology allowed for concentrated, single-dose radiation focused just on the tumor bed, leaving the normal adjacent brain tissue for the most part undamaged. In the old days, a patient such as EH would often undergo whole brain radiation for up to several weeks, with often serious, and permanent, cognitive loss.

Prior to the radiation, during the second week of September 2011, EH underwent both an MRI and a CT of the brain, which showed no residual or additional metastatic disease. When we talked about the findings, she again repeated what she had said before, that she was determined to stay compliant with my therapy.

After the single dose of radiation, EH's husband faxed me a note, informing me that EH had experienced no discomfort and none of the side effects about which she had been warned by the radiation oncologist. And she had fully resumed her nutritional therapy. They had also scheduled an appointment in my office for the third week of November 2011. He ended the note with, "Many thanks for your ongoing assistance. It really is very much appreciated."

I include these thoughts not to show how wonderful I am, but to show how wonderful EH and her husband are. Fighting bad cancer is never easy, for patient or for doctor. Even with the best of outcomes, along the way there will be detours and bumps in the road as in this case—sometimes frightening bumps. With a patient like EH and her devoted husband, it is so much easier to maneuver through such crises successfully. Certainly EH and her husband were rightfully anxious about the new developments, but they were determined to work with me to find a solution.

In late October 2011, several weeks before her appointment in my office, Patient EH's doctors arranged for repeat MRI of the brain and CT scanning of the chest, abdomen, and pelvis. The MRI did show an area of abnormality in the tumor bed, thought to be postoperative change, as described in the radiology report:

> The resection cavity in the right frontal love is involuting. In its deep aspect is a non-enhancing 0.5 cm high signal area…which may well represent some positive operative change.…
>
> Comment: Considerable improvement. The residual area of high signal should be followed up closely.

The CT scans of the chest, abdomen, and pelvis showed the following:

> No evidence of metastatic disease in the chest. The small lung nodules are unchanged.
>
> In the upper abdomen the subtle low-density in segment 6 [of the liver] is unchanged. No other focal abnormality in the liver.

When I met with EH and her husband in mid-November 2011, she had completed fourteen months on her therapy, seemed as before to be determinedly compliant, looked healthy, and reported feeling very well. She had experienced as I had expected a drop in energy around the time of the surgery, but she was back to her normal excellent health. She reported no residual neurological symptoms of any kind, informing me that her memory and cognition were excellent. She and her husband had brought their children with them on their trip to New York, which they had decided to turn into a vacation for the family.

In the months that followed, I hardly heard from EH. When I next saw her and her husband, in late March 2012, she seemed compliant with her therapy as before and looked and felt very well. She described no neurological symptoms, and in fact no symptoms of any type. She informed me that some weeks earlier, in February 2012, her oncologist had sent her for repeat scans of the brain, chest, abdomen, and pelvis—all of which came out clear. However, she was upset with the British National Health Services, which administers health care in Scotland, because of the enormous delays in getting results back on any test. She had to wait ten days to learn that the scans were fine, during which time she experienced considerable, and understandable, anxiety.

When EH and her husband returned to my office, during the last week of October 2012, again she seemed to be doing well and reported overall feeling "great." She reported that at that time, she was seeing both her dermatologist and oncologist every six months. Repeat MRI of the brain in August 2012 had been clear. She continued on the higher dose of enzymes as well as the twenty-five-day cycle of pills, all of which she tolerated without difficulty.

Thereafter she continued doing well. In late February 2013, she underwent repeat CT scans of the chest, abdomen, and pelvis, which, according to her husband, were "clear." However, her oncologist was concerned about the MRI of the brain, which this time showed no distinct mass in the treated tumor bed, but an "area of brightness." Her oncologist would be discussing the findings with the melanoma group at his hospital, to determine what the next step should be. EH was concerned of course, but I couldn't reassure her because I did not have a copy of the actual MRI report; I was going only on what she and her husband told me over the phone. Eventually, as I was to learn, the radiologist would conclude that the findings, in his best judgment, most likely reflected only radiation change, not recurrent tumor.

When I next saw EH and her husband, in early April 2013, EH seemed as compliant as ever, as determined as ever, and as healthy as before. She described excellent energy, stamina, and concentration, reporting no neurological symptoms of any kind. She was anxious about the recent brain findings, even though the radiologist argued against recurrent disease. Her oncologist, at the radiologist's urging, had ordered a SPECT scan for the week following her visit with me, as well as a repeat MRI.

After returning to Scotland, Patient EH proceeded with the SPECT scan as planned, but there were the usual bureaucratic delays in getting results. Then, during the second week of April 2013, the MRI revealed what was thought to be definitive recurrent tumor: "Findings: At the site of the previous noted abnormality in the right frontal lobe, adjacent to the resection site, there has been an increase in the abnormal enhancing mass which now measures 9 × 6 mm compared to the small ill-defined lesion previously. The appearances are consistent with recurrent tumor."

I was somewhat surprised to say the least when I read the official report, because clinically EH had been doing so well, with complete absence of any neurological symptoms. But in my conversations with her and her husband, and as evident in an email exchange between her husband and the oncologist, the general consensus was that, to everyone's disappointment, EH was experiencing recurrent tumor, adjacent to but outside the original tumor bed. Her oncologist and surgeon proposed excision of the lesion, followed by "conformational radiation," a somewhat more intense approach than pinpoint stereotactic, but not as diffuse as whole brain radiation.

When we talked in late April 2013 about these recent developments, Patient EH was clearly downhearted, and as disappointed as I was because she felt so well and was experiencing no neurological symptoms. But she had resigned herself to surgery, which unfortunately couldn't be scheduled until the second week of May 2013 because of her surgeon's prior scheduling commitments. Regardless, I admired her determination to resume her nutritional treatment as soon as possible after the procedure.

The operation went ahead as planned, and two days afterward Patient EH's husband faxed me a note, informing me the pathologist could find no sign of cancer in the surgical specimen, only residual damage from the prior radiation treatment: "The good news is that her brain operation went well. We got the results yesterday and it was radio necrosis and not melanoma. She is absolutely delighted and doesn't need any further treatment so back on your program harder than ever. She is still very tired from the operation, but the result was good."

When I spoke with EH later that day, she told me her local doctors were "dumbfounded" by the benign findings. She sounded very pleased with the results, as was I. There had been no recurrence.

Several days later, I received a faxed copy of the formal pathology report, which went on for some length. In summary, it reported, "The appearances are consistent with reactive and necrotic changes associated with radiotherapy. There is no evidence of tumor in the submitted sample."

Now more than seven years from her original diagnosis of melanoma, more than three years from her diagnosis of extensive metastatic disease in the abdomen and possible lung metastases, and more than two years from her diagnosis of brain metastases, Patient EH appears to be in excellent health with no evidence of recurrent disease. Her survival at this point is already quite remarkable in view of the dismal statistics for recurrent, stage IV melanoma. *Harrison's* has reported that "metastatic melanoma is generally incurable, and median survival ranges from 6 to 15 months."[7] Patients with visceral metastases, as in the case of Patient EH, fare far worse than cutaneous or lymph node recurrence.

The website UpToDate has provided an extensive discussion of standard drug treatment approaches to metastatic melanoma, none of which appears effective. The only FDA-approved drug for the treatment of metastatic melanoma, dacarbazine, yielded a response rate of 8 to 20 percent in clinical trials, but nearly all of these were short lived, with 50 percent of patients showing progression at six months, and only 2 percent at best surviving six years.

In a clinical trial of the drug temozolomide, chemically related to dacarbazine, of 305 patients enrolled, investigators reported an overall median survival of 7.7 months with temozolomide compared with 6.4 months for those receiving dacarbazine. Although interleukin-2, a very aggressive immune modulator, has been proposed as a treatment for metastatic melanoma for nearly three decades, results in clinical trials have not been impressive, and it is still not considered standard of care.

Although Patient EH never received chemotherapy or immunotherapy of any type, I provide these statistics to show the deadly nature of metastatic melanoma.

7   Longo et al., *Harrison's Principles*, 18th ed., 729.

For patients diagnosed specifically with brain metastases from melanoma, the website UpTo-Date has reported a "general grim prognosis." The authors of this section described a combined analysis of two clinical studies with a total of 1,400 patients, in which the median survival was four months, with one-year survival rates of 9 and 19 percent.

Although Patient EH was diagnosed with brain metastases after she had completed a year on her nutritional therapy, it's possible as discussed earlier that this tumor began growing in the interval between her clear MRI of the brain in August 2010 and the time she first began her nutritional therapy in early October 2010. Regardless, I have found over the years that it does take some time before the therapy controls a cancer, particularly with very aggressive disease as in this case, but usually over time, if the patient remains compliant, the situation will be controlled.

I find this case history particularly instructive about the nature of my approach, because it shows the contribution of a patient's attitude toward, and faith in, the therapy in achieving ultimate success. Even when it appeared that the treatment hadn't controlled the disease after nearly a year, EH only wanted to know what we could do, working together, to make the situation better. She didn't quit treatment in disappointment or in a huff, but only incorporated my suggested changes without a second thought. Such patients in my experience usually come through their crises nicely.

*IMPORTANT EDITOR'S NOTE:
According to Dr. Isaacs' patient files, Patient EH last communicated with Dr. Isaacs in January 2017.

SARCOMA

Experts recognize some twenty varieties of sarcoma, all of which originate in the connective tissue, muscle, fat cells, fibrous tissue, peripheral nerves, and blood vessels. Such tumors thus differ from the common solid tumors of the lung, colon, breast, or pancreas that form in the epithelial lining of organs, or the immunological malignancies such as leukemia or lymphoma that affect the white blood cells. Sarcomas are rare, accounting for only 1 percent of all adult malignancies according to the Liddy Shriver Sarcoma Initiative website, sarcomahelp.org. In 2012, about 13,900 cases were reported in the United States. Many cases appear first in the extremities, and, when localized, surgery can be curative. Once metastatic, this cancer type—notoriously resistant to chemotherapy and radiation—usually proves fatal within a year.

Case 1: Patient AQ
*A Minimum 11.2-Year Survivor**

Patient AQ, a farm woman in her late fifties, has survived eight years with a diagnosis of high-grade leiomyosarcoma. Her family history is pertinent because of a single case of cancer, primary unknown, in her maternal grandmother.

Prior to her diagnosis of cancer, Patient AQ had experienced a number of significant health problems, including gastritis and two episodes of severe chronic fatigue. The first occurred in 1987, when without any precipitating event or prodrome she woke up one day with severe fatigue. In the ensuing weeks, she experienced persistent tiredness, night sweats, and a chronic low-grade fever. Patient AQ consulted with her primary care physician a number of times, but blood tests showed no evidence of any infectious agent or metabolic abnormality. When the symptoms persisted, Patient AQ began treating herself with a variety of nutritional supplements and consulted with a local nutritionist. She stuck strictly to a whole-foods diet, incorporating juicing, and with her various interventions after six months her symptoms gradually abated.

She subsequently did well until 1997, when she experienced a recurrence of her symptoms after moving with her family to a new farmhouse that apparently was contaminated with mold. Once again, she developed severe fatigue, malaise, fevers, and night sweats, along with arthralgias, myalgias, and chronic diarrhea. This time around, the symptoms were considerably worse than during her first episode some twelve years earlier. At one point, after developing jaundice, she was hospitalized. Blood tests, including liver function tests, were within the normal range, and an abdominal ultrasound revealed only "a few gallstones," which her doctors thought inconsequential.

Once again, Patient AQ began treating herself with a whole-foods diet along with a variety of nutritional supplements. This time around, after some two years of significant illness, she began to improve, eventually returning to generally good health. However, after the second febrile episode resolved, three to four times each month she would experience bouts of tingling and numbness on the right side of her face associated with a racing heart, lasting several hours before subsiding.

Since 1997, she had experienced intermittent episodes of irregular heart rhythm, severe enough to warrant visits to the local emergency room. She was eventually diagnosed not with heart disease, but with acid reflux that apparently would, through neurological reflexes, set off the irregular rhythm. At that point, Patient AQ began a self-designed supplement program, with good results and resolution of both her reflux and her irregular heartbeat.

Patient AQ had been feeling quite well when, in January 2005, she experienced unusually heavy menstrual bleeding persisting throughout the spring of 2005. Over a period of weeks and months, she felt herself growing weaker and more fatigued. Initially, she did not seek medical attention, but in early May 2005, after detecting a mass in her pelvis, she returned to her primary care physician. On routine blood screening, her hemoglobin was extremely low at 8.0. She was referred for an ultrasound, which showed what was thought to be a large uterine fibroid. She was referred to a gynecologist, who biopsied the uterine lining, but when no malignancy was found, the uterine mass was again assumed to be a benign fibroid. However, because of its size and the bleeding, Patient AQ's physician still advised that a hysterectomy be done.

After agreeing to the plan, a week before the hysterectomy scheduled for mid-June 2005, she received a transfusion. Subsequently, at a local hospital Patient AQ underwent the hysterectomy and left salpingo-oophorectomy for what her doctors still thought was a large, but benign, fibroid, measuring some 10 cm in largest diameter. Assuming this to be a benign lesion, Patient AQ's gynecologist did not resect out any lymph nodes to search for malignant disease, collect pelvic washings as is routinely performed with a suspicion of cancer, or examine the abdominal viscera such as the liver.

The initial pathology evaluation seemed to confirm the noncancerous nature of the lesion, described in the official report as a "LARGE CELLULAR LEIOMYOMA," the official terminology for a benign fibroid. Just to be on the safe side, the pathologist sent the microscope slides to the laboratories of Genzyme, a nationally recognized biotech company based in New England. There, the pathologist saw something completely different, a very aggressive, rare form of sarcoma, as described in the formal pathology report from early July 2005: "HIGH-GRADE LEIOMYOSARCOMA WITH FOCALLY ABUNDANT MYXOID DIFFERENTIATION."

With the diagnosis of poor-prognosis cancer now confirmed, Patient AQ's gynecologist recommended a consultation with a local oncologist and the institution of intensive chemotherapy, which, the doctor said, was absolutely necessary. But Patient AQ, with her long interest in nutrition and alternative-type medicine, was adamantly against chemotherapy and declined the suggestion to meet with an oncologist. Instead, on her own she began reviewing the available medical literature about her particular type of cancer, which indicated that neither radiation nor chemotherapy improved survival. She then contacted a cancer consultation service, whose report on her situation confirmed that neither radiation nor chemotherapy, or even a combination of both, would offer her any real advantage.

From this group, she learned about my work, applied to be a patient, passed the screening, and was first seen in my office, with her husband, the first week of September 2005. At that time, she seemed to have recovered from surgery without a hitch and reported feeling quite well, with good energy, stamina, and concentration. A recent blood test showed her hemoglobin had moved into the normal range, and all blood chemistries were fine.

When Patient AQ and I first met, I had no idea of the actual stage of her disease because her doctors, initially believing, incorrectly, the mass to be benign, had not recommended CT scanning before surgery. Nor did they suggest such testing in the period immediately after her hysterectomy and hospitalization, because the initial pathology report confirmed a supposedly nonmalignant lesion. Once the correct diagnosis had been made, Patient AQ never did follow up with the recommended oncologist or proceed with a staging workup. So to this day, she has never undergone CT scanning to determine the extent of her disease.

During our first session together, as we discussed conventional options such as chemotherapy, I could see that indeed she had done her homework. As a start, she told me she was interested only in an alternative approach and would never submit herself to either chemotherapy or radiation—which she knew didn't work for her type of cancer in any event. She seemed very satisfied with her decision and very determined to proceed with my treatment.

Patient AQ informed me that once the diagnosis of cancer had been confirmed, she had begun a largely plant-based, near-vegan diet, with very limited animal protein. I explained to her that for our sarcoma patients we generally prescribed a quite different diet than the one she had chosen to follow, with large amounts of red meat, some poultry, fish, and dairy products, along with fruits, lots of vegetables, and whole-grain products. She said, smiling, she would have no problem adjusting her diet according to my determination, and actually admitted, as our sarcoma patients generally do, that she enjoyed red meat and missed it from her diet.

Thereafter, Patient AQ proved to be a very determined, vigilant, compliant, and grateful patient, grateful that I provided this nutritional approach to cancer. Initially, she did experience some difficulties adjusting to the program. During the first weeks of therapy, her gastritis seemed to act up. She developed persistent burning upper epigastric pain and consulted her local primary care physician, who graciously had agreed to help her as she pursued her nontraditional cancer regimen. This physician thought she might have an ulcer. After talking about the situation with her over the phone, I made some changes in her therapy, suggesting as well eight ounces of freshly made green or white cabbage juice each morning, an old and very effective treatment for ulcers. With these adjustments and the cabbage juice, her symptoms relented, and she was able to continue her therapy without a problem.

In early October 2005, after a month on treatment, Patient AQ sent me a note reporting that her stomach pain was "90% resolved." However, she also noted that she had experienced some of the symptoms that I had told her, during our initial session, were typical for patients on the therapy, such as achiness and some nausea. I attribute such side effects to the process of repair and rebuilding of damaged tissue, with the associated release of stored environmental toxins and metabolic wastes. Otherwise, she already seemed to be improving nicely, as she described in her note to me:

> I had a few days of achiness, headache, and nausea, but most of the time I feel great with lots of energy and very little fatigue....

> My family doctor says she is willing to work along with me and order any tests that you would ever prescribe

> Please advise and accept my thanks.

I was happy that Patient AQ seemed to be responding to treatment, and that her local doctor would work with us, despite the unconventional nature of my treatment. The famed Dr. Gerson, who sixty years ago utilized his own aggressive nutritional program in patients diagnosed with poor-prognosis cancer, wrote in his book *A Cancer Therapy* that an unsupportive family member can often sabotage his treatment. An unsupportive local physician, I have found, can do the same, with negativity and derision. On the other hand, a local doctor on board with the treatment can help enormously.

When I saw Patient AQ in my office in late March 2006 for a regularly scheduled six-month follow-up appointment, she seemed very compliant and reported overall feeling "wonderful," with "terrific" energy and stamina. About a month prior to her appointment, she had presided over a large wedding for her daughter, an event she had supervised without any difficulty.

Thereafter, Patient AQ continued her treatment. When she next returned to my office, in late October 2006, she had completed more than a year on her therapy. She reported occasional midabdominal burning pain relieved by drinking a glass of water, and occasional palpitations. But overall, she said she had continued to improve since her previous visit to my office, in March 2006. Her blood tests, which I ordered periodically, were normal except for a moderately elevated cholesterol—a long-standing issue in her case, and not one I thought particularly worrisome.

When I saw her in late April 2007, after she had completed some nineteen months on her therapy, she appeared compliant and again told me her health had continued to improve. She said she felt "great," with "excellent" energy and no symptoms. When I gently suggested she consider CT scanning to assess her status, she declined, stating that she would not change her treatment whatever a CT showed, so there was no point in undergoing such an expensive test that would exposure her to significant radiation.

When she returned to my office in October 2007—after two years of treatment—she had recently recovered from a severe upper respiratory infection. Her doctor had prescribed a round of antibiotics, which Patient AQ never took, instead choosing to manage her illness with herbal remedies that proved quite effective.

Thereafter, she returned to my office every six months, remained compliant with treatment, and continued doing well. In June 2008, she sent me a letter, explaining that she had been under considerable personal stress at home because of her husband's health problems, which we subsequently discussed at length in a phone conversation. When she next came to my office with her husband, during the last week of October 2008—now three years on treatment with me—she didn't mention the issues we had discussed, reporting only that she continued to feel "terrific." During the session, I suggested that maybe, after all this time, it wouldn't be a bad idea to go back to her surgeon, whom she hadn't seen since her follow-up visit immediately after her hysterectomy. She graciously declined my suggestion.

Everything seemed to be going well when, in late February 2009, a family member called, to elaborate somewhat on the nature of the stress in Patient AQ's life. The family member was concerned that Patient AQ seemed despondent, to the point that after complying so well with her nutritional regimen, she might be losing her motivation to continue.

Two days later, I spoke to Patient AQ, and she opened up about the nature of the stress, which we again discussed at length. She admitted she had been somewhat depressed, but her great faith in God and the support of her church and family had helped her through the difficult time. She remained determined to stay on her therapy and do well.

When the stress worsened in late March 2009, I suggested she add some St. John's wort to her supplement regimen. Though commonly thought of as an antidepressant—and though usually discounted as useless in the conventional medical world—I find this herb to be an enormous help with patients going through periods of personal stress.

During our next visit, the last week of April 2009, Patient AQ seemed much happier. She remained very compliant and physically seemed to be doing well. In terms of her depression, she thought that the St. John's wort had helped her mood considerably. She did complain of restless and painful legs at night, for which I prescribed additional vitamin E at bedtime, often helpful with this condition.

Six months later, during our late October 2009 session together, Patient AQ again appeared to be doing quite well, with the stress in her life apparently under control. She told me an interesting story, about which I had previously known nothing. Three friends, all members of her closely knit church group, had been diagnosed with the exact same type of uterine cancer, high-grade leiomyosarcoma, and at the same time as Patient AQ in 2005. But unlike AQ, all three had chosen to proceed with aggressive radiation and chemotherapy after hysterectomy— and all three were now dead, with the last one dying only recently. Patient AQ said these horrific outcomes had only convinced her how right she was to refuse chemotherapy when originally diagnosed.

Unfortunately, less than two months later, the stress again worsened, and this time her church seemed less supportive. In a phone conversation, she reported some anxiety with associated physical symptoms. I encouraged her as best I could, urging her to concentrate on her program and remember how well she had been doing physically.

To make matters more complicated, in late April 2010 Patient AQ had a terrible fall in her barn, injuring her ankle and neck. When she called me the day of the incident for my advice, I urged her to go to the local emergency room for x-rays. After our call, she consulted with a physician member of her church, who felt the situation did not require aggressive treatment, just conservative care. Subsequently, x-rays done at the office of a local chiropractor did confirm a mild fracture in her cervical spine, for which again conservative treatment was recommended. When she returned to my office, during the third week of May 2010, she seemed to be doing much better, reporting no residual neurological symptoms.

Thereafter, I continued seeing Patient AQ every six months, she remained compliant with her treatment, and she continued doing well with no clinical evidence of cancer—though as before, she expressed no interest in pursuing CT scan studies to confirm what she already knew, that she was doing fine. Fortunately, the home stress appeared to be under control finally, for which I was grateful. There were times I thought the stress was severe enough that she would lose the motivation to stay on treatment, but, I thought, hopefully these problems had finally resolved.

Subsequently, at times Patient AQ reported to me that she was experiencing intermittent neurological problems, particularly severe neck pain, which I related to her neck injury. Though she seemed happy with her progress under the care of her local chiropractor, when I last saw her in early June 2012, her neck problems had worsened once again, despite the treatment. I mentioned to her my friend Dr. Roy Sweat of Atlanta, Georgia, whom I first met in 1986 while I was completing my investigation of Dr. Kelley's treatment. I consider Dr. Sweat to be the finest and most scientific chiropractor who has ever lived.

Dr. Sweat developed his own system of adjusting, based on the methods of his mentor, Dr. John Grostic, a pioneering chiropractor who died in 1959, and who believed—as today Dr. Sweat believes—that the key to structural health, and in turn, neurological health, is the atlas bone, the first bone of the cervical spine. Named after the god Atlas, whom the Greeks believed held up the Earth, the atlas essentially "holds up," or stabilizes the skull. Any type of head trauma, even seemingly mild in nature, can jar the atlas out of its normal position, which should be parallel to the ground. Once out of its proper alignment, the atlas stays that way, unless properly treated.

This is not an insignificant concept; when the atlas remains out of its ideal position, it can exert direct pressure on the lower brainstem, which regulates many essential "autonomic" physiological processes, such as respiration and cardiovascular activity. In addition, with the atlas tilted, it can torque the two vertebral arteries that course through the cervical spine bones and feed the back third of the brain—not a good outcome. To make matters worse, an out-of-kilter atlas bone causes the skull bones to shift, placing additional and abnormal pressure on the brain at large. The end result can be all manner of problems, from simple issues such as numbness and tingling in the extremities, to headaches (very common), fatigue, malaise, cloudy thinking, mental fogginess, memory deficits, and at its worst even seizures.

Dr. Sweat developed a very precise method of adjusting the atlas that requires he first take a series of special x-rays of the neck, which allow him to determine, with mathematical precision, the precise angle of misalignment. With this information in hand, he then adjusts only the atlas, not using his hands, but a specially designed and very sophisticated instrument he developed with the help of engineers and mathematicians. With the patient lying on a specially designed table, a complex stylus is maneuvered into the correct position, and then a percussion wave courses through the stylus and through vector mechanics pushes the atlas back into place with minimal discomfort. Because the system is so precise, Dr. Sweat needs no hard force; in fact, patients usually cannot even tell they have been adjusted. Though trained as a classical chiropractor, Dr. Sweat never uses his hands; he believes hand adjusting is imprecise and more often than not leaves the patient worse off than before treatment.

Dr. Sweat's approach is so precise that at times a single adjustment, or a small series of adjustments over several days, can realign the atlas and resolve the symptoms. Often, patients hold their adjustment for years, with no further treatment unless they happen to reinjure their skull, neck, or back. In my own case, after I carelessly walked into a glass door that I thought was open space and banged my head very hard—to the point that I saw stars—an adjustment by Dr. Sweat the following weekend took care of all symptoms, and I have not needed another adjustment in the ten years since. Dr. Sweat has told me that over the past twenty-five years that I have been in practice, I have referred more than 250 patients to him from all over the country—with nearly every one experiencing a dramatic improvement, whatever the nature of their injury or symptoms

In the case of Patient AQ, I didn't initially push her to follow up with Dr. Sweat, or one of his protégés who practices in New Jersey, Dr. Angelo Colavita, because she invested considerable trust in her local hand-adjusting chiropractor and seemed to be improving under his care. But with her symptoms worsening, I encouraged Patient AQ to make the trip to Georgia and consult with Dr. Sweat.

A misaligned atlas bone is not an esoteric or trivial problem; if that vertebra is out of place, all bets are off in terms of nervous system efficiency. And because the nervous system controls every aspect of metabolism in the body, a poorly functioning set of nerves can seriously impede the progress of any treatment for any disease, including mine.

In any event, other than her neurological symptoms, Patient AQ remains compliant with her nutritional treatment and continues doing well, now more than seven years since her original diagnosis in June 2005.

According to the National Cancer Institute website, uterine sarcomas are quite rare, representing less than 1 percent of all gynecological malignancies and only 2–5 percent of all uterine cancers. Pathologists recognize three distinct categories of uterine sarcomas, of which leiomyosarcoma is the most aggressive. Even with disease limited to the uterus, the overall 5-year survival for women diagnosed with leiomyosarcoma runs about 50 percent for those with purely localized, stage I disease, but it falls to 0–10 percent for all other stages.

In terms of stage I disease, many experts believe the size of the tumor at diagnosis represents the most important prognostic indicator for leiomyosarcoma, with tumors greater than 5 cm—as in the case of Patient AQ—predicting a much poorer outcome than tumors smaller than 5 cm. In addition, we know that, based on the pathology report from Genzyme, AQ's tumor, defined as "HIGH-GRADE," was the most aggressive form of this very aggressive sarcoma. So even if Patient AQ was at stage I at the time of diagnosis, with her very large tumor and aggressive histology, her chances for long-term disease-free survival were not good.

But, in truth, we have no way of knowing the actual stage of Patient AQ's cancer at the time of diagnosis, whether it was limited to the uterus or not, because no CT scan was ever done, either before or after surgery. And, as mentioned earlier, during the hysterectomy her gynecologist, thinking the tumor benign, did not sample lymph nodes, perform pelvic washing, or undertake the usual search for metastases. But with an aggressive-histology tumor 10 cm in diameter, it would seem unlikely to have been limited just to the pelvis.

And of the four members of Patient AQ's religious community who were diagnosed at the same time with exactly the same disease, only she has survived. The other three, who chose to pursue conventional treatment including chemotherapy, died within a period of several years. The demise of these patients illustrates just how aggressive, and deadly, leiomyosarcoma of the uterus can be.

*IMPORTANT EDITOR'S NOTE:
Dr. Gonzalez died before updating this case report. According to Patient AQ's medical file, she last contacted Dr. Gonzalez in June 2014. Patient AQ last met with Dr. Isaacs in November 2016.

Case 2: Patient JZ
*A Minimum 8.4-Year Survivor**

Patient JZ is a woman chiropractor in her early fifties who has survived now five years with a history of unresected synovial sarcoma of the plantar surface of the right foot.

Her family history is pertinent because of her mother and a maternal aunt, both of whom survived breast cancer. A maternal first cousin survived colon cancer and testicular cancer, each treated conventionally. Prior to developing cancer herself, Patient JZ had long-standing allergies to pollens and animal dander and had experienced multiple sprains to her right ankle. In a skiing accident as a teenager, she had torn her right medial meniscus. Subsequently, after a serious motor vehicle accident in 1998 with multiple rollovers, she developed hypertension, which was treated with an angiotensin-converting enzyme inhibitor.

A health-conscious athlete who had jogged for many years, Patient JZ had practiced yoga on a regular basis, followed a whole-foods diet, and since chiropractic college had consumed a variety of nutritional supplements.

Her current problem dates back to 2000, when she first developed pain in the plantar surface of her right foot that persisted and gradually worsened in intensity over a period of months, to the point that walking could be difficult. In her office, she performed x-ray studies on her foot, which she interpreted as completely normal. Patient JZ assumed that the problem must be plantar fasciitis, a very painful inflammatory condition of the sheaths of the foot muscles. With that as the working diagnosis, Patient JZ tried a number of anti-inflammatory nutritional supplements, with some temporary improvement, but invariably the pain would return, only more intense than before. In 2003, a repeat x-ray in Patient JZ's office was again read as normal.

At that point, Patient JZ pursued a number of alternative-type treatments, including release therapy; acupuncture; LEFT, a form of laser therapy; standard chiropractic adjustments; and even orthotics, without any improvement. As her situation worsened, she consulted with a number of conventional medical doctors, including orthopedists, none of whom had any idea what might be the source of the persistent pain and none of whom could offer a solution.

In 2004, Patient JZ first noticed a lump in the plantar surface of her right foot, which she assumed must be due to muscle hypertrophy or spasm, the result of her ongoing pain. None of the many doctors she consulted seemed to think much of the finding, because the x-rays had all been normal.

In 2006, with the situation deteriorating, Patient JZ consulted her primary care physician, who referred her to a specialist in lower limb disease. Patient JZ would later tell me the meeting was a disaster, with the physician suggesting no scans, offering no diagnosis, and providing no treatment plan.

In the spring of 2007, the pain increased to the point that Patient JZ began to limp when she walked and found it difficult to function as a chiropractor standing over patients for hours each day. Though even mild pressure could bring on severe pain, Patient JZ powered through her long days in the office with sheer determination. In the summer of 2007, she consulted with a podiatrist, who, like the previous physicians Patient JZ had seen, was unconcerned about the lump in Patient JZ's right foot, though it had gradually been increasing in size. He suggested a new set of orthotics, which failed to remedy the situation. In fact, the situation worsened to the point that in the fall of 2007, Patient JZ returned to her primary physician with severe, unrelenting pain that was beginning to interfere with sleep. She was referred to a physiatrist, who, during the first consultation, was not as blasé about the growing plantar mass and insisted that an MRI—which had not been recommended before—needed to be done as soon as possible.

During the first week of November 2007, the MRI clearly showed a large tumor in the plantar surface infiltrating into the surrounding tissues, as described in some detail in the radiology report:

> A multilobulated focus is present adjacent to the plantar aspect of the cuneiform bones, which is difficult to accurately measure but measures approximately 3.5 cm in anterior-posterior diameter, 2 cm in craniocaudad diameter, and 2.7 cm in coronal diameter.... Linear extensions of the mass are present entering between the middle and lateral cuneiform bones as well as along the plantar aspect of the distal cuboid bone and bases of the fourth and fifth metatarsals. A lobule of the mass extends into the superior portion of the adductor hallucis muscle and quadratus plantae muscle. The extensor plantar tendons are mildly deformed by the lesion.

In the "Impression" section of the note, the summary of the findings, the radiologist seemed unsure as to the nature of the mass, offering a number of possibilities including a benign growth such as myxoma or a benign venous tumor such as a cavernous hemangioma.

In mid-November 2007, Patient JZ met to discuss the findings with the physiatrist, who recommended nerve conduction studies of the right lower extremity. This testing turned out completely normal, but with a malignant lesion now a possibility, the physician ordered a bone scan, performed during the third week of November 2007. This revealed a nonspecific abnormality in the plantar surface of the right foot, as stated in the report:

> Increased activity of radionuclide noted, projected over the cuneiform bones of the right foot, seen during the perfusion.... The findings are non specific....
>
> No other abnormality is noted.

During the first week of December 2007, Patient JZ then underwent "BILATERAL FOOT/ PLANTAR FASCIA ULTRASOUND," which also demonstrated a large right plantar mass, as recorded in the radiology report:

IMPRESSION:

A solid lesion within the deep portion of the plantar surface of the right foot measuring 2 cm × 1.4 cm × 2.7 cm. Although the lesion is quite nonspecific diagnostic considerations would include a fibroma [a benign tumor].

Patient JZ was then referred to an orthopedic oncologist at Mt. Sinai Hospital in Toronto for an evaluation, biopsy of the lesion, and a discussion of potential surgical approaches. During the first session with Patient JZ, this physician assumed the tumor to be malignant based on the various radiology reports but also expressed his opinion that the tumor as it stood was inoperable because of its size and infiltration into various foot muscles.

Assuming the biopsy confirmed a malignant lesion, the surgeon suggested Patient JZ proceed with amputation of the foot, which most likely would be curative, or perhaps as an option chemotherapy and radiation initially to shrink the lesion, followed by a more local surgical procedure to save the foot. But the physician emphasized that the more conservative approach might not work, so amputation might still be required.

During the second week of February 2008, Patient JZ underwent core needle biopsy of the tumor. Because of the inevitable delays in the Canadian health care system, Patient JZ did not immediately learn the results, but expecting the worst and with her long history of interest in nutritional practices, she began to investigate alternative approaches. She already knew about our work from friends, so she decided that if the biopsy confirmed a malignant lesion, she would forgo all standard treatments and begin our therapy.

Patient JZ did not learn of the biopsy findings until the second week of March 2008, nearly a month after the procedure. The pathological evaluation had confirmed a malignant lesion, specifically an aggressive sarcoma, as described in the official report:

DIAGNOSIS:
Soft tissue (right foot), needle core biopsies
Synovial sarcoma, grade II/III

With the diagnosis now certain, Patient JZ arranged for a CT scan of the chest to assess possible metastatic disease, as had been previously ordered by her doctors. Sarcomas notoriously tend to spread to the lungs first, hence the suggestion for a CT scan limited to the chest. However, Patient JZ had already decided she would not be returning to her orthopedic oncologist, nor would she consult with any of the recommended medical oncologists. She intended to follow up only with me.

Patient JZ's initial note to my office described her history and situation in great detail and with great passion. She explained that for years she had lived her life according to health-promoting principles and wanted none of the recommended treatments, particularly amputation. When I assessed her records, I realized that surgery could be curative for this aggressive cancer that has a tendency to spread. As a fundamental rule in my office, if a standard conventional approach can be curative for a patient applying to my practice, I feel ethically obligated to encourage that patient to proceed along those lines. So, in keeping with this policy, my office faxed Patient JZ a note expressing my belief that if the CT scan showed no evidence of metastatic disease, she should seriously consider the surgery, as horrific as it might seem, because it offered a very high potential for cure in her case.

The following day, Patient JZ faxed us back, arguing her case and asking me to reconsider:

> I have been advised about chemotherapy and radiation and I am not in agreement with its use since it is so destructive both short and long term. The tumor is not a good candidate for surgery as is either [sic] since it has diffuse tumor margins.
>
> Please consider me for a consult and I can travel on a moment's notice.

That same day, my office faxed Patient JZ back, asking her to send me a copy of the CT scan as soon as it might be available.

Several days later, Patient JZ underwent the CT, which showed "no evidence of metastatic disease." She faxed a copy of the report to me, again stating her wish to begin my treatment.

Because Patient JZ seemed so determined to proceed with my regimen, I provisionally accepted her into the practice if she were willing to send a brief note expressing her understanding that she had chosen to refuse the standard-of-care treatments, which in her case—as dreadful as they might be—could cure her. She complied, and with all the needed documents in hand, I accepted her as a patient.

As she awaited her appointment, scheduled for the second week of April 2008, Patient JZ did continue her radiological evaluation, searching for possible invasion of the tumor in the foot bones. During the third week of March 2008, x-ray studies of the foot revealed that "there does appear to be some neoplastic tissue extending between the cuneiform bones and basis of the metatarsals." However, a CT scan performed during the first week of April 2008 showed no definitive evidence of cortical bone invasion.

Subsequently, Patient JZ traveled to my office for her first consultation. From the start, I found her to be wonderfully intelligent and passionate about her work, her patients, her profession, and natural living. She had clearly made an informed decision about her choice of treatment, expressing her absolute resolve to keep her leg and avoid any toxic interventions such as chemotherapy, which, as she had read, really didn't provide any proven benefit. She hoped that my regimen might reduce the pain and shrink the tumor so that a limited surgical excision might be possible.

I warned her that my program works slowly and gradually, and oftentimes tumors stabilize for years—or even initially increase in size due to the inflammatory effect of the enzymes. She understood my explanation but still wanted to proceed. I did cautiously suggest during our initial session that she might consider at least meeting with a medical oncologist, to hear the conventional perspective—a suggestion she rejected outright.

Otherwise, she looked well and said she generally felt well except for the persistent and gnawing pain in her right foot, which made her long days in the office unpleasant, to say the least. As she explained, her work as a chiropractor required that she spend hours a day standing as she tended to her patients, a situation, we both agreed, that was not ideal with her tumor located where her right foot touched the floor. Even minor pressure on the lesion could elicit "excruciating" pain. I suggested she consider cutting down on her patient load, to minimize the time spent on her feet, a suggestion she agreed to consider. I emphasized to her that she needed to concentrate on her treatment, minimize the stress in her life, and try to keep pressure off the right foot.

Thereafter, Patient JZ proved to be a very determined, very enthusiastic, and very compliant patient. In subsequent months, she would occasionally call with a minor question about the regimen, but in general she adjusted to the program without any major difficulty. In early August 2008, we did an "office visit" by phone, in which she said that the pain, which had been such a consistent nightmare for her, had already improved "substantially"—the first time the discomfort had lessened in years. She told me that the pain was at least "50–60 percent" reduced, indeed a major step in the right direction, and that the tumor was "definitely" smaller by her own evaluation.

Several days after our phone conversation, Patient JZ underwent repeat MRI studies of the right foot, which showed "little if any interval change in the previously described mass, which was biopsied and apparently represents a synovial sarcoma. I question whether the plantar portion of the medially situated lobule of the mass has slightly increased by 1–2 mm in size, however, this is a very subtle finding."

When I next saw Patient JZ in my office, for her six-month follow-up appointment during the first week of October 2008, she again seemed very determined and very compliant, and she reported that overall she had improved substantially since our first meeting together, in April 2008. She had wisely cut down her practice hours and was now working only three days a week as opposed to six. When she was on her feet, the pain would increase, but she remarked that at other times, when she could sit, the pain essentially "was gone." However, Patient JZ, who I learned was quite well known in her profession, had been lecturing frequently around Canada and the US, and she found that when she stood on her feet during a presentation—which sometimes lasted hours—the effort could take a toll. I suggested that she sit when lecturing, an idea she thought perfectly feasible.

During our meeting together, she reported that her overall energy and stamina had improved substantially. During my exam, I measured her tumor, which I thought was somewhat reduced in size, though we discussed the MRI findings showing essentially no change. Regardless, she was glad that the tumor at least seemed to have stabilized.

Subsequently, Patient JZ continued on her therapy and overall seemed to be doing well. In preparation for her next visit with me, scheduled for early April 2009, she faxed me a note describing her current state of health. She remarked that on the days when she worked in her office, the tumor seemed to swell and the pain worsened, and at these times she felt exhausted. She wondered if she might be "doing too much, expecting my body to do more than it should right now."

When I saw her some days later, a year since she had begun her treatment with me, she still reported that the pain overall had substantially improved from when she had first walked into my office a year prior. She did report recent episodes of new-onset heavy vaginal bleeding associated with fatigue, but because of the Canadian health care system, she had to go through her primary care physician for a referral to a gynecologist, a process that she explained can take weeks. I wondered if she might not be anemic from the blood loss, a situation that might certainly explain the tiredness she reported. I encouraged her to get the appointment with the gynecologist set up as soon as possible.

On my exam, I thought the lesion was certainly no bigger, and perhaps slightly smaller, and to my relief, it seemed much less tender on palpation. She had scheduled a repeat MRI scan of her foot for early June 2009, so we would be able to assess the state of the tumor more thoroughly.

Back home in Canada, some eight days later, the bleeding worsened and blood testing showed her hemoglobin had dropped to 7.0, indicating severe anemia. After these results came back, she was admitted to her local hospital, transfused with packed red blood cells, and started on the birth control pill, which, in such situations, often helps stop abnormal uterine bleeding. When we spoke on the phone some days later, she reported feeling much better, and I recommended she begin a natural iron supplement that I find works very well in such situations.

A subsequent ultrasound revealed two uterine fibroids and a thickened endometrial lining, which her doctors decided required biopsy. A biopsy was then scheduled for July.

Unfortunately, in mid-May 2009 Patient JZ slipped on a rock at her summer home, landing very hard on the right foot. She was so disabled she had put herself in a wheelchair and used crutches when she walked. Patient JZ was concerned that she might have torn her right knee meniscus and medial collateral ligament in the fall, but because of the Canadian health care system, she told me it would take some time to get an MRI of her knee to assess the damage. When the tests were finally done, she actually had ruptured her left anterior cruciate ligament, not the right.

Several weeks later, in early June 2009, Patient JZ underwent MRI scanning of the right foot, but nearly a month passed before she obtained a copy of the report, which she then sent on to me. By that point, she had also undergone the endometrial biopsy, which fortunately showed no evidence of cancer, as well as ablation of the endometrial lining to stop the bleeding.

According to the radiologist, the MRI of the foot showed that the tumor might have increased slightly, though his report was very indefinite: "It is somewhat difficult to objectively measure the lesion, as it has a somewhat of a lobulated infiltrative appearance, however, subjectively I do feel that there has been some very slight increase in size of the lesion, compared with the previous and more remote studies."

During the first week of July, we discussed both the MRI and endometrial biopsy findings. Since her knee injury, she had been forced to place considerable pressure on the right foot when she walked, a situation that she believed contributed to increased inflammation around the tumor and in the foot. When we discussed the situation, she made it clear to me that she had no intention of abandoning her nutritional therapy.

For her endometrial bleeding and thickening, I suggested low-dose natural progesterone cream, which when used properly can be of use. Fibroids and endometrial thickening have been associated with long-term estrogen excess, and a relative progesterone deficiency, so supplementation with progesterone often helps—though not always. In any event, after the ablation procedure and once Patient JZ began treatment with low-dose bio-identical progesterone, the bleeding would not be a problem again.

When Patient JZ returned to New York for a follow-up appointment, during the third week of October 2009, she admitted that the previous six months had been quite difficult, with the episode of heavy bleeding, now resolved, and her fall at her summer home with damage to her left knee. She continued to have pain in the left knee, so when she walked she found herself favoring her right leg and right foot. The pressure had exacerbated pain in the tumor area. Further testing of the left knee confirmed a dislocation severe enough to warrant surgery, scheduled for late November 2009.

For all these reasons, Patient JZ had finally taken a disability leave from her chiropractor practice, which she had turned over to chiropractor relatives. She had decided that in the future she would concentrate on lectures and giving seminars. In a sense, I was relieved that she would not be working ten hours a day on her feet treating patients, a situation, I explained to her, that was hardly conducive to healing her right foot.

Despite the recent trauma and the added stress when walking, Patient JZ had remained compliant with her therapy and overall reported the right plantar pain was still "30–49 percent" better than when she had first arrived at my office eighteen months earlier. Because of her significant anemia brought on by the persistent bleeding, she reported feeling quite fatigued, although her energy and stamina were beginning to rebound. I made some changes in her supplement program, and she returned home to Canada, as determined as ever.

In the ensuing months, when I didn't hear from Patient JZ, I assumed her November 2009 knee surgery had gone well. When I next saw her in my office, during the second week of April 2010, she explained that the procedure had turned out to be more complicated than she initially thought it would be, though ultimately it had proven a complete success. As it turned out, the surgeon found a left torn meniscus and cruciate ligament, for which he had transplanted some right leg muscle to allow for reconstruction.

Since the surgery, she had been undergoing fairly intensive rehabilitation and physical therapy. Unfortunately, she had been instructed to avoid placing any pressure on the left foot for the time being, so when walking she had to rely on her already compromised right foot with the plantar tumor. In consequence, she said the right foot pain—which previously had been improving steadily—had worsened, at times reaching a "10" on a 1–10 scale, with 10 being the worst pain possible. The pain had been pretty constant since the surgery, at times severe enough to once again interfere with sleep. But, she emphasized, the left knee was gradually healing, with a program of intensive physical therapy. Fortunately, through all these difficulties she had remained very compliant with all aspects of her nutritional regimen.

Patient JZ informed me that she had sold her practice to two relatives, so the pressure of dealing with patients on a daily basis had come to an end. She felt somewhat relieved, she told me, now realizing how stressful her life had been trying to manage a heavy daily patient load while in severe foot pain. With her patient responsibilities at an end, she planned to do some writing and continue her lecturing.

Despite the surgery and long rehabilitation process, she reported her energy and stamina to be quite good. Her Canadian doctors planned to repeat the MRI of the right foot within the next couple of weeks, and she told me with some resignation that she expected the tumor to be bigger because when she walked, because of the left knee situation, she had been putting considerable force on the right foot. She was relieved, as was I, when the MRI two weeks later showed no change, as described in the formal radiology report:

IMPRESSION

The known synovial sarcoma in the sole of the foot is essentially unchanged.

Thereafter, she continued on her therapy with great determination. When she returned to New York for her next visit, in early October 2010—after completing two and a half years on her regimen—she reported the previous summer had been quite stressful. During the second week of July, she dropped a glass jar while standing in her kitchen. The jar had shattered, slashing her right medial malleolus area and cutting through a small vein. When she couldn't completely stop the bleeding, Patient JZ ended up in the local emergency room and required four stitches to close the wound. Some days later, unfortunately, she decided to go swimming at her summer house, and the wound, not yet fully healed, became infected, now requiring a course of antibiotics. To make her life more complicated, during that time a family member had suddenly become quite ill, though by the time we talked that situation seemed to be improving.

During the previous few months, I had been in repeated communication with Patient JZ's Canadian insurance company handling her disability claim. After several letters from me, the company had decided that Patient JZ must return to work as a chiropractor at a reduced pace, but for at least two to three days weekly—not an ideal situation, certainly. Now that she had to again spend long days on her feet treating patients, the right foot pain had worsened, though she was certain the tumor itself had not grown at all. At times, the pain could be severe enough to interfere with sleep. Patient JZ had tried bromelain, an anti-inflammatory enzyme derived from pineapple, but the supplement hadn't helped much, though she was reluctant to use any pharmaceutical anti-inflammatories such as ibuprofen.

Regardless of her ongoing difficulties, both clinical and personal, she remained faithful to her program. In November 2010, after discussing the idea with me, she decided to begin a course of photodynamic therapy, hoping it might help with the pain. This largely experimental treatment involves intravenous application of any number of supposedly anticancer substances that presumably concentrate in the tumor, then activate when a specialized light source is directly applied to the area. Though the treatment has generated considerable enthusiasm in recent years within both the alternative and the conventional medical world, the data to me overall seems flimsy. In any event, I didn't argue against the approach, which I did not think would interfere with my treatment. Patient JZ eventually would continue the treatment until taking a break from it in February 2011, when she told me the treatment hadn't helped with the pain at all.

During the first week of March 2011, after completing nearly three years on her nutritional therapy, a repeat MRI of the right foot showed the lesion might have increased in size slightly, though the radiologist wrote in his report, "It is somewhat challenging to give exact comparison." In the summary section, he wrote the following:

IMPRESSION

Again, there is a multilobulated, enhancing mass along the sole of the foot, as described. It demonstrates similar signal characteristics compared with the previous study, however is measuring slightly larger.

When I saw Patient JZ again, in mid-April 2011, she informed me she had again relinquished all direct patient care, to concentrate on lecturing and teaching. The stress of practice, she came to realize, was simply too much of a drain on her energy, whatever her insurance company might think. In recent months, she had traveled abroad considerably to speak at various chiropractic seminars, a change of pace she enjoyed, though I was concerned about the stress of travel and the difficulties of compliance. She emphasized that wherever she might be, she always remained adherent to her regimen.

Patient JZ had become actively involved in helping two of her siblings deal with their own serious health issues. To complicate her life, she was still recovering from her left knee surgery and undergoing physical therapy on a regular basis for postsurgical rehabilitation. So while she might no longer be treating patients, from my vantage point it seemed that her life remained quite stressful.

During our meeting together, we discussed the recent March 2011 scan, which showed some minor borderline enlargement of the tumor. Patient JZ reported that at the time of the test, her pain had actually worsened, but since that time it had improved considerably. The photodynamic therapy, she also reported, really hadn't done much but would be resumed for another four-month cycle. I had no objection, other than that I thought it wouldn't do much for her, but I didn't think it would interfere with my treatment.

In early May 2011, Patient JZ underwent repeat MRI scanning, which this time showed "no interval change," so once again the situation seemed to have stabilized.

When she returned to my office in early November 2011, now having completed three and a half years on her nutritional regimen, she remained as before extremely dedicated to the therapy—and extremely grateful. She reminded me that when she had first been diagnosed, the expert doctor she consulted was insistent that she would require amputation of the foot. So even though her progress as my patient had been at times erratic and the pain occasionally problematic, Patient JZ was very happy to still have her right foot intact.

At this point in her life, she seemed to be extremely busy in her new career as a full-time lecturer. She was in great demand as a teacher and had been to Australia, England, and elsewhere in Europe in the previous months. I advised her if at all possible to try to minimize the long-distance travel, which I find physiologically disruptive. But, at least, she did seem to manage her therapy well even on the long-distance trips.

PARASYMPATHETIC-DOMINANT CANCERS

Patient JZ had finally completed the eight-month course of photodynamic therapy in June 2011, which she admitted really hadn't done anything. In fact, as she remarked, it was while on this treatment that her tumor had actually grown in size, as documented in the March 2011 MRI.

Her pain for the most part was at a tolerable level, but she acknowledged that when she traveled to exotic new places such as Australia she liked to walk and explore. This activity invariably placed a strain on her right foot, particularly because she still had not completely recovered from the left knee surgery so her gait was hardly normal. At one point, after a day of considerable walking, her right foot pain had reached a "9 out of 10" and had interfered with sleep. In recent weeks, she hadn't been traveling, and not surprisingly, the pain had again improved. Otherwise, she reported that despite her hectic schedule and hectic life, her energy, stamina, and concentration were all excellent. Even with the bouts of pain, she seemed quite happy with her life and its new direction.

I didn't hear from her again until she returned to New York during the second week of April 2012 for her next regularly scheduled visit. She had by this time completed a full four years on her therapy, and she remained compliant with all of its various aspects. She thought four years with me represented a major milestone, with her foot still intact, because, as she again reminded me, the orthopedic experts had insisted that she required amputation as soon as possible after she was first diagnosed.

She had no questions, expressed her gratitude for the treatment I offered, and told me that her energy, stamina, concentration, and overall well-being were "excellent."

In late June 2011, a repeat MRI of the foot indicated "no interval change since the recent study." Clinically, at this time she seemed to be doing quite well, with far less pain. She had continued her busy lecture schedule, frequently giving all-day seminars on various health-related topics.

The term "synovial" comes from "synovium," which in anatomy refers to a membranous sheath around a tissue or organ, like a nerve or muscle. However, in the case of synovial sarcoma, the use of the word is somewhat of a misnomer, because for this particular cancer, the cell of origin has not been definitely determined.

Of the many different types and subtypes of connective tissue malignancies, synovial cell sarcomas represent one of the most common, accounting for 8 percent of all sarcomas according to the website sarcomahelp.org. Though initially synovial cell sarcoma grows slowly, as in the case of Patient JZ, it can transform into an aggressive cancer with a tendency to invade local tissues and metastasize.

Experts consider the histologic grade, that is, the aggressive nature of the tissue, as well as the tumor size at the time of diagnosis to be the most important prognostic indicators for those diagnosed with synovial cell sarcoma. Typically, patients with tumors less than 5 cm have a ten-year cancer-specific survival of 100 percent with treatment, as opposed to survival rates of 32 percent and 0 percent for patients with tumors between 5 and 10 cm and greater than 10 cm.

Surgery for localized disease remains the optimal conventional approach. Because of the rarity of this specific tumor, controlled clinical trials evaluating the benefit of radiation and chemotherapy are lacking, though both are frequently recommended as adjuvant treatment after surgery. Oncologists often recommend chemotherapy as in this case, to shrink tumors that are too large for initial surgical resection, though no definite data exists to support this approach.

Patient JZ's orthopedic oncologist, based on the MRI findings, believed that her tumor could not be locally resected because of its extensive invasion into the complex tissues of the palmar surface of the foot. In Patient JZ's mind, the two recommended options, either immediate amputation or chemotherapy to shrink the tumor to allow for more limited local surgery, seemed unappealing to say the least, particularly because the surgeon admitted that even with chemotherapy as a first-line treatment she very likely would still require amputation. Understandably, she wanted to keep her foot, and so she has done, now more than four years since beginning treatment with me.

Though the tumor hasn't regressed, it has stabilized nicely over the years and has not metastasized; Patient JZ still has her foot, and she functions at a high level. Certainly, her course hasn't been simple; until she retired from practice, her patient schedule required she be on her feet up to ten hours a day, placing considerable pressure on her foot. Her unfortunate fall in 2009 and the subsequent left knee surgery created additional stress on her right foot. But despite these complications, she has done generally well and continues to enjoy her new career as a lecturer and teacher. Though she isn't yet "cured," I too am quite pleased we've been able to save her foot and keep this potentially aggressive disease under control.

*IMPORTANT EDITOR'S NOTE:
Dr. Gonzalez died before updating this case report. According to the office medical files, Patient JZ last met with Dr. Gonzalez in April 2015. This patient met with Dr. Isaacs in September 2016.

Case 3: Patient OR
A Minimum 5.4-Year Survivor

Patient OR is a twenty-six-year-old white male who is more than five years from diagnosis of evolving chondroblastoma of the right foot.

His family history is pertinent because of his maternal grandfather, with a history of lung cancer; his maternal grandmother, who died from some form of cancer; and a maternal aunt with thyroid cancer.

Patient OR's orthopedic problems actually began at age twelve, when he experienced repeated problems with right foot sprains, even with only minor exertion on the foot. He would describe to me a feeling of weakness in the right foot, though no lesions or masses were evident.

The problem continued. When he was fourteen, his parents brought him to a local chiropractor, who suspected that one of his foot bones was "out of place." However, the weakness and repeated sprains did not improve after a course of chiropractic adjustments and heat therapy.

At age fifteen, he first noticed a small nodule on the right outer ankle that initially seemed insignificant and that grew only slightly over the next year. The lesion did affect his gait, and for the first time, he experienced pain in the foot with walking along with worsening weakness and more frequent "sprains."

Over the next several years, the nodule continued to grow, though slowly, and the pain gradually worsened. In November 2005, when he experienced a quite serious sprain in his right ankle, he consulted a local chiropractor, who again thought a foot bone remained out of its normal alignment, a situation that placed pressure on the respective ligaments. After another series of chiropractic adjustments had no effect and with the pain more quickly worsening, Patient OR decided to seek the advice of a local orthopedic surgeon who practiced in his rural area. X-rays at a local hospital revealed an expansile lesion in the anterior half of the calcaneus bone of the right heel.

Despite the suspicious findings, the physician, according to what Patient OR later told me, suspected only that the ligaments in that region of the foot might be congenitally loose because of a possible "genetic" problem. The orthopedist, however, did not seem particularly concerned about the lesion, which he thought had resulted from repeated injury to the ankle.

The surgeon suggested an intensive three-month course of physical therapy, two to three times weekly, but despite the treatment Patient OR experienced no improvement. In fact, the pain only continued to worsen. Several times during the physical therapy, Patient OR actually sprained his ankle, causing him only more discomfort and disability. Overall, Patient OR felt the treatment had left him worse off than when he had started.

At that point, a discouraged Patient OR did not follow up with this orthopedist but instead avoided all doctors for about eighteen months. He found that he could tolerate the pain, though the nodule continued to enlarge. However, during 2006, he sprained his ankle five times, to the point that walking became difficult and quite painful. Fortunately, he was able to continue his work as a truck driver, which did not require him to spend much time on his feet.

In June 2007, he was working on a home construction project and slipped through some boards, landing hard on his right foot. Subsequently, the pain became excruciating to the point that for two weeks he was unable to walk. The ankle itself was quite swollen, and he experienced frequent painful muscle spasms in the right foot. At times, the pain was so severe that he had to crawl from his bed to the bathroom, to avoid exerting any type of pressure on the right foot.

Through family, he learned of a highly regarded surgeon at a local orthopedic center, with whom he consulted in late June 2007. X-ray studies at that point revealed what was thought to represent "heterotrophic ossification," that is, calcification of the cartilage in the ankle brought on by the initial severe injury Patient OR had experienced when he was twelve years old. The physician thought the tendons and ligaments were not loose, but had been pushed out of place, explaining the repeated sprains and weakness in the joint. He suggested a conservative approach, expecting that with rest and protection of the right foot, the problem would resolve itself. The lump, he told Patient OR, probably formed as a reaction to the repeated injuries and most likely didn't represent a serious problem. However, to be cautious, the orthopedist did recommend a referral to another surgeon, who specialized in feet, with the thought of removing the nodule to relieve pressure on the nerves.

Patient OR was aware of my work, because I had been treating a close friend of his family. I had referred this patient of mine to the Hospital for Special Surgery (HSS), the renowned orthopedic hospital in New York, after she had experienced a severe fall and dislocation of her shoulder. Consequently, Patient OR learned of Dr. John Kennedy at HSS and consulted with him in early July 2007. After reviewing the records, Dr. Kennedy agreed the problem might be heterotrophic ossification from the previous injuries.

During the second week of August 2007, Patient OR underwent repeat MRI scanning of the foot, which revealed, as documented in the summary of the radiology report, a large tumor invading into the underlying bone of the foot:

CONCLUSION

Marrow replacing expansile lesion involving the anterior half of the calcaneus expanding laterally into the sinus tarsi and extending to the subcutaneous soft tissue. The lesion contains cystic spaces within it, with some fluid-fluid levels and has an appearance most consistent with an aneurysmal bone cyst or giant cell tumor. However, the possibility that this represents a chondrosarcoma, although less likely, cannot be entirely excluded, and a biopsy is recommended.

Dr. Kennedy then sent the MRI films to an orthopedic oncologist across the street from HSS at Memorial Sloan Kettering Cancer Center. This expert agreed a biopsy needed to be done to rule out a possible malignant lesion. At that point, with the level of suspicion increasing among the doctors, Patient OR decided to decline the biopsy and contact my office with the hope of becoming my patient. He was quite familiar with my approach, had been raised on organics in a family dedicated to wholesome eating, and occasionally had even done coffee enemas. When he explained to Dr. Kennedy that he was more interested in pursuing my therapy than proceeding with further conventional diagnostic testing or treatment such as surgery, Dr. Kennedy wrote a lengthy, thoughtful letter to me, summarizing the situation to date and explaining the need for biopsy:

> [Patient OR] is a 21-year-old gentleman who is complaining of ankle problems. There is evidence on plain film of some heterotropic ossifications about his ankle joint: however, of more concern on the MRI films, which we had arranged for him, there is a large mass within his calcaneus. This mass it seems is traversing at certain points the joint line, and although the working diagnosis from the MRI report was of a giant-cell tumor, the radiologist made a point of noting that it would be important to investigate it further to rule out a more sinister lesion, such as a chrondral sarcoma.
>
> With this in mind, we got a second opinion from an orthopedic oncologist in Memorial Sloan Kettering Cancer Center, who also believed it was imperative that a biopsy was performed, given the extent of the tumor and the pattern of its growth. We have informed the patient and his wife of this, of the necessity and importance for sampling of the tissue in order to clarify definitively the diagnosis and establish whether this is indeed a benign or malignant lesion.

Meanwhile, Patient OR did send a long and thoughtful note to my office, summarizing his situation to date and requesting that I accept him into my practice. His letter explained how serious the situation had become:

> Currently, I am unable to walk more than a few blocks without extreme discomfort, and have had to give up many of my favorite pastimes, including hiking, an amateur Ukrainian dance troupe and various sports....
>
> I am currently in touch with Dr. Kennedy's office, who recommends a bone biopsy as soon as possible to rule out a more malignant bone tumor. Dr. Kennedy seems a very capable and considerate surgeon, but I am very strongly opposed to using radiation or chemotherapy and am wholly convinced of the efficacy of your therapy.
>
> I can hardly imagine what it would be like to be able to walk and run without pain, and want very much to have a definite diagnosis for the tumor in my foot. I have seen

several friends and family members recovering through your therapy, and hope for the same experience.

Because I had treated friends and family members, I called OR and spoke to him at some length about his situation. I suggested strongly that he follow Dr. Kennedy's advice and proceed with biopsy, so all of us would know definitely the nature of this tumor. He agreed to the plan, and in late September 2007 at HSS he underwent biopsy of the lesion, which revealed a "chondroblastoma," a locally aggressive benign tumor originating in the cartilage that can at times evolve into a malignant lesion.

Subsequently, during the second week of October 2007, Patient OR returned to HSS to discuss the findings with Dr. Kennedy. According to what Patient OR later told me, Dr. Kennedy explained that the pathologist thought this was an aggressive form of chondroblastoma that might be evolving into a malignant tumor and required surgery as soon as possible.

Dr. Kennedy then discussed in great detail the proposed surgical procedure, which would be quite extensive and complicated, because the tumor was large and already invading surrounding tissues. He proposed using nitrogen and a sealant to try to prevent a recurrence down the road. Postsurgery, Patient OR was warned, he would require months of intensive physical therapy, with a gradual period of recovery. Dr. Kennedy emphasized the procedure would of necessity be a major operation, though he discounted chemotherapy and radiation as beneficial.

The conversation with Dr. Kennedy left Patient OR somewhat distressed. He tentatively agreed to surgery during the first week of November at HSS, but after thinking about the situation, he decided he wanted to cancel the procedure and instead begin treatment with me. In our phone conversations during that period, he explained that to make matters more complicated, he did not have health insurance—a serious issue, because Dr. Kennedy suggested when asked that his fee alone might be $60,000. This did not include the additional costs of the anesthesiologist, hospital stay, and subsequent intensive physical therapy that would be needed. Though Patient OR had begun to look into the possibility of Medicaid coverage, he and his wife had decided they just didn't want to do the surgery anyway, above and beyond the cost issue, because of their belief in my approach.

I actually encouraged him to seriously consider surgery despite the insurance issue, because the procedure could be curative. But when Patient OR seemed determined to proceed with us only, I told him I would take him on only if he agreed to leave the surgical option open as a possibility. So ultimately, Patient OR canceled the surgery and came to my office for his initial visit during the third week of October 2007. I could see immediately that he was in pain, as he walked down the hall of my office, limping and guarding his right foot.

During that first session together, I brought up surgery again, and he agreed he would consider it if his situation didn't seem to be improving under my care. We agreed to give my therapy a three-month window; if the situation seemed to be deteriorating at that point, he would reconsider surgery. Because he seemed to have made an informed and reasonable decision, we proceeded as planned.

During my exam, I could see the obvious tumor in the calcaneus area on the outer aspect of the right foot, measuring as least 6 cm in its widest diameter. It was very hard, though not particularly tender when I palpated the lesion.

Thereafter, Patient OR seemed to adjust well to his program, despite his long hours as a truck driver. I next saw him for an office visit in late January 2008, after he had completed three months on treatment. When we walked down the hall from the waiting room to my office, to my great relief I could see that his walking had improved, to the point that in fact he was walking normally.

As he explained once we were in my office, Patient OR had with great diligence worked his program into his work schedule and managed to be compliant with all aspects of the therapy, as rigorous as it is. He knew the seriousness of his situation and seemed determined to follow the program appropriately.

This was an important visit, because we had decided when we first met to give the program a three-month trial run, before reconsidering the surgical option. Fortunately, Patient OR reported that he himself could already feel the benefits of the treatment. His energy and stamina had improved substantially, and he acknowledged that the pain in his right foot had diminished considerably, at least by 20 percent, since beginning the nutritional regimen. He could walk long distances with greater ease, his balance was better, and he didn't have to think about moving and protecting his foot. Though the pain had not resolved, this was the first time in many years it had actually improved.

On exam, I thought the tumor had stayed about the same size, 6 cm in widest diameter. But because his symptoms had improved, we agreed to continue working together and hold off on any thoughts about surgery.

Many of my patients, when they begin treatment with me, arrive with very advanced cancer, often with multiple serious medical problems brought on by the disease itself as well as the damage caused by the various intensive conventional therapies such as chemotherapy and radiation that might have been previously employed. Often, my new patients will be on the phone repeatedly during the initial months of therapy, worried about this symptom or that symptom, reporting this problem or that, as I try to work them through their often life-threatening situations. Patient OR, on the other hand, proved to be, from my perspective, a very low-maintenance patient, who knew what he needed to do, followed the therapy, and rarely if ever called with a question or problem. In fact, between his office visit in January 2008 and that scheduled for late April 2008, he didn't call once.

When I saw him in April, he walked with no limp and no difficulty down the long hall of my office. As before, he seemed quite compliant with his program and appeared to be an extremely determined young man. I was concerned that he seemed to be working far too hard, reporting twelve-hour days as a trucker. He had in fact taken on a second job as a trucker, working for another company on his "off days." He felt the need to take on extra work because his wife was pregnant, so he anticipated increasing expenses. I certainly admired his work ethic, but I advised him to try to cut down the workload. I repeated to him, as I have repeated to many patients over the years, that the body heals best at rest—not during stressful activities running throughout the day.

Despite his work schedule, he reported that he had continued to improve. When he first arrived in my office, he could walk only very short distances before he would have to stop because of the pain. Now, he told me, there was "no limitation." His mobility had improved considerably, as his wife happily confirmed, and his limp, as I had noticed myself, was gone. The pain overall, he informed me, was substantially reduced, at least by 60 percent from when he had started with me. In fact, he and his wife, who had stayed in a hotel the night before the visit with me, had walked without difficulty or pain, to my office for their appointment with me from Grand Central Station, a distance of some six long city blocks. Prior to beginning my program, such a jaunt would have been impossible.

In addition, his energy, stamina, and overall well-being had all improved as well. He himself felt the tumor was "smaller," and by my measurements, it appeared to have reduced in size, from 6 cm to 5 cm in widest diameter, a 16 percent reduction. We were both happy with his progress and agreed once again to keep surgery in the background.

When over the next five months I didn't hear from Patient OR, I assumed he had to have been doing well. He called my office at the end of the summer asking if it would be possible to conduct the next visit scheduled for early September 2009 by phone. I agreed to the plan, and when we did speak, during the first week of September, he explained rather sheepishly that in July he and his wife went down South for a vacation. Unfortunately, he was feeling so well it became easy to be careless with his program, and for a period of some three weeks he didn't take any supplements at all, became erratic with the enemas, and was reckless, as he said, with the diet.

Not surprisingly, his right foot pain had returned with a vengeance, and walking had become difficult. During this time, the tumor itself, he said, had grown quickly. He was amazed, he said to me, how rapidly things got worse off the enzymes and other supplements. He said he had learned his lesson, and once back home he had resumed the full program with rapid improvement in his symptoms.

By the time of his visit with me, the pain had completed resolved, and he was walking normally. He emphasized that the right foot pain, which had plagued him for so many years was, after the summer flare-up, "completely gone." He also noted, despite the brief relapse during his vacation, that his foot and leg muscles seemed to be getting stronger. In recent weeks, he felt so much improved he actually had been playing some sports with friends and running, for the first time in years. His relatives and friends had remarked to him how much improved he seemed to be, in terms of his walking and overall mobility.

He reported excellent energy, stamina, endurance, and concentration, despite his long hours working as a truck driver.

I didn't hear from Patient OR until he returned with his wife for a re-evaluation during the first week of February 2009. Since our last consultation, he seemed to have been quite compliant with all aspects of the therapy, despite some unexpected stress in his life. His wife had delivered a healthy son in October, who was a joy to Patient OR. Right before Christmas, he had lost his job, but he actually seemed relieved as he talked about the situation, because he could now spend time with his new son. Some four weeks earlier, his grandfather, with whom he was quite close, had died suddenly.

Clinically, he continued improving. He felt that the tumor had regressed further, he reported absolutely no pain in the foot, and he had resumed folk dancing, a hobby he had been forced to give up because of the pain. He explained that he had no problems at all with the foot, even with the more aggressive steps involved with folk dancing. During this visit, he also expressed his gratitude that he had successfully avoided the aggressive surgery suggested by Dr. Kennedy, along with the $100,000 in medical expenses the procedure would have incurred.

On exam, the tumor did appear to have regressed again, measuring some 4 cm in diameter. I then mentioned repeating the MRI, but because he had no insurance and would have to pay for the test, because clinically he was doing very well, and because the tumor seemed smaller, I didn't press the issue when he said he would prefer to avoid any expensive testing.

When Patient OR next returned to my office, in late September 2009, now nearly two years on treatment, he again reported continued improvement. In fact, he said he had no problems at all. His wife and the new son were doing great, and he had gotten a job in construction. As a testament to the effect of my regimen, he explained that he was able to do difficult work remodeling kitchens and redoing roofs, all requiring considerable use of his right foot, without any difficulty. His mobility and foot strength had never been better.

He admitted that at times, when he might get lax with the therapy, the pain would return, but it would then quickly resolve with improved compliance. Patient OR again expressed his admiration for the pancreatic enzymes and their obvious effect on his tumor. In turn, I again lectured him about the need for vigilant compliance with all aspects of the therapy.

Our last contact was in March 2013; however, Patient OR never returned to my office, though I have heard from friends of his who are my patients, and from his grandmother, who is also my patient, that he and his family continue to thrive. Apparently, he continues aspects of the program, though not the complete regimen, and has no disability whatsoever. He has continued his sports activities and his folk dancing, with no limitation and, as has been reported to me, no pain. Of course, I am not happy that he has been absent from my office now for many years, but I am pleased that he is doing so well.

Though pathologists consider chondroblastoma to be a benign tumor, in some respects it behaves like a malignancy, able to invade into and through local tissues. And at times, though rarely, it can evolve into a cancer. In Patient OR's case, his orthopedic surgeon at the Hospital for Special Surgery thought he had a more aggressive type of chondroblastoma that might actually be transforming into something more nasty. Consequently, in his October 2007 meeting with Patient OR and his wife, Dr. Kennedy emphasized the need for aggressive surgery as soon as possible. Patient OR did agree initially to proceed with the operation, which had been scheduled for early November 2007. But after thinking about the situation carefully, Patient OR canceled the procedure, choosing instead to follow my nutritional approach as his only treatment.

Certainly, over the past five years Patient OR has done remarkably well, with resolution of his pain and regression of his tumor. At this point, from all reports he is leading a normal, happy life, having avoided aggressive and expensive surgery.

WALDENSTRÖM MACROGLOBULINEMIA

Waldenström macroglobulinemia plasma cell dyscrasias are abnormal proliferations of the cells that make immunoglobulins, which are proteins involved in the immune response. Normally, these cells produce a variety of immunoglobulins as needed in response to an immune challenge, such as an infection. But if an individual cell reproduces in an uncontrolled manner, it creates many clones, all of which produce an identical immunoglobulin—a monoclonal gammopathy.

Depending on the number of abnormal cells present, the volume of protein made, and the impact of the disease process on the body, a spectrum of disease can result, from the least severe, monoclonal gammopathy of unknown significance (MGUS), to the asymptomatic but more serious "smoldering myeloma," to the most severe form, multiple myeloma. Multiple myeloma–defining events include hypercalcemia, renal (kidney) damage, anemia, and bone lesions, frequently described by the acronym CRAB. Any of the CRAB events may be life threatening. Some but not all patients with MGUS or smoldering myeloma will progress to multiple myeloma. While patients with full-blown multiple myeloma are treated with various chemotherapeutic agents, the role of treatment in smoldering myeloma is less clear.

Immunoglobulins come in different classes—IgG, IgA, and IgM—and any of these can be the clonal protein in a plasma cell dyscrasia. However, the IgM immunoglobulin specifically can form aggregates or clumps, so patients with an IgM disorder may develop hyperviscosity syndrome, with symptoms such as dizziness or blurred vision caused by the thickened blood. IgM gammopathies bear the name Waldenström macroglobulinemia, named after the Swedish oncologist Jan Waldenström, who first described this illness in 1944.

Case 1: Patient IO
A Minimum 18-year Survivor

In 1995, at age fifty-four, Patient IO began to notice numbness in his right heel, which over weeks gradually spread to involve his toes as well. He was seen by his physician and by a podiatrist; anti-inflammatory medications and custom insteps for his shoes did nothing to help. He then consulted a neurologist, who did blood work in late June 1997 that showed a low platelet count at 106 K/uL and an elevated total serum protein of 10.3 g/dL, felt to be compatible with a monoclonal gammopathy.

A bone marrow biopsy was done in mid-July 1997. The pathologist reported the following: "Sections reveal a cellularity of 70–95%. The marrow has a relatively monomorphous appearance due to the presence of space filling aggregates of small cells containing round densely hyperchromic nuclei with a thin rim of cytoplasm. Other hematopoietic elements are present; however they are relatively rare."

The pathologic diagnosis was "HYPERCELLULAR MARROW WITH MONONUCLEAR AGGREGATES SUGGESTIVE OF MALIGNANT LYMPHOMA," but when blood testing revealed an elevated IgM at 5230 mg/dL, the diagnosis was changed to Waldenström macroglobulinemia. CT scans of the abdomen and pelvis showed no enlarged lymph nodes and were normal except for gallstones. His case was discussed at the tumor board meeting of his local hospital, and no treatment was initiated. Patient IO then called someone he knew who had done well under Dr. Kelley's care some years earlier, who suggested he contact my office.

I first saw Patient IO in early September 1997, at which time he reported that he felt some minimal shortness of breath with exertion, along with numbness in both feet and occasionally in his hands. After returning home, he began his nutritional program. Blood work a month later showed an elevated IgM of 4790 mg/dL.

In late March 1998, he returned to my office. He told me that he was feeling stronger and better, with improvement of stamina and endurance. He did, however, report that he had not been taking his supplements quite as regularly as recommended. In October 1998, during a subsequent visit, he said that his adherence to his supplement protocol had improved, but he had started to compromise with his diet. Patient IO told me that part of his problem was that he felt "fantastic." His energy, stamina, and endurance had substantially improved, though his neuropathy persisted.

In December 1998, his IgM level was 5430 mg/dL. Patient IO reported that his local doctors were pleased that the IgM values were essentially stable. Over the following years, he continued his protocol and continued to feel well. His adherence to his protocol varied due to frequent travel needed to promote his business. His work was also dependent on tourist travel to the vacation spot where he lived, so after the events of September 11, 2001, with decreased air travel in general, he reported severe financial constraints and could not come to the office as frequently.

He stopped seeing his hematologist during this time and was followed by his local doctor and me with total serum protein levels, a less precise but less expensive test than that measuring IgM levels. His platelet count remained low, and his total serum protein levels gradually went from 9.3 g/dL in March 1999 to 10.7 g/dL in January 2002.

In February 2003, he noticed blood in his urine. His urologist did cystoscopy, which showed dilated veins in his bladder that were cauterized. During this time, he became anemic and required transfusions. In March 2003, he was seen by a hematologist; IgM levels were ordered, and they returned at 5720 mg/dL, with a platelet count of 128 K/uL. The hematologist believed that Patient IO's bleeding from his bladder was caused by a low platelet count due to his Waldenström macroglobulinemia, even though he had been clinically stable for years, the IgM level was not much changed from the time of diagnosis, and the platelet count was actually slightly improved. The hematologist strongly suggested treatment with Rituxan, a medication that targets the type of cell that produces immunoglobulins.

Patient IO began Rituxan in April 2003 and completed four cycles. During this time, he felt terrible and his neuropathy worsened. In June 2003, he sent me the results of blood work showing his IgM level was 5970 mg/dL, along with a note: "Here are results of blood tests before and after Rituxan—which apparently did not work at all!" His doctor suggested thalidomide, but the patient's response to that was, "I feel they are shooting in the dark."

In July 2003, his serum IgM was 7470 mg/dL. His panicked doctors wanted to start thalidomide. But by that time, off the Rituxan and back on his protocol, Patient IO felt great and opted to delay, while continuing to follow up with his hematologist. I adjusted his enzyme dose, and he promised me he would follow the protocol "religiously."

Over the next few months, his IgM level was slightly improved at 6870 mg/dL in September, 7140 mg/dL in October, and 6910 mg/dL in November, on no orthodox treatment. In November, his hematologist ordered a bone marrow biopsy; the final diagnosis was "lymphoplasmacytic cell infiltrate consistent with Waldenström macroglobulinemia."

In the discussion, the pathologist reported the following: "The section reveals a core biopsy of bone with 80% cellularity. The marrow is diffusely infiltrated by lymphoid cells exhibiting lymphoplasmacytic morphology as well as mature lymphoid cells.... The lymphoid cell infiltrate constitutes 65% of the nucleated cells."

My chart notes from November 2003 read as follows: "I had a long talk with [Patient IO]. . . . He said his oncologist is very perplexed about [Patient IO's] case because he has not certainly followed the normal course of Waldenström. . . . He is feeling fine except for the numbness in his left foot, which he has had for years."

The year 2004 for Patient IO was notable for the development of gout, with an elevated uric acid and an episode of swelling in his left foot. In early 2005, he told me that his hematologist once again wanted to start Rituxan, because of an elevated serum viscosity of 3.5 CP (normal 1.5 to 1.9 CP), but he opted not to proceed. Then, in February 2005, his IgM returned at 8270 mg/dL with a serum viscosity of 4.8 CP. Patient IO reported he was feeling well, had been traveling extensively, and had not completely adhered to his protocol. Repeat blood work in March 2005 showed an IgM of 7030 with a viscosity of 3.6 CP, improved from the previous reading.

His IgM levels continued to fluctuate, and in October 2005 he came to see me in my office. He reported compliance with his protocol. My notes read, "At this point, he does not want to go back to his hematologist. He said they had him dead and buried two years ago. He said he is not and he had never been more productive."

Subsequently, his IgM levels gradually improved, from 8010 mg/dL in January 2006 to 5750 mg/dL in March of 2007. In April 2007, Patient IO and I spoke at length by phone. He reported continued financial stress and a need to travel to promote his work. In the previous month, he had had another gout attack, followed by pneumonia.

Later in 2007, his IgM went up to 7910 mg/dL, and his serum viscosity went up as well, to 4.3 CP. His IgM gradually increased during 2008, and in January 2009 his IgM reached 10,000 mg/dL with a serum viscosity of 5.0 CP. He felt fine, he reported, with continued mild neuropathy, unchanged, and no other symptoms.

Throughout 2009, his IgM gradually improved, reaching 8320 mg/dL by November. Subsequently, over the next few years, his IgM levels remained in the 7000–8000 mg/dL range. He had another episode of blood in the urine in November 2009 and developed some cardiac problems, with worsening of chronic atrial fibrillation followed by a mild heart attack with no residual damage in April 2010. In May 2011, he called to report he was feeling "wonderful" on his protocol, plus some medications for his heart.

During 2012, his IgM dropped from 8110 mg/dL in February to 7510 mg/dL in November, with slight improvement in viscosity as well, from 3.7 CP to 3.6 CP. He contacted me briefly in 2013 and 2014 to report that he was feeling well. Then, in January 2015, he had more blood work done, which he sent me in a note in March. His IgM had dropped to 5640 mg/dL. In our subsequent conversation, he expressed his gratitude for his nutritional protocol.

Patient IO was given the diagnosis of Waldenström macroglobulinemia in 1997, based on the presence of an IgM monoclonal gammopathy in the blood along with bone marrow involvement of 10 percent or more of the bone marrow sample. Around 20 percent of patients with Waldenström macroglobulinemia have a peripheral neuropathy and 2 percent have low platelets, the two issues Patient IO consistently had.

Patient IO's condition would be defined as "smoldering Waldenström" based on the absence of symptoms. In a series from the Mayo Clinic of forty-eight patients with smoldering Waldenström macroglobulinemia followed for a median of 15.4 years (range 0.4 to 24.6 years), the authors reported a cumulative rate of evolution to symptomatic Waldenström macroglobulinemia or other conditions requiring treatment of 6 percent at one year, 39 percent at three years, 59 percent at five years, and 68 percent at ten years.[1] However, in this report, patients with more than 50 percent involvement of the bone marrow by abnormal cells, such as Patient IO, were found to have a 92 percent chance of progression at five years.

The risk of progression at five years was 61 percent in those whose monoclonal protein was ≥ 3 g/dL at presentation; Patient IO's IgM was 4.79 g/dL at diagnosis. Patient IO also had a low platelet count, which is considered to be a poor prognostic indicator. Finally, and most recently, Patient IO's IgM has improved dramatically, from 8110 mg/dL in November 2012 to 5640 mg/dL in March 2015.

Patient IO's eighteen-year survival with poor-prognosis smoldering Waldenström macroglobulinemia is by any standards unusual. In Patient IO's mind, there is no doubt; in our last conversation, he thanked me repeatedly for helping him outlive the dismal predictions of his hematologists, and for the productive and vigorous life he has led since starting his nutritional program.

1   Robert A. Kyle et al., "Progression in Smoldering Waldenström Macroglobulinemia: Long-Term Results," *Blood* 119, no. 19 (2012): 4462–66.

APPENDIX

A Case of Insulin-dependent Diabetes
Publisher: Alternative Therapies in Health and Medicine
The Gonzalez Protocol

The treatment of cancer with pancreatic enzymes according to the Gonzalez protocol has been well-described[1-3], as has the trophoblast model of cancer on which the protocol is based[3]. A trial of gemcitabine versus pancreatic enzymes for the treatment of pancreatic enzymes[4] is so flawed methodologically that its findings, which suggest that the Gonzalez protocol is ineffective for pancreatic cancer, should be ignored[5,6]. Gonzalez and Isaacs have reported individual cases and a small case series in which patients with advanced, MRI and biopsy-confirmed pancreatic cancer have had remarkably long survival times, often exceeding a decade[1,3,5].

To date, however, the use of the Gonzalez protocol for medical problems other than cancer has not been reported. The purpose of this case report is to describe the case of a man with insulin-dependent diabetes, extreme fatigue and insomnia, paresthesias, and a host of other symptoms, who improved dramatically on the Gonzalez protocol.

Case Report:

Patient G is a 44-year-old white male medical device salesman from the Northeast who first presented for consultation in late June, 2011. Family history was notable for paternal grandmother with fatal myeloma, paternal grandfather, a smoker, with fatal lung cancer, and a paternal uncle with fatal liver cancer. Multiple family members had been diagnosed with hypertension. At the time Patient G first presented, his mother was being treated for adult onset non-insulin dependent diabetes, while his maternal grandmother had developed the insulin dependent form of the disease as an adult.

Patient G presented with a complicated history over the four years previous to his first consultation, though the genesis of his problems seemed to have occurred much earlier. A serious athlete in college, he played hockey, ran track, and lifted weights regularly. After graduation, he continued playing "aggressive" contact hockey in a local adult league. During a game in 2007, he experienced a serious fall and injury around the net, twisting his back as he fell and immediately developing "excruciating" lower back pain. The pain persisted for some four weeks during which time he was unable to work full time. When his situation did not improve, he consulted with his primary care physician, who arranged for an extensive diagnostic workup complete with a CT scan of the abdomen as well as colonoscopy. All testing was within normal limits. Eventually, when his pain improved and he was able to resume his vigorous work schedule, he assumed the problem was resolved.

In June 2008, one year after his accident, Patient G's general health suddenly worsened over a period of several weeks; he developed persistent, chronic fatigue that he would describe later as "incredible fatigue all the time." His eyes felt heavy, and his muscles, in all muscle groups, became uncharacteristically weak, which for this weight lifter was an unusual circumstance.

When the symptoms persisted, Patient G returned to his primary care physician who ordered blood studies that came back within normal limits except for a slightly elevated TSH, thought to be due to an autoimmune thyroiditis. Lyme and a variety of other infectious markers were all negative. Patient G's physician prescribed levothyroxine for the hypothyroidism but suggested no other treatment at the time.

Despite the thyroid supplementation, Patient G's severe fatigue persisted, though he "pushed" himself through his work, and forced himself to continue his vigorous exercise regimen. However, his work, which demanded increasingly long hours each day and standing for hours in operating rooms, became increasingly difficult to sustain.

By July 2008, Patient G was falling asleep easily during the day, while experiencing what he would describe to me as "brain cloudiness or fog." To complicate the situation he developed persistent, "terrible" insomnia, as well as episodes of anxiety and obsessive worrisome thoughts. All the while his muscle weakness continued to worsen.

Through his own contacts he learned about a well-known internist at Hahnemann Medical College in Philadelphia known to handle "difficult" and enigmatic cases, who could be seen only by referral, which G's primary care physician provided. After an initial consultation at Hahnemann this physician began an intensive workup, checking for all manner of common as well as rare illnesses. The testing revealed a single abnormality, an elevation in acetylcholine receptor antibodies indicating possible myasthenia gravis. With that finding, Patient G then underwent continued evaluation at Hahnemann including: muscle resistance testing which was negative; a CT scan of the chest to rule out thymoma, (also negative); and endoscopy to check esophageal function, which proved to be normal. A multi-fiber EMG to assess muscle firing activity in patients with presumed myasthenia gravis revealed no abnormality consistent with the disease. Importantly, in terms of what would eventually play out, his blood sugars throughout this period were all within the normal range.

Despite the negative results, the Hahnemann physician decided, because of the borderline acetylcholine receptor antibodies, to start a course of the anti-cholinesterase pyridostigmine, the standard treatment for myasthenia. Patient G dutifully took the medication for three weeks but discontinued the drug when he could see no positive effect.

As he continued to deteriorate, Patient G took a leave of absence from work to concentrate on finding a solution to his condition. At that point, his insomnia had progressed to such a degree that his primary care physician prescribed zolpidem. With growing frustration at the lack of answers, on his own he decided to consult at the Myasthenia Gravis Specialty Center at Jefferson Medical College in Philadelphia. There, a single fiber EMG test, the most sensitive for neuromuscular disorder, showed nothing, so the doctors ruled out myasthenia as a diagnosis. Instead, deciding his whole problem to be psychological in nature, they referred him for psychiatric evaluation and treatment. Desperate for any solution, Patient G agreed to the plan and subsequently, as he would later tell me, he was prescribed "every different anti-depressive medication on the market," none of which led to improvement in any of his symptoms and most of which left him feeling much worse.

Through sheer dint of will he returned to work, though he experienced relentless exhaustion complicated by the continuing insomnia unresponsive to sleep medication. His muscles throughout his body chronically ached and he felt perpetually weak. He reported that during this time he was constantly "miserable from not being able to get any answers about my condition." Though depressed, he felt more anger than depression because no one had any solution to his situation.

In January, 2009, for the first time he developed daily severe headaches, but nonetheless continuing pushing himself in his work. In frustration, he then decided to consult with a local neurologist who did extensive titers for Lyme and other infectious agents. This physician ruled out myasthenia, but despite the negative antibodies decided Patient G's problems were due to Lyme disease. After placement of an IV port, Patient G began a six-week course of intravenous high dose ceftriaxone, learning to administer the antibiotic himself at home and even on the job so he could continue working. But at the end of the six weeks, he experienced no improvement, in fact, he only felt worse.

By September 2009, he had deteriorated to such a degree that he could no longer work. December 2009, proved to be a particularly difficult time for him, to the point that he began feeling he might be dying because of the severity of his muscle weakness, fatigue, and diffuse muscle pain. In desperation he began looking into unconventional medical approaches, eventually consulting with a well-known alternative physician in New Jersey whom he found open-minded and sincerely concerned about his situation. This physician once again raised the issue of myasthenia gravis because of the persistent muscle pain and weakness, though extensive blood testing this time around revealed only borderline positive Lyme titers. The physician started patient G on an intensive supplement program, then admitted him to a local hospital for three days of intensive antibiotic treatment. After completing the course of IV antibiotics, Patient G was discharged with plans for him to continue oral antibiotics. Despite the therapy he would experience "absolutely no improvement" in any of his symptoms.

Nonetheless, Patient G continued under the care of this alternative physician for three months before discontinuing the relationship because of his lack of improvement and his ongoing decline. During this period he developed new symptoms, including eyelid twitching and bags under his eyes so severe that it appeared, as he would later report, that he had swollen cheeks. His hands began to "shake" with tremors, he developed severe burning pain bilaterally in his feet, and he rapidly lost all the hair on his arms, legs, and chest, and even his eyebrows began to thin. Additionally, he developed acute onset severe periodontal disease and potency issues.

 He then decided to consult with another well-known alternative practitioner in New Jersey, who prescribed a course of IV vitamin C and weekly testosterone injections after blood testing revealed low levels of the androgen. In addition, under this doctor's direction, Patient G underwent extensive allergy testing, all of which proved negative. Patient G continued under the care of this physician for about five months before stopping the aggressive treatment when he felt no improvement.

Throughout the early part of 2010, Patient G continued his downward spiral, developing new onset paresthesias in his feet, worsening muscle weakness and pain, ongoing terrible insomnia, and debilitating persistent exhaustion. Finally, during the latter part of 2010, he consulted with yet another "difficult case" internist, hoping this physician might have a solution to his situation. Because of the patient's family history of diabetes, this physician ordered a Hemoglobin A1C. This time around testing revealed a blood sugar close to 500 mg/dl associated with a very high Hemoglobin A1C near 10%. Oddly, all prior blood sugars had been normal.

Because of the very high blood sugars, Patient G was hospitalized for two days with the goal of aggressive supervised insulin treatment of his apparent diabetes along with diabetic teaching, but when discharged his blood sugars remained unstable. At that point, he began experiencing polydipsia, polyphagia, and polyuria. He said that he was thirsty all of the time without ever having a break.

Patient G believed the diabetic teaching given to him in the hospital for self-management of his condition, including the dietary instructions, to be inadequate. Once home he continued the recommended insulin schedule and tried to incorporate the prescribed eating plan into his life, but nonetheless he could not regulate his sugars properly. He simply didn't know how to administer the insulin because the protocol given him seemed unduly complicated, nor was he consistent with the recommended diet. Apparently his doctors did not insist on close medical supervision.

After his hospitalization, Patient G continued experiencing "terrible polyuria and polydipsia" as well as new onset mood swings; at times his temper would go out of control, a new experience for him and his family since he was normally quite mild-mannered. During that period the burning and paresthesias in his feet worsened considerably, particularly if he stood for any length of time.

By the end of 2010, his condition was no better despite the insulin and dietary treatment. Then in January 2011, Patient G developed a severe flu-like illness with fevers, chills, and sweats, so severe he could barely get out of bed. His throat hurt so badly he could only consume fluids; at one point his breathing became labored and he developed new-onset severe mid-abdominal pain.

In late February 2011, after recovering from his acute flu symptoms he remained so weak he could barely walk, and at one point he passed out when attempting to stand up. When he awoke, he felt as if he had "a ton of bricks on his chest." After calling 911, he was admitted to a local hospital with a body temperature of under 90 degrees, in what turned out to be, according to doctors at the hospital, diabetic ketoacidosis with respiratory failure, pneumonia, metabolic acidosis as well as acute pancreatitis secondary to diabetic ketoacidosis and acute renal failure with secondary acute tubal necrosis from the diabetic ketoacidosis. He was diagnosed as well with mastoiditis, and uncorrected hypothyroidism, and began a 13-treatment course of emergency dialysis for his renal failure. Comorbidly, he developed Clostridium *difficile* pseudomembranous colitis as a result of antibiotic treatment for his pneumonia.

After a difficult two-week hospitalization, Patient G continued the dialysis as an outpatient. This time around the endocrinologist (with a history of diabetes himself) assigned to his case prescribed insulin lispro 4 units three times a day with meals and insulin glargine 50 units at night, and insisted on close monitoring of his condition. Patient G was also placed on a variety of supplements for his kidney failure including calcium acetate, magnesium oxide, and vitamin B complex. He underwent a course of oral metronidazole for the Clostridium, and was prescribed furosemide 40 mg a day, escitalopram 10 mg daily, levothyroxine 100 mcg daily and a probiotic. With careful management, Patient G's diabetes seemed finally under if not ideal, at least better control.

In early June 2011, two weeks before his first consultation with this MD, Patient G consulted an ophthalmologist who found, fortunately, no damage to his eyes.

My evaluation of all new patients, whatever their underlying problem might be, involves two lengthy sessions. The first, the intake history and physical, usually takes two hours since the majority of our patients tend to present to us, as in this case, with complicated medical histories. During the second session, again usually lasting two hours, I review the recommended nutritional protocol in some depth.

At the time of our first meeting together, Patient G appeared very fatigued, and worn out, and pale. He did not smile once through the two-hour session and at times talking seemed to be an effort. He still was out of work, but did explain that in recent weeks, with close medical management, better dietary compliance, and a regular program of insulin lispro and insulin glargine, his blood sugars had been fairly well regulated and some of his symptoms had lessened in severity. He reported that the hair on his arms and legs had begun re-growing; his gums showed some improvement, but he still required zolpidem for persistent severe insomnia and the paresthesias in his feet had actually worsened. He described burning in his feet so intense he could not stand for any length of time and he experienced persistent odd "electrical-shock" type symptoms in various places in his body.

His endocrinologist had arranged teaching for intensive foot care, which Patient G followed to the letter, washing his feet 3–4 times daily. His sexual function, though improved, remained problematic, perhaps, as he said, 20% of his former self. He had some time earlier discontinued the testosterone prescribed by one of his alternative doctors because he felt it did nothing. He still could not exercise because of his persistent weakness and fatigue as well as the paresthesias in his feet that made activity like running or walking impossible. He described chronic loose, watery stool associated with some urgency maybe twice a day, some lower back pain, and muscle cramping at night in his calves.

He reported occasional chills but no sweats, and bouts of nausea, which he related to low blood sugars. Because Patient G could go from hyperglycemia to hypoglycemia very quickly, his endocrinologist had advised him not to use the insulin lispro if he had not eaten.

His most recent blood work from early May 2011, showed a hemoglobin A1C high at 7.8%, a normal TSH at 4.01 mIU/L, a high glucose at 133 mg/dl, and normal BUN, creatinine, electrolytes and liver function. A CBC from March indicated a low hemoglobin at 9.8 g/dl with a hematocrit at 29.4%. A recent CT scan of his brain had revealed some cerebral edema.

Under Past Medical History, the following problems were listed:

1. Insulin-dependent diabetes.

2. Acute renal failure requiring 13 treatments of dialysis in February/March 2011.
3. Hypothyroidism.
4. Diabetic ketoacidosis.
5. Pancreatitis.
6. Pseudomembranous colitis.
7. Periodontal disease.
8. Occasional migraines.
9. Hypoglycemia with syncope if he does not eat. Two MRI scans have been negative.
10. Pneumonia when he was admitted into the hospital in February 2011.
11. Chronic diarrhea.
12. Borderline hypertension.

At the time of his first visit with this MD, Patient G's medications included hydrochlorothiazide 20 mg a day, duloxetine 30 mg a day for muscle pain, insulin lispro 4 units 3 times a day with meals and insulin glargine 50 units at bedtime. He remained on levothyroxine 100 mcg each morning.

On physical examination, Patient G's blood pressure was mildly elevated at 136/100 mm Hg. Other than lack of hair on his extremities, he appeared otherwise normal.

Notably, despite a family history of diabetes, this patient's dysglycemia is likely of traumatic/mechanical etiology related to his injury in 2007 that most likely had damaged his pancreas significantly, setting the stage for his subsequent decline.

During the second session, we reviewed at length the proposed treatment plan. In general, our therapy can be broken down into three basic components: individualized diet, individualized supplement protocols, and detoxification routines such as coffee enemas. Unlike many alternative practitioners, we don't prescribe one diet for everyone, but recommend very detailed and individualized eating plans based on our assessment of each patient's underlying metabolism. Our prescribed diets can range from largely raw food plant-based—though we never recommend a purely vegetarian diet—to an Atkins' type diet emphasizing multiple courses of fatty red meat daily, with all manner of diets in between. Similarly, we prescribe a variety of supplements, including vitamins, minerals, trace metals, enzymes and glandular products (made for us in New Zealand), the doses, forms, and proportions varying, again depending on our assessment of the patient's metabolic needs. For all patients, whatever their problem and whatever their prescribed diet and supplement regimen, we require the coffee enemas as well as other procedures such as a liver flush, colon cleanses, juice fasts, and various baths.

Nutrition and the Autonomic Nervous System

We base our dietary and supplemental prescriptions on the state of the patient's autonomic nervous system (ANS), whose two branches, the sympathetic and parasympathetic, regulate all or most all metabolism including respiration, cardiovascular function, digestion, endocrine activity and immunity. Certain patients we believe have a genetically determined tonically active, even hyperactive, sympathetic nervous system (SNS) and a correspondingly weak parasympathetic nervous system (PNS). In these patients, all those tissues, organs, and glands normally stimulated by the SNS such as the organs of respiration, cardiovascular function and endocrine secretion, tend to be highly developed and overly efficient, while those tissues, organs, and glands normally stimulated by the weak parasympathetic system, such as all the digestive organs including the liver and pancreas as well as the immune system, tend to be weak and inefficient. These patients, we find, respond best to a plant based diet, though the exact composition varies depending on the degree of what we call "sympathetic dominance."

Other patients, we find, possess an overly strong, genetically determined parasympathetic system, and a correspondingly weak sympathetic system. In these patients those tissues, organs, and glands normally stimulated by the PNS, particularly those of digestion and immunity, tend to be highly active, even overactive, while those tissues, organs, and glands normally stimulated by their weak SNS such as the lungs and heart, tend to be inefficient.

The third category demonstrates a balanced autonomic system, with both branches equally developed and equally efficient. In this group all the various physiological systems and their associated tissues, organs, and glands, work equally effectively.

Such a construct is of more than just esoteric interest, and in our model it helps explain the origins of much disease while providing insight into beneficial treatment approaches. Fundamentally, we perceive that much if not most illness including malignancy develops either because of autonomic imbalance, or in the case of "balanced metabolizers," combined inefficiency in both the SNS and PNS divisions.

The concept that autonomic imbalance or autonomic inefficiency underscores much disease did not originate in our office, but to the contrary has a long and well-researched history going back nearly 100 years. Francis Pottenger Sr., MD, son of the famed Pottenger medical family with now four generations of American physicians to its roster, described the critical role of autonomic activity, autonomic imbalance, and autonomic inefficiency in his classic text *Symptoms of Visceral Disease* with six editions beginning in 1922, and the last dating to 1944[7].

The great University of Minnesota physician and neuroscientist, Ernst Gellhorn, MD, PhD., with over 400 papers and eight books to his credit spent decades investigating the role of autonomic imbalance and inefficiency as the root cause of much human illness[8]. Succeeding

Pottenger and Gellhorn, the more unconventional alternative practitioner, the dentist William Donald Kelley, combined the work of these two scientists into a complex nutritional therapy based on autonomic dysfunction[9].

It was Kelley who first proposed that the typical solid epithelial tumors, that is tumors of the breast, lung, pancreas, colon, liver, uterus, ovaries, and prostate tend to develop in those with a strong sympathetic system and weak parasympathetic system. In contrast, immune malignancies such as leukemia, lymphoma and multiple myeloma, and the embryologically related connective tissue cancers such as the sarcomas, occur in those with a strong PNS and a weak SNS. Balanced autonomic metabolizers tend to avoid cancer, though they can experience other illnesses and syndromes such as chronic fatigue if both branches weaken.

In these models of Pottenger, Gellhorn, and Kelley, restoration of health, whatever the underlying problems, requires bringing an out-of-balance autonomic system into balance and homeostatic equilibrium, or in the case of balanced metabolizers, improving efficiency and synergy in both autonomic divisions.

Both Pottenger and Gellhorn, independently of each other, had discovered that certain nutrients, particularly minerals such as calcium, magnesium, and potassium, whatever else they might do in the body have an enormous influence on autonomic firing. For example, Pottenger discovered that calcium stimulates the SNS, magnesium blocks sympathetic firing at the ganglion, and potassium stimulates the PNS in central nuclei. By judicious use of nutrients such as these, Pottenger, in his clinical work with patients, could successfully bring an out-of-balance autonomic system into balance, or improve the efficiency of each. Gellhorn, in his research, further confirmed the profound influence of various nutrients on autonomic function, showing again, as had Pottenger, that by their precise use autonomic balance and autonomic efficiency would improve, with often startling positive results in his clinic patients.

Though these pioneering researchers concentrated on certain nutrients, it was Kelley who would more thoroughly investigate the effect of foods and the various individual nutrients—the vitamins, minerals, trace elements, fatty acids, etc.,—on autonomic activity. And in his dietary and supplement prescriptions, Dr. Kelley always sought to bring an out-of-balance ANS into efficient equilibrium—or with his "balanced metabolizers," strengthen both branches equally.

Dr. Kelley believed that his "sympathetic dominant" patients, whatever the underlying problem, required for improvement a plant-based diet that included a wide variety of fruits, vegetables, nuts, seeds, organic whole grain products but limited animal protein—eggs, yogurt and cheese, with some additional food from animal sources depending on the extent of sympathetic activity; the stronger the SNS, the fewer animal products he would allow.

As more conventional nutritional scientists know, vegetables and fruits have an alkaline ash, and an alkaline extracellular fluid environment tends to suppress sympathetic, while increasing parasympathetic, firing. Further, fruits and vegetables provide significant amounts of the minerals magnesium and potassium, which as Pottenger had shown, respectively suppress sympathetic tone while increasing that of the parasympathetic nerves.

Red meat and to some extent poultry provide certain nutrients in relatively high amounts such as phosphates, sulfates, the amino acids phenylalanine, tyrosine, aspartic acid, glutamic acid, and saturated fats, all of which, via unique pathways, stimulate the SNS while suppressing the PNS. The phosphates and sulfates, for example, convert in the body into phosphoric and sulfuric acid, acidifying extracellular fluids and in turn activating the SNS while suppressing the PNS—a scenario what would be counterproductive for a sympathetic dominant metabolizer. Phenylalanine and tyrosine, which serve as the precursors to the sympathetic neurotransmitters norepinephrine and epinephrine, similarly have a SNS stimulating effect. So in a sympathetic dominant patient we restrict these animal foods, the amounts allowed again depending on the degree of sympathetic dominance. In an extremely strong sympathetic dominant we forbid all red meat and poultry; for a patient only slightly on the side of sympathetic dominance we might allow small amounts of both weekly.

In summary, a largely plant-based diet specifically suppresses the sympathetic division while activating the parasympathetics.

In his day, Dr. Kelley prescribed, and we recommend today, precise forms, doses, and proportions of the various vitamins, minerals, trace elements, at times herbs and often glandular products from New Zealand animals, again designed, like diet, to bring about autonomic balance and efficiency. ANS balance is always our main concern in any of our dietary or supplement prescriptions. Of course all the various individual nutrients have multiple metabolic roles—magnesium for example serves as a cofactor in over 300 reactions—but our concern is always their effect on the autonomic system.

Specifically, Kelley found and we find that beta carotene, the B vitamins thiamine, riboflavin, niacin, pyridoxine, folic acid, and vitamins C and D either suppress the SNS or stimulate the PNS. Certain minerals and trace elements including magnesium, potassium, manganese, and chromium, have a similar SNS inhibiting, PNS activating action as does the plant-based omega-3 essential fatty acid, alpha linolenic acid.

For the parasympathetic-dominant patients, Kelley prescribed—and we prescribe today—a diet high in animal fats and protein, sometimes red meat twice daily, which with its specific complement of nutrients such as the phosphates sulfates, phenylalanine, tyrosine, aspartic acid, glutamic acid and saturated fatty acids, will stimulate the weak SNS and suppress the strong

PNS, helping to bring the out-of-balance ANS in the parasympathetic dominant patients into more efficient equilibrium. With their acid-forming, sympathetic stimulating activity, meat and poultry represent ideal foods for this group of patients—again the frequency and amounts varying according to the degree of parasympathetic dominance; the more parasympathetic a patient, the more fatty red meat we prescribe.

Parasympathetic dominant patients do well with certain vegetables, particularly root vegetables and those in the cruciferous family, which we find to be not particularly alkalinizing, but the diets limit or forbid leafy greens which, because of their high magnesium content, will suppress the SNS. For our parasympathetic patients we allow varying amounts of whole organic grains, again the amount depending on the extent of PNS dominance; the more parasympathetic a patient, the fewer servings of grains we allow. The diet does permit beans, but limited or no fruit. Fruit, with its alkaline ash, its high content of potassium and other SNS-suppressing nutrients, would be counterproductive for this group. For a patient with an extremely strong PNS we restrict fruits and grains to the point that, at times, we allow none at all.

Parasympathetics do best with certain nutrients, specifically preformed vitamin A; certain B vitamins including B12, choline, inositol, PABA and pantothenic acid: and the calcium salts of vitamin C and vitamin E. Appropriate minerals include large doses of calcium, which we find stimulates strongly the SNS (but minimal amounts of magnesium and potassium); the trace minerals selenium and zinc; and the animal-derived omega-3 fatty acids EPA and DHA which we find best suited to their metabolic needs.

Balanced metabolizers do best with a diet and supplement regimen that provides all the food classes and nutrients but in moderate doses that will effectively stimulate and support both autonomic branches equally, helping to promote and maintain efficient autonomic function and autonomic balance. For this group the diet allows all the various fruits, vegetables, nuts, seeds, whole grains, eggs daily, organic raw milk and raw cheese, fish 2–3 times weekly, poultry 2–3 times weekly, and red meat 2–4 times weekly. In terms of supplements, for these patients we prescribe all the various vitamins, minerals, trace elements, essential fatty acids (from both plant and animal sources) but in moderate doses so as not to excessively stimulate or suppress either autonomic branch.

Our Approach to Diabetes

Kelley recognized, as do endocrinologists, two forms of diabetes, an insulin deficient type and an insulin excess variety, what we would today call insulin resistance. But his approach, as does ours today, differed considerably from conventional wisdom, always focusing as he did on autonomic activity and imbalance as the underlying culprit needing to be addressed.

If for a moment we think of diabetes in autonomic terms, indeed when the sympathetic system fires it does suppress both the exocrine and endocrine pancreas while at the same time stimulating gluconeogenesis, leading to a combination of diminished insulin secretion, increased glucose production and consequently chronically low blood insulin, elevated blood sugars and elevated hemoglobin A1C. In Kelley's model, a sympathetic dominant individual who might follow the typical American eating plan including 150 pounds of white sugar a year, and an additional regular intake of refined and processed grains and food, will end up with an insulin deficient form of the disease prompted by carbohydrate excess in the absence of beta cell reserve.

When the parasympathetic nerves fire, they increase both the synthesis and the release of insulin, while stimulating the storage of glucose either as glycogen or in adipocytes as triglycerides. In these patients, an intake of white sugar and refined grains leads first to reactive hypoglycemia due to the hyperinsulinemia, followed by classic insulin resistance. In this situation the excessive blood levels of insulin provoke insensitivity in the insulin receptor of target cells, which when functionally normal will activate the downstream glucose membrane receptor so the sugar can enter cells to be used for energy,

In the world of mainstream diabetic thinking physicians believe the "insulin dependent, Type 1" or childhood diabetes, results from alleged autoimmune attack on and destruction of, the insulin-secreting beta cells of the pancreas often occurring at quite young ages. Kelley believed this type of insulin deficient diabetes could occur in adults as well as children, and even in the group of child patients, the real culprit remained an excessively active SNS, perhaps beginning during fetal growth and development. The traditional "Type II" form, more easily regulated by diet, would be consistent with Stanford researcher Dr. Gerald Reaven's concept of insulin resistance, persistent insulin excess in response to a high intake of poor quality refined carbohydrates, leading eventually to receptor insensitivity and the paradoxical situation of high blood insulin and high blood glucose.

In the case of Patient G, the initial evaluation of his autonomic status indicated that he fell moderately into sympathetic dominance but not extremely so. For him I prescribed what we call the "Balanced Vegetarian Metabolizer Diet" designed for those patients who are essentially balanced in terms of autonomic efficiency but leaning toward sympathetic dominance.

Case Report Continued: Patient G's Specific Diet

As a first principle for all our patients, whatever their autonomic state and whatever their prescribed diet, we strongly advise that their food be organic, as clean as possible, and always non-GMO. Studies going back to the great English agronomist Sir Albert Howard repeatedly have demonstrated the superior nutritional value of "organically" raised foods and livestock. Such agricultural practices provide additional benefit to the soil and the various soil organisms such as earthworms and the micro-organisms of the soil; this microbiome forms the foundation of all agriculture and is susceptible to damage from pesticides and herbicides. To make matters worse, pesticides, at least most of them, act as neurotoxins, which we believe should be avoided at all costs.

I recommended for Patient G that approximately 50% of his food be consumed in the raw, uncooked state, while 50% should be cooked. Researchers such as the late Edward Howell proposed that raw food contains all the vitamins, minerals, and trace elements in a completely undamaged, and usually more accessible form than does cooked food[10]. In addition, Howell pointed out that every cell, whether from a plant or animal, contains hundreds of different enzymes as part of the cell's normal metabolic machinery. These enzymes, Howell maintained, based on his clinical and laboratory studies, could be absorbed like a vitamin or mineral to assist in various metabolic reactions, and help in the repair and rebuilding of damaged tissue.

However, these "food enzymes," as Howell called them, denature and deactivate above 117 degree Fahrenheit so even mild cooking will render them useless as beneficial nutrients. Because of this finding, Howell became a great proponent of raw food therapeutic diets, projecting him into the role of grandfather of the current "raw foods" movement.

Though Kelley acknowledged the benefits of raw food, he also learned, through his extensive clinical experience, that some patients did best with mostly cooked food. For those who might have been ravaged by cancer and aggressive conventional treatments such as chemotherapy and radiation, Kelley found their digestion to be so inefficient they could not tolerate an excess of raw food. Though cooking does neutralize certain nutrients like folic acid and vitamin C, make certain minerals like calcium less available, and inactive the "food enzymes," the process does break down cell walls and membranes in plant and animal food products respectively, in a sense "predigesting" the food, thereby making it more easily assimilated. To make up for any nutrient loss in the cooking process, Kelley would always prescribe—as we do today—large doses of accessory nutrients and an enzyme product developed by Dr. Howell himself. In any event, we find balanced metabolizers particularly, such as Patient G, do best with a diet equally proportioned between cooked and raw.

In terms of specific food types, the diet prescribed Patient G allowed all the different vegetables, encouraging the intake of at least 3–4 servings a day with a mix of both cooked vegetables and raw vegetables in salads and freshly made juice, with no limit whatsoever on serving size or frequency. The diet did recommend frequent servings from the cruciferous family which have an anti-cancer effect, as well as dark leafy greens, which provide a significant amount of magnesium and a sympathetic-suppressing effect, ideally suited for a patient like G who fell, if only mildly, on the sympathetic dominant side.

The prescribed diet also included a glass of freshly made carrot juice daily, which we find provides a host of useful nutrients and enzymes. We find that, in a patient such as this with a strong SNS and what we consider an "insulin deficient" form of diabetes, the sugar content in a single glass of carrot juice does not affect the blood glucose to any great extent; the benefit, we believe, far exceeds any small risk.

Despite current recommendations in some camps that diabetics of any ilk should avoid all fruit, Patient G was allowed as much *whole* as desired, but restricted fruit juice and dried fruit whose concentrated sugar content would be initially excessive. Additionally, Balanced Vegetarian Metabolizers diagnosed with diabetes tolerate grains, even gluten, well, as long as they consume non-GMO organic forms, preferably sprouted such as the Ezekiel line of breads and grain products. Such grain foods tend to be not only more nutritious as the sprouting process increases the enzyme content, but also less allergenic. In any event, we do not find that these foods significantly and negatively affect blood glucose levels in this specific group of patients as long as they stick to the organic, non-GMO, preferably sprouted forms.

The diet also allowed as much, or as little of the nuts, seeds, and bean categories as Patient G might wish to consume, though again emphasizing organic non-GMO varieties in all cases, while forbidding peanuts and soy. Peanuts, technically a legume, can grow the Aspergillus mold which produces the liver toxin, aflatoxin. Though there remains ongoing debate about the potential problem this is in US-grown peanuts, we err on the side of caution. And we forbid for all our patients soy products, even though they are widely promoted as a "health food," for two reasons. First, a regular intake of soy will, over time, block thyroid function, eventually leading to hypothyroidism. Second, soy contains the protein Bowman-Birk Inhibitor, named for the scientists who isolated it, that interferes with the action of trypsin, the main pancreatic proteolytic enzyme so important in our anti-cancer programs.

Though Patient G tended toward the sympathetic dominant side, because he fell close to balance I did allow in his diet a fair amount of animal protein, including two organic eggs daily, cooked anyway he preferred, and raw milk to drink as well as raw milk cheese, yogurt, and butter. Evidence dating back to the famed cat studies of Francis Pottenger Jr, son of the previously mentioned neuroscientist Pottenger, that he conducted over ten years beginning in 1932 rather forcefully documented the dangers of cooked milk and as opposed to the health-promoting qualities of raw milk. Today, the current industry practice of heating milk to 230 degrees Fahrenheit, separating, recombining, and homogenizing the fat and watery liquid effectively destroys all the important enzymes and many other nutrients as well. Kurt Oster of Bridgeport, Connecticut long argued that the cherished process of homogenization changed the milk into an atherosclerosis-provoking food[11]. Of course, most states forbid the retail sale of raw milk, but even in those locales patients can often obtain raw milk from local farmers or buyer's groups.

I also recommended 2–3 servings of seafood weekly. We fully recognize the increasing problems of pollution of our major and minor waterways, which affects the quality of the fish living in these waters. But there are still areas, as in the Alaskan inlets and waterways and in the North Atlantic, that provide clean fish, or as clean as one can find in this day and age. For all our patients we do forbid the large predatory fish such as tuna and swordfish that accumulate mercury over time, as well as farm raised fish, much of which now comes from South Asia and China, where there are lax environmental regulations and questionable growing methods.

The diet allowed 2–3 servings of organically-raised poultry a week, and 2–4 servings of grass-fed fatty red meat. For the fish, poultry and red meat, I prescribed a specific frequency per week, but in all cases left the actual serving size up the patient. I learned a long time ago from Dr. Kelley that a patient's brain will be a far more accurate guide in determining appropriate serving sizes than some preconceived arbitrary rule.

I thought, based on my experience, that the weekly servings of acid-forming, sympathetic stimulating red meat were necessary in this case to help achieve balance in the autonomic branches. A diet too heavy in fruits and vegetables in a patient like this, and lacking sufficient animal foods, would in our experience push him too strongly into parasympathetic dominance, excessive production of insulin, and down the road, an insulin resistance type of diabetes. We find that the recommended servings of animal products in a slightly sympathetic dominant patient keep the pendulum from swinging too far into the parasympathetic realm, preventing a whole other set of problems.

The supplement protocol I designed for Patient G totaled 26 capsules with breakfast and dinner, and 37 with lunch. His program included what we call the "Moderate Vegetarian Multi Min" providing those minerals and trace metals such as magnesium, potassium, chromium, and manganese that we find suppress the SNS and activate the PNS. A separate supplement, the "Moderate Vegetarian Multi Vit," as it is called, contains those vitamins we find similarly suppress the SNS while increasing parasympathetic tone, such as beta carotene, the B vitamins thiamine, riboflavin, niacin, folate, and pyridoxine, and vitamin C and vitamin D. Additionally, I also included a "Glucose Tolerance Factor" supplement consisting of chromium and associated nutrients that have been documented to help regulate sugar metabolism, and which we find particularly useful for our sympathetic dominant patients. For added benefit, Patient G's program included the anti-oxidant alpha lipoic acid and the amino acid N-acetyl cysteine, a duo that together increases levels of glutathione in the body and, like chromium, assists in glucose regulation. For all patients, we also recommend a probiotic, most commonly "Vital 10" from Klaire Labs. In addition, in Patient G's particular case I also added a capsule of Saccharomyces boulardii, a specific bacteria found useful in those patients recovering from Clostridium difficile infection.

Patient G's supplement protocol provided a number of "glandular" products in capsule form including adrenal medulla, hypothalamus, liver, and orchic (testicle), derived from animals and made for us in New Zealand by exacting technology. Such supplements we believe provide certain growth factors that target like tissues, enhancing repair and regeneration of damaged cells. With each meal I also prescribed six capsules of our Pancreas enzyme product, which contains the various digestive enzymes but also homeopathic doses of insulin. In the whole pancreas glandular concentrate, we find that the insulin seems to be absorbed active into the blood stream, in contrast to purified preparations of insulin which denature in the stomach when taken orally. In the 1920s, before the wide availability of manufactured insulin, physicians at times would prescribe whole pancreas supplements that seemed to keep the disease in check.

As part of the third component of G's treatment regimen, the detoxification routines I prescribed included daily coffee enemas, which we believe are as important to treatment success as the recommended diet and supplement protocols. We find that as a patient's body repairs and rebuilds, regardless of the underlying problem, large amounts of toxic debris will be released from stored sites within the various cells. These wastes include sequestered toxic chemicals from environmental sources such as heavy metals, pesticides, hydrocarbons, etc., that sit in the cells waiting to cause genetic and cytoplasmic damage. In addition, wastes from normal cellular metabolism can also accumulate, adding to the deleterious load. In our program, with all the good nutrition provided, it appears that the various cells get the signal to begin molecular "house cleaning," gradually dumping the stored toxins and metabolic wastes into the blood stream for eventual processing and excretion primarily through the liver, and secondarily through the kidneys. Because of inefficiency in our natural detoxification systems due to chronic overexposure to environmental chemicals and processed food, we find adjunctive "detoxification" a critical component of the therapy.

The mainstay of the detoxification routines remains for all patients the daily coffee enemas, which have long been belittled by the conventional medical world. However, I have found few physicians aware that esteemed medical texts, including the *Merck Manual*, and many conventional nursing texts, recommended coffee enemas as a treatment modality for decades during the 20th century. In addition, there exist dozens of papers from the academic peer-reviewed literature beginning in the 1920s documenting the effective use of coffee and other forms of enemas in syndromes as variable as septic shock and arthritis to bipolar illness. One memorable paper from the *New England Journal of Medicine* in 1932[12] reports the successful treatment of hospitalized psychiatric patients with a variety of "colonic irrigations."

We believe that the coffee enemas, through activation of a parasympathetic reflex, stimulate both Phase 1 and Phase 2 detoxification systems in the liver, whose efficient function is so important in the treatment of just about any disease. For Patient G, I also prescribed other procedures such as a liver flush and a colon cleanse, to be alternated on a monthly basis.

For most of our patients we usually recommend any of a number of juice fasts, but in this patient's case, because of the unstable blood sugar picture, I thought any juice fast would be too strenuous early on in the treatment process.

Because of G's terrible chronic insomnia, I prescribed the "blue light blocking glasses" available from Photonic Developments, Walton Hills, Ohio (www.lowbluelights.com). This intervention is based on the discovery that all light, whether natural sunlight in origin or artificial from light bulbs, TV screens, computers, smart phone screens, etc., contains a blue wave length, which is most commonly invisible to the eye. This particular light wavelength stimulates the alert centers in the brain as a survival benefit to keep us awake and aware in daylight. Like any daytime creature, our circadian rhythms dictate that we should be alert during daylight, and sleepy at night, when under natural conditions with the setting of the sun, the stimulating blue light wavelength disappears. But we creative humans with our synthetic lights and electronic devices expose our brain to an ongoing barrage of blue wavelength light that keeps us in an "unnatural" state of vigilance in preparation for activity, even well into late night. An outcome of disrupted sleep cycles and chronic insomnia often follows.

My patient's research group designed eyeglasses, akin to sunglasses, with a rose colored lens that blocks specifically and only the blue light, in effect tricking the brain into thinking it is pitch dark even when surrounded by light. With the activating centers of the brain turned off, we can fall asleep normally, even if living in a light-rich environment and continuing our activities, such as television-watching or computer work—as long as we wear the blue light blocking glasses. In clinical trials, the glasses worked well, bringing on sleepiness quickly, often in the most hardened of insomniacs. For years, I have been prescribing the blue light blocking glasses for patients with a history of insomnia, usually with satisfying outcomes.

During the second two-hour session with Patient G and his wife, I reviewed in great detail the various aspects of the prescribed protocol. By the end of that meeting, when he expressed his gratitude that I was willing to take him on as a patient, I suspected he would be compliant with all aspects of the treatment. As we parted, after the second part of the consultation, the patient expressed understanding of the treatment and was encouraged to call with any questions he might have, also suggesting, since he lived fairly close to New York City, that he return for an office visit in three months.

Patient G's Progress on the Therapy

For all my patients, wherever they may live, we require that they return for an extended re-evaluation every six months. More local patients like G, I like to monitor initially closely, usually every three months, but after our initial two sessions together Patient G disappeared for an extended time. In the months that followed our initial sessions together not once did he call with a question. There was no contact until he sent a Christmas card in late December 2011, adding to the printed message, "Thank you for getting my life back in order." I assumed he must be doing well, but I wouldn't hear from him again until he came in for an appointment in mid-June 2012—a year after he had first consulted with me.

At that time, he walked in, again with his wife, looking like a completely different individual from a year earlier. First of all he was smiling, in stark contrast to his pained visage during our first sessions and he had what might be best described as a "glow" of good health. He expressed gratefully that the "the program has changed my life." He apologized for not coming in sooner as I had recommended, but he had been out of work until recently, so money had been tight. But he was pleased to inform me that now he had a good job he enjoyed and his newfound excellent energy, stamina, and concentration he attributed to the nutritional regimen allowed him now to work long hours under stress without any difficulty.

Over the previous 12 months, Patient G had been vigilantly compliant with all aspects of the prescribed nutritional program, including the diet, supplements, and detoxification routines. When we talked about his apparent good compliance, he had a very simple answer—I had told him what he needed to do, and he just went ahead and did it all, without complaint or need for constant support from me.

My note from the day sums up his current situation:

> He said that he is doing so much better. He said that when he walked in here he could barely function. He said that his functionality is extraordinary. He has been extremely compliant with all aspects of the problem… He does the whole program.
>
> In addition, he is on insulin lispro, which he takes three times a day. He varies the dose according to his blood sugars. He is also on insulin glargine and down to about 25 to 30 units at bedtime. He was on 50 units when he first came in… He is off the duloxetine.
>
> He basically emphasized that the program has changed his life…
>
> He is enjoying his work and working long hours.
>
> He said that when he came in here one year ago he could not exercise at all. He is exercising regularly. He is going to the gym. He is lifting weights…
>
> He said that he is enjoying his life. He is enjoying his children. He said that it is just wonderful to be alive. He said that the program has made "an unbelievable difference" in his life. His energy is substantially improved. He is able to enjoy life, go out, and be with his children. He said that he could not do that one year ago when he came in here because he was so weak, exhausted, tired, and sick. He is using much less insulin. His endocrinologist, who knows he sees me, is extremely happy with how he is doing…

He said that for so long he was not exercising but he is now feeling so good that he can exercise. He does not need the duloxetine anymore for the muscle pain.

The blue light blocking glasses helped enormously with his sleep. He said that they were "miraculous." He is sleeping soundly and sleeping well.

His energy is "unbelievable." Stamina is "great." Concentration is "very good."

His kidneys are fine. They did kidney function tests three months ago that were perfect, as if he had never been sick. Nephrologist has discharged him as he does not need to see him anymore.

In addition, Patient G's periodontal disease had completely resolved, he had not experienced any further episodes of pancreatitis, his gastrointestinal function was now completely normal, and he rarely felt hypoglycemic.

Based on my testing, my experience, and his excellent clinical situation, no changes were made to his prescribed diet, and only very minor alterations in his supplement protocol. He was to continue the detoxification routines as before.

Subsequently, Patient G continued as a "low maintenance" patient. Over the next six months he didn't call once with a question or problem, and I would not hear from him again until he and his wife returned to my office in mid-December, 2012, some 18 months after his first beginning treatment with me.

Again he looked well, reported feeling well, and remained very compliant with his nutritional regimen. My note from the session recorded his situation at the time:

> He looks great. He said that he is feeling great. His job is going well … He is busy and he is doing well financially. When he first came in here, as he said today, he did not have a job and he said that he could not work. He had lost his job because he could not function…
>
> He said that he is really doing fine. He continues on the insulin lispro but is adjusting the dose downward. He does not need as much… He is really exercising quite vigorously…
>
> He said that his stamina is "fantastic." Energy is "fantastic…" He is sleeping well. He said that the blue light blocking glasses really changed his sleep…
>
> The only doctor he is seeing at this point is his endocrinologist… He has not done blood work so I suggested that we need to do that. He agreed. He said that he just does not want to see any other doctors other than me. His endocrinologist… is just monitoring his blood sugars. His hemoglobin A1C last time was 12…

Although I had given him an order for extensive blood testing at our December, 2012 meeting, he wouldn't get the test done until late June, 2013 in preparation for his upcoming re-evaluation scheduled for the second week of July, 2013—now two years since he had begun treatment with me. At that time, his blood sugars seemed less controlled, coming in at 328 mg/dl with a significantly elevated HgbA1C at 14% (normal 4.8–5.6%). His TSH was also elevated at 6.24 mIU/L (normal 0.45–4.50 mIU/L). Though he had remained on levothyroxine, clearly he needed more thyroid replacement, or a different form of medication.

Upon follow up, he looked well, seemed as before completely compliant with the therapy, and expressed, once again, his heartfelt gratitude for the treatment. He informed me that he felt so well he had taken on a second full-time job because of his family's financial needs, but felt terrific despite the added workload. I thought it a sign of great progress that he could manage two stressful jobs successfully, since when he had first consulted me he couldn't work at all. He also explained that he, his wife, and his children had just returned from a two-week vacation out West, including a trip to the Grand Canyon which he had enjoyed immensely. As my note recorded, "He said that it was really very relaxing and he really enjoyed it."

Regarding blood sugar instability, he reported that his daily blood sugar monitoring generally indicated a level no higher than 200 mg/dl, Based on clinical experience, it was suspected that the problem might be stress brought on by his second job. Compliance with diet and the prescribed supplements did not seem to be an issue, since he appeared to be as dedicated as ever to the treatment. But he did acknowledge recent significant additional stresses in his life.

As my note from the visit reported:

> He has been under a lot of stress, and I could tell from the metabolic report. He took a second job. He is a salesman for medical products… They are completely different products so he is able to do that without a conflict of interest. He is working anywhere from 10 to 16 hours a day. His territory… goes from Washington D.C. up to New Hampshire.
>
> He said that he just needed the extra money with his three kids… It is a lot of stress. He said that the miracle is that he is able to do it. He is able to work 12 to 16-hour days. He has good energy, stamina, and endurance. We talked at length about the fact that this is really too much considering where he came from as he was really burnt out when he first walked into my office. He said that he really feels "great."
>
> His blood sugars at home range around 200 mg/dl.
>
> He has been working out three to five times a week. He said that the miracle is that when he first came in [sic] could not work at all… His energy, he said, is great. Stamina is "great." Concentration is good. He is sleeping great. He said that the blue light blocking glasses really made a difference.

Because of his high TSH, I increased his kelp supplement, a good source of iodine, and the thyroid glandular we use with patients experiencing hypothyroidism. Since he was due to see his endocrinologist in two weeks, adjustments to levothyroxine dose were deferred.

It was not surprising, based on increased work stress, that his blood sugar picture had become a problem; as patients improve on our therapy and start feeling truly well after long periods of severe ill health, they may take on more activities and responsibilities than I would normally recommend. Particularly with Patient G's autonomic profile, increased stress was almost guaranteed, at least at this still early point in his therapy with me, to worsen his blood sugars. Stress in any form in a patient such as this with a dominant SNS, whether it be physical, psychological, spiritual, or as in this case, work-related, turns on the sympathetic system more strongly, turns off the parasympathetic system, and reduces insulin synthesis and secretion.

In preparation for Patient G's next visit with me in mid-January 2014—2.5 years after his first consultation—blood testing indicated some improvement, with his blood sugar down to 280 mg/dl, and HgbA1C at 12.4%. His TSH had actually worsened to 8.43 mIU/L. Despite these results, when he was examined, he looked well, remained compliant with all aspects of his therapy, and reported that he was "doing great." After seeing me in July, 2013, and despite his misgivings, he had consulted again with his endocrinologist who had doubled his levothyroxin dose to 200 mcgs daily.

Fortunately, he had quit the more demanding of his two jobs, the one which required considerable travel, which he didn't enjoy, and which he admitted had affected his sense of well-being. Instead, he had taken on another second full time job, but one that required only local travel and which he found more intellectually stimulating while at the same time less stressful. As I wrote in my note, "…he is very happy with his job and felt my advice was really very useful."

He continued his regular strenuous workouts, which he acknowledged did help control his blood sugar levels, enabling him to reduce his insulin dosing still further. He also remarked that through trial and error he realized that when his blood sugar went below 120 mg/dl, he did not feel well at all, observing that a level between 120 and 150 mg/dl seemed most suitable, leaving him feeling most energetic and alert. We do find that our sympathetic dominant patients in general, and our sympathetic diabetic patients in particular, not only tolerate what would be considered higher than normal blood sugars, but, as in this case, feel best with moderately elevated blood glucose and feel terrible with sugars in the so-called "optimal" range.

My note described his continuing good health: "Overall his energy is excellent. Stamina is good. He gets through the day fine. He is sleeping "great." He does not even have to use the blue light blocking glasses anymore as sleep as improved so much. Concentration is good."

After discussing his worsening TSH result, I decided to up his dose of our non-prescription thyroid support supplement, to two at breakfast, two at dinner, and one at lunch.

When I next saw Patient G in mid-July, 2014, he had completed three years of treatment with me, remained compliant, and continued improving. Again he reported that the therapy "has changed my life."

Though he had not gone for the blood testing I had requested for the visit, he reported that with increasing vigorous exercise, over the past six months his blood sugars had further stabilized, rarely going below 120 or above 150 mg/dl. The levels tended to be highest in the AM, then improved throughout the day. As before, with these levels he seemed to feel clinically the best.

His assessment in comparison to his original set of health problems was as follows:

> He has had no recurrences of any of the diarrhea or pseudo-membranous colitis type symptoms. He said his gut is "fine."
>
> He has been to his dentist and his gums and teeth are fine.
>
> He has been to his ophthalmologist and there is no damage at all to his retina. His ophthalmologist is very pleased.
>
> He has very rare hypoglycemic symptoms. He knows how to manage them well…
>
> He has also had no further recurrences of any of his pancreatitis type symptoms… He is really doing very well.
>
> He has had no blood work done the last six months… We will get some blood work done.

I last saw Patient G in my office in mid-July, 2015, more than four years after his first visit. Patient G remains fully compliant with his therapy, continues doing well, and continues enjoying his work, his life, and his family. He remains grateful to the therapy we offer. His blood sugars had been falling steadily in the range of 120 mg/dl in the mornings, ideal for him, rising only slightly throughout the day. He was on the lowest doses of insulin since starting treatment with me.

He described his two-job routine as demanding, but he felt so well he had no problem meeting his responsibilities. His career, in fact, seemed to be going quite well, better than ever. He and his wife had purchased a new larger home, but even the stress of selling his old house and moving he handled without difficulty. I doubt in this particular case that Patient G will ever be free of all supplemental insulin. However, I have learned not to underestimate the ability of any organ to regenerate at least to some extent. In any event, Patient G continues experimenting with lowering his insulin dose, with ongoing success in improving his blood sugar regulation.

As a final note to Patient G's complex history before his doctors finally diagnosed diabetes, repeated extensive blood testing did not show elevated blood sugars for two and a half years.

Conclusion

Patient G provides an interesting example of how a precisely targeted, precisely prescribed diet designed according to a patient's autonomic state, can lead to substantial improvement in serious illnesses other than cancer. In this case, in contradiction to current recommendations in both the conventional and more alternative medical worlds, Patient G's specific diet recommended a considerable daily intake of carbohydrates, though mostly complex, always as part of a whole food, and always from organic sources. In this way, along with the complementary supplement protocol, we were able—at least in our model of physiology—to reduce his sympathetic tone, increase parasympathetic firing, increase beta cell activation and his own insulin production with resulting significant improvement not only in his blood sugars but also in his overall health.

Nicholas Gonzalez, MD

REFERENCES

1. Gonzalez NJ, Isaacs LL. *The Trophoblast and the Origins of Cancer. One Solution to the Medical Enigma of our Time.* New York: New Spring Press; 2009.

2. Ross CA. The trophoblast model of cancer. *Nutr Cancer.* 2015;67:61–67.

3. Gonzalez NJ, Isaacs LL. Evaluation of pancreatic proteolytic enzyme treatment of adenocarcinoma of the pancreas with nutrition and detoxification support. *Nutr Cancer.* 1999;33: 117–124.

4. Chabot JA, Tsai WY, Fine RL, et al. Pancreatic proteolytic enzyme therapy compared with gemcitabine-based chemotherapy for the treatment of pancreatic cancer. *J Clin Oncol.* 2010;28: 2058–2063.

5. Gonzalez NJ. *What Went Wrong. The Truth Behind the Clinical Trial of the Enzyme Treatment of Cancer.* New York: New Spring Press; 2012.

6. Ross CA. Methodological flaws in the Chabot trial of pancreatic enzymes for pancreatic cancer. *Int J Cancer Prev Res.* 2015;1:1–4.

7. Pottenger FM. *Symptoms Of Visceral Disease—A Study Of The Vegetative Nervous System In Its Relationship To Clinical Medicine.* New York: CV Mosby; 1922.

8. Gellhorn E. *Autonomic Imbalance and the Hypothalamus: Implications for Physiology, Medicine, Psychology, and Neuropsychiatry*. Minneapolis: University of Minnesota Press; 1957.

9. Gonzalez NJ. *One Man Alone. An Investigation of Nutrition, Cancer, and William Donald Kelley*. New York: New Spring Press; 2010.

10. Howell E. *Enzyme Nutrition*. New York: Avery Publishing Group; 1995.

11. Oster K. *Homogenized Milk and Atherosclerosis*. Lawrence, KS: Sunflower Publishing; 1970.

12. Marshall JK, Thompson CE. Colon irrigation in the treatment of mental disease. *N Engl J Med*. 1932;206:454–457.

About the Author

———— ⟞⟋⟍⟞ ————

Nicholas James Gonzalez, MD, age sixty-seven, passed away suddenly at his home in New York City with his wife, Mary Beth, at his side. Born in Flushing, New York, he graduated from Brown University, Phi Beta Kappa, magna cum laude, with a degree in English literature. He subsequently worked as a journalist, first at Time, Inc., before pursuing premedical studies at Columbia.

He then received his medical degree from Cornell University Medical College in 1983. During a postgraduate immunology fellowship under Dr. Robert A. Good, considered the father of immunology, he completed a research study evaluating an aggressive nutritional therapy in the treatment of advanced cancer.

Dr. Gonzalez had been in private practice in New York City since 1987, treating patients diagnosed with cancer and other serious degenerative illnesses. His nutritional research received substantial financial support from Proctor and Gamble and Nestlé. Results from a pilot study published in 1999 described the most positive data in the medical literature for pancreatic cancer.

Dr. Gonzalez is the author of several books published by New Spring Press:

- *The Trophoblast and the Origins of Cancer*
- *One Man Alone: An Investigation of Nutrition, Cancer, and Dr. William Donald Kelley*
- *The Enzyme Treatment of Cancer and Its Scientific Basis by Dr. John Beard, foreword by Dr. Gonzalez*
- *What Went Wrong: The Truth behind the Clinical Trial of the Enzyme Treatment of Cancer (Independent Book Publishers Association 2013 Silver Award Winner)*
- *Conquering Cancer: Volume One—50 Pancreatic and Breast Cancer Patients on The Gonzalez Nutritional Protocol*

- *Conquering Cancer: Volume Two—62 Patients on The Gonzalez Protocol*
- *Nutrition and the Autonomic Nervous System: The Scientific Foundations of The Gonzalez Protocol*

Dr. Nicholas Gonzalez leaves a legacy of faith, healing, and genuine love for the truth, people, and the pursuit of medicine. For more information about Dr. Gonzalez and The Gonzalez Protocol, visit The Nicholas Gonzalez Foundation website at www.thegonzalezprotocol.com.

Summary

Nicholas Gonzalez, MD's series of books have provided both a theory about cancer and the scientific evidence.

In *The Trophoblast and the Origins of Cancer*, Dr. Gonzalez reveals Dr. John Beard's theory for the likely origin of cancer and his pioneering use of pancreatic enzymes for cancer treatment. In **One Man Alone**, Dr. Gonzalez summarizes his assessment of Dr. William Donald Kelley's fifty patients and their remarkable recoveries. In *Nutrition and The Autonomic Nervous System: The Scientific Foundations of The Gonzalez Protocol*, Dr. Gonzalez explains why one diet doesn't suit all.

Then, in *Conquering Cancer: Volume One—50 Pancreatic and Breast Cancer Patients on The Gonzalez Nutritional Protocol*, Dr. Gonzalez details the evidence through his own pancreatic and breast cancer patient case reports. Now *Conquering Cancer: Volume Two* completes the case reports with an additional 17 types of cancer and 61 cancer patients. Plus a peer-reviewed published case report of a Gonzalez diabetes patient.

Together, these revolutionary books answer the question of which alternative therapy is most effective in treating and reversing cancer. Cancer patients and their families throughout the world owe it to themselves to demand increased access to the appropriate pancreatic enzymes and The Gonzalez Protocol to reduce the severity and incidence of cancer. The solution to cancer is here, and you can recommend these books to those who do not believe it.

For more information, visit
www.dr-gonzalez.com